MCSE Guide to Microsoft® Windows® 2000 Active Directory Certification Edition

Will Willis
Tillman Strahan
David Watts
Barry Shilmover
Kevin Hilscher
John Hales

THOMSON
✳
COURSE TECHNOLOGY™

Australia • Canada • Mexico • Singapore • Spain • United Kingdom • United States

THOMSON

COURSE TECHNOLOGY

MCSE Guide to Microsoft® Windows® 2000 Active Directory Certification Edition

by Will Willis, Tillman Strahan, David Watts, Barry Shilmover, Kevin Hilscher, and John Hales

Managing Editor:
Stephen Solomon

Product Manager:
Charlie Blum

Associate Product Manager:
Elizabeth Wessen

Production Editor:
Catherine G. DiMassa

Text Designer:
GEX Publishing Services

Editorial Assistant:
Janet Aras

QA Manuscript Reviewer:
Nicole Ashton

Composition House:
GEX Publishing Services

BRIEF
Contents

TABLE OF
Contents

CHAPTER NINE
Active Directory Maintenance and Recovery   211

CHAPTER TEN
Implementing Group Policy   233

Preface

Welcome to the *MCSE Guide to Microsoft Windows 2000 Active Directory Certification Edition*! This book provides in-depth coverage of the knowledge and skills required to pass Microsoft certification exam #70-217: *Implementing and Administering a Microsoft Windows 2000 Directory Services Infrastructure*. This course of study prepares a network professional to work in medium to very large computing environments that use the Windows 2000 network operating system. Organizations place greater and greater demand on their networks and the services those networks deliver, often providing round-the-clock services to both internal and external clients. Therefore, there is increased demand for network professionals who can design flexible, usable directory service implementations that can properly advertise and support all necessary network services, as well as the users and groups who make use of them.

The Intended Audience

The goal of this book is to teach directory services implementation and administration to individuals who desire to learn about that topic for practical purposes, as well as those who wish to pass Microsoft certification exam #70-217. This book provides the content for all the skills measured on that exam, but also provides related information that is not directly tested.

Chapter 1, "Introduction to Active Directory," provides an overview of the concepts and capabilities inherent in Microsoft's Active Directory directory services environment, so essential to the proper design and delivery of network services on large, complex networks. Chapter 1 explains the logical and physical structures of Active Directory, and introduces the basics involved in working with Active Directory from initial directory design, through the installation process, and in working with and maintaining Active Directory thereafter. **Chapter 2**, "The Structure of Active Directory," explores the server roles involved in operating an Active Directory environment, the various components that appear within Active Directory databases, and the physical structures into which Active Directory installations fall. **Chapter 3**, "Planning an Active Directory Implementation," focuses on understanding an organization's physical and political structures and explains how to map them into appropriate namespaces, site designs, domain structures, and organizational units (OUs).

Chapter 4, "Domain Name System (DNS),"explores the structures, functions, and relationships among name servers, and how those servers interact to maintain an up-to-date distributed DNS database. Chapter 4 also explores how to integrate and manage DNS alongside Active Directory, particularly to support a Dynamic DNS (DDNS) environment. **Chapter 5,** "Installing Active Directory," zeroes in on preparations for and installation of Active Directory, including domain creation and working with Active Directory Wizards. Chapter 5 also explains how to properly understand the Active Directory database and Active Directory domain modes.

Chapter 6, "Active Directory Configuration," picks up where Chapter 5 leaves off, as it describes the requirements for and activities involved in configuring Active Directory for any specific installation. Chapter 6 covers all the necessary details involved in site creation and in implementing organizational units and using them to delegate authority and manage groups. **Chapter 7,** "Administering Active Directory," focuses on the ongoing maintenance and upkeep involved in managing an Active Directory environment, including how to query the database, working with permissions, managing resources, moving objects around a directory tree or forest, and delegating authority.

Chapter 8, "Performance Monitoring," begins with a basic overview of Windows 2000 performance monitoring terms, tools, and techniques. Chapter 8 continues with coverage of the Windows 2000 System Monitor, along with objects and counters relevant to Active Directory, as well as event logs, specific instrumentation, and tools specific to monitoring Active Directory per se. **Chapter 9,** "Active Directory Maintenance and Recovery," looks at what's involved in protecting the Active Directory database, and in recovering from errors or failures that affect this vital service. Topics covered include a review of the Active Directory Data model, discussion of key Active Directory files and dependencies, plus issues related to backing up, cleaning up, and restoring Active Directory itself.

Chapter 10, "Implementing Group Policy," covers key concepts related to the Group Policy Object, and explains how to plan and implement effective Group Policies. **Chapter 11,** "Managing User Environments with Group Policy," picks up where Chapter 10 leaves off, as it explores how to use scripts and administrative templates to control the user environment, and how to use folder redirection to relocate user files on some server. **Chapter 12,** "Deploying and Managing Software by Using Group Policy," explores further use of the Group Policy Object, along with system components like IntelliMirror, to prepare, distribute, and manage software deployment in an Active Directory based environment.

Chapter 13, "Deploying Windows 2000 Using Remote Installation Services," explores what RIS can do, and how it works with DNS, DHCP, and Active Directory to enable easy remote installation of Windows 2000 clients and servers. **Chapter 14,** "Active Directory Replication," explores the replication process in an Active Directory environment, including its intra- and inter-site behavior. **Chapter 15,** "Security," addresses security matters relevant to Active Directory, including auditing, security templates, and the Security Configuration and Analysis Tool.

FEATURES

To ensure a successful learning experience, this book includes the following pedagogical features:

- **Chapter Objectives:** Each chapter in this book begins with a detailed list of the concepts to be mastered within that chapter. This list provides you with a quick reference to the contents of that chapter, as well as a useful study aid.

- **Illustrations and Tables:** Numerous illustrations of server screens and components aid you in the visualization of common setup steps, theories, and concepts. In addition, many tables provide details and comparisons of both practical and theoretical information and can be used for a quick review of topics.

At the end of each chapter is a Chapter Summary, a bulleted list is that gives a brief but complete summary of the chapter.

Appendix B includes the following features to reinforce the material covered in each chapter:

- **Key Terms List:** A list of all new terms and their definitions for each chapter.

- **Review Questions:** A list of review questions tests your knowledge of the most important concepts covered in each chapter.

- **Hands-on Projects:** Hands-on projects help you to apply the knowledge gained in each chapter.

- **Case Projects:** Case projects take you through real-world scenarios for the material covered in each chapter.

- **CoursePrep ExamGuide:** Provides the information you need to master each exam objective. The ExamGuide devotes an entire two-page spread to each certification objective for the exam. In addition, there are several practice test questions for each objective on the right-hand page.

- **On the CD-ROM:** On the CD-ROM you will find **CoursePrep®** exam preparation software, which provides 50 sample MCSE exam questions mirroring the look and feel of the MCSE exams.

TEXT AND GRAPHIC CONVENTIONS

Wherever appropriate, additional information and exercises have been added to this book to help you better understand what is being discussed in the chapter. Icons throughout the text alert you to additional materials. The icons used in this textbook are as follows:

 The Note icon is used to present additional helpful material related to the subject being described.

 Each Hands-on Project in this book is preceded by the Hands-On icon and a description of the exercise that follows.

 Case project icons mark the case project. These are more involved, scenario-based assignments. In this extensive case example, you are asked to implement independently what you have learned.

INSTRUCTOR'S MATERIALS

The following supplemental materials are available when this book is used in a classroom setting. All of the supplements available with this book are provided to the instructor on a single CD-ROM.

Electronic Instructor's Manual. The Instructor's Manual that accompanies this textbook includes:

- Additional instructional material to assist in class preparation, including suggestions for classroom activities, discussion topics, and additional projects.
- Solutions to all end-of-chapter materials, including the Review Questions, Hands-on Projects, and Case Projects.

ExamView® This textbook is accompanied by ExamView, a powerful testing software package that allows instructors to create and administer printed, computer (LAN-based), and Internet exams. ExamView includes hundreds of questions that correspond to the topics covered in this text, enabling students to generate detailed study guides that include page references for further review. The computer-based and Internet testing components allow students to take exams at their computers, and also save the instructor time by grading each exam automatically.

PowerPoint presentations. This book comes with Microsoft PowerPoint slides for each chapter. These are included as a teaching aid for classroom presentation, to make available to students on the network for chapter review, or to be printed for classroom distribution. Instructors, please feel at liberty to add your own slides for additional topics you introduce to the class.

Read This Before You Begin

To the User

This book was written with the network professional in mind. It provides an excellent preparation for the Microsoft certification exam #70-217, and also for the real-life tasks involved in implementing and administering directory services for today's networks, which must support an ever-increasing variety of users, services, and applications . To fully benefit from the content and the projects presented here, you will need access to a classroom lab containing computers configured as follows:

- **Windows 2000 Server or Windows 2000 Advanced Server.** In a classroom lab situation each student or pair of students should have a computer capable of running Windows 2000 Server or Windows 2000 Advanced Server.

- An Internet connection is helpful, and will be required for some of the case projects.

Visit our World Wide Web Site

Additional materials designed especially for you might be available for your course on the World Wide Web. Go to *www.course.com*. Search for this book title periodically on the Course Technology Web site for more details.

To the Instructor

When setting up a classroom lab, make sure each student workstation is capable of running Windows 2000 Server. Students will need access to the Windows 2000 source files when they install Windows 2000 Server and when they require access to various services during the hands-on projects. Detailed setup instructions for the labs are contained in the Instructor's Manual.

1

INTRODUCTION TO ACTIVE DIRECTORY

After completing this chapter, you will be able to:

♦ Discuss the main goals Microsoft set for Windows 2000 development

♦ Describe the different versions of Windows 2000

♦ Describe the main purpose for each version for Windows 2000

♦ Describe and define some of the key new features that have been introduced in Windows 2000

♦ Define and describe the goal and purpose of a directory service

♦ Describe the ways in which networks have used directory services in the past

♦ Describe the main areas of improvement for system administrators

♦ Describe how Active Directory achieves better scalability than previous versions of Windows NT

♦ Describe some of the key open standards that have been adopted in Windows 2000

♦ Describe some of the logical components that make up Active Directory

The release of Microsoft Windows 2000 gives us a lot to be excited about. Along with an operating system (OS) that is more stable, more scalable, and easier to maintain than previous operating systems, we have new features and possibilities that we have not seen before. Some of these new features are fairly minor (although none is insignificant). Others require you to change the way you think about your networks and the way you work with them in an enterprise.

In this chapter, we will start by giving you a brief overview of Windows 2000 and its features. We won't spend too long going through each feature in detail, because the focus of this book is Active Directory (which represents the most significant new element). However, knowing some of the new features and the way each one leverages Active Directory can help you see both the importance and significance of this new Microsoft technology.

Once we have finished with the new features, we will spend a little time going through the significant elements that represent Active Directory and allow it to work. This discussion is not intended to be exhaustive. Rather, it acts as an introduction to the topics that follow in this book.

Active Directory represents a monumental leap for Microsoft and its family of network operating systems (NOSs). Although some of the older concepts remain, their foundation is entirely different. This difference will affect the way you design and administer your networks, how you secure and delegate administrative tasks throughout your enterprise, and the troubleshooting techniques that you employ. This book will go into each of these details in turn, arming you with the knowledge you need to be effective with Windows 2000 and also to prepare for the 70-217 exam.

WINDOWS 2000 OVERVIEW

Windows 2000 is the latest release from Microsoft. Previous versions of Microsoft NOSs were called Windows NT. **NT** is an acronym for **new technology**. For this new release, Microsoft has changed the naming scheme and has appended *Built with NT technology* to the CD. The name change might seem like a minor detail, but the marketplace has initially shown some confusion over what product Windows 2000 is intended to replace. Windows 2000 can replace earlier desktop OSs such as Windows 98—but it is important to note that the change is not minor. Windows 98 users who upgrade to Windows 2000 thinking that the change is on the same scale as a Windows 95 to Windows 98 upgrade will be in for quite a shock. This OS is radically different from an architectural point of view. The most natural succession is a move from Microsoft Windows NT Workstation 4 to Windows 2000 Professional.

It is true that any experience you have had with Microsoft Windows NT 4 will help you become familiar with Windows 2000. However, it is important that you do not overlook the changes that have occurred under the covers of this important OS. In the following sections, we will take a brief look at the additional features that have been integrated into Windows 2000.

The main focuses of Microsoft for this new version are:

- Increasing stability
- Increasing scalability
- Increasing security
- Reducing total cost of ownership (TCO)
- Supporting standards-based technologies

No single feature can achieve these goals. Microsoft has achieved these goals through a mix of features and new technologies. We'll outline each of them in a moment.

Before we go any further, we should take a look at the different flavors of Windows 2000 that are currently on the market. Four different versions of the OS are currently available, each with a designated purpose. Knowing what the versions are—and what issues they have been designed to address—will help you understand where Active Directory and its associated technologies fit in.

The Windows 2000 Family of Operating Systems

The previous version of Microsoft's NOS has three versions: NT Workstation, NT Server, and Enterprise Server. Each of these versions is intended to fit a niche within the enterprise. Windows 2000 has now added a fourth version to accommodate the new network functionality and performance that are demanded in enterprises today. The following list describes all four versions:

- *Windows 2000 Professional:* The replacement for Windows NT 4 Workstation. It incorporates many of the new Windows 2000 features and is fully compatible with Active Directory. In designing Windows 2000 Professional, Microsoft addressed issues such as stability, performance, and manageability. It addresses concerns with earlier Workstation products in the NT line by supporting a host of power management features in laptop and desktop computers. Windows 2000 Professional can also replace Windows 9.*x* on your users' desktops. Windows 9.*x* is a surprisingly lenient OS—it's seemingly able to run most anything thrown at it. This characteristic has been both a blessing and a curse. The OS works, so users want it; it is also difficult to manage and support, however. Windows 2000 Professional addresses this issue by increasing compatibility and offering extensive management capabilities. Windows 2000 Professional can operate as part of a network or as a standalone OS, making it suitable for all areas of your organization.

- *Windows 2000 Server:* A replacement for Windows NT 4 Server. The main difference between this product and Windows 2000 Advanced Server is scalability. Most of the other features are equal (with some notable exceptions). You can use Windows 2000 Server for file and print sharing. It also supports terminal services and applications. Its support for Internet Information Server 5 means that it can serve as a Web server on both the Internet and your intranet. It can also be useful in workgroups. Microsoft has been clear that this version of the OS is intended for small to medium-sized organizations. However, the company is not so clear on what this range constitutes. It is safe to assume that any place you currently have Microsoft Windows NT 4 is a good candidate for an upgrade to Windows 2000 Server.

- *Windows 2000 Advanced Server:* Like Windows 2000 Server, the advanced server product can operate as a file and print server, can host terminal services and applications, and can also operate as a Web server. In addition to these common features, Advanced Server also offers additional functionality in the areas of clustering, load balancing, and larger memory and CPU capacities. Because these advanced features are not important to the topics in this book, we will not cover them in detail.

- *Windows 2000 Datacenter Server:* The highest end of Microsoft's Windows 2000 family of OSs. It is designed with data warehousing in mind. That means even more memory capacity and more CPUs are supported. This product is intended for high-end, large-scale analysis projects. Its use and feature set are outside the scope of this book, and we will not be looking at this OS in detail.

As you can see, Microsoft has targeted all levels of enterprise with its new line of OSs. A full deployment of Windows 2000 will touch upon every level and desktop in your organization. To fully benefit from the new features offered by Windows 2000 and Active Directory, you will need to deploy Windows 2000 fully in your environment. Doing so means that every workstation and every server must be upgraded to the new OS. Let's take a look at some of the specific features that make a compelling argument as to why this comprehensive upgrade is a good idea.

The New Features in Windows 2000

What good would Windows 2000 be if nothing was new? No need to worry—Microsoft has added brand-new features that you have not seen before, and has also tweaked many of the older tools. In this section, we will take a brief look at some of these features. By becoming familiar with them, you will grow more acclimated to using the new OS.

The list of features shown in Table 1-1 is not (despite its length) exhaustive. Windows 2000 is packed with new features that may be significant from a development point of view but that do not have a huge impact on the work of system administrators.

Table 1-1   New features in Windows 2000

Feature	Description
Active Directory	Microsoft Windows NT 4 has been criticized because it does not scale well in an enterprise. Microsoft has addressed this criticism with Active Directory. Active Directory is the main focus of this book. Windows 2000 is fully integrated into Active Directory and was very much built with it in mind. It might surprise you to learn that Active Directory is not all Microsoft's idea. Indeed, it is largely built upon industry standards, which makes it both robust and compatible with other directories and systems. Active Directory addresses the scalability, security, and maintenance issues that will ensure a lower TCO. It also acts as a foundation for many Windows 2000 technologies such as Remote Installation Services, Group Policy, and Delegation of Authority.

Table 1-1   New features in Windows 2000 (continued)

Feature	Description
Active Directory Service Interface (ADSI)	Microsoft OSs have become known partly because of the familiar Graphical User Interface (GUI). Although this interface has been a useful tool for administrators, familiarity has bred contempt. Sometimes it just gets in the way. To address this situation, Microsoft has defined ADSI. ADSI is a set of Component Object Model (COM) components that open up Active Directory features to programmers. This feature is useful not only to development staff, but also to system administrators. ADSI is outside the scope of this book, but it is a safe bet that top-of-the-line Windows 2000 administrators will gain a familiarity with ADSI and what it can do.
Disk quota support	It has taken Microsoft a long time to recognize the need for disk quotas. However, they have finally arrived. Disk quotas allow you to designate a finite amount of space for a group or user on your Windows 2000 network. This assignment is done at the volume level on a server. The user can then be prevented from exceeding this limit. Disk quotas allow administrators to manage their disk resources and to ensure that no single user can monopolize a server.
Encrypted File System (EFS)	Windows 2000 supports the use of all the traditional methods of securing data, such as Access Control Lists (ACLs), user logon, and permissions. In addition, it supports EFS, which is a method to further encrypt data on an NTFS disk. EFS means that although hackers may be able to gain access to your system, they will not have access to the underlying data files. This is a useful feature for laptops or other computers that are often on the road (and therefore are more likely to be vulnerable to such attacks).
Group Policy	Group Policy is one of the key new features of Windows 2000. It allows you to both secure and maintain Windows 2000 Professional and Server computers in your enterprise. It leverages Active Directory for all of its features. Some of the key concepts of auditing and analyzing security rely upon Group Policy. Group Policy allows you to have a policy-based system that can be applied both at a high level and to many different systems at the same time. It is centrally managed and can be targeted at IP subnets, specific groups of computers or users, or an entire domain.
Internet Connection Sharing (ICS)	ICS allows you to refine the use of the Internet in small organizations or in the home office. Traditionally, home offices had a single point to the Internet: a dial-up connection. Each computer that required access to the Internet required its own dial-up connection. This setup was tedious and time consuming (not to mention rather expensive, because every system required its own modem). ICS allows you to make a single connection to the Internet and then share that connection among all the computers on your network. Although ICS would not work well for large organizations (which require a more robust system with better security options), for the home office this feature alone might be worth the price of admission.

Table 1-1 New features in Windows 2000 (continued)

Feature	Description
Internet Information Server (IIS)	This new version of IIS allows you to integrate your intranet site with the new multimedia features of Windows 2000 and Exchange 2000. It supports Active Server Pages (ASP) and document sharing across the Internet. In addition, it is now possible to limit the amount of processing time a Web site uses (**process throttling**); and IIS provides an extended reporting functionality that will help you identify which processes on the IIS system are using a disproportionate amount of CPU time.
Lightweight Directory Access Protocol (LDAP)	LDAP defines an industry standard method of accessing Active Directory data. By making Active Directory LDAP compliant, Microsoft has aided in the integration of Active Directory with other established systems. Microsoft has also enabled administrators who are already familiar with LDAP to get up to speed quickly on Active Directory integration.
Microsoft Management Console (MMC)	The MMC is the pervasive tool used to administer Windows 2000. The MMC is a flexible tool that can be customized to meet a specific customer's needs. It uses consoles to perform its tasks. You can create and combine consoles so they work the way you like. These custom consoles can then be distributed much the same as Microsoft Office documents.
Plug and Play	Most administrators are familiar with this functionality, which has been part of the Windows 9.x product for a long time. It has finally arrived in all its glory in Windows 2000. The idea behind Plug and Play is simple: Plug in a new piece of hardware (such as a network or video card), and Windows 2000 will detect its presence and load the necessary drivers without any interaction from the administrator. Plug and Play (in combination with the Hardware Compatibility List) should ensure that administrators no longer have to fight with complex configurations when adding new hardware to servers or Windows 2000 professional systems.
Remote Installation Services (RIS)	Microsoft has been supporting systems management for a long time, but one area has proven difficult to support: the initial installation of the operating system. RIS works by booting a computer from a Pre-Boot Execution Environment (PXE) read-only memory (ROM) chip. These chips are commonly found on network cards. Once the system has been booted, it is directed to an RIS server that contains images for installations of Windows 2000 professional. (Note that the current version of Windows 2000 does not support the installation of other OSs through RIS.) The image is then pulled down from the RIS server to the client. Because this is a scripted installation, no administrative interaction is required. Combined with ADSI, RIS is a powerful tool in your deployment arsenal.

Table 1-1 New features in Windows 2000 (continued)

Feature	Description
Windows Media Services	Windows 2000 now supports an extensive array of multimedia features, including streaming media and voice over IP. As bandwidth availability increases, video conferencing can finally become a reality. And because it is integrated into Windows 2000 and IIS 5, we can expect to see it adopted quickly.
Windows Scripting Host (WSH)	WSH is a powerful scripting language that can be used to configure systems or to apply changes to Windows 2000 systems on your network. Although it has been around for quite some time, the additional interfaces provided to Active Directory mean that its use has been extended dramatically. WSH is a host that can run scripts. It does not define the language that is being used for the scripts. As a result, you can write the scripts in whatever language you find most appropriate, including VBScript or JavaScript.

We will concentrate on some areas that are likely to have an impact on system administrators or deployment staff working with Windows 2000.

As you can see, this subset of new features opens up a whole new world for those just starting out using Windows 2000. Taken on their own, these features represent a wealth of new ideas for working—taken together, they represent a new way of looking at networking in your enterprise.

WINDOWS 2000 DIRECTORY SERVICES

This book concentrates on Active Directory, which is the directory service employed in Windows 2000. Although Active Directory is interesting within itself, you also need to understand how other Windows 2000 features leverage the functionality it provides to perform specific tasks.

Before we can get to these topics, let's look at a definition of what a directory service really is—and, more specifically, what Active Directory brings to the table. At the same time, we will explain the specific benefits, terminology, and introductory concepts that you will need to understand in order to be successful with Active Directory.

A **directory** is a collection of data that is related, in one way or another, to other pieces of data. In other words, a directory is a database. You probably use a directory in your everyday life without thinking too much about it. One of the most commonly used directories is the telephone directory, which keeps an alphabetized list of telephone subscribers.

A telephone directory is useful, but sometimes the data is not stored in a way that is useful for a particular function. For instance, if you want the telephone number of a Mr. Powell, it is an easy matter to look up his name in the P section. If you need a list of computer suppliers, however, things get more difficult. In order to use a simple telephone directory, you must know the names of the computer suppliers before you can look them up.

To solve this problem we have another directory, commonly known as the Yellow Pages. This directory also contains names and telephone numbers, but instead of being ordered by the names of subscribers, the list is sorted by category based around the jobs or tasks the subscribers perform. In this case, you could look up Computer Suppliers and then examine the list of names to find the one nearest you.

This directory is more useful; but it's a little inefficient, because it requires that you have two books on hand to find the information you commonly need. Sounds like a job for a computer, doesn't it? By keeping all this data in a database, you can easily sort or search on any criteria.

Telephone directories are a good way to present data on all subscribers to the telephone service. In fact, they are so useful that it did not take long for someone to realize that computer networks should be organized the same way. After all, if you think of your users and computers as subscribers to your network service, the analogy works quite well.

Networks have grown beyond the original vision of those who built the foundation of our industry. At the outset, no one could imagine that even single computers would want to talk to one another. Now, hundreds of thousands of computers need to share resources and to exchange data and processing cycles. Gaining control of these dispersed resources is not easy—but doing so is much simpler with a directory service in place.

So, a directory service is simply a central repository for data that describes the resources on your network. This data includes information about computers, users, user groups, printers, servers, and a whole host of other resources. A directory service both stores data and provides it to other systems. It allows various components on your network to identify themselves and to interact. In Windows 2000, this fundamental concept powers many of the new features.

In the past, things were very different. On early networks, each computer had its own directory service (a list of user accounts). They stored far less data than today's systems, because there wasn't as much to know. From these individual directory services, networks shifted to central repositories stored on server machines. Each of the servers in an organization had its own directory. So, if a user needed access to two servers, a user account (or, in Windows 2000 terms, a **user object**) had to be created on both machines, quite independent of each other.

Microsoft Windows NT 4 employs a different method. In this case, it uses a directory service based around the domain model. All data about objects within the domain is stored in a single database. One server in the organization has a special task—that task is to accept changes to the directory, and then to distribute those changes to other machines in the domain so they can service directory requests (such as validation for logon purposes).

As we move into the twenty-first century, computer networks have grown exponentially. The older model used in Microsoft Windows NT 4 has proven successful, but it is unlikely to survive the move to global networking that is currently under way. It is time for something different—an evolution of directory services. It is time for Active Directory.

Windows 2000 and Active Directory

Active Directory is the name given to the directory service employed in Windows 2000. Naming aside, the goal of Active Directory is as we just outlined. Active Directory is a central source of data about resources on a Windows 2000 network. It is both a repository (or storage area) and a service that can provide data to applications and features outside of Active Directory. This dual purpose is illustrated in Figure 1-1.

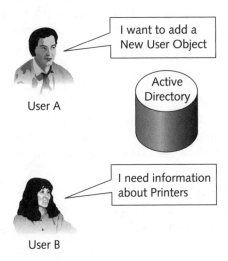

Figure 1-1   The dual nature of Active Directory

When reading about Active Directory and Windows 2000, you will often see general terms thrown about. You might wonder how Active Directory specifically addresses them. Let's take a brief look at some of the terms used and see how Active Directory works to help in these areas.

We will examine the following areas:

- Ease of administration
- Scalability
- Standards support

By understanding the fundamental ways in which Windows 2000 and Active Directory address these issues, you can better understand the significance of what you read in this book.

Ease of Administration

Microsoft Windows NT 4 goes a long way toward simplifying administrative tasks. As we described earlier in this chapter, there was a time when each server on a network operated as though it existed in its own little world. The concept of **domains**, introduced in Windows NT, simplifies this concept by having a single point of authentication for everyone.

The concept of domains has been retained for Windows 2000. As a result, the skills you have developed in designing and implementing domains are still valuable. However, there are some subtle differences in Windows 2000. For instance, for a user to access data in another Windows NT domain, an administrator must create what is known as a **trust**. A trust basically means that users and groups in one domain are trusted to access data or resources in another domain. This system works well, but in multinational organizations, it can result in a complex web of trusts. By default in Windows 2000, these domain trusts are created automatically. What's more, they are **transitive**, which means that if domain A trusts domain B, and domain B trusts domain C, then A in effect trusts C. This feature very much simplifies administration and the assignment of access to resources in an enterprise.

Scalability

One of the problems that became apparent in Windows NT 4 is the limited size of the security database. At the time NT 4 was introduced, a 40MB database seemed huge; as networks have grown, however, it has become clear that this arbitrary size is a factor in limiting potential growth.

Fortunately, Microsoft has addressed this issue by effectively removing limits from the size of the Active Directory database. Of course, there is a physical limit; because it can be defined as more than 16 million different objects, however, it is unlikely that we will run out of room any time soon.

Another scalability issue came about when widely dispersed organizations began to implement Windows NT 4. In this earlier iteration of Microsoft's NOS, one server acts as the keeper of the data. It is unique in that it is the single place on the network that accepts changes to the data. This server is known as the Primary Domain Controller (PDC). All other domain controllers exist only to service local requests for directory data. These servers are known as Backup Domain Controllers (BDC) because they back up the functionality of the PDC.

This system works well, except that the position of the PDC in an infrastructure can affect the amount of traffic moved across the network cable. What's more, a single point of failure exists, because if the PDC goes down for some reason, things can get pretty hairy. It's possible to promote a BDC and make it the new PDC, but that BDC is unlikely to be in an optimal location. To solve this problem, Microsoft has made all domain controllers in a Windows 2000 domain equal. They all act as though they are PDCs. Now a new problem has been introduced: If any domain controller can accept changes to the directory, how are all copies of the directory updated with the changes? The answer is Active Directory replication, which we will cover in detail in Chapter 14.

Open Standards Support

Microsoft has introduced support for Internet standards into its core OSs, which should lead to earlier adoption and even better scalability over time. An example of

1

open standards support is the adoption of Domain Name System (DNS) as the underlying naming format for domains. In fact, DNS is so fully integrated into Windows 2000 that you simply cannot install Active Directory without it.

Active Directory can share its data through LDAP, which we described earlier. The LDAP standard was designed to overcome some of the overhead associated with the original Directory Access Protocol. LDAP is not the only protocol that can be used to gather data from Active Directory—Microsoft also supports Hypertext Transfer Protocol (HTTP). Because HTTP is supported in all Web browsers, you can see that the door is wide open for tools that can utilize the directory information.

Windows 2000 has taken a big step to being more open and scalable by using these proven industry standards. By removing the OS's reliance on more proprietary protocols, such as NetBIOS, Microsoft has ensured that Windows 2000 will work efficiently and be more integrated with other networks, such as Novell NDS and the Internet than ever before.

THE PHYSICAL AND LOGICAL STRUCTURE OF ACTIVE DIRECTORY

We will take a closer look at the elements that make up Active Directory in Chapter 2. Before you start on your journey, however, let's briefly describe some of the terms you will see, and let's explain conceptually how Active Directory works.

Active Directory is a database, pure and simple. Databases are stored in rows and columns, and Active Directory is no different. In fact, Active Directory is a single (albeit very large) table. This table resides in a single file that is essentially copied to all domain controllers. Once the database is copied, only changes are sent from domain controller to domain controller (this is a process known as **replication**).

Each row of data in the Active Directory database describes a resource on the network. In Active Directory terms, the many different types of resources are known as **objects**. Objects have properties, which are defined by each column in a row; they are also called **attributes**. Anyone familiar with a database application such as Microsoft Access or Microsoft SQL Server should be familiar with the concepts detailed here. This structure is illustrated in Figure 1-2.

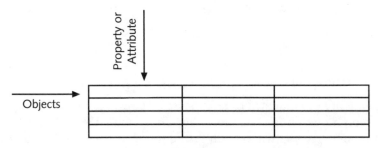

Figure 1-2 A view of Active Directory as a database table

Of course, Active Directory cannot accept just any kind of object. In fact, each object type has to be defined before it can be used. The **Active Directory Schema** defines which objects can be stored within Active Directory and which properties or attributes they can have. This schema is very flexible. Although it is not possible to completely remove the various object types that Microsoft has defined for you, it is entirely possible to define new object types. These object types are then replicated along with all other Active Directory data in the replication process.

You might also see the term **metadata** in your travels around the world of Windows 2000. In fact, in the terminology we're using here, each attribute is considered to be Active Directory metadata. Metadata is data about data. In this case, it means that the properties of an object in Active Directory describe something about that object.

Although it is convenient to alter the Active Directory Schema and add object types and attributes that you want, you should also exercise caution. Definitions can be added to Active Directory, but they can never truly be deleted—instead, they can be **deactivated**, which means they are not used but still exist within the directory data.

The Active Directory Schema is a second table that exists on every domain controller. Once again, it is a simple table of rows and columns, just like a Microsoft Excel spreadsheet or simple database file. This concept might confuse you, because all representations of Active Directory show this simple table in a hierarchical fashion. That's the case because part of the Windows 2000 OS takes what is essentially a two-dimensional representation of the data and gives it to you in the form you require.

Logical Components

How is Active Directory data organized? It is all well and good to be told that a database contains all the data about each object in your organization, but how does that help you, the system administrator, do your job?

We can answer this question by taking a look at a logical view of a Windows 2000 network. A **logical view** means that you are looking at representations, or interpretations, of the underlying data. The data itself is not changed—it is simply your view of the data that is changed.

In the following paragraphs we will give you brief descriptions of the following:

- Domains
- Groups
- Organizational Units

These descriptions are not intended to be exhaustive. However, by becoming acquainted with the concepts now, along with how they fit in with the older style Microsoft Windows NT 4 concepts, you will be well placed to move ahead to more advanced definitions and other new features of Windows 2000.

The first logical structure will be familiar to you: the *domain*. Domains really have not changed very much from previous versions of Microsoft Windows NT 4. A domain operates as a single entity and boundary for security purposes. Domain administrators have ultimate power over the domain; they can create new user accounts, printers, and groups.

Of course, Windows 2000 is bigger than a single domain—it is now an enterprise-level directory service. Although in previous versions the domain administrator could be thought of as the ultimate authority, this is no longer the case. The ultimate authority in a Windows 2000 network is an enterprise administrator, because he or she has exclusive rights over Active Directory and permissions in all domains.

 You will often see Active Directory described as both a Directory, and as a Directory Service. The context dictates the usage of these terms. When we talk about a Directory Service, we are actually talking about two different things—the storing of the data (in the Directory) and the ability to supply that data to applications (offering a Service.)

Microsoft Windows NT 4 has the concept of **groups**, and this concept has been extended into Windows 2000 with a couple of new twists. The first twist is that a fully deployed implemented Active Directory includes a new type of group: the Universal group. It is used to assign permissions throughout an enterprise. The second twist is the addition of another level of organization: an Organizational Unit (OU).

You cannot assign access permissions to members of an OU simply through their membership, because OUs don't have security tokens. However, OUs serve as a way to organize resources and to apply Group Policy to them. Group Policy is covered in detail in Chapter 10; it forms a foundation for much of what you will do on your network.

As you can see, these basic concepts are based on what you are used to, with some new twists and turns that give you more flexibility and control. Many more new terms and definitions will be necessary for you to get a good understanding of Active Directory. These, along with a more detailed discussion of the elements covered in this chapter, will be presented in Chapter 2.

WORKING WITH ACTIVE DIRECTORY IN YOUR ENTERPRISE

Having a new directory service in place is one thing, but what exactly does it do for you? It is useful to know how to define Active Directory and to see some of the ways it can help you maintain and administer your network—but you may wonder what other day-to-day tasks will be affected by enabling Active Directory on your network.

That is the topic of the rest of this book, and it could ultimately lead to your acceptance and use of Active Directory. Active Directory can help you directly with many tasks or problems, and in other, more subtle ways, it can aid you in getting your job done. This section will briefly outline the ways Windows 2000 and this book can help you. Each option will be illustrated in far greater detail in later chapters. This section simply aims to define highlights of both Windows 2000 and the new features you will want to implement.

Working with DNS

One of the first things you will need to consider is the impact of the adoption of the aforementioned standards. Microsoft Windows NT 4 relied heavily upon NetBIOS for both name resolution and naming standards. Windows 2000 has now moved toward using the industry standards of DNS. What's more, an increasing number of organizations have moved some of the name resolution work to the Internet.

The Internet also uses DNS as its name-resolution scheme. As a result, you will have to be careful how you name your Windows 2000 domains. It's important to be aware of the possible consequences of naming your domains in such a way that they conflict with someone who already has an Internet presence.

You may deliberately decide to share an Internet name, or you may have an Internet presence and want to keep Windows 2000 as a separate entity (by choosing a different name). Whichever route you choose, careful planning will be key to your success. Don't forget, Internet names are regulated and must be registered. If your Windows 2000 network will be connected to the Internet, you cannot use a domain name that already exists or that has already been registered.

DNS is a complex system—it is at the very heart of the Internet, and it alone allows you to find all the Web sites you are familiar with. There has never been a better time to get acquainted with the details of DNS than now. Windows 2000 does not function without it, and you will not be able to implement Active Directory without a good understanding of all its components. Your clients will perform name resolution all the time—they will be searching for network services and resources, and this process is taken care of by DNS. You will have to scale DNS servers in your enterprise and be aware of methods you can use to place DNS servers in remote locations to handle the load and avoid slow network bandwidths.

The Installation Process

Given the nature of Active Directory, it is not likely that you will be lucky enough to simply install it throughout your enterprise in one swoop. Not only would it be complex to do so, but you probably already have a network infrastructure in place.

Moving from a Microsoft Windows NT 4 system to a Windows 2000 system is not too complicated. However, adding Active Directory involves more than simply installing the core OS. In fact, as you will see in Chapter 5, there is no way to install Active Directory along with the core OS. The step to install Active Directory is performed afterward. This flexibility allows you both to promote systems to operate as domain controllers in your organization, and also to demote them back to plain old servers (something sorely missing in previous Windows NT versions).

It should also be noted that not all Active Directory installations are created equally. When you're moving an older domain into the new style with Active Directory, you have two different levels of functionality, also known as **modes**. The first is known as **mixed mode**; essentially, it means you have older OSs operating on your new Windows 2000 network. Once you have fully upgraded, you can move to **native mode**. You should know about some significant differences as you move from one mode to the other; these will be covered in Chapter 5.

New Overhead

The additional functionality of a Windows 2000 implementation with Active Directory does not come without some overhead. Most of that overhead is in the increased knowledge you must have on the inner workings of Active Directory. For instance, in previous versions, you really don't care much about how data is copied from the PDC to the BDC. The process is largely automatic, with few configurable options. In Windows 2000, this process has changed. You will need to gather data on your TCP/IP network and get accurate data on the amount of network bandwidth available to you. Designing a Windows 2000 network suddenly became more complex—but, fortunately, the rewards are greater.

Delegating Tasks

Of course, where would we be without our user community? Once you have Windows in place and working, you will find that most of the everyday tasks are much the same as you have experienced previously: They include adding users, creating groups, and assigning permissions to network resources. We will take a look at these processes in detail later. With the new delegation-of-authority options, however, you will be able to assign people permission to perform some of the most common functions. We'll show you how to do this in Chapter 7 and tell you why it is a good idea to take advantage of this feature (believe me, you'll be busy enough).

Active Directory Maintenance

It should come as no surprise to find that Active Directory itself will need some maintaining. We're not talking about the users and groups—we mean the underlying files that allow it to work. Because Active Directory is a database, that database must be backed up and restored in the event of failure. Because every domain controller is a peer, a lot can change between the time a domain controller goes offline and the time it is once again made functional. You must be aware of how Active Directory deals with such circumstances, and how you can both maintain and optimize Active Directory in your environment.

Group Policy

We have not spoken much about Group Policy in this chapter. This is not because it isn't going to be significant in your enterprise—actually, quite the opposite is true. Group Policy is a huge part of what will make Windows 2000 a significant upgrade for your organization. It is so important that this book includes no fewer than three chapters (Chapters 10, 11, and 12) that discuss both the core functionality of this feature as well as two specific areas in which it can be of help.

Group Policy builds upon the functionality of Active Directory to make Windows 2000 a more controlled and manageable environment. It enables much of the TCO savings that we talked about earlier. These features include setting security at clients and servers along with software distribution. Group Policy uses the Active Directory database along with the logical elements of a Windows 2000 network as outlined earlier. This fact should help reinforce in your mind just how important the planning aspects of your Windows 2000 rollout will be. Without a solid foundation, you cannot successfully implement these features.

Replication and Security Templates

You should also know about two other areas of interest. The first is the method Active Directory uses to replicate all this enterprise data from one point to another. Microsoft has the responsibility not only of making sure that all changes are available at all times, no matter where you are on the network, but also of ensuring that the replication of this data does not overwhelm slow links or the servers themselves. We will walk you through the replication process in some detail in Chapter 14. Once you have an understanding of how it works, you should be able to follow replication throughout your organization and design an infrastructure that can support the amount of data that must be replicated.

Finally, you must know how to secure your network through security templates and Group Policy. **Security templates**, discussed in Chapter 15, are merely predefined groupings of settings that can be applied to all machines that are grouped in a logical way (through domains or OUs, for instance). By applying security policies this way, you can ensure that they are applied consistently and that all Windows 2000 systems are treated equally.

CHAPTER SUMMARY

- In this chapter, we looked at some of the new features offered in Windows 2000. We also introduced some of the concepts that will be discussed in the rest of this book. We began by examining Microsoft's main Windows 2000 design goals. Microsoft has stated that its goals are increased stability, scalability, security, reduced TCO, and adherence to industry standards.

- We also defined the different versions of Windows 2000 that are currently available, describing how each compares to previous versions of Microsoft Windows NT 4

1

and providing information to help you decide which version is right for your organization. We saw that four versions currently exist: Windows 2000 Professional, Windows 2000 Server, Windows 2000 Advanced Server, and Windows 2000 Datacenter Server.

❏ Windows 2000 Professional is the heir to the Microsoft Windows NT 4 Professional throne. It can also replace Windows 9.*x* in corporate environments. Windows 2000 Server replaces Microsoft Windows NT 4 Server and can act as a file and print server for small to medium-sized organizations. Windows 2000 Advanced Server includes additional functionality, such as clustering and load balancing. It is intended for large organizations. Datacenter Server is intended for large database applications, such as data warehousing. Microsoft has added scalability functionality to the Advanced Server and Datacenter Server products, including support for more RAM and CPUs.

❏ We then looked at some of the new features introduced in Windows 2000. The list was not intended to be complete—rather, it attempted to show some of the ways in which Windows 2000 can improve the workload of a system administrator. These features include Active Directory, disk quotas, EFS, and Group Policy. They combine to make Windows 2000 far more useful than older versions of Windows NT in your enterprise.

❏ We then defined the term **directory services**. We explained that a directory service—and therefore the Active Directory component of Windows 2000—is simply a database containing information about the resources available in your enterprise. You learned that similar to a telephone directory, every user, computer, and group (among other things) has an entry in the Active Directory database. We explained that these different types of information are known as **objects**.

❏ Each object in Active Directory has **attributes**. You can query Active Directory for these attributes using the administrative tools in Windows 2000 or by using LDAP or ADSI and the WSH. You learned that a common term used to describe these attributes is **metadata**; metadata is data about data.

❏ We briefly looked at the older-style directory service that shipped with Microsoft Windows NT 4, and how it fails to scale to today's multinational organizations. You learned that the old-style PDC and BDC arrangement has been replaced with a new type of domain controller. All domain controllers in a Windows 2000 network operate as though they were PDCs, which helps increase the scalability of Windows 2000.

❏ We saw that some of the most common administrative tasks, such as creating trust relationships across domains, have been virtually eliminated in Windows 2000. Trusts are automatically configured as domains are created.

❏ We then examined some of the physical and logical objects that help a Windows 2000 network function. These objects include domains, objects, attributes, groups, and OUs. These objects allow the administrator to better define and assign permissions throughout the enterprise.

❏ We next explored several topics that will be covered in more detail as you work your way through this book. These topics include DNS, installing Windows 2000 domain controllers, and the different modes (**mixed mode** and **native mode**) in which Windows 2000 must operate when older-style OSs participate on the network.

❏ We introduced the concept of Group Policy and why it will be a large part of your enterprise. We discussed several areas where it will be important, including the assignment of security settings along with software deployment.

❏ Finally, we took a brief look at some security issues and how they might be solved. We defined security templates in order to prepare you for later chapters of this book.

❏ This chapter set out to introduce you to some new terms and to prepare you for what is to come. We laid the groundwork for a good understanding of both Windows 2000 and Active Directory. We also introduced key features and functionality.

2

THE STRUCTURE OF ACTIVE DIRECTORY

After completing this chapter, you will be able to:

♦ Understand the purpose and role of sites in Active Directory

♦ Understand the purpose and role of Organizational Units within Active Directory

♦ Understand the purpose and role of containers within Active Directory

♦ Understand the purpose and role of domain trees and forests within Active Directory

♦ Understand the purpose and role of DNS and DDNS within Windows 2000

♦ Understand the logical structure of Active Directory

♦ Understand the physical structure of Active Directory

This chapter will discuss the major components of Active Directory, including sites, containers, Organizational Units, domain trees and forests, bridgehead servers, and more. The purpose of each of these components and their roles within the Active Directory structure will be covered. In addition, we will discuss both the logical and physical structure of Active Directory and the implications of these structures on the domain design.

ACTIVE DIRECTORY TERMINOLOGY

With the advent of Windows 2000, everything about Windows domains has changed. Rather than the simple domain structures of Windows NT, Windows 2000 supports the Active Directory service. The increased complexity of Active Directory naturally requires a richer vocabulary. In addition to the domains and trusts familiar to Windows NT administrators, new terms such as *sites, schema, forests,* and *containers* are included within an Active Directory structure. We'll discuss these new terms, precisely how each is used, and the implication of these new structures to the traditional Windows NT network environment. First, let us begin by defining some terms.

Domains

A **domain** is a selection of computers, user accounts, or other objects that share a common security boundary. This means that every item within a domain is controlled by the same security policies and access restrictions. The concept of a domain as the core of the networking structure was introduced in Windows NT. A Windows NT domain is a self-contained unit, and security policies do not extend beyond the borders of the domain. However, Windows 2000 has extended the concept of a domain somewhat beyond that of Windows NT.

The components of a Windows 2000 domain are as follows:

- A hierarchical structure of containers and objects (we'll define these terms shortly).

- A unique Domain Name System (DNS) domain name. As we will discuss in Chapter 4, the NetBIOS name resolution and naming conventions used in earlier Microsoft operating systems are no longer required in a native Windows 2000 environment. Instead, Windows 2000 uses DNS names exclusively for name resolution, and the DNS domain name is used as the Windows domain name.

- A security boundary that controls authentication of users, access to resources, and any trusts with surrounding domains.

A Windows 2000 domain includes every object within a domain. An **object** is anything within the network that has been defined and can be uniquely identified within the Windows 2000 hierarchy. Although this may seem to be a recursive definition, it really is not. An object can represent a wide range of items: Computers, network users, printers, shared folders, and individual files are all examples of objects. A domain is simply a collection of these objects, all of which are controlled via a central security policy. The administrator of the domain defines the security policy for the domain and the access rights relating to the objects in the domain. Each domain has its own security policy; access to resources across domains is accomplished via security relationships called **trusts**.

Domain Controllers

The rights of a particular user or group of users within a domain are determined by the security policy within that domain. Likewise, resources and the access to those resources are defined by that security policy. When a user logs in to a domain, he or she is authenticated and assigned the appropriate rights. Servers known as **domain controllers** (DCs) provide this authentication.

DCs are servers that are running Windows 2000 and on which the Active Directory service is installed. Each DC possesses a copy of the domain's security policy, lists of domain users and passwords, and the access requirements for each object within the domain. The information about the domain is stored in a database called the **data store** on each DC. The data store is contained within the file ntds.dit. The default location for this file is *%systemroot%*\NTDS, but it can be relocated during the installation of the Active Directory service.

In a homogenous Windows 2000 domain, each of the DCs acts as an equal peer and can send updated domain objects or rights to other DCs. DCs can also interoperate with earlier versions of Windows NT, such as NT 4 and NT 3.51. In these mixed-mode environments, the earlier versions of Windows NT operate as backup DCs and act as passive receivers of updates from a Windows 2000 DC. One specific Windows 2000 DC takes on the role of the Primary Domain Controller (PDC) for the downlevel operating systems (Windows NT, Windows 9*x*, and Windows 3.*x*). This *PDC emulation master* is assigned to act as the Windows NT PDC and replicates directory changes to Windows NT DCs. In addition, the PDC emulation master provides network services for network clients that cannot access Active Directory. These clients include Windows NT Server and Workstation, Windows 98 and 95, and Windows 3.*x*/DOS operating systems.

Trust Relationships

Windows NT domains are independent entities. The security policies and rights within a domain are limited to the resources within the domain. Although this structure made sense during NT's early role as a workgroup and small local area network (LAN) server, the same structure became a limiting factor as Windows NT evolved into an enterprise network operating system (NOS). Massive network environments strain the capacities of the Windows NT security database and can require multiple domains to contain all the computer accounts and user accounts.

Because the security policies within a domain are limited to that domain only, Windows NT administrators are forced to use relationships called *trusts* to enable cross-domain access to resources. Trusts allow network administrators to assign rights and resources to users that are authenticated within another domain. A trust relationship consists of two domains: a trusted domain that authenticates a user, and a trusting domain that accepts users authenticated by another domain. As shown in Figure 2-1, Domain 2 trusts the authentication of Domain 1 and will allow Domain 1 users to access resources within Domain 2.

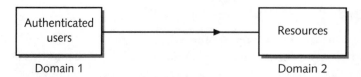

Figure 2-1   One-way trust relationship

 The actual access rights within Domain 2 are still controlled by the security policy enacted by the administrator of Domain 2.

In a traditional Windows NT trust scenario, the trusts can be either one way or two way. A one-way trust works as just described: One domain accepts (trusts) the authenticated users from a second (trusted) domain. If both domains accept each other's authenticated users, the relationship is described as a two-way trust relationship. An example of a two-way trust is shown in Figure 2-2.

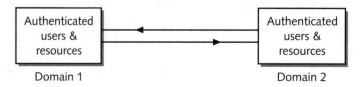

Figure 2-2   Two-way trust relationship

Trust relationships are effective in providing cross-domain resource access, but limitations with the implementation of trust relationships within NT 4 and earlier resulted in excessive administrative overhead in larger environments. The main problem with Windows NT trusts is the lack of transitive trusts. If Domain 1 trusts Domain 2, and Domain 2 trusts Domain 3, no trust relationship exists between Domain 1 and Domain 3. If Domain 3 users need access to Domain 1 resources, a separate trust relationship must be established between the domains.

As you might suspect, the trust relationships within a large network environment can easily become very complicated. Furthermore, each trust relationship requires administrative intervention at both ends to form the relationship. In some environments, adding a new domain requires that trusts be configured with every other domain within the network. Windows NT administrators developed several methods to improve the efficiency of the trusts, including the master/resource domain model and the multimaster model. Ultimately, however, these methods are merely elegant workarounds for an inherent problem.

Windows 2000 extends the capability of trusts by allowing transitive trusts. With a transitive trust, if Domain 1 trusts Domain 2, and Domain 2 trusts Domain 3, then a trust relationship automatically exists between Domain 1 and Domain 3. This relationship is illustrated in Figure 2-3. These transitive trusts eliminate much of the web of trusts required within a Windows NT environment. Furthermore, the two-way transitive trusts are created automatically when a new domain is added to a domain tree. We will discuss domain trees and the roles of trusts within those trees shortly.

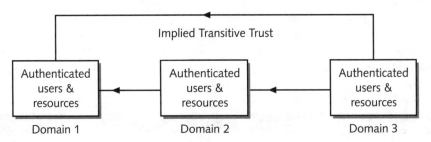

Figure 2-3　Transitive trust relationship

Namespace

Windows 2000 uses a different method of name resolution and domain organization than earlier versions of Windows NT. Rather than the NetBIOS-based name resolutions, Windows 2000 uses DNS name resolution. The DNS system is the same as that used for resolving Internet domain names to Internet Protocol (IP) addresses; most people will recognize www.microsoft.com as an example of a DNS-resolvable name.

DNS is a hierarchical naming system, with the names becoming more specific to the left and more general towards the right. Let us examine a DNS name in more detail first, and then look at the implications for the Windows 2000 domain structure.

We'll use a hypothetical company for our study. Texas Pinball and Cattle Company sells and services pinball machines to homes and businesses. As do most businesses these days, the company has a Web site and e-mail connectivity. Traditionally, the company has used a Windows NT domain named Corporate for its internal network, and its main file servers are known as Flipper and Bumper. See Figure 2-4 for the structure of the network.

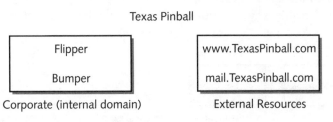

Figure 2-4　Texas Pinball (traditional NT structure)

Texas Pinball has two Internet-accessible resources: the Web site at www.TexasPinball.com and the mail server at mail.TexasPinball.com. The DNS system translates these names into IP addresses that remote computers use to connect to the servers. Taking the names from right to left, the .com represents a top-level domain (TLD). Top-level domains are used to distinguish the type of organization represented by the domain. The traditional uses of TLDs are listed in Table 2-1. Over the past few years, the traditional demarcation between the .com, .net, and .org addresses has faded as the number of .com addresses has increased. Many organizations now register .net and .org names for a variety of reasons, such as protecting their .com address from similar names, a lack of desirable names in the .com namespace, and duplicate organization names.

Table 2-1   Top-level domain uses

Type	Meaning
.com	Commercial entities
.net	Internet infrastructure services
.org	Nonprofit organizations
.edu	Universities, colleges, and other educational institutions
.mil	United States military
.gov	United States government

 In addition to the TLDs listed in Table 2-1, each country has been assigned a country code that also functions as a TLD. Although use of a country code is rare within the United States, organizations within other countries use country codes regularly. An example of this is www.microsoft.co.uk.

The next section of the domain name is TexasPinball. This portion is commonly known as the second-level domain name, and it is indicative of the company or organization. Everything to the left of the second-level domain name is under the control of the organization that owns that domain name, including servers and subdomains. If the name to the left of the domain name is a server, then it is referred to as a **hostname**. If the name to the left of the domain name refers to another collection of computers, it is considered a **subdomain**. Figure 2-5 shows the relationship between the levels of a domain name.

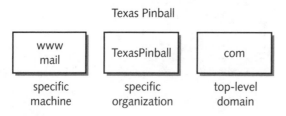

Figure 2-5   A diagram of DNS space

As we mentioned earlier, a company or organization controls the naming within its second-level domain name. Every host and subdomain within the domain name is considered part of the domain's **namespace**.

To bring this discussion back to our example, Texas Pinball and Cattle Company controls the namespace that is associated with the TexasPinball.com domain. With the traditional NT domain structure and the NetBIOS naming associated with it, no direct relationship exists between NT domain names and DNS domain names. Therefore, Texas Pinball and Cattle Company has only two objects within its namespace: www.TexasPinball.com and mail.TexasPinball.com. The servers and workstations within the Corporate domain are not considered part of the TexasPinball.com namespace.

With Windows 2000, DNS is now the primary method of name resolution; as a result, Windows domains now map much closer to DNS domains. Let's take a look at how our example company might look with Windows 2000.

Texas Pinball and Cattle Company can use its existing DNS domain name for internal use, or the company can choose to use a separate DNS domain for its internal network. For now, we will assume that the company will use its existing TexasPinball.com domain for both the internal and external network.

Remember that both subdomains and hosts are part of the namespace controlled by a company. As a result, it is possible to design a domain structure that incorporates both the internal network and the externally accessible resources within the same DNS domain. In the example shown in Figure 2-6, the internal network is designated by the Corporate.TexasPinball.com subdomain. The two fileservers mentioned earlier are named Flipper.Corporate.TexasPinball.com and Bumper.Corporate.TexasPinball.com.

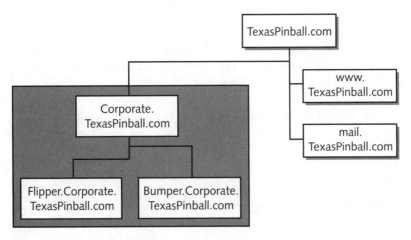

Figure 2-6 Windows 2000 namespace

Dynamic DNS

With the move from NetBIOS naming to DNS naming, a significant change has occurred in the way clients interact with the name servers. With previous versions of Windows NT, client operating systems register themselves with a Windows Internet Naming Service (WINS) server that maintains a database of NetBIOS names and IP addresses. WINS clients automatically reregister themselves whenever the IP address changes.

On the other hand, computers running the Windows 2000 operating system can register themselves with a server running the DNS service. The ability of a client to register itself into a DNS host table as it joins the network environment is a hallmark of the Dynamic DNS (DDNS) system. In addition, if the IP address of a computer changes, the computer can automatically register the change with the DNS server.

In a homogenous Windows 2000 environment, DDNS replaces the WINS services required in earlier Windows NT environments. If the network includes downlevel operating systems such as Windows NT, Windows 95 or 98, or Windows 3.*x*, a WINS server is still required for name resolution.

Domain Trees

The use of DNS namespace and the Active Directory structure require us to rethink the traditional use and structures of Windows domains. Remember that Windows 2000 will automatically form two-way transitive trusts between domains if they have the same DNS root (i.e., Corporate.TexasPinball.com and Sales.TexasPinball.com). Remember also that the use of DNS for naming within Windows 2000 allows the use of hierarchical domain names, such as Home.Sales.TexasPinball.com.

The combination of these two elements creates domain trees. A **domain tree** is a group of Windows 2000 domains that share the same namespace, a common schema, and a Global Catalog. (We will discuss the schema and Global Catalog later in this chapter.) In addition, the domains within a domain tree will usually share an automatic transitive trust with other domains within the tree. The result is that permissions and rights flow down throughout the tree and allow for administrative control throughout the domain. Figure 2-7 shows the relationships and structure within a domain tree.

The elements of a domain tree are as follows:

- The domains share a common namespace. Usually, the domain tree consists of parent and child domains.

- All domains share a common schema.

- All domains share a common Global Catalog.

- Implicit two-way transitive trusts exist between domains.

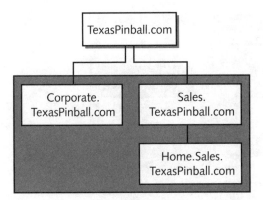

Figure 2-7   Windows 2000 domain tree

Domain Forests

Just as a normal forest is a collection of trees, so too is a **domain forest** a collection of domain trees. Recall that a domain tree is a collection of domains that share a common schema, Global Catalog, and namespace. However, if the domains do not share a common namespace, but they still share a common schema and Global Catalog, they are considered part of a domain forest. All domains within a domain forest share implicit two-way transitive trusts with the other domains within the forest.

The elements of a domain forest are as follows:

- The domains have a noncontiguous namespace and differing name structure.

- All domains share a common schema.

- All domains share a common Global Catalog.

- Domains operate independently, but cross-domain communication is enabled by the forest.

- Implicit two-way transitive trusts exist between domains and domain trees.

Domain forests often arise in situations where companies have different internal and external domain names, or in cases where mergers, acquisitions, or other elements have resulted in multiple root domains within an organization. As an example, let us imagine that Texas Pinball and Cattle Company decides to acquire an Internet-based pinball service dispatching company. The pinball service company is called Pinball.nu ("We make your Pinball like NU"), and naturally it uses the Pinball.nu namespace. Rather than force a migration to the TexasPinball.com namespace, the network administrators instead choose to form a Windows 2000 domain tree that includes both the TexasPinball.com domain and the Pinball.nu domain, as shown in Figure 2-8. Once the domains are associated within a tree, the resources of all the domains are accessible by the users of the two organizations.

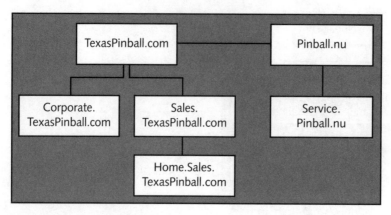

Figure 2-8   Domain forest

ACTIVE DIRECTORY COMPONENTS

The Active Directory service allows administrators to create a network structure that matches the needs of the organization. You do so by defining objects and their related attributes within a directory structure. The directory and all its components are replicated to all the DCs within the domain. Each DC stores a copy of the directory and the security policy of the domain, and metes out access as defined by the security policies.

Active Directory Objects

Within Active Directory parlance, an **object** is simply a defined element within the directory. Each object refers to a specific, distinctive, named network resource. Each resource is defined by a set of attributes that are characteristic for that resource, such as computer names or user passwords.

Almost everything within Active Directory is considered an object. User accounts, computer accounts, printers, shares, servers, containers, and the like can all be viewed as objects within the Active Directory tree. Many types of objects are predefined, such as user accounts and computer accounts.

Objects can be collected and organized within the directory. Logical groupings of similar objects are considered **classes**. Some objects can contain other objects, and are naturally known as **containers**. One example of a container object is the domain, which contains user accounts, servers, computers, and other objects.

Active Directory Schema

Recall from when we were discussing domain trees and forests that one of the defining elements of a forest or tree was a common schema. The **schema** is simply a definition of the types of objects allowed within a directory and the attributes associated with those objects. As you can see, these definitions must be consistent across domains in order for the security policies and access rights to function correctly.

Two types of definitions exist within the schema: **attributes** and **classes**, also known as **schema objects** and **metadata**. Attributes are defined only once, and then can be applied to multiple classes as needed. The object classes, or metadata, describe which attributes are used to define objects. As an example, the Users class requires certain attributes such as user name, password, groups, and so on. A particular user account is simply an object that has those attributes defined.

As shown in Figure 2-9, a class is simply a generic framework for particular objects. That framework is generated by a collection of attributes, such as Logon Name and Home Directory for users, or Description and Network Address for computers. Windows 2000 ships with a predefined set of attributes and classes that fit the needs of many network environments. In addition, you can expand the schema by defining additional attributes and extending the classes within the directory.

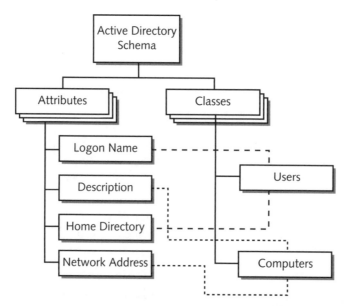

Figure 2-9 The relationship between attributes and classes within a schema

Extending a schema by developing additional attributes and classes is an advanced function that should be performed only after careful planning. Remember that the changes are automatically replicated within the directory, and that a schema cannot be deleted.

Organizational Unit

One of the enhancements within Active Directory is the ability to organize your network in a logical manner and hide the physical structure of the network from the end users. Active Directory uses a special container known as an **Organizational Unit** (OU) to organize objects within a domain in administrative groups. These OUs can be used to divide a domain into groups that mirror the functional or physical separations within the company. OUs are limited to a single domain; each domain can implement its own OU hierarchy, as illustrated in Figure 2-10.

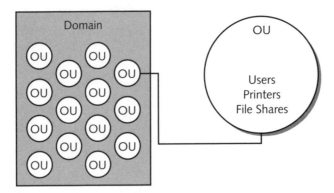

Figure 2-10   Organizational Units within a domain

An OU can contain user accounts, computers, printers, file shares, applications, and any other objects within the domain. OUs can be used to separate administrative functions within a domain without granting administrative rights to the whole domain.

An OU is the smallest element to which you can assign administrative rights. Therefore, OUs can be used to delegate authority and control within a domain; in essence, OUs allow the functionality of subdomains without your actually having to create additional domains.

Global Catalog

Domain controllers keep a complete copy of the Active Directory database for a domain, so that information about each object in the domain is readily available to the users and services. This arrangement works well for the local domain, but what about information about other domains and the objects within those other domains? Remember, one of the design goals for Windows 2000 was a unified logon, no matter where a user was located within the domain tree. Obviously, for such a unified logon to work, the local DCs must have some information about the other domains within the tree and forest. However, replicating all the information about all the objects in all the domains within a forest is simply not feasible.

Windows 2000 solves this issue through the use of a special limited database known as the **Global Catalog**. The Global Catalog stores partial replicas of the directories of other domains. The catalog is stored on DCs that have been designated as Global Catalog Servers. These servers also maintain the normal database for their domain.

Function of the Global Catalog

The Global Catalog has two primary functions within Active Directory. These functions relate to the logon capability and the queries within Active Directory. We will next examine each function in detail.

Within a native-mode multidomain environment, the Global Catalog is required for logging on to the network. The Global Catalog provides universal group membership information for the account that is attempting to log on to the network. If the Global Catalog is not available during the logon attempt, and the user account is external to the local domain, the user will only be allowed to log on to the local machine.

Obviously, if the account is part of the local domain, the DCs for the local domain will handle the authentication request. The Global Catalog is required only when a user account or object needs to be authenticated by another domain.

Queries make up the majority of Active Directory traffic, and queries for objects (such as printers and services) occur much more often than database updates. Within a simple single-domain environment, the directory is readily available for these queries. However, imagine for a moment a highly complex multidomain environment. It doesn't make sense to require every query to search through each domain.

The Global Catalog maintains a subset of the directory information available within every domain in the forest. This arrangement allows queries to be handled by the nearest Global Catalog, and thus saves time and bandwidth. If more than one DC is a Global Catalog Server, the response time for the queries improves. Unfortunately, each additional Global Catalog Server increases the amount of replication overhead within the network.

 The Global Catalog is a read-only database, unlike the normal directory database.

Global Catalog Servers

Windows 2000 automatically creates a Global Catalog on the first domain controller within a forest. Each forest does require at least one Global Catalog. In an environment with multiple sites, it is good practice to designate a DC in each site to function as a Global Catalog Server. Remember, native-mode Windows 2000 domains require a Global Catalog to allow users to complete the authentication process and log in to the network. A mixed-mode domain does not require a Global Catalog server.

If you need additional Global Catalog Servers, you can add the service to any DC within the forest. You do so through the AD Sites and Services snap-in. The Global Catalog can also be moved off the initial DC if additional DCs are available.

Although any and all DCs can be configured as Global Catalog Servers, a sense of balance is necessary when designating these servers. As the number of Global Catalog Servers increases, the response time to user inquiries decreases. However, the replication requirements within the environment increase as the number of Global Catalog Servers increases.

Operation Masters

Much of the replication within an Active Directory environment is multi-master replication, which means that the DCs are all peers. This is in contrast to earlier versions of Windows NT, in which a Master DC is responsible for recording all changes to the security policy and replicating those changes to the backup DCs.

Several types of operations are impractical for a multi-master environment, however. Windows 2000 handles these operations by allowing only a single DC to make these types of changes. This DC is known as an **operations master**. Actually, five different operation master roles can be assigned to DCs: schema master, domain naming master, relative ID master, PDC emulator, and infrastructure master. Each of these roles will be discussed in detail later in this chapter.

By default, Windows 2000 assigns all five of these operations master roles to the first DC installed in a forest. In a small network environment, these roles may very well stay with that first DC. As the network environment gets larger, some of the roles will need to be reassigned to other DCs. Two of the operations master roles must appear in each domain forest, and the remaining three must appear in each domain.

The two operations master roles assigned on a forestwide basis are the schema master and the domain naming master. Only one of each of these operation masters can exist within a forest. The schema master controls all the updates and modifications to the schema itself. As you will recall, the schema controls the definition of each object in the directory and its associated attributes. The domain naming master controls the addition of domains to or removal of domains from the forest.

The three operations master roles assigned for each domain are the relative ID master, the PDC emulator, and the infrastructure master. Each domain within a forest must have one of these masters.

The relative ID (RID) master controls the sequence number for the DCs within the domain. The master assigns a unique sequence of RIDs to each of the DCs. When a new object is created by a DC, the object is assigned a security ID (SID). The SID must be unique within the domain. The SID is generated by combining a domain security ID and a relative ID. The domain security ID is a constant ID within the domain, whereas the relative ID is assigned to the object by the DC. When the DC uses all the RIDs that the RID master has assigned, the DC receives another sequence of RIDs from the RID master.

The PDC emulator is used whenever a domain contains non–Windows 2000 computers. It acts as a Windows NT PDC for downlevel clients and for Windows NT backup DCs. The PDC emulator processes password changes and receives preferential treatment within the domain for password updates. This preferential treatment continues even if the domain is operating in native mode. If another DC is unable to authenticate a user due to a bad password, the request is forwarded to the PDC emulator.

The infrastructure master is responsible for maintaining all interdomain object references. It informs certain objects (such as groups) that other objects (such as users in another domain) have been moved, changed, or otherwise modified. This update is needed only in a multiple domain environment. If there is only a single domain, then all DCs already know of the update, and this role is unnecessary. Likewise, if all DCs are also Global Catalog servers, the DCs are aware of the updates and do not need the assistance of the infrastructure master.

PHYSICAL STRUCTURE OF ACTIVE DIRECTORY

The primary goal of the Active Directory service is to allow users to access resources throughout the domain structure without necessarily knowing precisely where those resources are located. Active Directory hides the physical structure of the network from the end user and shows instead a logical topology that focuses more on the resources than their location. Within this section, however, we will focus on the physical structure of a Windows 2000 network and its related elements: sites, bridgehead servers, DCs, and site links.

Sites

The core concept of the physical structure of a Windows 2000 domain is the site. A **site** is a collection of computers connected via a high-speed network. Typically, the computers within a site are connected via LAN-style technology, and are considered to be well-connected. **Well-connected** generally means constant high-speed connectivity within an IP subnet, although a site can include multiple subnets.

It is important to understand that sites and domains do not have a direct relationship. Domains map the logical structure of your organization, whereas sites relate to the physical layout of the network. The domain namespace is likewise unrelated to the physical sites, although many times administrators will choose to align the namespace and the physical sites during the planning phase of a Windows 2000 rollout or migration.

A site can contain multiple domains; likewise, a domain can cross several sites. In most cases, sites will mirror the actual physical layout of the network, with a site at each of the major business locations of a company. If a company is using a single-domain structure, then that domain will cross the sites as shown in Figure 2-11.

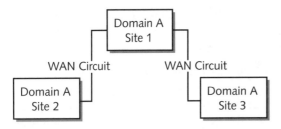

Figure 2-11   A single domain across multiple sites

Because of the separation of the physical and logical structure, a site can also support multiple domains. In Figure 2-12, Site 1 has computers in both Domain A and Domain B.

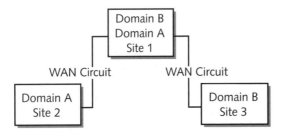

Figure 2-12   Multiple domains across multiple sites

Why Use Sites?

If you are a network administrator who has supported wide area network (WAN)-connected Windows NT domains, you may wonder about the purpose of defined sites within Windows 2000. After all, the use of remote networks, backup DCs, and WAN circuits certainly is nothing new, nor is the concept of multiple domains at a particular location. The problem with the older Windows NT network lies in the replication of security information between the DCs. Whenever changes occur to the security policy within a domain—such as new user accounts, new groups, or even group membership changes—the entire Security Accounts Manager (SAM) database must be replicated across the WAN link. In large or active network environments, this replication can consume a majority of the bandwidth between locations.

Windows 2000 corrects this issue by replicating data between DCs differently depending on the relationship between the DCs. Within a site, the primary goal of replication is to keep the DCs updated with as little latency as possible. Between sites, the replicated data is compressed and sent periodically. The compression helps save bandwidth, but does require more processing overhead on the part of the DCs.

The primary function of a site is to consolidate directory service requests within a high-speed connection area and to control replication with external DCs. Sites provide the following benefits:

- Directory services are provided by the closest DC, if one is located within the site.

- Latency is minimized for replication within a site.

- Bandwidth utilization for replication is minimized between sites.

- Replication can be scheduled between sites to better suit network utilization.

Sites and Domain Controllers

A domain controller is automatically placed within a site during the server promotion process. DCPromo checks for the defined sites during the promotion process; if the server's IP address falls within the range of a defined subset, the server is automatically placed within the site associated with that subnet.

If no subnets are associated with site objects, the server is placed in the default site, which is named Default-First-Site. If the IP address of the server does not fall within a range that is defined, the server is placed in the Default-First-Site. Sites are automatically assigned only during the initial promotion; if a DC configuration or physical location changes significantly, the DC must also be moved to another site via the AD Sites and Services snap-in.

Multihomed servers can belong to only a single site. When a multihomed server is promoted, DCPromo selects the site at random from the ones that the server matches. If you do not agree with the selection, you can move the DC to another site via the AD Sites and Services snap-in.

Creating a Site

Sites are created via the AD Sites and Services snap-in, shown in Figure 2-13. Windows 2000 creates the first site automatically when Active Directory is installed. This site is named Default-First-Site, and it includes all the DCs. Additional sites must be created manually. To create a site, open the snap-in, and then open the context menu of the Sites folder. Select the New Site option to create a new site.

The New Object–Site screen, shown in Figure 2-14, allows you to enter the name of the remote site and to select the site link for the site. Windows 2000 creates a default site link called DEFAULTIPSITELINK that you can use to establish the replication process of the Active Directory service. This default site link uses remote procedure calls (RPC) over TCP/IP and will use any available route to the remote site for replication. If explicit site links have been previously defined, those site links will show up in the lower portion of the New Object–Site screen.

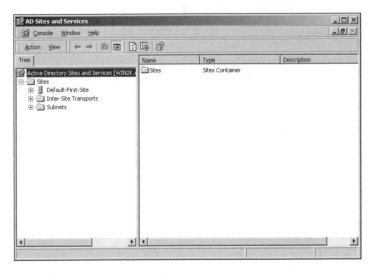

Figure 2-13   AD Sites and Services snap-in

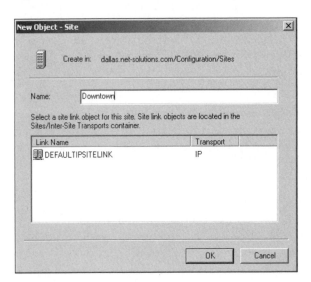

Figure 2-14   Creating a new site

Once the site is defined, you must undertake several other steps before the site can be activated within the Active Directory structure. These steps are nicely delineated in the dialog box that follows the creation of a new site, as shown in Figure 2-15. To finish configuring a site, you must do the following:

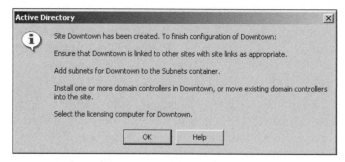

Figure 2-15   Required configuration steps for a new site

- Add appropriate IP subnets to the site.

- Install or move a DC or DCs into the site. Although a DC is not required for a site, it is strongly recommended.

- Connect the site to other sites with the appropriate site link.

- Select a server to control and monitor licensing within the site.

Once you've completed these steps, the site is then added to the Active Directory structure and the replication is automatically configured by Windows 2000.

Site Links

A site is a subnet or selection of subnets that are connected via a high-speed connection. The sites themselves are connected via site links. **Site links** are low bandwidth or unreliable/occasional connections between sites. In general, any connection between locations slower than LAN speeds is considered a site link. WAN links (such as frame relay connections) are examples of site links, as are high-speed links that are saturated and have a low effective bandwidth.

Site links are not automatically generated by Windows 2000. Instead, you create the site links through the AD Sites and Services snap-in. The site links are the core of Active Directory replication. The links can be adjusted for replication availability, bandwidth costs, and replication frequency. Windows 2000 uses this information to generate the replication topology for the sites, including the schedule for replication.

Windows 2000 DCs represent the inbound replication through a special object known as a **connection object**. Active Directory uses site links as indicators for where it should create connection objects, and connection objects use the physical network connections to replicate directory information. Each DC creates its own connection objects for replication within a site (**intrasite replication**). For replication between sites (**intersite replication**), one DC within each site is responsible for evaluating the replication topology. The DC creates the connection objects appropriate to that topology. The server that is responsible for evaluating and creating the topology for intersite replication is known as the Inter-Site Topology Generator (ISTG).

Site links, like trusts, are transitive. This means that DCs in one site can replicate with DCs in any other site within the enterprise through these transitive links. In addition, explicit links can be created to enable specific replication paths between sites.

Creating a Site Link

Windows 2000 creates a default site link named, naturally enough, DEFAULTIP-SITELINK. This site link can be used to connect sites in simple network environments, but in more complicated enterprise environments, you should establish explicit site links.

To create a site link, first open the AD Sites and Services snap-in, as indicated in Figure 2-16. Open the Inter-Site Transports folder and then right-click on the appropriate transport protocol. Select New Site Link from the context menu to form a new link.

In our example, the name of the new site link is Uptown Frame Link. Although the name of the link is arbitrary, good administrative practice dictates the name should be something that identifies the link, the connected sites, and the type of link. Of course, the link could be named Bob, but that name would tend to confuse successors and co-workers.

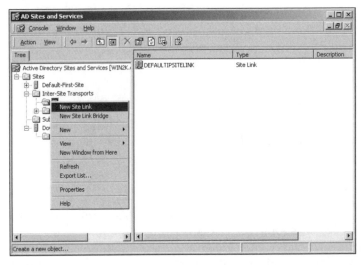

Figure 2-16   Creating a new site link

The next step is to select the linked sites from the left column in the New Object–Site Link dialog box. Click on Add to associate them with the link, as shown in Figure 2-17. A link must contain at least two sites; in general, a link will connect only two sites. If multiple sites exist at one physical location or are connected via a particular network path, however, then those sites could all share a single site link.

Figure 2-17 Naming the site link and associating the sites

Each site link has four properties that are important, as well as an optional descriptor. The properties are:

- *Name:* A name that uniquely identifies the site link. As discussed earlier, this name should clearly indicate the sites being linked and the speed/type of circuit.

- *Cost:* The relative speed of the link in relation to the other links within the topology. The cost has nothing to do with the actual monetary cost of the bandwidth. Links with a lower cost are faster, whereas links with higher costs are slower. The cost defaults to 100 on a new circuit.

- *Transport:* Indicates the type of transport used to replicate the directory information between the DCs. There are two options: synchronous RPC over a routed TCP/IP connection, and an asynchronous Simple Mail Transfer Protocol (SMTP) connection over the underlying mail transport network. This property is not set within the link properties, but is instead determined when the site link is first created.

- *Schedule:* Determines when the directory information is replicated between sites. This is determined by two elements: the replication frequency and the available times. The replication frequency is adjusted within the properties of the site link, as shown in Figure 2-18. The schedule is a listing of times that the site link is available to pass replication data. This schedule is adjusted through the Change Schedule option within the site link properties.

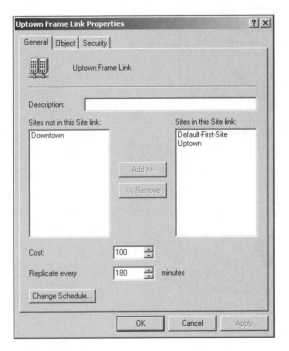

Figure 2-18 Site link properties

Bridgehead Servers

The replication topology between and among sites is generated automatically by Windows 2000. This topology is generated via a service known as the Knowledge Consistency Checker (KCC). The KCC service tries to establish at least two inbound replication connections to every DC; therefore, if a server becomes unavailable or uncommunicative, replication can still occur.

Within a site, all DCs are treated equally, but replication between sites is another matter. Windows 2000 prefers to funnel intersite replication to only a single DC. These preferred servers are known as **bridgehead servers**. The replicated data is first sent to the bridgehead server of a site, and is then replicated from that bridgehead server to the other DCs within the site.

 If the preferred bridgehead server is unavailable, Active Directory will use an alternate replication path.

CHAPTER SUMMARY

- Active Directory brings a whole new element to Windows domain functionality, and also brings with it new terminology and concepts. The core concept of Active Directory is that everything within the network environment is defined as an **object**. The directory is simply that—a database that stores the object, information about the object, and that object's relationship to the other objects. The types of objects that are allowed in the directory are defined by the schema. Windows 2000 automatically installs a default schema, but you can make modifications to those default definitions if desired.

- The basic unit of Windows networking through the years has been the **domain**. A domain is simply a collection of computers, users, and other objects that share a common security boundary and policy. The traditional Windows NT domain is a standalone entity. If users require access to resources within another domain, a special connection must be created between the domains. These special connections are known as **trusts**. Windows 2000 treats domains somewhat differently: An underlying relationship exists between Windows 2000 domains that share a common schema.

- Windows 2000 domains that share a common schema, namespace, and Global Catalog share **transitive two-way trusts**. These transitive trusts form a structure known as a **domain tree**. If a combination of domains share a Global Catalog and common schema, but occupy a different namespace, then the structure is actually a collection of domain trees. This structure is known as a **domain forest**.

- Each domain requires at least one domain controller. The DCs within a domain contain the Active Directory database and use that database to authenticate users, services, and computers. DCs record changes to the database and replicate these changes to the other DCs. Every DC has the ability to pass changes to other DCs. This process is known as **multi-master replication**.

- One of the design requirements for Windows 2000 was the ability to log in throughout the domain tree. Obviously, this requirement means that the DCs for one domain need to know which users, computers, and other objects are defined in the other domains. However, replication of all directory information in all domains throughout a domain tree or forest would be cumbersome and very bandwidth intensive. Windows 2000 resolves this issue through the use of Global Catalog Servers. Global Catalog Servers are DCs that contain a subset of information from other domains in a domain forest. The subset contains the most commonly used objects and greatly speeds both searches within the domain forest and logon services.

- Despite the use of multi-master replication, several functions of Active Directory replication need to be controlled from a single point. These functions are handled by specially designated DCs known as **operations masters**. Operations masters handle five functions: the schema master, domain naming master, relative ID master, primary DC emulator, and infrastructure master. Windows 2000 assigns each of these roles to the first DC installed in a domain forest, but the roles can be adjusted as desired by the administrator.

❑ Windows 2000 handles replication over a WAN very differently from earlier versions of Windows NT. Windows 2000 groups well-connected computers into sites. A **site** is an area of high-speed connectivity. Sites are linked by slower links, usually WAN links. Sites are associated with a particular subnet or subnets, and usually include a DC. Replication within a site is optimized to prevent latency; replication between sites is optimized to conserve bandwidth. The timing of the replication can be adjusted to take advantage of periods of lower network utilization.

❑ Replication topology between and among sites is controlled by the Knowledge Consistency Checker (KCC). The KCC attempts to connect each DC to two other DCs for replication purposes. The KCC runs every 15 minutes to verify connectivity and to adjust the replication structure as needed. Intersite replication is handled via preferred DCs that replicate between sites and then pass the replicated data to the DCs within the sites.

❑ One important thing to recall is that no direct relationship exists between sites and domains. A site can encompass multiple domains, and a domain can encompass multiple sites.

3

PLANNING AN ACTIVE DIRECTORY IMPLEMENTATION

After completing this chapter, you will be able to:

♦ Choose an appropriate organizational model within Active Directory

♦ Plan the DNS namespace for the Active Directory enterprise

♦ Understand the use of sites and site boundaries within Active Directory

♦ Design for flexibility of organizational or geographic changes

♦ Understand the use of Organizational Units within Active Directory

♦ Design an appropriate infrastructure for the Active Directory enterprise

Planning has always been a large part of any network design. It is particularly crucial for you to understand the business needs driving the creation of the network and the capabilities of the technology that is implemented. It seems simplistic to state that "planning is the first job," but too often network systems are built in a haphazard manner. Windows NT seems particularly vulnerable to "evolution networking" due to the standalone character of domains. In addition, the ease of installation and administration within Windows NT often leads to inexperienced administrators controlling the systems.

The integration of directory services with Windows 2000 places a much higher premium on planning and analysis skills. Some factors simply must be resolved before the first CD is placed in a drive—for example, DNS namespace issues, whether to implement a single domain or a multiple-domain tree, and how best to organize the company structure. We will examine some of these issues throughout the course of this chapter.

Namespace

One of the most significant issues surrounding the implementation of Active Directory is how best to implement the new namespace. Windows 2000 uses Domain Name System (DNS) as a primary method of name resolution, and the specific Windows 2000 implementation of DNS is tied directly to the directory services within Windows 2000. This use of DNS leads to two separate but intertwining issues: how best to integrate Active Directory into an existing DNS namespace, and how best to implement Windows 2000 DNS.

The specifics for installing and implementing Windows 2000 DNS are covered in Chapter 4 of this book. Our discussion in this chapter will cover planning and the impact of the various methods of namespace design.

Essentially, you have two options when it comes to planning an Active Directory implementation. The first option is to create an entirely new namespace specific to the Active Directory. The second option is to integrate Active Directory into an existing DNS namespace. Both approaches offer advantages and disadvantages, as detailed in the following sections.

New DNS Namespace

Companies often create a new DNS namespace when they have not been using DNS for internal name resolution. This is very often the case when you are upgrading a Windows NT environment, because of the use of Windows Internet Naming Service (WINS) name resolution within Windows NT networks. A new DNS namespace is also useful when you need internal and external resources to be clearly delineated. A separate namespace for internal and external resources allows a clear separation of administrative and logical structures.

 DNS namespaces must be registered with an Internet Corporation for Assigned Names and Numbers (ICANN)-approved registrar—even namespaces that you will be using for internal use only. Registration of the domain name (microsoft.com, for example) allows your company to control the namespace and prevents others from using that namespace.

 Often, companies will use different namespaces for internal and external resources. Resources available to the public (such as HTTP or FTP servers) will be part of a public namespace, whereas domain controllers (DCs) and file servers will be part of a second, private namespace. In most cases, at least two DNS servers will be involved: The DNS server that provides resolution for the external namespace either will be hosted by a connectivity provider or will be located outside a company's firewall, whereas the server for the internal DNS will be located within the firewall and maintained by the network administrators. An example of this form of configuration is shown in Figure 3-1. Usually, the second namespace is not published to the external world. The advantages of this configuration are the following:

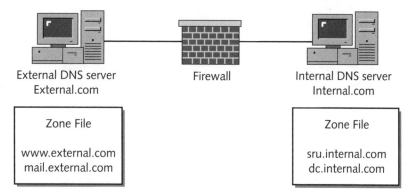

External DNS server
External.com

Firewall

Internal DNS server
Internal.com

Zone File

www.external.com
mail.external.com

Zone File

sru.internal.com
dc.internal.com

Figure 3-1   Separate DNS namespaces

- You can easily separate internal and external resources. The domain name makes it easy to differentiate between internal and external servers.

- Administration is separated for internal and external namespaces. For many businesses, the connectivity provider administers the external DNS namespace, whereas network administrators handle the internal DNS namespace.

- You can easily secure the internal resources. Firewalls, proxy servers, or other security devices can disallow external traffic bound for the internal namespace, and the internal namespace does not need to be published outside the company.

- If your company has a restrictive Internet access policy, clients can be granted access only to the internal resources through several methods: firewall filtering rules, proxy server configurations, publishing only internal DNS namespaces, or Web browser configurations.

Naturally, maintaining separate internal and external DNS namespaces has disadvantages. Most of the disadvantages are administrative issues:

- *The company must maintain seperate DNS name tables for each name space.* Although the automated features of Windows 2000 Dynamic Domain Name Service (DDNS) help alleviate that burden on the internal namespace, someone must maintain and administer both namespaces individually.

- *The company must maintain and pay for multiple domain name registrations.* Although the cost of registering and maintaining domain name registrations has fallen lately, a slight administrative cost is related to this activity.

- *Logon names will be different from Internet e-mail addresses.* This difference can be an issue if it confuses the user base. You may need to provide some user education.

Integration with an Existing Namespace

Sometimes a new namespace is not a viable option for a company. A company may already be using DNS for internal name resolution, or it may simply resist the idea of multiple namespaces. In this case, Windows 2000 name servers can be integrated into the existing namespace.

You can use two separate methods to integrate Active Directory into an existing DNS environment:

- *Integrate Active Directory at the root level.* For example, using this approach, server.domain.com and workstation.domain.com are included within the same zone as the publicly accessible resources such as **www.domain.com**.

- *Define a subdomain of the root domain and then install the Active Directory tree within that subdomain.* Doing so would result in server.subdomain.domain.com and workstation.subdomain.domain.com, and would allow the administrator to use firewall filtering and custom zone files to protect these machines from external attack. In most cases, Windows 2000 installations that are integrated with existing DNS structures will be configured as subdomains of the existing DNS namespace.

Just as a separate, nonpublic namespace helped protect the internal resources in our earlier example, a separate, nonpublic zone helps protect internal resources when extending a namespace. As shown in Figure 3-2, two DNS servers are separated by a firewall, proxy server, or other security device. The externally accessible DNS server has a zone file that includes information only about resources that the public should be able to access. The internal DNS server has a zone file that also includes information about the internal structure of the network and the locations of the internal resources.

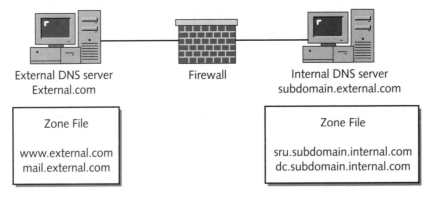

External DNS server   Firewall   Internal DNS server
External.com   subdomain.external.com

Zone File

www.external.com
mail.external.com

Zone File

sru.subdomain.internal.com
dc.subdomain.internal.com

Figure 3-2   Extending a namespace

Using a contiguous namespace for both internal and external resources offers several advantages:

- Logon IDs and e-mail addresses are the same for the user base, thus eliminating that area of confusion.

- Internal and external resources can be accessed seamlessly by the user base.

- The Active Directory tree is the same for internal and external corporate resources.

Naturally, there are also some disadvantages:

- Administrators must be cautious not to accidentally publish internal resources on the external DNS server.

- Firewalls or other security products must be put in place to protect the internal network.

The ultimate decision about whether to create or extend a namespace will depend on the existing DNS configuration and the needs of the company. Regardless, a Windows 2000 DNS server is required for integration with Active Directory.

SITE DESIGN

As mentioned in Chapter 2, **sites** are areas of high-speed connectivity. Frequently, a site matches the physical location of a local area network (LAN). Within an enterprise network environment, these physical locations are connected via slower wide area network (WAN) links. Windows 2000 uses sites to control the bandwidth used by Active Directory replication. Active Directory tries to minimize latency within a site, and tries to minimize bandwidth utilization between sites.

The administrator for a network determines the number of sites and which domain controllers and IP subnets are associated with those sites. The actual implementation of the site structure is covered in Chapter 6 later in this book; this section will focus on the planning of sites. As an example of site planning, we will look at a real enterprise network environment and examine different site designs that may be applied to the environment.

The first element in site planning is determining which needs are the most important to the company. For example, if the ultimate goal is absolute ease of administration, perhaps a single site design is the most appropriate. If the design goal is controlling bandwidth utilization over every link, then it makes sense to generate a site for every physical location.

Let's take a look at the following network. The company (we will call it Rayco) manages stores in several cities and has a corporate office in Fort Worth. As shown in Figure 3-3, the company has 1.54 Mbps frame connections between Fort Worth, Dallas, Denver, and Houston. Several secondary sites exist within Houston and Denver: the Houston sites are all connected to the hub site via 384 Kbps metro frame connections, and the Denver sites are connected via 128 Kbps frame connections.

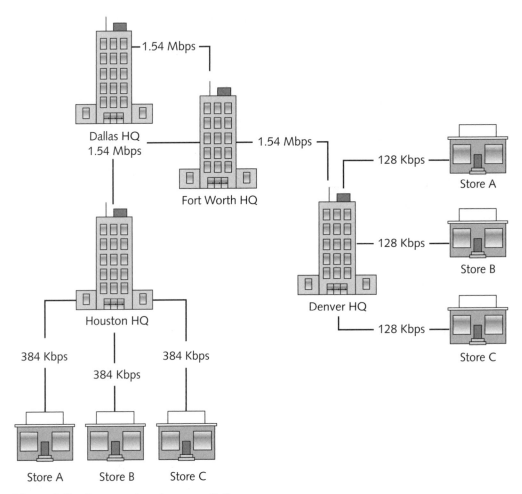

Figure 3-3   Rayco network connectivity

So, what possibilities are available with this environment? At a quick glance, it appears that many possibilities exist; the company could have from one to nine sites. Let's take a look at some of the more likely possibilities:

- *Single site:* One potential answer is to include the entire network within a single site. This approach would do much to ease administration, because there would be no need to create additional sites and site links. There would also be no need to move DCs between sites, because all the DCs would be part of the single default site. The problem with a single site is that domain replication traffic and authentication traffic are not controllable, and they could easily overwhelm some of the smaller WAN links. Even if a DC was placed at each physical location to handle authentication, the Active Directory replication alone could impact the remote sites in Denver.

- *Four sites:* Some elements of site design are impacted by the locations of the DCs. If the DCs were located only at the sites connected via the 1.54 Mbps links, the best configuration would generate four sites: Fort Worth and Dallas would each constitute a site, the Houston area locations would form the third site, and the Denver area locations would form the fourth. This design allows for better use of the long-haul links, while requiring a bare minimum of DCs.

- *Seven sites:* Even though a 1.54 Mbps connection is much slower than a LAN link, it still offers enough bandwidth that the physical location could be configured as a single site connected via frame connections. Obviously, with this structure the concern would be bandwidth utilization at the slower remote sites in Houston and Denver. Placing a DC at each of the slower locations and defining each of those locations as a site can overcome this issue. Doing so would allow the administrator to schedule replication with each of those slower sites. The administrator can schedule the replication to occur only at specified times, such as after business hours.

- *Nine sites:* If the company has the resources to place a DC at each site, then the optimal solution is to define each physical location as an independent site. Although doing so requires administrative overhead in order to define and maintain each site, the ability to control the replication and to authenticate locally result in the best performance for the Active Directory structure. Placing a DC at each physical location in our example results in nine sites. Of course, a site does not require that a DC be at that physical location—a site can consist of client machines only, which will then authenticate across the WAN link to the nearest DC.

 A DC can be placed in multiple sites, if you wish to force clients to authenticate against a particular DC. To place a DC in multiple sites, first create the sites. Next, edit the Registry on the DC. Find the HKLM\SYSTEM\CurrentControlSet\Services\Netlogon\Parameters subkey, and then add a REG_MULTI_SZ value named SiteCoverage. The names of the sites should be entered within the value.

In general, it is best to create as many sites as you have physical locations. In addition to the advantages we have already discussed, many of the services within Windows 2000 are **site aware**. A site-aware service will adjust its actions based upon the site from which the user logged in. This adjustment helps provide a seamless network experience regardless of the physical location of the user.

DOMAIN STRUCTURE

Once the decisions have been made regarding name resolution and site design, it is time to think about domain structures. In the past, Windows NT domain structures have been influenced by two issues: First, any trust relationships were on a domain-by-domain basis and were not transitive; and second, no way existed to grant administrative control over a section of a domain. As a result, any need to delegate administrative control almost always resulted in the creation of yet another domain.

The issues surrounding administrative control and resource allocation resulted in environments such as master logon domains with multiple trust relationships to the resource domain; or the ever-popular multi-master environment, in which multiple logon domains maintained a complex web of trust relationships with many resource domains. Windows NT administrators had their hands full designing and maintaining these trust relationships and troubleshooting problems with access rights.

Windows 2000 removes both of those limitations. Trusts are now automatic and transitive, so that the complex trust relationships common to NT environments are no longer required. In addition, a new structure known as an **Organizational Unit** (OU) allows Active Directory objects to be grouped together for administrative or policy purposes (we'll discuss OUs a bit later in the chapter).

From a strict technical perspective, you have very little reason to use multiple domains within a Windows 2000 environment. Because the OUs can function as a type of sub-domain, the master-resource model is no longer needed to allow administrative control of a group of computers. This model was the most common reason for creating a multiple-domain environment when creating a domain from scratch.

Basically, a multiple-domain environment may be necessary under Windows 2000 for three reasons:

- *A very slow link exists between two or more physical locations.* Even though Windows 2000 is efficient at managing replication over site links, at absolute minimum a 128 Kbps connection is still needed for synchronous replication to operate effectively. If the physical locations are connected at a slower speed than 128 Kbps, it makes sense to create separate domains.

- *You must maintain a legacy Windows NT network structure.* Because Windows NT domains are not capable of a transitive trust, nor are they aware of Active Directory, the existing domain structure will need to stay in place until all the domains are upgraded.

- *Political considerations exist.* Although there may be no valid technical reason to create a separate domain, political considerations will play a role in the structure of the Windows 2000 environment. If domains that double as fiefdoms dominate the current network environment, it is unlikely that a single Windows 2000 domain will replace that structure.

A single-domain strategy is highly recommended. This strategy minimizes administrative overhead.

USES OF ORGANIZATIONAL UNITS

Earlier, we defined an Organizational Unit as a grouping of Active Directory objects. We will discuss the implementation of OUs in Chapter 6; right now we will look at how OUs can be used within your domain structure.

It is important to understand two things about OUs before beginning to implement them within your environment:

- They are not required within a Windows 2000 environment. Access rights can be managed through security groups, much as they are in Windows NT.

- An OU is a domain object and cannot contain objects from another domain.

OUs function much like resource domains in Windows NT structures. Objects such as user accounts, computers, shares, printers, services, and more can be grouped together in an OU, and administrative rights can be granted to that OU by the domain administrator. This arrangement allows a departmental or geographical split on the security rights, while still avoiding the cumbersome and often unreliable trust links that joined the domains in a master-resource structure.

You can use several methods to implement OUs within a domain structure. Although OUs can be created and deleted with ease, proper planning will result in a structure that serves both the technical and business needs of the company. This planning process should include input from other departments within the company to help formulate the proper units and structure. A little extra time spent in planning will go a long way toward reducing problems after implementation. Some of the possible OU models are the following:

- *Object model:* Involves creating an OU for each type of object within the domain. This model is already implemented somewhat by default; the Users and Computers folders are simply OUs that are created automatically. Additional OUs can be created that contain printers, groups, and other objects. If necessary, secondary OUs can be created for more granularity, such as color printers or laptop computers. The advantage of this model is that it can easily be extended as new object types are added to the domain. The disadvantage is that usually no direct relationship exists between the object model and business processes within a company.

- *Departmental model:* Uses OUs to separate objects based upon the business departments associated with those objects. The departmental model groups users and the resources they most frequently use, such as shares, printers, and file servers. The advantage of this structure is the close integration of resources and the people who use them.

- *Geographic model:* Uses OUs to group objects based on the geographic location of the resources. Because OUs can be nested, the OUs can be as specific as a city or building, or as wide as a country. The geographic model can be used to cope with rapid changes in corporate structure, because user accounts and resources can be moved within the OUs as things change.

- *Administrative model:* Mimics the administrative structure within your organization. This model can be used to show the organizational structure of a company and can be nested through several levels to indicate the various levels of management. This model does not cope well with rapid changes within the company. If the changes are radical enough, many OUs may have to be scrapped and new ones built as replacements.

- *Business unit model:* Similar to the departmental model, but is based upon a much higher scale. Business units are usually divisions of a corporation that have a specific role and that often include multiple departments. A business unit model is generally used in conjunction with a departmental model to form a mirror of the corporate structure.

OUs can be used for many purposes within a Windows 2000 network structure. Primarily, you'll use OUs to provide structure for the resources within the Active Directory. If OUs are not used, the objects will be stored in a single list that can eventually become unmanageable. OUs also provide a flexible and easily managed way to handle permissions, especially if the company often undergoes structural changes. OUs can also be used to grant administrative control of resources such as computers or user accounts to a particular person or group or people, such as a departmental IT support organization.

DESIGNING THE INFRASTRUCTURE

The underlying structure of a network impacts the placement of servers, DCs, and other resources. Likewise, the amount of resources at a physical location often impacts decisions about the allocation of bandwidth.

Windows 2000 replicates data much more efficiently than Windows NT has in the past. This additional efficiency exists for two main reasons:

- The data is compressed with replicating across WAN links between sites, whereas Windows NT treated all replication the same regardless of the speed between the Primary Domain Controller (PDC) and Backup Domain Controllers (BDCs).

- Windows 2000 replicates only the changes in an object, rather than the entire record for the object. This means, for example, that a password change for a user will replicate only the new password, not the entire user object.

Because of this additional efficiency, you usually don't need to upgrade if your current network environment is meeting the business needs of the company. In fact, with intersite replication and the ability to limit the replication to non-business hours, the network may function a bit better with Windows 2000 DCs rather than Windows NT systems.

The additional efficiency comes into play only after sites and site links have been configured within the Active Directory structure. As mentioned earlier in this chapter, it is quite possible to create a multiple-location Active Directory structure that contains only a single site. However, a single site provides no advantage over the earlier versions of Windows NT—in fact, performance is likely to suffer, given that Windows 2000 attempts to minimize latency between DCs. However, we do not wish to form sites and throw DCs at random across the environment. Instead, you should follow a process to determine the proper placement of sites and to establish the impact on the existing infrastructure. The following sections describe this process.

Gather Data about the Network

The first element in any network planning exercise is to determine what elements the existing structure contains. Although this step may seem simplistic, many times an administrator will inherit a network that has little or no documentation. You must develop a map that includes all physical locations of a company, the current infrastructure layout between the locations, the speed and reliability of the infrastructure links, and the current utilization of those links. This map should also include information about the IP subnets in use on the network, if any exist.

Lay Out the Active Directory Sites

As we discussed earlier, best practices for Active Directory sites tell you to define a site for each physical location on the network. A site should be an area of high-speed connectivity, which usually means 10 Mbps LAN connections or higher. Take a look at the map created in the previous step and mark the areas that represent a concentration of computers or servers. These will be your sites.

 Remember, sites and domains have no direct relationship to each other. A site can contain multiple domains, and a domain can cross multiple sites.

Place the DCs within the Sites

Once the sites are defined, it is time to determine how many DCs are required and where they should be located. Remember that not all sites require a DC—a site can be composed entirely of client computers. Also remember that the more DCs exist, the more replication overhead the network will suffer.

The first step is to determine where the DCs should be located. It is tempting to simply install a DC in each site; but you should consider the following several reasons to locate a DC at a site:

- *A slow bandwidth link exists to the nearest DC.* If a site has a fast link to the nearest DC, then it is possible to authenticate across the link. However, if the site is connected via a low-bandwidth link, then authentication across that link will be slow. Placing a DC at that location will dramatically improve authentication times.

- *A domain is limited to a particular physical location.* In this case, you don't need to pass authentication traffic across a WAN link when the DC can be located at the physical site.

- *Users at a site perform a large number of cross-domain searches.* In this case, a DC doubling as a global catalog server would provide the best performance for these searches.

- *You want to speed authentication.* More-than-sufficient bandwidth may be available to access a central DC, but performance will always be quicker with a local DC.

A DC at a site may also be a poor idea for several reasons. Some of these reasons are listed here:

- *Hardware costs:* Although we hope this will not be an issue, it can be expensive to place a server-class machine at each site, especially when the site has few users.

- *Physical security:* If you can't physically secure a DC at the site, then it may be prudent not to locate a DC at that site. Many of the Windows NT security exploits require console access to a DC, and it is reasonable to expect similar exploits to arise with Windows 2000.

- *Administrative overhead:* Although Windows 2000 offers much more remote management capability than previous versions of Windows NT, every additional DC will result in an added load on the IT support staff. Consolidating the number of DCs will result in a more manageable environment.

- *Replication overhead:* As the number of DCs increases, so does the replication traffic for the domain.

Once you have decided where your sites and DC will be placed, you should have a good idea of the loads placed upon your network. Compare the locations of the DC and the large sites with the bandwidth links and speeds collected earlier. You should notice that the higher-speed links tend to be associated with the DC locations. If you find a major discrepancy, then you either need to increase the bandwidth at that site or revisit the decisions about sites and DCs.

Establish Replication Schedules

The replication schedule also impacts the infrastructure. Replication can be limited to particular times, so that the replication operation does not affect the users who need to use the bandwidth for business purposes. We will discuss the mechanics of limiting bandwidth later in this book; at this point, we are discussing strategies for optimizing replication traffic.

Forcing replication to occur outside of normal business hours increases the effective bandwidth of a remote site. For sites that are connected with high-speed links, the effect of replication every three hours (the default interval) may be minimal. Sites that are connected via slow links may see a degradation of performance, especially if many regular changes occur in the Active Directory objects.

A good rule of thumb for replication traffic is that the slower the link, the more restrictive the replication schedule should be:

- *High bandwidth (low cost):* Replication should be allowed throughout the day. The default interval is three hours between replication attempts.

- *Medium bandwidth (medium cost):* Replication may be restricted to evening hours. The default interval may be changed to lengthen the time between replication attempts.

- *Low bandwidth (high cost):* Replication should be restricted to a particular window of time. It is important that this window of time match the replication times available at the other end of the site link. If the replication windows do not match, replication cannot occur.

The combination of physical connectivity, site design, DC placement, and replication schedules will determine how well your network performs. Although a WAN never has enough bandwidth, judicious use of replication schedules can minimize the impact of replication on the network. Windows 2000's use of sites actually places a lighter load on the network infrastructure than an equivalent Windows NT structure. If the existing network infrastructure is supporting a Windows NT environment, then it will probably be able to support a Windows 2000 environment without problems. Naturally, it is important to verify the network structure before implementing any new network operating system.

CHAPTER SUMMARY

- Planning remains the most important element in designing and implementing a Windows 2000 networking environment. The Active Directory service requires much more planning than the Windows NT operating system, due to elements such as sites, site links, and replication scheduling.

- The namespace is the first issue you will face in planning the new Windows 2000 implementation. Windows 2000 uses DNS naming rather than the NetBIOS naming that dominates Windows NT networking. The DNS naming requires a fully qualified domain name for the Windows domain, such as Microsoft.com.

- Companies that have not used DNS previously must develop a DNS solution for internal name resolution. The domain that a company wishes to use must be registered with an ICANN-approved registrar to prevent it being used by some other company. Domain names can be registered either directly by a company or through an ISP or other connectivity provider. Once the name has been registered, it may be used.

❑ Several options are available for companies that previously had a registered DNS domain name for either internal or external resources. One option is to register another domain name for internal use only. This option provides additional security, because there is no need to publish the internal DNS information to the outside world. The negatives are minor: primarily, the need to maintain an additional domain name and the administrative overhead that comes with that additional name.

❑ A company can also extend a domain name to include the new internal resources. The most common method is to create a subdomain within the domain name and use that subdomain for internal resources. As an example, TexasPinball.com could use an internal subdomain such as Corporate.TexasPinball.com for its Active Directory structure. The problem with using a subdomain is maintaining a separation between internal and external resources through zone files and firewall configurations. It is important not to publish information about internal resources on any DNS server reachable from the outside world.

❑ Once the decision is made regarding the namespace, the next level of planning involves determining how many domains will be required in the new Windows 2000 structure. Windows 2000 offers some new elements that can minimize the number of domains. Organizational Units (OUs) can be configured to perform many of the same functions as resource domains. In general, strive for the fewest as possible domains in an environment. It is recommended that a single domain be used unless political or legacy issues require a multiple-domain structure.

❑ OUs are new with Windows 2000. An OU is essentially a container than can include other objects within the domain. An OU cannot include objects from another domain. OUs can be nested within each other as necessary. Administrative control over an OU can be granted to a domain user or to a group of domain users. Doing so allows an OU to function as a resource domain and to be controlled on an individual basis within the domain.

❑ You can use several OU models to organize OUs within a domain. Some of these methods include the geographic model, business unit model, administrative model, departmental model, and object model. Each model has advantages and disadvantages. In order to develop an OU structure that best fits your company, other departments should be allowed to provide significant input. Remember, the goal is to reduce the effort needed to maintain the structure and to allow for flexibility if the company reorganizes.

❑ Infrastructure issues are always a concern when a new product is introduced on a network. This is a great time to verify that the network infrastructure matches the information you have regarding speed, subnet allocation, and routes. The major concern is whether the additional load will adversely affect the ability of the company to perform its primary function. Fortunately, Windows 2000 is better at managing replication bandwidth than its predecessor, and replication can be scheduled so that it will not affect the users at a location.

❏ The amount of bandwidth used by replication is dependent upon a number of items. The primary factors are the number of sites and the number of DCs within the Active Directory structure. The structure of a company's network will determine the number of sites. In general, a site should be created for each subnet or physical location.

❏ The number of DCs will be determined by several factors. The first is the available bandwidth between the clients and the DCs. Not every site will require a DC, if sufficient bandwidth exists to allow reasonably quick authentication via another DC. If the bandwidth is restricted to a site, however, a DC at that site makes perfect sense. The second factor is the relative value of a DC versus the additional hardware costs and administrative headaches associated with additional servers at remote locations.

❏ Replication traffic can be controlled through properties of the site links. Links can be scheduled to be active only at certain times. Replication traffic will not flow while a site link is inactive, but normal network traffic will be allowed. Sites that are connected via high-bandwidth links should not be restricted, whereas sites that have very low bandwidth should be limited to a particular replication time.

4

DOMAIN NAME SYSTEM (DNS)

After completing this chapter, you will be able to:

♦ Understand DNS name resolution

♦ Understand the different types of name servers

♦ Configure and manage DNS zones

♦ Understand zone transfers

♦ Install DNS for Active Directory

♦ Configure DNS for Active Directory

♦ Monitor and troubleshoot DNS for Active Directory

The Domain Name System (DNS) is a name resolution database that is used on Transmission Control Protocol/Internet Protocol (TCP/IP) networks and is associated primarily with the Internet. Everyone who has used the Internet is familiar with DNS names—for example, www.InsideIS.com or ftp.Microsoft.com—whether they realize it or not. However, DNS also plays an integral role in an Active Directory implementation. Essentially, Active Directory cannot function without DNS (either an implementation of Microsoft DNS or third-party DNS server software).

In this chapter, you will learn not only what DNS is and how to set up, configure, monitor, and troubleshoot it, but also about the advantages and disadvantages of using Windows 2000 DNS. By the end of this chapter, you should be able to deploy DNS on your network for use with Active Directory.

UNDERSTANDING DNS NAME RESOLUTION

The Domain Name System originated from the Internet, which is based on the TCP/IP network protocol. Computers communicate with each other through numbers, and on TCP/IP networks that means IP addresses. An IP address is formed of four octets of numerals from 1 to 254. For example, **192.168.1.21** is a valid IP address. Part of the address refers to a network ID signifying the network the computer is on, and the remaining part is the host ID, which uniquely identifies a given host on a TCP/IP network. A process called **masking** determines where the network ID stops and the host ID begins, which is why you often see the term **subnet mask** used in conjunction with IP addresses.

HOSTS Files and Their Function

Unfortunately, humans are not as good at remembering numbers as computers are. In fact, we work much better with names. The process of **name resolution** was created to enable humans to work more efficiently with networked computers. Originally, all the host-to-IP address mappings were kept in a single file called HOSTS. Whenever a new computer was introduced to the Internet, a systems administrator would manually update the HOSTS file and send copies of it to all the other systems on the Internet.

Although this was an adequate solution in the early days of the Internet, when there were few systems and updates were infrequent, the manual process quickly reached its limit and became a burden. In addition, the HOSTS file provided only what is called a **flat** namespace. Because the namespace was flat, any change made to a rapidly growing HOSTS file—such as adding a single computer—had to be replicated to every system on the Internet. Every system was responsible for being able to resolve the name of every host to its IP address. To alleviate the growing problem of maintaining an up-to-date HOSTS file, DNS was born.

Name Resolution Beyond HOSTS: DNS

DNS created a **hierarchical** namespace, which allowed the namespace of the Internet to be partitioned and distributed. This arrangement eliminated the need to distribute the entire database to every host. Name servers could be set up that were responsible for only a portion of the namespace rather than all of it. For example, the DNS server ns1.InsideIS.com has to be responsible only for the InsideIS.com namespace, not the entire Internet. If a host on the InsideIS.com network needs to resolve the name of a host outside that domain, the name server knows how to contact other name servers that are responsible for different pieces of the overall domain namespace.

At the top of the namespace is the root, which is represented by a period (.). Below the root domain are the top-level domains. Table 4-1 illustrates the more popular top-level domains and the type of organizations with which they are associated.

Table 4-1 Common top-level domains

Top-Level Domain	Type
Com	Commercial organization
Edu	Educational institution
Gov	U.S. government department
Mil	U.S. military organization
Net	Network provider
Org	Nonprofit organization

4

Although the types listed are the traditional designations, the main domain name registrar—Network Solutions—allows just about anyone to register a Com, Net, or Org domain name without regard to how it will be used. Now you'll see commercial companies with **.org** names, and home users/consumers with registered **.net** names, simply because the **.com** equivalent is already taken. At one time, however, these designations were fairly strictly enforced, and to register a name you had to show the intended purpose of the site.

Second-Level Domains

Below the top-level domains are the second-level domains, which are the domain names that individuals and organizations register with a registrar such as Network Solutions. These are names like Inside-Corner.com, Examcram.com, Whitehouse.gov, and Army.mil. The domain namespace can be partitioned even further. InsideIS.com can yield www.InsideIS.com, ftp.InsideIS.com, and so forth. Figure 4-1 shows an example of the domain namespace.

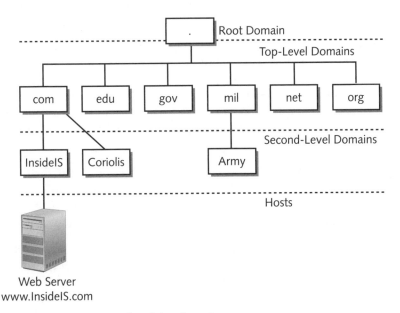

Figure 4-1 An example of the domain namespace

Fully Qualified Domain Names

In our previous example, the host computer www.InsideIS.com. is what is known as a fully qualified domain name (FQDN). Notice that the trailing period after .com is intentional. A FQDN describes the exact position of a host within the namespace. In this case, **www** is the computer, **InsideIS** is the second-level domain of which **www** is a member, **.com** is the top-level domain, and the trailing **.** represents the root domain. The DNS system uses a host's FQDN to resolve its name to an IP address.

Relative Distinguished Names

In situations where hosts are on the same network, using an FQDN to communicate between them is cumbersome. To compensate, DNS provides for a **relative distinguished name**, which is simply the host name. In our www.InsideIS.com FQDN example, **www** is the relative distinguished name. This name provides a more convenient means of communicating with other systems that belong to the InsideIS.com second-level domain, reducing redundancy.

Active Directory and DDNS

Windows 2000 is built to run on TCP/IP, and to utilize Active Directory you must forsake the older Windows Internet Naming System (WINS) technology for DNS. Probably the biggest downside to DNS is that, while distributed, it was still designed as a system that required manual updates. Whenever a new host was added to a domain, an administrator needed to update manually the zone database on the primary DNS server (zones are discussed later in this chapter) to contain the new host. If the network included secondary name servers, the changes were replicated in a zone transfer.

Recently, a dynamic updating feature was proposed in RFC 2136 that provides the means for updating a zone's primary server automatically. Windows 2000 supports this new Dynamic DNS (DDNS). The caveat is that it works only with Windows 2000 clients—older Windows NT, Windows 9x, and non-Windows clients must still be added manually. When DDNS is enabled and a Windows 2000 client logs into the network, the client automatically sends an update to the name server it has been configured to use, adding its A (address) record. This process greatly simplifies the administration of DNS on a Windows 2000 network.

Now that you have a basic understanding of what DNS is, let's look more closely at exactly how the name resolution process works.

Forward Lookup Queries

As we've said, part of the beauty of the DNS system is that the database can be distributed so that not every name server has to be responsible for resolving every host on the network. So, unlike the days when TCP/IP networks relied strictly on HOSTS files, no one server knows how to resolve every host name to an IP address on the Internet. A

DNS server could be all-knowing for a given company, but, unless that company does not communicate with any outside networks, eventually any DNS server will need to ask for help to resolve a name.

The standard method of name resolution with DNS is the **forward lookup query**. In this method, the client needing to resolve a host name to its IP address sends a query to its primary DNS server (configured on the client) asking for help. The DNS server checks its zone database to determine if it contains the host-to-IP address mapping to answer the client query. If so, it returns the information to the client to fulfill the query. If not, it forwards the request to another DNS server for resolution. This process continues until the FQDN is completely resolved; then the information is passed back the way it came.

For example, suppose we attempted to access www.examcram.com from our current computer, a host in the inside-corner.com domain:

1. When we enter "www.Examcram.com" into our browser, our system contacts our primary DNS server as configured on our system.

2. The local DNS server is authoritative only for the inside-corner.com domain, so it forwards the query to a root server on the Internet.

3. The root server responds by informing our primary DNS server that www.examcram.com is in the Com domain, and that it needs to talk to a Com DNS server.

4. Our DNS server contacts a Com DNS server with the query; this server in turn responds with a referral to the name server authoritative for the ExamCram.com domain.

5. Our DNS server contacts the name server authoritative for ExamCram.com, which finds the correct host-to-IP address mapping and returns the results of the query to our DNS server, which then returns the results to our host computer.

6. Communication can be established directly between our computer and www.examcram.com. In this case, the Web site would load into our browser.

Caching

As you can probably imagine, the name resolution process can result in a lot of network traffic, because a query can potentially be sent to numerous name servers in order to be resolved. To alleviate this problem, DNS servers use a process called **caching**: The DNS server will store the information it learns about host-to-IP address mappings outside of its zone for a configurable length of time. This way, client queries for the same host in the near future do not have to repeat the entire resolution process.

The configurable length of time a DNS server will cache the results of a query is referred to as Time To Live (TTL); in Windows 2000, it defaults to 60 minutes. Longer TTL values reduce network traffic for subsequent communication with remote hosts, whereas shorter TTL values ensure that information about the namespace is current. This happens because if a remote host's DNS information changes while information about it is cached, a client won't know about the changes until the TTL expires and the name server initiates a new name resolution query.

Reverse Lookup Query

In some cases (most notably, troubleshooting) you need to be able to query in reverse—that is, to resolve a name from an IP address. The regular forward lookup query process that DNS uses is much like a phone book: You look up someone's name and find the phone number. Typically, you don't start with a phone number and want to find the name associated with it. However, some applications implement security based on being able to resolve a name from an IP address, and troubleshooting tools like the **nslookup** command use **reverse lookup queries** to report host names from IP addresses.

Because the DNS namespace is distributed as host-to-IP address (like a phone book), a reverse lookup query would require exhaustively searching every domain name until the correct host was found. To get around this problem, a special second-level domain was created that contains only IP address-to-host mappings. This second-level domain is called in-addr.arpa, and it follows the same hierarchical structure as the rest of the DNS namespace. Subdomains in the in-addr.arpa domain are named in reverse dotted-decimal format. For example, the network ID **192.168.1.0** would be represented as **1.168.192.in-addr.arpa**. Troubleshooting with nslookup is covered later in this chapter, when we'll show you reverse lookup queries in action.

UNDERSTANDING THE DIFFERENT TYPES OF NAME SERVERS

In our previous discussion, we've really considered only one type of DNS server: a primary DNS server. However, there are other types of name servers. We'll cover the following types in this section:

- Primary DNS servers
- Secondary DNS servers
- Caching-only name servers
- Forwarding DNS servers

Primary DNS Servers

There are two main types of DNS servers: primary servers and secondary servers. As we briefly mentioned earlier, the DNS namespace is partitioned into what are known as **zones**. We discuss zones in detail later in this chapter, but for now you should just understand that a zone is the part of the overall DNS namespace that is controlled by a primary server. There can be only one primary server in a zone, and that primary zone is said to be **authoritative** for the zone. It is the master, and any changes to the DNS domain must be made on the primary server. The exception is an Active Directory–integrated zone, which is also discussed later in this chapter.

Secondary DNS Servers

A secondary server is basically a backup server for the primary server. It is important to note that during the name resolution process, if a primary server cannot resolve a host name, the query is *not* submitted to a secondary server (if one exists in the zone). Essentially, the secondary server is used as a failover, which means it does essentially nothing until the primary server fails, at which time the dormant secondary server picks up where the failed server left off with no interruption in service to the user. If a client is unable to contact the primary DNS server, it will attempt to use the secondary server, if one has been configured. Another potential use of a secondary server is load balancing. If you have 1,000 network clients, for example, you could configure half of them to use the primary server first and half of them to use the secondary server first. This setup would reduce the load on the primary server.

Changes are never made directly to a secondary server, which receives a copy of the master zone file from the primary name server in a zone. This process is called **zone transfer** and is covered in more detail later in this chapter. Unlike with primary servers, a zone can have multiple secondary servers.

Caching-Only Name Servers

A caching-only name server does pretty much what the name implies: It functions only to cache queries. The caching-only name server does not maintain a zone database file, nor does it receive updates from a primary server. It simply performs queries, caches the results, and returns results to querying clients.

The advantage of using a caching-only name server is a twofold reduction in network traffic. First, no replication traffic is generated between the primary name server and the caching-only server, as happens between a primary and secondary. Second, a caching-only server reduces name resolution traffic by reducing the need for subsequent queries to go through the entire name resolution process.

Caching-only servers are still bound by TTL rules, although the TTLs are often set longer than they are on primary and secondary servers. TTLs are set longer on caching-only servers since the goal of having this type of DNS server is to build up a substantial cache to reduce name-resolution traffic. The disadvantage of caching-only servers is that, if a server is rebooted, the cache is flushed and the server must build its cache again from scratch.

Caching-only servers can also perform what is called **negative caching**, which caches failed results. This reduces the timeout process when a client queries for a site that does not exist or is unavailable.

Forwarding DNS Servers

Forwarding DNS servers exist solely to communicate with DNS servers outside the local zone. By default, any DNS server that receives a query it cannot resolve will contact an outside DNS server in order to resolve the name for the client making the query. A DNS forwarder functions like a proxy, becoming the only DNS server in a zone that can communicate outside the zone. For example, if the primary name server cannot resolve a name, it will send the query to the forwarding DNS server for resolution. Figures 4-2 and 4-3 show a DNS infrastructure not using a forwarder and one using a forwarder, respectively.

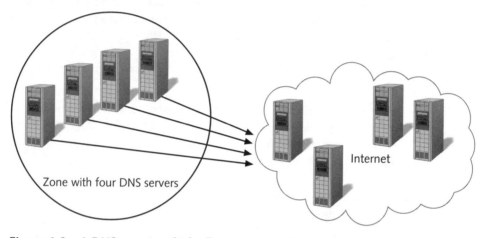

Figure 4-2   A DNS zone in which all name servers communicate outside the local zone

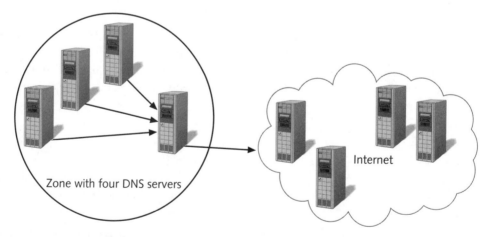

Figure 4-3   A DNS zone that uses a forwarding name server to communicate outside the local zone

4

Forwarding servers can be configured to use either nonexclusive or exclusive mode. In nonexclusive mode, a name server can attempt to resolve a query through its own zone database files if a forwarder cannot resolve the query. In exclusive mode, if a forwarder cannot resolve a query, the server that sent the query to the forwarder does not attempt to resolve the name itself, and simply returns a failure notice to the client that originated the request.

CONFIGURING AND MANAGING DNS ZONES

We've mentioned zones a few times so far, but we haven't taken the time to talk about them in much depth. As we've said, a zone is a partitioned portion of the overall DNS namespace. Zones make managing the namespace much easier than the flat namespace of HOSTS files did. Figure 4-4 shows an example of the InsideIS.com domain divided into two zones.

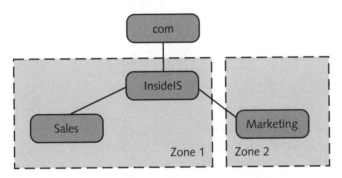

Figure 4-4 An example of DNS zones

At the simplest level, a single zone contains the entire namespace of a second-level domain. In our example, a single zone could be authoritative for all of InsideIS.com without dividing it into two zones. A zone must encompass contiguous namespace, however, which means a single zone could not be authoritative for both InsideIS.com and ExamCram.com. Those two domains are not part of the same namespace.

In our example, we divided our namespace into two zones, in which one zone is authoritative for Sales.InsideIS.com and a second zone is authoritative for Marketing.InsideIS.com. You will use multiple zones primarily to distribute administrative responsibilities. In many corporations, political boundaries must be managed, with different divisions/departments having their own administrators. Multiple zones allow multiple administrators to be responsible for their individual pieces of the namespace.

Another reason to partition the namespace into zones is to reduce the load on a DNS infrastructure. Consider a megacorporation such as Microsoft, with more than 100,000 nodes on the network, spread across the globe. A single zone would place a tremendous burden on the primary DNS server (remember, a zone can contain only one primary server), and the replication traffic to secondary DNS servers would make a significant impact on network performance. Dividing the Microsoft.com namespace into multiple zones distributes the load, which increases performance and eases administration.

Windows 2000 Zones

Windows 2000 supports two types of zones: forward lookup zones and reverse lookup zones. These zones are associated with the types of name resolution queries they enable. We will discuss these zones in greater detail later in this chapter when we look at installing and configuring Windows 2000 DNS.

UNDERSTANDING ZONE TRANSFERS

Zone transfer is the process by which changes made on the primary server are replicated to all of the secondary servers in the zone. There are three types of zone transfers to consider:

- Full zone transfer
- Incremental transfer
- DNS Notify

Full Zone Transfer

Originally, the only method of replication between primary and secondary servers was the full zone transfer. With this method, the entire zone database file is transferred whenever an update is made. Zone transfer is performed through a "pull" mechanism rather than a "push"—that is, the secondary servers initiate a zone transfer. The process is as follows:

1. The secondary server waits a predetermined amount of time before contacting the primary server. When it does establish contact, it requests the primary server's SOA (Start of Authority) record. Record types are discussed in depth below.

2. The primary server responds to the secondary server with its SOA record.

3. Whenever a change is made to the primary name server, the serial number held in the SOA record is incremented. When the secondary server receives the SOA record from the primary server, it compares the serial number to its own. If the serial number in the SOA record sent by the primary server is higher than the serial number in the SOA record currently on the secondary server, the secondary server knows its zone database is out of date. It then sends a request back to the primary server for a full zone transfer. This full transfer is done through an AXFR (or Full Zone Transfer) request.

4. The primary server sends its full zone database file back to the secondary server. After the update is complete, the process begins again with the waiting period.

Incremental Transfer

As you can probably imagine, performing a full zone transfer every time a change is made to the primary server is inefficient. It also can generate a lot of network traffic if the primary server receives frequent updates and there are multiple secondary servers. To get around this problem, RFC 1995 allowed for incremental zone transfers. As the name implies, with an incremental transfer only the portion of the database that has been changed is replicated.

The process with an incremental transfer is basically the same as a full zone transfer. The difference lies in the type of request. During an incremental transfer, the secondary server sends an IXFR (or Incremental Zone Transfer) request signifying an incremental transfer, rather than an AXFR request signifying a full zone transfer.

Version History

So, how do the name servers keep track of the changes in order for incremental transfer to work? The primary server maintains a version history, which keeps track of all changes that have been made since the last version update was transferred to a secondary server. When a secondary server requests an IXFR transfer, the primary server begins sending the recent updates, starting with the oldest updates and progressing to the most recent updates.

When the secondary server begins receiving the updates, it creates a new version of the zone and begins applying the updates to that copy. After all the updates are committed to the copy of the zone database, the original database is replaced with the copy.

If the primary server does not support incremental transfers, it will simply ignore the incremental request of the secondary server and perform a full zone transfer. A primary server that supports incremental transfers can also arbitrarily decide to perform a full zone transfer even if an incremental transfer is requested, if conditions indicate that a full zone transfer would be better. For example, if a large number of updates have been made since the last transfer, an incremental transfer would consume more bandwidth than a full zone transfer.

DNS Notify

DNS Notify was proposed in RFC 1996 as an update to incremental transfer. With DNS Notify, rather than waiting for a secondary server to contact the primary server to see if there are any changes, the primary server notifies secondary servers in its notify list whenever an update is made. The notify list is maintained on the primary server; it contains a list of IP addresses of secondary servers that should be notified whenever an update is made. This process helps the zone database stay more consistent across the enterprise. The DNS Notify process works as follows:

1. When the zone is updated on the primary server, the serial number in the SOA record is updated to reflect a newer version of the zone.

2. The primary server consults its notify list and contacts members of that list, informing them of a newer zone database version.

3. Similar to the process with a full zone transfer or an incremental transfer, the secondary server contacts the primary server and requests the SOA record.

4. When the SOA record is received, the secondary server compares the serial numbers of the primary server's SOA record and its own SOA record.

5. If the serial number of the primary server is higher, the secondary server knows its version of the database is out of date. It then requests a zone transfer (AXFR or IXFR).

INSTALLING DNS FOR ACTIVE DIRECTORY

So far, we've discussed a lot of DNS theory, but not much of the practical side of things. In this section, we'll cover actually installing and configuring the DNS service for Windows 2000.

DNS Preinstallation

We must consider a few preinstallation tasks before starting the installation procedure. The first of these tasks is making sure your server is ready for DNS. A DNS server, for obvious reasons, must have a static IP address. If the server that is to run the DNS service currently has a Dynamic Host Configuration Protocol (DHCP)–assigned IP address, you must reconfigure that before continuing. To configure the IP address in Windows 2000, perform the following steps:

1. Right-click on My Network Places and click on Properties. A window similar to that in Figure 4-5 will appear.

2. Right-click on the network adapter that the DNS service will use and click on Properties. A window similar to that in Figure 4-6 will appear.

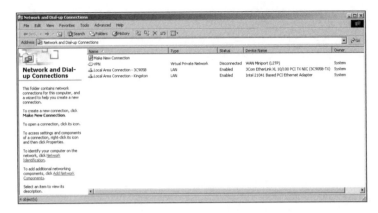

Figure 4-5   You can configure network settings through Network and Dial-up Connections Properties

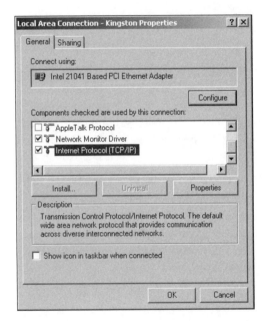

Figure 4-6   You can configure settings for your network adapter through its property page

3. Navigate down the Components list until you see Internet Protocol (TCP/IP). Right-click on TCP/IP and click on Properties to open the property sheet where you can configure the IP address, or left-click to highlight and then choose the Properties button at the bottom of the screen. This window is shown in Figure 4-7.

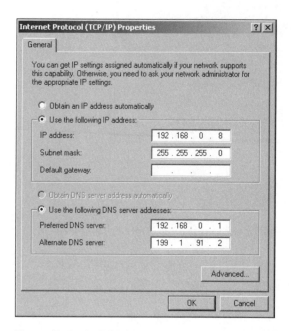

Figure 4-7   In TCP/IP Properties, you can configure TCP/IP settings for your network
adapter

4. In our example, our internal network is using the standard reserved class C
network ID. You should configure your server to use an IP address that is
valid for your subnet.

5. Before exiting this dialog box, you must perform an additional step: configuring the DNS server IP address under the Advanced TCP/IP Settings. Click
on the Advanced button, and then click on the DNS tab. You will see a window similar to that shown in Figure 4-8.

In our example, the first listed DNS server is primary and the second server is secondary.

DNS Installation

For the sake of this discussion, we will assume that you did *not* choose to install the DNS
service when you initially set up Windows 2000. It is not installed by default, so if you
installed DNS during setup you probably don't need to be reading this section.

With Windows 2000 already installed, adding the DNS service is accomplished through
Control Panel|Add/Remove Programs|Add/Remove Windows Components. When
the Windows Components Wizard launches, navigate to Networking Services. Highlight
it and click on Details. Select Domain Name System (DNS) and click on OK.

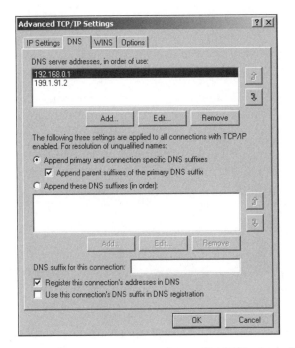

Figure 4-8   You must configure the DNS server IP address in TCP/IP Properties on the server on which you are installing the DNS service

CONFIGURING DNS FOR ACTIVE DIRECTORY

With the DNS service installed, the next step is to configure it for use on your Windows 2000 network. You must consider several configuration issues when setting up DNS, such as:

- Root servers
- Forward lookup zones
- Reverse lookup zones
- Resource records
- Dynamic DNS

Root Servers

When you initially launch the DNS Microsoft Management Console (MMC) snap-in, a configuration wizard opens. You first have the option of configuring your server as a root server. As you may recall from earlier in the chapter, root servers on the Internet are authoritative for the entire DNS namespace. Obviously, you would not be able to create a root server that is authoritative for the entire Internet, so you should create a root server only if your network is not connected to the Internet. If your local area network (LAN) is not connected to the Internet and you create a root server, the root server will be authoritative for any namespace you create.

Forward Lookup Zones

For DNS services to work, at least one forward lookup zone must be configured on your server. Forward lookup zones enable forward lookup queries—the standard method of name resolution in DNS—to work.

To create a forward lookup one, right-click on Forward Lookup Zones in the DNS MMC console and click on New Zone. A configuration wizard will launch. The first choice you have to make when configuring a new zone is what type of zone it will be. The choices are:

- Active Directory Integrated
- Standard Primary
- Standard Secondary

Active Directory Integrated

An Active Directory-integrated zone uses Active Directory to store and manage all zone information. Recall from earlier in the chapter, when we discussed primary and secondary name servers, that a zone can contain only one primary name server, where all updates must be made. This configuration provides a single point of failure, because, if your primary server goes down, you cannot promote a secondary server to become the primary server à la Primary Domain Controllers (PDCs) and Backup Domain Controllers (BDCs) in Windows NT. With an Active Directory-integrated zone, however, all domain controllers (DCs) essentially become primary name servers. Through Active Directory, all DCs are replicated a fully writeable copy of the zone database. This process provides a level of fault tolerance unavailable with a standard primary zone. Also, Windows 2000 clients can register dynamic updates with the nearest available DC, rather than having to contact a single primary server.

Being able to contact any available DC provides additional flexibility. If your network spans several slow wide area network (WAN) links, you would have to set up secondary name servers at the remote locations in order to provide name resolution services with a decent response time. With an Active Directory-integrated zone, your DCs at the remote locations would automatically be able to handle DNS functions.

Standard Primary

A standard primary zone was discussed previously in the chapter—a single primary server that is authoritative for the zone. Whereas in an Active Directory-integrated zone the zone database is stored within the Active Directory, the zone database in a standard primary zone is stored in a text file per RFC standards. If your network will have non-Windows 2000 name servers, you must choose one of the standard zone types for communication between the Windows 2000 and non-Windows 2000 name servers to take place.

When you go through the configuration wizard to create a standard primary zone, the first step is to create a zone name. Here, you define the namespace for which the zone will be authoritative. After designating the zone name, you are prompted to enter the name of the text file the zone will use. By default, the filename will be *zone*.dns, where *zone* is the zone name you assigned on the previous screen. Notice that you also have the option to use an existing file. If you specify an existing zone database file to use, make sure to copy it to the \winnt\system32\dns directory.

At this point, the zone is configured. You are given the opportunity to review your settings before clicking on Finish.

Standard Secondary

A standard secondary zone was discussed previously in the chapter—it draws its zone information from one or more primary name servers. A secondary zone can contain the zone databases of multiple DNS zones. After specifying the name of the zone in the configuration wizard, you will see the dialog box shown in Figure 4-9.

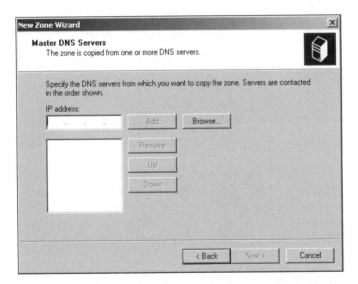

Figure 4-9   When configuring a standard secondary zone, you can specify multiple primary DNS servers from which to draw zone information

After entering the IP addresses of the primary name servers with which this secondary zone should communicate, click on Next. You can review your settings, and then click on Finish.

Reverse Lookup Zones

A reverse lookup zone is not required for DNS services to function; however, you will want to create a reverse lookup zone to allow reverse lookup queries to function. Without a reverse lookup zone, troubleshooting tools such as the **nslookup** command (which can resolve host names from IP addresses) cannot work.

As with forward lookup zones, you have the option of creating Active Directory–integrated, standard primary, or standard secondary zones. No matter which zone type you choose, you name your zone in the window shown in Figure 4-10.

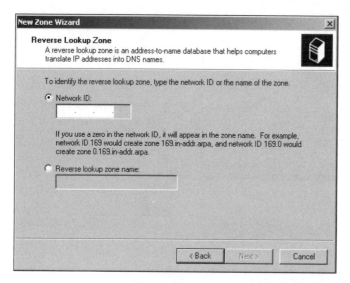

Figure 4-10   Naming a reverse lookup zone to translate IP addresses into host names

Unlike naming a forward lookup zone, you name a reverse lookup zone by its IP address. You can either type your network ID into the first field and watch the reverse lookup zone name automatically be created for you, or you can type the reverse lookup zone name into the second field, following RFC conventions. The on-screen information between Network ID and Reverse Lookup Zone Name describes how to name a reverse lookup zone.

As with forward lookup zones, if you are creating an Active Directory–integrated zone, you are done after supplying the zone name. With standard primary and standard secondary zones, you must also supply the zone filename, which defaults to adding a .dns extension to the end of your zone name. With a standard secondary zone, you must list the IP addresses of the primary DNS servers with which the secondary zone should communicate.

With your zones configured and DNS services functioning, let's look at the entries known as **resource records** that you'll find within the server.

Resource Records

Resource records (RR) are the basic units of information within DNS. When the Windows 2000 DNS service starts up, a number of records are registered at the server. Figure 4-11 shows an example of the netlogon.dns file, which contains a listing of server resource records that are registered with DNS upon startup. The netlogon.dns file is located in the \winnt\system32\config directory.

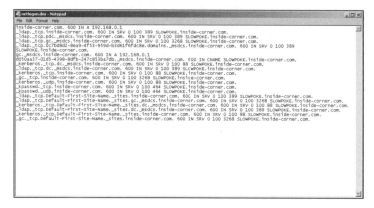

Figure 4-11   A number of resource records are registered with DNS when the service first starts

Okay, so you're probably thinking that the file looks like some foreign language you slept through in high school. The file is actually very structured, so let's look at the first entry:

```
inside-corner.com. 600 IN A 192.168.0.1
```

The structure of the entry's fields is as follows:

- Owner
- TTL
- Class
- Type
- RDATA

Breaking down the first entry in netlogon.dns, **Inside-Corner.com** is the owner. **600** is the TTL, in seconds (10 minutes). **IN** is the class, which is Internet System. You'll find that the class is practically always **IN**. The type identifies the resource record, in this case **A** for address (more on that in a minute). Finally, RDATA is the resource record data. This is a variable whose value depends on the type of record. In an A record such as this, the RDATA entry is the IP address of the system registering the entry.

A number of common resource records are used with Windows 2000 DNS, as follows:

- Start of Authority (SOA)
- Name Server (NS)
- Address (A)
- Pointer (PTR)
- Mail Exchanger (MX)
- Service (SRV)
- Canonical Name (CNAME)

Start of Authority (SOA) Record

The SOA record is contained at the beginning of every zone, both forward lookup and reverse lookup. Its fields define a number of details for the zone, such as:

- *Owner:* Previously defined.
- *TTL:* Previously defined.
- *Class:* Previously defined.
- *Type:* Previously defined.
- *Authoritative Server:* The primary DNS server that is authoritative for the zone.
- *Responsible Person:* The e-mail address of the person who administers the zone.
- *Serial Number:* The serial number of the zone. Remember that the serial number is incremented whenever an update is made, and that secondary servers use serial numbers to determine whether their copy of the zone database is out of date.
- *Refresh:* How often secondary servers check to see if their zone database files need updating.
- *Retry:* How long a secondary server will wait after sending an AXFR or IXFR request before resending the request.
- *Expire:* How long after a zone transfer a secondary server will respond to zone queries before discarding the zone as invalid, due to no communication with the primary server.
- *Minimum TTL:* The minimum TTL a resource record will use if the SOA record does not explicitly state a TTL value.

Name Server (NS) Records

NS records show all servers that are authoritative for a zone: both primary and secondary servers for the zone specified in the SOA record, and primary name servers for any delegated zones. The NS record uses the Owner, Class, Type, and Authoritative Server fields just described.

Address (A) Records

The A record is the most basic entry in DNS—it maps the FQDN of a host to its IP address. When a client sends a standard forward lookup name resolution query, the server uses A records to resolve the name.

Pointer (PTR) Records

PTR records are the opposite of A records—they provide reverse lookup services for DNS. That is, a PTR record maps an IP address to a FQDN. When a reverse lookup query is sent to a DNS server, such as through the **nslookup** utility, PTR records are consulted to resolve the address.

Mail Exchanger (MX) Records

The MX records designate a mail exchanging server for a DNS zone, which is a host that will process or forward e-mail. In addition to the standard Owner, Class, and Type fields, MX records also support a fourth field: Mail Server Priority. This field is used when your domain has multiple mail servers—mail exchangers with lower values are preferred over mail exchangers with higher values when determining which server to use to process an e-mail message.

Service (SRV) Records

SRV records allow you to specify the location of servers providing a particular service, such as Web servers. You can create SRV records to identify hosts in the zone that provide a service; a resolver can then find the A record of a service to resolve the name. The SRV record format looks like this:

```
_http._tcp.inside-corner.com.  IN   SRV 0  0  80
www.inside-corner.com.
```

The fields are as follows:

- *Name:* Designates the name of the service. In this case, **_http.** indicates a Web server.

- *Protocol:* **_tcp.** indicates that TCP protocol is being used. Options are TCP or UDP.

- *Domain:* The domain name to which the resource record refers. In our example, the domain is Inside-Corner.com.

- *Class:* In this case, the value is **IN** (the standard Internet System designation).

- *Type:* The standard Type field. Our example value, **SRV**, indicates an SRV record.

- *Priority:* The first value after the Type (in this case, **0**). As with MX records, hosts with lower priority levels are contacted first.

- *Weight:* The second value after the Type (in this case, **0**). This field is used in conjunction with Priority. When two records have the same priority, the Weight field indicates which server should be tried more frequently. The higher the weight, the more frequently a host will be used.

- *Port:* In this case, **80** is the standard port for the HTTP protocol.

- *Target:* The last field, which is the FQDN of the Web server (in this case, www.inside-corner.com).

Canonical Name (CNAME) Records

A CNAME record creates an alias for a specified host. This type of record is used most commonly to hide implementation details of your network. For example, suppose you have a Web server running at www.mycorp.com. The Web site might really be running on the server server1.mycorp.com. You don't want users to have to use the real server name; and you want the flexibility of being able to move the Web site to a newer, faster server in the future as traffic grows, without having to change the address of your Web site from server1.mycorp.com to server2.mycorp.com. CNAME provides the ability to alias the host name so such problems do not occur.

Other Record Types

There are many other, less common record types besides those listed here. Some are listed in RFCs and some, like WINS and WINS-R, are specific to Windows 2000. In most cases, you will not need to use resource records other than the common ones.

Dynamic DNS

For all of the improvements DNS added over HOSTS files, in essence the update process didn't change. Whenever a new host needed to be added to the network, an administrator had to manually add the appropriate resource records to the primary name server. Fortunately, a relatively recent RFC (RFC 2136) defined a means of dynamically updating the primary server. This RFC relieved a tremendous burden from DNS administration— with the caveat that it works only with Windows 2000 clients. Legacy clients, such as Windows NT 4 and Windows 9*x*, do not support dynamic updates. If you have systems running those operating systems, or other non–Windows 2000 operating systems on your network, you must still add the resource records for those hosts manually.

Dynamic DNS in Windows 2000 is used in conjunction with DHCP. When a Windows 2000 client boots up and receives addressing information from DHCP, it can register itself with DNS, automatically adding the requisite resource records. DDNS is enabled and disabled through zone properties. Simply right-click on your forward or reverse lookup zone and click on Properties. On the General property sheet are the Allow

Dynamic Updates? choices: Yes, No, and Only Secure Updates, as shown in Figure 4-12. When DDNS is enabled, DHCP manages the resource records for DHCP clients. When a DHCP lease expires, the DHCP service cleans up the A and PTR records from DNS.

4

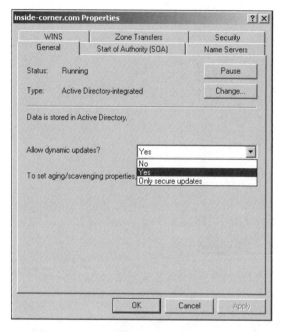

Figure 4-12   Windows 2000 DDNS is configured on a per-zone basis, through zone properties

MONITORING AND TROUBLESHOOTING DNS FOR ACTIVE DIRECTORY

As with any network service, eventually there will be some sort of problem. Windows 2000 provides some tools to monitor and troubleshoot DNS, however, so you can take steps when the DNS service is not behaving as expected.

In Figure 4-13, you can see the monitoring options in Windows 2000. To reach this window, right-click on the DNS server you want to monitor in the DNS MMC snap-in, and then click on Properties. Once there, click on the Monitoring tab. The options and their descriptions are listed in Table 4-2.

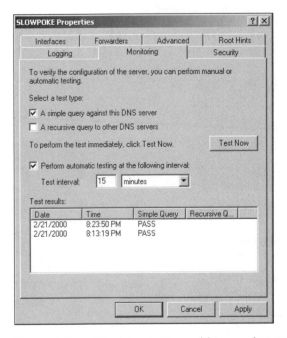

Figure 4-13   Windows 2000 enables an administrator to monitor the DNS service

Table 4-2   Windows 2000 monitoring options and descriptions

Option	Description
Simple Query	As the name implies, a simple forward lookup query is passed to the server for resolution. The result is either PASS or FAIL (as shown in Figure 4-13), and it is time and date stamped in the Test Results box at the bottom of the window.
Recursive Query	This option runs a more complex query, where the server queries other servers until it can resolve the query or runs out of options and fails. With a recursive query, the name server cannot simply refer the client query to another name server.
Perform Automatic Testing	This option tells the server to run the tests you choose at the interval you specify. Doing so is helpful in troubleshooting intermittent server problems.

DNS Logging

In addition to monitoring, you can also enable logging of selected DNS events. You configure logging through the Logging property sheet in the DNS server's properties. In fact, the Logging tab is right next to the Monitoring tab previously discussed. Logging should be performed only for debugging or troubleshooting purposes, because the act of logging will have a negative impact on server performance and hard disk space. The Logging property sheet is shown in Figure 4-14.

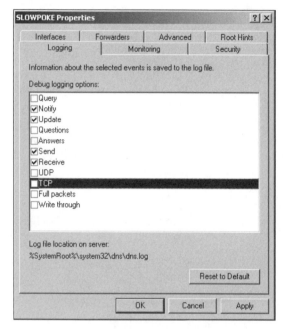

Figure 4-14   Logging is a useful troubleshooting tool when a DNS server is not responding as expected

nslookup

The primary command-line tool for troubleshooting DNS, **nslookup** also makes a handy security tool for tracing hackers back to their source. This basic TCP/IP tool is already on your system if you have the TCP/IP protocol installed.

Remember that if you want nslookup to be able to resolve host names from IP addresses, you must have already configured a reverse lookup zone. nslookup has two modes: noninteractive and interactive. In noninteractive mode, you simply enter a command such as

```
C:\> nslookup 192.168.0.1
```

If nslookup is successful, it will return the host name associated with the IP address in question. There are a number of options for nslookup in noninteractive mode; you can access them by typing "nslookup /?" at a command prompt. One of the more common options is **–server**, which allows you to specify a name server to test other than the current primary DNS server configured on the client.

You enter interactive mode by typing "nslookup" and pressing Enter. To leave interactive mode, type "exit" at a prompt. Typically, you'll use interactive mode when you want more than a single piece of information returned, or when you are running multiple queries one after another.

35

CHAPTER SUMMARY

DNS is an essential ingredient in a Windows 2000 Active Directory environment. You need to know a lot of theory about how DNS works before you can confidently sit down and configure a DNS server on your network. With the information in this chapter, you should now feel more comfortable with the name resolution process, configuring zones, managing zone transfer for Active Directory–integrated and standard zones, and monitoring and troubleshooting the DNS service if it doesn't function correctly.

Key points to remember from this chapter are as follows:

◻ DNS is a hierarchical namespace that replaces the flat namespace provided by HOSTS files.

◻ DNS is a distributed database, meaning a single name server doesn't have to hold the entire database of host-to-IP address mappings.

◻ The most basic name resolution query is a forward lookup query.

◻ Reverse lookup queries resolve host names from IP addresses.

◻ Caching-only servers are not authoritative for any zone and do not hold a zone database file.

◻ DNS forwarders are used so that only one name server in a zone communicates with DNS servers outside of the local zone.

◻ A secondary server can be updated by a full zone transfer, incremental transfer, or DNS Notify.

◻ At least one forward lookup zone must be configured for DNS services to work.

◻ Resource records are the basic units of information stored in DNS.

◻ Dynamic DNS requires Windows 2000 clients using DHCP.

◻ **nslookup** is the primary troubleshooting tool for the DNS service.

5

INSTALLING ACTIVE DIRECTORY

After completing this chapter, you will be able to:

♦ Create a Windows 2000 domain

♦ Understand the role of DCPromo.exe and the Configure Your Server wizard

♦ Use the Active Directory Installation Wizard

♦ Promote a member server to a domain controller

♦ Demote a domain controller to a member server

♦ Understand the role of the Active Directory database

♦ Understand the role of the shared system volume

♦ Understand Active Directory domain modes

♦ Install Active Directory on a Windows 2000 server

♦ Add additional domain controllers to a domain

♦ Change the mode of a Windows 2000 domain

This chapter discusses installing and configuring the Windows 2000 Active Directory. We will discuss the various tools available for installing Active Directory, the components of Active Directory that are installed, and the different domain modes that Active Directory supports. Through examples and projects, you will learn how to create Windows 2000 domains, manipulate domain controllers, and remove domains from the network.

As mentioned in an earlier chapter, the Windows 2000 Active Directory uses domain controllers (DCs) to store the database of objects and containers that create the domain tree. Each DC contains the complete records of that domain's objects, containers, and organizational units. Each of these DCs is a **peer**, meaning that it is capable of providing domain logon, security, and management functionality.

When we speak of installing Active Directory, we really mean installing the Active Directory service on the DCs themselves. Many Windows 2000 servers are installed as member servers of a domain, and although they participate in the domain, they are not running Active Directory service itself. Rather, the member servers are Active Directory clients.

Member servers can be upgraded to DCs, and DCs can be demoted to member servers. This is a significant change from Windows NT 4 and earlier. We will discuss changing the role of a server later in this chapter.

Before we launch into a discussion of the actual installation of Active Directory within a Windows 2000 environment, we first need to discuss some preinstallation issues. Although some of this material will be a review of previous chapters, the importance of planning the initial installation of Active Directory cannot be overemphasized.

PREPARING FOR ACTIVE DIRECTORY INSTALLATION

It is extremely tempting to jump into Windows 2000 at full speed. In fact, the initial installation almost encourages that approach, with the Configure Your Server wizard launching immediately after the first installation. If you accept all the defaults while installing the first DC, however, the resulting configuration may not be suitable for your environment. For example, the default initial installation will configure your server to run on the 10.x.x.x network with a 255.0.0.0 subnet mask; it will also install the Dynamic Host Configuration Protocol (DHCP) and Domain Name System (DNS) services on the server. This configuration probably will not match your company's needs. Although the server can be reconfigured later, it is more efficient and effective to configure it correctly the first time.

Preparing IP Addressing Schemes and DNS

Unless you are creating a network from scratch or migrating from another network protocol, your environment probably has an existing TCP/IP addressing scheme and naming convention. Your naming convention is likely to be a NetBIOS naming style, with server names like Exchange01 and FileSrv01 or even Hermes. Although Windows 2000 servers provide backward compatibility with NetBIOS naming, a native Windows 2000 network environment operates entirely upon a DNS name resolution.

Domain Context

Unlike previous versions of Windows NT, a Windows 2000 domain does not stand alone. Instead, every domain exists within a **context**, or relationship, with every other domain in a domain tree. Windows 2000 automatically creates the required two-way and transitive trusts required to allow the newly created domain to function within the tree. During installation of the first DC, the Active Directory Installation Wizard uses the provided information to install the DC and create the domain within the existing context of other domains and DCs. If no other domains exist, then the newly created domain functions as the root domain.

Your planning will determine the context in which the new domain should be installed. For some network environments, organizing and installing domains along business lines will be appropriate. For others, a geographical breakdown makes much more sense. As an example, let us look at a fictional company and some ways to organize its domain tree.

Texas Pinball and Cattle Co. is a company that specializes in the sale and service of pinball machines to home and business markets. This company has offices scattered around Texas, but primarily it focuses in the Dallas/Fort Worth, Houston, and San Antonio markets. Each market has a home office and branch offices. Each office both sells and supports pinball machines.

Assuming that the company needs multiple domains, there are several ways to divide the organization. First, let's look at a geographical split. The company can be broken into a northern region that encompasses the Dallas/Fort Worth area and a southern region that encompasses San Antonio and Houston. For our purposes, we will call these the North region and the South region. If TexasPinball.com is the root domain owned by the Texas Pinball and Cattle Co., then each region could have a child domain: North.TexasPinball.com and South.TexasPinball.com. Naturally, these domains could be broken down even further by cities, if needed. The resulting structure would look something like Figure 5-1.

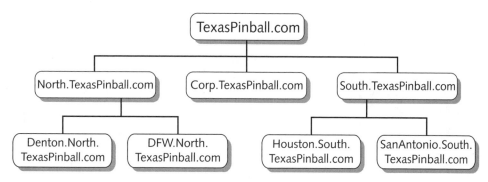

Figure 5-1   Geographical domain organization

Another method of organization is to split along business divisions. Once again, assuming that the company needs multiple domains, a natural division exists between the Sales and the Service departments. For our purposes, we will call these the Sales division and the Service division. If TexasPinball.com is the root domain owned by the Texas Pinball and Cattle Co., then each division could have a child domain: Sales.TexasPinball.com and Service.TexasPinball.com. Naturally, these domains could be broken down further if necessary—for example, home and business sales, electromechanical, and solid-state repairs. The resulting structure could look something like Figure 5-2.

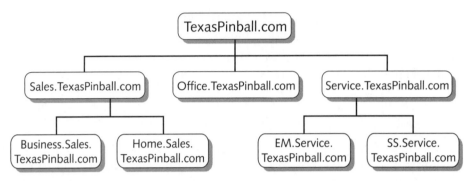

Figure 5-2 Business model domain organization

INSTALLING ACTIVE DIRECTORY

Once the planning for the Active Directory is finished, it is time to move on to the actual installation. Windows 2000 uses guides called **wizards** to perform many of the administrative and configuration tasks. The Active Directory service is installed using one of these wizards. The Active Directory Installation Wizard can be used to install Active Directory, upgrade a member server to a DC, or demote a DC to a member server. You can use two methods to launch the wizard—the Configure Your Server wizard and a program named dcpromo.exe—depending upon whether the server is newly built or has been previously configured. We will be looking at both of these methods and how to use them in this section.

Configure Your Server

If the server is newly built, a configuration wizard will follow the initial installation. This Configure Your Server wizard will allow you to install Active Directory on a server and configure it as the initial server in a domain. As mentioned earlier, the default configuration will result in a server running on the 10.x.x.x network with a 255.0.0.0 subnet mask and will also install the DHCP and DNS services on the server. Naturally, you can adjust each of these elements to meet your needs; for many administrators, however, canceling the initial configuration wizard and later configuring only the needed services will be the most appropriate choice, as displayed in Figure 5-3.

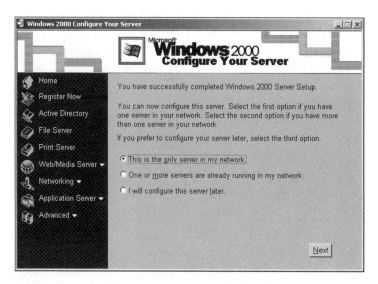

Figure 5-3   Initial Configure Your Server wizard

Dcpromo.exe

The Active Directory service can also be installed on a server that has been previously configured as a member server. The Active Directory Installation Wizard is activated via the dcpromo.exe program. To start the wizard, select Start|Run and enter "dcpromo.exe". The wizard will detect that Active Directory is not installed and will prompt whether to install the server as a domain controller in a new domain or as a new controller within an existing domain, as seen in Figure 5-4.

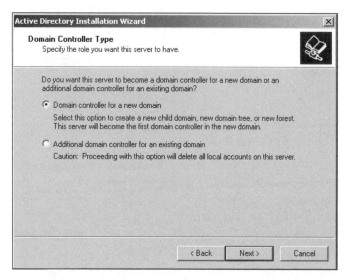

Figure 5-4   Installing Active Directory with dcpromo.exe

You also use dcpromo.exe to remove the Active Directory service from a DC and demote it to a member server. As you can see in Figure 5-5, the wizard detects the DC status of the server. If the server is a DC, the only option presented is to demote the server to a member server status.

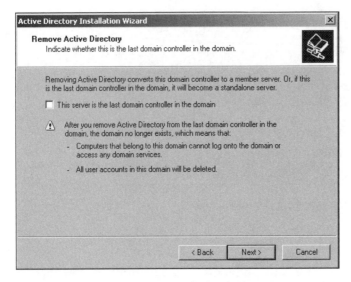

Figure 5-5   Demoting a DC with dcpromo.exe

 If the last DC in a domain is demoted, the domain itself is destroyed and removed from the network. All domain user accounts and services are also removed.

In most cases, dcpromo.exe is the method you should use to invoke the Active Directory Installation Wizard. You should use the initial Configure Your Server wizard only when installing the first DC within a domain—and even then, the best technique is to configure any prerequisite services manually and then use dcpromo.exe to install the Active Directory services.

CREATING WINDOWS 2000 DOMAINS

According to Microsoft, a Windows 2000 **domain** is a selection of computers or resources that share a single security boundary. In other words, everything within a domain shares the same security settings, rights, and relationships. Domains are not necessarily related to a geographical boundary; in fact, many companies have domains that consist of multiple physical locations. Conversely, multiple domains can serve a single physical location.

When multiple domains are interconnected via trust relationships, the domains can form a domain tree. A **domain tree** shares a common schema, Global Catalog, and contiguous namespace. Domains within a domain tree automatically form trust relationships that allow network resources to be shared throughout the tree. If several domain trees share a common schema, configuration, and Global Catalog, but do not share a contiguous namespace, then the trees are considered to form a **forest**.

Installing the Active Directory service on at least one DC forms a Windows 2000 domain. As mentioned earlier in this chapter, the Active Directory Installation Wizard can be invoked either through the initial Configure Your Server wizard or through dcpromo.exe, depending upon your needs and whether the Active Directory service has been previously configured on the server. In the next section, we will look at using the wizard to create a Windows 2000 domain, add an additional DC to the domain, and remove a DC from the domain.

5

USING THE ACTIVE DIRECTORY WIZARDS

After Windows 2000 is installed, the first screen presented to an administrator on the initial login is a Configure Your Server wizard, as seen in Figure 5-6. Due to the importance of the Active Directory service to a Windows 2000 network environment, that service is the first one presented by the configuration wizard.

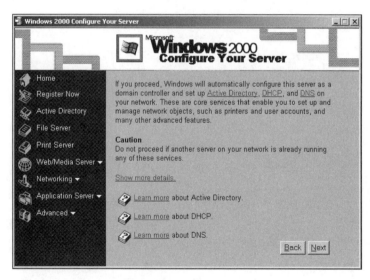

Figure 5-6   The Configure Your Server wizard

Installing the First Domain

In this section, we will look at the default installation of the first Windows 2000 domain on a network. For the purposes of this section, we will install Active Directory on the server as if it were the first and only server on the network. This process will install the

DHCP and DNS services in addition to the Active Directory service. In most real-world scenarios, some or all of these additional services will already be present within the network environment. If these services are already present, then Active Directory will need to be installed separately using the dcpromo program.

Beginning the Wizard

The Active Directory installation starts with the Configure Your Server wizard. After the initial installation of Windows 2000, this wizard walks you through the main configuration elements. The Configure Your Server wizard allows you to choose several different options, based on the role of the server within the network and whether an existing domain is already present (as was shown in Figure 5-4).

Installing the Domain

To install the first domain of a domain tree, first select the This Is The Only Server In My Network option from the opening screen in the wizard, and then click on the Next button as shown in Figure 5-7. The Active Directory Installation Wizard will automatically configure the server as a DNS and DCHP server, and it will also configure the server as a DC for the new domain. The wizard will inform you of these options, and it will also allow you to check the help files if you have any questions about the services it installs.

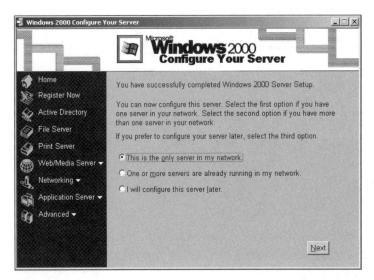

Figure 5-7   Beginning configuration with the Configure Your Server wizard

 If DNS and DHCP services are already available on your network, the default configuration of the Configure Your Server wizard is likely to cause issues. You may wish to cancel from this wizard and use the DCPromo.exe utility as an alternative.

Role of the Domain Controller

When a server is promoted to a domain controller and the Active Directory service is installed on it, the Active Directory Installation Wizard will prompt for the role of the DC. The DC can be installed as the first DC in a new domain or as an additional controller within an existing domain. For our purposes, we wish to install this computer as the first DC within a new domain. To create a new domain, select Domain Controller For A New Domain, as shown in Figure 5-8, when prompted by the wizard.

5

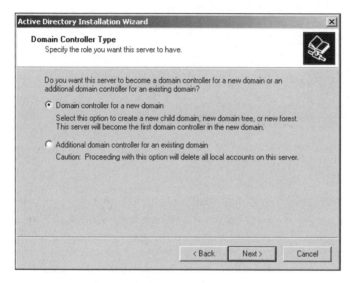

Figure 5-8   Selecting the DC role

Selecting the Domain Context

With the advent of transitive trusts in Windows 2000, the traditional NT domain structures are no longer relevant. Rather than implementing master and resource domain relationships, or creating a web of one-way and two-way trusts, domains are now structured in domain trees. As a member of a domain tree, a domain has a structured relationship with every other domain within the tree.

During the installation of a new domain, the wizard will prompt whether the new domain is a child domain within an existing domain tree, or whether the new domain forms the basis for a new domain tree. If the new domain is a child domain, you will be prompted for the placement of the domain within the tree. If you select a new tree, the wizard will assume the new domain is the root of the new tree.

For the purposes of this section, we will choose to create a new domain and new domain tree, as displayed in Figure 5-9.

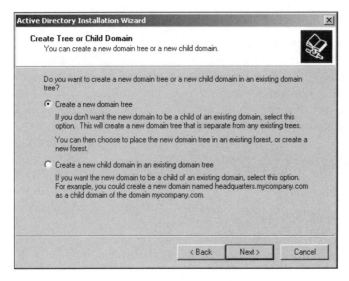

Figure 5-9   Selecting the domain context

The Domain Name

Unlike previous versions of Windows NT, Windows 2000 uses DNS rather than WINS for name resolution. One interesting effect is the need for fully qualified domain names rather than the shorter NetBIOS domain names of the past. Many times, a company will already have registered a DNS domain name for use on the Internet. If so, the internal network can be a subset, or **subdomain**, of that Internet domain name. If your company does not have a registered domain, it is best to use local as the root, to avoid name conflicts with external resources. Some companies will register two domain names and then use one for external servers and the other for internal domain structures. Doing so helps minimize the chances of internal data leaking to the outside network.

For our purposes, we will install the new domain tree for a mythical company, Net-Solutions of North Texas. Net-Solutions owns the Net-Solutions.com domain and is currently using it for external purposes only, such as maintaining a Web presence and receiving e-mail. The company's ISP currently provides DNS services for the external network. The MIS manager has decided to use the Net-Solutions.com domain name for the internal network also.

Because the company's corporate headquarters is located in Dallas, a decision is made to create a subdomain of the net-solutions.com domain and name it Dallas.Net-Solutions.com, as shown in Figure 5-10. This domain is for internal use only, and should not be registered with the external DNS server. The first server is imaginatively named Win2K, and thus the computer name is Win2k.Dallas.Net-Solutions.com.

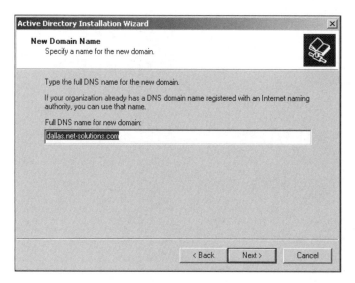

Figure 5-10   Creating the domain name

The NetBIOS Domain Name

As mentioned earlier, Windows 2000 no longer uses NetBIOS name resolution, but rather resolves names via DNS. Earlier versions of Microsoft operating systems rely on NetBIOS naming, however. These downlevel operating systems include Windows NT version 4 and previous versions, Windows 95 and 98, and Windows 3.*x*. In order for these operating systems to access a Windows 2000 domain, the domain must also be given a NetBIOS name.

In this case, we'll choose the NetBIOS domain name to match the DNS subdomain. As shown in Figure 5-11, because the DNS name of the domain is Dallas.Net-Solutions.com, the NetBIOS name of the domain is DALLAS. The domain will appear as Dallas in the domain lists when viewed by a downlevel operating system.

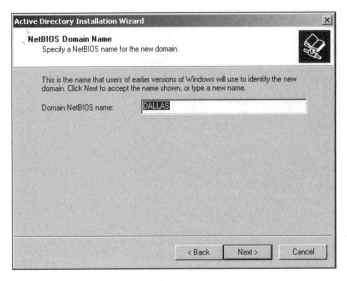

Figure 5-11   NetBIOS domain name

 The NetBIOS domain name does not have to be the same as the Windows 2000 DNS domain name. However, matching the names can help ease recordkeeping and troubleshooting.

Active Directory Database and Logs

Windows 2000 uses both a database and database log files to maintain the directory within a domain. The default location for both the database and the log files is within the *%systemroot%*\NTDS directory, as seen in Figure 5-12. The **systemroot** directory is the installation location of Windows 2000; in a default Windows 2000 install, the directory will be C:\WINNT.

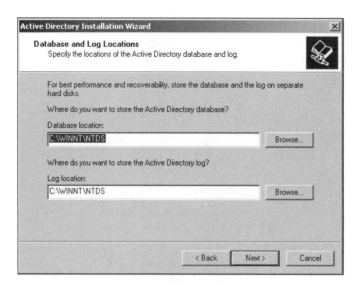

Figure 5-12   Active Directory database and logfile locations

To maximize performance on a Windows 2000 server, the log files and the database should be separated onto different physical hard drives or drive arrays. If you desire, you can split the Windows 2000 operating system, the Active Directory database, and the Active Directory log across three separate physical drives or drive arrays.

The Shared System Volume

All domain controllers within a Windows 2000 network contain a series of folders that contain the logon scripts and some policy objects for both the enterprise and the local domain. The SYSVOL share is roughly analogous to the NETLOGON share in earlier versions of the Windows NT operating systems. However, only Windows 2000 clients will read logon scripts and policies from a DC's SYSVOL share. For compatibility with downlevel systems, Windows 2000 still supports the NETLOGON share.

As shown in Figure 5-13, the default location for the shared system volume is within the *%systemroot%*\SYSVOL directory. The *systemroot* directory is the installation location of Windows 2000; in a default Windows 2000 installation, the directory will be C:\WINNT.

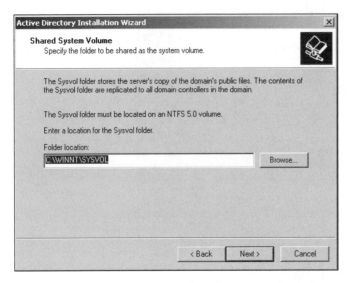

Figure 5-13   Active Directory shared system volume location

 The shared system volume must be located on an NTFS 5 partition or volume. NTFS 5 is the new implementation of the NT File System that is part of Windows 2000.

Installing DNS

Windows 2000 uses DNS as a method of locating the domain controllers for a domain. A client on a Windows 2000 network queries the DNS server, and the DNS server returns the address for the DC closest to the client. The client then contacts and is authorized by the DC, and uses the Active Directory database on the controller to locate objects within the domain.

Microsoft's latest implementation of DNS extends the traditional capabilities of DNS somewhat, with the integration of Dynamic Domain Name Service (DDNS). DDNS allows DCs to automatically change the records for the domain as computers join and leave the network. Due to the integration of DDNS and Active Directory, a Windows 2000 environment will require at least one server running Microsoft DNS. If the Active Directory Installation Wizard cannot communicate with a Microsoft DNS server, it will prompt you to install the DNS services, as shown in Figure 5-14.

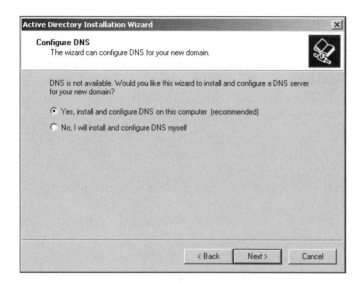

Figure 5-14 Installing DNS on the Windows 2000 server

 If another DNS solution is already in place on the network, you need to plan carefully before activating the first Windows 2000 DNS server on the network. Failure to plan the implementation of DNS may result in incorrect name resolution for both internal network clients and external clients.

The DNS installation will automatically install the forward and reverse lookup zones for the domain and populate the zones with the Start of Authority (SOA) records, name server records, and known hosts. The default installation assumes that it is the root DNS server. DNS records can be viewed and modified via the DNS snap-in, as seen in Figure 5-15.

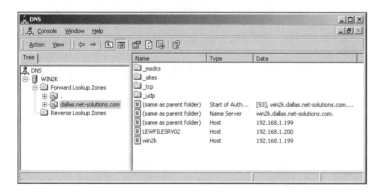

Figure 5-15 Viewing DNS records on the Windows 2000 server

Directory Services Restore Mode

The Directory Services Restore Mode is a safe-mode option that allows an administrator to restore the SYSVOL directory and Active Directory database from backup if needed. The Directory Services Restore Mode requires a special local administrator logon, because the server will not be able to access the Active Directory database and thus will not be functioning as a DC in this mode.

The Restore Mode administrator account and password are similar to the local administrator role within an NT 4 member server. As seen in Figure 5-16, the Active Directory Installation Wizard will prompt for the password of the account during the installation. It is important to remember this password, because the Active Directory cannot be restored without it.

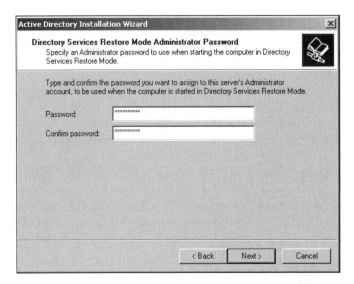

Figure 5-16 Entering the Active Directory Restore Mode password

 If you forget the Directory Services Restore Mode password, the Active Directory cannot be recovered on a DC. You will have to demote the server to a member server via dcpromo.exe and then reinstall Active Directory services on the server.

Final Review and Installation

After all the selections have been made, Windows 2000 will show a summary screen of your choices, as shown in Figure 5-17. If any selections need to be changed, click on the Back button to make the necessary modifications. If the selections are correct, click on Next to begin the installation of the Active Directory service and to create the Windows 2000 domain.

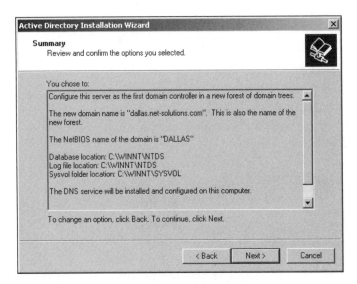

Figure 5-17   Verify final installation selections

Promoting a Server to a Domain Controller

Once a Windows 2000 domain has been created, you can add domain controllers to the domain to improve redundancy and provide additional logon points. The additional DCs contain a complete copy of the Active Directory database and replicate changes to that database to other DCs.

Windows 2000 uses a **multi-master** domain model, which means that each DC is a peer. The multi-master method provides fault tolerance by allowing any DC to process changes and updates to the Active Directory database. This process is in contrast to earlier versions of Windows NT, which required the Primary Domain Controller (PDC) to be online before modifications could be made to the domain security information.

An additional contrast to earlier versions of Windows NT is the ability to promote normal servers to DCs, and the ability to demote DCs to normal servers. Windows NT 4 and earlier required that the operating system be reinstalled if a server was to be promoted to a DC or demoted to a member server. Windows 2000 offers that ability without reinstalling the operating system.

The process of upgrading a server to a DC is similar to installing the first DC. The dcpromo.exe utility is used to promote or demote a server.

Beginning the Wizard

Start the Active Directory Installation Wizard by launching dcpromo.exe from a command line or by selecting Start|Run and entering "dcpromo.exe". Once the wizard begins, it will recognize that the server is not a DC. The wizard will give you the option of creating a new domain or adding an additional DC to a domain.

To upgrade the server to a DC within the domain, select Additional Domain Controller For An Existing Domain, as shown previously in Figure 5-4.

Network Credentials

In order to upgrade a server to a domain controller, you must have administrative rights on the server and within the domain. As shown in Figure 5-18, the wizard will prompt you for the username, password, and domain of the account you wish to use while installing the Active Directory service.

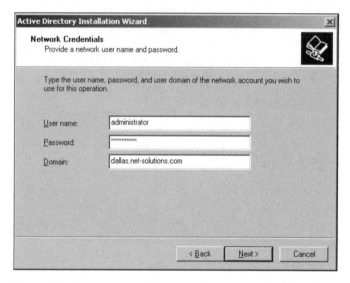

Figure 5-18   Entering the network account for the installation

Selecting the Domain

The Active Directory Installation Wizard will prompt you for the domain to which the new DC will be added. As shown in Figure 5-19, the domain name will default to the domain of which the server is currently a member. If you wish the server to become a DC within a different domain, then click on the Browse button to choose another domain.

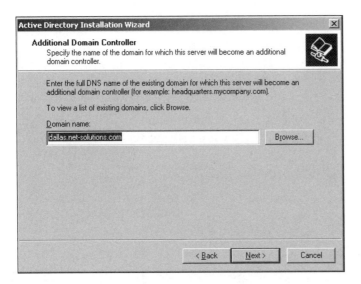

Figure 5-19   Selecting the domain for the new DC

The remainder of the wizard is nearly identical to the steps used in creating a new domain. You select the locations of the SYSVOL, Active Directory database, and Active Directory logs, and choose the Directory Services Restore Mode password. After that point, the directory service is installed and the domain information is replicated to the new DC. Once the database has been replicated to the server, it is ready to function as a DC on the network.

Demoting a Domain Controller

Unlike previous versions of Windows NT, Windows 2000 offers the ability to demote a domain controller to a member server without forcing an operating system reinstallation. This ability can also be used to completely remove a domain from a network.

You use dcpromo.exe to demote a DC. The program launches the Active Directory Installation Wizard. The wizard detects that the server is already a DC and offers the option to remove the Active Directory service from the server. If other DCs exist within the domain, the server will become a member server within the domain. If there are no other DCs within the domain, removing the Active Directory service will dissolve the domain and result in a standalone server.

Removing the last DC within a domain will result in the deletion of all domain accounts and removal of domain services. Any computers that belong to the deleted domain will be unable to log in to the domain; only local user accounts on those computers will function.

Removing Active Directory

Start the Active Directory Installation Wizard by launching dcpromo.exe from a command line or by selecting Start|Run and entering "dcpromo.exe". Once the wizard begins, it will recognize that the server is a DC. The wizard will give you the option to remove the Active Directory service and demote the server to a member server.

Select This server is the last domain controller in the domain, as shown in Figure 5-20, to remove the domain from the network and convert the server to a standalone server.

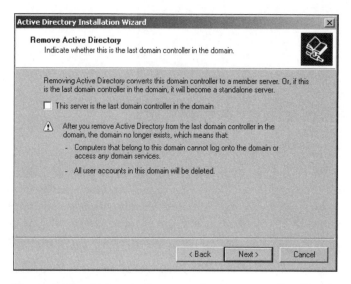

Figure 5-20   Using dcpromo.exe to remove Active Directory

Local Administrator Password

Once the Active Directory service is removed, the server will function as a member server. As with earlier versions of Windows NT, member servers have a local administrator account that applies to that particular server. The Active Directory Installation Wizard will prompt you for the password that the local administrator account should use, as shown in Figure 5-21.

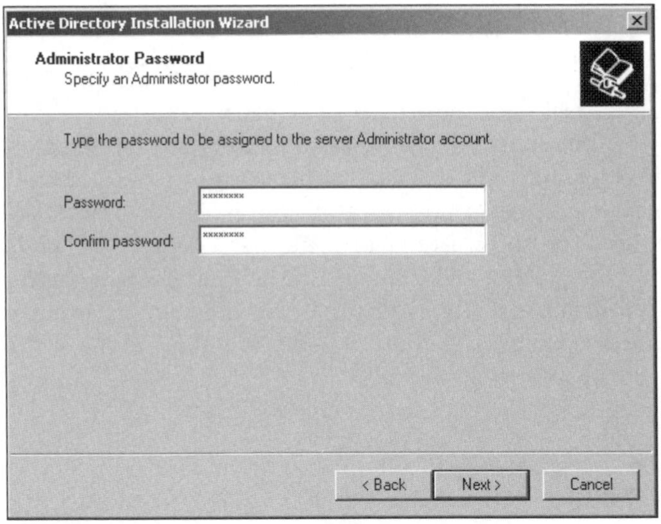

Figure 5-21   Set the local administrator password

Final Review and Removal

After all the selections have been made, Windows 2000 will show a summary screen of your choices. If you need to change any selections, click on the Back button to make the necessary modifications. If the selections are correct, click on Next to begin the removal of Active Directory service. Figure 5-22 shows an example of this verification.

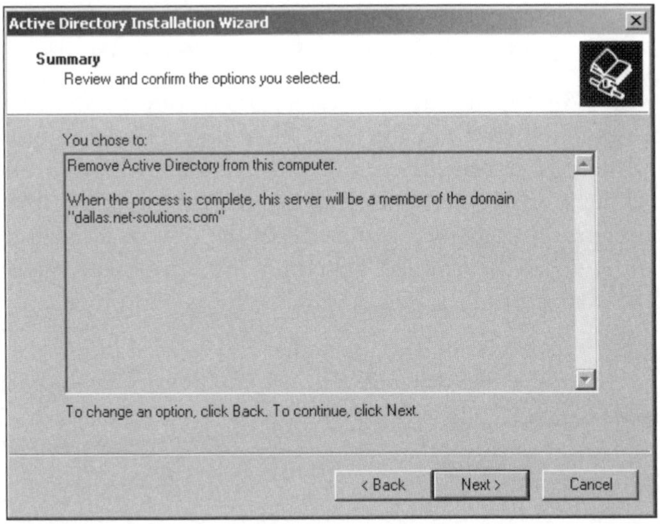

Figure 5-22   Final verification of Active Directory removal

UNDERSTANDING THE ACTIVE DIRECTORY DATABASE

Windows 2000 uses both a database and database log files to maintain the directory within a domain. The default location for both the database and the log files is within the *%systemroot%*\NTDS directory. The *systemroot* directory is the installation location of Windows 2000; in a default Windows 2000 installation, the directory will be C:\WINNT. The database itself—the record of all the users, computers, printers, and other objects within the domain—is stored in a file named ntds.dit. This database is updated whenever an object within the domain is modified. Each of these changes is also logged, so that the database's integrity can be verified in the event the Active Directory service terminates abnormally. Both the database file and the log file are discussed in more detail in the following sections.

ntds.dit

ntds.dit is a Windows 2000 Jet database that is improved over previous versions of the Jet database engine. It is based on the same database engine used in Exchange 5.5. Two copies of the database are stored on a DC, as follows:

- *%systemroot%\NTDS\ntds.dit:* This file is the current database that is used by the DC. It contains the values for the objects within the domain and the values for the domain forest. This location can be modified during the installation of the Active Directory service.

- *%systemroot%\System32\ntds.dit:* This file is a default directory that is used by dcpromo.exe during the installation of the Active Directory service. During the installation of Active Directory, this file is copied to the location specified within the wizard. Once Active Directory is installed and started, replication from other DCs replaces the default information with the current domain information.

The ntds.dit file size will vary depending on the number of objects within the directory and the attributes associated with those objects. Each object in the directory is represented as one row in the data table, and each attribute is represented as one column in the table. Windows 2000 offers the ability to store more than 1 million objects within a directory. Microsoft has performed tests on the size of the ntds.dit file based on various numbers of objects, and has determined that most installations of Windows 2000 should not exceed 3GB of space; in fact, 500,000 user objects consumed only 1.8GB.

The size of the ntds.dit file will vary as objects are added and removed from the directory. However, the apparent size of the file will not change. This occurs because of the way NTFS reads the size of the file. NTFS records the file size when it is first opened, and will not update the size until the file is closed. Because the Active Directory service opens the ntds.dit file when the DC boots, the file size is never refreshed. You can determine the current size of the ntds.dit file in two ways:

- Reboot the DC and observe the size of the file immediately after boot.
- Use explorer.exe to determine the available space on the partition, and calculate the size of the ntds.dit file from that available space.

The ntds.dit file can be located on NTFS, FAT, or FAT32 partitions. For best results and increased redundancy, it is recommended that the database be on at least a RAID 1 (Disk Mirroring) partition.

5

The drive containing ntds.dit must be configured for basic storage, not dynamic storage.

Database Logging

Windows 2000 Active Directory uses a log-based recovery method, in the event that the directory service is not shut down gracefully. Whenever a change is made to the directory, the change is first made dynamically within the memory of the DC, and immediately logged to the edb.log file. When the level of activity drops to an acceptable level, the changes are written permanently to the ntds.dit file and replicated across the enterprise.

If the directory service is stopped abruptly, such as in the case of a power failure, the log file is used to recover any changes that have not been written to the directory. The database reads the log files and reapplies changes in order until the database and log files are synchronized. The default location for the log file is %systemroot%\NTDS. This location can be changed during the installation of Active Directory. For best performance and increased redundancy, the Active Directory database and log files should be on separate partitions, and if possible separate physical drives.

Windows 2000 can either create a new log file when the current one is full, or it can overwrite the existing entries beginning with the oldest. If the system is configured to create a new log file, it is performing **noncircular logging**. If it overwrites the existing entries, it is performing **circular logging**. Circular logging saves space, but noncircular logging provides additional protection against losing database changes.

By default, Windows 2000 uses noncircular logging and creates additional files as needed. Editing the Registry can change this behavior. Modify the value of the key HKEY_LOCAL_MACHINE\CurrentControlSetServices\NTDS\Parameters\ CircularLogging and set the value to 1 for circular logging or 0 (default) for non-circular logging.

Registry editing should be performed with care. Incorrect modification of the Registry can result in a system that is unstable or even unbootable, and it is recommended that you have a current Emergency Repair Disk (ERD) before editing the registry.

UNDERSTANDING ACTIVE DIRECTORY DOMAIN MODES

Windows 2000 supports two modes of operation: native mode and mixed mode. A Windows 2000 domain is originally formed in a mixed mode style to provide backward compatibility with Windows NT DCs. The interoperability allows Windows NT DCs to receive replicated account updates and script or policy changes. Native mode does not support replication with Windows NT DCs, but it does allow for use of the more advanced security and grouping functions available in Windows 2000. Both mixed mode and native mode operation, including the advantages and limitations of each, are discussed in more detail in the following sections. In addition, we will discuss how to manually switch a Windows 2000 domain into native mode operation.

Mixed Mode

Mixed mode provides interoperability with domain controllers running earlier versions of Windows NT. This mode affects only the interoperability of the DCs; client computers and member servers of the domain that are running earlier versions of Windows NT or Windows 9*x* can function within a native mode domain. A network environment that has varied client or server operating systems is known as a **mixed environment**.

Mixed mode supports Security Accounts Manager (SAM) replication of both Windows 2000 and downlevel DCs such as Windows NT 4– or 3.51–based servers. A Windows 2000 domain can operate in mixed mode indefinitely, but it will not have all the capabilities of a native mode domain, such as universal groups and group nesting. Although many environments will eventually switch to native mode, there are several reasons to remain in mixed mode. Let's examine those reasons.

Inability to Upgrade Domain Controllers

In some cases, it is not feasible to upgrade a Windows NT domain controller to Windows 2000. Such cases may include unsuitable hardware for an upgrade or application incompatibilities with Windows 2000. If the DCs cannot be upgraded to Windows 2000 or cannot be downgraded to a member server, then the domain must remain in mixed mode.

Inability to Secure Domain Controllers

Due to the multimaster update method of the Active Directory service, physical security of the domain controllers is more important than ever. A physically insecure DC potentially could be used to modify accounts illicitly throughout the domain tree. If the servers cannot be secured, then leaving the DCs with a previous version of Windows NT may help minimize the potential security issues within the domain structure.

Lack of Resources to Upgrade Domain Controllers

One potential issue that is often overlooked is the cost involved in upgrading the domain controllers. In addition to any needed hardware changes, your company will have to pay Microsoft for the upgrade of the operating system. Depending on the size of the company, this may be a significant cost. Client licensing will also have to be verified with the new operating system, because some of the licensing modes have changed in Windows 2000. For some companies, any migration to Windows 2000 will have to be taken piecemeal.

5

Need for Fallback to Windows NT

Although proper testing will minimize any problems, there is always the possibility of problems with any new operating system. Maintaining the Windows 2000 domain as a mixed mode domain allows some degree of fallback. If it's necessary to switch back to a Windows NT–based domain, you can add a Windows NT backup DC to the domain, synchronize the SAM database, and then promote the Backup Domain Controller (BDC) to the Primary Domain Controller (PDC) of the domain. Doing so would allow for the removal of the Windows 2000 DCs without adversely affecting the clients and member servers of the domain.

Native Mode

After all DCs have been upgraded to Windows 2000, the domain can be switched to native mode. This change switches the domain from a single-master replication system to the Active Directory multi-master replication method. In addition, this change disables the NETLOGON replication, so that Windows NT DCs can no longer be added to the domain.

Switching to Native Mode

An administrator must manually perform the change from mixed mode to native mode. Dcpromo.exe does not have the capability to change a domain to native mode. The change is made using the administrative tools available in the Start menu or through Control Panel.

 The change to native mode is irreversible without the reinstallation of the OS. Once the domain has been changed to native mode, Windows NT DCs will not be able to receive account updates. Domains should not be changed to native mode if downlevel DCs are still participating in the domain.

To change a domain to native mode, first open the Active Directory Domains And Trusts snap-in, as shown in Figure 5-23, and then select the domain you wish to change.

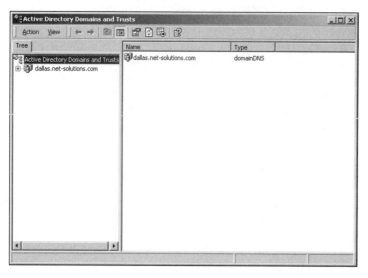

Figure 5-23   Selecting a domain to convert to native mode

Right–click on the domain to bring up the context menu, or click on the Action menu. Select Properties for the domain. The General tab of the property sheet will show the mode in which the domain is operating. In the example shown in Figure 5-24, the domain is running in mixed mode.

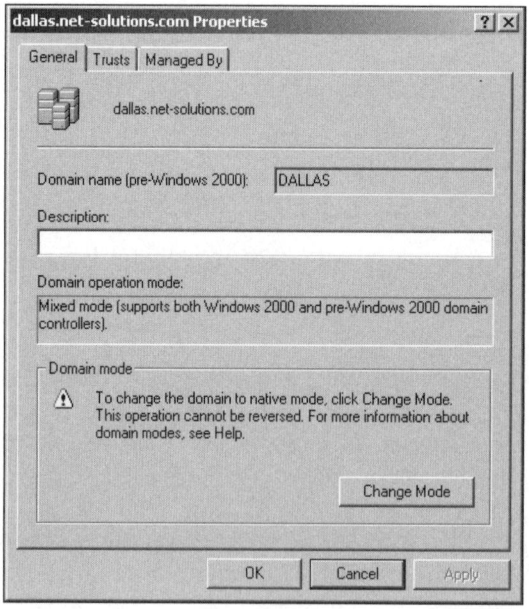

Figure 5-24   Domain operating in mixed mode

Click on the Change Mode button at the bottom of the General tab to switch the domain to native mode. This operation cannot be reversed. You will be prompted to verify the change before the domain is changed to native mode. Verify the change by clicking on Yes in the confirmation dialog box, as seen in Figure 5-25.

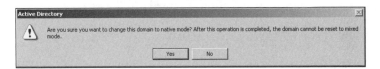

Figure 5-25   Final verification of the change to native mode

After verification, the domain will change to native mode operation. This may take some time, depending on the size of your domain and the connection speeds between your DCs. Once the domain has been changed, you can check the operational mode by again opening the property sheet of the domain. Note in Figure 5-26 that there is no longer an option to change the mode of the domain.

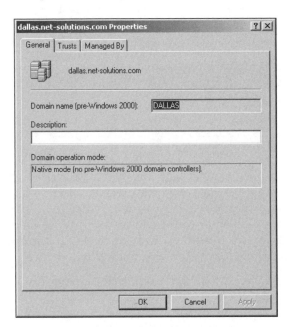

Figure 5-26   Domain operating in native mode

Native Mode Operation

Native mode operation modifies several aspects of the replication methods and group types. Some of the changes include:

- The domain uses Active Directory multimaster replication exclusively.
- Support for NETLOGON replication is halted.

- Windows NT DCs can no longer join the domain.
- All DCs now can perform directory updates.
- Windows 2000 group types are enabled, such as universal groups.
- Windows 2000 group nesting is now enabled.

Advantages of Native Mode Operation

The greatest advantage of native mode operation is the multi-master replication of directory changes, which allows any DC to propagate a change to the rest of the DCs within the tree. This replication is in marked contrast to the single-master method used in previous versions of Windows NT.

The second advantage to native mode operation is the automatic transitive trusts within a domain tree. With these automated transitive trusts, the administrator of the network no longer has to keep track of a web of trusts, nor is the administrator required to create the trusts manually. Instead, the Active Directory service automatically creates two-way transitive trusts when a new domain is brought into a domain tree. The result of these trusts is that users can log in to the domain from any location on the network and gain access only to their resources.

The new universal group capability is available only after a domain is operating in native mode. Additionally, all predefined security groups within Windows 2000 are available in native mode.

CHAPTER SUMMARY

□ Windows 2000 domains are designed around the Active Directory service, which is an enterprise-class directory service designed to provide seamless domain integration. With Active Directory, a client can log in to the network at any physical location and gain access to the correct information and resources. In addition, Active Directory automatically creates any necessary trusts between domains, freeing administrators from the manual intervention required by earlier versions of Windows NT.

□ Windows 2000 uses Domain Name Service (DNS) to perform name resolution, unlike the NetBIOS name resolution of previous Microsoft operating systems. In order to provide name resolution for an ever-changing selection of client computers, Active Directory integrates closely with Dynamic Domain Name Service (DDNS). This extension of the traditional capabilities of DNS allows for dynamic updates to the DNS records as computers register themselves with the DCs. Due to this integration, a Windows 2000 domain will require at least one Microsoft DNS server within the environment.

□ Windows 2000 domain structures require more planning than earlier versions of Windows NT. Because the domains are integrated within a single namespace and are automatically connected via transitive trusts, the domain space looks much like a tree. The first domain within a Windows 2000 domain is called the root domain, and each successive domain afterwards is a child of that root domain.

❑ Active Directory is installed via the Active Directory Installation Wizard. This wizard can be invoked in two ways. The first method is with the Configure Your Server wizard that begins automatically after the installation of Windows 2000. The implications of this method should be considered carefully, because it also will install DHCP and DNS on the server. If these services are provided elsewhere on the network, this method should not be used, in order to avoid conflicts.

❑ The second method to install the Active Directory service is to use the dcpromo.exe program. This program is invoked by entering "dcpromo.exe" on the Run line of the Start menu. This method runs only the Active Directory Installation Wizard.

❑ You can also use dcpromo.exe to promote a member server to a DC, or to demote a DC to a member server. Unlike previous versions of Windows NT, a change in DC status does not require a reinstallation of the operating system. If the last DC in a domain is demoted, that server becomes a standalone server, and all domain accounts and services are deleted.

❑ The Active Directory information is stored in the ntds.dit file. This file can be located on a FAT, FAT32, or NTFS partition. The default location for this file is the %systemroot%\NTDS directory. This location can be modified during the Active Directory installation process. For best performance, it is recommended that this file be located on a partition that is separate from the operating system.

❑ Changes to the Active Directory database are logged to provide redundancy and recovery capabilities in the event that the Active Directory service is terminated abnormally. The default location for this log is the %systemroot%\NTDS directory. This location can be modified during the Active Directory installation process. Due to the journaling capabilities on NTFS 5, the database logs must be located on an NTFS 5 partition. The logs work in a noncircular mode by default and create new log files when the current log file is full. Modifying a Registry entry can change this behavior. The log files should be stored on a separate partition from the database files, to increase the chances of recovery in the event of a hard drive failure.

❑ Windows 2000 domains run in a special mode to provide interoperability with Windows NT DCs. This mode is known as mixed mode operation. Although many of the features of Windows 2000 are functional in this mode, certain capabilities—such as multi-master replication and universal groups—are not. To enable this functionality, you must switch the domain to native mode operation. This change is performed manually by the network administrator via the Active Directory Domains And Trusts snap-in. Once the domain has been switched to native mode, Windows NT DCs can no longer participate in domain security. The switch to native mode is not reversible.

6

ACTIVE DIRECTORY
CONFIGURATION

After completing this chapter, you will be able to:

- Create sites within Active Directory
- Create subnets within Active Directory
- Create site links within Active Directory
- Create site link bridges within Active Directory
- Create connection objects within Active Directory
- Create Global Catalog Servers within Active Directory
- Move server objects between sites within Active Directory
- Transfer operations master roles within Active Directory
- Implement an Organizational Unit structure

This chapter discusses the steps necessary to create an Active Directory structure for an enterprise network environment. The Active Directory elements that we will examine in this chapter include sites, subnets, site links, site link bridges, connection objects, Global Catalog Servers, operations masters, and more. We will look at how each element is configured within Windows 2000 and how these elements interact.

CREATING A SITE

As we discussed in Chapter 2, **sites** are collections of computers that are connected via a high-speed network. Typically, the computers within a site are connected via local-area network (LAN)–style technology and are considered to be well connected. **Well connected** generally means constant high-speed connectivity within an IP subnet, although a site can include multiple subnets.

Windows 2000 creates the first site automatically when Active Directory is installed. This site is named Default-First-Site, and it includes the initial domain controller (DC). For a small LAN, the single site will be sufficient. For larger environments, however, additional sites must be created manually. To create a site, open the AD Sites and Services snap-in, shown in Figure 6-1, and open the context menu of the Sites folder. Select the New Site option to create a new site.

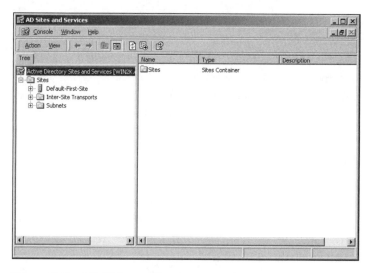

Figure 6-1   AD Sites and Services snap-in

The New Object–Site screen, shown in Figure 6-2, allows you to enter the name of the remote site and to select the site link for the site. Windows 2000 creates a default site link called DEFAULTIPSITELINK that can be used to establish the replication process of the Active Directory service. This default site link uses remote procedure calls (RPCs) over TCP/IP, and will use any available route to the remote site for replication. If explicit site links have been previously defined, those site links will show up in the lower portion of the New Object–Site screen.

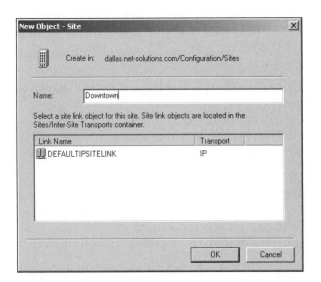

Figure 6-2   Creating a new site

Once the site is defined, you must undertake several other steps before the site can be activated within the Active Directory structure. These steps are nicely delineated in the dialog box that follows the creation of a new site, as shown in Figure 6-3. To finish configuring a site, you must do the following:

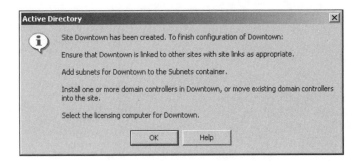

Figure 6-3   Required configuration steps for a new site

- Add appropriate IP subnets to the site.
- Install or move a domain controller or controllers into the site. Although a DC is not required for a site, it is strongly recommended.
- Connect the site to other sites with the appropriate site link.
- Select a server to control and monitor licensing within the site.

After these steps are completed, the site is added to the Active Directory structure, and the replication is automatically configured by Windows 2000. We will discuss each of these steps in this chapter.

Adding Subnets to Active Directory

Defined sites within Windows 2000 allow for a more efficient replication process than previous versions of Windows NT provided. Replication within areas of the network that are connected via high-speed connections is optimized to minimize latency and to minimize the time required to update records within the Active Directory. In contrast, replication across slower wide area network (WAN) links is optimized to reduce the required bandwidth and avoid flooding the link to a remote location, although Active Directory updates may require more time to take effect. In order for this more efficient replication process to function, Windows has to understand the network topology.

Because every network environment is different, Active Directory does not attempt to create sites nor to associate the subnets with the sites. Instead, the network administrator is tasked with creating these sites and associating IP subnets with the sites. We have already discussed creating a site, so we will now look at associating a subnet with these sites.

To associate a site with a subnet or a group of subnets with a site, first select the Subnets folder from the AD Sites and Services snap-in. Choose New Subnet from the context menu, as shown in Figure 6-4.

Figure 6-4   Adding a new subnet in the AD Sites and Services snap-in

The new subnet requires the subnet address and the network mask. You enter these items in dotted octet format, which is automatically translated into the network/bit-mask format. You select the site that will be associated with the subnet in the lower section of the property page, shown in Figure 6-5.

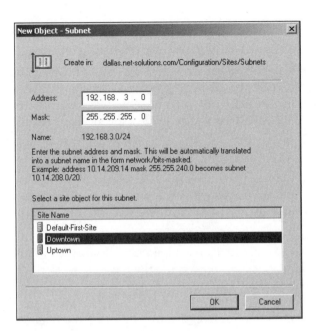

Figure 6-5   New subnet properties

Once the subnet is created and associated with a site, it and other sites will appear in the Subnets folder in the AD Sites and Services snap-in, as shown in Figure 6-6. The properties of each subnet can be manipulated by selecting a subnet and then selecting Properties from the context menu.

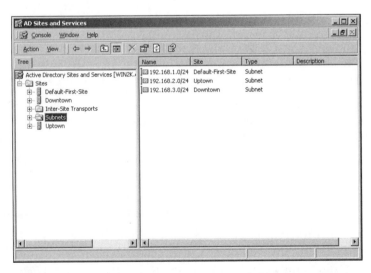

Figure 6-6   Subnets within the AD Sites and Services snap-in

Site Connections

A site is a subnet or selection of subnets connected via a high-speed connection. The sites themselves are connected via site links. **Site links** are low bandwidth or unreliable/occasional connections between sites. In general, any connection between locations slower than LAN speeds is considered a site link. WAN links such as frame relay connections are examples of site links, as are high-speed links that are saturated and have a low effective bandwidth.

Site links are not automatically generated by Windows 2000. Instead, the administrator creates the site links through the AD Sites and Services snap-in. The site links are the core of Active Directory replication. The links can be adjusted for replication availability, bandwidth costs, and replication frequency. Windows 2000 uses this information to generate the replication topology for the sites, including the schedule for replication.

Windows 2000 DCs represent the inbound replication through a special object known as a **connection object**. Active Directory uses site links as indicators for where it should create connection objects, and connection objects use the physical network connections to replicate directory information. Each DC creates its own connection objects for replication within a site (**intrasite replication**). For replication between sites (**intersite replication**), one DC within each site is responsible for evaluating the replication topology. The DC creates the connection objects appropriate to that topology. The server that is responsible for evaluating and creating the topology for the intersite replication is known as the Inter-Site Topology Generator (ISTG).

Site links, like trusts, are transitive. This means that DCs in one site can replicate with DCs in any other site within the enterprise through these transitive links. In addition, explicit links can be created to enable specific replication paths between sites.

Creating a Site Link

Windows 2000 creates a default site link named, naturally enough, DEFAULTIP-SITELINK. This site link can be used to connect sites in simple network environments, but in more complicated enterprise environments, you should establish explicit site links.

To create a site link, first open the AD Sites and Services snap-in. Open the Inter-Site Transports folder and then right-click on the appropriate transport protocol, as shown in Figure 6-7. Select New Site Link from the context menu to form a new link.

In our example, the name of the new site link is Uptown Frame Link. Although the name of the link is arbitrary, good administrative practice dictates that the name should be something that identifies the link, the connected sites, and the type of link. Of course, the link could be named Bob, but that name would probably confuse successors and co-workers.

The next step is to select the linked sites from the left column in the New Object–Site Link dialog box and click on the Add button to associate them with the link, as shown in Figure 6-8. A link must contain at least two sites; in general, a link will connect only two sites. If multiple sites exist at one physical location or are connected via a particular network path, however, then those sites could share a single site link.

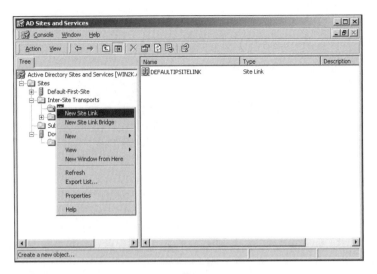

Figure 6-7   Creating a new site link

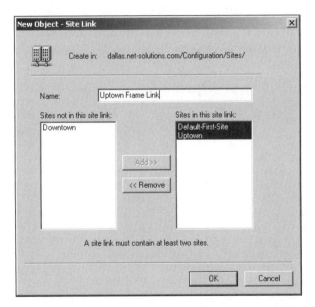

Figure 6-8   Naming the site link and associating the sites

Each site link has four properties that are important, as well as an optional descriptor. The properties are as follows:

- *Name:* A name that uniquely identifies the site link. As discussed earlier, this name should clearly indicate the sites being linked and the speed/type of circuit.

- *Cost:* The relative speed of the link in relation to the other links within the topology. The cost has nothing to do with the actual monetary cost of the bandwidth. Links with lower costs are faster, whereas links with higher costs are slower. The cost defaults to 100 on a new circuit.

- *Transport:* Indicates the type of transport used to replicate the directory information between the DCs. You have two options: synchronous RPC over a routed TCP/IP connection, or an asynchronous Simple Mail Transfer Protocol (SMTP) connection over the underlying mail transport network. This property is not set within the link properties, but is instead determined when the site link is first created.

- *Schedule:* Determines when the directory information is replicated between sites. This property is determined by two elements: the replication frequency and the available times. The replication frequency is adjusted within the properties of the site link, as shown in Figure 6-9. The schedule is a list of times that the site link is available to pass replication data. It is adjusted through the Change Schedule option within the site link properties.

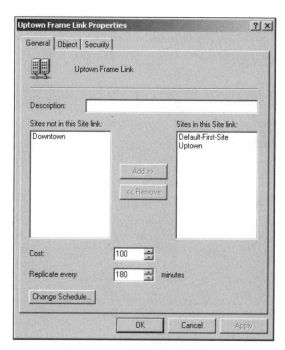

Figure 6-9   Site link properties

Site Link Bridges

Within a fully routed network, site links are transitive. As a result, all the site links for a particular transport are bridged together, and the replication can route between sites as needed. By default, Windows 2000 bridges all the site links for a particular transport.

If the network is not fully routed, then site link bridges must be explicitly defined for each transport. The transitive link feature can be turned off within each transport. You do so by unselecting the Bridge All Site Links option within the property sheet of each transport, as seen in Figure 6-10. Once the option is unselected, site link bridges allow transitive replication routing within the bridged links, but not outside the bridge.

6

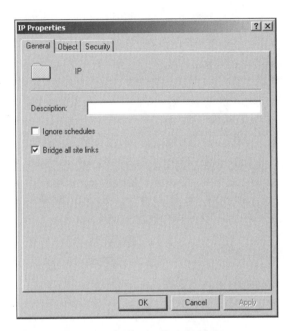

Figure 6-10   Default site link bridging

To create a new site link bridge, first you must have defined the site links themselves, as discussed earlier. Then, open the Inter-Site Transports folder and select the desired transport. This transport can be either IP or SMTP. From the context menu of the selected transport, choose New Site Link Bridge, as shown in Figure 6-11.

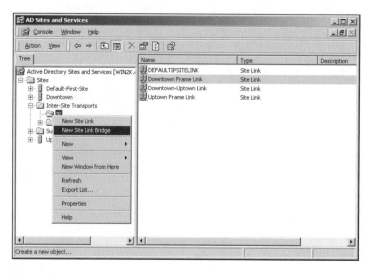

Figure 6-11   Creating a new site link bridge

The new site link bridge requires at least two site links. When these site links are bridged, a transitive replication link is generated across both links. In the case of our example in Figure 6-12, the downtown link connects the corporate center with the downtown center, and the uptown link connects the corporate center with the uptown center. Through the site link bridge, the uptown site can now replicate directly with the downtown site, even though no direct physical link exists between the sites.

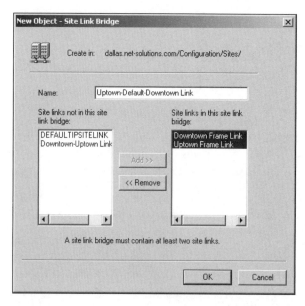

Figure 6-12   The downtown link connects the corporate center with the downtown center, and the uptown link connects the corporate center with the uptown center

Connection Objects

As we explained earlier, Windows 2000 DCs represent inbound replication through a special object known as a **connection object**. In general, connection objects will be automatically generated both within sites and between sites. If you don't use the Knowledge Consistency Checker (KCC) to generate replication topology, however, then you will have to generate the connection objects manually. To generate these objects, first open the AD Sites and Services snap-in, and then navigate to the DC on which you wish to form a connection object. Select NTDS Settings, and then choose New Active Directory Connection from the context menu, as shown in Figure 6-13. The next screen, shown in Figure 6-14, lists the DCs that can be used for inbound replication.

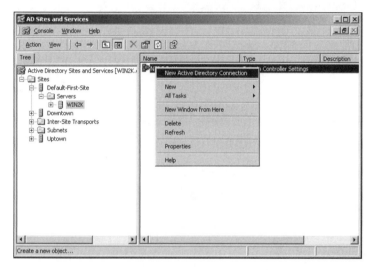

Figure 6-13   Creating a new connection object

Figure 6-14   Available DCs for replication

Choose the desired DC and then click on OK. The selected DC appears in the next screen, as shown in Figure 6-15. If this is the correct DC for inbound replication, click on OK to finish creating the site connector.

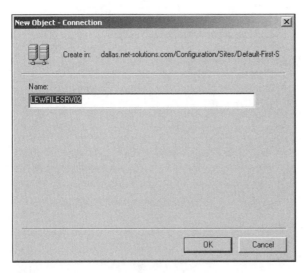

Figure 6-15   Finish creating the connection object

Once the connection object is created, you can view it through the NTDS Settings for each DC, as seen in Figure 6-16. Remember that connection objects are usually created automatically, and they can be dynamically modified to change replication if new DCs and sites are created. A connection object should be manually created only if you are absolutely confident that it will be needed on a permanent basis.

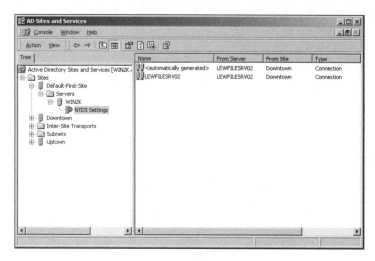

Figure 6-16   Viewing connection objects

 Manually created connection objects will remain until manually deleted.

Both manually and automatically created connection objects can be viewed through the NTDS Settings for each of the DCs. In the previous example, you will notice that the manually created object and the automatic object are identical, because we had only two DCs to work with.

Moving Domain Controllers between Sites

We discussed earlier how subnets can be associated with particular sites. After a site has been associated with a subnet, any new DC with an IP address within that subnet will automatically be assigned to the site. For example, if site Downtown has the subnet 192.168.1.0/24 associated with it, a new DC with the IP address 192.168.1.5 will automatically become part of the Downtown site. If a DC is assigned an IP address that is not associated with a particular site, the new DC will be assigned to the default site.

In some situations, the automated assignment does not fit the needs of the network environment, or pre-existing DCs need to be moved to the correct sites. Fortunately, this is a very easy process.

To move a DC between two sites, first open the AD Sites and Services snap-in. Navigate to the server that you wish to relocate, and then open the context menu for that server, as shown in Figure 6-17.

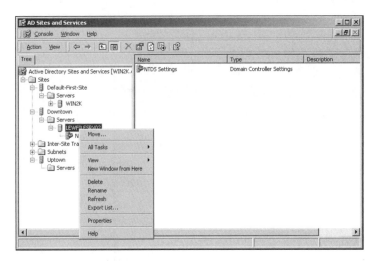

Figure 6-17   Moving a DC between sites

Select Move from the context menu, and then select the destination site, as shown in Figure 6-18.

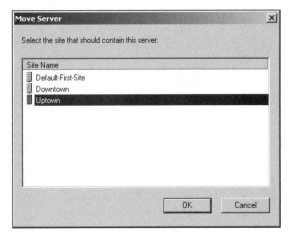

Figure 6-18   Select the destination site for the DC

Click on OK to move the server to the destination site. Obviously, doing so does not change the actual network settings on the DC itself. If IP address changes or other network configuration changes are necessary, those changes will need to be made on the DC before it will be able to communicate with the rest of the network environment.

The new configuration of the site will automatically be displayed within the AD Sites and Services snap-in, as shown in Figure 6-19. Note the new location of the moved DC.

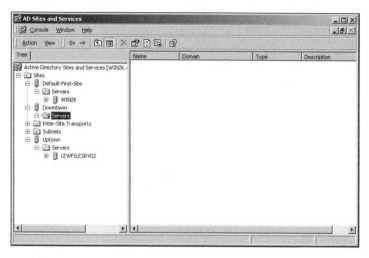

Figure 6-19 New site location for the DC

Global Catalog Servers

DCs keep a complete copy of the Active Directory database for that domain, so that information about each object in the domain is readily available to the users and services. This setup works well for the local domain, but what about information for other domains and the objects within those other domains? Remember, one of the design goals for Windows 2000 was a unified logon, no matter where a user was located within the domain tree. Obviously, for such a unified logon to work, the local DCs must have some information about the other domains within the tree and forest. However, replication of all the information about all the objects in all the domains within a forest simply isn't feasible.

Windows 2000 solves this issue through the use of a special limited database. This database is known as the Global Catalog. The Global Catalog stores partial replicas of the directories of other domains. The catalog is stored on DCs that have been designated as Global Catalog Servers. These servers also maintain the normal database for their domain.

Function of the Global Catalog

The Global Catalog has two primary functions within Active Directory. These functions relate to the logon capability and the queries within Active Directory. We will examine each in detail next.

Within a native-mode multidomain environment, the Global Catalog is required for logging in to the network. The Global Catalog provides universal group membership information for the account that is attempting to log on to the network. If the Global Catalog is not available during the logon attempt and the user account is external to the local domain, the user will be allowed to log in to only the local machine.

Obviously, if the account is part of the local domain, the DCs for the local domain will handle the authentication request. The Global Catalog is required only when a user account or object needs to be authenticated by another domain.

The majority of Active Directory traffic consists of queries, and queries for objects (printers, services, and so on) occur much more often than database updates. Within a simple single-domain environment, the directory is readily available for these queries. However, imagine for a moment a highly complex multidomain environment. It doesn't make any sense to require every query to search through each domain.

The Global Catalog maintains a subset of the directory information available within every domain in the forest. This process allows queries to be handled by the nearest Global Catalog, and thus saves time and bandwidth. If more than one DC is a Global Catalog Server, the response time for the queries improves. Unfortunately, each additional Global Catalog Server increases the amount of replication overhead within the network.

The Global Catalog is a read-only database, unlike the normal directory database.

Creating Global Catalog Servers

Windows 2000 automatically creates a Global Catalog on the first DC within a forest. Each forest requires at least one Global Catalog. In an environment with multiple sites, it is good practice to designate a DC in each site to function as a Global Catalog Server. Remember, native-mode Windows 2000 domains require a Global Catalog to allow users to complete the authentication process and log in to the network. A mixed-mode domain does not require a Global Catalog Server.

If additional Global Catalog Servers are desired, the service can be added to any DC within the forest. You do so through the AD Sites and Services snap-in. The Global Catalog can also be moved off the initial DC if additional DCs are available.

To create a Global Catalog Server, first open the AD Sites and Services snap-in. Then, navigate to the DC that you wish to be a Global Catalog Server. Highlight NTDS Settings for the desired server and then select Properties from the context menu, as shown in Figure 6-20. Doing so will bring up the screen shown in Figure 6-21.

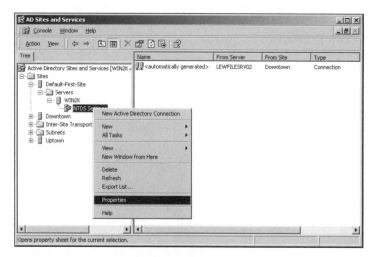

Figure 6-20   Creating a Global Catalog

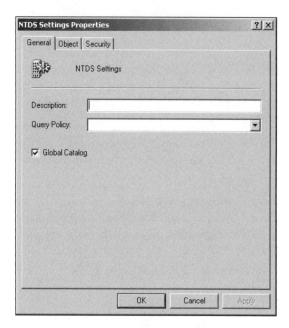

Figure 6-21   NTDS Settings

To enable the DC as a Global Catalog Server, simply check the box labeled Global Catalog. Deselecting the box will remove the Global Catalog from the DC.

Although any and all DCs can be configured as Global Catalog Servers, a sense of balance is necessary when designating these servers. As the number of Global Catalog

Servers increases, the response time to user inquiries decreases. However, the replication requirements within the environment increase as the number of Global Catalog Servers increases.

Operations Masters

Much of the replication within an Active Directory environment is multi-master replication, which means that the DCs are all peers. This is in contrast to earlier versions of Windows NT, in which a Master Domain Controller was responsible for recording all changes to the security policy and replicating those changes to the backup DCs.

Several types of operations are impractical for a multi-master environment, however. Windows 2000 handles these operations by allowing only a single DC to make these types of changes. This DC is known as an **operations master**. Five different operations master roles can be assigned to DCs: the schema master, domain naming master, relative ID master, Primary Domain Controller (PDC) emulator, and infrastructure master. Each of these roles will be discussed in detail a bit later.

The schema master and domain naming master operations master roles are assigned on a forestwide basis. Only one of each operations master can exist within a forest.

Schema Master

The schema master controls all the updates and modifications to the schema itself. As you will recall, the schema controls the definition of each object in the directory and its associated attributes.

To change the schema master, begin by opening the Active Directory Schema Manager. If this tool has not been installed on the DC, install the Schema Manager from the Windows 2000 CD-ROM.

Select the Active Directory Schema Manager. Right-click on it and choose Change Domain Controller, as shown in Figure 6-22, to select the desired schema master. You will have two options: The first allows Active Directory to select the new DC/schema master, and the second allows you to select the target DC. For our purposes, we will designate the new schema master. Enter the name of the target DC, as shown in Figure 6-23.

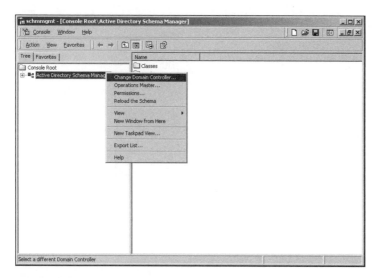

Figure 6-22   Changing the schema master

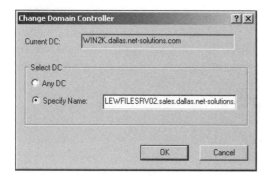

Figure 6-23   Selecting the desired DC

Doing so will change the focus of the Active Directory Schema Manager to the newly chosen DC. To complete the change, select the Active Directory Schema Manager from the left pane and then choose Operations Master from the context menu, as seen in Figure 6-24.

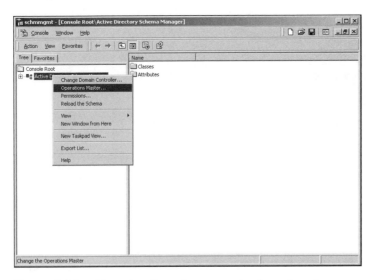

Figure 6-24   Changing the schema master for a forest

Doing so will bring up the property sheet shown in Figure 6-25, which shows the current focus of the Active Directory Schema Manager and the current operations master for the forest. Click on Change to move the schema master to the server listed at the top of the property page from the server listed at the bottom of the property page.

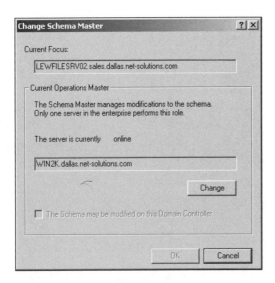

Figure 6-25   Final selection for the schema master

Domain Naming Master

The domain naming master controls the addition of domains to or removal of domains from the forest. As with the schema master, only one domain naming master can exist within a forest.

To modify the domain naming master, begin by opening the Active Directory Domains and Trusts snap-in. This modification is much like the schema master modification. First, connect to the DC to which you wish to transfer the operations master. You do so by selecting Connect To Domain Controller from the context menu, as shown in Figure 6-26.

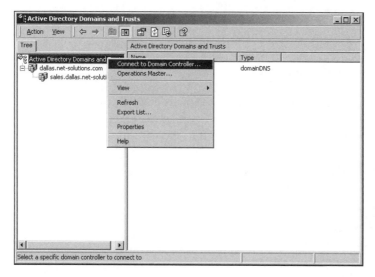

Figure 6-26   Changing the focus of the Active Directory Domains and Trusts snap-in

Select the target domain via the Browse button, and then choose an available DC from the list at the bottom of the screen. Selecting Any Writable Domain Controller will allow Active Directory to choose the target DC. If you wish, you can select a particular DC to which to connect. In Figure 6-27, we chose the DC for sales.dallas.net-solutions.com.

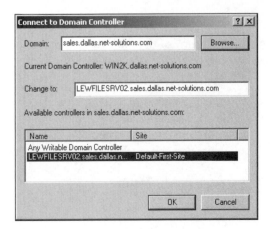

Figure 6-27   Selecting the target DC

Selecting the new DC automatically changes the focus of the Active Directory Domains and Trusts snap-in to the new DC. To change the domain naming master for the forest, select Operations Master from the context menu within the snap-in, as shown in Figure 6-28.

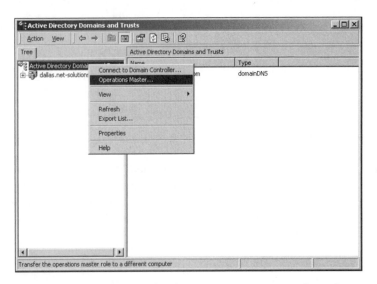

Figure 6-28   Changing the domain naming master for a forest

This selection will bring up a sheet that shows the current domain naming operations master and the targeted DC. Clicking on Change, as shown in Figure 6-29, will move the domain naming master operations role to the DC shown within the second box on the screen. The change takes place instantly, although replication of that change to the other DCs will naturally depend upon the replication topology and schedule.

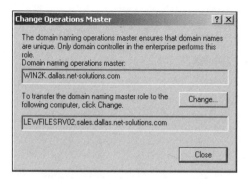

Figure 6-29   Final selection for the domain naming master

Relative ID Master

The relative ID (RID) master controls the sequence number for the DCs within the domain. The master assigns a unique sequence of RIDs to each of the DCs. When the DC uses all the RIDs that the RID master has assigned, the DC receives another sequence of RIDs from the RID master.

By default, the RID master is the first DC installed within a domain. To modify the RID master, first open the Active Directory Users and Computers snap-in. Select Connect To Domain Controller from the context menu, and then navigate to the target DC.

Once the target DC becomes the focus of the Active Directory Users and Computers snap-in, select Operation Masters from the context menu, as shown in Figure 6-30. Doing so will bring up the property sheet shown in Figure 6-31.

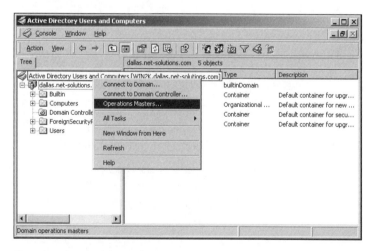

Figure 6-30   Changing operation masters within a domain

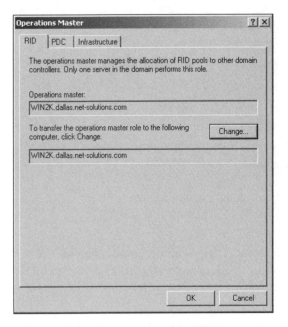

Figure 6-31   The RID master settings

The current operations master for the RID service should appear in the upper field, and the target DC will appear in the bottom field. In the case of a domain with only a single DC (not recommended!), the operations master cannot be changed. Click on Change to move the selected role to the new operations master.

PDC Emulator Master

The PDC emulator is used whenever a domain contains non–Windows 2000 computers and acts as a Windows NT PDC for downlevel clients and for Windows NT backup DCs. By default, the first DC installed in a Windows 2000 domain will be the PDC emulator, but this role can be modified if desired.

To change the PDC emulator master, first launch the Active Directory Users and Computers snap-in and change focus to the target DC as described earlier. Then, open the Operations Master properties from the context menu, as shown in Figure 6-30.

Click on the PDC tab to bring the PDC emulator to the forefront of the properties screen, as seen in Figure 6-32. The current operations master will be listed in the upper field, and the target DC will be listed in the lower field. Click on Change to complete the process.

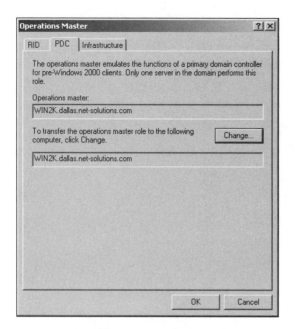

Figure 6-32   The PDC emulator settings

Infrastructure Master

The infrastructure master is responsible for maintaining all interdomain object references. That is, the infrastructure master informs certain objects (such as groups) that other objects (such as users in another domain) have been moved, changed, or otherwise modified. As with the other domainwide operations masters, this role is initially performed by the first DC within a domain. The infrastructure master role can be moved to another DC via the Active Directory Users and Computers snap-in.

To do so, change the focus to the target DC as discussed earlier, and open the operations master property sheet. Click on the Infrastructure tab, as shown in Figure 6-33.

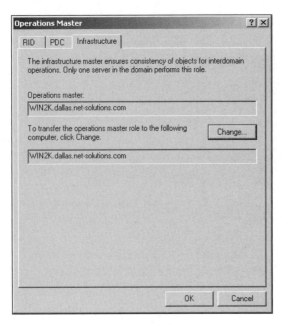

Figure 6-33 The infrastrusture master settings

The current operations master will be listed in the upper field, and the target DC will be listed in the lower field. Click on Change to complete the process.

IMPLEMENTING ORGANIZATIONAL UNITS

One of the primary advantages of Windows 2000 and the Active Directory service over Windows NT is the ability to control administrative powers more discretely. Under Windows NT, the base unit of administrative power is the domain. There is no way to grant someone administrative power over a subsection of the domain, such as a sales division or geographical office. This limitation means that either you are forced to make every required change to user access rights, or administrative power is granted to a larger circle of people.

Some workarounds exist to this problem, including the user of master domain/resource domain structures; but even these require careful planning and additional infrastructure to function correctly. Particularly annoying is the fact that competing network operating systems offer the ability to segregate administrative roles to a particular element of the network.

Fortunately, Active Directory introduces the Organizational Unit (OU) to the Windows networking environment. An OU is essentially a subset of a domain that can contain any Active Directory object. The network administrator can designate control of and access to each OU and the objects it contains. In addition, policies can be designated on the OUs in order to manage user policies and rights.

Essentially, two main uses exist (so far) for OUs. They are:

- Allow subadministrators control over a selection of users, computers, or other objects.
- Control desktop systems through the use of Group Policy Objects associated with an OU.

We will look at each of these uses in the following sections.

Delegating Control of Part of a Domain

One of the most common administrative needs is the ability to allow others to manage user accounts. A fine line always exists between maintaining security and delegating power to others. Windows NT offers the ability to grant the right to change passwords and other limited administrative control, but these rights apply on a domainwide basis.

Windows 2000 offers a capability to delegate various levels of control on only parts of a domain. You do so using OUs. As discussed earlier, an OU is a container that can contain various objects, including user accounts, computers, printers, shares, services, and much more. An OU can be treated as a subdomain for practical purposes—administrators of a domain retain control of the OU, but specific rights can also be granted to other users or groups.

Follow along as we create an OU and delegate control of it. In our scenario, the marketing department is almost like a separate organization, and its employees have decided that they need the right to change passwords for the division. Tired of changing passwords for marketing people at 2:00 A.M., the IT department agrees.

First, an OU must be created to contain the user accounts and other objects for the marketing department. All OU implementation and administration is accomplished through the Active Directory Users and Computers snap-in. Once the console is started, navigate to the domain within which the OU should be located. From the context menu, choose New | Organizational Unit, as shown in Figure 6-34.

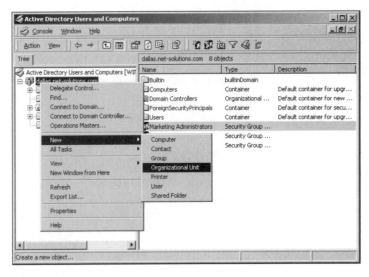

Figure 6-34   Creating a new OU

The first property screen for the new OU asks for a name. This name should be descriptive and should clearly show the role of the OU. Enter it in the Name field, as shown in Figure 6-35.

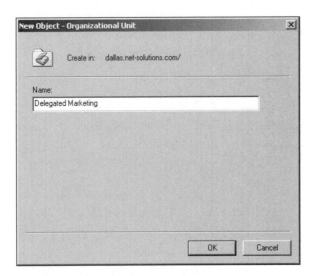

Figure 6-35   Enter the name for the OU

Once the OU is created, it must be populated. To move users, computers, or other objects to an OU, simply open the proper folder and highlight the desired objects. From the context menu, click on Move, as shown in Figure 6-36.

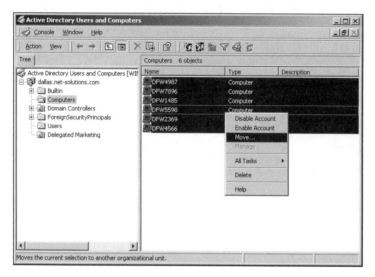

Figure 6-36   Moving objects to an OU

The next step is to select the destination OU for the objects, as shown in Figure 6-37.

Figure 6-37   Selecting the destination OU

After the various objects are moved into the OU, the contents of that OU can be viewed through the Active Directory Users and Computers console. You can see in Figure 6-38 that we placed in the OU both the Marketing group and the computers the marketing group uses. The computers are placed here for future use; the delegation would work just as well without those objects. The Marketing group contains the user accounts for the marketing department.

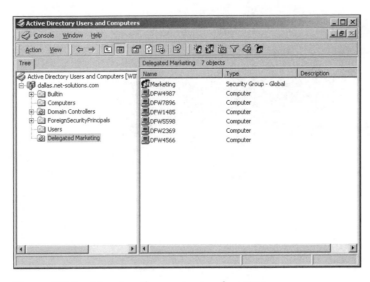

Figure 6-38   Viewing the contents of an OU

Once the OU is created, it is time to delegate control of the OU to a selected few marketing users. Begin by opening the Active Directory Users and Computers console and selecting the desired OU. From the context menu, select Delegate Control, as shown in Figure 6-39.

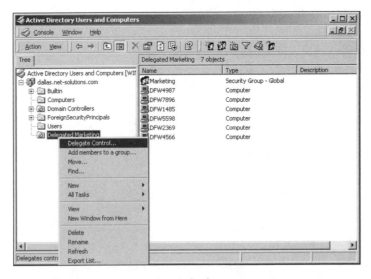

Figure 6-39   Delegating control of an OU

This action will launch the Delegation of Control Wizard, as seen in Figure 6-40. As with most wizards, just click on Next to pass the startup screen.

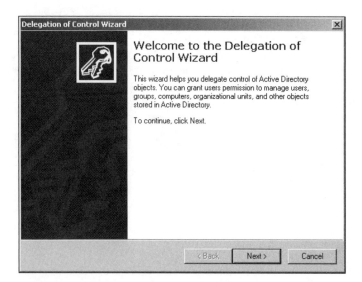

Figure 6-40   The Delegation of Control Wizard

Next, choose the group and/or users to whom the control is being delegated. In our case, we'll choose a group called Marketing Administrators, as shown in Figure 6-41. This group, which we created earlier, contains the user accounts of the two people trusted to change the passwords.

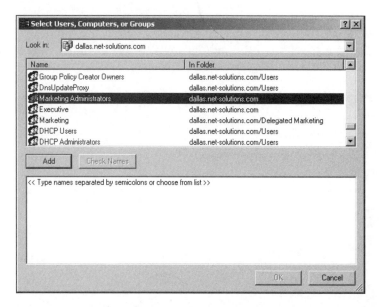

Figure 6-41   Select the group or users to whom control will be delegated

After this selection, choose the rights that the delegate should exercise over the OU. The options you choose here determine the abilities of the delegated administrator. Selecting Reset Passwords On User Accounts will allow the administrators for the OU to reset user passwords. As you can see in Figure 6-42, several other options are available.

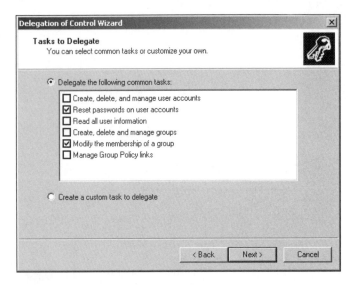

Figure 6-42   Assigning permissions

The last step merely confirms the rights granted to the delegates. You should always double-check and verify that the rights granted actually match the intended purpose. Remember, the rights are inherited throughout the OU. If the rights granted are correct, click on Finish, as shown in Figure 6-43.

Figure 6-43   Verifying the delegated rights

Group Policies and OUs

A second major use of OUs is to assign group policies to particular computers and users. Group policies are used to define default settings for computers and users, such as folder locations, what software can be installed, desktop appearance, and much more. In general, group policies are applied at a domain or site level, but they also can be applied at an OU level in order to generate a specific combination of user and computer environmental factors.

Although the many details of group policies are beyond the scope of this chapter, we will discuss how to associate a new or existing Group Policy with an OU.

First, open the Active Directory Users and Computers management console and navigate to the desired OU. After highlighting the OU, select Properties from the context menu. Doing so will bring up a property sheet like the one shown in Figure 6-44. Select the Group Policy tab to view and modify group policies relating to the OU.

6

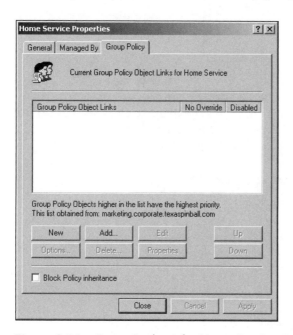

Figure 6-44   Property sheet for Home Service OU

To define a new Group Policy for this OU, begin by clicking on New at the bottom of the screen. A policy called New Group Policy Object will appear. Rename this policy to something memorable and descriptive. In Figure 6-45, the new policy is named Service.

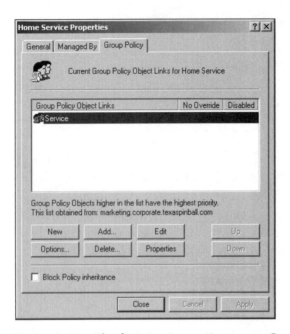

Figure 6-45   The first step in creating a new Group Policy

After the new Group Policy is named, it must be defined. Click on Edit to bring up the Group Policy editor, shown in Figure 6-46. After the policy is modified and saved, clicking on OK on the OU property sheet will finish linking that OU to the policy.

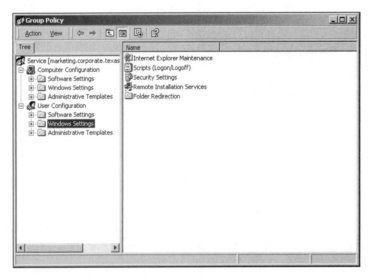

Figure 6-46   The Group Policy editor

OUs can also be linked to group policies that have been previously defined. To link to an existing policy, click on Add from the OU Group Policy properties. Doing so will bring up the screen shown in Figure 6-47. Navigate to the desired policy and select it. Click on OK to link the policy to the OU.

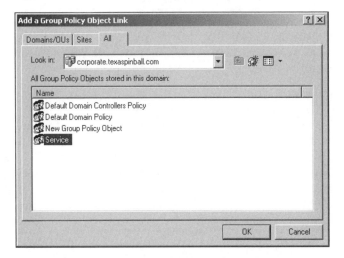

Figure 6-47   Selecting an existing group policy

Naturally, OUs can be unlinked from group policies, as well. To remove a Group Policy from an OU, open the properties of the OU within the Active Directory Users and Computers console. Click on the Group Policy tab, highlight the policy, and click on Delete. Active Directory will offer two options: to unlink the Group Policy from the OU or to delete the Group Policy from the Active Directory environment.

CHAPTER SUMMARY

❒ The most important element in designing and implementing a Windows 2000 networking environment remains planning. The Active Directory service requires much more planning than the Windows NT operating system due to elements like sites, site links, and replication scheduling.

❒ Once the planning is finished, it is time to actually implement the Active Directory structure. The core tool for configuration of the Active Directory services is—not surprisingly—the AD Sites and Services snap-in.

❒ Sites are areas of high-speed connectivity; typically sites correspond to a physical location and a LAN. Sites are connected via slower links. These links are typically WAN links or, more rarely, heavily utilized LAN links. A site is defined within the AD Sites and Services snap-in through the Sites folder. Windows 2000 creates an initial site called Default-First-Site.

❐ Once a site is created, an IP subnet or multiple subnets must be associated with the site. You do so through the Subnets folder within the AD Sites and Services snap-in. Now, any new computers created with IP addresses within that subnet are automatically assigned to the site. Subnets are entered with standard dotted octet notation, but are identified in a network/bit-mask format within the Subnets folder.

❐ Servers created before the sites and subnets are associated are placed in the Default-First-Site. The same is true for servers that have IP addresses outside the ranges associated with particular sites. These servers can be moved between sites through the AD Sites and Services snap-in.

❐ Sites are linked via site links. A site link is a network connection of some type between at least two sites. As with everything else related to sites, the links are created within the AD Sites and Services snap-in. The cost (relative speed) of the network link can be defined by the network administrator, as well as replication frequency. You also have the option of making the site link active only at certain times. By default, all site links are bridged to allow replication throughout the network environment. If the replication path needs to be controlled, then the default site link bridging can be disabled and specific site link bridges defined. Once specific site link bridges are defined, replication will travel only over the specified links.

❐ Global Catalog Servers keep a minimal database containing the users and rights from every domain within a forest. The Global Catalog is required to complete the logon process within a native mode, and it also serves to reduce query and logon times. Any DC can be a Global Catalog Server. This arrangement is accomplished by checking the Global Catalog option in the NTDS Settings for that server.

❐ The multi-master replication process eliminates many of the performance bottlenecks that affect replication in earlier versions of Windows NT, but it leads to additional problems. Active Directory corrects these issues by creating operations masters that have the sole responsibility for several tasks. By default, the first DC created within a forest controls all these roles, but all the functions can be moved to other DCs.

❐ Organizational Units are groups of users, computers, and other objects that can be administered as a unit. An OU can be used to form a type of informal subdomain within a Windows 2000 domain. You can delegate administrative control of an OU to a particular group or user via the AD Users and Computers console.

❐ OUs can also be used to assign particular policies to selections of users and computers. You do so through the Group Policy tab in the OU properties. An OU can be linked to a new or existing Group Policy, or unlinked from a policy.

7

ADMINISTERING ACTIVE DIRECTORY

> **After completing this chapter, you will be able to:**
> ◆ Identify common Active Directory object types
> ◆ Find objects within Active Directory
> ◆ Control user access to objects through permissions
> ◆ Understand how inheritance works with permissions
> ◆ Understand how to publish shared folders
> ◆ Move objects within a domain
> ◆ Move objects between domains using MoveTree and Netdom
> ◆ Understand how to delegate control to users and groups
> ◆ Explain the implications of delegating control

Active Directory is the new directory service that ships with Windows 2000. Many people would agree that it is the single-most significant new feature to arrive with this operating system. It affects not only the design aspects of a Windows 2000 network, but also the way administrators will interact with the network.

In the chapter, we will look at some of the ways in which Active Directory will affect administrators directly. We will show how you can use the directory service to query for information in ways that were impossible with previous versions of Windows. We will examine how the architecture of Active Directory will affect the way you control access to Active Directory objects, and how objects can be moved from one location in Active Directory to another.

One of the features that will require planning in your organization is the assignment of administrative permissions to other users or groups. This feature is called **delegation of control**, and it represents a shift in how our networks will be administered. In the past, system administrators bore most of the responsibility of adding users or creating groups, because it was difficult to assign administrative privileges on a granular basis. This situation has changed with Windows 2000 and Active Directory—it is now possible to compartmentalize users or groups and then to assign permissions over that specific group of computers or people.

This chapter focuses on some of the common tasks administrators will be asked to perform when working with Active Directory. As such, it forms a foundation for those tasks you must perform after you have an operational network. Although many people think that system administration consists of simply designing and installing a network and then adding the users and groups, you are about to find out that much more must be considered during this process.

QUERYING ACTIVE DIRECTORY

Active Directory is nothing more than a database. When you realize this simple fact, you can consider all the tasks you usually perform with a database, and you can begin to use Active Directory to help you with your administrative tasks. One of the most common tasks performed against a database is searching it for data.

Active Directory stores data about each object on your network, including your users, groups, and computers. These objects have unique and distinct names, and they also have attributes. It is possible to query Active Directory for this data either with the tool provided by Microsoft or by using a third-party program or script. In this chapter, we will take a look at one of the built-in tools that ships with Windows 2000. This tool allows you to search for objects within Active Directory.

Before we examine the tool itself, however, we should first describe some of the most common objects stored in Active Directory. This list is not exhaustive, partly because Active Directory is **extensible**—you can create your own objects within Active Directory. We will concern ourselves here only with the default object types that are created. The general principles of querying for custom objects are the same as those outlined.

Common Objects

When we refer to **common objects**, we are talking about objects that have been defined in the Active Directory schema. The initial set of objects has been defined by Microsoft. If an object exists in Active Directory, then every domain controller in the enterprise will have an entry that represents it. Therefore, queries can be run against any copy of the Active Directory (or domain controller). This feature makes searching for data very efficient, because queries do not have to cross your network to be resolved.

When you add a resource to Active Directory, you create an object to represent it. Every resource that has been added to Active Directory is an object, and can therefore be returned as part of a search request. Table 7-1 lists the common objects that are created. Along with the name of the resource, the table gives a brief description of what the object represents.

Table 7-1   Common objects in Active Directory

Object Type	Description
User Account	This object represents a user who has the ability to log on to a Windows 2000 network. You can search for the object (or user name) or you can use some of the optional fields available for this object, such as Home Address, Employee ID, Email Address, or Title.
Contact	This object type defines a person who has a connection with an organization, such as a supplier. Along with the contact name, you can also search for optional data such as Company Name, Division, or Fax Number.
Group	A group represents a grouping of user accounts, computers, or other groups. Groups are used for administrative purposes or security assignments. Along with group names, you can also search for optional properties such as Description, Members, Web Page Address, and Office Location.
Computer	This objects stores information about computers that are part of the domain. Along with the computer name, you can search for optional information such as the role the computer plays in the domain (Workstation, Server, or Domain Controller). You can also query specific fields such as Operating System, Operating System Version, and Managed By.
Printer	This object is a printer on your network. Printers that are added to Windows 2000 Professional systems must be manually added to Active Directory; printers added to a domain controller are automatically added. Along with a printer name, you can search for optional fields and features. Fields include Asset Number, Contact, Location, and Model. Additional features include the ability to print double sided, print in color, or staple.
Shared Folder	This object gives a pointer to a shared folder. It is only a pointer, because shared folders exist in the Registry of the computer where they are made. Therefore, a shared folder pointer in Active Directory points to the machine and entry only, not to the actual shared folder. Along with the name of a shared folder, you can also search for optional fields such as Description, Network Path, and Managed By.
Organizational Unit	An Organizational Unit (OU) is used to organize other Active Directory objects for administrative purposes. Along with the OU name, you can also search for optional fields such as Description and Managed By.

7

These common objects will probably make up most of your searches within Active Directory. Knowing the different types of objects is one part of the equation; without an easy-to-use interface to Active Directory, however, it will still be difficult to get the data you want. With this is mind, Microsoft has provided a Find dialog box in which you can quickly enter the data you want to search for and see the results returned.

Finding files and folders has been a common feature in Microsoft operating systems for quite some time. Microsoft has taken this familiar interface and extended it to accept the optional parameters and attributes of Active Directory objects. By using this interface, you can quickly search for objects within the directory.

Finding Active Directory Objects

You can quickly find objects within Active Directory by using the Find dialog box. This dialog box resembles the search tools used to search local hard disks in previous versions of Microsoft Windows 9.*x* and Microsoft Windows NT. This dialog box is shown in Figure 7-1.

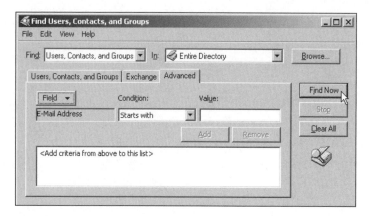

Figure 7-1   The Find dialog box

The Find dialog box's appearance may change slightly depending on the type of object you are searching for. For instance, when you choose Users, Contacts, And Groups in the Find drop-down box, an additional Exchange information tab allows you to limit the search to Microsoft Exchange recipients. Other object types might add items or remove certain options.

Table 7-2 defines and describes the various options available within the Find dialog box. The list given is extensive and attempts to offer you an explanation for every possible option. This dialog box is deceptively simple.

Table 7-2   The Find dialog box's options

Option	Description
Find	The Find drop-down list allows you to choose the object type you wish to search for. These object types include users, computers, groups, printers, shared folders, and more, as defined in Table 7-1. One of the most important options is Custom Search, which allows you to search for a combination of object types using Lightweight Directory Access Protocol (LDAP).
In	This drop-down box allows you to limit the scope of your search. You can choose to search the entire directory, a specific domain, or an OU.
Browse	The Browse button displays a hierarchical list of the folders and objects available. You can then specify a specific path to search.

Table 7-2   The Find dialog box's options (continued)

Option	Description
Advanced tab	This tab is context sensitive, meaning that the contents of this tab will change depending on the object type you have elected to search. This tab displays many different options, which are defined in the following entries of this table. You can use the Advanced tab to construct queries based on drop-down boxes or to enter queries manually. In order to do so, you must be familiar with LDAP queries. (A discussion of LDAP queries is beyond the scope of this book.)
Field	Located on the Advanced tab, the Field button displays a list of optional fields that are available to be searched. The list of fields will vary depending on the object type you have elected to search. Some of these optional fields were listed earlier in Table 7-1.
Condition	The Condition drop-down list is located on the Advanced tab. Once you have selected a specific field to search, you can further limit the search by defining a condition. Condition elements include Starts With, Ends With, Is Not, and Not Present.
Value	The Value text box is located on the Advanced tab. If you use a specific attribute to limit your search, then you must also enter a specific value to search. You don't need to use wildcards in this field. For instance, if you want to search for all user objects that start with the letter A, you can simply choose Starts With in the Condition field and enter "A" in the Value field.
Search Criteria	The Search Criteria box is located on the Advanced tab. This text box contains each of the search options you have defined. A single search can contain a combination of custom searches. As you create these custom searches, they are listed in this box.
Find Now	This button causes the search to occur.
Stop	This button causes a search to stop. You might use the Stop button if the search you created is taking too long (probably meaning it is too broad in scope) or if the search results being displayed are not what you want. When you click on the Stop button, the results returned up to that point are displayed. You should note that this may not be a complete list of success matches for your criteria.
Clear All	Once you have completed a specific search with custom criteria, you may want to perform a second search. In order to do this, you should first clear the criteria you configured previously. You do so by clicking on the Clear All button.
Results	When you perform a search, the Results window is added to the Find dialog box. This window displays the results of your search. If your search's results are too large to fit in the window, scrollbars appear and allow you to scroll through the result set. Columns are returned along with the result set. By clicking on the column names, you can sort the result set.

7

The Find dialog box offers a relatively simple interface for searching Active Directory. By using a combination of standard searches and custom searches through the Advanced tab, you should be able to find just about any piece of information you want.

PERMISSIONS AND ACTIVE DIRECTORY OBJECTS

Administrators of Microsoft Windows NT 4 will be familiar with the concept of **permissions**. Permissions are used extensively in NTFS to grant or deny access to files and folders at the user or group level.

Windows 2000 and Active Directory extend this model to the object level. As a result, you can assign permissions to perform tasks at a specific object or attribute level. This process is known in Windows 2000 as **access control**. Each object within Active Directory has a security descriptor. This descriptor allows users or groups to be assigned specific permissions to an object. In the following sections, we will investigate this feature and how it can help you as a Windows 2000 administrator.

Introduction to Active Directory Permissions

You must consider two things when assigning permissions to objects: who should be allowed to access an object; and what permissions, or **actions**, users should have once they have gained access to an object.

You will find that assigning permissions to Active Directory objects is a balance between ease of use and the amount of administrative work for which you want to be responsible. For instance, it is possible to assign specific permissions to every object within Active Directory. However, although doing so would make the objects highly secure (you would have examined each object and assigned only the precise permission required), it would also increase the overhead of supporting your Active Directory implementation—almost certainly beyond what would be considered reasonable.

You must consider two levels: Active Directory security and object permissions. These levels work in tandem to define the security model that best fits your organization. Let's define these two terms in a little more detail.

Active Directory Security

You use Active Directory permissions to determine who does or does not have access to an object. By denying a user or group permissions on an object, you are effectively hiding this object from them. Only administrators or object owners can assign permissions on an object, thereby preventing unauthorized users from assigning permissions.

The list of users and groups that are allowed access to an object is stored in the object's Access Control List (ACL). Each object has an ACL. The ACL lists everyone who has been granted access to an object along with the actions that users or groups can perform.

One of the most common ways you will use ACLs is to assign administrative permission to OUs. In Windows 2000, it is possible to create an OU for a group of objects—perhaps users in the Finance department—and then to assign a user full administrative permissions over that OU. Doing so would have the effect of making the Finance department autonomous for day-to-day operations such as adding users or assigning permissions to shared folders within its own organization. Although some users might have administrative control over objects within that specific OU, they would not automatically gain administrative permissions over other objects. This arrangement keeps your Active Directory secure.

Object Permissions

Different types of objects have different permissions. Therefore, it is difficult to make blanket statements about what is and what is not allowed for a given object. We will take a look at some of the most common permissions in a moment.

You can assign object permissions at the specific user level or at the group level. If you decide to assign permissions at the user level, then you will increase the complexity of your security infrastructure. You should make sure that you document your permissions and that you keep this list in a secure place (perhaps on your hard disk using Encrypted File System [EFS]).

You may assign a specific user permissions on an object when the user also has default permissions from group membership. This situation can occur when you are using a combination of object permissions at the user and group levels. In such cases, the user will have a combination of both sets of permissions. For instance, if a specific user has the right to reset a password on an object, and at the same time he is a member of a group assigned permission to change a user name, the user will have a combination of both permissions—he has the ability to both reset the password and rename the object.

The one exception to the combination-of-permissions rule occurs when you deny access to an object. If a user is a member of a group, and you assign that group Full Control permissions on an object, then the user has Full Control through group membership. However, if you then specifically deny that user access to the object, the Deny permission overrides any other permissions. The net result is that the user does not have any permissions over the object. It is important to remember that Deny overrides all other permissions.

Be sparing in your use of Deny. It can be difficult to troubleshoot problems if you have been busy denying access to certain objects at the user level. It is almost always better to assign or deny permissions at the group level. You will have to create far fewer sets of permissions this way, and undoing mistakes and making changes to your security plan are much simpler if you use groups.

Here's one final caveat: It is possible for you to deny everyone access to an object. As a result, no one will have access to the object—including administrators. The object is effectively orphaned until an administrator takes ownership of it. Taking ownership of an object should be done sparingly; make sure you understand the consequences of performing an action before you change permissions on an object.

Permissions and Special Permissions

Active Directory uses two sets of permissions: standard permissions and special permissions. **Standard permissions** are the most common set of permissions assigned to a user or group. **Special permissions** offer a finer degree of control and are used infrequently. Using special permissions will increase your administrative overhead.

Each object type has its own set of permissions. For instance, a shared folder allows you to assign permissions for users to execute files and traverse the folder structure. This permission is not available for User objects because these actions are not applicable.

Rather than attempt to list every possible permission available, we will define a few of the most common permissions that can be assigned. Table 7-3 lists the permissions that are considered standard.

Table 7-3 Standard permissions

Permission	Description
Full Control	Assigns all the standard permissions along with Full Control and Take Ownership. It should be used sparingly.
Read	Enables users or group members to view the object and its attributes. This permission also lets you view the object owner and any permissions that have been assigned in Active Directory.
Write	Allows the user or group member to change the attributes of an object. Note that this permission does not assign Full Control or Take Ownership.
Create All Child Objects	When assigned as a permissions on a OU, allows the user or group member to create objects as children of that OU. Doing so creates a hierarchy of OUs or objects.
Delete All Child Objects	Allows the user or group member to delete objects from within a specific OU. This permission is most often assigned along with Create All Child Objects so that objects can be both created and removed.

Assigning Permissions

Now that you have an idea of some of the permissions that can be assigned and what they do, we can examine how a system administrator assigns permissions to a user or group. This is a common task that you will perform when working with Windows 2000.

You can assign permissions in several different places, but the end result is the same. For instance, to assign permissions to a User object or OU within Active Directory, you use the Active Directory Users and Computers console. On the other hand, to assign permissions to a shared folder, you use Explorer. Which tool to use largely depends upon the types of objects the tool lists. Explorer does not list users and groups—therefore you cannot assign permissions on those objects using that tool.

Figure 7-2 shows a typical Properties dialog box. In this case, we have chosen to show you the standard permissions that can be assigned to a folder. Note that the list of permissions given here is limited.

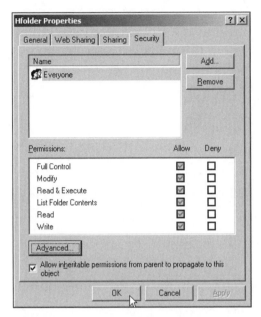

Figure 7-2   Standard permissions for a folder

The list of permissions shown in Figure 7-2 is a subset, also known as the **standard permissions** for this object type. By clicking on the Advanced button and choosing a group or user to assign permissions to, you can also view the advanced permissions for this object type (see Figure 7-3). Notice that the standard permissions are not duplicated in this list, and that many more options are available.

The checkboxes next to the permissions allow you to either grant or deny permissions to the selected user or group. Windows 2000 uses **inheritance** extensively. If the checkbox in the Allow or Deny column is grayed out, then that permission has been inherited from a parent object. (We will take a closer look at inheritance in a moment.) If you wish to prevent an object from inheriting permissions from its parent, you should uncheck the Allow Inheritable Permissions From Their Parent To Propagate To This Object checkbox (not shown in the figure).

To fully understand the net effect of assigning permissions, you should have a good understanding of inheritance. Let's take a look at inheritance and how it works.

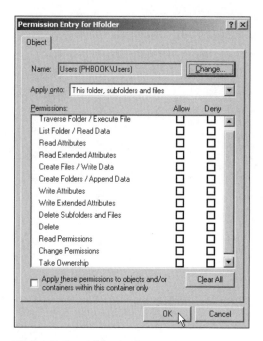

Figure 7-3   Advanced permissions

Permission Inheritance

Permissions are inherited by child objects by default. As a result, if you have a hierarchy of objects and you assign permissions to the object at the top of the hierarchy, all objects beneath it will be assigned the same permissions. This behavior can be overridden. It works much the same as inheritance works with files and folders. Inheritance was designed to simplify the administration of objects—by assigning a default set of permissions in a single place, all objects can be assigned the same default set.

Permission inheritance is useful with OUs. OUs are designed to simplify administration; you can achieve this goal by grouping together objects that have similar administrative needs, such as printers. By grouping all printers into a single OU called Printers, you can easily assign permissions to a group of users. For instance, if all printers are part of a single OU, you can create a group called Printer Administrators and assign that group Full Control permissions on the Printers OU. Through inheritance, all Printer objects within the OU will inherit this permission, and all members of the Printer Administrators group will have the Full Control permission.

We spoke earlier of the Allow Inheritable Permissions From Their Parent To Propagate To This Object option, which allows you to block inheritance from a parent object. This option lets you prevent the flow of permissions. It gives you a finer degree of control over objects, while at the same time increasing the amount of administrative overhead; it should therefore be used sparingly. When you uncheck this checkbox, you are presented with the Security dialog box shown in Figure 7-4.

As you can see in Figure 7-4, you are presented with three choices. The first choice is to copy the permissions from the parent object; this option means that the starting point for permissions for this object will be whatever is inherited from its parent. The second option is to remove the inherited permissions; this option allows you to remove the default permissions and to apply your own set. Finally, you can cancel the operation.

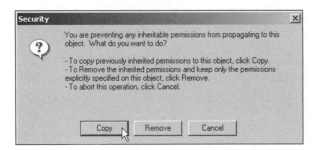

Figure 7-4   The Security dialog box

The choice you make here will depend on the amount of work it will take to adjust the inherited permissions to match the set you wish the object to have. If you want to change only one or two settings, then it might be better to copy the settings. However, if the changes will be extensive, then you should remove the permissions and start from scratch. Understand that if you choose to remove permissions, the object will have no permissions set—by default, only administrators and the object's owner will be able to access the object.

Permission inheritance is an important concept, and you should take it into account when designing your security infrastructure. By using it wisely, with the maximum amount of inheritance left in place, you can design quite complex security plans with a minimum of work. That is not to say assigning individual permissions to an object is a bad thing to do—just be aware such a setup will take more planning and maintenance.

MAKING RESOURCES AVAILABLE

Adding objects to Active Directory and then assigning permissions to those objects are among the main functions of a system administrator. Active Directory stores information about objects and then returns the results of queries to users.

When Active Directory makes data available for display as query results, it is (in Windows 2000 terminology) *publishing* the data. **Publishing** means making the data available for viewing. You can publish many different kinds of data from Active Directory, including information about users, computers, printers, and files.

Some pieces of data are published automatically. For instance, User objects are published automatically so they can be returned in queries and used in groups. As you have seen, objects have a number of associated attributes. You should note that only a subset of attributes is published along with the object. The attributes that are automatically published include the most commonly searched-for items, including the login name of the user.

Other pieces of information either are not published at all or are published to a limited subset of users. For instance, security information about a User object is published but can be viewed only by administrators.

Publishing Resources

Some resources are published automatically, whereas others must be published manually. In order to publish manually, you must use the Active Directory Users and Computers console. Until a resource is published, users will not be able to see it on the network. Active Directory makes resources visible to your user community.

Don't forget, if a printer is installed on a domain controller, it is automatically published. If a printer is shared from a Windows 2000 Professional machine or a standalone server, then it must be published manually. You will be creating a share and publishing it in the Real-World Projects at the end of this chapter.

Publishing Network Services

Because Active Directory is so flexible, you probably will not be surprised to find that users, computers, and shared folders are not the only network resources that can be published. In fact, it's useful to make a host of other resources available for searching in Active Directory.

Imagine being able to search for a specific network service in Active Directory and then being able to administer that service once it is found. Doing so could save the administrator a lot of time. Of course, if you knew the server name, it might be just as easy to search for the server that is offering the service. By publishing the service itself, however, you can gain some administrative flexibility. In effect, you have divorced the service from the server; as a result, if the server that is offering the service changes, the service can still be found.

For example, you might publish the Certificate Services network service in Active Directory. This essential service requires periodic administration. By publishing the service, your administrators will be able to find it by querying Active Directory through the Active Directory Sites and Services Console. This process allows your administrators to concentrate on the service rather than on both the service and the server.

When to Publish Services

Before you publish every network service under the sun, let's examine some of the best reasons to publish this information. Once you understand the reasons that exist for doing so, you will be ready to design your own publishing criteria. You should publish the following kinds of data:

- *Data that is stable*—You should not integrate into Active Directory any data that will change constantly. The data you publish in Active Directory is replicated to every domain controller in Active Directory (see Chapter 14 for details). Because this replication can take some time to occur (with a maximum period of 15 minutes), it is possible for data returned from one replica of the Active Directory to be out of date. This situation will self-correct when replication takes place, but it is still an inconvenience. You should also take into account that replication requires network bandwidth. Data that changes frequently will generate additional network traffic, and the convenience of having the service published may be outweighed by the cost of network bandwidth. If you are not careful, services can appear and then disappear from Active Directory (if they are deleted). Also, users connect to some services via TCP/IP ports. If a port changes and this change has not had time to replicate to all domain controllers, then it might appear to users and administrators as though the service is not available.

- *Properties with a small amount of data*—Do not replicate large pieces of data within Active Directory. You must consider not only the frequency of a change, but also the size of the changed data. Active Directory will replicate data based on the entire property, not on part of a property. If a Description property is 50 bytes long and you change one word, then the whole 50 bytes must be replicated.

- *Useful information*—The information that you decide to replicate should have widespread significance. That is, replicate only the data that will be of some use to a large number of clients. If you have a property such as Asset Number, and that asset number is used by only five people in a network of thousands, then it makes little sense to replicate this data to every domain controller. Choose data that is commonly searched by a large number of people. Doing so ensures that you get the maximum benefit from the necessary network bandwidth and disk space.

MOVING OBJECTS

Objects within Active Directory can be moved to accommodate administrative tasks. For instance, you might have built a host of OUs around your departmental structure. User objects are stored within the respective departments' OUs. If a user is then transferred to a different business unit, you should move that User object from one OU to another.

Some significant differences exist between moving objects *within* a domain and *between* domains. We will take a look at each task in turn. When you're moving large numbers of objects, consider using a scripting engine such as Windows Scripting Host (WSH). WSH is discussed in more detail in Chapter 11.

Moving Objects within a Domain

Moving objects within a domain is a fairly simple task. Most commonly, you might do this when you want to move a user object from one OU to another OU—perhaps during an organizational restructuring. You use the Active Directory Users and Computers console to perform this task.

When moving objects within a domain, take the following factors into account:

- Permissions will be inherited from the new OU. The permissions that were inherited from the previous OU will no longer be applied. This change can affect access to shared folders and administrative permissions to other user objects.

- Permissions that have been assigned to the specific object will be retained. This fact can be both a blessing and a curse. It also illustrates perfectly our earlier point regarding the complexity of administration when you assign permissions at the object level. If you no longer want the User object to have a specific permission, then you must remove the permission from the object after the object has been moved. It is better to assign permissions at the OU level, so a user is automatically assigned permissions.

- It is possible to move multiple objects at the same time. To do so, simply highlight one of the objects you want to move, hold down the Ctrl key, and select additional objects.

- You must initiate the move on the domain controller acting as the relative ID (RID) master of the domain that currently contains the object.

Moving Objects between Domains

Moving objects between domains is a little more complicated, partly because Microsoft has failed to provide us with a Graphical User Interface (GUI) for this purpose. More significantly, though, moving an object from one security boundary to another is technically complex.

In order to move an object from one domain to another, you must use a command-line utility called MoveTree. This utility is not installed by default. In fact, it is sometimes preferable to delete an object and re-create it rather than move it. In order to install the MoveTree utility, you should execute the Setup program in the \Support\Tools folder on your Windows 2000 CD.

Moving an object within a domain is a fairly simple process; however you must consider many more factors when moving objects from one domain to another. An example is a security identifier (SID) that is assigned to an object when it is created. An object's SID is based partially upon the domain in which it exists. If the domain then changes, the SID is incorrect. Windows 2000 will go ahead and create a new SID for the object and store a copy of the old SID information in a new field called SIDhistory. Whenever a

User object logs on to a Windows 2000 network, the current SID and all entries in the SIDhistory field are included in the security token for the object. As a result, the object retains some of its permissions even though it has been moved.

Each object in a Windows 2000 network also has a unique Globally Unique Identifier (GUID), which is a reference number to an object. Because this number is universally unique, you don't need to change it—moving an object from one domain to another will not affect the object's GUID.

It is also possible to move other types of objects, such as OUs. When you're moving OUs, any Group Policy Objects (GPOs) that have been assigned to the OU will remain intact. This feature can be useful when you want the same settings to be applied. The GPO data is not replicated to the new domain controllers, however. As a result, the data for the GPO remains in the old domain and must be pulled from there. You should consider the traffic associated with this data transfer and with re-creating Group Policy settings in the new domain.

As you can see, MoveTree supports many different types of operations. Some additional operations you might want to consider are as follows:

- You can move an object or objects between domains even if the object contains child objects. This action is supported only if you are moving objects within the same Active Directory forest.

- You can move both local groups and global groups between domains if they do not have any members. If a group contains members, however, it can be moved only between containers within the *same* domain.

- You can move Universal groups both within and between domains, regardless of whether the group has members.

MoveTree Restrictions

Some restrictions come with the list of tasks that can be performed with the MoveTree utility. Some operations are considered unsupported, which is another way of saying they cannot be performed successfully.

Let's take a look at some of the objects that cannot be moved using the MoveTree utility:

- Local and global groups that have members.

- Some object data. This data includes users' personal data (documents and spreadsheets), their encrypted files, and public key certificates. Logon scripts are not copied, either. As a result, a user being moved from one domain to another may end up having a very different user experience. Keep this fact in mind when you plan to move users.

- System objects. Any objects that belong to the system cannot be moved, including any objects stored within the Configuration or Schema containers.

- Objects that are stored in special containers such as LostAndFound, Builtin, and System.

- Domain controllers. If you want to move a domain controller, you must demote the domain controller and then promote it into the new domain using the DCPromo utility.

- Any object with the same fully qualified domain name. Every object within Active Directory must have a unique name within the hierarchy. If an object has the same name, then the move will fail.

Along with these restrictions, you should be aware of some significant items regarding the moving of User and Group objects:

- When you're moving a User or Group object, the object must not have any objects beneath it. Such an object is known as a **leaf object**.

- If the User or Group object's name already exists in the context to which you are trying to move it, then the move operation will fail. You should also note that some security settings can also cause the move to fail. An example would be the minimum password length setting. If the User object does not have a password of at least the minimum length, the move operation fails.

- If the User object is a member of any global group, then the move operation fails because a global group can contain members only from its own domain. The one exception is the Domain Users global group when it is the primary group for the User object (default behavior). User objects are automatically added to the group when they are created, and can therefore be removed.

Using the MoveTree Command

The MoveTree utility is run from the command line. Currently, no GUI is available for this utility. That does not mean the utility is not feature rich—in fact, this command-line utility is a boon. You can include it quite easily in batch files or scripts.

Figure 7-5 shows the **MoveTree** command when run with the **/?** parameter. Notice that this command displays all the available options with descriptions and examples.

MoveTree generates three log files when it is run; these files are stored in the folder where the command is run. The log files supply you with a list of errors and statistics and can be useful for troubleshooting possible problems. The three files are:

- *MoveTree.err*—Lists errors that were encountered.

- *MoveTree.log*—Lists statistics for the move operation.

- *MoveTree.chk*—Lists any errors that have been found during the test phase of the command. This log can alert you to possible errors that might occur, so you can address them before performing the actual command. Use the **/check** option to create this file.

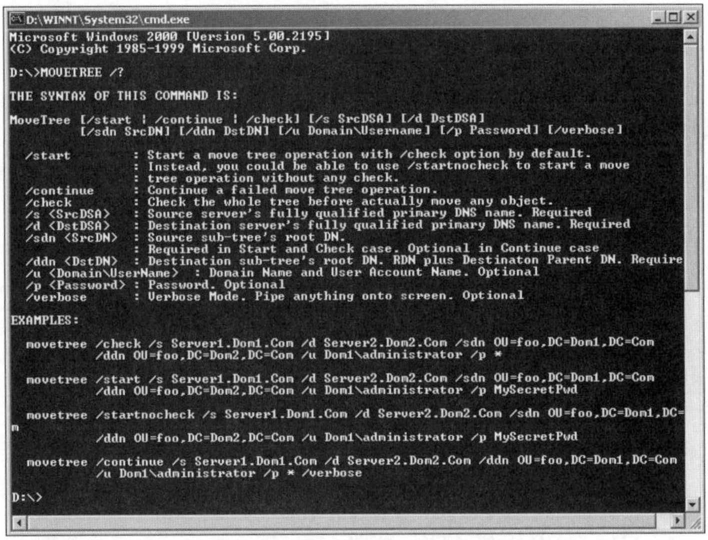

Figure 7-5   The MoveTree command-line utility

The MoveTree utility is useful for moving users, groups, and OUs between domains. You might also want to move other significant objects, however. These objects cannot be moved with MoveTree—instead, you must use a different utility. This utility is discussed in the next section.

Moving Workstations and Member Servers

When you install support tools such as MoveTree, as outlined in the previous section, you also install a command-line utility called Netdom. This utility is used to move workstations and member servers between domains. Use of this command-line utility is very much the same as we saw with the MoveTree utility.

The command-line options and syntax are shown in Figure 7-6. You can get more detailed information from the Windows 2000 Resource Kit help file. Unfortunately, detailed information about the Resource Kit utilities is outside the scope of this book. However, it is highly recommended that any administrator of Windows 2000 purchase the full kit; it contains a host of utilities and information.

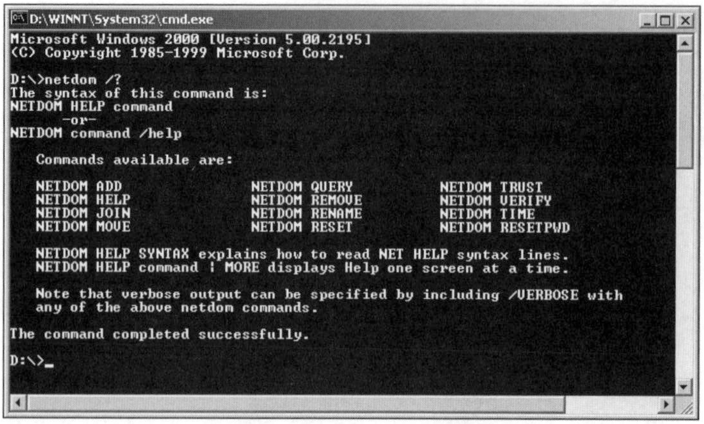

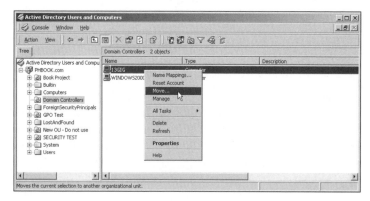

Figure 7-6 The Netdom command-line utility

Moving Domain Controllers between Sites

The easiest move operation involves moving domain controllers between sites. In the Real-World Projects at the end of this chapter, you will move a shared folder from one location in Active Directory to another. You can use this same technique to move domain controllers between sites. In short, you can simply right-click on a domain controller object within the Active Directory Users and Computers console to bring up the context-sensitive menu; then select the Move command. This command (shown in Figure 7-7) enables you to choose the container to which the domain controller will be moved.

Figure 7-7 The context-sensitive menu with the Move command

Moving Objects to the LostAndFound Container

Some objects cannot be successfully moved from one domain to another. For example, some child objects will fail to move. If a parent object of a child is moved, then the parent is no longer available, and the child is considered to be **orphaned**. An orphaned object is moved to the LostAndFound container, which is visible in the Active Directory Users and Computers console. You should periodically take a look at the LostAndFound container and move any objects you want to keep into another parent object. The LostAndFound container can be seen in Figure 7-8.

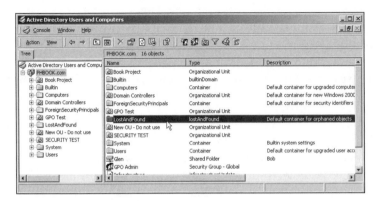

Figure 7-8   The LostAndFound container

By default, you will not be able to see the LostAndFound container in the Active Directory Users and Computers console. In order to see this container, you must be in Advanced Features view. To enter this view, choose View | Advanced Features in Active Directory Users and Computers.

DELEGATING AUTHORITY

Wouldn't it be nice if some of the more routine tasks that a system administrator performs could be offloaded to someone else? Although it can sometimes be tempting to make sure that no one but the administrator can perform certain tasks, doing so means that everything must go through that one person or team—and often the team becomes a bottleneck.

What's more, some administrative tasks can be quite routine. If you could assign permissions to perform these tasks and be assured that no other permissions were being assigned, wouldn't it be nice to let a departmental staff member add Printer objects to and remove them from Active Directory?

This is the goal of **delegation of control**: Certain administrative tasks are assigned to a user or group. The interface for performing the delegation task is the Delegation Of Control Wizard. This wizard has several options, which we will look at in a moment.

The following list shows the types of tasks that can be assigned with the Delegation Of Control Wizard:

- Allow a User object the permissions to change the properties of a particular container, including such items as the container name or description.

- Allow a User object to create, delete, or modify objects in a particular OU or container. You can set this feature at the object-type level, which means you can allow a User object to create printers but not user accounts, or vice versa. Note that the ability to assign this permission at the OU level means you can give departments within your organization a level of administrative autonomy.

- Allow a User object to modify the properties of objects in an OU or container.

Notice that the implications of these tasks are quite far reaching. In large organizations, creating and deleting User objects for temporary workers can generate a lot of administrative work. By delegating authority for these types of functions, the administrators can concentrate their efforts on large, more complex efforts.

As we saw earlier, you should be careful when delegating authority. What starts out as a method of reducing the amount of work for your IT administrative staff may end up creating more work for them. For instance, delegating authority at the object level (rather than at the container or OU level) can cause an increase in the amount of administrative overhead, because someone will have to track what has been delegated and to whom.

It is far better to delegate authority at the container or OU level; however, doing so can have effects that are farther reaching. If you delegate the authority to create objects of a certain type in an OU, then the User object can create as many objects as it wants. Make sure that the user who will get this new authority has been well trained in the consequences of performing an action.

You should take delegation of authority into consideration when designing your OU structure. Your OU design should match your administrative needs, and delegation of authority is likely to be a large part of your future plans. Delegation allows you to decentralize some of the administrative work that takes place in every organization. Although you must strike a balance when delegating (you do not want to allow departmental administrators to have permissions outside the realm of their responsibilities), delegation can have many benefits when used wisely.

If you are going to upgrade to Windows 2000, you may be consolidating domains. In Microsoft Windows NT 4, you may have had more than one domain. In Windows 2000, it is possible—and even desirable—to have a single domain. In the process, you must face a political issue: You should severely restrict the members of the Domain Admins and Enterprise Admins groups. Staff members who were previously members of Domain

Admins may feel that their jobs have been reduced in importance. You can alleviate this situation by using delegation of authority to give them Full Control permission over an OU that contains all objects relating to their line of business.

Follow these guidelines when using delegation of authority:

- Always assign permissions at the OU or container level. It is possible to assign permissions at the object level, but doing so is discouraged.

- If you want to assign permissions at the object level, then you cannot use the Delegation Of Control Wizard. Instead, you must use Active Directory Users and Computers console.

- Maintain a record of who has been assigned permissions. Windows 2000 does not do a good job of recording what has been assigned. Although you can always get the properties of an OU or container, doing so can be cumbersome when you're searching multiple objects. Keep a record in a database and make sure it is available to all administrators.

7

Using the Delegation Of Control Wizard

As you will see, the Delegation Of Control Wizard is fairly straightforward. You should use the wizard whenever possible, because Microsoft has streamlined the commands required to make delegation work. In order to start the wizard, you must use the Active Directory Users and Computers console. For instance, if you want to delegate authority to an OU, you start the Active Directory Users and Computers Console and then right-click on the OU name in the right-hand panel. Doing so brings up the context-sensitive menu. Select Delegate Control to start the wizard, which is shown in Figure 7-9.

When you click on the Next button, you can select the users or groups to which you will delegate control. Be careful when selecting users and groups—make sure you limit the number of users that will be granted permissions for the OU or container.

Once you have selected the users or groups, click on Next again. This time, the wizard prompts you to enter the tasks to be assigned to the user or group, as shown in Figure 7-10.

Figure 7-10 shows the options when you're delegating common tasks such as creating and deleting groups or resetting passwords. If you want to assign more granular permissions, then click on the Create A Custom Task To Delegate button. (The options presented, if you do this, are outside the scope of this book.) Once you have selected your permissions, click on Next; the wizard will display a summary screen. That is all there is to the Delegation Of Control Wizard!

Don't forget that all data affecting Active Directory must be replicated to every domain controller in the domain. As a result, a time lapse often occurs between performing a task—such as running the Delegation Of Control Wizard—and the permissions' actually being assigned. You should take this time lapse into account. It is not likely that permissions granted with this wizard will be immediately available. The permissions can take up to 15 minutes to be granted.

Figure 7-9   The Delegation Of Control Wizard

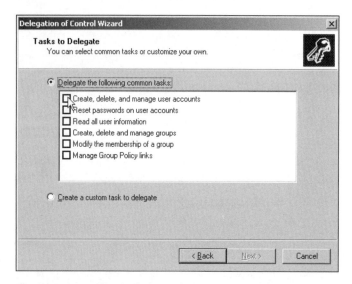

Figure 7-10   The Tasks to Delegate screen of the Delegation Of Control Wizard

Delegating authority is a key feature of Windows 2000. When it's used in conjunction with a good OU design, you can save yourself a lot of work. However, don't forget that ultimately, the system administrators are responsible for the network. Do not overuse the Delegation Of Control Wizard, but don't forget about it, either.

CHAPTER SUMMARY

- In this chapter, we looked at some of the aspects you need to be aware of when administering Active Directory. We started by examining ways you can query the data stored in Active Directory. You can query Active Directory for any data that it contains, if you have sufficient permissions to do so (some objects, such as system objects, are visible only to administrators).

- You learned that several common objects exist. These objects include User Accounts, Groups, Computers, and Printers. We also noted that you can create custom objects.

- We then discussed the Find dialog box. This dialog box can perform complex searches against Active Directory data. The attributes that are available to be searched vary among the different object types. You learned that although the most common options (such as object name) are displayed by default, you can also use the Advanced tab to access optional fields and narrow a search.

- We then discussed Active Directory permissions. Each object has a security descriptor that contains, among other things, a list of users or groups that have some level of control over the object. You learned that there are two types of permissions: Active Directory permissions and object permissions. The latter determine what action can be performed on an object, whereas the former determine whether an object is visible to a user or group.

- We saw that it is possible to allow or deny permissions on an object. When a user or group is denied access, this setting overrides all other assigned permissions. Other than the Deny permission, all permissions assigned to a user through direct assignment or group membership are cumulative.

- We took a brief look at some of the available permissions. There are two sets of permissions: standard permissions and special permissions. Standard permissions are commonly granted. Special permissions offer more granularity but also increase the complexity of your environment.

- We then examined permission inheritance. We saw that permissions for Active Directory objects operate in much the same way as permissions assigned to files and folders. When permissions are granted to a container object, the user or group gains rights over any Active Directory objects within that container. Also, any child container will, by default, inherit any permissions assigned to its parent container. It is possible to stop this from happening by blocking inheritance.

- Before network resources can be seen by users, they must be published. Some objects, such as printers installed on domain controllers, are published automatically. Others must be published manually. You also learned that you can publish network services, such as Certificate Services. When doing so, you should exercise caution and publish only data that is fairly static and small. This is the case because Active Directory must replicate all data to domain controllers, and doing so takes time, processing, and bandwidth.

❑ We took a look at objects and how they can be moved within Active Directory. This task can be quite difficult when objects such as OUs and groups must be moved from one domain to another. We noted that the tools built into Windows 2000 work only when moving objects within the same tree or forest.

❑ You learned that moving an object within a domain is a fairly simple process using the Active Directory Users and Computers console. However, moving objects between domains requires you to install the support utilities from the Windows 2000 compact disk. (These utilities are not installed by default.) To move User, Group, and OU objects between domains, you must use the MoveTree command-line utility. To move workstations or member servers, you must use the Netdom command-line utility.

❑ Finally, we examined delegation of control, which allows you to delegate certain administrative tasks within a container object to users or groups. Doing so has the benefit of decentralizing day-to-day administrative tasks and reducing the workload of busy system administrators.

❑ We saw that you can delegate control quite simply by using the Delegation Of Control Wizard. This wizard walks you through the process of assigning common tasks to users and groups with a minimum of fuss. We explained that it is a good idea to be sparing with this feature, and to make sure that users who are given administrative permissions receive adequate training.

8

PERFORMANCE MONITORING

After completing this chapter, you will be able to:

♦ Describe the tools you can use to monitor system performance

♦ Describe the function and purpose of System Monitor

♦ Describe and use counters in System Monitor to analyze system performance

♦ Describe the purpose of the Event Viewer

♦ Configure alerts in System Monitor

♦ Define the logs that exist on a Windows 2000 domain controller

♦ Describe the tools available to monitor Active Directory performance

Domain controllers (DCs) have a significant role to play on your Windows 2000 network. What's more, problems that occur at DCs can show up in the strangest places. Perhaps you are getting calls from your users, complaining that the network is slow; or maybe users are having trouble saving documents to a particular share or logging on. DCs have such an important role to play that problems with a single one can manifest itself in hundreds of different ways.

In this chapter, you will learn about monitoring your domain controllers. You will see that making sure they are operating correctly is a common task that must be performed on a regular basis. We will discuss the tools and techniques you can use to maintain an efficient network.

INTRODUCTION TO PERFORMANCE MONITORING

If you asked 10 professionals what characteristics a fast computer should have, you would probably get 10 different answers—what is important to one person has no meaning to another. When it comes to Information Technology (IT) professionals, the truth is that we are not particularly good at defining what a good system really is.

There are several reasons for this. First, a system configured to operate in one environment, to answer one specific need, may not meet the requirements of another environment. This fact explains why a Web server may work well until you install Microsoft Exchange or some other messaging system on it—what works for one function just won't work for another. Second, applications have their own stress points and things you can do to optimize them. Without an awareness of these features, you cannot possibly make intelligent design decisions.

For some administrators, the goal is always to have the least amount of work going on at a particular server. The Nirvana is assumed to be processors that are never stressed beyond 10% utilization and memory capacity that is never stretched beyond 50% usage. We would like to dispel that myth. Think of it in terms of a car. What is the point in buying a Maserati sports car, if you're going to coast in the slow lane at 20 miles per hour? You are essentially doing the same thing when you buy a multiple-processor-enabled server, with RAID controllers and gigabytes of RAM, only to use it for file sharing.

That is not to say that a neat list exists of what is acceptable and not acceptable. If a server is operating at 40 percent of processor capacity all day and night, however, is that really a bad thing? As long as it is fulfilling its role, the answer may very well be "no." You should strive to get a handle on your servers and what they are doing. But the goal is not to eliminate load completely—it is to control the load, and to identify when something out of the ordinary is taking place.

Many different things can affect the performance of a computer. Most people concentrate their efforts in the areas of processors and memory. We have been sold this approach for years now in magazine articles and white papers: Add processors (or put in a new processor with better performance), add some more Random Access Memory (RAM), and things should be fine. Many of us have found, after filling our Windows 95 and Windows 98 boxes with 256 MB of RAM, that at a certain point, more does not equal better.

Of course, we are not talking about Windows 95 or Windows 98 here; we are talking about Windows 2000. Like all new operating system releases, this latest release requires newer hardware to fully reach its potential. Although minimum requirements do not look dissimilar from previous versions of Microsoft Windows NT, don't be fooled into thinking that a fast Pentium III with at least 256MB of RAM won't make things run a lot faster—because they will!

So, in a world where finances are finite, and where your managers are asking you to cut costs, what can the system administrator do to make sure you are getting the best bang for the buck? To begin with, you can get a better understanding of how systems perform, and why they react the way they do to various events.

Performance monitoring is an important skill, because by using it you can get a **signature** for the servers in your environment. A signature is also known as a **baseline**, which can be further defined as a level of performance on a normal working day. The baseline defines how the server will operate when things are running normally. Once you have this information, you can then run performance statistics periodically and compare the results. Are things running efficiently? Are there deviations from the baseline? Are problems developing, and in what areas are you having problems? All these questions and more can be answered if you know which performance statistics are available to you, what they mean, and how to use them. Introducing you to these statistics is the purpose of this chapter.

Furthermore, we are going to look at several of the tools at your disposal. One of the most important tools is System Monitor. System Monitor allows you to access counters that can report on system performance.

We could list every counter available to you and define what they do, but doing so would simply fill a lot of pages with boring lists. Instead, we will define some critical counters for a DC operating in a Windows 2000 environment. We'll define some important terms in a moment so you don't get lost.

Performance monitoring (which, incidentally, goes beyond simply using the System Monitor tool in Windows 2000) hardly ever gets its due attention. All those counters can be perplexing; once you have the data, moreover, you have to make sense of it. This chapter will walk you through what performance monitoring really is, how it works, how it differs from what we have seen in previous versions of Windows NT, and how you can use these tools to predict problems before they occur, thus avoiding costly outages. This may not be the most exciting chapter in this book, but the rewards you can get from understanding this topic could pay you back many times over.

WINDOWS 2000 SYSTEM MONITOR

System Monitor, also commonly known as simply perfmon, has been included with Microsoft Windows NT for a number of years. The version that ships with Windows 2000 has been improved in some significant ways, so even if you are familiar with the tool, you should take time to read through this section. The default System Monitor display is shown in Figure 8-1.

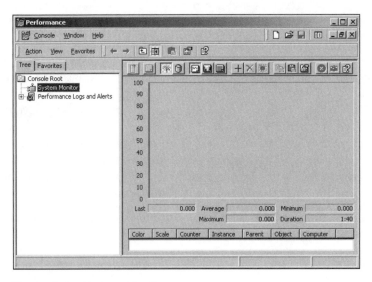

Figure 8-1   System Monitor

Before we dig into the details, let's define what it is that you want to monitor. A server is a complex mix of components, and simply monitoring the hardware characteristics won't be enough. In fact, you need to be concerned with all aspects of a server's performance including hardware, applications, the operating system, and anything else that has been enabled for monitoring.

The true measure of a system's performance is usually a combination of all of these things. You can have state-of-the-art hardware with horrible software, and you will be unhappy with performance. Or, you can buy and install the latest and greatest operating system and put it on an older piece of hardware, and you just won't get that cutting-edge feel you hoped for.

When you examine a server to determine its performance, you'll look in four key areas:

- Memory
- Processor
- Disk
- Network

These areas obviously are key to a server—if any one of them is significantly lacking, then you can expect to see degraded performance. Measuring them will become an important part of your skill set. Let's briefly describe each of these areas.

Memory

Memory is the RAM inside the server (or any other machine being monitored). Memory usage is actually quite complex. When you look at memory usage on a Windows 2000 server, you generally simply glance at the Physical Memory counter on the Performance tab of Task Manager. However, this value provides a very high-level view of memory and how it is being used. It can let you know immediately whether a server needs more RAM, but it does nothing to tell you about memory usage over time, or what process is using the memory.

For the purposes of setting a baseline or discovering the performance characteristics of a given server during normal use, you need to become more familiar with processes that are running on a server and how they are used. We'll take a closer look at some of the important memory counters later in this chapter. They will give you an idea of some common areas of concern, and how you can monitor potentially problematic situations. Figure 8-2 shows some of the counters available for the Memory object, as shown in System Monitor.

8

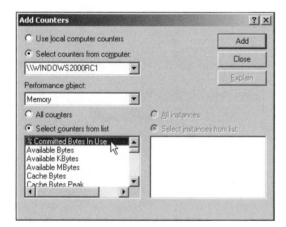

Figure 8-2   The counters of the Memory object

When a server runs low on memory, it begins to use hard disk space as though it were physical memory. This process is called **paging**. If you ever had a bad day when everything on your system was slow and saving documents to your hard disk took forever, you were probably paging. Paging is efficient, in that your system does not crash simply because you have a lack of memory; but it is also very slow. Think of paging as a cry for help. We'll show you how to identify this common problem.

Processor

As often as you will hear technical support cry, "Have you tried rebooting it?" you will hear your IT staff say "I need a faster processor!" There is no denying the fun in having the latest and greatest technology from Intel or AMD—but the fact is, we underutilize most processors.

An underpowered processor that is straining to keep up with all the work you throw at it is going to hold up every other component on a system, however. Of course, you can upgrade processors, or add more than one. We will take a look at processors later.

Disk

The disk subsystem of your server is probably the most overlooked component you have. However, if you corner a database person (maybe a Microsoft SQL Server 2000 or Oracle DBA expert) and ask him where most performance issues can be solved, he'll start to talk at length about disk subsystems.

Data is read into a computer's memory, worked on by code and the processor, and then generally written somewhere on the local hard disk before being either transported somewhere else or saved permanently. Two of those three processes—the reading into memory and manipulation by the processor—are extremely fast. Writing out to disk, however, is a mechanical process, and you can quickly run into a lot of trouble.

You must know how quickly data is being written to and read from the disk. Are things waiting to be copied to the disk? How quickly does the disk respond? These aspects will have an enormous impact on the performance of a server. Often we balance fault tolerance against disk reads or disk writes. Regardless of these compromises, the faster you can make the disk subsystem on your computer, the better performance you will see. Examining the disk subsystem does not immediately spring to mind when performance has been questioned, but, as a Windows 2000 professional, you should keep it in the back of your mind. Even though you have plenty of RAM and a fast processor, a disk-intensive application loaded on top of a slow disk subsystem can spell disaster or, at the very least, disappointment.

Network

Networks are fast; networks are efficient—and I have a bridge to sell you in Brooklyn. When examining performance-related issues, you must take everything into account, and you should not assume that the speed of a given network is fast.

Take a 10MB network. That network can theoretically transport 10MB of data per second. A remote office is connected to that network via a T1 connection. A T1 connection has a maximum bandwidth of 1.54MBps. Let's imagine that users on the other end of that T1 line want to connect to a server on the network. Our example is illustrated in Figure 8-3. How much bandwidth do the users have available?

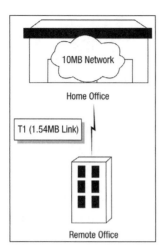

Figure 8-3   Connecting a remote office to the home office

If you think about it for a moment, you imagine that the thinnest pipe, in this case the T1 line, is the limiting factor. So, the answer might well be 1.54MB. But maybe the 10MB network is drowning in data—perhaps it has only 1MB of bandwidth remaining, even if the T1 line is operating at its most efficient. Now, suppose the network card at the server is taking a beating because of a new database application that has been installed, and it's processing data very slowly, effectively cutting the data throughput even more.

As you can see, there is no simple answer to the question, "How much bandwidth is available on the network?" You cannot simply look at a network diagram and get any idea of what is going on. Instead, you must measure bandwidth. This ability is going to be in your arsenal of monitoring tools by the time you reach the end of this chapter.

System Monitor Terminology

When dealing with System Monitor, you basically need to be familiar with three key terms:

- Throughput
- Queue
- Response time

You will see these terms time and again as you work with System Monitor, so it is a good idea to get a clear definition for each of them before we move on.

Throughput

When we talk about **throughput**, we are really talking about how much gets done in a given period of time. As more tasks are thrown at a server, more will get done, and therefore throughput will increase. Then comes the time when the server (or a component on the server) begins to be overwhelmed. At that point, throughput will decrease.

When throughput begins to decrease, either less activity is going on at the server (old requests have been processed and no new requests need attention) or a component is getting behind. This second condition is often known as a **bottleneck**.

Measuring throughput is obviously very important, but do not make any assumptions about the amount of work a component is doing and whether that component is the cause of a bottleneck. The fact is, a component can be humming along 99 percent utilized but still keep up, whereas a hard disk might have one thing to do—say, write a 5GB file—and fall on its knees. Careful monitoring will help keep you on track regarding which components are truly causing problems.

Queue

When a server (or a component in a server) begins to fall behind, things have to wait to be processed. This line of things waiting to be processed is known as a **queue**. When you have a queue, you essentially have a wait state—nothing can proceed until the data is dealt with. This wait can cause performance issues.

Queues can be created by a continuous stream of data hitting a server or server service, when the process simply cannot keep up. They also can be caused by a large amount of data hitting a server at the same time. The data might not be too much to handle if it were broken up into parts, but in bulk it simply overwhelms a system. Zero queues are good; lots of long queues are bad.

Response Time

As you might suspect, **response time** is a measurement of elapsed time from the beginning of a process to its conclusion. Most of the time, you might be looking at small processes; but response time can also be applied to end-to-end processes, such as a request originating in an accounting system and being returned from the server.

Windows 2000 has several different methods of looking at response time. We will examine them later.

 Previous versions of Microsoft Windows NT include Performance Monitor, which is a tool very similar to System Monitor. Some might say it is the same program under the guise of a Microsoft Management Console (MMC) snap-in. But there have been some changes, and some of them are significant. What follows applies equally to both versions, though—except where noted.

SYSTEM MONITOR DATA COLLECTION

Before we begin really digging into examples of using System Monitor in Windows 2000, we need to work through one more section of definitions in the area of data collection. We'll answer two very good questions: "What can you monitor?" and "How is data collected from a Windows 2000 server?"

First, let's take a look at how System Monitor (and Performance Monitor before it) captures data from a Windows 2000 machine. To answer the first question, data can be collected from something called **system resources**, which consist of memory, processors, disks, and network components. (These components were defined earlier in the chapter.)

Of course, these are very general areas. When you drill down on any one of the resources, you will find all kinds of information. You can obtain data on hundreds of parameters for each of the four general categories.

In addition to the four key areas already specified, it is worth noting that a software vendor can also add parameters that can be monitored. For instance, a database vendor might add a counter that allows an administrator to view the efficiency of queries against a database. This capability equally applies to any service on a Windows 2000 server.

To answer the second question, the parameters that can be monitored are stored in the Registry in a performance key for each service, application, or operating system component. The counters are stored in DLLs that are installed on your system. This chapter will give you a general overview, with some drill-down into the more useful parameters before concentrating in the area of Active Directory.

 Each parameter that can be monitored is defined in a performance counter library—a DLL. The Active Directory performance counter library is NTDSPERF.DLL.

You can also use another method to get data supplied to System Monitor, but we will talk about it later in this chapter, in the section "Windows Management Instrumentation."

We're next going to define three key terms that are used to describe how you can configure System Monitor to gather data for you. Once you understand these terms, you will be ready to move on to using the tool. The three terms are:

- Objects
- Counters
- Instances

These terms form a type of hierarchy of objects, which have counters, which in turn have instances. This relationship is shown in Figure 8-4.

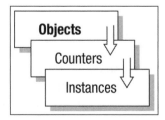

Figure 8-4 The relationship among objects, counters, and instances

Objects

An **object** is a system resource. Some of the most common objects you will use include Network Interface, Paging File, and Processor. There are literally hundreds of objects. You can think of an object as a container for counters and instances.

Any application or service can also appear as an object, so you should not think of objects as being just server or hardware related. Objects can be any measurable item defined within the system.

Counters

A **counter** is used to measure various aspects of an object. The Processor object includes counters for Processor Time, User Time, and Interrupts/Sec, among others. Every object will have at least one counter associated with it, but, as illustrated here, most have more than one.

The trick to successful performance monitoring is figuring out which counters are important in a given situation. We will show you some basic counters in a moment, but this book isn't long enough to discuss every counter in detail.

Instances

An **instance** is a specific counter that is in use. For example, there is an object called Thread. Processes running on a system use threads, and you can monitor each of them by using the Thread object. When you have more than one process running on a system, you can monitor one thread or multiple threads on the system. If you are monitoring Processor Time for two threads, each thread is considered an instance of the counter.

RECOMMENDED COUNTERS

Now that you have a good idea of the terms relating to System Monitor, it is time to mention the names of specific counters that can help you troubleshoot issues on a server. Of course, we cannot imagine all the types of issues you might be troubleshooting, or list every available counter. Instead, we will list counters that are most commonly used for each of the four key areas mentioned earlier: memory, processor, disk, and network.

Counters for Memory Troubleshooting

A lack of memory is most evident when a server is beginning to perform poorly (which in simple terms means more slowly). Although this can be an easy issue to identify through other methods (such as Task Manager), a good system administrator should be able to give more detail than simply saying, "All the memory is being used." The counters described in the following sections will help you gather additional data.

Pages/Sec (Memory Object)

Windows 2000 performs a lot of caching, because accessing data that is in physical memory is far faster than fetching it from the hard disk. When a process attempts to gain access to the data that is not held in memory, the result is a **hard page fault**. Hard page faults cause a system to perform more slowly. The Pages/Sec counter helps you track the number of times a hard page fault occurs. The lower this number is, the better. The solution to a high value might be to add more memory, but a high value can also be caused if a slow hard disk causes reads from the disk to be too slow.

Committed Bytes (Memory Object)

If a system is running low of physical memory, it writes out to the hard disk. This process is known as **paging**. A process can actually reserve space in the page file in case it's ever needed; doing so increases performance, should the page file be needed. The Committed Bytes counter records the amount of space that has been reserved.

Pool Nonpaged Bytes (Memory Object)

The physical memory in a Windows 2000 system is assigned specific tasks. One of these areas is the **nonpaged pool**. As suggested by its name, the nonpaged pool contains data that cannot be paged—that is, it must always be in memory while it is being used. Needless to say, because this data cannot be paged, if a lot of data exists in the nonpaged pool you can quickly run out of physical memory. A high reading in the Pool Nonpaged Bytes counter suggests that you need additional physical memory.

Pool Nonpaged Allocs (Memory Object)

The unfortunate term **Allocs** is actually a shortening of **Allocation**. The Pool Nonpaged Allocs counter tells you how many times a request occurs to allocate memory from the nonpaged pool. This counter allows you to determine (in conjunction with the Pool Nonpaged Bytes counter) whether you are making lots of calls to allocate memory from the nonpaged pool. If you are receiving many calls to allocate memory, especially after installing a new application, then the system may have a memory leak.

Available Bytes (Memory Object)

The Available Bytes counter allows you to view quickly how much physical memory is still available. Windows 2000 has a pretty sophisticated way of using physical memory. Say a program loads and needs 1MB of memory. Windows 2000 goes ahead and allocates it. Now, after 10 more processes have started up, the system finds that it doesn't have enough memory to satisfy new requests. First Windows 2000 tries to take memory back from the processes that are already running; if that fails, it begins to page to the hard disk. This process obviously has an impact on the performance of a server. A higher number is better here.

8

Avg. Disk Queue Length (Physical Disk Object)

A queue is a line of information that is waiting to be processed. Computer processes are busy, and any time they are made to wait is bad for the system. The Avg. Disk Queue Length counter shows the average wait length for both disk reads and writes. The higher this number is, the worse performance is going to be.

Avg. Disk Sec/Transfer (Physical Disk Object)

The Avg. Disk Sec/Transfer counter records the average amount of time for a disk transfer. A **disk transfer** is a transfer of data from memory to disk, or from disk to memory. If you do a little math, you can figure out the percentage of time your system is paging: Simply multiply the value generated by the Memory object counter Pages/Sec (defined above) by this value. For example, a value of 0.2 indicates that paging is taking place 20 percent of the time. This behavior would cause poor performance if it continued for an extended period.

% Usage (Paging File Object)

You may have guessed that the % Usage counter tells you what percentage of the page file is currently in use. What might surprise you is that any value less than 100 percent is acceptable, but higher values are better than lower values. For instance, if you have allocated 100MB to a page file, it is a waste of disk space if you are using only 4 percent of that space for actual paging. Basically, anything up to 99 percent is acceptable—but tuning a system to use 99 percent and never more is extremely difficult.

Pool Paged Bytes (Server Object)

The Pool Paged Bytes counter records the amount of space that has been allocated on the server for paging purposes. The higher this value is, the slower your system will be. However, setting this value too low can cause a system to become virtually inoperable. This counter allows you to see how much of the page file is actually being used. This information is useful when you're optimizing a server. If you install a new application on a server, you should review all the counters in the memory section.

Pool Nonpaged Bytes (Server Object)

The Pool Nonpaged Bytes value will tell you the size of the nonpaged memory pool. We just defined this pool as a memory area where data that must not be paged out to hard disk is stored. If this area of memory is too large, there may not be enough memory for other services and processes. This situation would indicate a need to add more physical memory to the system.

Counters for Processor Troubleshooting

The system processor is, obviously, the heart of your system. A poorly performing processor will bring a system to its knees. The problem is that it is not always clear precisely what is overwhelming a processor. The most obvious guess would be that too many processes are running on the server (applications, users, and services). But this might not be the case—hardware failures in other components can also cause the processor to max out. The following counters will help you determine how your processor is doing.

Processor Queue Length (System Object)

The Processor Queue Length counter tells you the number of threads waiting to be processed. This counter should never have a sustained value of two or greater. If it does, then you probably need a faster processor in your server.

Interrupts/Sec (Processor Object)

Various processes and pieces of hardware on a server generate interrupts. These interrupts are basically calls to the processor, telling it that the process of a piece of hardware needs attention. It might be that a task is about to begin, or that a task has ended. Such processes should also cause system activity to increase. If the number of interrupts increases, but system activity does not increase, you could have a hardware problem. An example would be a bad network card that is sending a constant stream of interrupts.

% Processor Time (Processor Object)

The % Processor Time counter tells you the percentage of time your processor is in use. A high sustained value means your system needs either a faster processor or an additional processor.

Counters for Disk Troubleshooting

As we mentioned earlier in this chapter, system administrators often jump to assumptions regarding system performance. The first consideration is often the amount of memory. If that is not the problem, then they point to the system processor. You need to be aware of the importance of the disk drives in your system. This component can have an enormous impact (both positive and negative) on how well your system performs. What follows are some counters that can help you track the efficiency of disk subsystem.

Current Disk Queue Length (Physical Disk)

The Current Disk Queue Length counter can be a little tricky because, to make sense of it, you need to know how many spindles exist on your hard disk. Usually there is one; this counter can become complicated when your system has multiple disks, however, especially when they are configured to use RAID 5. (RAID 5 is a set of disks—a minimum of three—that have been configured to act as one.) This counter records the number of system requests that are queued (waiting) to be processed. Its value should never be more than two times the number of spindles in your system. The actual number will vary from server to server, depending on the disk configuration.

% Disk Time (Physical Disk)

As you might have guessed, the % Disk Time counter simply gives you a reading of the percentage of the time your disks are being used. A value of up to 90 percent can be considered good. If the value is higher, you might want to consider a faster disk or a different disk configuration. If your server has a RAID device, this counter can give false readings. You can use % Disk Time in conjunction with Current Disk Queue Length to determine if a disk subsystem is having problems.

Avg. Disk Bytes/Transfer (Physical Disk Object)

The Avg. Disk Bytes/Transfer counter tells you the average amount of data that is transferred from a disk during read and write operations. This value should be greater than 20KB. If it is not, then an application on your system is probably using the disk drive inefficiently. A low value does not necessarily indicate that you need a new hard disk.

Disk Reads/Sec (Physical Disk Object)

Although it is useful to get the big picture view of how well a disk drive is transferring data, averages do not always give you all the information you need. For instance, a hard disk might be overwhelmed with work—but the situation could be caused by a memory problem that is increasing the number of writes to the disk or by an application that is constantly reading from the disk (such as in video streaming). The Disk Reads/Sec counter can identify the rate that disk reads are occurring on a disk.

Disk Writes/Sec (Physical Disk Object)

Disk Writes/Sec is a partner to the previous counter. This counter records the rate at which disk writes are occurring.

Counters for Network Troubleshooting

The network and the network operations on a system can have a direct effect on the perceived speed of a system. If you have a dial-up Internet connection at your office or home, then you know what we're talking about. If you take the fastest system in the world and hook it up to the Internet, but your dial-up connection is slow due to congestion caused by a failure somewhere else, you will begin to think that your system is running slowly. In fact, the memory, processor, and disk subsystem on your system may not be stressed at all—the network connection is causing the slowdown. The following counters will help you determine whether you have a network problem.

Bytes Total/Sec (Server Object)

The Bytes Total/Sec counter is not directly related to memory usage; however, you should periodically check it. This counter records the number of bytes that a server receives from the network and is putting onto the network. If this value is consistently high, and you are having performance issues, you might want to increase the amount of memory on the server.

Work Item Shortages (Server Object)

As items are received, they need to be processed. The Work Item Shortages counter will increase when incoming requests are being received but no work items are available to process the requests. This situation will cause the network to appear slow.

Bytes Received/Sec (Network Interface Object)

Servers have different roles. It can be useful to know if a server is receiving a lot of data, or whether it is sending data out onto the network. The Bytes Received/Sec counter shows you how much data is being received per second. Compare this to the counter that follows.

Bytes Sent/Sec (Network Interface Object)

The Bytes Sent/Sec counter indicates how much data a server is putting back onto the network. A server filling the role of a read-only database application might have a very high Bytes Sent as opposed to Bytes Received.

Packets Outbound Errors (Network Interface Object)

The Packets Outbound Errors counter tells you how many packets are being discarded at a server because they contain errors. A high number could indicate a problem with the network card. If you have multiple network cards on your machine, then there is an instance for each card; you can check each one.

Counters for Active Directory Troubleshooting

So far, this chapter has concentrated on making sure that you have a good understanding of System Monitor. Without a firm foundation of what it is and how it works, it is impossible for you to use the tool effectively to identify performance and other problems.

We have concentrated on the four main areas with which System Monitor is concerned. These four areas relate to system performance and allow you to determine whether a system has enough memory, whether you have a bad network interface, and so on. It is now time to zero in on how you can use System Monitor to help troubleshoot issues with Active Directory.

When Active Directory is installed on a server, a set of counters is added to System Monitor. These counters work in the same way as other counters. What follows is a list of some significant counters you will use when monitoring the various elements of Active Directory. Once again, it is not possible to list every counter.

DRA Inbound Bytes Total/Sec (NTDS Object)

DRA stands for Directory Replication Agent. The DRA Inbound Bytes Total/Sec counter tells you the sum of the number of bytes received by the DRA for replication. The DRA receives both uncompressed data (for instance, intrasite replication data) and compressed data (such an intersite replication data). However, the counter's sum is for data in uncompressed format—so, in the case of intersite replication traffic, the counter does not necessarily indicate the amount of physical data sent (because the packets are compressed).

DRA Inbound Full Sync. Objects Remaining (NTDS Object)

The DRA Inbound Full Sync. Objects Remaining counter indicates how many objects remain to be replicated when a full synchronization is taking place. This counter can help you determine how long a process is likely to take, and what percentage of objects have already been completed.

DRA Inbound Objects Applied/Sec (NTDS Object)

The DRA Inbound Objects Applied/Sec counter tells you the number of objects that have been received and written to the local Directory Service. These objects are received from replication partners. By looking at this counter, you can quickly find out how many replication updates are taking place due to changes that are being processed by other servers.

DRA Inbound Object Updates Remaining in Packet (NTDS Object)

Replication updates are received in packets. The DRA Inbound Object Updates Remaining in Packet counter tells you how many objects are waiting to be written to the local Directory Service. If this number remains high, then the server is taking a long time to process updates. This situation could indicate problems on the server, and you can use other counters to find out where the problem lies.

DRA Pending Replication Synchronization (NTDS Object)

The DRA Pending Replication Synchronization counter records the number of directory synchronization requests that are currently queued at a server, waiting to be processed. Essentially, this queue becomes a backlog of replication traffic. If this counter begins to climb, it might indicate that the server is slow to process objects. The larger the number, the worse the situation.

We will make configuration changes and use System Monitor in the Real-World Projects that appear at the end of this chapter. System Monitor is a complex tool that provides you with a lot of data. Mastering its use is key to your success as a system administrator of a Windows 2000 network.

System Monitor Logging Options

Before we conclude our discussion of this important topic, we should spend a little time discussing the various options that are available to you when creating logs from System Monitor. System Monitor can provide you with a lot of data, and these configuration options can help you organize it; these options also allow you to zero in quickly on the pieces of data that are most important to you.

Three options are available from within the System Monitor console: Counter Logs, Trace Logs, and Alerts. These options are shown in Figure 8-5. As you can see, the three options are accessible by clicking on Performance Logs and Alerts in the console.

Figure 8-5   The Performance Logs And Alerts option of System Monitor

The three options allow you to set various logging options, such as log names and the format of the log file. We will take a brief look at these options. Before we do, let's define each of them.

Counter Logs

Counter logs are simply ways of creating templates for your performance monitoring tasks. Once you have come up with a group of counters you would like to monitor, you can save them in a template for later use. That way, if you ever want to go back and use the same counters, you do not have to add them one at a time.

The counter logs option dialog box is illustrated in Figure 8-6. The dialog box has various tabs; let's take a closer look at some of the options, so you can see what they do.

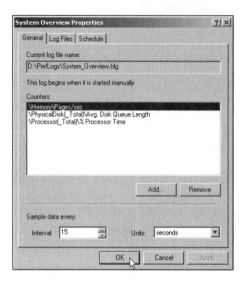

Figure 8-6   The counter logs option dialog box

The General Tab

The General tab allows you to define which counters will be part of this counter log. By clicking on Add, you can add counters to the list.

Other options include the ability to set a sample rate. A **sample rate** is the frequency at which data is sampled. If you want to determine how much data is being transferred to a hard disk, you can set this counter log to sample the transfer rate for a duration of seconds, hours, minutes, or even days. The more frequent the sampling, the more load is put onto the system you are monitoring, because the system now needs to read this data in addition to its existing workload.

The Log Files Tab

Figure 8-7 shows the Log Files tab. The log file allows you to set the properties for the physical file that is used to capture the performance data. These properties include the file location and the filename. Other options allow you to choose the file format; format options include whether the file should be a text format or binary. Text files are easier to use in third-party applications—in fact, you read these log files in Notepad. Binary files require an application to be designed to read them. Of course, System Monitor can read its own binary file format.

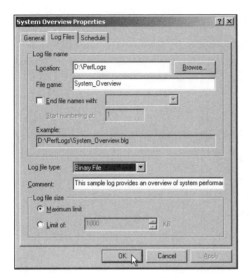

Figure 8-7 The Log Files tab

The final important option on this tab is Log file size. This option allows you to set the maximum size for the log file you are creating. You should consider two things here: Data is constantly being sampled (at the frequency set on the General tab), and the associated log file can grow to be enormous. In fact, unfettered, it would be only a matter of time before the log file filled up the entire hard disk. By default, note that the Maximum Limit option is checked. This option allows the log to grow to the size of available disk space. You should change this setting if you are going to leave logging turned on overnight, or at least make sure you understand the amount of data that your options will generate.

The Schedule Tab

The Schedule tab is shown in Figure 8-8. This tab allows you to configure System Monitor to start gathering data at a specific time. By default, this is a manual process—you configure the options you want to monitor and then tell System Monitor to start. However, this procedure may not always meet your requirements.

Let's say that you want to know the effect on a server of Active Directory replication. The server you are looking at is a bridgehead server between two sites. Because the link between these two sites is busy during the day, the replication is set to take place between 2:00 A.M. and 3:00 A.M. You want to monitor this traffic. Without a scheduling capability, you would have to be at the office at 2:00 A.M. to start the log. With scheduling, however, it is quite easy to set the options you want to monitor, and then have them start automatically.

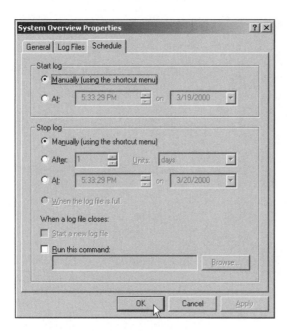

Figure 8-8 The Schedule tab

Another option allows you to decide what will happen when a log file closes. You can either start another log file or execute a program or batch file. The latter choice enables you to have the files copied to another location once they are full, or to perform some other maintenance task.

Trace Logs

Trace logs are a new option that has been added to the monitoring tool since Windows NT 4. Trace logs allow you to configure samples of data to be collected from providers on the system. These providers use Web-Based Enterprise Management (WBEM). WBEM is an industry initiative that defines how data should be collected and also the schema for data collection. We will discuss the architecture of WBEM later in this chapter, in the section "Windows Management Instrumentation."

The data collected from the trace logs is in binary format, and before it can be read it must be parsed. This is another way of saying that you need a special program to read the logs. Unfortunately, Microsoft chose not to include such a tool with Windows 2000. You will have to seek out third-party vendors to use this feature. At the time of this writing, no tools were available.

Alerts

Alerts are a way of making some of the performance data come to life. They do this by allowing you to configure system messages, start a log file, or run an application (perhaps a paging application to alert you to a significant event). The alert configuration dialog box is shown in Figure 8-9.

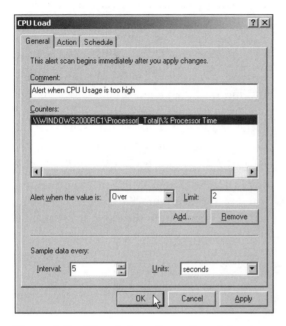

Figure 8-9 The alert configuration dialog box

Alerts can be configured to begin immediately or to occur at specific intervals (such as after work hours). Alerts are essentially triggers; that is, an event will occur if a particular performance monitor counter falls within a certain range. The events that can be triggered include:

- Logging the event to the Application Log

- Sending a network message

- Starting a log file

- Running an external application

System Monitor is a powerful tool that will take some time to master, but it is an important skill that will pay many dividends when you are stuck in front of a server that is not performing correctly. The information in this section will give you a good basis from which to increase your knowledge.

EVENT LOGS

As you have seen in our discussion of System Monitor, you can monitor many different operations on a system. After reading the previous section, you may think that all monitoring takes place in realtime—but this is not the case. Sometimes, it is simply important that events be recorded. You can read the logs to be aware of what has been going on.

Event logs have existed in all versions of Microsoft Windows NT, but you will find that Microsoft has extended their use in Windows 2000. There are now logs for specific functions, which is particularly important for a domain controller in a Windows 2000 environment. We will take a closer look at the logs that are available on a DC, along with some tips on how to read them. You probably will spend a lot of time in the Event Viewer tool, so familiarity is essential to your being an effective administrator.

Event Viewer in Windows 2000 looks a little different from what you might be familiar with from previous versions, as you can see in Figure 8-10. Each available log file is shown in the left pane. The data in the log is shown on the right. Let's take a closer look at the each of these log files, so you understand what data they contain.

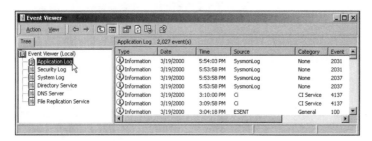

Figure 8-10   Event Viewer

Application Log

The Application Log records events for applications that exist on the system. An example of the use of the Application Log is troubleshooting a failure of an e-mail system or system management application.

The Application Log can quickly become full. In a moment, we will look at how you can control that growth. On standalone systems, it is a safe bet that you will spend much of your time in the Application Log, because most of the day-to-day operations are reported to it. If you are having a problem and want to see if something is wrong, this is the place to start.

Security Log

By default, the Security Log is essentially turned off. The systems are configured by default to be fairly loose—that is, to have a minimal amount of logging occurring.

The Security Log responds to auditing events that are configured via the Computer Management MMC snap-in and Group Policy settings. These options are not turned on by default because they cause a lot of logging to take place. They should be used sparingly, and only when needed. For instance, it is possible to configure a log event to occur every time a user logs on to the network. In an enterprise, this logging will cause a lot of data to be written to the Security Log, a load to be generated at the server, and disk space to be consumed.

You can also audit object access, such as a user's accessing a file or a folder. Doing so might be useful if you think users are trying to access parts of the network from which they have been excluded. Again, you should use these options only when they are needed.

System Log

The System Log is the location to which all messages generated by the system are reported (with the exception of those components that now have their own logs). Messages from applications such as Microsoft Exchange are recorded in the Application Log. The components that report to the System Log include services and components such as Netlogon and the File Replication Service (FRS).

If you are having difficulties starting a service on a system, this log would be a good place to start your search for the cause of the problem. It is worth noting that a system often has dependencies that can cause long strings of errors. For example, if TCP/IP fails on a system, the server and workstation services also fail. This failure, in turn, will cause Netlogon to fail, and so on. The key to troubleshooting such an issue is to locate the operation that caused the dependency to fail and then troubleshoot it from there. The component reporting an error condition might not have a problem at all—the problem may exist elsewhere in the system and be reported elsewhere in the log.

Directory Service

Messages generated by Active Directory have their own log, because the volume of messages would make it difficult to find them all if they were recorded elsewhere. The Directory Service log records events that relate to all aspects of Active Directory operation, including the failure of a replication event or the stopping and starting of the database engine.

This log also records events for the Knowledge Consistency Checker (KCC) and the automatic maintenance processes. (If these terms are unfamiliar to you, you should read Chapter 14, which discusses each of them in detail.)

DNS Server

The DNS Server log records all events that have to do with the Domain Name System (DNS) operations on a DC with the DNS service installed. DNS is an important part of Windows 2000; without it, Active Directory will fail to function.

Because DNS is such an important component, it stands to reason that you will need to monitor it specifically—and that is why DNS now has its own log. You will find entries in this log for such events as being unable to write to Active Directory (because DNS can now be integrated into Active Directory, this occurrence can be fatal).

File Replication Service

The File Replication Service has many different tasks within Windows 2000. One of these tasks is to replicate data between SYSVOLs on DCs. This folder is an essential part of many aspects of Windows 2000, including Group Policy.

Group Policy is not the only time this service is used, however; it is also used for domain Distributed file system (Dfs) and for the replication of source files for software distribution functions of group policy. This log will contain data such as an inability to replicate data from one DC to another. This problem could be due to an error at the server that is instigating the replication (the one reporting the error) or at the destination location.

On standalone and Windows 2000 Professional systems, you will see only the Application, Security, and System logs. On DCs, you will see all six logs, because the role of the server is that much greater. You should understand that the role of system administrators will generally cause them to spend their time in the three most common logs, because they contain data that is more concerned with day-to-day operations (such as application failures).

Event Types

You will see three event types in the various event logs. Each type has its meaning, and you should have different levels of concern regarding them. The three types are:

- Information
- Warning
- Error

Each event type has its own associated icon; these icons make the events easy to see when you are glancing quickly at a full log. These icons are shown in Figure 8-11.

Figure 8-11   The icons for the three event types. You should be most concerned about error messages, because these types of log entries indicate that something has failed.

Table 8-1 gives you a quick definition for what each type of event means, and why the events can be generated. As you will see, many events are purely informational and exist only to let you know that processes are occurring and whether they are successful.

Table 8-1   Event types

Event Type	Description
Information	This type of message records the successful operation of a task or application. For instance, when services successfully start on a system when it is booted, informational messages will appear.
Warning	A warning is an event that may or may not be significant. For instance, when hard disk space begins to get low on a system, the condition is logged as a warning message. It alerts you to the fact that you might have a space problem developing, but for the moment other things are working fine.
Error	Error messages demand immediate attention. They signify a problem that can be anything from the failure of a service to start, to the loss of data. All error messages should be investigated to see how they affect your system. For instance, a single service can cause multiple services to fail. You should seek out errors and eliminate them as soon as possible.

Viewing Remote Event Logs

Event Viewer is a flexible tool. Event logs contain a lot of key information, and you can also view the logs on remote systems. It is simply a matter of connecting to a remote system.

Figure 8-12 shows how you can view the Application Log of a remote machine. As you can see, you simply right-click on the Event Viewer (Local) option and choose Connect To Another Computer. Once you have done this, simply enter the name of the system you want to connect to. As you might imagine, you need sufficient access rights to read another system's logs. For instance, you must have at least administrator access to read the Security Log.

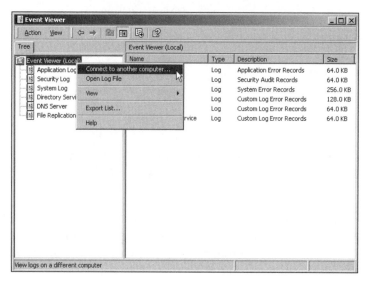

Figure 8-12   Connecting to a remote computer

Managing Event Logs

Event logs are essential to your monitoring techniques; however, although the data is undoubtedly important, you should make sure that you are only keeping data that will be useful. Several options are available when it comes to configuring the log files; they apply to each log equally. You can:

- Provide an upper size limit for the log files
- Set the number of days that data should be kept
- Save the events for archival purposes

Although it might seem like a good idea to collect data for as long as you can, the truth is that you are not going to have time to go through endless logs looking for significant events. It is far better to put some time aside each day to view the event logs and see what has occurred. If you do this regularly, then there will be no need to keep archives going back weeks or months.

The exception would be if you are trying to discover trends on a new server that has been installed on your network. It can be a good idea to monitor a new server a little more closely, to make sure that it is completely functional. Logs for these types of servers can be archived for later analysis.

The Log Properties dialog box is shown in Figure 8-13. As you can see, several options are available. These include the maximum size of the log file (by default, 512K) and actions to take if the log file reaches its maximum size.

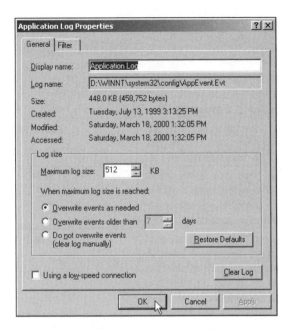

Figure 8-13   The Log Properties dialog box

These options are described in the following:

- *Overwrite Events As Needed*—Causes events to be deleted from the log once it has reach its maximum size. This happens regardless of the number of days an event has been in the log. If a lot of logging is occurring in a system, it is possible that events from the same day could be overwritten. In systems that are used less, it could be days or weeks before events are overwritten.

- *Overwrite Events Older Than*—By default, set to seven days. With this option set, events older than the specified number of days will be overwritten, even if maximum log size is not reached. This option can be useful when you never want to review log data that is older than a given length of time.

- *Do Not Overwrite Events (Clear Log Manually)*—Causes events to be never deleted from the log file. This option can cause problems if you forget you have set it and the log file fills up. (Windows 2000 will stop logging events if this occurs, with the exception of security events.) This is also the most secure of all the options, because no event is ever lost (overwritten or deleted).

The Event Viewer application is an important tool that you can use to monitor the actions and functions occurring at a particular system. Because the Security Log can contain information regarding security breaches, you should pay close attention to the data it contains. Viewing these log files should become part of your everyday activities as a system administrator.

WINDOWS MANAGEMENT INSTRUMENTATION

A key new feature has been added to System Monitor (it was not available in previous versions of Window NT). This feature is the integration between System Monitor and the Windows Management Instrumentation (WMI). WMI is a key industry initiative, and it is worth spending a few paragraphs defining it and explaining why it is so significant.

WMI first made an appearance in a significant way with the release of Microsoft Systems Management Server 2.0 (SMS). Earlier versions of SMS were fairly good at getting hardware inventory data from clients on a network. The amount of data was arbitrary and limiting, however. Also, some of the most important data (such as serial numbers of computers) could not be collected.

Along came Intel and many other hardware vendors, who decided that there should be a way to pull data from a computer. Not only that, but if the method were industry defined, then the information from (say) a Compaq machine ought to be the same as the information from a Dell.

Sometimes, however, things don't work out the way everyone wants. This group of vendors did come up with something called the Desktop Management Interface (DMI), which is basically an Application Programming Interface (API) that allows generic (or at least well-known) function calls to be made to gather data. DMI worked well, but it fell down a little when it came to the agents that had to be installed to make it work. An agent was needed because some piece of code had to run on each machine to make those API calls; and, over time, getting agents from all manufacturers for all machines was time consuming. In addition, the data they returned was not always the same.

Over time, networks have become more complex. Many more things need to be monitored, and the agent piece of the equation had to be simplified. The industry got together again, and came up with a standard on which monitoring and data collection can be based: Web-Based Management Instrumentation (WBEM). Microsoft agreed to implement WBEM on its operating systems, but it also changed the name. Microsoft's implementation is known as Windows Management Instrumentation (WMI).

Because DMI was dogged by agent issues, that problem required a solution. Microsoft came to the rescue by shipping in every copy of Windows 2000 what is essentially the middleware between the applications that display data and the underlying data providers. In fact, Microsoft went a step further and added it to Windows 9.x and Windows NT 4, as well. (Service Pack 4 for Windows NT 4 installs the necessary components.)

Now, all that is needed is for vendors to write the piece that collects the data. In WMI terms, this is a combination of providers and Management Object Files (also known as MOF files). Some of these have already been installed in your copy of Windows 2000.

You will find the WMI files in the *<Systemroot>*\system32\Wbem folder. The MOF files can be found in *<Systemroot>*\system32\Wbem\Mof. You should not delete these files from your system—it will become unstable if you do. You can read more about DMI at **http://www.dmtf.org/**. For information on WMI, go to **http://www.microsoft.com/management**.

WMI extends to many places that DMI never did. For instance, Intel has demonstrated systems that can detect whether a screw had been removed from the back of a case, or if a BIOS chip begins to heat too rapidly. It remains to be seen what will happen to WMI, but we expect it to play a significant role in future generations of reporting and monitoring tools. You read it here first!

Just for clarity, Figure 8-14 presents the architecture for WMI. In the figure, you can see the role of an application, the middleware, and the providers that supply the data. System Monitor is an application like any other, utilizing the data providers.

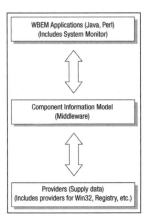

Figure 8-14   WMI architecture

To allow System Monitor to use WMI counters to display data, simply choose Start | Run and type "perfmon /WMI". Press Enter, and System Monitor will start.

TOOLS FOR MONITORING ACTIVE DIRECTORY

Along with the standard set of tools that exists in every installation of Windows 2000, some command-line and Graphical User Interface (GUI) tools are optional. These tools are for the advanced Active Directory administrator and are not to be taken lightly. It is worth mentioning them here, however, so you have a well-rounded view of the available tools.

We will take a brief look at some of the additional monitoring and informational applications available on the Windows 2000 CD. To use some of these tools, you must first install them—

they are not installed by default. To install these tools, you need the Windows 2000 CD. When you insert this CD, you are presented with the Microsoft Windows 2000 CD dialog box (if autorun is not enabled on your system, you will not see this screen; you will have to navigate to the necessary folder manually). Click on Browse This CD to open the folder for the CD contents. Navigate to the SUPPORT\TOOLS folder. Once there, execute the SETUP.EXE program to install the tools we are about to discuss.

When the installation has completed, you will have a new program group called Windows 2000 Support Tools. You can start most of these tools from this group. When there is an alternative method of starting them, we will discuss it in the definition.

What follows are brief descriptions of some of the most important tools. We won't spend too much time on this topic, because these tools are rarely used and are intended for advanced users.

LDAP Diagnostic Tool (LDP.EXE)

The Lightweight Directory Access Protocol (LDAP) diagnostic tool allows you to run LDAP queries against the Active Directory. LDAP is a protocol, and queries within a Windows 2000 tree are made via this protocol. If you are having problems performing queries against the directory on your network, then you can use this tool to confirm that LDAP is functioning. You can perform add, modify, search, and compares on data within the directory.

The graphic tools within Windows 2000 do not necessarily let you see every object that is stored within Active Directory. This includes metadata that is included with some objects. Tools like LDP allow you to expose this information. However, unless you are intimately familiar with the underlying data, these objects might not have much meaning.

Unlike many of the other tools, there is no inline help for this tool. You must also have a firm grasp of LDAP syntax before the tool will be much use. Unfortunately, a detailed discussion of LDAP is beyond the scope of this book. A typical LDP display showing Active Directory data is shown in Figure 8-15. To start this tool, follow the installation directions given at the beginning of this section. Then choose Start|Run, type "LDP", and click on OK.

Active Directory Replication Monitor (REPLMON)

The Active Directory Replication Monitor (REPLMON) allows you to view the status of replication between partners. You can also view some performance information. This application offers a lot of information, such as the directory partitions stored on a server and which direct replication partners are relevant to each. It will display both direct partners and also partners through transitive trusts. Icons within REPLMON quickly show you whether a partner is operational.

Along with replication data, REPLMON can display the roles that a server is playing in the enterprise. For instance, if a server is also the PDC Emulator, this status would be displayed.

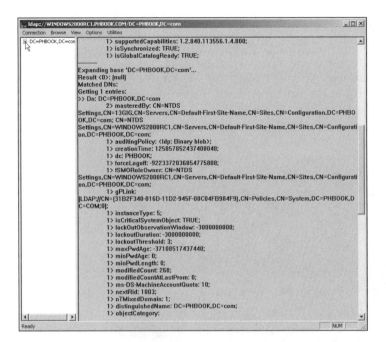

Figure 8-15   The LDP tool

For direct replication partners, you can see the Update Sequence Numbers (USNs) of the servers and the number of failed replication attempts that have occurred. You can also view the Globally Unique Identifier (GUID) for the partner and the protocol the partner is using to replicate data.

Finally, you can trigger replication manually within this tool. Doing so might be necessary if you know a server is out of date, or if you want to monitor the effect of replication traffic on a particular segment of your network or at a DC.

REPLMON is a powerful tool, and despite all the good points mentioned here, you can do a host of other things with it. We suggest (once you have mastered everything else in this book) that you take a closer look at REPLMON. When you want to have a better understanding of replication in your enterprise, there isn't a better tool.

REPADMIN

Just because it does not have a fancy name, don't be fooled into thinking that the REPADMIN command-line tool is not powerful. (In fact, Windows 2000 has introduced a whole host of command-line tools for many functions. If you are coming from a Unix environment, you might very well be more comfortable working outside of the standard GUI tools provided by Microsoft.) This utility can display the names of replication partners. This information is useful when you want to know how a server fits into the overall replication topology.

The one drawback of this command is that it does not see the connection objects created in Active Object. Instead, it shows only the connections made by the KCC. (If you do not remember what these terms mean, go back to Chapter 6 for a review.)

The list of command-line switches available within REPADMIN is shown in Figure 8-16. As you can see, many options are available for you to use. For example, open a command prompt on a DC, type "REPADMIN /showrep", and press Enter. Doing so will display the replication partners for the server according to the KCC.

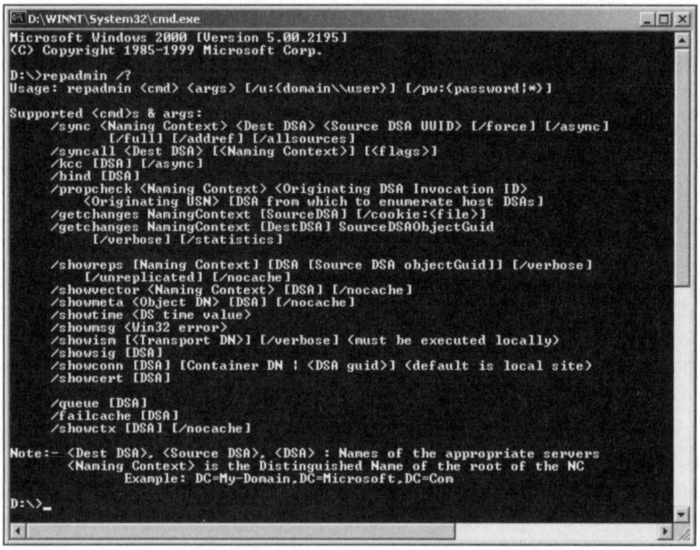

Figure 8-16   REPADMIN command-line switches

These tools, and many others, are useful when troubleshooting and monitoring Active Directory and Windows 2000. It would take an entire book to discuss each of them in detail. Once you have learned everything in this book, you will be ready to tackle the other tools. Here, we have presented a good overview of the tools, both for real-world use and for the Microsoft 70-217 exam.

CHAPTER SUMMARY

❑ In this chapter, we looked at methods you can use to monitor the performance of domain controllers on your network. Some of the tools and strategies can also be used on Windows 2000 Professional systems, but they will not work on Windows 9.x machines.

❑ We first examined what constitutes a system that is performing poorly. It is fairly common to underutilize systems and to aim for unrealistic goals (such as 0 percent CPU usage). We discussed all the major steps administrators take to improve a system, such as adding a new hard disk, memory, or processor. We also warned against simply throwing additional resources at problems without first performing some kind of analysis.

❑ We introduced the term **baseline** to describe what normal operation should be for a system. A baseline is a set of statistics that describes the performance level for a system on a normal working day. You use a baseline as a standard, and then compare subsequent statistics against it to identify problems or to compare the performance of a system after a change has been made.

❑ The first built-in tool we looked at is System Monitor. System Monitor is an MMC snap-in that allows you to access counters for various components (also known as **objects**) available on a system. System Monitor is a new and improved version of the Performance Monitor that shipped with Microsoft Windows NT.

❑ You should be concerned about four main areas when performing baseline analysis or examining a system for variations from the baseline: memory, processor, disk, and network. These areas work together to determine the overall performance of a system. System Monitor gives you the ability to collect statistics for each of these key areas. In System Monitor, these areas are known as *objects*. Many other objects are available, but these are the basic four.

❑ Memory includes statistics for the RAM inside your machine (including usage and amount free) and counters for the swap file. The swap file is an area of hard disk space that acts like RAM, should the system require additional memory space.

❑ The Processor object includes counters that allow you to see how busy the system processor is. You can view this information as a percentage of capacity (processor is working at 90 percent of capacity, for instance) or in more sophisticated ways by viewing the number of requests waiting to be serviced by the processor. If your system has more than one processor, you can view each of them individually.

❑ The Disk object allows you to view a large range of information, including the amount of space free on a disk, how quickly data is being written to the disk, and how quickly the disk is able to perform reads. When performing system monitoring of disks, you should take into consideration the fact that your servers are likely to be using a fault-tolerant system (such as RAID 5)—such a system can skew the results.

❑ The Network object concerns itself with the performance of the communication components on a system, including the amount of data being put onto the wire by the system and being read off the wire. If a system appears to be performing poorly, it might be because data cannot be written to or from the network quickly enough.

❑ Performance of a system is usually discussed using the following three terms: throughput, queue, and response time. Throughput measures the amount of work that takes place in a given period of time. Queue defines the line of waiting requests that need to be processed. Response Time measures how quickly a process is completed (a measurement of start to finish).

8

❏ Each of the four objects discussed (Memory, Processor, Disk, and Network) has statistics you can use to measure performance. These statistics are called objects, counters, and instances.

❏ An object is a representation of a system resource. Each object has associated counters and instances. The object level is the catch-all where you can view every statistic available in a particular area. It is worth noting that a complete analysis of a system will include analysis of data from many different object types.

❏ A counter is a specific area of statistics for a given object. For instance, the Processor object has counters for User Time and Interrupts/sec. A specific counter can generate statistics for every occurrence of a resource in a system, via instances. In order to measure a counter, you must measure an instance.

❏ An instance is a specific occurrence of a counter. A counter can have multiple instances. For instance, the Processor object has a counter that generates statistics for the percentage of time a processor is being used. This counter is the % Processor Time. If your system has more than one processor, there will be multiple instances of this counter for you to monitor.

❏ System Monitor in Windows 2000 includes hundreds of counters—far too many for us to list in this book. As well as supporting the built-in counters, it is also possible (and probable) that third-party vendors will add their own objects and counters to System Monitor. We listed some of the most commonly used counters in each of the four areas we have identified. These counters should be used before a problem occurs, to define the baseline for a system.

❏ These counters work together to form a description of a system and how it performs. We also discussed counters that are specific to Active Directory. This is an example of a vendor adding counters to System Monitor to help you view the performance of a newly installed service (in this case, Directory Services).

❏ System Monitor data is very important, and you should run it periodically so you can compare results over time. Rather than setting up the options individually each time, you can configure counter logs. Counter logs allow you to choose counters once and then reuse them. The results can be saved to a file on disk for later analysis, and you can choose from several different file formats. Once you have configured the options for your counter logs, you can schedule when (and how often) the counters should run.

❏ System Monitor works by reading data from the system Registry. Each counter is defined in a Dynamic Link Library (DLL) on the hard disk. System Monitor also allows you to use WMI (Microsoft's implementation of WBEM). WBEM is an industry-defined method of collecting data. It helps define which data can be collected, and how it should be presented.

❏ Another important tool is Event Viewer. Event Viewer allows you to view the event logs that are recorded on every Windows 2000 system. The number of logs will vary, depending on the services and functions installed on a system. The three standard logs that appear on every system are the Application Log, Security Log, and System Log. In addition, on Windows 2000 DCs, you will find a Directory Service log, DNS Server log, and File Replication Service.

❑ Each of these logs displays data on various events. There are three event types: information, warning, and error. These should elicit varying levels of concern. Information messages are probably not of concern; error messages mean something has failed, and should therefore be examined carefully.

❑ Event logs can become very large (and the more logs on a system, the more space is used). You can set options for event logs that include the maximum size of the logs, the number of days data is stored in the log, and how events should be saved.

❑ Finally, we took a brief look at some tools that are available specifically for monitoring Active Directory. These tools are often rather obtuse and complex, and are not installed by default. They include the LDAP Diagnostic Tool, the Active Directory Replication Monitor, and REPADMIN. You can use these tools to view the details of Active Directory replication or to determine if you have problems with queries to the directory.

8

CHAPTER

9

ACTIVE DIRECTORY
MAINTENANCE AND RECOVERY

After completing this chapter, you will be able to:

♦ Describe how data is stored in Active Directory

♦ Define key Active Directory terms such as System State Data

♦ Perform a non-authoritative restore of Active Directory data

♦ Understand the security permissions required to perform a backup and restore

A ctive Directory is a key part of your Windows 2000 network. A lot of time is spent designing its architecture, both from a logical and physical standpoint. But when you get down to it, Active Directory is simply another set of files that exist on a server in your enterprise. As part of your plans, you should make sure that you have the ability to perform both a backup and a restore of Active Directory data.

In this chapter, you will learn about the data structure of Active Directory. Once you understand how data is stored and where the physical files are stored on the hard disk, we will show you how to perform system maintenance, backup, and restore operations.

RECOVERY AND MAINTENANCE OVERVIEW

When things are working well, the network is humming, and your servers are operating without a single critical message in your event logs, it is easy to forget how difficult the situation can become in a relatively short period of time. A simple call to a help-desk technician saying, "You know, I can no longer save my documents" can quickly turn the life of a system administrator into a turbulent race against time.

When it comes to disaster recovery, it is not a matter of "if"—it is a matter of "when." I can guarantee that at some time in the future, you will be standing before a server that has either crashed outright or has ceased to perform its function sufficiently. If it happens to be a server that is home to a mission-critical piece of software (such as an e-mail server), people will be buzzing around you like flies, pleading with you to bring the server back online as soon as you can. You must understand what files and data need to be backed up—and you must execute that backup plan—or you might very well never be able to bring your server back online. We will cover everything you need to know to make sure that Active Directory operates on your network, even if one of your domain controllers goes belly up.

As you have worked through this book, you have no doubt noted the way Windows 2000 domain controllers (DCs) differ from those in previous versions of Microsoft Windows NT. One of the key differences (although not the only difference) between these two sets of DCs is that in Windows 2000, DCs are peers. That is, the whole concept of a Primary Domain Controller (PDC) and Backup Domain Controller (BDC) no longer exists. In the old world, if a BDC went down, it was not a disaster. If the PDC went down things could get pretty scary, but the situation was easy enough to fix.

You can be forgiven for thinking that because DCs in Windows 2000 are peers, it should not be quite so catastrophic if one of them dies. Actually, that may or may not be the case. Don't forget that Windows 2000 has a concept of **sites** (see Chapter 2), and sites affect much of the normal operations on your network. For instance, sites are used to optimize logon traffic on your network, to give access to the nearest Distributed file system (Dfs) share, and for Active Directory replication traffic, among other things. If a carefully placed DC goes down, the effects on your network can be unpredictable and obscure. Although this event would probably not prevent users from doing their work, the balance of your network can suffer considerably.

So, the same rules we have used for user data still apply. The only ways to protect yourself are with fault-tolerant hardware (such as Redundant Array of Independent Disks, or RAID 5) and careful backup and restore policies. That is one of the purposes of this chapter: to make sure that you have an understanding of what constitutes a reasonable backup of a DC in Windows 2000.

Before we begin looking at the mechanics involved, you need to have an understanding of how Windows 2000 stores data. By understanding this process, you will be able to see how Windows 2000 DCs are able to survive if a DC is suddenly turned off. We will then locate the critical Active Directory files and tell you how to back them up.

ACTIVE DIRECTORY DATA MODEL

Active Directory is a lot of things, but if we were asked to come up with a two-word definition, it would be this simple: a database. (Given three words, we'd say it is a distributed database.) Along with databases such as Microsoft SQL Server, the underlying database of Active Directory has built-in mechanisms that ensure data is written in a uniform, guaranteed way. If this were not the case, then there would be a good chance that the data would become corrupt. Figure 9-1 shows the basic structure of the Active Directory data store model. As you can see, it has three distinct layers.

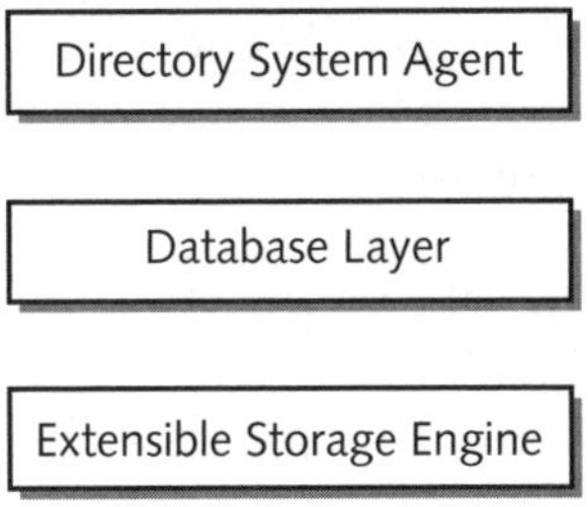

Directory System Agent

Database Layer

Extensible Storage Engine

Figure 9-1   Three layers of the Active Directory data store model

Let's take a look at each of these items in turn, and present a clear definition for each.

Directory System Agent (DSA)

When you use an application to access data within Active Directory, the data must first go through the Directory System Agent (DSA). The DSA sits at the top of Figure 9-1, and it creates an instance of the directory service. When an application wants to access data within the directory, the DSA makes it available.

You should note that applications within Windows 2000 do not have direct access to the underlying data in the directory. Instead, the DSA impersonates applications, retrieves the data itself, and then passes it back to the calling application. This process offers an extra level of security. Because applications and users are not able to access the underlying data, the data does not have to be secured through countless access control lists.

The DSA has many tasks to perform. Because Active Directory is a fairly complex process, it is not enough for the DSA simply to make data available. It must also enforce security settings within the directory and facilitate Active Directory replication.

The Database Layer

Some key concepts regarding the physical storage of Active Directory data might surprise you. When looking at Active Directory, and when studying topics such as the schemas and domain design documents, you are used to viewing the data in a hierarchical form—that is, like a tree with the trunk at the top and roots spreading out beneath it.

The physical data as it is stored in the database is not like that. In fact, the data within the physical file is **flat**. A hierarchical view is simply a representation of what actually exists.

The database layer takes that flat data and makes it hierarchical for you. It applies the defined schema for Active Directory against the data to show you what you expect to see. It manages all the parent-child relationships in your management tools and provides a better way of seeing your data. After all, looking at one huge table is certainly not conducive to easy learning!

Extensible Storage Engine (ESE)

The Extensible Storage Engine (ESE) is the underlying engine that physically stores the Active Directory data. This engine scales to enormous proportions. We will be taking a closer look at how the integrity of the data is ensured in a moment.

 It might surprise you to learn that Active Directory data is stored in just two tables. The first table, which is known as the **object table**, holds the data. The other is the **link table**, which implements the links between objects that help build relationships.

It turns out that this underlying database engine is not new. In fact, it has been used in production networks for quite some time. It is the same engine that is used in Microsoft Exchange 5.5. Because it was thoroughly field-tested prior to the existence of Windows 2000, Microsoft is assured of performance and scalability issues. This database was designed to handle up to 16 terabytes of data—so you can be confident that it will scale across your enterprise.

HOW DATA IS WRITTEN TO THE DATABASE

Now that you have a good idea what the structure of the underlying engine is like, it is time to walk through the process of how data is written to Active Directory. The method Active Directory uses is very much like that used in Microsoft SQL Server. Data is never written directly to the database; instead, it is held temporarily in a log before the physical write takes place. This log can then be used to fix problems, should they occur.

A change being made to the database is called a **transaction**. Transactions can come from many places: from the administrative tools provided with the operating system, from scripts written by users and administrators, or from third-party software vendors who wish to integrate their products with Active Directory. Regardless of where they come from, the process of moving the data from the interface to the physical data store (the object table in the ESE) is a regimented and efficient process.

The following paragraphs walk you through the process of how a change is made in a console and is eventually written to the object table. As you will see, it is a simple yet effective way of ensuring that data is written to the database efficiently, and with a level of fault-tolerance necessary in such a critical application. Figure 9-2 shows an administrator sitting at a console ready to make that change.

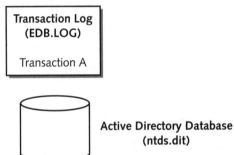

Figure 9-2   An administrator making a change using an administration tool

After the administrator selects the necessary options, the change is made on the DC. First, the change is accepted and a transaction is created. This transaction encompasses the changes that will be made to the underlying database records. Next, this transaction is written to a **transaction log**. A transaction log is a file stored on disk that contains a list of all the transactions that have been applied to the Active Directory database. It is important to realize that all proposed changes to Active Directory are written to a transaction log *before* actually going to disk. Figure 9-3 shows this data being written to the transaction log.

In the case of a failure on a DC, Active Directory can look at the list of changes stored within this file and quickly determine which changes it has stored in the physical database and which changes have been lost due to the failure. It uses this information either to undo changes that have not been fully written to the database file (known as **rolling back** a transaction, because it undoes an incomplete change) or to apply all outstanding transactions (known as **fully committed** transactions).

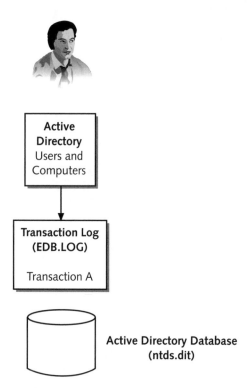

Figure 9-3   Data is written to the transaction log

The next step is completed when the transaction is written to the database stored in memory on the DC. The entire database is not stored in memory (so you don't have to worry about the enormous amounts of Random Access Memory [RAM] your DC will need); instead, a small piece of the database is stored and written to memory. These pieces of the database are known as **pages**. (A discussion of pages is outside the scope of this book, and the topic is not important to pass the 70-217 certification exam. Readers are nevertheless encouraged to read about the topic for their general knowledge.)

Finally, the change is written to the physical file on the disk. This step is shown in Figure 9-4. The transaction can now be removed from the transaction log, because the data is no longer needed. The transaction log uses a pointer system to determine which entries have been physically written to the data store on disk and which are still waiting to be written. The most up-to-date view of Active Directory data is the physical data store, along with any entries in the transaction log that are waiting to be written to that physical store.

When is data written from the transaction log to the physical data store? The answer varies. The official answer is that the data is written during idle times on the DC. So, you cannot count on the preceding steps occurring at the same intervals for each transaction.

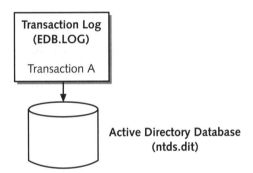

Figure 9-4 Data is written to the database

 Have you noticed that after you make your computer a DC, it seems to perform more poorly than before? Not only does Active Directory place an additional burden on DCs by installing a host of new services and processes, it also disables write caching to the hard disks. It does so to ensure data integrity of the Active Directory data files. With write caching enabled, Windows 2000 cannot be sure precisely when data is written to the hard disk.

You might be thinking that once the data within a transaction log has been committed to the database, there is little point in keeping it around forever—and you would be right. A short archive period is probably a good idea, because you never know when a failure will take place; but storing information for days is not a good use of the finite resources on the DC (meaning the hard disk space). In fact, Windows 2000 periodically performs what is known as **garbage collection**. This process runs every 12 hours on DCs; it cleans up the transaction logs, getting rid of entries that are no longer of any use. (We will talk more about this process later in this chapter.)

9

THE FILES OF ACTIVE DIRECTORY

Having taken a look at the process that enables data to be written to Active Directory, let's examine the actual files that are affected. The following sections give the location and names of both the database and transaction files that are used by Windows 2000. These are the files you should back up for disaster-recovery purposes.

The Database File (ntds.dit)

The ntds.dit file contains both the object and link tables. This is obviously a critical file that must be saved for disaster-recovery purposes. ntds.dit can be found (by default) in the *<systemroot>*\NTDS folder on each DC. In addition to information on all the objects of the directory, this file stores the schema and configuration partitions of the directory.

If you do a search of your hard disk, you will turn up two copies of ntds.dit. In addition to the copy in the \NTDS folder, another version of the file is stored in *<systemroot>*\system32. This copy exists on all Windows 2000 servers and is used as a template, should the server ever be promoted to a DC. If this file is missing, then the Windows 2000 CD is needed during the promotion.

 The DIT file extension stands for Directory Information Table.

The Log Files (EDB.LOG, RES1.LOG, and RES2.LOG)

The EDB.LOG file is the transaction log that we looked at earlier in this chapter. It is used to store transactions before they are committed to the database file (ntds.dit). After that process has taken place, these logs have a record of which transactions have occurred on a DC.

The log file has a predetermined maximum size. Once that size is reached, the file is renamed, and a new transaction log is created. The approximate maximum size of this log is 10MB. Older transaction log files are stored in the same folder as the EDB.LOG file, which by default is the same location as ntds.dit. The older logs are named EDB*****.LOG, where the asterisks are replaced by a hexadecimal value.

It can be difficult to calculate how quickly transaction logs will grow. Transactions are of differing sizes, depending on the amount and number of changes that need to be committed. So, it is virtually impossible to determine precisely when one log file will be considered full and another will be created.

As you have seen, the transaction logs play a vital role in the maintenance and integrity of Active Directory data. But what happens if the hard disk runs out of disk space, and there is no longer enough space in the current transaction log to record all the changes that need to be made to the directory? Two transaction logs are standing by to take over if such a disaster should occur: RES1.LOG and RES2.LOG. These files are 10MB each (not coincidentally, the default maximum size for the EDB.LOG file). In effect, they reserve space on the hard disk, should that space ever be needed by Active Directory.

Circular Logging

You may wonder how much disk space the transaction logs will take up on your DCs. We hope that each of your DCs has enough disk space to perform its intended role; but if you are particularly concerned about this topic, you might want to consider **circular logging**.

Circular logging is a method whereby transaction logs are not archived when they are full. Instead of having a slew of EDB*****.LOG files on your DC, the same file is used repeatedly—when the EDB.LOG file is full, it is overwritten. This mechanism can help you maximize the space on your DC's hard disks, but it offers less fault tolerance.

 Unfortunately, turning on circular logging requires a Registry hack. I don't want to go through the usual warnings about editing the Registry—just keep in mind that if you mess up the Registry on a Windows 2000 machine, it's probably going to be toast! The Registry key for turning on circular logging can be found at HKEY_LOCAL_MACHINE\CurrentControlSet\Services\ NTDS\Parameters\CircularLogging. A value of 0 means that it is turned off; changing the value to 1 turns the feature on.

Checkpoint Files (EDB.CHK)

So, how does Active Directory recover when power is suddenly lost to a domain controller? As you have seen, Active Directory is maintained through the interaction of a database file and transaction logs. The transaction logs store all changes that need to be made to the underlying database.

The checkpoint file EDB.CHK, on the other hand, is simply a file that contains pointers to where transactions begin and end in the transaction log file. Active Directory does not really *need* this file, because it could work out the information simply by reading the transaction logs directly; but doing so would be less efficient.

By looking at the checkpoint file, Active Directory can write any uncommitted transactions to the database. This process takes place at system startup. So, if a server is suddenly turned off and then turned back on, Active Directory reads this file to make sure the database file is up to date.

PATCH FILES

Patch files, which have a PAT extension, are used during online backups. An **online backup** means that you can perform a backup operation even though the underlying data is still being used. Doing so introduces additional complexity that is taken care of by patch files.

9

For instance, what happens if a transaction is recorded during the backup process, and the underlying data in ntds.dit that will be changed by that transaction has already been backed up to tape? The transaction is written to the patch file. This file is backed up along with all the other Active Directory files. It is then deleted from the server (which means you will not get to see the patch file). A typical folder listing for the *<systemroot>*\NTDS folder, from which the patch files have been deleted, is shown in Figure 9-5.

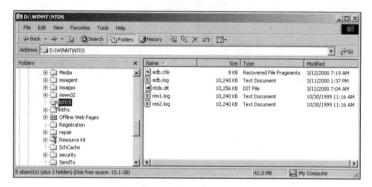

Figure 9-5   Listing for the NTDS folder

ACTIVE DIRECTORY DEPENDENCIES

It is important to understand that Active Directory does not exist in a vacuum. We have so far talked about a set of files that are an integral part of Active Directory and that must be backed up if you are to have any chance of salvaging a server that has crashed. If you have only those files, however, you will quickly find that you do not have enough information to restore a server fully.

The additional files and services that you need are collectively known as the **system state data**. This data should be backed up regularly.

System State Data

For an Active Directory restore to be successful, you need to return the server to the state it was in prior to the condition that caused it to fail. To do so, you must restore dependent services along with the Active Directory files. In fact, this information is so important that you cannot restore Active Directory without it.

What is this system data? First, consider that if Windows 2000 will not boot, restoring the Active Directory data won't do you any good. You must be sure you back up the system startup files—without them, the system is not operational.

Second, don't forget the system Registry. The Registry in Windows 2000, much as in previous versions, is the most important file if you want to maintain the settings on a server. A corrupt or missing Registry is fatal to a system.

Some other services and components must be backed up if they're installed on a Windows 2000 DC. These include DNS, Certificate Server, and all File Replication Service settings. These elements work on your network to both support and implement various pieces of Active Directory; if they are not working, you will not be able to restore a DC to an operational state.

 You cannot restore a DC in Windows 2000 unless you have a backup of the system state data. Failure to back up this data will prevent you from performing a restore.

TYPES OF RESTORE

You can perform a restore of a Windows 2000 DC using two different modes: non-authoritative and authoritative. This choice is due to the additional complexities of Active Directory and its replication model. If you think about how replication works for a moment, you can quickly identify the problems.

All DCs in a Windows 2000 domain are peers of one another. That is, changes can be made at any DC, and those changes will be replicated to all the other DCs in the domain. If a DC crashes and has to be restored, the Active Directory data that is pulled from backup media (usually tape) is by its very nature out of date. What happens when you have a fully operational DC, but its data is inaccurate?

You have two choices in such a circumstance: You can perform a restore that simply gets a DC up and running, and then let Windows 2000 take care of the rest; or you can dictate a precedence for the data. We will define these types of restore next. As well as being useful for disaster recovery purposes, knowing about them will enable you to recover from accidental mass deletions—so this information can be very useful!

Non-Authoritative Restore

A **non-authoritative restore** is the most common method of performing a restore of a Windows 2000 DC. In this case, a restore is performed, and then Active Directory replication takes care of the rest. Because the data on the backup media will be out of date, normal replication processes make sure that all changes not currently recorded at the replica are made.

Don't forget that a restore procedure restores much more data than simply the Active Directory files. Because of this fact, the DC must be brought offline for a restore to take place.

Because you cannot be sure that the Active Directory data is consistent, its integrity must be checked before the DC is operational. To take care of this task, the restore operation writes a Registry key that causes the DC to perform both a consistency check and a re-indexing of all Active Directory data. You will not see this key, because once the operation is completed the key is deleted from the Registry.

Once these tests have taken place, the server can be brought back online. Normal Active Directory data replication processes now kick in, and the DC is able to receive all changes that were made after the backup was run.

In the case of non-authoritative restores, a DC is simply brought back online; it then accepts changes from other DCs and conforms to their view of the directory. Any changes made are recorded on the replica. This is the default mode for restores.

Authoritative Restore

In the case of an **authoritative restore**, data that has been restored is given precedence over data stored on every other DC in the domain. This might sound like a strange thing to do—let's go through a scenario to explain why such a restore is sometimes useful.

Joe the system administrator is having a bad week. The network has been slow all day, and e-mail is down. People are running in and out of his office, complaining and asking him to hurry up, he has not had lunch, and it's four in the afternoon. About this time, his boss comes in, saying, "You have to delete that Temp group right now—they have all left the company, and it's a security problem!"

Joe is already quite flustered, and now he's also annoyed that his boss doesn't realize he is very busy. So, he pulls up the Active Directory Users and Computers administration tool, highlights what he thinks is the Temp group, and presses Delete. Then he goes back to the tasks at hand.

A little while later, he starts getting further complaints from many different departments. They no longer have access to certain network resources—and some of their desktop settings have disappeared. Joe opens his administration tool again and finds, much to his surprise, that he didn't delete the Temp group—instead, he inadvertently deleted an entire Organizational Unit (OU)! He frantically looks for the Undo function, and then realizes Windows 2000 doesn't have one. Joe breaks into a cold sweat, wondering how he's going to fix this problem.

Luckily for Joe, he performed an up-to-date backup this morning. A non-authoritative restore, as we have just seen, will do nothing to help him in this circumstance—but an authoritative restore will. An authoritative restore allows you to perform a restore and then tag certain objects to be authoritative. When they are marked as authoritative, changes to those objects will not be accepted from other DCs when the restored DC is brought online. In fact, the opposite process takes place: The flagged objects replicate to all other DCs.

Joe performs an authoritative restore for the OU he created and lets replication take care of the rest. Within an hour, his users are back at work. All the DCs have accepted the replication from the restored server, he's finally able to eat lunch, and life is good again. An example of the conversation between DCs when an authoritative restore is performed is shown in Figure 9-6.

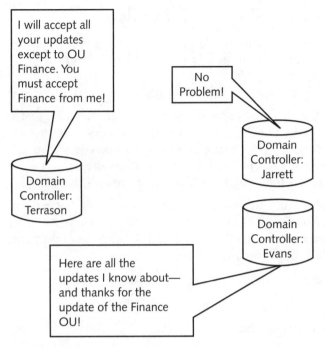

Figure 9-6   An authoritative restore

In order to perform an authoritative restore, you must use a command-line tool called NTDSUTIL. This tool is somewhat complex, but useful.

STRATEGIES FOR ACTIVE DIRECTORY BACKUP

Most people are quick to realize that performing a backup of data on a DC is a good idea. After all, if something can go wrong, it will, and many of us have experienced a hard disk failure.

In order to facilitate a solid backup strategy, you should include certain things in your backup plan. The first of these is an optimal hardware configuration. Running a Windows 2000 DC on a system with a single Integrated Disk Electronics (IDE) drive will not provide you with optimal backup and restore conditions (not to mention performance).

It is also important that you come up with a comprehensive backup plan, *and then stick to it*. It is no good having all the hardware in the world and a great plan on paper, if you never execute that plan. You must commit to performing backups regularly, and yet hope you never need those backups. If you do need them, however, they mean the world.

9

Hardware Configuration of Domain Controllers

When you get down to it, the bigger the box, the better. In this section, we will talk about some basic disk configuration information that will enable you to optimize your domain controllers. Although this information does not directly relate to backup and restore procedures, it is a key concern when making your recovery plans.

We all know we should have fault tolerance on our servers. Usually, that equates to RAID 5, but, although RAID 5 has a lot going for it, it does not achieve everything we would hope for in the way of performance tuning. It can certainly save you if a disk goes bad—perhaps enough to prevent you from ever having to resort to your backups—but you can do some other things that will yield better performance.

For the best performance, you must ensure both fault tolerance and separate physical disks for various files. RAID 5 supplies the former, but not the latter. Although separate disks will undoubtedly increase the hardware costs and complexity of the hardware configuration on your servers, the performance gains can be considerable.

Three sets of files should exist on their own physical disks. They are:

- Windows 2000 operating system files (\WINNT)
- Active Directory database file (ntds.dit)
- Transaction logs (EDB.LOG)

This arrangement will give you optimal performance on your servers. Even if you can achieve only part of your goal—perhaps putting the operating system files on one physical disk and the Active Directory files on another—doing so will give you superior performance over having all the files on a single set of disks. Anything you can do in this area is beneficial.

ACTIVE DIRECTORY MAINTENANCE

Now that we have looked at backing up and restoring Active Directory, let's turn to the topic of how to maintain it. As you have seen, once you strip out all the magic that Active Directory can perform, you are left with a database and a set of files. Like most files on a hard disk, some periodic maintenance is required to keep them working at peak efficiency.

Maintenance is important for several reasons. As objects are deleted from Active Directory, space is not necessarily reused; and as with many databases, this can cause fragmentation. A database that takes up more space on the physical disk than necessary is obviously a problem, and a fragmented database is inefficient and causes processing overhead.

Although some of these issues are dealt with automatically on a regular schedule, we will show how you can perform them manually. This information will give you the flexibility to decide when these processes take place.

Automatic Maintenance

Fortunately, Microsoft has taken care of two of the most pressing issues that can occur on a Windows 2000 DC: fragmentation and the deletion of objects. This process has a rather stern name—it's called *garbage collection*. The garbage collection process kicks off on each DC every 12 hours.

This process performs three key tasks, which are outlined in the following sections. (Don't forget that you can also perform these tasks manually, as we will discuss a little later.)

Deleting Transaction Logs

As you saw earlier, the transaction log (EDB.LOG) can be 10 MB in size by default. When the log file gets full, it is renamed, and a new EDB.LOG file is created. After all transactions in a log file have been written to the database, the log is no longer required. Garbage collection identifies these log files and deletes them.

Deleting Objects from the Database

The dynamic nature of Active Directory replication introduces a few complications into database maintenance. Let's take object deletion as an example.

When changes are made to Active Directory (such as deletion of a user), this information originates at one DC and then must be replicated to all other DCs. Before the object can be physically deleted from the database on each DC, Active Directory must be sure that all replicas are aware of the deletion and are in fact going to make the deletion, as well. This process ensures consistency of Active Directory data. Without it, one Active Directory database might think an object exists when in fact it has been deleted from every other replica.

To deal with such situations, Microsoft has implemented a system known as a **tombstone lifetime**. When an object is deleted from Active Directory, it is flagged with a tombstone lifetime; the default value is 60 days. This period gives Active Directory time to copy the deletion request to all replicas. In the meantime, the deleted object does not show up in user queries, giving the impression that it is gone.

Tombstoning is a key element of Active Directory design because it involves the permanent deletion of data from the directory. Once the data is gone, it is permanently removed—you can't get it back. The date for the deletion will be the same on each DC, so when the data is removed, it no longer exists anywhere on the network.

You might think that you could get the data back, even if the tombstone lifetime has expired and the data has been deleted, simply by performing a restore. You'd be wrong. Because all references—on all DCs—are removed, it is not possible to use a tape that is older than the tombstone lifetime setting in Windows 2000. You should take into account the default time period of 60 days when making your backup plans. You cannot restore data from tape once the data's tombstone lifetime has expired. If doing so were allowed, replication would fail.

When garbage collection is taking place, each object in the directory is checked to see if its tombstone lifetime has expired. If it has, the object is deleted from Active Directory.

Database Defragmentation

As objects are deleted from Active Directory, fragmentation can occur. For example, suppose a 4K object is deleted from the database, and then an 8K object is created. Active Directory, like most file systems, will copy half of that new object's data to the 4K space and the remaining data to a different location within the file. This process should not be considered a problem, because all current file systems work this way.

The automatic cleanup process performs a defragmentation of the database. Doing so ensures optimal performance of database queries. Because the cleanup process operates every 12 hours, the database is kept finely tuned.

 It is important to note that performing a defragmentation does not decrease the size of the database. To decrease the physical size of the database, you must run the manual cleanup process. The database can require resizing when a large number of objects have been deleted.

MANUAL DATABASE CLEANUP

By now you should be convinced that maintenance of the Active Directory database is a good idea. You have seen how a process kicks off on each domain controller every 12 hours and performs most of the necessary tasks to ensure that things run smoothly and that your servers perform to the highest degree of efficiency.

There are a couple of tasks that the automatic process does not perform, however. These tasks should be taken care of in a manual process. The key points to know are:

- Manual cleanup reduces the size of the database; automatic cleanup cannot.
- Manual cleanup involves taking the DC offline.

We will briefly discuss these points in the section that follows. It is important to note that although some automatic processes take place, periodically you will have to schedule a manual maintenance process to ensure that your directory is performing at its best.

Offline Defragmentation

Unlike the automatic cleanup process (online defragmentation), the offline version of this process can actually reduce the size of an Active Directory database file. Microsoft has stated that you should never need to run an offline defragmentation; however, if there have been many deletions from your directory, it is the only way to reduce the physical database file to a more reasonable size.

We highly recommend that you perform a test of this process in a lab before you take a production DC offline. Doing so will enable you to make sure that the process works on your system, and to see the benefits of running it. These benefits will vary depending on how your directory is being used.

You should not be concerned that a DC that is taken offline will no longer be up to date when it is turned back on. The Active Directory replication process will ensure that any changes made after the DC was shut down will be replicated.

BASIC BACKUP PRINCIPLES

Effective backup is accomplished through two tasks. First, you must have an understanding of the underlying technical issues, have a clear idea of *what* should be backed up, and understand the situations that might prevent you from performing a restore operation. These concepts were covered in the first part of this chapter.

Second, you should keep in mind some basic but important points that must be addressed in order to ensure that no matter what happens, a restore operation will be a viable option. You can do some simple things to make sure everything runs smoothly, as we will explain in the following sections.

9

Hardware Requirements

Generally, the media used for backup is tape. Many different manufacturers make tape drives and tape media, and we will not try to rate them. However, you need to be aware of several considerations:

- Make sure you have sufficient capacity on your tape drive. If you have 10GB of data to back up, and your tape drive has a capacity for only 2GB, then you will need five tapes in order to perform a backup. This need involves far greater interaction from the system administrator (and wastes the administrator's valuable time). It will also increase the amount of time a backup takes.

- If the backup process is slow and cumbersome, it may never get done. The number one problem with backups is that often they are not performed, because the process is time consuming and difficult.

- Be wary of hardware vendors' claims about the capacity of their tape drives. Often, a drive that claims to store 20GB of data is actually a 10GB-capacity drive with compression turned on. Compression is an effective way of getting more data into a smaller space, but, like much advertising, the reality rarely meets the expectations set by marketing and sales departments. Assume the worst when buying hardware—you can never have too much capacity.

- Don't forget that performing a backup causes a lot of network traffic. On most corporate networks, you won't want this process to occur in the middle of the afternoon. Schedule the backup to occur when a minimal number of users are on the network. For many organizations, this is some time in the early hours of the morning.

Media Storage

You need two sets of backup media. You must have a set close at hand, so when someone asks you to restore a file or DC, you can do so quickly. However, a second set of media should be stored at an off-site location, to protect you from acts of God, such as fire and flood. If your entire office burned to the ground, what would you lose? When it comes to data, the answer should be "nothing." (You have probably heard this warning many times, but are you actually heeding it?)

It does not matter where the media are taken, as long as they are not in the same physical building as your other media. Everyone should know the storage location, so they can retrieve media if needed. Don't forget that data is the lifeblood of a business; so, the storage area must not only be distant from the location of the servers, but it also should be both secure and media friendly. **Media friendly** means a controlled environment. There is little point in throwing the media into a box at the back of your garage, if the temperature there reaches 110 degrees every day.

Finally, don't forget that the tombstone lifetime is set by default to 60 days. Tapes containing Active Directory are no longer much use after that time.

Testing Restore Operations

Do not assume that the shiny new tape drive and media, along with perfect error logs from your backup software, are doing everything they say they are doing. You should plan to perform test restores periodically, to make sure that data is retrievable. If you do not, there is a chance that your backup will fail when you need it most—after a system failure.

You should also have redundant backup hardware. The media backed up with one device should be used for restore purposes in the opposite hardware. This process ensures not only that the media is good, but also that the hardware is working properly. Although this setup obviously increases the costs involved with performing backup operations, there is no substitute when the chips are down and the network is on its knees due to a server crash.

BACKUP AND RESTORE SECURITY

The data on your network is critical, not only because it needs to be available at all times, but also because it must be protected from unauthorized access. The only real way to make a server secure is to provide for physical security. That is, the server must be in a locked room, and only a small number of people should have physical access to it.

Of course, this arrangement becomes somewhat complicated when you are talking about backups. The media you are using must be secured—particularly the off-site media. Always make sure there is accountability for this media.

It would also not make much sense if anyone could perform a backup and restore of Active Directory data. Toward this end, Microsoft has defined two sets of built-in groups for this purpose: one for performing backups and one for performing restores. As a result, you can assign these two important tasks to different groups of people.

The only people who can perform backup and restore operations are members of the Domain Administrators and Backup Operators groups. Alternatively, you can create groups yourself. For this to work, you must assign the groups both the Backup File And permissions and Restore Files And Directories permissions.

To perform a restore when a DC is offline, you must be a member of the Local Administrators group. This requirement runs somewhat contrary to previous Microsoft Windows NT behavior. In versions prior to Windows 2000, DCs had no local account. You will need to know this account name and password to perform a restore.

THE MICROSOFT BACKUP UTILITY

Microsoft has been kind enough to provide a Backup utility with Windows 2000. Do not confuse this with a full-fledged enterprise-level backup program, however. The utility provided by Microsoft lacks some significant features, and you should be looking for a more fully featured application to use on your own production servers. For example, not least of the missing features is the utility's inability to back up data on remote servers; the backup utility can back up data only on the local machine.

The Backup utility provided is actually a scaled-down version of Backup Exec, a product from Veritas Software (www.veritas.com). Despite its lack of enterprise-level features, this utility can perform all of the necessary functions mentioned in this chapter.

CHAPTER SUMMARY

- In this chapter, we examined both recovery and maintenance of Active Directory. We looked at how you can protect your network from catastrophic loss of a domain controller in Windows 2000. In order to fully recover from a crash, you should have a full backup of your data.

- To help you fully understand how Active Directory operates, we first took a look at the architectural model. This model enabled us to show how a DC is able to guarantee consistency of data and allow for recovery from simple failures such as a power loss. More specifically, we examined the three-layer model, including the Directory System Agent (DSA), the database layer, and the Extensible Storage Engine.

- These three layers have distinct roles, and understanding each of these roles enables you to gain a better understanding of how data is stored in Active Directory (and why some files are more important than others for backup purposes). The DSA is responsible for retrieving data for client applications. Clients never directly access the data store of Active Directory.

❑ The database layer is simply a view of the data. The actual data is stored in a flat file; data in Active Directory is often viewed in a hierarchical fashion, but the physical storage is simply a table with rows and columns, much like a spreadsheet. The database layer organizes the data into a hierarchical form, so it is easier to read and understand.

❑ The ESE is the underlying data engine that powers Active Directory. We learned that this engine has been tested extensively in the real world—because it is the same engine used in Exchange 5.5.

❑ In order to understand how Windows 2000 maintains resiliency on DCs, we took a close look at how data is written to the database. This process involves interaction among several different files. The process might appear to be overly complex, but it is designed to ensure that DCs can recover, should there be a simple failure such as power outage.

❑ We learned that data is not written directly to the Active Directory database. Instead, data is first written to a transaction log. Once the entire transaction is written to the log, it is written to a piece of the database that is buffered in memory. Finally, it is written to the database on the disk. If any one of these steps fails, then the transaction is rolled back, which means it is undone at every level.

❑ In order to understand which files you should be certain to back up, we took a look at the physical files that support Active Directory and discussed which files would be important, should you need to perform a restore operation. We began with ntds.dit, which contains all of the Active Directory data. We learned that two copies of this file exist: one is used for installation purposes only and is stored in the <*systemroot*>\system32 folder, and the other is the actual Active Directory data file.

❑ Next, we examined the various log files used by Active Directory. Only one of these files, EDB.LOG, is used all the time. This file is a transaction log, which means all transactions are first written to this file before being applied to ntds.dit. A transaction log is useful because a Windows 2000 DC can quickly read this file to find out if it missed any transactions. This process occurs during each system boot-up. The default size for this log file is 10MB.

❑ There are two other log files: RES1.LOG and RES2.LOG. The main purpose of these two files is to reserve space on a DC's hard disk, in case the disk drive that stores Active Directory data becomes full and transactions can no longer be written to EDB.LOG. In this case, transactions are written to these two placeholders. Each of these files is 10MB in size.

❑ Logging is an important task for any DC. We learned that when a log file reaches its maximum size (10MB), a copy of the log file is made, and a new one is created. This behavior affords maximum recoverability; however, it requires additional disk space (10MB multiplied by the number of backup files created).

If you do not have the necessary resources, you can turn on circular logging. With circular logging, backup copies of old transaction log files are not made.

◻ As data is written from the transaction log to the underlying database, the transaction is considered **committed**. A pointer is written to indicate the last transaction that has been committed in the log file. This information is in turn stored in a checkpoint file named EDB.CHK.

◻ We also took a brief look at patch files. These files are used during online backups. An online backup takes place while the DC is being used for its normal, everyday purposes. Patch files ensure that data changed during the backup operation is recorded on the backup media. Without these files, you would find inconsistencies in the data, should it be used for a restore.

◻ Active Directory does not work alone. We learned that fully restoring a Windows 2000 DC also requires a full copy of the system state data. This data includes everything needed to bring a server back to the same state it was in before the failure, including operating system files, the Registry, and any services installed on the DC (such as DNS services and the File Replication Service). These services are integral to Windows 2000, and failure to back them up will cause you to be unable to achieve a completely operational state even if you have backed up the Active Directory files.

◻ You can use two types of restore operation: non-authoritative, which is the default operation; and authoritative. With a non-authoritative restore, once a restore operation is complete, normal Active Directory replication takes place to bring the DC up to date. With an authoritative restore, you are able to flag certain objects to replicate to every DC within the domain. In essence, the restored data becomes the master data, and each DC will accept it. This operation is useful when you have accidentally deleted an object, and you need to get it back.

◻ Backup is only one of several ways you can protect data on your DC. We briefly discussed other methods, such as using RAID 5. For optimal configurations, you should try to ensure that the three sets of essential files—ntds.dit, EDB.LOG, and the operating system files—are stored on different physical disks.

◻ We discovered that several maintenance tasks take place periodically on a DC. They occur without user interaction every 12 hours by default. This maintenance procedure defragments the NTDS.DIT file, deletes any objects from the database, and removes transaction log files that are no longer needed.

◻ Objects are physically deleted from the Active Directory database only after a tombstone lifetime flag has expired. This flag is set to 60 days by default. It is set because Windows 2000 needs to ensure that all DCs are aware that the object should be deleted. If this did not happen, there would be inconsistencies in Active Directory data. Tombstoning has a significant effect on system restores, because media older than the tombstone life (60 days) cannot be used.

❐ We learned that although this maintenance process takes place automatically, you might sometimes want to perform it manually. Performing manual maintenance also enables you to shrink the size of the Active Directory database. For manual maintenance tasks, however, the DC must be taken offline (the automatic maintenance process does not need to take the server offline).

❐ Finally, we examined a few important considerations to keep in mind when designing your backup strategy. You should ensure that you have sufficient hardware to perform the necessary backups. We also discussed keeping a copy of backup media off-site, to protect you in case of a catastrophic failure in which you lose your storage area at the local office. We also suggested that you perform periodic test restores to make sure that restore operations are possible, and to ensure that the backup hardware, the backup software, and the physical backup media are all functioning properly.

10

IMPLEMENTING GROUP POLICY

After completing this chapter, you will be able to:

♦ Understand Group Policy concepts

♦ Plan an effective Group Policy design

♦ Implement Group Policy

Windows 2000 dramatically improves the ability of systems administrators to exert control of the user environment, compared to Windows NT 4. With Group Policy, an administrator can define a large number of detailed settings that are applied throughout the organization. In fact, in Windows 2000, Group Policy is now the primary means of applying, to users and computers, changes that are enforced across an organization.

In this chapter, we will look at the basics of implementing and administering Group Policy. In subsequent chapters, we will expand our discussion to include managing user environments and deploying software with Group Policy.

UNDERSTANDING GROUP POLICY CONCEPTS

Group Policy is a power tool for network administrators to control any number of environment settings across an enterprise. Implementing Group Policy can greatly reduce the administrative overhead for a network, reducing total cost of ownership (TCO) and increasing return on investment (ROI) for Windows 2000. Although TCO and ROI issues might sound more like business terms than technological terms, increasingly MIS departments are being expected to function as business units rather than just as cost centers. The enlightened information systems professional learns to understand how to apply technology from a business perspective, and how to maximize a corporation's investment in technology systems.

Before we can delve into implementing Group Policy, however, we must examine some basic concepts such as:

- Windows 2000 Group Policy versus Windows NT 4 system policies
- Group Policy Objects (GPO)
- The Group Policy Microsoft Management Console (MMC) snap-in
- Group Policy namespace
- Startup, shutdown, logon, and logoff
- Active Directory structure and Group Policy
- Group Policy inheritance
- Group Policy processing

Windows 2000 Group Policy versus Windows NT 4 System Policies

With Windows NT 4, Microsoft introduced system policies. These policies are edited through the poledit.exe utility; they give the administrator the ability to define user environment settings stored in the Registry. System policies allow specific configuration settings to be enforced on any Windows NT 4 workstation or server in a domain.

With Windows 2000, Group Policy provides all of the functionality of system policies and more. You use the Group Policy MMC snap-in rather than poledit.exe, although poledit still exists for backward compatibility. It is important to note, however, that poledit.exe has been updated for Windows 2000; the format of the POL files created in Windows 2000 is different from the format of the files created in Windows 9x and NT 4. Policies created with the Windows 9x or NT 4 policy editor cannot be applied to Windows 2000 systems—but policies created in Windows 2000 with poledit.exe *can* be applied to Windows 9x and Windows NT 4 clients.

For Windows 2000 workstations and servers, however, Group Policy all but replaces system policies. Group Policy provides a more flexible means to apply and enforce configuration settings; even more important, it allows for a much more granular approach. Whereas system policies can be applied only to domains, Group Policy can be applied to sites, domains, and Organizational Units (OUs). The following sections compare and contrast NT and Windows 9x system policies with Windows 2000 Group Policy.

Windows NT 4 and Windows 9x System Policies

System policies have the following features:

- They are applied only to domains.

- They are limited to Registry-based settings an administrator configures.

- They are not written to a secure location of the Registry. Hence, any user with the ability to edit the Registry can disable the policy settings.

- They often last beyond their useful life spans. System policies remain in effect until another policy explicitly reverses an existing policy or a user edits the Registry to remove a policy.

- They can be applied through NT domain security groups.

Windows 2000 Group Policy

Group policies have the following features:

- They can be applied to sites, domains, or OUs.

- They can be applied through domain security groups, and can apply to all or some of the computers and users in a site, domain, or OU.

- They are written to a secure section of the Registry, which prevents users from being able to remove a policy through the regedit.exe or regedit32.exe utility.

- They are removed and rewritten whenever a policy change takes place. Administrators can set the length of time between policy refreshes, ensuring that only the current policies are in place.

- They provide a more granular level of administrative control over a user's environment.

In addition, Windows 2000 Group Policy provides features not available through system policies, such as additional system startup/shutdown control and folder redirection. These features will be covered later in the chapter.

Group Policy Benefits

When properly implemented, Group Policy can reduce the TCO for a Windows 2000 network. One of the more common causes of lost productivity among corporate users is system downtime due to user-induced errors. These errors can result when users modify or

10

delete critical system files, or when they waste time playing with screen savers, games, wallpaper, and other operating system features. Through Group Policy, you can create a managed user environment that provides a consistent interface for users of certain experience levels.

Group Policy can also be used to enhance the end user's computing experience by providing customized environments to meet the user's work requirements. Such customization might include putting specialized application icons on the desktop or Start menu, or redirecting the My Documents folder to a network drive so the user's files are available no matter what computer they log on to. In addition, an administrator can execute such tasks as startup, logon, logoff, or shutdown to meet the user's needs. In this light, Group Policy can create a positive working environment for users.

Managing User Expectations

From the end user's perspective, system policies/group policies are often viewed negatively. Many users see managed desktops as a sign of distrust from management, or they feel they are not being allowed any individuality. This viewpoint is an important aspect of desktop management to consider, especially if Group Policy will be applied to desktop systems that have been open to user configuration in the past. Although few would argue that the computers belong to the company and therefore they can be managed in any way that will best suit the company, the psychology of the situation must be handled delicately. If it is not, any efficiency gains from desktop management may be offset by lost productivity from declining employee morale. Restrictive services such as policies, e-mail mailbox limits, and disk quotas are better implemented from the beginning rather than in midstream, to minimize the impact on morale. But if they must be implemented after the network is initially set up, be sure to consider the employee mindset and keep communication channels open between users and management.

Group Policy Objects

The collection of Group Policy settings are stored in what are known as Group Policy Objects (GPOs). There are two types of GPO: local and non-local. Local GPOs are stored on each Windows 2000 computer, whereas non-local GPOs are stored at the domain level within Active Directory.

Local GPOs

A local GPO exists on each Windows 2000 computer, and by default only the settings under the Security node of Group Policy apply. Local GPOs are stored in the \winnt\system32\GroupPolicy folder. Through discretionary access control lists, the following permissions are set:

- *Administrators*—Full Control
- *Operating System*—Full Control
- *Authenticated Users*—Read

The easiest way to prevent local GPOs from applying to a computer is to remove Read permissions from the Local Administrators group. Even if Apply Group Policy is set to Allow, this setting cannot be applied if the GPO cannot be read.

Non-Local GPOs

Non-local GPOs are stored at the domain level within Active Directory. As such, they apply at the site, domain, and OU level. Two locations are used to store non-local GPOs: a Group Policy container and a Group Policy template. A globally unique identifier (GUID) is used in naming the GPOs to keep the two locations synchronized.

A Group Policy container is an Active Directory storage area for GPO settings for both computer and user Group Policy information. The Group Policy container includes the following information:

- Version information, ensuring that the information in the Group Policy container is synchronized with the Group Policy template information

- Status information, indicating whether the GPO is enabled or disabled

- The list of extensions that have settings in the GPO

- The policy settings defined by the extensions

An example of an extension would be the Software Installation snap-in. The Group Policy container stores information used by the snap-in to describe the status of software available for installation. A server-based repository contains the data for all applications, interfaces, and Application Programming Interfaces (APIs) used in application publishing and assigning.

In addition to the Group Policy container, Active Directory stores information in a Group Policy template, which is contained in a folder structure in the System Volume (SYSVOL) folder of domain controllers. Figure 10-1 shows this directory structure, located under \winnt\SYSVOL\sysvol*domain_name*\Policies.

When a GPO is created, the Group Policy template is created with the folder structure shown in Figure 10-1. The folder name given to the Group Policy template is the GUID of the GPO. In our example, the GUID and folder name is {31B2F340-016D-11D2-945F-00C04FB984F9}. Table 10-1 shows a breakdown of the Group Policy template subfolders.

10

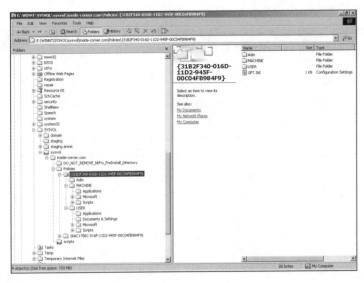

Figure 10-1 Group Policy template information is stored under the SYSVOL folder structure

Table 10-1 The structure of Group Policy template subfolders

Subfolder	Contents
\ADM	The ADM files (administrative templates) for a Group Policy template. The ADM file consists of a hierarchy of categories and subcategories that together define how the options are displayed through Group Policy.
\Machine	A Registry.pol file that includes the Registry settings to be applied to computers. When the computer boots up, the Registry.pol file is applied to the HKEY_LOCAL_MACHINE portion of the Registry.
\Machine\Applications	AAS files (application assignment scripts) used by Windows Installer. These files contain instructions associated with the assignment or publication of a package.
\Machine\Microsoft\ Windows NT\SecEdit	The GptTmpl.inf Security Editor file.
\Machine\Scripts\Startup	Scripts that apply to the computer during startup.
\Machine\Scripts\Shutdown	Scripts that apply to the computer during shutdown.
\User	Includes a Registry.pol file that applies to users as they log on. The Registry.pol file is applied to the HKEY_CURRENT_USER portion of the Registry.
\User\Applications	AAS files used by the Windows Installer.
\User\Documents & Settings	Files to deploy to all desktops for all users utilizing this Group Policy template.

Table 10-1   The structure of Group Policy template subfolders (continued)

Subfolder	Contents
\User\Microsoft\IEAK	Information about settings the Internet Explorer Administrator Kit uses for deploying IE settings to the desktop.
\User\Microsoft\RemoteInstall	The oscfilter.ini file, which includes policies about Remote Installation Services (RIS).
\User\Scripts\Logoff	Scripts that apply to the user during logoff.
\User\Scripts\Logon	Scripts that apply to the user during logon.

In the contents pane of Figure 10-1, you will notice a file called GPT.INI. The root folder of each Group Policy template contains this file, which includes information about whether the local GPO is enabled or disabled, the version number, and which client-side extensions of Group Policy contain user or computer data in the GPO.

How does Windows 2000 determine what to store in a Group Policy container versus a Group Policy template? Data that is small in size and that changes infrequently is stored in Group Policy containers, whereas data that is either large in size or that changes frequently is stored in Group Policy templates.

The Group Policy MMC Snap-in

In order to edit Group Policy Objects, you will need to open the Group Policy Editor. By default, there is no single Group Policy administrative tool. The Group Policy Editor can be invoked at a number of different levels depending on your needs. For example, to edit Group Policy settings for a site, launch the Active Directory Sites and Services management console. From there, right-click on the site you want and choose Edit; then, click on the Group Policy tab and click on Edit. Doing so will start a new MMC console, with the Group Policy ready to edit site settings.

Typically, you will edit GPOs at the domain level rather than the site level; you do so through Active Directory Users and Computers. Right-click on the domain and choose Properties to bring up a window similar to that shown in Figure 10-2. Select Default Domain Policy and click on Edit.

When you click on Edit, you will see a console similar to that shown in Figure 10-3. You will use this Group Policy console most of the time.

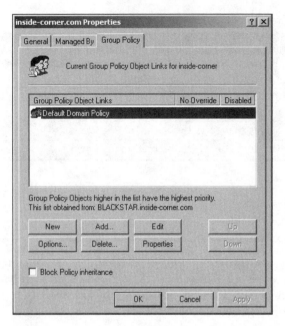

Figure 10-2   The Active Directory Users and Computers utility can be used to invoke the Group Policy Editor at the domain level

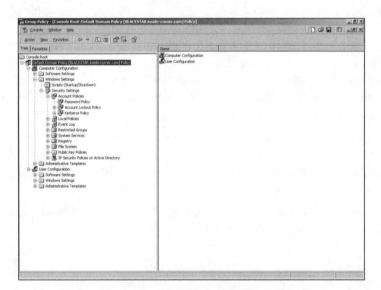

Figure 10-3   The Group Policy MMC snap-in allows you to configure GPOs

You also have the option of creating a custom MMC console with the Group Policy focus you will use most often. By doing so, you can save yourself the time of going through another tool in order to get to Group Policy.

Group Policy Namespace

The Group Policy snap-in displays the root node as the name of the GPO and the domain in which it is stored. In our earlier example, the node is written as

```
Default Domain Policy [BLACKSTAR.inside-corner.com] Policy
```

The next level of the namespace has the Computer Configuration and User Configuration nodes. Each of those nodes contains the following subnodes:

- Software Settings
- Windows Settings
- Administrative Templates

Let's look at the Computer Configuration and User Configuration nodes and their subnodes in more detail.

Computer Configuration

The Computer Configuration folders contain all computer-related policy settings that you can use to customize the user's environment at the computer level. These settings can include such things as operating system behavior, desktop behavior, security settings, computer startup and shutdown scripts, and application settings. Policies assigned to computers apply to every user who logs on to the computer.

User Configuration

The User Configuration folders contain all policy settings that you can use to customize the user's environment at the user level. These settings can include such things as desktop appearance, application settings, logon and logoff scripts, assigned and published applications, and folder redirection settings. Policies assigned at the user level apply only to the specific user when he or she logs on to a computer. In general, computer policies will override user policies.

Software Settings

The Software Settings node is a place for independent software vendors to add further extensions to Group Policy. Initially, only a single Software Installation node will appear under Software Settings—this extension is included with Windows 2000.

Windows Settings

The Windows Settings node contains extensions provided by Microsoft and included with Windows 2000. These extensions include Scripts (startup/shutdown for Computer Configuration, logon/logoff for User Configuration) and Security Settings that apply to both computers and users, and Internet Explorer maintenance that applies specifically to users.

10

In addition, folder redirection settings are configured under Windows Settings for the User Configuration container, as are Remote Installation Services (RIS) if RIS is installed.

Many administrators find themselves most often in the Security Settings area of Group Policy. This area in Computer Configuration is extensive, covering three core areas:

- Password Policy
- Account Lockout Policy
- Kerberos Policy

The Password Policy settings, shown in Figure 10-4, contain many of the settings you may remember from the Windows NT 4 Account Policies utility.

Figure 10-4   You can configure policy settings that affect password requirements

In NT 4, these settings are configured by opening the Policies menu and choosing Account from the User Manager For Domains administrative tool. Administrators of NT 4 systems will notice two new additions in Windows 2000:

- Passwords must meet complexity requirements
- Passwords are stored using reversible encryption for all users in the domain

The first of those options is a great new feature for administrators who struggle with users who undermine password policies by repeatedly choosing a simple password whenever they are required to create a new one. Windows 2000 can now force a password to contain alphanumeric or other characters in addition to remembering a password history and requiring passwords to be a certain length.

From a Group Policy perspective, you as the administrator can employ password policies that apply either to your entire enterprise or locally on a machine-by-machine basis. For example, you may have a few computers in a sensitive area that need more stringent password policies than ordinary domain users require.

Account lockout policies, shown in Figure 10-5, are the same as in NT 4. You can choose how many bad passwords a user can enter in a certain time frame before the account is locked—for example, you might allow three bad passwords in 30 minutes before locking the account. In addition to these settings, you can set the length of time the account remains locked out. The default lockout setting is 30 minutes, at which time the account reverts to its normal state. For better security, we recommend setting the lockout duration to zero, which requires a locked account to be manually unlocked by an administrator. Not only will a potential intruder be unable to pick on a single account unnoticed, but this setting ensures that an administrator is aware of any instances where multiple bad passwords are entered for a user account in a short period of time. Even if such an occurrence is not a sign of malicious activity, it could indicate either a user training issue or a system problem that needs to be addressed.

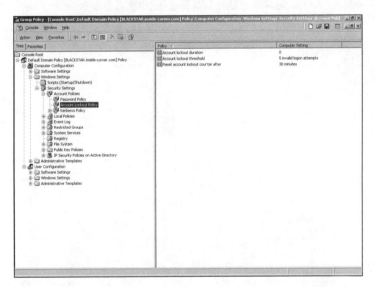

10

Figure 10-5   Account lockout policies are much the same in Windows 2000 as they were in Windows NT 4

Windows 2000 uses the Kerberos security protocol. You can use Group Policy to configure the various Kerberos security and ticketing policies that apply to a Windows 2000 domain.

Administrative Templates

As in Windows NT 4, administrative templates have an .adm extension in Windows 2000. Administrative templates provide a source for Group Policy to generate the policy settings that you can configure. These files provide information about the Registry settings to be modified when an administrator makes a change, the specific settings that correspond to the GPO entry, and (in some cases) a default value if such a value is automatically assigned when a setting is enabled.

Administrative templates created with the NT 4 System Policy Editor can be read and changed with the Windows 2000 System Policy Editor, because Windows 2000 uses a superset of the language supported by NT 4. Because the languages are not the same, however, administrative templates created in Windows 2000 cannot be read by the NT 4 System Policy Editor.

In the Computer Configuration and User Configuration containers, administrative templates are provided with Windows 2000 for the categories and subcategories shown in Table 10-2.

Table 10-2   The Group Policy categories and subcategories available for computers and users in Windows 2000

Container	Category	Subcategory	Subcategory
Computer Configuration	Windows Components	Netmeeting	
Computer Configuration	Windows Components	Internet Explorer	
Computer Configuration	Windows Components	Task Scheduler	
Computer Configuration	Windows Components	Windows Installer	
Computer Configuration	System		
Computer Configuration	System	Logon	
Computer Configuration	System	Disk Quotas	
Computer Configuration	System	DNS Clients	
Computer Configuration	System	Group Policy	
Computer Configuration	System	Windows File Protection	
Computer Configuration	Network	Offline Files	
Computer Configuration	Network Connections	Network and Dial-up	
Computer Configuration	Printers		
User Configuration	Windows Components	Netmeeting	
User Configuration	Windows Components	Netmeeting	Application Sharing
User Configuration	Windows Components	Netmeeting	Audio & Video
User Configuration	Windows Components	Netmeeting	Options Page
User Configuration	Windows Components	Internet Explorer	
User Configuration	Windows Components	Internet Explorer	Internet Control Panel

Table 10-2   The Group Policy categories and subcategories available for computers and
users in Windows 2000 (continued)

Container	Category	Subcategory	Subcategory
User Configuration	Windows Components	Internet Explorer	Offline Pages
User Configuration	Windows Components	Internet Explorer	Browser Pages
User Configuration	Windows Components	Internet Explorer	Toolbars
User Configuration	Windows Components	Internet Explorer	Persistent Behaviors
User Configuration	Windows Components	Internet Explorer	Administrator Approved Controls
User Configuration	Windows Components	Windows Explorer	
User Configuration	Windows Components	Windows Explorer	Common Open File Dialog
User Configuration	Windows Components	Microsoft Management Console	
User Configuration	Windows Components	Task Scheduler	
User Configuration	Windows Components	Windows Installer	
User Configuration	Start Menu & Taskbar		
User Configuration	Desktop		
User Configuration	Desktop	Active Directory	
User Configuration	Desktop	Active Desktop	
User Configuration	Control Panel		
User Configuration	Control Panel	Add/Remove Programs	
User Configuration	Control Panel	Display	
User Configuration	Control Panel	Printers	
User Configuration	Control Panel	Regional Options	
User Configuration	Network	Offline Files	
User Configuration	Network Connections	Network and Dial-up	
User Configuration	System		
User Configuration	System	Logon/Logoff	
User Configuration	System	Group Policy	

10

Some overlap exists among items that can be configured at both a computer level and a user level, such as certain Windows components, because policies can apply to a computer as a whole or only to certain users of a computer, depending on specific needs. In many cases, there appears to be overlap; however, different sets of policy settings are available depending on whether the configuration is set at the computer or user level. For example, the policy settings under the System root in Computer Configuration and User

Configuration are completely different, because different types of system policies apply to computers than apply to users. In this case, the apparent overlap is *not* an example of the same policies just applied at a different level.

Startup, Shutdown, Logon, and Logoff

Group Policy can be used to affect the user or computer environment in different ways at different times. Computer policies can be applied at both system startup and shut-down, whereas user policies can be applied at logon and logoff. The combination of the four events can be used to create complex policy configurations for Windows 2000 users. For example, a common script might be run on the computer at startup to affect certain settings that should apply to anyone who uses the computer. User-specific scripts can be run when a user actually logs on to the computer. When a user logs off, you can designate a script to run that performs certain actions such as disconnecting any mapped network drives. In addition, a computer can execute a shutdown script to perform any required actions before it is turned off.

The ability to run scripts at any of these four times offers much more flexibility over Windows NT 4, which allows only for logon scripts. This flexibility gives the Windows 2000 administrator increased control over the user and computer environment.

Active Directory Structure and Group Policy

As we touched on earlier, there are two types of GPO: local and non-local. GPOs are the basic units of Group Policy, and they can be linked or filtered. Because they are the basic units, only a GPO in its entirety may be linked to another target. That is, you can-not link only a subset of a GPO. The effects of GPOs are actually applied through links, as they are linked to sites, domains, or OUs. If no link exists between a GPO and any other target, then the policy settings will not have any effect.

The exception to linking is that GPOs cannot be linked to generic Active Directory containers, such as the Users container in Active Directory Users and Computers. They receive domain-linked Group Policy through inheritance, however. Inheritance is dis-cussed later in this chapter.

The structure of Group Policy in Active Directory is as follows:

- GPOs linked to a site apply to all domains within the site.

- GPOs applied to a domain apply to all users and computers within the domain, and through inheritance apply to all users and computers in OUs further down the domain structure.

- GPOs applied at the OU level apply to all users and computers within the OU, and through inheritance apply to all users and computers included within OUs that are contained within the OU that is linked to the GPO.

- Local policies are applied first, followed by non-local policies.

- Non-local policies are applied in the following order: site level, domain level, and then OU level, beginning at the highest OU level within the Active Directory tree and ending with the lowest level OU within the Active Directory tree that contains the user or account.

It is important to make note of this structure, because, by default, policy applied later overrides earlier policies. For example, a policy applied at the domain level would be overridden by a conflicting policy applied at the OU level. This precedence is true for policy settings set to Enabled or Disabled. Policies set to Not Configured are ignored and do not overwrite anything. Also note the exception to lower-level settings overriding higher-level settings: Computer policies will generally take precedence over user policies when there is a conflict.

This default inheritance behavior can be changed, however, as we will see next.

Group Policy Inheritance

The default inheritance settings of Windows 2000 Group Policy can be changed via two settings:

- No Override
- Block Policy Inheritance

The following sections examine these settings.

No Override

No Override is set on a link, and not on a site, domain, OU, or specific GPO. In contrast, Block Policy Inheritance applies to a domain or OU, and therefore applies to all GPOs linked to that level or higher in the Active Directory tree. When in conflict, No Override will take precedence over Block Policy Inheritance.

No Override is used to prevent policies at lower levels in the Active Directory tree from overwriting policies applied at a higher level. For example, say you linked a GPO to a domain and set the GPO link to No Override, and then configured Group Policy settings within the GPO to apply to OUs within the domain. GPOs linked to OUs would not be able to override the domain-linked GPO.

Block Policy Inheritance

Block Policy Inheritance will also prevent policies from higher in the Active Directory tree from being applied at lower levels of the tree. For example, if you had an OU policy and wanted to leave all settings unconfigured that weren't explicitly defined for that GPO, you would use Block Policy Inheritance to prevent a domain-level policy from applying settings to that OU. Block Policy Inheritance is enabled through a checkbox on the Group Policy tab of the specific domain or OU. Figure 10-6 shows an example.

10

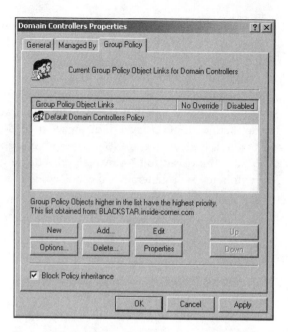

Figure 10-6 You can block policy inheritance of Group Policy settings at the specific domain or OU

To see GPO links, open the GPO in the Group Policy console, view the properties by right-clicking on the root node, and choose Properties. Click on the Links tab and click on Find Now after choosing the appropriate domain.

Group Policy Processing

So far, you have learned that group policies are processed in the following order:

- Local
- Site
- Domain
- Organizational Unit

You have also learned that processing order can be affected through the No Override and Block Policy Inheritance options. The order of processing cannot be modified, even through No Override and Block Policy Inheritance, although the use of filtering can remove or block an individual part of the processing order, such as the OU.

Now that you know how Group Policy is processed in general, it is important to look at the processing of Group Policy as it applies to computer and user policies.

Computer versus User Policy Processing

In addition to the processing order we just outlined, computer policies are processed before user policies. When the computer is booted up, the computer policy will process first. That processing will include any startup scripts that have been configured, as well as policy settings defined in the Computer Configuration container. Once computer policies have been applied, user policy begins. When a user logs on to the computer, any logon scripts that have been configured will execute. The logon scripts will be followed by policy settings configured for the User Configuration container.

Synchronous versus Asynchronous Processing

So far, we have been discussing what is known as **synchronous** processing, which waits until one action is complete before beginning another. For example, computer policies are applied before the logon dialog box is displayed to the user, and then user policies are applied before the Explorer shell and desktop are presented to the user. This is the default behavior in Windows 2000.

The opposite behavior is **asynchronous** processing, which allows policies to process without waiting for the outcome of other policies. Computer and user policies will attempt to apply themselves at the same time, which can lead to undesirable side effects in many cases. Unless you have a specific reason to process Group Policy asynchronously, we recommend that you leave the default settings in place. Synchronous processing provides a higher degree of reliability.

In Case of Conflict

In the event of conflict, a computer policy set in Computer Configuration will generally have precedence over a user policy set in User Configuration. In some cases, such as the Windows Installer policy Always Install With Elevated Privileges, the policy must be set on both the Computer Configuration and User Configuration nodes in order for it to be enabled.

Periodic Policy Processing

Consider for a moment the following situation. You are the Group Policy administrator for 10,000 Windows 2000 systems on your corporate wide-area network (WAN). What happens if you modify a domain-linked GPO and you need to have it take place within a short period of time—say, two hours? Do you send out a global e-mail asking everyone to reboot? How do you handle the offices on the other side of the globe, where it might be the middle of the night and computers might be left on?

The answer lies with periodic refresh. System policies in Windows NT 4 can be changed only when a user reboots, at which point the new policy overwrites the old policy settings. But with Windows 2000, you can choose to have group policies processed periodically without requiring a reboot. The default settings process group policies every 90 minutes, with an offset of up to 30 minutes. An **offset** is a random amount of time applied to

10

the 90-minute setting so that not every computer tries to process policy updates at the same time. If 5,000 computers all log on to the network at roughly 8:00 A.M. when work starts, you don't want all those machines hitting the servers simultaneously throughout the day to process Group Policy updates (even if no changes are made). The offset ensures that Group Policy requests are staggered, which eases the load on the servers.

In addition to the default setting of 90 minutes for workstations and servers, the default for domain controllers is 5 minutes. It is important not to specify too frequent a refresh policy in hopes of keeping the domain always up to date. Whenever a policy refresh occurs, the Windows shell refreshes as well. This action causes a momentary interruption in any user activity, which can range from annoying to intolerable depending on the refresh interval. It is best to balance carefully between regular policy refreshes and user inconvenience.

Exceptions to policy refreshes include:

- Software installation
- Folder redirection

For these two policies, periodic processing typically is not appropriate. For example, you wouldn't want a software installation to remove a particular application that might be in use. You also wouldn't change the location of folders when there might be open files from the old location.

In the event that you need to refresh Group Policy immediately, Windows 2000 offers a command-line Security Editor. The commands to refresh computer and user policies are

```
secedit /refreshpolicy MACHINE_POLICY
secedit /refreshpolicy USER_POLICY
```

These commands are useful when the refresh interval is set to a large amount of time and you need changes to take place right away.

Now that you have an understanding of the general concepts of Group Policy, it is time to look at some of the more concrete issues that you will face as an administrator of Group Policy. The first issue is possibly the most important: planning.

GROUP POLICY PLANNING

As with most things in life, proper planning is the key to implementing a project successfully. Group Policy is no different in that regard. In this section, we will look at some of the design and planning issues you will face as you prepare to deploy Group Policy on your Windows 2000 network. These issues include:

- Change control procedures
- Structuring domains and OUs for Group Policy
- Segmented versus monolithic GPOs

- Cross-domain GPO links

- Managing network bandwidth

- Best practices

Change Control Procedures

As you can probably already imagine, and as will become increasingly clear as we focus on specific policies, the effects of GPOs across a domain can be very complex. Therefore, one of the most important aspects of Group Policy administration is change control management.

With change control management, Group Policy administrators maintain records of all GPOs for an organization, including the following information:

- Name of the GPO

- Settings that the GPO applies

- Whether the settings apply to computers or users

- Specific sites, domains, and OUs to which the GPO applies

- Creation and modification dates

- List of specific changes that have been made since the GPO was created, and the names of the administrator(s) who implemented the changes

- Descriptions of changes and why they were made

10

Documentation is often tedious, and it is usually one of the first aspects of systems administration to be forgotten when your work queue is piling up with things that needed to be done yesterday. However, proper documentation will actually save you time in the long run, because you will be able to trace problems and procedures easily to their source. If you make a change to a GPO that doesn't take effect for several days, and you don't document the change, you may not realize at first the source of a problem that occurs because of the change. Even worse, in larger corporations with multiple administrators, much time can be wasted tracing problems if one administrator doesn't know about changes another administrator has made. With better efficiency, you'll spend less time in the fire-fighting mode in which systems administrators too often find themselves.

Structuring Domains and OUs for Group Policy

Planning a domain and OU structure for Group Policy ties in very closely with your Active Directory planning in general—in fact, they go hand in hand. Two key issues face Group Policy planning:

- Delegation of permissions

- GPO location

Let's examine these issues in more detail.

Delegation of Permissions

We will discuss delegating Group Policy administration a bit later in this chapter, but in this section we're referring to the delegation of administration for Active Directory in general. Whether you decide to administer Active Directory centrally or to distribute the administrative functions among a group of administrators in different locations will have an impact on how you should set up your domain and OU structure. For instance, if you are centrally managing your organization, you might want to have only a few GPOs implemented at the domain level. Note that a centrally managed infrastructure has a lot of flexibility at the OU level. Because you don't delegate administration of OUs, you have less restriction on how you place them in your organizational structure.

If your network spans multiple locations, however, and administrative functions are distributed among multiple administrators, it would make sense to look at a domain/OU structure that is more suited to that setup. If network administration is decentralized, permissions must be delegated to other Group Policy administrators. This setup can be less flexible, because the layout of administrative duties across the network may necessitate certain OUs existing in specific locations. The delegation of administrative responsibilities to multiple Group Policy administrators will play a role in determining the types of OUs you create and where you place them in the domain structure.

GPO Location

Although we have touched briefly on the idea that the domain structure affects GPO placement, we haven't been very specific about the reasons. Consider a network that has 10,000 users in a single domain over four cities. The company has the standard collection of business units and a centralized MIS department that is responsible for all technology needs and services. The OU structure can take on any number of forms, depending on organizational needs. Each department can have its own OU, each physical location can be an OU, or even each city can be an OU, if some cities have multiple offices. Inherent flexibility is afforded to administrators of the centralized model because of the ability to assign OUs based on a variety of organizational models.

Now consider the same network—except that for political reasons, each physical location has its own administrator. In some cases, individual departments have their own administrators. This type of decentralized control suggests that certain OUs will exist in specific locations. For example, each location could have an OU, plus separate OUs can be created for specific departments required to maintain their own control. GPOs can be created that apply to the individual OUs, and administrative responsibility for them is delegated to local administrators. This scenario represents the decentralized approach to managing Group Policy.

Whether you choose centralized or decentralized management, it is important to design a structure that minimizes the amount of administrative overhead necessary to manage the network. Taking our previous examples, you can implement an OU structure in which you put all 10,000 users and computers in a single OU and assign permissions to that OU in such a way that local administrators control only the users and computers for which they are responsible. This is a terribly cumbersome approach. It's much better to create an OU for each administrator's area of responsibility and to give each administrator control over his or her particular OU.

This approach to OU structure applies to GPOs, as well. It makes more sense to create multiple smaller GPOs and delegate permissions to the GPOs rather than try to put the policy settings for the entire network into a few very large (monolithic) GPOs. This brings us to a point where we need to discuss the advantages and disadvantages of segmented versus monolithic GPOs.

Segmented versus Monolithic GPOs

The type of OU structure that is implemented on your network may dictate whether to choose a segmented or a monolithic approach to designing GPOs. Centralized environments will tend to lean toward a monolithic design, whereas decentralized environments will lean toward a segmented design. Let's examine what these terms mean.

Monolithic Design

A monolithic design uses a few very large GPOs, and is often implemented at the site or domain level. The GPOs apply to all users and computers on the network, regardless of OU membership. Group Policy processes more quickly because there are fewer objects to process. The downside is that delegation is difficult, because the few GPOs contain a large number of settings.

10

Segmented Design

A segmented design is most often associated with decentralized administrative control, because that type of environment is more likely to have multiple administrators and delegated control over Group Policy. Segmenting GPOs creates smaller GPOs that contain fewer settings than those in a monolithic design. This design is much more flexible with respect to the delegation of administrative functions; however, performance is impacted because Group Policy takes longer to process an increased number of GPOs.

Quite possibly the best design for your organization will be a mix of monolithic and segmented GPOs. Keep in mind the advantages and disadvantages of each as you are planning your design, and use the appropriate type of GPO when implementing Group Policy.

Cross-Domain GPO Links

With Group Policy, you must note a few considerations for networks that consist of multiple domains and possibly multiple sites. It is possible to create GPOs in one domain and have them apply to users and computers in another domain. However, doing so is not recommended in most cases, because computer startup and user logon are slowed—sometimes dramatically—if authentication must be processed by a domain controller from another domain. GPOs, you'll remember, reside within Active Directory. To apply a GPO, the target of the policy must be able to read the GPO. The overhead of additional authentication mechanisms to validate the computer or user account in the remote domain means that reading a GPO in a remote domain will not be as fast as reading a GPO in the same domain. Therefore, normally it is better to create duplicate GPOs in multiple domains rather than attempt to cross-link GPOs to other domains.

Other than the performance issue, there's no real reason not to cross-link domain GPOs rather than create multiple duplicate GPOs. In fact, a cross-linked single GPO is actually easier to manage—if you make a modification to the GPO, the change automatically applies to all users and computers in the sites and domains that link to the GPO. Otherwise, you will have to make the same change on every GPO that you created to perform the same functions in other domains.

Cross-domain GPO links work because the GPO links are contained in Active Directory, within the Global Catalog. All DCs in a forest share a single Global Catalog.

Managing Network Bandwidth

Along the lines of domain-linked GPOs is managing site boundaries and network bandwidth. If your sites are set up correctly, you shouldn't have any problems; this area should be taken care of during the planning stages.

As with cross-domain linking, cross-site linking is possible because site objects are stored in the GC and replicated to all DCs in a domain. Because a site can span multiple domains, any GPO linked to a site will be replicated and applied to all computers and users within the site, regardless of domain or OU membership. Only the link information is replicated, though—not the entire GPO. Therefore, performance issues that apply to cross-domain linked GPOs will apply to cross-site linked GPOs, as well.

Proper site design holds that all subnets within a site are well connected—that is, connected by fast links. If a site does not follow those rules, however, and includes subnets connected by WAN links, then GPOs will be accessed across the WAN links and performance will suffer. Fortunately, Windows 2000 provides some built-in safeguards.

When Group Policy detects a slow link, rather than processing policy settings as normal, the following rules apply:

- Security Settings are always processed regardless of link speed.
- Administrative templates are always processed regardless of link speed.
- Folder Redirection is turned off.
- Software Installation is turned off.
- Internet Explorer maintenance is turned off.

Windows 2000 provides a policy template so that you can adjust these settings, with the exception that Security Settings and administrative templates cannot be disabled.

The default threshold for whether Windows 2000 considers a link to be slow or fast is 500Kbps. That speed is user configurable, however, so you can adjust the setting up or down, depending on your needs. A slow link can be either a WAN connection, such as a 384Kbps Frame Relay connection between sites, or a dial-up Remote Access Service (RAS) connection. Windows 2000 uses a complex formula to determine the current bandwidth, unlike Windows NT 4, which simply measures file-system performance. The formula for determining if a link is slow or fast for users and computers is as follows:

1. Using 0 bytes of data, ping the server and time the number of milliseconds. This value is time #1. If it is less than 10 milliseconds, then assume the connection is a fast link, and exit.

2. Using an uncompressible 2K of data, ping the server and time the number of milliseconds. This value is time #2. The algorithm uses a JPEG (.jpg) file that is already compressed. (If a compressible file was used, hardware compression on the adapter would compress it and make the network appear faster than it is.)

3. DELTA equals time #2 minus time #1. This value removes the overhead of session setup by assuming any time associated with time #1 is overhead (because it transferred 0 bytes). DELTA is the time in milliseconds to move 2K.

4. DELTA is measured three times, and the average of the three values is called AVG. Measuring three times provides a value that is more reliable and less susceptible to a temporary line condition that would skew the numbers.

5. The connection speed Z, measured in kilobits per second (Kbps), is figured as

   ```
   Z = 32000/AVG
   ```

The formula for this entire process is as follows:

```
(Z kilobits / second) = 2 * (2 kilobytes) * (8 bits/
byte) * (1000 milliseconds / second) / ( AVG milliseconds)
```

It sounds complicated, but the goal is to provide a reliable means of determining the real performance of the network connection.

In addition to the speed settings for Group Policy, you can also set the speed that should be considered a slow or fast link for User Profiles. You configure this speed through Group Policy, in the Computer Configuration\Administrative Templates\System\Logon node. The user profile algorithm will attempt to ping the server first; however, if the client does not have support for the TCP/IP protocol, it will revert back to measuring the file system performance as in NT 4.

Group Policy Best Practices

When planning your Group Policy implementation, there are some best practices to keep in mind. These are not hard-and-fast rules that you must follow, but rather they are some guidelines that could make your administrative life a lot easier. In this section, we'll give each tip its own heading with a description of why it is important.

Disable Unused Portions of a GPO

As you browse through the Group Policy console, you can see that many settings are set to Not Configured. If you find that you do not need to use either the Computer Configuration or User Configuration portion of a GPO, you can disable one or both nodes to prevent Group Policy from processing it. For example, maybe you have created a GPO that applies specifically to user accounts in a domain. You are not using any of the computer policy settings in that particular GPO. By disabling the Computer Configuration node, you can speed up the processing of Group Policy, which won't process the node if it is disabled. Figure 10-7 shows the options to disable the computer or user policies; to reach this dialog box, right-click on the GPO root and choose Properties. If you decide to disable a node, you will receive the warning, shown in Figure 10-8, that asks you to confirm your choice.

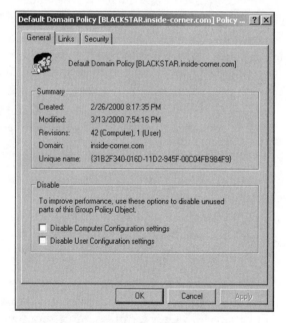

Figure 10-7   Disabling usused portions of a GPO can speed up Group Policy processing time

Figure 10-8   Windows 2000 provides a stern warning about loss of settings before letting you disable a node

Restrict the Number of Policies

It is important to note that the more policies you have applied to computers and users, the slower the logon startup process is. The guidelines are rather vague, and only through testing in your own environment will you know how many GPOs are too many. Faster machines and network connections can handle more policy settings in a shorter amount of time than slower machines or slower network connections. In general, be prudent with your policy decisions, and apply policies only where you specifically need to.

Avoid No Override and Block Policy Inheritance When Possible

The No Override and Block Policy Inheritance settings can make it difficult to troubleshoot policy problems on a network, so it's best to avoid them when possible. They can also add a lot of complexity to your Group Policy setup. For example, suppose you block policy at a node, and then find that some areas need to have that policy overridden. Then, you put in some No Overrides to compensate. You quickly end up in a mess that is difficult to manage. This is not to say you should never use No Override and Block Policy Inheritance, only that you should use them cautiously.

Use Group Policy Rather than System Policies

Windows 2000 corrects many of the shortcomings of NT 4's system policies, including the undesirable trait that system policies persist beyond their useful lives. Group Policy cleans up after itself whenever it refreshes (administrator configurable), and provides a wealth of new features.

10

Filter Group Policy with Security Groups

As discussed in the next section of the chapter, "Group Policy Implementation," **filtering** is the process by which you allow or deny GPO access to individual computers or users or to groups of computers or users. As with general security management in Windows NT and Windows 2000, you should use security groups rather than apply policy settings directly to individual users and computers. It is much simpler to manage a single security group object than it is to configure dozens of user accounts individually, especially when modifications are made after the initial setup.

Avoid Cross-Domain GPO Links when Possible

As previously discussed, creating cross-site and cross-domain GPO links has performance implications. If a slow link exists between domains or sites, the policy information will still have to pass over it during replication and user logons. Unless you have sufficient bandwidth, it is best to create duplicate GPOs in the other domains and sites.

Limit the GPO Refresh Period

Having Group Policy settings refresh too often can put a serious damper on user productivity, because the Windows shell refreshes when the policy is updated. In most environments, policy settings are not constantly updated; so, choose a refresh interval that won't put too much of a burden on your computing environment.

Now that we have discussed the planning issues involved with Group Policy, it is time to shift our attention to the actual implementation.

GROUP POLICY IMPLEMENTATION

With concepts and planning under our belts, we turn to examining the implementation of Windows 2000 Group Policy. In this section we won't walk through all of the procedures, such as actually creating a GPO. Instead, in most cases we will simply describe the implementation details.

In this section, we will discuss the following topics:

- Creating a GPO
- Creating a GPO console
- Specifying Group Policy settings
- Filtering Group Policy
- Delegating administrative control of Group Policy
- Linking a GPO

Creating a GPO

Before you do anything else with Group Policy, you must first create a GPO. In fact, without any GPOs created, you cannot even access the Group Policy Editor. Fortunately, Windows 2000 creates a GPO by default when you install Active Directory. It is the Default Domain Policy.

You create a GPO primarily through the Active Directory Users and Computers management console. From within the console, right-click on a domain or OU and select Properties. You will notice the options such as Add, New, Edit, and Delete. Those are the major commands, and they perform the following functions:

- *Add*—Add a Group Policy Object link
- *New*—Create a new GPO
- *Edit*—Modify an existing GPO
- *Delete*—Remove a GPO, a GPO link, or both

Creating a GPO Console

In order to edit Group Policy settings, you must open the Group Policy Editor. The Group Policy Editor is the Graphical User Interface (GUI) for configuring GPOs; and, as you have learned, it provides the Computer Configuration and User Configuration nodes. You can open the Group Policy Editor in two primary ways: as a standalone tool or by editing a GPO.

Using the Group Policy Editor as a standalone tool, you can execute mmc.exe from a Run line and add the Group Policy snap-in. In Figure 10-9, we have opened a new blank console by executing mmc from a Run line. To begin the process of adding the Group Policy snap-in, choose Console | Add/Remove Snap-in.

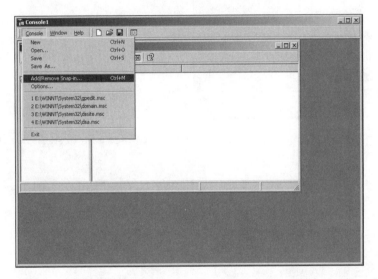

Figure 10-9   Click on Add/Remove Snap-in to get a list of standalone snap-ins to add to your console

Next you'll see the window displayed in Figure 10-10. It shows that currently you have not added any snap-ins to the console, and you have no available snap-ins to remove. Click on Add to add a snap-in.

10

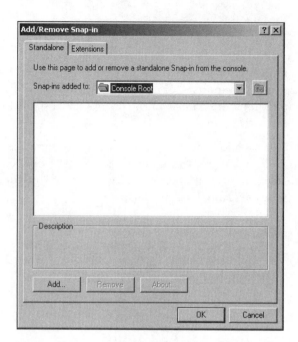

Figure 10-10   In the Add/Remove Snap-in window, you can see a list of snap-ins currently associated with the console

When the Add Standalone Snap-in dialog is displayed, as in Figure 10-11, navigate to the snap-in for Group Policy. Highlight it and click on Add.

Figure 10-11   You can select one or more standalone snap-ins to add to your blank console

Once you add the Group Policy snap-in, you are presented with the window shown in Figure 10-12. The snap-in will default to Local Computer. You can change it by clicking on Browse and choosing a different GPO for the focus, as shown in Figure 10-13.

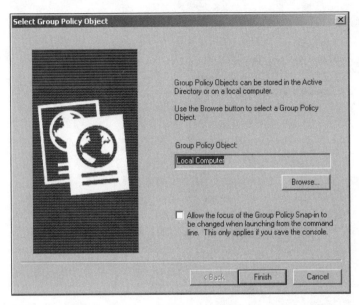

Figure 10-12 The Group Policy standalone snap-in defaults to the Local Computer for its focus

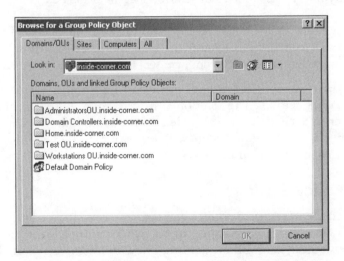

Figure 10-13 You can change the focus of the Group Policy snap-in by choosing a different GPO from the available list

10

Once you've chosen your GPO, click on OK. You'll then see, as in Figure 10-14, that you have a snap-in to manage in the Add/Remove Snap-ins window. You can simply click on OK at this point to return to the console window and edit Group Policy settings.

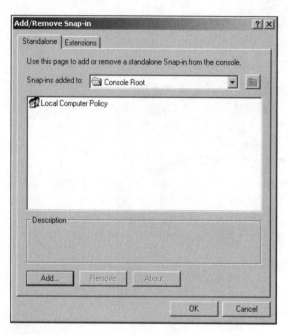

Figure 10-14   An entry now exists in the Add/Remove Snap-in dialog box

The other way to get a Group Policy Editor console with the focus on a GPO of choice is to go into the properties of a domain or OU in Active Directory Users and Computers and select the Group Policy tab. Editing a GPO from here will launch the Group Policy Editor.

Obviously, either of these methods is a tedious process to go through every time you want to edit Group Policy settings. The solution is to save your console by using the Console | Save As command. Give the console a descriptive name—like "Group Policy-*name of GPO*"—and OK it. Windows 2000 will save your custom console to the Administrative Tools folder, where you can access it easily in the future.

Specifying Group Policy Settings

Once you have created your GPO and a GPO console, you're ready to edit the Group Policy settings. In Figure 10-15, we have created a Workstation OU to include all Windows 2000 Professional systems in our domain. The GPO name is reflected in the root node of the console.

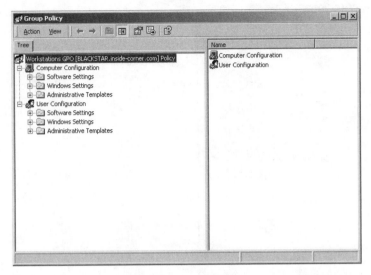

Figure 10-15   With the Group Policy Editor focused on our new GPO, we're ready to start configuring settings

10

To configure settings, start expanding the nodes of the tree and exploring the settings you have available. Previously in the chapter, we discussed the Computer Configuration and User Configuration nodes and the subnodes beneath each of them: Software Settings, Windows Settings, and Administrative Templates.

Filtering Group Policy

As we briefly mentioned earlier, Group Policy can apply only to users and computers that have Read permission for a Group Policy object. In fact, the easiest way to prevent certain users or OUs from receiving policy settings is simply to remove the Read permission to the GPO. This process is known as *filtering*, whereby you affect the groups of users and computers over which a GPO has influence. As discussed previously, a Group Policy object is the smallest unit in Group Policy; therefore, any filtering applies to the whole GPO. You cannot use security groups to filter only a portion of the settings in a GPO.

In order to filter GPOs through security groups, use the Security tab of a GPO's Property sheet. Figure 10-16 shows the Security tab for a Default Domain Policy GPO.

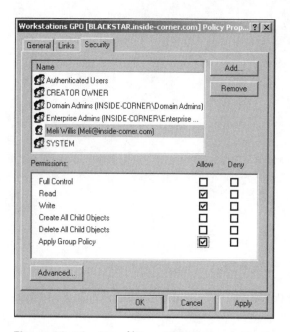

Figure 10-16   You filter a GPO through the Security tab of a GPO's Property sheet

When filtering the effects of a GPO by security group, you are essentially editing the discretionary access control list (DACL) on that GPO. Using the DACL, you allow or deny access for users and computers to the GPO based on their memberships in security groups. In addition to DACLs, you also have access control entries (ACEs), which are the permission entries within a DACL. ACEs are permissions such as Full Control, Read, Write, and Apply Group Policy.

The Apply Group Policy permission, along with Read, allows users and computers to execute Group Policy settings. By default, all authenticated users have Read and Apply Group Policy permissions, but not Full Control or Write. This setup prevents ordinary users (non–administrators) from being able to modify GPOs. Microsoft recommends removing the Apply Group Policy permission from security groups that have had Read permission removed, because Group Policy will process more quickly if both settings are taken away. Apply Group Policy cannot function without Read permission to the GPO; keep that in mind as you are filtering Group Policy settings.

Delegating Administrative Control of Group Policy

In decentralized environments, it is usually necessary to delegate some administrative control of Group Policy to other locations' administrators. Even in a large centralized environment, multiple administrators may be responsible for Group Policy administration.

Three Group Policy tasks can be delegated individually, as follows:

- Managing Group Policy links for a site, domain, or OU

- Creating GPOs

- Editing GPOs

Local Group Policy applies to standalone computers only, whereas non-local Group Policy requires a Windows domain controller. The rights to administer Group Policy can be found under the *<GPO name>*\User Configuration\Administrative Templates\Windows Components\Microsoft Management Console node in the Group Policy Editor.

Managing Group Policy Links

In order to delegate control to someone to manage GPO links, you must use the Delegation Of Control Wizard. To access this wizard, right-click on the domain or OU in Active Directory Users and Computers and select Delegate Control.

When the wizard starts, you are asked to select users or groups to which you want to delegate control. Once you have selected the appropriate personnel, click on Next. Then, you will see a window such as that in Figure 10-17, which shows a list of tasks to be delegated. Simply click on Finish after you have made your settings, and then click on Next; the wizard requires no other settings.

10

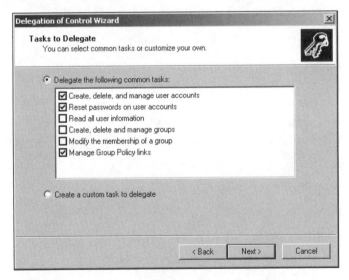

Figure 10-17   Windows 2000 allows you to choose the tasks you want to delegate using the Delegation Of Control Wizard

Creating GPOs

You delegate the ability to create GPOs through Active Directory Users and Computers, as well. In order to create a GPO, a user account must belong to the Group Policy Creator Owners administrators group. Double-click on the Group Policy Creator

Owners group in the Users container, and click on the Members tab. Add the users who should be able to create GPOs.

Editing GPOs

The ability to edit a GPO comes from being delegated administrative control of a specific GPO. To do this, open the GPO in the Group Policy Editor. Right-click on the GPO name and choose Properties, and then click on the Security tab. Add the user(s) you want to have administrative control and set the appropriate permission levels. At minimum, they will need Read/Write permissions, although you could go so far as to give Full Control.

Linking a GPO

Before you can link a GPO, you must have at least the permissions listed previously to edit a GPO: Read/Write or Full Control.

To link a GPO, open Active Directory Users and Computers (or Active Directory Sites and Services, if you wish to link a GPO at the site level) and right-click on the domain or OU to which you want to link a GPO. Choose Properties, and then click on the Group Policy tab. Click on Add and navigate to select the GPO you want to link to the particular domain or OU. Click on OK when you are done. The GPO is now successfully linked to this domain or OU.

CHAPTER SUMMARY

Group Policy, as you have learned, is a powerful new feature of Windows 2000 for systems administrators. Its feature set far surpasses the system policies available in Windows NT 4, although Windows 2000 provides for backward compatibility with the older policies.

As we moved through the chapter, we discussed concepts of Group Policy such as:

❐ Windows 2000 Group Policy versus Windows NT 4 system policies

❐ Group Policy Objects (GPO)

❐ The Group Policy MMC snap-in

❐ Group Policy namespace

❐ Startup, shutdown, logon, and logoff

❐ Active Directory structure and Group Policy

❐ Group Policy inheritance

❐ Group Policy processing

In addition, we covered planning issues such as:

❐ Change control procedures

❑ Structuring domains and OUs for Group Policy

❑ Layered versus monolithic GPOs

❑ Cross-domain GPO links

❑ Managing network bandwidth

❑ Best practices

Finally, we finished up with a discussion of Group Policy implementation, covering the following topics:

❑ Creating a GPO

❑ Creating a GPO console

❑ Specifying Group Policy settings

❑ Filtering Group Policy

❑ Delegating administrative control of Group Policy

❑ Linking a GPO

Some of the key points to remember from this chapter include:

❑ GPOs can be applied at the site, domain, or OU level.

❑ Group Policy can help reduce TCO on networks, while increasing ROI for technology expenditures.

❑ Group Policy is processed in the following order: local, site, domain, Organizational Unit.

❑ The Group Policy Editor is the primary interface for modifying Group Policy settings.

❑ Policy settings can be blocked or overridden, if necessary.

❑ The use of Group Policy can impact the Active Directory domain and OU design process.

❑ Group Policy administration can be filtered or delegated.

❑ GPOs can be linked to other sites, domains, and OUs.

❑ When planning a Group Policy design, it is important to consider employee morale issues as well as technical issues.

In the next few chapters, we will expand on the knowledge of Group Policy that you've gained from this chapter, and explore managing the user environment with Group Policy, as well as deploying and managing with Group Policy. Windows NT 4 provides desktop management functionality through system policies, but it offers no equivalent for software management. And software management is a great new feature of Windows 2000.

10

11

MANAGING USER ENVIRONMENTS WITH GROUP POLICY

After completing this chapter, you will be able to:

♦ Use scripts to apply configuration settings to users and computers

♦ Control the user environment through administrative templates

♦ Use folder redirection to move user files to a server

U p to this point, we've examined Group Policy concepts and showed you how to create and implement Group Policy objects. In this chapter, you'll expand on that knowledge by putting what you've learned into practice. For many corporations, the key benefit of Group Policy is the ability to exercise control over the user environment. That's what this chapter covers: We'll discuss the options Group Policy provides for creating a customized computing environment for your users, including scripts, administrative templates, security settings, and folder redirection. Windows 2000 Group Policy also provides software management features to complement the desktop configuration features, which we'll cover in Chapter 12.

Configuring the user environment consists of using settings that apply to specific users, as well as computer settings that apply to the computer itself (and therefore to all users of the computer). As you learn to apply policy settings to administer the user environment, it will be important to keep track of which settings apply at the computer level versus the user level, and which settings will take precedence when a conflict situation exits. We'll start by examining scripts.

USING SCRIPTS TO APPLY CONFIGURATION SETTINGS TO USERS AND COMPUTERS

One of the most common ways to apply configuration settings in the past was through login scripts. Essentially, when a user enters a username and password to log on to the network, a login script that was associated with the user account is executed. Login scripts have traditionally been simple batch files (with a .bat extension), and the commands within the login scripts tended to be fairly basic. An administrator might include commands to map various network drives or to set the computer's clock against a local time server. Scripts have changed in Windows 2000, though, not only in the command set they support, but also in the times at which they can be run. In this section, we'll discuss:

- Overview of scripts
- Windows Scripting Host
- Assigning scripts through Group Policy

Overview of Scripts

Batch files are limited by nature. In addition, traditional scripts could be run only at logon. With Windows 2000, however, scripts can be run at any or all of the following times:

- *Startup*—Computer scripts that run under the Local System account and apply settings during computer startup, before the user logon dialog box is presented.

- *Logon*—Traditional user login scripts that run when the user logs on to the system. The scripts run under the user account with which they are associated. Login scripts are executed only after computer startup scripts have been processed by Windows 2000.

- *Logoff*—User scripts that run when the user either chooses Start|Logoff or chooses to shut down or restart the computer. Logoff scripts are executed before computer shutdown scripts.

- *Shutdown*—Computer scripts that run when the computer is shut down. As with startup scripts, shutdown scripts run under the Local System account to apply settings at the computer level.

As we touched on in Chapter 10, by default, Group Policy processes synchronously. Because of this processing, computer startup scripts will process completely before the user login script is even given an opportunity to begin processing. You can change this behavior to asynchronous processing through the Group Policy Editor, although doing so is not generally recommended.

Most systems administrators will already be familiar with the concept of scripts, so we will not spend much time discussing the traditional batch filescripts. Suffice it to say that

Windows 2000 supports everything you might have done with NT 4 login scripts, except that now scripts can be run at the times we just discussed rather than just during user login. Windows 2000 flexes its muscles, however, when you get beyond MS-DOS commands and into ActiveX scripting using the Windows Scripting Host, VBScript, and JScript.

Windows Scripting Host

Windows Scripting Host (WSH) is a scripting host that allows you to run VBScript (.vbs) and JavaScript (.js)—or JScript, as it is also known—natively on 32-bit Windows platforms. This means you can execute VBScript or JScript scripts just as you would MS-DOS batch files. WSH is extensible, so in the future you might be able to run third-party scripts such as PERL or Python natively, as well.

Two versions of WSH exist. Version 1 shipped with Windows 98 and was available as a download for Windows 95. It also shipped as part of the Windows NT 4 Option Pack for use on NT systems. Version 2 shipped with Windows 2000. As you would expect, version 2 has added numerous new features. It is fully backward compatible, however, so any scripts designed for version 1 will run on version 2 without modification.

WSH comes with two executable files:

- WScript.exe
- CScript.exe

11

WScript

WScript.exe is the graphical version of WSH; it allows you to run VBScript and JScript scripts inside of Windows by double-clicking on the filename. You can also execute WScript.exe from the Start|Run line. The syntax is

```
wscript <script name>
```

You must be sure to specify the path to the script in *<script name>* in order for it to execute properly. WScript provides the following configurable properties:

- *Stop Script After Specified Number Of Seconds*—Specifies the maximum length of time a script can run. By default, no time limit is placed on script execution.
- *Display Logo When Script Is Executed In A Command Console*—Displays a WSH banner while running the script. This setting is turned on by default.

CScript

CScript.exe is the command-line version of WSH. It is useful when you need to specify parameters at runtime. CScript is great for the types of scripts we are dealing with in this chapter: computer and user scripts that are executed during startup, logon, logoff, and shutdown. The syntax of CScript.exe is

```
cscript <script name> <script options and parameters>
```

The definitions for the options are as follows:

- **<script name>**—The full path and filename of the script to be executed by CScript.exe.

- **<script options and parameters>**—Enable or disable various WSH features. Options are preceded by two forward slashes, as in **//logo**. Table 11-1 summarizes the host options.

Table 11-1   Windows Scripting Host options and their definitions

Option	Definition
//B	Batch Mode. Suppresses script errors and user prompts that might display. Computer and user scripts that we discuss in this chapter will typically have this option specified.
//I	Interactive Mode. The opposite of Batch Mode. Interactive Mode is the default if neither mode is specified.
//Logo	By default, displays a logo banner during script execution.
//Nologo	Disables the logo banner from displaying during script execution.
//H:WScript	Changes the default script host to WScript. This is the default setting if no host is explicitly specified.
//H:CScript	Changes the default script host to CScript.
//E:engine	Specifies which engine to use in executing the script. Either the VBScript or JScript engine can be specified.
//T:nn	Time out in seconds. The maximum amount of time the script is allowed to run before it is terminated by the script host.
//D	Debugger. This setting enables active debugging.
//X	Executes the script in the debugger.
//S	Save. Saves the current command-line options for this user.
//Job:<jobID>	Runs the specified *jobID* from a WSH 2 WSF file.
//U	Tells WSH to use Unicode for redirected I/O from the console.
//?	Displays the help file for syntax and options.

It is beyond the scope of this chapter to explore in depth the differences between WSH versions 1 and 2, other than to point out a couple of important ones.

Windows Scripting Host 1

In WSH 1, VBScript and JScript scripts used a WSH file containing per-script settings that were applied when the script was executed. For the IT old-timers who might be reading this, the WSH file functioned much like a PIF file did in Windows 3.*x* in supporting 16-bit DOS applications running in Windows. The format of the WSH file is similar to a Windows INF file. A sample WSH file is as follows:

```
[ScriptFile]
Path=C:\WINNT\Samples\WSH\showprop.vbs
[Options]
Timeout=0
DisplayLogo=1
BatchMode=0
```

Windows creates the WSH files automatically when you edit the properties of a VBS or JS file and click on OK. To edit the properties, simply right-click on the script file and select Properties. Make your changes and click on OK.

Benefits of WSH Files

You can create a per-script WSH file that specifies settings the script will use when executed. Multiple versions of the WSH file can be created for deployments to a variety of users in a domain. In addition:

- You can apply a WSH file to a specific group of users within the organization. Doing so allows you individual control over specific scripts that can be executed.

- You can create individual WSH files for individual users within the organization. Doing so allows you control over specific scripts used at the user level within the organization.

- You can use specific WSH files for login scripts when users log on to their systems. Doing so provides you individual control over specific script properties executed on client machines when users log on.

When you double-click on a WSH file or execute it from the command line, WScript.exe or CScript.exe reads the WSH file to determine the specific script settings that should be used to execute the specific script file. The script host will execute the original script, passing in the properties that are defined within the WSH file. It is important to note that the original script file must be present when you execute the WSH file. If the original VBS or JS file is not present, an error will result.

Windows Scripting Host 2

Whereas WSH 1 uses a WSH file that works in conjunction with the VBS or JS script file, WSH 2 scripts use a WSF file that replaces the VBS or JS file altogether. Rather than the INF-style formatting of Windows Scripting Host 1 WSH files, the WSF file contains Extensible Markup Language (XML) code that defines more than just the formatting and options of the script output. Windows Script Files (WSF) are not engine specific, offering increased flexibility to the administrator who is writing scripts.

Benefits of WSF files

WSF files offer the following benefits over WSH files:

- *Multiple engine support*—You are not limited to using only a single script engine within a WSF file. Because some scripting languages are stronger than others for certain tasks, you can mix and match scripting engines as you choose.

- *Multiple jobs*—You can create multiple jobs within a single WSF file; doing so allows you to use a single file to store all your code. When you execute the WSF file, you can use the **JobID** parameter (discussed previously) to specify the individual job within the WSF file that you wish to run.

- *Support for **include** statements*—WSF files allow you to use the programming technique of including previously written functions within your scripts.

- *Support for type libraries*—You can use constants within your script code, thereby increasing the code's power and flexibility even more over that of limited MS-DOS batch files.

- *Support for tools*—You can edit your WSF files with any standard XML editing utility. You can also use any standard text editor, such as Notepad, to edit a WSF file.

Generally, it is recommended that you use WSH 2 WSF files rather than WSH 1–style scripts with complementary WSH files. Microsoft, like many companies, is making a strong push toward standardizing on XML. You'll be ahead of the game if you make the move now rather than later.

The XML nature of WSF files adds a bit of complexity to the script file, compared to a standard VBS or JS script. This is the case because you include settings about the script that in WSH 1 would reside in the WSH file. Because WSF files by definition are language and engine independent, you must include settings that tell WSH how to process the file.

The following is an extremely simple VBScript example: the standard "Hello World" application that everyone learns to write the first day of any introductory-level programming class:

```
MsgBox "Hello World"
```

When you execute this code, you get the result shown in Figure 11-1.

Figure 11-1   A simple VBScript example

That same basic VBScript example, written in XML for a WSH 2 WSF file, looks like this:

```
<job>
<script language="VBScript">
MsgBox "Hello World"
</script>
</job>
```

When this code is executed, the output is a message box identical to that seen in the previous example.

In a simple example like this, the only real difference between the two scripts is that the Example.vbs script has a corresponding Example.wsh file residing in the same directory as the script, whereas Example.wsf is a standalone file. The power of the second example shines through, however, if you add multiple jobs to the WSF file and/or increase the complexity of the scripts by adding **include** statements or type libraries. (These additions are beyond the scope of this book. For more information on Windows Scripting Host and using it to write administrative scripts, see Microsoft's Web site at http://msdn.microsoft.com/scripting/default.htm.)

Writing scripts could be the topic of an entire book on its own—and is, in several cases. There are some outstanding programming books, and I particularly recommend *VBScript Programmer's Reference* (ISBN, 1861002718; 1999) and *Windows Scripting Host Programmer's Reference* (ISBN, 1861002653; 1999), both published by Wrox Press. These two books, along with Microsoft Developer Network (MSDN), will take you a long ways toward writing complex scripts for all sorts of systems and network administration tasks.

11

Assigning Scripts through Group Policy

Fortunately, the hardest part about implementing scripts on a Windows 2000 network is the actual writing of the scripts. Group Policy makes it easy to deploy computer and user scripts.

As we've touched on previously, startup and shutdown scripts apply to computers, and logon and logoff scripts apply to users. The Group Policy Editor divides the Group Policy Objects (GPOs) into two main nodes: Computer Configuration and User Configuration. Startup and shutdown scripts are under Computer Configuration, whereas login and logoff scripts are under User Configuration. These nodes are illustrated in Figure 11-2.

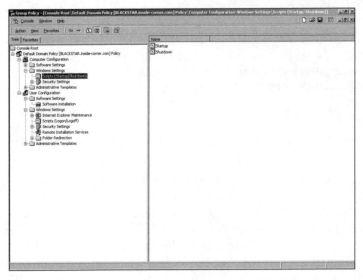

Figure 11-2   The Group Policy Editor divides GPOs into Computer Configuration and User Configuration nodes

To apply a script, click on the Scripts node under the appropriate container (Computer Configuration or User Configuration). Double-click on the desired script, such as the startup script, to bring up the dialog box shown in Figure 11-3.

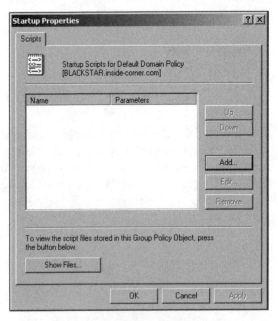

Figure 11-3   Double-clicking on a script brings up a Properties dialog box

In the script's Properties dialog, click on the Add button to add a new script. Doing so will bring up the dialog box shown in Figure 11-4.

If you know the name of the script you want to use for computer startup for this GPO, simply type in the name. Otherwise, click on Browse. Figure 11-5 illustrates the location of the script files for computer startup. Select the script you want to use, as in Figure 11-6, and click on Open. Doing so will return you to the dialog box shown previously in Figure 11-4. Enter any parameters, such as "//Nologo", and click on OK.

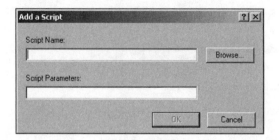

Figure 11-4   The Add a Script dialog box allows you to specify a script name and script parameters

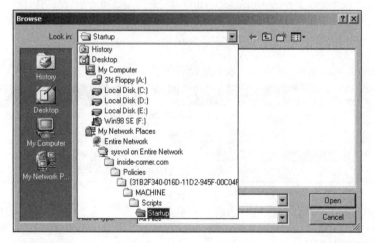

Figure 11-5   The default directory structure leading to computer startup scripts

11

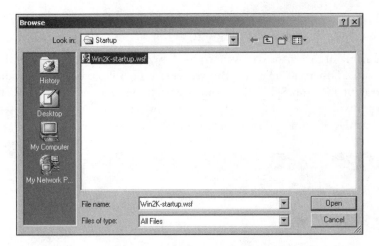

Figure 11-6 After selecting the script that you want to assign, click on Open

It is important to note that when you're assigning a script through Group Policy, the script can be located on any drive and folder the system can read. This is in stark contrast to Windows NT 4, which requires that login scripts be located in the NETLOGON share, located at \winnt\system32\repl\import\scripts. Table 11-2 shows the Windows 2000 default script directories for the different types of scripts. It is not recommended to use locations other than these defaults for storing scripts.

Table 11-2 The default directories for Windows 2000 scripts

Script	Directory
Startup	\winnt\sysvol\sysvol*domain*\Policies*GUID*\MACHINE\Scripts\Startup
Shutdown	\winnt\sysvol\sysvol*domain*\Policies*GUID*\MACHINE\Scripts\Shutdown
Logon	\winnt\sysvol\sysvol*domain*\Policies*GUID*\USER\Scripts\Logon
Logoff	\winnt\sysvol\sysvol*domain*\Policies*GUID*\USER\Scripts\Logoff

The File Replication service (FRS) has replaced the NT 4 and earlier Directory Replication service, and now replicates the entire SYSVOL directory tree across all domain controllers.

The exception to the recommendation about not changing the default location for scripts occurs if you are supporting legacy clients on your network (Windows 9*x* or Windows NT 4). For these clients, you should copy the relevant logon scripts to the NETLOGON share, which in Windows 2000 is located under the \winnt\sysvol\sysvol*domain*\scripts directory. Legacy clients cannot use the Windows 2000 features of startup, shutdown, and logoff scripts, so the NETLOGON share exists for backward compatibility with their logon script capabilities.

Let's make one more note about scripts before we move on to administrative templates. When you go into the properties of a script, such as a logon script, you'll see a Show Files option. Clicking on Show Files brings up the dialog box shown in Figure 11-7, which shows all the logon script files that have been associated with this GPO.

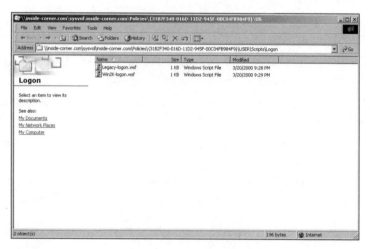

Figure 11-7   Show Files presents a list of all the scripts of the type you selected that are associated with the current GPO

11

CONTROLLING THE USER ENVIRONMENT THROUGH ADMINISTRATIVE TEMPLATES

Administrative templates provide the majority of the settings that you will configure in order to control the user environment. The Administrative Templates node exists under both the Computer Configuration and User Configuration nodes. Combined, the administrative templates form the core of the settings that the Windows 2000 administrator uses to control the desktop.

In this section, we will look at the following topics:

- ADM files
- Computer templates
- User templates

ADM Files

Administrative templates that reside within a GPO consist of a set of ADM files that exist for each GPO and are contained within the system volume (SYSVOL). Windows 2000 includes several ADM files, as follows:

- *System.adm*—Installed by default in Group Policy. System.adm is used for Windows 2000 clients.

- *Inetres.adm*—Installed by default in Group Policy. Inetres.adm contains Internet Explorer policies for Windows 2000 systems.

- *Windows.adm*—Contains user interface options for Windows 9x systems; used with the System Policy Editor (poledit.exe).

- *Winnt.adm*—Contains user interface options for Windows NT 4 systems; used with the System Policy Editor (poledit.exe).

- *Common.adm*—Contains user interface options common to both Windows NT 4 and Windows 9x systems; also used with the System Policy Editor.

Administrative templates are text files that define Registry settings containing the desired configurations and that define how Group Policy settings are displayed under the Administrative Templates nodes in the Group Policy Editor. As such, you can create your own custom administrative templates through this extensible system.

The following is an example from Inetres.adm, showing how an administrative template is constructed. Due to page-formatting limitations, some lines have been broken up into two lines. Typically, an entry such as KEYNAME= would have its entire value written on one line, which isn't always the case in the following example. When creating your own .adm files, put in a return only at the end of a line, not in the middle of a line.

```
#if version >= 3
CLASS USER
CATEGORY !!WindowsComponents
 CATEGORY !!InternetExplorer
  POLICY !!Search_NoFindFiles
    KEYNAME "Software\Policies\Microsoft\Internet Explorer
\Restrictions"
    EXPLAIN !!ExplainSearch_NoFindFiles
    VALUENAME "NoFindFiles"
    END POLICY
  POLICY !!Branding_NoExternalBranding
    KEYNAME "Software\Policies\Microsoft\Internet Explorer
\Restrictions"
    EXPLAIN !!ExplainBranding_NoExternalBranding
    VALUENAME "NoExternalBranding"
    END POLICY
```

```
    POLICY !!FavImportExport
    KEYNAME "Software\Policies\Microsoft\Internet Explorer"
      EXPLAIN !!ExplainFavImportExport
      VALUENAME "DisableImportExportFavorites"
       END POLICY
CATEGORY !!EnableTabs
   POLICY !!ControlPanel_RestrictGeneralTab
     EXPLAIN !!ExplainControlPanel_RestrictGeneralTab
     KEYNAME "Software\Policies\Microsoft\Internet Explorer
\Control Panel"
     VALUENAME GeneralTab
      END POLICY
   POLICY !!ControlPanel_RestrictSecurityTab
      EXPLAIN !!ExplainControlPanel_RestrictSecurityTab
      KEYNAME "Software\Policies\Microsoft\Internet Explorer
\Control Panel"
      VALUENAME SecurityTab
      END POLICY
END CATEGORY

   POLICY !!ControlPanel_RestrictAdvanced
      EXPLAIN !!ExplainControlPanel_RestrictAdvanced
      KEYNAME "Software\Policies\Microsoft\Internet
Explorer
\Control Panel"
      VALUENAME Advanced
      END POLICY

      KEYNAME "Software\Policies\Microsoft\Internet Explorer
\Control Panel"   POLICY !!RestrictHomePage
      EXPLAIN !!ExplainRestrictHomePage
      VALUENAME HomePage
      END POLICY

   POLICY !!DialupSettings
      EXPLAIN !!ExplainDialupSettings
      KEYNAME
"Software\Policies\Microsoft\Windows\CurrentVersion
\Internet Settings"
      VALUENAME DialupAutodetect
      VALUEON NUMERIC 1
      VALUEOFF NUMERIC 0
      END POLICY

  END CATEGORY ;; Internet Explorer
END CATEGORY ;; WindowsComponents
```

11

```
CLASS MACHINE

CATEGORY !!WindowsComponents
 CATEGORY !!InternetExplorer
  POLICY !!Security_HKLM_only
    EXPLAIN !!ExplainSecurity_HKLM_only
    KEYNAME "Software\Policies\Microsoft\Windows
\CurrentVersion
\Internet Settings"
    VALUENAME Security_HKLM_only
    END POLICY

  POLICY !!Security_options_edit
    EXPLAIN !!ExplainSecurity_options_edit
    KEYNAME "Software\Policies\Microsoft\Windows
\CurrentVersion
\Internet Settings"
    VALUENAME Security_options_edit
    END POLICY
 END CATEGORY ;; Internet Explorer
END CATEGORY ;; WindowsComponents
#endif

[strings]

GPOnly_Tip1="The Inetres.adm file you have loaded requires
Group Policy"
GPOnly_Tip2="in Windows 2000. You cannot use the System
Policy Editor"
GPOnly_Tip3="to display Windows 2000 Group Policy settings."
GPOnly_Tip4=" "
GPOnly_Tip5="Enabling or disabling this policy has no
effect."
GPOnly="Unsupported Administrative Templates"
GPOnlyPolicy="Inetres.adm"
WindowsComponents="Windows Components"
InternetExplorer="Internet Explorer"
GeneralTab="General Settings"
General_RestrictHomePage = "Disable home page settings"
General_RestrictCache="Disable Temporary Internet files
settings"
General_RestrictHistory="Disable history settings"
General_RestrictColors="Disable color settings"
General_RestrictLinks="Disable link color settings"
General_RestrictFonts="Disable font settings"
General_RestrictLanguages="Disable language settings"
General_RestrictAccessibility="Disable accessibility
settings"
RestrictHomePage = "Disable changing home page settings"
```

```
DialupSettings="Use Automatic Detection for dial-up
connections"
AutoProxyCache="Disable caching of Auto-Proxy scripts"
DisplayScriptFailureUI="Display error message on proxy
script
download failure"
RestrictCache="Disable changing Temporary Internet files
settings"
RestrictHistory="Disable changing history settings"
ConnectionTab="Connection Settings"
RestrictConnectionWizard="Disable Internet Connection wizard"
RestrictConnectionSettings="Disable changing connection
settings"
RestrictProxy="Disable changing proxy settings"
RestrictAutoconfig="Disable changing Automatic
Configuration settings"
Menus="Browser menus"
File_Menu="File menu"
File_NoBrowserSaveAs="File menu: Disable Save As... menu
option"
File_NoFileNew="File menu: Disable New menu option"
File_NoFileOpen="File menu: Disable Open menu option"
File_NoBrowserSaveWebComplete="File menu: Disable Save As Web
Page Complete"
File_NoBrowserClose="File menu: Disable closing the
browser and
Explorer windows"
View_Menu="View menu"
View_NoViewSource="View menu: Disable Source menu option"
View_NoTheaterMode="View menu: Disable Full Screen menu
option"
Favorites_Menu="Favorites menu"
NoFavorites="Hide Favorites menu"
Tools_Menu="Tools menu: Disable Internet Options... menu
option"
Search="Search"
NoSearchCustomization="Disable Search Customization"
NoFindFiles="Disable Find Files via F3 within the browser"
Search_NoSearchCustomization="Search: Disable Search
Customization"
Search_NoFindFiles="Search: Disable Find Files via F3
within
the browser"
AdminApproved="Administrator Approved Controls"
Media_Player = "Media Player"
ActiveMovie_Control = "ActiveMovie Control"
Windows_Media_Player = "Windows Media Player"
Menu_Controls = "Menu Controls"
MCSiMenu = "MCSiMenu"
PopupMenu_Object = "PopupMenu Object"
```

11

```
Security="Security Page"
PolicyName="Security Tab Settings"
Security_HKLM_only="Security Zones: Use only machine
settings "
Security_options_edit="Security Zones: Do not allow users
to change policies"
Security_zones_map_edit="Security Zones: Do not allow
users to
add/delete sites"
UserProxy="Make proxy settings per-machine (rather than
per-user)"
HKLM_only="Use only machine settings for security zones"
options_edit="Do not allow users to change policies for
any security zone"
zones_map_edit="Do not allow users to add/delete sites
from a security zone"
ExplainSecurity_options_edit="Prevents users from changing
security zone settings. A security zone is a group of Web
sites with the same security level.\n\nIf you enable this
policy, the Custom Level button and security-level slider
on the Security tab in the Internet Options dialog box
are disabled.\n\nIf you disable this policy or do not con-
figure it, users can change the settings for security
zones.\n\nThis policy prevents users from changing secu-
rity zone settings established by the administrator.
\n\nNote: The "Disable the Security page" policy (located
in \User Configuration \Administrative Templates\Windows
Components\Internet Explorer\Internet Control Panel),
which removes the Security tab from Internet Explorer in
Control Panel, takes precedence over this policy. If it is
enabled, this policy is ignored.\n\nAlso, see the
"Security zones: Use only machine settings" policy."
ExplainControlPanel_RestrictGeneralTab="Removes the
General tab from the interface in the Internet Options
dialog box.\n\nIf you enable this policy, users are unable
to see and change settings for the home page, the cache,
history, Web page appearance, and accessibility. \n\nIf
you disable this policy or do not configure it, users can
see and change these settings.\n\nWhen you set this pol-
icy, you do not need to set the following Internet
Explorer policies (located in \User Configuration\
Administrative Templates\Windows Components \Internet
Explorer\), because this policy removes the General tab
from the interface:\n\n"Disable changing home page
settings"\n" Disable changing Temporary Internet files
settings"\n"Disable changing history settings"\n"Disable
changing color settings"\n"Disable changing link color
settings"\n"Disable changing font settings"\n"
Disable changing language settings"\n"Disable changing
accessibility settings""
```

The above file has been edited for length, because the actual file is approximately 50 pages long. Various important features of the ADM file are explained here:

- **CLASS**—The first entry in an ADM file. The valid classes are **USER** and **MACHINE**; they refer to policies that apply under the User Configuration or Computer Configuration node of a GPO.

- **CATEGORY**—The category name, which follows the class. The category is displayed as a node in the Computer Configuration or User Configuration node of a GPO (depending on whether **CLASS** is defined as **MACHINE** or **USER**). One of the sections in the sample inetres.adm file is User Configuration\Administrative Templates\Windows Components\Internet Explorer. Figure 11-8 shows what this section looks like in the Group Policy Editor.

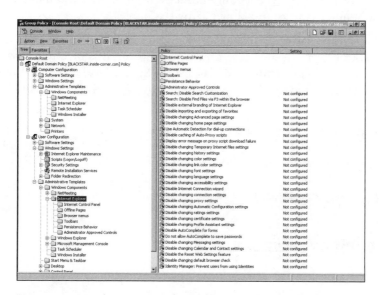

Figure 11-8   The Group Policy Editor graphically displays the settings defined in an ADM file

- **POLICY**—The heart of the ADM file: the defined policies that can be modified through the Group Policy Editor. Common values you will specify under **POLICY** include **VALUENAME**, which defines the options available within a policy, and **KEYNAME**, which references the Registry key that holds the current state of the value.

- **EXPLAIN**—Used to provide contextual help for a particular policy. You can specify a short text string contained within quotation marks, or reference a different explanation section. Notice in the inetres.adm example that the **EXPLAIN** referenced within the policy simply points to a longer explanation section contained at the end of the file.

- **STRING**—Can be used in an ADM file to define text strings for the user interface. For example, notice in the sample inetres.adm file how the **[strings]** section is used to provide text that appears in the user interface referenced by the **POLICY** keys earlier.

- **PART**—Although not used in inetres.adm, can be used to specify various user interface options, such as text boxes and drop-down lists.

- **PartTypes**—Used in conjunction with **PART**. **PartTypes** include advanced user interface items such as combo boxes, checkboxes, alphanumeric text boxes, drop-down lists, and list boxes.

- **NUMERIC**—Can be used to enhance the configuration options that can be performed through the Group Policy Editor user interface. **NUMERIC** displays an edit field that accepts only numeric input. It can also include an optional spinner control (up-down arrows).

In most cases, the administrative templates included with Windows 2000 provide a sufficient level of control over the user environment. However, it is nice to know that, as an administrator, you can add custom templates for a higher level of control over specific aspects of your environment. Adding (or removing) administrative templates is an easy process:

1. Right-click on the appropriate Administrative Templates node (Computer Configuration or User Configuration) and choose Add/Remove Templates. Doing so brings up the dialog box shown in Figure 11-9.

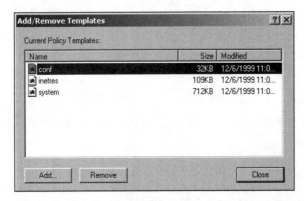

Figure 11-9 It is easy to add or remove administrative templates through the Group Policy Editor

2. Click on the Add button to bring up the dialog box shown in Figure 11-10.

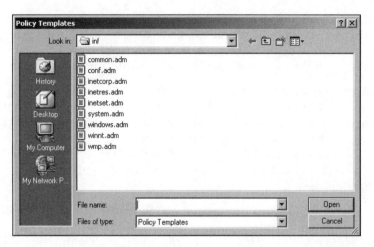

Figure 11-10   Adding an administrative template is a matter of browsing for and choosing the desired ADM file

3. Once you have browsed for and found the desired ADM file, simply select it and click on Open. The nodes will be added under the Administrative Templates nodes as defined by the **CATEGORY** keys within the ADM file.

Computer Templates

The Administrative Templates node under the Computer Configuration node of a GPO stores changes affecting the HKEY_LOCAL_MACHINE portion of the Registry. As you saw previously, the node is built from ADM files that define the appearance of the administrator-configurable settings in the Group Policy Editor. In this section, we will define the default nodes within the Computer Configuration Administrative Templates node. They are:

- Windows Components
- System
- Network
- Printers

Windows Components

The Windows Components node contains policies that can be configured for several items, as follows:

- *NetMeeting*—Contains settings for the collaborative NetMeeting utility that apply to the entire computer. The administrator can disable the ability to remotely share the desktop in the NetMeeting program.

- *Internet Explorer*—Contains computer-based settings for Internet Explorer (IE), including whether IE should automatically check for updates, automatically install missing components, make proxy settings apply at the machine level rather than the user level, and control security zones.

- *Task Scheduler*—Contains policies that allow you to exercise control over what a user can do with the Task Scheduler. The Task Scheduler enables regular users of a computer to configure tasks that are run at a specified time. For example, you might want to configure certain tasks on the machine and prevent the user from modifying or deleting the tasks. In addition, policies can be set to disallow the creation of new tasks and to prevent access by users to specified features such as the Advanced menu.

- *Windows Installer*—Contains settings for the Windows Installer program that will apply to all applications on the computer. Some of the settings include whether Windows 2000 should always install programs with elevated privileges (allows non-administrators to execute and install Windows Installer packages), whether the rollback feature should be enabled or disabled, how much logging should be performed, and so on. Windows Installer is discussed in detail in the Chapter 12, where we talk about managing software with Group Policy.

System

The System node is sort of a catchall for policies that don't quite fit into other sections. The root of the System folder contains settings for autoplaying CDs; displaying the Welcome screen when logging in to Windows; displaying messages during boot, logon, logoff, and shutdown; and enabling the Run Once and Legacy Run features. In addition to these settings, the following subnodes appear under the System node:

- *Logon*—Contains policy settings that influence how the system operates during user logon. Settings include whether to run scripts synchronously or asynchronously, whether scripts should be run visibly, and how the system should respond if it detects a slow network connection or previously cached profiles.

- *Disk Quotas*—Contains settings related to disk quotas, such as whether they should be enforced, default quota limits for the computer, and what kind of logging should be performed when quotas are reached.

- *DNS Client*—Contains settings that are applied to the Domain Name System (DNS) clients of the computer (specifically, the primary DNS suffix to be applied).

- *Group Policy*—Contains settings that control how Group Policy behaves and is applied to the computer. Figure 11-11 illustrates the Group Policy options.

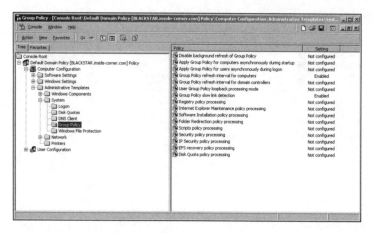

Figure 11-11   The Group Policy node of Administrative Templates contains important settings for how Group Policy behaves on a system

- *Windows File Protection*—Contains settings that control how often protected files are scanned and allow you to specify cache settings for protected files.

Network

The Network node of Administrative Templates contains settings related to network functionality. Two subnodes appear below Network, as follows:

- *Offline Files*—Contains settings that control how the Offline Files feature of Windows 2000 works. Offline Files is a feature that makes local copies of user files stored on a network file server for use when the system is disconnected from the network. This feature is most useful for mobile users who work in the office during the day, and then take their laptops home so as to work during the evenings and on weekends. By default, Offline Files is enabled on Windows 2000 Professional and disabled on Windows 2000 Server.

- *Network And Dialup Connections*—In the Computer Configuration node, this Administrative Templates subnode defines whether connection sharing is allowed on the machine.

Printers

The Printers node, shown in Figure 11-12, contains settings governing the behavior of printers. This node has no subnodes, although you can configure a number of policy settings. These settings include whether printers can be published to Active Directory, whether Web-based printing should be enabled, and whether printer browsing is allowed, among others. These settings apply mainly to printers' ability to be networked and shared.

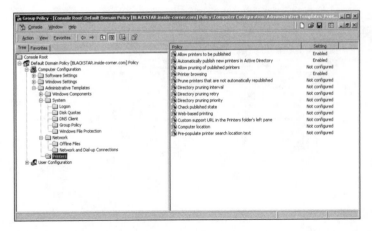

Figure 11-12   The Printers node allows an administrator to configure policy settings for printers

User Templates

Even more than computer templates, the administrative templates found under the User Configuration node in the Group Policy Editor will aid you as an administrator in configuring desktop settings. The settings within this node are geared toward helping you lock down the user environment in various ways. Let's take a look at the available nodes. In some cases, the names of nodes are the same as under Computer Configuration; however, the settings are aimed at users rather than at the computer as a whole.

The following nodes exist by default in Administrative Templates under the User Configuration node:

- Windows Components
- Start Menu & Taskbar
- Desktop
- Control Panel
- Network
- System

As you can see from Figure 11-13, many more subnodes appear under Administrative Templates in the User Configuration container than in the Computer Configuration container.

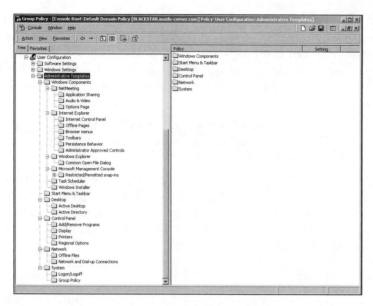

Figure 11-13   A plethora of settings are available in Administrative Templates under the User Configuration container

Windows Components

Windows Components serves much the same function as it does in the Computer Configuration node of Group Policy. It contains settings related to the following components:

- *NetMeeting*—Contains settings related to the NetMeeting application. Three subnodes (Application Sharing, Audio & Video, and Options Page) contain additional settings for the program.

- *Internet Explorer*—Contains settings that govern the ability of the user to modify browser settings and configurations. In addition to policy settings in the root of this node, there are several subnodes: Internet Control Panel, Offline Pages, Browser menus, Toolbars, Persistent Behavior, and Administrator Approved Controls.

- *Windows Explorer*—Policy settings that relate directly to the look and feel of the shell and desktop. With these settings, you can configure such items as the ability to map network drives, view domain computers in My Network Places, use the File menu in Windows Explorer, access drives in My Computer, and search for files or computers, among others. A subnode under Windows Explorer lets you configure Common Open File Dialog settings.

- *Microsoft Management Console (MMC)*—Contains settings that specify the level of control a user can exercise over the MMC environment. Settings include whether the user can enter author mode in a console and if they can use more than the explicitly listed snap-ins. A subnode for Restricted/Permitted snap-ins allows you to define—on a snap-in by snap-in basis—what a user can and cannot use.

- *Task Scheduler*—Similar to the Task Scheduler settings under Computer Configuration, except that the settings apply at the user level rather than the machine level.

- *Windows Installer*—Contains user policy settings for the Windows Installer feature of Windows 2000, including whether packages can be rolled back and whether they should be installed with elevated privileges. This node is similar to the Windows Installer node under the Computer Configuration container, except that settings apply at the user level.

Start Menu & Taskbar

The Start Menu & Taskbar node contains settings that have the potential to strongly limit what a user can do with the Start menu and taskbar. You can lock down settings such as the Programs, Documents, and Favorites folders, the Run and Search commands, and the user's ability to log off or shut down the computer. The user can also be prevented from making changes to the Start menu and taskbar, and you can remove context menu items from the taskbar and control personalized menus. Through this node, you can wield tremendous power over what a user can do.

Desktop

The Desktop node, as the name implies, contains settings related to the desktop. The root of the node contains settings for actions such as removing icons from the desktop, preventing users from changing the My Documents path, and preventing user changes from being saved when they log off. Two subnodes appear below the Desktop node:

- *Active Desktop*—Contains settings to enable or disable various features of Active Desktop, such as the ability to add, remove, modify, or close items. You can also specify the wallpaper that the user should use.

- *Active Directory*—Contains settings related to the user's ability to interact with Active Directory, such as disabling the Find utility and hiding the Active Directory folder.

Control Panel

Along with the policy settings in Start Menu & Taskbar and Desktop, the settings in Control Panel combine to form the heart of a desktop-lockdown configuration. The settings in the root of Control Panel include the options to hide Control Panel altogether or simply to show or hide certain applets. In addition, there are several subnodes:

- *Add/Remove Programs*—Contains settings related to the Add/Remove Programs Control Panel applet, from whether the applet should be displayed at all to how functions within the applet behave, such as Change or Remove Programs or Add/Remove Windows Components.

- *Display*—Contains settings related to the Display applet in Control panel, such as whether the user can configure the appearance of the desktop and change video settings. You can force a particular look on the user's environment, including what screen saver to use (if any—it can be disabled, as well) and if it should be password protected.

- *Printers*—Contains settings that can prevent the user from adding or deleting printers and for specifying default Active Directory paths to begin searching for printers.

- *Regional Options*—Contains settings that govern the ability to change regional settings in Windows 2000.

Network

The Network node is very similar to its counterpart under the Computer Configuration node. It contains no settings in its root node, but has two subnodes:

- *Offline Files*—Contains settings that apply on a per-user basis with regard to offline file policies. This node is very similar to the Offline Files node in Computer Configuration.

- *Network And Dial-up Connections*—Contains settings that control what level of access users have to local area network (LAN) and Remote Access Service (RAS) settings. These settings include a user's ability to add, modify, or remove connections; and whether the user can configure advanced settings or preferences.

System

The System node contains policy settings that don't really fit into any other category. In the root of the node are options such as disabling Registry-editing tools, running only specified applications, and whether to display the welcome dialog box at logon. There are two subnodes, as follows:

- *Logon/Logoff*—Contains settings not only for logon/logoff behavior, but also for options available when you press Ctrl+Alt+Del. These include the ability of the administrator to disable the Lock Computer and Task Manager options, and limiting the user's ability to use various Run features during logon/logoff. You can also choose to make scripts run synchronously, which is generally not advised.

11

- *Group Policy*—Contains settings for the behavior of Group Policy as it applies to slow connections and refresh intervals, and whether the ability to create new Group Policy Objects should be disabled.

Using Folder Redirection to Move User Files to a Server

One of the powerful new features of Windows 2000 is folder redirection. Folder redirection comes as an extension within Group Policy; unlike other Group Policy nodes, however, the settings are not listed in the folders to be double-clicked. Instead, you access the settings by right-clicking on the folder and choosing Properties. The Folder Redirection node is located in the Group Policy Editor under the User Configuration container, below the Windows Settings node.

Folder redirection is essentially the process by which the operating system changes the location of certain Windows 2000 folders from the local hard drive to a specified network share. Only the following folders can be redirected:

- Application Data
- Desktop
- My Documents
- My Pictures
- Start Menu

When you right-click on one of these special folders in the Group Policy Editor and choose Properties, the first dialog box you see contains the target setting. By default, this setting is No Administrative Policy Set. You can change it to either of the following:

- *Basic—Redirect Everyone's Folder To The Same Location*—As the description implies, this policy will redirect all folders to the same network share. You can individualize the path by incorporating the *%username%* variable, such as specifying *server**share*\%*username*%\My Documents. Figure 11-14 shows an example of the Basic configuration redirecting My Documents to a server share.

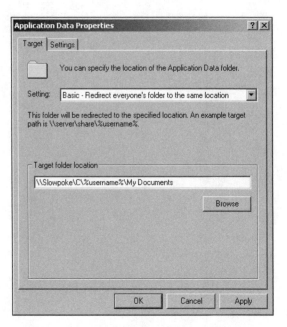

Figure 11-14   The Basic folder redirection policy allows you to specify a single location for everyone's redirected folders

■ *Advanced—Specify Locations For Various Groups*—The Advanced policy allows you to redirect folders based on security group memberships. Folders of members of one group can be directed to one share, and folders of members of another group can be redirected to a different share. Again, you can use the *%username%* variable in your path to establish individual folders for each user. Figure 11-15 shows an example of the Advanced folder redirection policy, and Figure 11-16 shows the dialog box that appears when you click on Add in Figure 11-15 to add a security group and its redirection path.

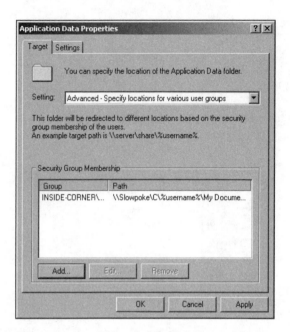

Figure 11-15 The Advanced folder redirection policy allows you to specify settings based on security group membership

Figure 11-16 When adding security groups to the Advanced policy, you can assign different target locations for redirection to different groups

Whether you're configuring a Basic or Advanced policy, you can configure additional settings for the folder redirection. Figure 11-17 shows these settings, which you access by clicking on the Settings tab.

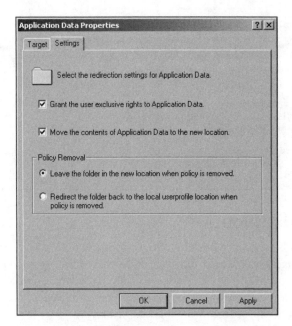

Figure 11-17   Additional settings can be configured for folder redirection

The following settings are available:

- *Grant The User Exclusive Rights To* <special folder>—This setting is enabled by default. It gives the user and the local system account full control, and gives no permissions to anyone else (even administrators).

- *Move The Contents Of* <special folder> *To The New Location*—This setting is enabled by default; <*special folder*> is the name of the folder being redirected.

- *Policy Removal*—You have the option either to leave the files in the new location when the policy is removed (default) or to have the files redirected back to their original location.

Folder Redirection Notes

As you've learned, only a few special folders can be redirected in Windows 2000. You need to consider a few things, however, when redirecting folders. Table 11.3 provides additional information about some of the special folders.

Table 11-3 Notes about special folders

Special Folder	Notes
Application Data	This folder is controlled by the Group Policy User Configuration setting under Administrative templates\Network\Offline Files when caching is enabled.
My Documents	My Documents contains a subfolder called My Pictures, which can be redirected independently of My Documents or follow along with it (default).
Start Menu	If you choose to redirect the Start menu, all subfolders will automatically be redirected, as well.

Advantages of Folder Redirection

In general, folder redirection is beneficial when the redirection will take place over a fast network connection, because users will always have access to their files no matter where they log on. This is especially true of the My Documents folder. Combined with offline files technology, even mobile users can enjoy the benefits of having network folder redirection along with synchronized copies stored on their hard drives.

Another benefit of folder redirection from an administrative perspective is backups. Most environments do not back up user hard drives. When a drive crashes, data is typically lost if the user hasn't proactively backed up to a Zip drive, floppy disk, or similar removable media. By having folders redirected to the servers, the data is backed up and can be restored if a user accidentally deletes a file.

In most environments, folder redirection is a practical way to enhance the availability and integrity of user data. In the Real-World Projects at the end of the chapter, you'll put folder redirection into practice.

CHAPTER SUMMARY

In this chapter, you learned about scripts, administrative templates, and folder redirection—all features that allow an administrator to exercise a high level of control over the user environment. Using Group Policy, you can force settings on the desktop to provide a consistent look and feel across an enterprise. We also discussed the following:

◻ Windows 2000 includes Windows Scripting Host, a powerful engine for running VBScript and JavaScript scripts natively.

◻ WScript is the graphical version of WSH.

◻ CScript is the command-line version of WSH.

◻ WSH 2 WSF files support XML natively for building scripts.

❏ Windows 2000 supports executing scripts at computer startup and shutdown, and at user logon and logoff.

❏ Scripts can be assigned through the Group Policy Editor.

❏ Administrative templates are the primary mechanism for applying Group Policy settings to control user environment settings.

❏ Administrative templates can apply at the computer or user level.

❏ You can create custom ADM files to extend the scope of administrative templates.

❏ Start Menu & Taskbar, Desktop, and Control Panel administrative templates are the primary means of controlling the desktop through Group Policy.

❏ Folder redirection allows you to redirect Windows 2000 special folders from the local hard drives of users to network shares.

11

12

DEPLOYING AND MANAGING SOFTWARE BY USING GROUP POLICY

After completing this chapter, you will be able to:

♦ Understand IntelliMirror components and change and configuration management concepts

♦ Understand the phases of software management

♦ Create and configure Windows Installer packages

♦ Manage software deployment through the Software Installation MMC snap-in

♦ Patch software using the Windows Installer Package Editor

To this point, we have discussed a couple of the key components of change and configuration management: user data management (folder redirection) and user environment management. In this chapter, we move into the final phase: software installation and maintenance.

Windows 2000, unlike its NT predecessors, provides the ability to manage software throughout an organization by using a centralized Group Policy–based management system. This management system reduces total cost of ownership (TCO) for an organization, because it allows software to be efficiently managed remotely, without you having to go to every separate computer in order to make changes. Remote management reduces the number of support personnel that must be kept on staff, which translates into cost savings for a company.

In this chapter, we will examine the components of a software installation and management strategy, from basic concepts through best practices. In between, you'll learn how to build Windows Installer packages and how to install, patch, and remove software through Group Policy. Without further ado, let's begin!

INTELLIMIRROR COMPONENTS AND CHANGE AND CONFIGURATION MANAGEMENT CONCEPTS

The last several chapters have focused extensively on topics that make up the area known as **change and configuration management**, which is a collection of ideas and strategies for reducing TCO and increasing return on investment (ROI). Although these may sound like topics better suited for the bean counters in the company, it has become increasingly important for the IT professional to be business savvy and to be able to evaluate IT needs from business perspectives. Change and configuration management includes tasks such as documentation and (as the name implies) managing changes and configurations within an organization. That may sound a little redundant, so let's examine this concept further.

From an IT perspective, change within a company usually refers to new hardware and software being deployed; configuration generally refers to the standard configuration of hardware and software. Managing change involves strategic planning for prepared change (rolling out new equipment) and responsiveness for unplanned change (for example, the server network interface card [NIC] goes bad and is replaced by a newer model NIC). Managing configurations typically involves maintenance and support—for example, responding to a help desk call when a user inadvertently deletes several key system files. Why is change and configuration management so important? The answer is easy to find: Just look at the bottom line of the general ledger.

As we said previously, the goal of change and configuration management is to reduce TCO and increase ROI. An example of a real-world situation dealing with TCO issues can help illustrate why these objectives are so important.

Hard versus Soft Costs

Many IT professionals never consider the **soft costs** of an IT infrastructure, but rather look only at the **hard costs** (the initial cost of the equipment). For example, say you buy 500 new systems at $2,500 each. The hard cost is $1.25 million for those systems. But also consider that users are being paid to utilize the systems, and a staff of IT professionals is being paid to support them. Say one of your systems crashes, for whatever reason, causing an IT staff member to have to go to the user's office and fix the computer. A cost is associated with this event, because the user's salary is paid during the downtime when he cannot work, and the IT staff member's salary is paid even though she is unavailable for work on other projects while spending time fixing the computer. Depending on the type and number of problems a company has on any given day, the number of IT staff required to support the computers grows. The costs of support and lost productivity increase the TCO of the computer to a number far higher than the initial $2,500 spent on each computer. These are the soft costs associated with information technologies, and it is often extremely difficult to place an exact dollar figure on these costs.

Many businesses now demand that IT departments function more as business units and less as cost centers. Therefore, although IT doesn't generate direct revenue like a sales staff, it can dramatically reduce expenditures and increase productivity through change and configuration management.

Windows 2000 supports a number of new change and configuration management features that enable a company to realize tremendous savings in TCO. The entire next chapter is devoted to one of the features, Remote Installation Services (RIS). The other tool is a collection of features collectively referred to as **IntelliMirror**.

IntelliMirror

IntelliMirror is a feature of Windows 2000 that seeks to increase the availability of Windows 2000–based computers while decreasing TCO. In the past, you may have heard of IntelliMirror as Zero Administration Windows (ZAW), which was Microsoft's original initiative to create a managed desktop environment under Windows. IntelliMirror relies on a combination of Active Directory and Group Policy in order to be deployed, and it consists of three key features. We have already discussed two of these features at great length, and the third feature is the focus of this chapter.

The features of IntelliMirror are:

- *Data management*—Data management is implemented in Windows 2000, as we have seen, through folder redirection. When folder redirection and offline folders are used, user data can be synchronized between a server copy and a local copy, ensuring that data files are accessible no matter where users are and what computer they log on from.

- *Desktop settings management*—Desktop settings can be stored in profiles that roam with a user so that they are applied whenever a user logs in to a networked computer. Group Policy is used to control what settings should be stored and can control a user's ability to make changes to desktop settings.

- *Software installation and maintenance*—The focus of this chapter, this feature of IntelliMirror allows applications to be published by an administrator for use by defined users, computers, and groups. Windows Installer applications can even be set up to replace corrupt or missing files automatically. Doing so reduces downtime associated with broken applications that would ordinarily require an IT staff member to go to a workstation and manually reinstall the application.

The great advantage of using IntelliMirror technologies is that usually users don't know what is happening behind the scenes. The automation that IntelliMirror provides often avoids problems that would otherwise require intervention from a desktop support technician. In addition, IntelliMirror can provide a consistent computing experience for users no matter what computer or location they log on from, which is something that could not be done in the past.

12

A Real-World Example

To illustrate the effectiveness of IntelliMirror technologies, here's a real-life example of how employing IntelliMirror dramatically enhanced the end-user experience and decreased TCO for a company.

The company I work for is a fairly standard Microsoft shop, using BackOffice on the back end and a mixture of NT 4 Workstation and Windows 98 on the front end. We had about a dozen outside sales people who would come into the office periodically; usually, at least two or three would be in the office each day. When meetings were held, they took place in the office. Because the sales staff was outside sales, they worked from their homes rather than having cubicles or offices at the corporate location. When they were in the office, however, they needed to be able to check their e-mail from whatever computer they could beg, borrow, or steal for a few minutes.

Our e-mail environment uses Exchange Server and Outlook 2000, and with Outlook one must configure an e-mail profile in order to access the e-mail account. Dealing with e-mail profiles was a constant support issue. Either a salesperson would configure and change the default profile of a computer, causing the regular users of the PC to get an error when they came back to their PC, or the salesperson would not know how to create a profile and would require assistance. Because a particular salesperson did not always use the same computer when in the office, it was difficult to ensure that the salespeople could always access their e-mail, short of going to each computer and creating e-mail profiles for every salesperson. If we had done this, we would have had to train both the sales staff and the regular users on how to manipulate profiles, in order to ensure that the correct profile was selected for a given user. In addition, whenever there was a personnel change, the process would have to be repeated. This would definitely be a high-maintenance process, which would have driven up TCO for our e-mail system.

Our initial solution, before Windows 2000, was to attempt to use the Outlook Web Access (OWA) feature of Exchange Server and Internet Information Server (IIS), which allows users to access their e-mail accounts through Internet Explorer. Because of certain performance and security issues with OWA, however, that solution was abandoned.

After upgrading our network to Windows 2000, we were able to use IntelliMirror to create a situation in which the IT staff did not have to intervene to ensure that whoever logged into a computer got the correct e-mail profile. Sales staff members, regular users, or anyone else with a valid domain account could log on to any computer on the network, and their settings would automatically be applied. The specific IntelliMirror technologies we used to make this happen were:

- *Active Directory*—The cornerstone. Without AD, none of the rest would be possible.

- *Group Policy*—Through Group Policy, we could manage desktop settings and determine what to apply and where.

- *Roaming user profiles*—Through roaming profiles, we were able to ensure that when users logged in to a computer, their settings were applied. This was the key to having e-mail profiles follow their owners.

- *Folder redirection*—In addition to profiles, we redirected user folders to a network share so they would be backed up. As you learned in Chapter 11, folder direction is not applied over slow links; so it was not in effect for the sales staff when they dialed in from home over 56Kbps modems.

- *Offline folders*—In addition to the outside sales staff, some users work both in the office and at home or on the road. These users have laptops, and we were able to use offline folders in conjunction with folder redirection to ensure they have full access to their files regardless of whether they are in the office on the LAN or working offline on an airplane.

As you can see, IntelliMirror technologies increased the availability of resources to a variety of types of users, while reducing the support burden on the IT staff at the same time. Since implementing IntelliMirror, the IT staff has been able to focus on more time-intensive projects that were difficult to complete in the past due to the support volume. Because we are able to better use our staff's time, we have translated the increased productivity into cost savings, which ultimately has led to better bonuses for each of us (the company uses a profit-sharing pool). Both users and IT staff members are happier on a day-to-day basis, as well. The users are happier because they get a consistent computing experience and do not have to call the help desk as often, and the IT staff is happier because they don't have to perform as many desktop support tasks and can spend time on more interesting projects.

Having already covered data management and settings management, we will spend the rest of this chapter discussing the software installation and management aspect of IntelliMirror.

12

UNDERSTANDING THE PHASES OF SOFTWARE MANAGEMENT

This section will present a high-level overview of software management by taking you through the stages—or phases—of the deployment of a new software application. Breaking down software management into phases provides a systematic, repeatable method for upgrading and deploying software in an organization. Your high school science teacher probably talked frequently about systematic methods for scientific experiments, in which the goal is to perform an experiment in a way that can be repeated each time and provide consistent results. That is essentially what we are doing in the IT world: We want to devise procedures that we can follow every time we roll out a new application and that will give us the positive results we are looking for.

The phases of software management that we will discuss here are:

- Preparation phase
- Distribution phase

- Targeting phase
- Pilot phase
- Installation phase

Preparation Phase

The preparation phase of software management consists of the initial information collecting process. This phase includes analyzing your organization's structure to determine its software requirements. In addition, you will need to determine how many licenses you must purchase in order to be legal, and decide how users will access the software. The following are some of the questions you will need to answer during the preparation phase:

- Will the software be loaded on a central server that users will access, or will the software be installed locally on users' computers? The answer to this question will help determine capacity requirements on the servers and workstations, and will dictate how the application is set up for distribution.

- What users will need access to the new application? If not everyone needs access, you must arrange through Active Directory and Group Policy for the required users to have access while ensuring that users who shouldn't have the application do not have access. You might have to create additional Organizational Units (OUs) based on software needs.

- Do you have enough licenses or will you need to purchase additional ones? This is an important question, because you do not want to get caught in a situation where you are short on software licenses. There are plenty of horror stories about companies paying extensive fines for using unlicensed software, and you don't need or want your company to become one of them.

- Will the network infrastructure support the deployment design you are considering? For example, if you have multiple locations connected by wide-area network (WAN) links, you won't be able to run server-based applications from one or more central servers at one location. You will need to deploy these applications to remote servers so that all users who should have access to the application are running it over a local-area network (LAN) connection. If applications will be installed directly to users' hard drives, you will need to plan for local distribution points so that software is not installed over a slow WAN connection.

Assigned or Published?

One other key question to consider is whether the application will be assigned directly to users or published into Active Directory. When an application is assigned, its icons appear in the Start menu or on the desktop of the user's computer according to criteria defined by the administrator. The first time a user attempts to launch an assigned application, the software is automatically installed without user or administrator intervention. If a user later uninstalls the application through the Add/Remove Programs applet in Control Panel, the software will still be available to the user the next time he or she logs on. If a user attempts to launch a program he or she thought had been uninstalled, the software will simply reinstall itself and open. Because the software has been assigned to the user, the user cannot get rid of it. The advantage to this arrangement is that users cannot break assigned applications; rather, the software is self-healing, without requiring a traditional visit from an IT staff member to repair it through manual reinstallation.

On the other hand, administrators can also choose to simply publish applications into the Active Directory rather than assigning them directly to users. Assigned applications are typically used when users need a particular application to do their job. Published applications are not necessarily required by users to do their jobs, but they are beneficial applications that the administrator wants to make available. A published application shows up in Add/Remove Programs but must be explicitly installed by the user. No icons appear in the Start menu or on the desktop in advance to inform users of the application's availability, and if a user uninstalls the application, it is removed from the computer just as an application would be after a traditional uninstall procedure.

In addition to answering the previous questions, during this preparation phase an administrator prepares the software for distribution. This process includes creating any necessary Windows Installer packages (discussed later in this chapter).

Distribution Phase

Once all of the planning and preparing has been completed, you are ready to move on to the distribution phase. In this phase, you define network locations, called **distribution points** in Windows 2000, which will hold the software you want to deploy. Essentially, the main task of the distribution phase is to get the software to the distribution points from which they can be installed.

Distribution points are simply network locations from which users can install software. Creating a distribution point is a matter of creating network shares with the appropriate permissions, and then copying the installation files for an application to the share. For ease of administration and ease of use, you should create subfolders for each application you are making available.

After creating your distribution points, you must either copy the installation files to the distribution points or (in the case of some applications) perform an administrative installation to the distribution points. Administrative installations usually involve invoking a special switch to the command line, such as **setup /a** in the case of Microsoft Office 97. This type of installation allows you to customize certain options as an administrator when you distribute the installation files to a distribution point.

In general, administrators should have full control permissions over the distribution points, and users should have read permissions.

12

Software Deployment Options

Windows 2000 can distribute Windows Installer packages through the Software Installation snap-in in Group Policy. The limitation, of course, is that Group Policy is supported only on Windows 2000 clients. In addition, Software Installation can support only the deployment of Windows Installer packages. Because not all applications are Windows Installer compatible (and hence Windows 2000 certified), you will often run into applications that cannot be deployed through these means. If you want to distribute non–Windows Installer applications or to distribute to Windows 9x or Windows NT 4 clients, you can use Microsoft Systems Management Server (SMS). The use of SMS is outside the scope of this book, but suffice it to say that it provides a wealth of software deployment features well beyond what Windows 2000 can offer out of the box. In many environments, a combination of Windows 2000 Software Installation and SMS is appropriate.

Targeting Phase

Once the software has been distributed through copying or administrative installation to the various distribution points, you are ready to begin the targeting phase of software management. The emphasis during this phase is on determining the scope of management— that is, to determine the needs of the users.

To this point, you have analyzed to whom you want the software to go, and you have established the distribution points that hold the software to be deployed. Now, in the targeting phase, you use Group Policy to create and/or modify Group Policy Objects (GPOs) in order to target the software to specific users and groups. In addition, you begin to create a pilot program to test your deployment before actually going live with your rollout. (We discussed creating and modifying GPOs in Chapters 10 and 11; you can refer back if you have any questions about using GPOs to target settings at specific users, computers, and groups.)

The targeting phase involves extensive use of the Software Installation snap-in, which is discussed in detail later in this chapter. So, we'll hold off on a more involved discussion of targeting software.

Pilot Phase

Of all the phases involved in software management, the pilot phase most often gets short-changed in small to medium-sized organizations. A pilot program is a trial run deployed first in a lab environment and then to a subset of users, for the express purpose of troubleshooting and debugging any application issues prior to the full-blown deployment. A good pilot program will also provide the foundation for the ongoing maintenance of the software, from being able to apply patches or upgrades to being able to remove the application.

The pilot phase is often skimped on by smaller companies due to resource availability. Often, small to medium-sized companies cannot afford or choose not to carry extra inventory that can be used as a research and development (R&D) or test lab. Perfectly good computer systems that are not being used for productive means are a poor investment, in the minds of many small companies. What they do not realize, however, is that having a lab for testing new software, whether full applications or just upgrades or patches, actually carries the cost benefit of reducing downtime associated with rolling out applications into a production environment and troubleshooting live systems on the fly as users wait impatiently. Successfully piloting an application first strongly increases the likelihood of a successful deployment. If you work for a company that is hesitant to devote resources for pilot programs, ask management if they would consider receiving medical treatment if someone developed a drug and offered it directly to the public with no prior testing (disregard FDA regulations for a moment). Chances are, they will say absolutely not. So, why risk the health of their computer networks, on which their business relies, to software that has not been tested in your environment?

Elements of a Pilot Program

A pilot program begins in the lab, on non-production machines. Then it does not matter if the software crashes the computer and forces you to have to reinstall the operating system. Once the software is proven to work in your lab environment, you are ready to deploy it to a subset of the users on your network. Why deploy to only a subset of users and not everyone? Well, one thing every good administrator learns (often from experience) is that application behavior in a lab environment, no matter how closely the lab simulates the production environment, is often different than in the production environment. When you deploy to live users, you will invariably discover strange new issues with the software. It is much easier to troubleshoot and fix a software deployment to 20 users than it is to 2,000.

12

User Types

When considering the target group for the pilot, it is important to select a group that will be representative of the organization as a whole. They should run all the regular applications in use by the company and be the very definition of the average users. If you have mobile users who work from both home and the office, you should include someone from that group in the pilot and test the software under both conditions. Assemble your pilot group so that all the types of users you have in the organization are part of the process.

How to Test

A good pilot should test every possible manner in which you will deploy the software application. Will you be publishing the application to some users and assigning the application to other users? Will you be adding any custom files to the installation, such as templates? All of these elements need to be tested to ensure that they function correctly before the rollout.

In addition, the pilot is the opportunity to carry out performance testing on the software. If the application is installed locally to user hard drives, does it perform adequately for the average computer systems used by the company? Will some systems need upgrades to run the application more efficiently? If it is a network application, can the network handle the stress of multiple users running the application at once? Will you need to add server capacity, or possibly replace hubs with switches or segment your network with routers in order to make more efficient use of bandwidth? For obvious reasons, it is much better to answer these questions during the pilot program than to make a guess and spend money unnecessarily for upgrades you don't need. Even worse would be overestimating your capacity and watching production grind to a halt when users can't access the necessary resources, or when the applications perform so slowly that they might as well be unusable.

Installation Phase

Once you are satisfied that you've answered all the questions in the pilot program and you are confident of the application's ability to function as expected in your environment, you are ready to proceed to the installation phase. In this phase, you roll out the software across your organization to all users and computers who are set up to receive it.

The installation phase is invoked whenever you need to install an application fresh, update an existing application, or patch an existing application. For Windows 2000, usually you will use the Windows Installer to install software and manage an installation, unless you are dealing with third-party, non–Windows 2000-certified software. The Windows 2000 CD comes with the VERITAS WinINSTALL Discover utility, which can be installed separately. (Seagate owned WinINSTALL Discover before VERITAS bought it.) In some Microsoft (and non-Microsoft) references and documentation, you will see WinINSTALL Discover referred to as WinINSTALL LE, although in this chapter we will refer to it simply as WinINSTALL.

WinINSTALL enables you, as the administrator, to create or modify Windows Installer packages and to repackage third-party software as Windows Installer packages. There are some limitations to this process, however, as we will see in the next section.

CREATING AND CONFIGURING WINDOWS INSTALLER PACKAGES

Later in this chapter, you will learn how to deploy software on your Windows 2000 network, but for now let's take a look at actually creating some software packages to deploy. Windows 2000 includes the Windows Installer file format as its default software installation packaging, a format first introduced with the Microsoft Office 2000 suite. In this section, we will discuss the following aspects of the Windows Installer:

- Windows Installer technology overview
- Managing Windows Installer settings with Group Policy
- Creating Windows Installer packages with WinINSTALL LE

Windows Installer Technology Overview

As we've briefly mentioned already, Windows Installer is a client-side technology that allows for a more intelligent software deployment than has been available in the past. Windows Installer technology is built in to Windows 2000; unlike many of the new technologies, however, it can also be used in Windows 9*x* and NT 4. Office 2000 was the first released product to incorporate the Windows Installer technology, and other applications have followed. In fact, in order for an application to be certified as Windows 2000 compatible, it must use the Windows Installer.

When a Windows Installer package is installed for the first time on a Windows 9*x* or NT 4 system, Windows Installer technology is installed and configured on the computer in order to support the software installation. Microsoft provides a freely redistributable installation program called instmsi.exe to enable Windows Installer support on these platforms. Because Windows Installer is already on Windows 2000 systems, no updates are needed prior to the application installation.

We say that Windows Installer allows for a more intelligent software deployment than has been available in the past because of the new features it provides. They are:

- *Software diagnostics and repair*—Windows Installer makes the concept of self-healing applications a reality. If a user accidentally deletes a critical application DLL file, for example, Windows Installer will automatically recognize this action and replace the missing file from the installation source files. In the past, this type of error would have been a show stopper, and almost invariably it would have resulted in a support call and a trip from a desktop support technician to reinstall the application.

- *Complete uninstallation of software*—Often in the past, uninstalling a program from your system resulted in numerous files, directories, and Registry settings being left behind by the removal program. These orphaned files were, at minimum, an annoyance that wasted disk space and memory resources. In some cases, orphaned DLL files could interact with other programs and cause problems that were difficult to diagnose. Sometimes, the uninstall process would remove shared files that were used by other programs, causing those programs to no longer function correctly. Windows Installer manages the entire installation process, so it is able to remove a program completely should you choose to uninstall it. Windows Installer also prevents shared files from being removed, because it knows which other Windows Installer applications might be using those files.

- *Multiplatform capability*—Unlike traditional installation programs that package software for a particular platform (such as Windows, MacOS, or Solaris), Windows Installer technology enables developers to create a single installation package that can install the software on different platforms and in different configurations. This ability reduces the amount of overhead associated with packaging an application for distribution.

12

Now you know what the Windows Installer is capable of. Let's see what a Windows Installer package is.

Windows Installer Packages

A Windows Installer package is an MSI file that contains instructions pertaining to the installation and removal of an application. The package comes in the format of a relational database, and it contains all the information necessary to manage the program's installation.

In addition to MSI files, a Windows Installer routine can also include MST files, which are known as **transforms**. A transform is used to customize the installation of an application, changing it from its default behavior. This file is put in the same installation directory as the MSI file, and it can be modified at any time.

Windows Installer uses a transaction-based system similar to that used in Active Directory and Microsoft Exchange Server. A transaction-based system writes changes one at a time, so that at any point of failure, the installation can be rolled back to its prior state. This is a great feature for administrators, who have long suffered the pain of having an application's installation program crash and leave temporary files and a half-installed application on the hard drive and in the Registry with no easy means of removing them. With Windows Installer, a failed installation will simply roll back to its state prior to the installation's beginning. You will learn how to package programs with third-party Windows Installer packager later in this chapter.

Windows Installer settings can be managed with the Group Policy Editor. We'll look at this process next.

Managing Windows Installer Settings with Group Policy

Windows Installer has global settings in Windows 2000 that affect the way it behaves when Windows Installer–compatible software is installed. These settings are managed on a GPO basis through the Group Policy Editor. As you will remember from the last couple of chapters, GPOs are assigned to computers, users, and groups. If you want to have Windows Installer settings that act globally in your Active Directory, edit the default domain policy GPO when configuring the settings.

As we've discussed previously, in many cases Group Policy settings can be applied either to computers (the Computer Configuration container) or to users (User Configuration). That is the case with Windows Installer, which uses different settings depending on whether you are configuring the policies for computers or users. Figures 12-1 and 12-2 illustrate these differences.

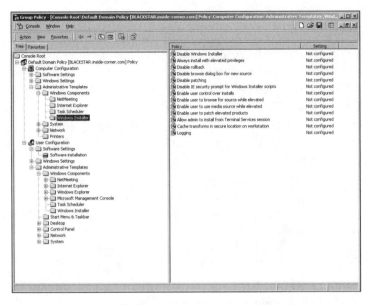

Figure 12-1   The Windows Installer settings for computers

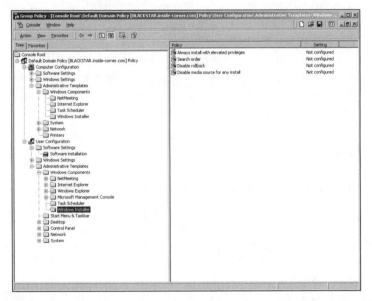

Figure 12-2   The Windows Installer settings for users

12

Some of the key settings include:

- *Always Install With Elevated Privileges*—Available under both the Computer and User Configuration containers; allows Windows Installer packages to be installed with administrator privileges. These privileges are usually required in order to install software on a Windows 2000 system, because an ordinary user account cannot make changes to the Registry.

- *Disable Media Source For Any Install*—When enabled, prevents ordinary user accounts from being able to install software from removable media drives (CD or floppy disk, typically).

- *Enable User To Use Media Source While Elevated*—Enables or disables a user's ability to install software from removable media under elevated permissions. This setting is used in conjunction with Disable Media Source For Any Install to prevent users from installing their own software from CD or floppy disk. The purpose is to keep users from loading unauthorized software on their systems (a common problem in many companies).

- *Disable Windows Installer*—Restricts a user's ability to install Windows Installer–packaged software. There are three settings: Never, which fully enables Windows Installer (the default setting); For Non-Managed Apps Only, which allows users to install only applications assigned or published by the administrator; and Always, which prevents users from installing any Windows Installer–based application at all.

Typically, you won't need to restrict Windows Installer settings unless you are working in a high-security environment. The only setting that we recommend configuring for the average environment is Always Install With Elevated Privileges. For most organizations, this convenience saves many support calls while posing a minimal amount of security risk.

In addition to managing Windows Installer settings, you can also create your own Windows Installer packages.

Creating Windows Installer Packages with Win INSTALL LE

As we discussed earlier in this chapter, Windows 2000 Server offers the third-party program WinINSTALL LE from VERITAS Software. This program can be installed from the \VALUEADD\3RDPARTY\MGMT\WINSTLE folder on the installation CD. Two components are installed: VERITAS Discover (WinINSTALL Discover) and VERITAS Software Console. The Software Console contains the Windows Installer Package Editor, which we will discuss later in this chapter. In this section, we will focus on WinINSTALL Discover, which will allow you to create a new Windows Installer package. In our example, we will create a package for WinZip 8.0. (WinZip 8.0 is available from WinZip Computing, Inc. WinZip is a registered trademark of WinZip Computing, Inc. [copyright 1991–2000], and is available from www.winzip.com. WinZip screen images are reproduced with permission of WinZip Computing, Inc.)

Before creating a package, you must keep in mind an important consideration. As a rule, you should use a clean operating system to create a package—that is, one that does not already have a bunch of other applications installed. The reason is that usually, a software installation program will not copy a file to a hard drive if a newer version exists. If you create a package on a system that has a particular application other systems do not have, and you then deploy the package to other systems, you might find that your package does not work on those other systems due to missing files. Also, for the package-creation process, you should use a system that is representative of the average computer on your network. The more like other computers your development system is, the more likely you are to end up with a good Windows Installer package that works flawlessly on other systems.

Creating a new Windows Installer package—an MSI file—first involves launching the WinINSTALL Discover application from the Start menu. Figure 12-3 shows the screen you will first see.

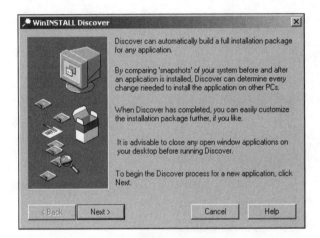

Figure 12-3   The WinINSTALL Discover welcome describes the Windows Installer package creation process

When you click on Next, you will be prompted to supply the filename for your new package. As a reminder, Windows Installer packages have an .msi extension. Supply a descriptive filename for your package and choose the directory the file will be saved in, as in Figure 12-4.

On the next screen, shown in Figure 12-5, you will find that the path and filename for the new package are already filled in from your choices on the previous screen. You can modify those choices now, if you want. In addition, you are prompted to name the application. This name will become the display title in the Add/Remove Programs applet. You can also change the language setting if necessary. Click on Next.

12

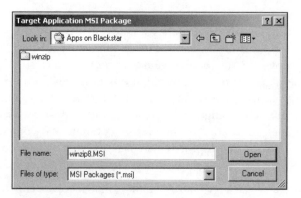

Figure 12-4 The first step in creating a package is to name the MSI file and choose an appropriate directory in which to store the new package

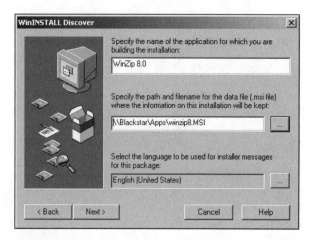

Figure 12-5 The next step in creating a new package is to name your application and verify that the path and filename are correct

After naming your application, you are prompted for the drive that WinINSTALL Discover will use to store temporary files during the package creation process. You should choose a drive that contains plenty of free disk space, depending on the application. Figure 12-6 illustrates this dialog box.

The next step is to determine what drives WinINSTALL should check for changes, as shown in Figure 12-7. In our example, we have chosen to have WinINSTALL scan drives C: and E:, because we intend to install our application to C:, and E: is the drive where our Windows 2000 operating system is installed. D: is strictly a data drive in our configuration, so we have chosen to skip scanning it for changes. In most cases, you will probably want WinINSTALL to scan all local hard drives just to make sure no changes slip by.

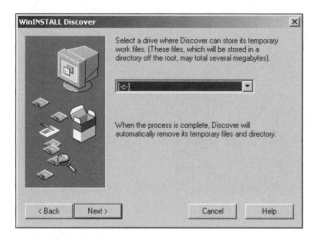

Figure 12-6   You must choose a drive to store temporary working files for
WinINSTALL Discover

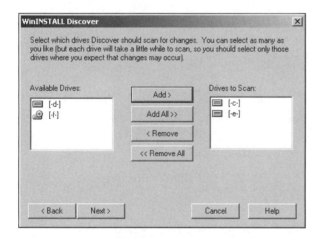

Figure 12-7   WinINSTALL Discover will scan the drives you choose for changes made
during the application installation

WinINSTALL then asks if you want to exclude any files or folders from the scan, as illustrated in Figure 12-8. You should choose to exclude obvious files like pagefile.sys, because they could change during the installation and you wouldn't want them included as part of your distribution. Another likely candidate to exclude would be the Recycle Bin. Make your choices and click on Next.

Next, WinINSTALL will begin to scan with the criteria you specified, as shown in Figure 12-9. Once the scan is complete, you will receive the dialog box shown in Figure 12-10. The initial "before" scan will look at every file on your hard drives (those that you specified for scanning) and every Registry setting. After the application is installed, an "after" scan will run on the same drives and Registry and compare the before and after states. The changes that occurred between the two scans are compiled into the Windows Installer package.

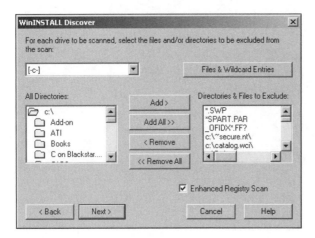

Figure 12-8   WinINSTALL allows you to exclude files and folders that could possibly change during installation but that should not be included with the distribution

Figure 12-9   WinINSTALL takes a snapshot of the current state of your system before running the application installation

Figure 12-10   Once the initial scan is complete, WinINSTALL will begin the application installation process

After you click on OK in the dialog box in Figure 12-10, you are prompted to choose your application's installation program. Figure 12-11 shows this dialog box.

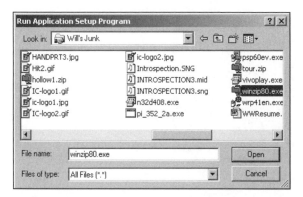

Figure 12-11   To begin installation of your application, simply navigate to the source directory and select its setup program

The application installation proceeds at this point, as it would if you were installing the application normally and not building a Windows Installer package. Install the program as you want it to be configured for your package, with any desired options. Once you have installed the program, *do not* reboot if you are prompted to. If you reboot, Registry changes or file updates might be committed that would not be possible later when you are installing the package on another machine, causing that installation to fail. If the program requires a reboot, it has Registry entries that execute and complete the updates upon reboot. You want future machines receiving this package to be able to make these updates as well, to ensure a successful installation.

Rather than reboot, choose to return to Windows or to restart later, whatever the wording might be. WinINSTALL has exited at this point, so relaunch it through the Start menu. You will then see the dialog box shown in Figure 12-12, which gives you the option of discarding your package or continuing with the "after" snapshot.

As shown in Figure 12-13, WinINSTALL repeats the scanning process to determine the differences between pre-installation and post-installation. Once the snapshot is complete, the dialog box in Figure 12-14 appears, advising you that your Windows Installer package has been successfully created.

With your package created, you are ready to use the Software Installation Group Policy snap-in to manage and deploy it.

12

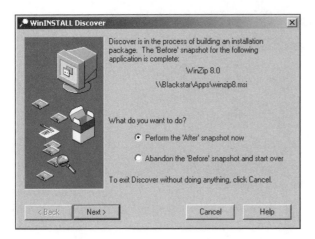

Figure 12-12 You can now continue your package creation by performing the "after" snapshot on your system

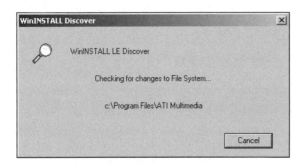

Figure 12-13 WinINSTALL repeats the earlier scan, checking for differences

Figure 12-14 WinINSTALL notifies you that your Windows Installer package has been successfully created

MANAGING SOFTWARE DEPLOYMENT THROUGH THE SOFTWARE INSTALLATION SNAP-IN

The Software Installation snap-in is an extension to Group Policy that allows you to establish a Group Policy–based software management system. As a component of IntelliMirror, Software Installation works to reduce TCO for your network and increases the efficiency of both end users and IT staff members. Through Software Installation, you can centrally manage each of the following:

- *Deploying applications*—These can be shrink-wrapped third-party software or custom-built applications developed in-house.

- *Applying upgrades and patches*—Through Software Installation, you can update existing software or even replace it in the case of a product upgrade. Deploying service packs for operating systems becomes much easier, as well.

- *Uninstalling software*—When a product is no longer in use or supported by the IT department, you can easily remove it from users' computers.

The goal of Software Installation is to deploy applications in such a way that whenever users log on to a computer, no matter where they are, their applications will always be available to them. When combined with the Windows Installer, this technology is often referred to as just-in-time (JIT), because deployment will occur either during user logon or when the user launches a particular application. For example, say you have assigned Microsoft Word to a particular user. Even though users have not explicitly installed Microsoft Word, they see the icon for it on their desktop or in their Start menu. The first time they attempt to use Word, the system installs the application automatically, with no user intervention, and launches the program.

Likewise, if users attempt to use a feature of the program that is not installed by default, the application will be smart enough to automatically install the missing feature on the fly from the network and allow users to use it. In the past, installing a missing feature invariably meant manually running the program's setup utility and either reinstalling the entire product to add the missing feature or simply selecting the missing feature and choosing to update the installation. In either case, it interrupted the user's workflow and very likely required a desk-side trip from a desktop support technician.

We will discuss assigning applications through Software Installation a bit later.

Requirements for Software Installation

In order to use the Software Installation snap-in, several prerequisites must first be met. In addition, some conditions apply, depending on what type of application you are attempting to manage. The following sections discuss these Software Installation topics.

12

Group Policy Dependency

In order to use the Software Installation snap-in, you must be using Group Policy on your network. Because Group Policy is limited to Windows 2000 computers, you will be able to manage software only for your Windows 2000 environment. Any legacy Windows 9x or NT 4 clients will not be able to receive applications through Group Policy and Software Installation.

Active Directory Dependency

Because Group Policy is dependent on Active Directory, it makes sense that you cannot use the Software Installation snap-in unless you have deployed Active Directory on your network. Software Installation relies on GPOs, which are stored in Active Directory, to determine who can access software that it manages. As with Group Policy, Windows 9x and NT 4 computers cannot participate in Active Directory. At this point, Microsoft has not determined whether it will include Active Directory support in its upcoming Windows Millennium operating system. Windows Millennium (sometimes written Windows ME or WinME) is the next-in-line consumer operating system that will replace Windows 98. Because Microsoft is aiming Windows Millennium at the consumer market and Windows 2000 at the business market, it has not decided for certain whether it will force all businesses using the Win9x line of operating systems to upgrade to the more expensive and hardware-intensive Windows 2000 in order to take advantage of the features of Active Directory.

Works Best with Windows Installer Applications

By combining Software Installation with Windows Installer–based applications, you can make JIT deployment of applications a reality. Rather than producing an error message or just crashing, applications can be self-healing and automatically replace missing features or files when they are accessed. Applications that are Windows 2000 certified will have been created as Windows Installer packages.

Works with Non–Windows Installer Applications

Although limitations exist, Software Installation can be used to deploy non–Windows Installer packaged software, as well. The main limitation is the lack of support for JIT delivery of application settings and features. Existing setup programs should be repackaged as Windows Installer packages, if for no other reason than the fact that installing software usually requires administrative privileges on the local system. Through Group Policy, you can have Windows Installer packages always install with elevated privileges, meaning ordinary users can install software without administrator intervention.

You can also deploy non–Windows Installer packages by creating a ZAP file, which is sort of like an old INI file. It contains settings relevant to controlling the program's appearance and behavior. You create the ZAP file in a text editor and place it in the shared folder with the application's setup program. Here is a sample ZAP file for deploying Microsoft Office 97:

```
[Application]
FriendlyName = "Microsoft Office 97"
SetupCommand = ""\\Server01\apps\Off97\setup.exe""
[ext]
DOC=
DOT=
RTF=
XLS=
XLA=
XLW=
MDB=
PPT=
```

This example file contains two sections: [Application] and [ext]. The [Application] section is the only required section within a ZAP file, and the entries shown in our example are the only required elements. FriendlyName is the descriptive name that is displayed in the Add/Remove Programs applet, and SetupCommand provides the universal naming convention (UNC) path to the application's setup file.

The second section, [ext], is strictly optional. It lists file extensions for the program that should auto-install into the Registry.

Other optional sections can be defined within a ZAP file, but they are outside the scope of this book. The Windows 2000 Resource Kit has an excellent section on creating ZAP files for software distribution.

Assigned versus Published Applications

As we discussed earlier, applications can either be assigned or published to users. Assigned applications appear in the Start menu or as desktop icons, and reappear even if users uninstall the applications through the Add/Remove Programs applet in Control Panel. Published applications are made available through Add/Remove Programs, but a user must explicitly install them in order to use them. Unlike assigned applications, published applications do not stick with the system if a user uninstalls them.

We'll discuss the method of assigning and publishing applications shortly.

Using the Software Installation Snap-in

To this point you've learned a lot about what the Software Installation snap-in is and does, but nothing about how to actually use it. In this section, we will explore the Software Installation snap-in, specifically the following topics:

- Configuring Software Installation properties
- Deploying a new package
- Configuring package properties

12

Configuring Software Installation Properties

Before we get into deploying packages to manage with the Software Installation snap-in, let's first look at the global settings that can be configured. The Software Installation snap-in is located under both the Computer Configuration and User Configuration containers of a GPO. Open the GPO to which you wish to assign a software package; as you can see in Figure 12-15, the Software Installation snap-in is located under the Software Settings node.

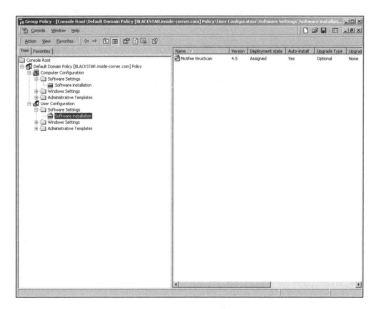

Figure 12-15   The Software Installation snap-in is located under the Software Settings node in both the Computer Configuration and User Configuration containers of a Group Policy Object

To configure the global properties of the Software Installation snap-in, simply right-click on the snap-in and choose Properties. Keep in mind that computer and user settings are independent of each other, so making changes to the computer policy for Software Installation will have no effect on the user policy, and vice versa.

The first dialog box you are presented with when you enter Software Installation Properties is the General tab, shown in Figure 12-16.

The first section allows you to define the default package location for new packages. This setting is useful if you collect all your packages to be deployed into a centralized location.

The next section defines the behavior of the snap-in with regard to new package creation. By default, the Deploy Software dialog box will be displayed when you choose to create a new package. This dialog box contains the choice to assign or publish a package, allowing you to choose how you want Software Installation to handle a package on a package-by-package basis.

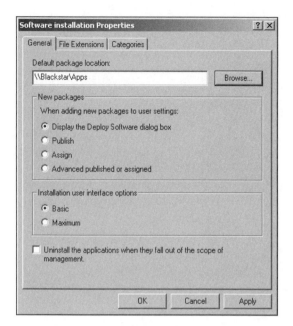

Figure 12-16   The General tab contains information about the default behavior of the
Software Installation snap-in

In addition, the General tab contains a setting to determine how much information is presented to the user during package installation. By default, only basic information and
options are supplied. Optionally, you can specify that a maximum amount of information
and options be shown to the user during installation.

Last, the General tab has the optional setting to define whether software should automatically be uninstalled when it falls outside the scope of management. That is, if Software
Installation no longer manages applications, they should no longer be available to users. By
default, this option is turned off.

After the General tab is the File Extensions tab, as shown in Figure 12-17. Often, more
than one application installed on your computer is capable of opening a given type of file.
This section allows you to pick a file type and set the order of precedence for applications
that are capable of opening the application.

The last tab is Categories, which is an organizational option. You create categories to help
keep track of where software is deployed. By default, there are no categories; you must create them if you want to use this feature. You name your categories according to personal
preference, although your environment will probably dictate the names. For example, you
might choose to create categories for your software based on department or location.
Figure 12-18 shows an example of the Categories property sheet.

12

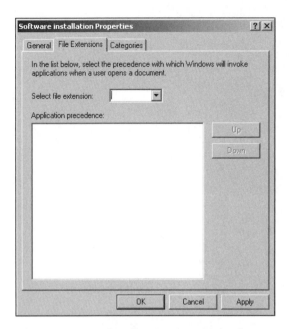

Figure 12-17 The File Extensions tab allows an administrator to set a precedence for programs that are capable of opening a given file type

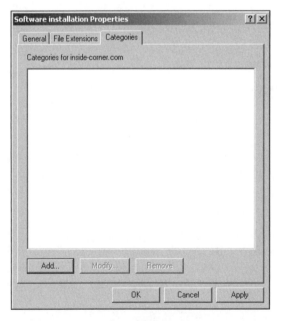

Figure 12-18 The Categories tab allows you to organize your managed software into custom-defined categories

Deploying a New Package

With the global options set for Software Installation, we will move on to deploying a new package. In order to deploy a new package, you must have first copied the installation files to a network share, otherwise known as a distribution point. Right-click on the Software Installation snap-in and choose New | Package. The dialog box shown in Figure 12-19 will appear.

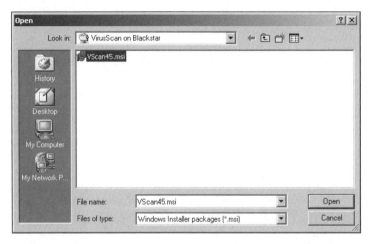

Figure 12-19   The first step in deploying a new package is to select the Windows Installer package or ZAP file that is to be deployed

12

In our example, we're selecting a Windows Installer package for McAfee VirusScan 4.5, which is located in the VirusScan share on the server Blackstar. This is our distribution point. When we select the file and click on Open, we are presented with the dialog box shown in Figure 12-20. We see this dialog box because previously we left the global setting for Software Installation to show us these choices when creating a new package, rather than to default to either publishing or assigning.

It is important to note that you can publish an application only if the package is being deployed under the User Configuration container. Software deployed to computers does not support publishing, and therefore those packages can only be assigned. If you deploy a package under the Computer Configuration container, when you reach the dialog box shown in Figure 12-20 the Published option will be unavailable.

If you select either Published or Assigned and click on OK, the package is deployed without any further prompting. If you select Advanced Published Or Assigned, the package will still be deployed, but you will be prompted with a dialog box similar to that shown in Figure 12-21. This is the same dialog box you can access later by going into the properties of a package, as discussed next.

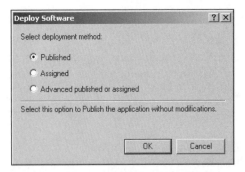

Figure 12-20   After choosing the software package to deploy, you must decide whether to publish or assign it

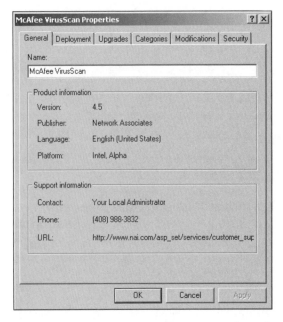

Figure 12-21   You can configure a number of advanced settings for an application once it has been deployed

Configuring Package Properties

To access the properties of a package once you've deployed it, simply right-click on the package and choose Properties. You will see the same dialog box you saw if you selected

Advanced Published Or Assigned during the new package deployment. A number of property sheets contain settings for the package. An overview of them is as follows:

- *General*—Contains product information such as the name and version number, as well as contact information.

- *Deployment*—Defines the deployment type (assigned or published), which can also be changed here. In addition, this property sheet contains settings for deployment options, including whether the package should be uninstalled if it falls outside the scope of management and if it should be displayed in the Add/Remove Programs applet. Advanced deployment options determine whether the language setting should be ignored when installing the software and whether previous installations of the product should be uninstalled if they weren't installed through Group Policy.

- *Upgrades*—Defines the applications that are to be upgraded by this package, and which packages can upgrade this package.

- *Categories*—Determines the categories under which the software will be displayed in the Add/Remove Programs applet.

- *Modifications*—Allows you to apply modifications or transforms to the package in order to customize the deployment.

- *Security*—Determines who has what level of access to the package. Through the Security property sheet, you control the deployment of the software to computers, users, and groups.

12

These are the basics of the Software Installation snap-in. With an understanding of the Windows Installer and Software Installation, you are ready to put both of them together to deploy software on your Windows 2000 network. However, sometimes an existing package will no longer work in a changing environment. A package may simply have to be re-created from scratch. In many cases, however, it is easier to patch an existing package.

PATCHING SOFTWARE USING THE WINDOWS INSTALLER PACKAGE EDITOR

After you've created a Windows Installer software package, a time may come when you need to modify it. Patching software is the process by which you modify a Windows Installer package to meet changing needs. You perform this task through the VERITAS Software Console utility (also called the Windows Installer Package Editor) that is installed as part of WinINSTALL LE. Figure 12-22 shows the WinZip 8 package that we just created opened in the Software Console for modification.

Figure 12-22   The VERITAS Software Console enables you to open and modify existing Windows Installer packages

You can see that Software Console is divided into three main sections. They are:

- *Tree view (top-left frame)*—Shows the Windows Installer Package Editor header with a listing of the current package (if any) open for editing.

- *List view (bottom-left frame)*—Contains the heart of the package information. The information about the package in this section includes:

  - *General*—Includes a summary of installed features.

  - *Files*—Shows a list of the files that will install with this package, as well as their size, version number, and target locations.

  - *Shortcuts*—Shows any shortcuts that will be created by the package during installation.

  - *Registry*—Shows a list of Registry keys and values that the installation will update. The example in Figure 12-22 shows the Registry updates for our WinZip package.

  - *Services*—Shows a list of new services that will be installed on Windows NT and Windows 2000–based computers.

  - *INI Edits*—Exists primarily for backward compatibility with 16-bit applications. This setting shows any INI files that will be updated during the installation, as well as the specific modifications to be made.

- *Advertising*—Contains COM settings for interaction with a COM server, and includes file types that will be registered by the package installation.

- *Data view (right frame)*—Shows the contents of the selections made in the list view. For example, if you select Services in the list view, the data view will show the services to be installed.

Patching Applications

Patching (modifying) a Windows Installer package is not too difficult, once you are familiar with the layout of the Software Console as described in the previous section. At the top of the data view frame is a tab for an Add property sheet for most list view settings, and a Remove tab for a few, as well. On the Add tab, for instance, are New, Properties, and Delete choices. These choices allow you to manipulate the contents in the data view, such as adding custom files to your installation that are not included by default or removing settings and features you no longer need.

In some cases, you might use the Windows Installer Package Editor to clean up a package before distributing it. Say, for example, you forgot to exclude the page file on your Windows 2000 system from the "before" and "after" scans, and it inadvertently ended up in your distribution file. Using the Software Console, you could remove the file from the package so it doesn't needlessly increase the file size of the package and potentially cause installation problems when it can't overwrite an existing page file during installation. You can also customize the package for different deployments if you wish, saving the modifications with different file names.

If you patch a package that has already been deployed to other users, you can use the Software Installation snap-in in Group Policy to automatically patch/upgrade the existing application on users' systems, as discussed previously in this chapter.

12

CHAPTER SUMMARY

In this chapter, you learned about the powerful software deployment and management features of Windows 2000, which are part of Microsoft's IntelliMirror technologies. Some of the key topics included the following:

- Change and configuration management is an increasingly important IT concern. The soft costs of supporting a network far exceed the hard costs of purchasing the actual equipment.

- IntelliMirror consists of data management, desktop settings management, and software installation and maintenance.

- IntelliMirror technologies are dependent on Active Directory and Group Policy in order to operate.

❐ The phases of software management can be broken down into preparation, distribution, targeting, pilot, and installation.

❐ Windows 2000 includes VERITAS WinINSTALL LE on the installation CD for creating and patching Windows Installer packages.

❐ Windows Installer packages end with an .msi extension.

❐ Windows Installer packages can be self-healing, automatically detecting missing files and settings and replacing them on the fly when combined with the Software Installation snap-in.

❐ The Software Installation utility requires Group Policy.

❐ Software can either be assigned or published to users through Software Installation.

❐ Windows Installer packages can be patched after they've been created, to remove incorrect files and settings, add additional customizations, and change the installation behavior.

13

DEPLOYING WINDOWS 2000 USING REMOTE INSTALLATION SERVICES

After completing this chapter, you will be able to:

♦ Understand what RIS is and how it functions

♦ Understand the requirements for RIS

♦ Identify RIS client and server components

♦ Set up and configure RIS

♦ Create RIS images

♦ Create RIS boot disks

♦ Manage RIS security

In the previous three chapters, 10, 11, and 12, we have discussed components of Microsoft's IntelliMirror technologies, which provide a desktop management solution for Windows 2000 networks. In this chapter, we focus on the last component involved in a complete change and configuration management strategy: Remote Installation Services (RIS). With RIS, administrators are able to automate the installation of Windows 2000 Professional workstations over the network.

At this point, NT 4 administrators might be asking, "So what? Couldn't I do the same thing with answer files in NT 4?" The answer is an unequivocal "No!" Through answer files, an administrator could automate an NT 4 installation by including in the text file the appropriate responses to the questions with which a user would be prompted during installation—network settings, computer name, and so on. However, if you had no installation CD and you needed to install a custom image from the network, or if you didn't have a boot disk with DOS network card drivers, you were pretty much out of luck.

With RIS, if you have a compliant client computer, you can get network connectivity and choose from any number of administrator-created images with which to install and configure Windows 2000. With that in mind, let's look at an overview of what RIS does and how it functions.

RIS OVERVIEW

The simplest way to define RIS is as follows: RIS is a Windows 2000 Server component that allows Windows 2000 Professional to be installed remotely onto a system without a support technician needing to actually touch the computer. Combined with the other IntelliMirror technologies we have previously discussed—such as data management (folder redirection, offline folders), desktop settings management (roaming profiles and Group Policy settings that follow a user, group, or computer), and software installation and management—RIS completes a total desktop management solution. Through these technologies included in Windows 2000, an administrator can effectively deploy new PCs and even reinstall existing PCs from a central location, without having to visit a user's office. This ability is a tremendous time saver for IT departments; it frees staff members from less productive work (reinstalling/repairing software) so that their talents can be used more efficiently elsewhere.

In addition, with IntelliMirror, users no longer have to sit and wait unproductively for an IT staff member to show up after they have placed a call to the help desk. With RIS, even the entire operating system (OS) can be reinstalled upon request: A preconfigured OS image can be applied to the computer, and the user needs to supply only logon information.

Before we get into the details of how RIS works, it is extremely important to note that the process of applying an OS image to a computer through RIS *erases all existing data on the hard drive*. For obvious reasons, it is important to ensure that any nonreplaceable user information is backed up prior to reinstalling the OS. Because RIS erases the hard drive, it cannot be used to upgrade an existing OS, such as Windows 98 or NT Workstation 4. Furthermore, RIS can be used to install only Windows 2000 Professional—you cannot install Windows 9x or NT with RIS. To automate an OS upgrade or install a non–Windows 2000 Professional OS on a client PC, you need to look at a full-blown systems management utility such as Microsoft Systems Management Server (SMS).

To realize the power of RIS and IntelliMirror fully, imagine a situation where the hard drive in a user's compliant PC has had a hardware failure. A desktop support technician must go to the user's office and replace the hard drive with a new one. So far, nothing out of the ordinary has happened. However, instead of having to sit there half a day reinstalling the OS and all the applications, the technician can activate an RIS installation and walk away. The user only needs to type in a username and password, and the rest of the process of installing Windows 2000 Professional proceeds automatically.

Once the OS is installed, the user logs on to the network. Group Policy runs, and through Software Installation and Maintenance settings (assigned and published applications) and desktop settings management, the user has access to all their applications and their desktop. Start menu settings return to the state they were in prior to the hard-drive crash. The user can begin productive work immediately—and all of this takes place automatically, without any intervention by an administrator or desktop support technician.

How RIS Functions

RIS works by creating a Pre-Boot Execution Environment (PXE), which enables a compliant client PC to gain basic TCP/IP network connectivity. PXE (pronounced "pixie") technology is not integrated into every network card, so you must ensure that you have a PXE-compliant adapter before you can use RIS. The client requirements for RIS are listed in the next section.

Once network connectivity is established, a series of scripts can be run to bring the client to the point of installing the OS. For NT 4 administrators, this ability makes RIS a must-have item. In the past, administrators often experienced the frustration of trying to reinstall an OS on a computer without a boot floppy or installation CD handy. You knew all the software you needed was on the network, and the computer on which you were trying to reinstall the OS had a network card, but you couldn't get network connectivity established. RIS ends that frustration, because network connectivity is established at the hardware level through the interaction of the network card with the network. The details of this interaction will be discussed later in the chapter.

With RIS, an administrator can choose to have a computer go through a CD-like installation of Windows 2000 Professional, as if a normal installation is taking place from a CD. Alternatively, you can customize the installation to the point of scripting it with an answer file, so that the user is not required to choose any options during setup.

Now that you have a basic understanding what RIS does, let's discuss the components required for RIS.

RIS REQUIREMENTS

13

In order for RIS to function, a number of components must already be installed and configured on a Windows 2000 network. They are:

- Remote Installation Services
- Domain Name System (DNS)
- Dynamic Host Configuration Protocol (DHCP) Server
- Active Directory

In the next sections, we will discuss each of these Windows 2000 components as they relate to using RIS.

Remote Installation Services

Windows 2000 includes RIS as an optional component that can be installed through the Windows Components Wizard of the Add/Remove Programs applet in Control Panel. RIS runs as a service on at least one Windows 2000 Server system on the network, listening for client requests. In addition, the RIS server stores the OS images that the client computer can choose from when it invokes RIS. You can use Group Policy to determine which images should be available to which users.

Setting up an RIS server is discussed later in this chapter.

Domain Name System (DNS)

DNS is the service that enables RIS clients to find RIS servers on the network. Windows 2000 RIS servers register themselves in DNS, so that when an RIS client establishes network connectivity, it has the name and Internet Protocol (IP) address of an RIS server from which to pull an image. Microsoft DNS is not required as long as the third-party DNS server you use supports Requests for Comments (RFCs) 2052 (SRV RR) and 2136 (dynamic updates).

Dynamic Host Configuration Protocol (DHCP) Server

In order to establish network connectivity, an RIS client must have an IP address. Because the process all takes place at the hardware level, there is nowhere to assign a static IP address. RIS therefore uses dynamic addressing in order to obtain an IP address and connect to the network. For an RIS client to obtain a dynamic address, a DHCP server must be running on the network. It can be either a Microsoft DHCP server or a third-party DHCP server.

Active Directory

RIS is dependent on Active Directory in order to function. The reason is twofold. First, RIS uses Group Policy, which is dependent on Active Directory, in order to determine permissions for user accounts and computer accounts prior to supplying RIS image choices to the user. Second, RIS uses network configuration settings stored in Active Directory to determine information such as which RIS server should be used in the case where multiple RIS servers exist on a network. In addition, Active Directory information is used for such things as implementing a standard naming convention for new computers and determining in which domain or Organizational Unit to place the new computers.

With an understanding of RIS's dependencies, let's look at the server and client components that make up RIS.

RIS CLIENT AND SERVER COMPONENTS

In addition to the RIS dependencies we just listed, components at both the client and server enable RIS to function. In this section, we will discuss the client and server components of RIS.

Client Requirements of RIS

A client computer must meet a number of requirements in order to use RIS. These requirements are:

- Computer must meet NetPC or PC98 standards
- Computer must have a compliant BIOS
- Computer must have a compatible network adapter

NetPC or PC98 Standards

A computer can meet the requirements of RIS by conforming to the NetPC or PC98 standard. A client computer that meets the requirements set forth by either the NetPC or PC98 standard will include PXE functionality. Compliant computers must have version 1.0b at minimum to work with RIS.

Additional standards exist within the NetPC and PC98 standards, but for the purpose of this book only PXE and Plug and Play requirements are discussed.

Compliant BIOS

A PC can also meet the requirements of RIS by having a compliant motherboard BIOS, which will include the necessary PXE functionality for RIS. If you don't currently have a PXE-capable motherboard, see the manufacturer about a possible flash upgrade (almost all motherboards are now upgradeable).

Compatible Network Adapters

In addition, a compliant client computer can simply have a compatible network adapter installed in order to use RIS. A compliant network adapter will be PXE compliant, meaning it supports the preboot execution environment standard. Due to Plug and Play requirements, a compliant network card will also be PCI based. This excludes Personal Computer Memory Card International Association (PCMCIA) network adapters typically found in laptops; so, if you want to use RIS with a laptop system, you must first connect the laptop to a docking station containing a Peripheral Component Interconnect (PCI) network adapter that also has PXE functionality.

If the motherboard is not compliant and the computer does not meet NetPC or PC98 standards, and you don't have a PXE-compliant network adapter, it might still be possible to still use RIS. Windows 2000 includes an RBFG.EXE utility that allows an administrator to create a bootable floppy disk that emulates the PXE environment. Creating boot floppies for RIS is discussed in detail later in this chapter.

Windows 2000 doesn't support a large number of non–PXE-compliant network cards, but Table 13-1 lists them.

13

Table 13-1 Compatible network adapters supported by the RIS boot floppy

Manufacturer	Model
3Com	3C900B-Combo 3C900B-FL 3C900B-TPC 3C900B-TPO 3C900-Combo 3C900-TPO 3C905B-Combo 3C905B-FX 3C905B-TX 3C905C-TX 3C905-T4 3C905-TX
AMD	AMD PCnet Adapters
Compaq	NetFlex 100 NetFlex 110 NetFlex 3
DEC	DE450 DE500
HP	Deskdirect 10/100 TX
Intel	Pro 10+ Pro 100+ Pro 100B
SMC	8432 9332 9432

Hardware Requirements

In order to use RIS on a client computer, the client must meet the following hardware requirements:

- Pentium 166 or faster CPU

- 32MB of RAM minimum (64MB recommended)

- 800MB or larger hard drive

- DHCP PXE-based boot ROM or network adapter supported by the RIS boot floppy

Client Installation Wizard

The Client Installation Wizard is the client-side piece for RIS, which is downloaded to the client and communicates with the RIS server. A default set of screens is presented to the user; these screens are provided by the Boot Information Negotiation Layer

(BINL) server-side service. They guide the user through the Client Installation Wizard to log on and select Windows 2000 Professional installation options that have been defined by the administrator. The user invokes the Client Installation Wizard by pressing F12 once the PC's power-on self-test (POST) process has completed and before the OS starts booting.

It is important to note that the boot process is not secure: Information is sent over the network in clear text that can be read with a packet sniffer. Therefore, you should ensure that only limited RIS servers are on the network, and that you have control over who is allowed to set up and configure RIS servers in general.

Now, let's look at the server components for RIS.

Server Components of RIS

The RIS services on a server are less dependent on specific hardware than are client computers, although you must make note of some hardware requirements. These requirements are:

- Pentium 166 or faster CPU (200+ recommended).
- 96 to 128MB of RAM required when running Active Directory, DNS, and DHCP services.
- 10MB Ethernet adapter (100MB recommended).
- Access to Windows 2000 Professional installation files (can be CD-ROM, network share, or local directory with a copy of the files).
- 2GB hard-disk space for the RIS servers folder tree. It is recommended that you devote an entire hard-disk partition to the directory tree for RIS.
- NTFS-formatted partition for RIS images. RIS cannot be installed on Distributed File System (Dfs) or Encrypted File System (EFS) volumes.

As we previously discussed, the requirements to use RIS from the server end include Active Directory, DNS, DHCP, and the Remote Installation Services service. When RIS is installed through Add/Remove Programs (RISetup.exe is the program that actually installs RIS, as discussed later), additional services are installed on the server. These services include:

- *Boot Information Negotiation Layer (BINL)*—As discussed previously, this service listens for client DHCP/PXE requests. In addition, BINL redirects clients to the appropriate files needed for installation during the Client Installation Wizard. The BINL service also verifies logon credentials with Active Directory.

13

- *Trivial File Transfer Protocol Daemon (TFTPD)*—RIS uses TFTP to initially download to a client all files necessary to begin the Windows 2000 Professional installation. Included in this download is Startrom.com, which is the bootstrap program that displays the message for the user to press F12 for Network Service. If the user does press F12 within three seconds, the Client Installation Wizard is downloaded through TFTP to the client computer.

- *Single Instance Store (SIS)*—The SIS service seeks to reduce disk space requirements for RIS images by combining duplicate files. The service contains an NTFS file system filter (RIS, as you will recall, can be installed only on an NTFS partition) and the service that manages images on the RIS installation partition.

Another server component, RIPrep.exe, is used to create RIS images. Creating RIS images is discussed later in this chapter.

Now that we have discussed the basics of RIS, let's get our hands dirty with an RIS installation.

SETTING UP AND CONFIGURING RIS

If you perform a typical installation of Windows 2000 Server at the time you run Setup, RIS is not installed. RIS is an optional component that can either be selected in a custom setup or added later through the Windows Components Wizard of the Add/Remove Programs applet in Control Panel. When you launch the Windows Components Wizard, as shown in Figure 13-1, you have a choice of components that you can add or remove. Put a check mark in the box for Remote Installation Services and click on Next.

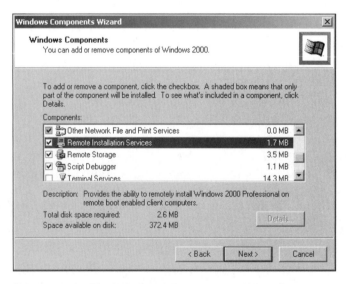

Figure 13-1   The Windows Components Wizard

Once you click on Next, the installation wizard begins configuring RIS, as shown in Figure 13-2. Windows 2000 installs RIS services, but it does not actually allow any configuration of RIS during this initial setup. After RIS is installed, you will see the window shown in Figure 13-3. Click on Finish, and restart your computer when prompted.

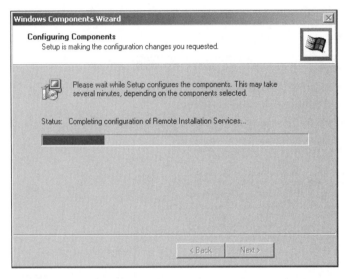

Figure 13-2 Windows 2000 installs the RIS service to the hard drive, updating the system in the process

Figure 13-3 After RIS is installed, click on Finish and then restart the computer

13

RISetup

Once RIS is installed and you have restarted your computer, it is still necessary to configure RIS. RISetup.exe is the utility used to configure RIS, and you can invoke it from the Run line. The Remote Installation Services Setup Wizard, shown in Figure 13-4, prepares the server to be an RIS server. In the following sections, we will walk through the setup and configuration of an RIS server.

Figure 13-4   The Remote Installation Services Setup Wizard is invoked through the RISetup.exe command

The first option you are presented with, shown in Figure 13-5, is the installation directory for RIS. Note that this directory must reside on an NTFS partition with sufficient disk space for your RIS images. If you attempt to install to a non-NTFS partition, the Setup Wizard will give an error message. Windows 2000 will provide a default drive and directory, but the drive may or may not be valid (the wizard does not check the drive for file system type and disk space before offering it as a choice). Therefore, you may have to choose a different drive for your RIS installation. In most cases, however, you should leave the default directory name.

The next step in your installation is to decide whether your RIS server will immediately begin servicing requests once you have completed Setup, as shown in Figure 13-6. By default, RIS services do not begin immediately after Setup. This is primarily a security measure. Because you really can't use RIS anyway, until you've created an RIS image, there is little sense in having the services running when—as we mentioned earlier—

RIS data is sent to and from the server in clear text. An unscrupulous individual could exploit your new RIS server if it were online before you were ready to start using it. In most environments, though, enabling RIS probably isn't much of a security risk.

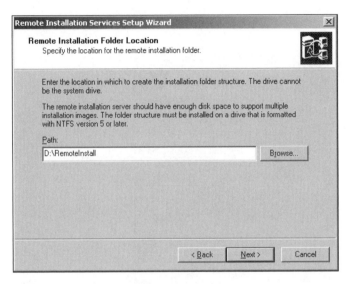

Figure 13-5   The first step in installing RIS is to choose an installation directory

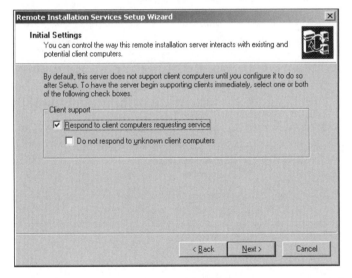

Figure 13-6   You can choose whether to start servicing RIS clients immediately, and whether RIS should respond to unknown computers

In addition to deciding whether to start RIS, you can choose whether RIS should respond to unknown computers. Select your choices, and then click on Next.

The next step in configuring RIS is to point Setup to the installation files for Windows 2000 Professional, as shown in Figure 13-7. This location can be a CD or a network path, as in our example. Once you have defined your directory, click on Next.

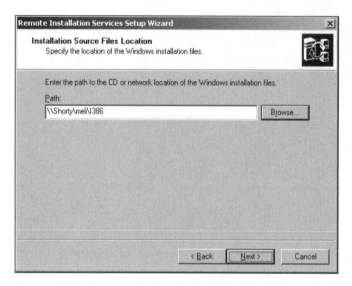

Figure 13-7   You can define the installation directory for Windows 2000 Professional as either a CD or a network path

Now, the Setup Wizard prompts you for the name of the folder to copy the Windows 2000 Professional setup files to on the RIS server. Unless you have a specific need to change it, the default directory supplied by RIS Setup, illustrated in Figure 13-8, should be fine.

The next step is to determine a friendly description for your RIS image, and the help text that will be shown in the Client Installation Wizard when the user presses F12 to start RIS on the client. Figure 13-9 shows an example.

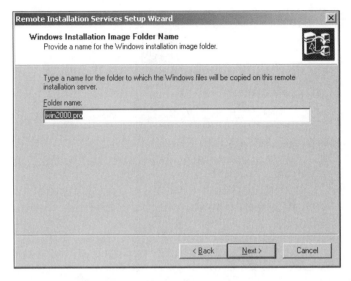

Figure 13-8   RIS Setup next offers a default directory to copy the Windows 2000 Professional setup files into on the RIS server

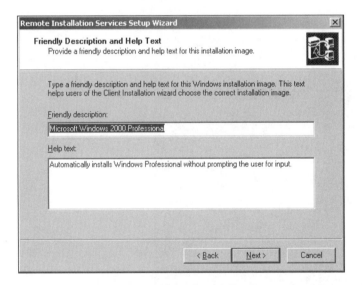

Figure 13-9   Assigning a friendly description to the RIS image makes it easier to determine what RIS image to use when choices are presented in the Client Installation Wizard

Before Setup actually begins, you are given the chance to review your settings and go back to change any settings. Once you click on Finish, as shown in Figure 13-10, installation begins. Figure 13-11 shows RIS Setup as it runs through its task list.

Figure 13-10   You have a chance to review your installation options before proceeding with the actual installation

After you have configured RIS, you can go into Windows Explorer and look at the new directory structure. It will look something like that shown in Figure 13-12 if you didn't make any changes from the defaults.

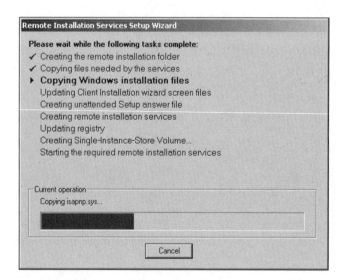

Figure 13-11   The Remote Installation Services Setup Wizard completes the list of tasks as it configures RIS

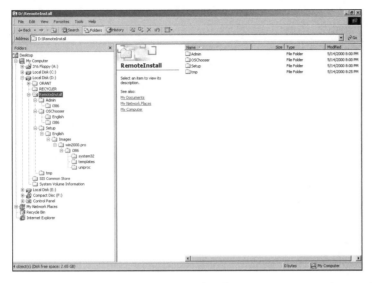

Figure 13-12   RIS Setup creates this directory structure during the Setup Wizard

Now that we have set up and configured RIS, let's look at creating additional RIS images and creating RIS boot disks.

CREATING RIS IMAGES

As we have seen, CD-based RIS images can be created through the RISetup utility. Additionally, the RIPrep.exe utility allows you to clone a standard corporate desktop for deployment to other systems. In this section, we will examine the RIPrep utility and also learn about creating RIS boot disks for compatible network adapters.

RIPrep

Unlike RISetup, which allows only an administrator to deploy a CD-based setup of Windows 2000 Professional (even a network-based installation is just a copy of the files from the CD shared on a network drive), RIPrep can be used to deploy the OS plus customized settings and even locally installed desktop applications. This process is not the true disk cloning that products like Norton Ghost provide, because it can be used only with Windows 2000 Professional. In addition, RIPrep does not support multiple hard drives or multiple partitions on the computer where the image is being created.

Other limitations of RIPrep include the requirement that a CD-based image with the same version and language as the RIPrep image also exist on the RIS server, and that the target system must have the same hardware abstraction layer (HAL) as the system used to create the image. By having the same HAL, an image created on a single processor system cannot be installed onto a dual-processor system. Because Windows 2000 does not support Alpha processors like NT 4 does, you won't have to worry about mixing up Intel (I386) and Alpha images.

Although RIPrep has limitations, it offers advantages over using RISetup to create images. Most notably, RIPrep allows an administrator to create a standard desktop image and then use RIS to deploy it to new computers as they come in from an original equipment manufacturer (OEM). In addition, reinstallation of the OS is much faster from an RIPrep image, because the image is applied as a copy operation to the target hard drive and not run though an actual Windows 2000 installation, as would happen with a CD- or network-based RISetup image.

Creating Images with RIPrep

Creating an image with RIPrep is a two-step process:

1. Install and configure a computer with Windows 2000 Professional and the specific applications and settings you want to include in the image.

2. Run RIPrep.exe from the RIS server.

You must keep clear an important distinction: The RIPrep.exe utility is located on the RIS server, but it is *executed* from the RIS client on which the image is being created. From the client, choose Start|Run and type

```
\\RISserver\reminst\admin\i386\riprep.exe
```

If you attempt to run RIPrep.exe from a non-Windows 2000 Professional system, you will receive an error message stating that the utility will run only on Windows 2000 Professional. When you run RIPrep from a valid system, however, the Remote Installation Preparation Wizard starts, as shown in Figure 13-13.

Even though you ran RIPrep.exe from one RIS server, you do not necessarily have to copy the image you are creating to that particular server. Figure 13-14 shows the next step in creating an image with RIPrep, where you choose the RIS server to which to copy the image.

Figure 13-13   The Remote Installation Preparation Wizard is started by executing RIPrep.exe from a Windows 2000 Professional client computer

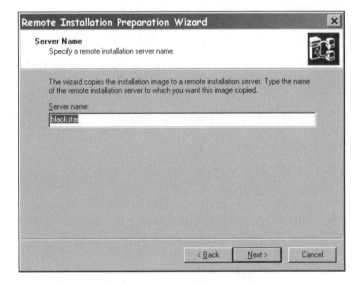

13

Figure 13-14   If you have multiple RIS servers on your network, you can choose which server should receive the image

The next step in creating the RIS image is to supply the name of the installation directory on the RIS server previously chosen. Typically, you would type the name of an existing directory only if you were replacing an existing image. If this new image will not be replacing an existing image, type in a new directory name as shown in Figure 13-15 and click on Next.

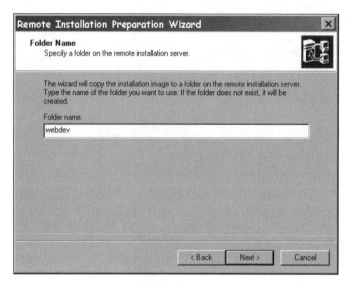

Figure 13-15   Supply a directory name on the RIS server for the Remote Installation
                    Preparation Wizard to copy the image

In our example, the image is being created for a corporate Web developer environment. For that reason, we gave the directory the descriptive name *webdev*, in order to identify the image it contains on the RIS server.

In Figure 13-16, you can see the next step in creating an image, which is assigning a friendly name to the image and creating the help text. The friendly name displays in the list of available images during the Client Installation Wizard. The help text provides an additional description to help the user identify the correct image to use when acting as an RIS client. In our example (an RIS image for a Web development system), we list the applications that will be installed on the system along with the Windows 2000 Professional OS as part of the imaging process.

If you have any programs or services running that could interfere with the imaging process, Windows 2000 will warn you. Figure 13-17 lists a number of programs and services that were running on the RIS image source workstation at the time we created this example image. Once you have closed the programs and stopped the necessary services, click on Next.

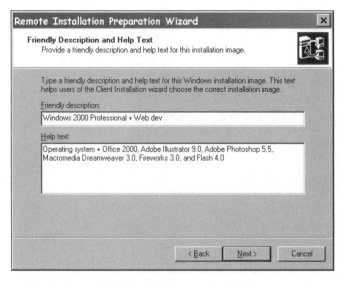

Figure 13-16   By assigning a friendly name and help text, users can identify the correct image to use during the Client Installation Wizard

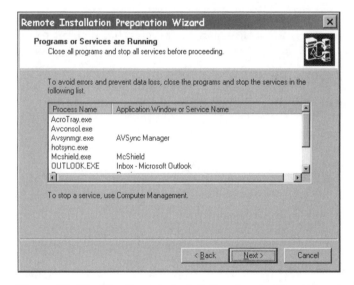

Figure 13-17   The Remote Installation Preparation Wizard prompts you to close any programs and services that might interfere with the imaging process

Before beginning the actual image creation, the wizard allows you to review your choices. Notice in Figure 13-18 that the folder name is incorrect. Initially, we created a generic folder that we intended to use for RIS images, only to decide later to create separate subfolders for each image. By reviewing the settings we had configured, we were able to back up through the wizard and change the folder name from *RISimages* to *webdev* before starting the actual image creation.

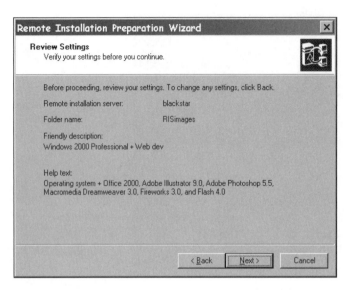

Figure 13-18 Before starting the actual image creation, take a moment to review your settings and ensure they are correct

The last step, shown in Figure 13-19, is an information dialog box from the Remote Installation Preparation Wizard that describes the process that is about to occur. Once you understand what is about to happen on your system, click on Next to continue. You can watch the RIPrep wizard image process taking place, as shown in Figure 13-20.

Figure 13-19 The RIPrep wizard informs you of how the image process will take place on your system before beginning

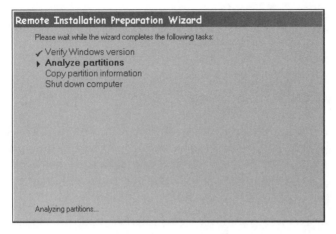

Figure 13-20   The RIPrep wizard displays the current status of the image process, showing the completed, current, and pending tasks

Images created by the RIPrep wizard are stored in the same subfolder as images created during RISetup. If you used the default settings when we examined the RISetup wizard earlier in this chapter, and you are using an English language version of Windows 2000 Server, your RIS directory structure will be as follows:

- *\RemoteInstall\Setup\English\Images\win2000.pro\i386*—The default image created during the RISetup wizard earlier. Subdirectories exist under i386 for this CD-based installation image for system32, templates, and uniproc.

- *\RemoteInstall\Setup\English\Images\webdev\i386*—The image directory we just created for our webdev image. A directory called Mirror1, which appears under i386, does not appear in the subdirectories of an RISetup-created image.

RIPrep Files

In addition to the directory structure created, you need to know what files are important to the RIPrep image. These files are as follows:

- *RIPrep.log*—This ASCII text file documents the Remote Installation Preparation Wizard image process, listing any errors and relevant information that might be of troubleshooting use to an administrator.

- *Bootcode.dat*—This file is located in the \Mirror1 subdirectory of the image's i386 folder. It contains the boot sector information for the client system.

- *Imirror.dat*—This file also is located in the \Mirror1 directory, and contains installation information about the image source computer, such as the installation directory and the HAL type.

It is worth repeating here that RIPrep can create images only for single-partition systems. If you have Windows 2000 Professional installed to a partition other than the boot partition, the RIS image process will fail.

CREATING RIS BOOT DISKS

Creating an RIS boot disk is necessary if you do not have a PXE-capable network adapter or motherboard, but you do have a network adapter that is supported by the RIS boot disk creation utility, RBFG.exe. We briefly touched on the Windows 2000 Remote Boot Disk Generator previously, but we did not discuss creating disks. In this section, you will actually create an RIS boot disk.

There is not much to the Remote Boot Disk Generator. Essentially, as you can see from Figure 13-21, you have the option to view the supported adapter list or create the disk. The About page contains program credits; and if you have multiple floppy drives (does anyone still have two floppy drives?), you can choose which one to use to create the disk. The RBFG utility will erase the floppy in the drive without warning you first, so ensure that you select the right disk and drive before continuing.

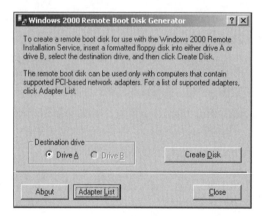

Figure 13-21   The Remote Boot Disk Generator allows you to create a network-bootable diskette for supported network adapters

Table 13-1, shown earlier, listed the supported adapters. To see the list on screen, click on the Adapter List button in the utility. The RIS boot disk emulates a PXE environment for these supported non-PXE-capable network adapters, and if you look, you will notice that the boot disk once created contains only a single file: RISDISK.

RISDISK has no file extension, and the file is only 90K in size. If you have a supported network adapter, however, this disk is all you will need to start the Client Installation Wizard.

MANAGING RIS SECURITY

Security is always an important issue when discussing computer networking topics, and this is no different with RIS. As you've been reading about how RIS functions on a network, you might have been asking yourself what steps you could take as a Windows 2000 systems administrator in order to prevent unauthorized individuals from setting RIS servers, creating images, or even gaining network connectivity through RIS and installing an image. Fortunately, RIS has some built-in safeguards that will allow you to maintain some control over who is able to use Remote Installation Services. Some of these security services include requiring RIS servers to be authorized before they can respond to RIS client requests, being able to use Group Policy to manage RIS client installation options, and editing configuration settings through the Active Directory Users and Computers administrative tool.

Authorizing an RIS Server

Before an RIS server can service client requests, it must first be authorized into Active Directory. Authorization can be done a few different ways. First, during the Remote Installation Services Setup Wizard, you can choose to have the RIS server start responding to client requests immediately upon completion of the wizard. This is not the recommended method of authorization, and, by default, the box to enable immediate authorization is not checked.

Second, if you install RIS onto a server that is not already an authorized DHCP server, you can authorize RIS through the DHCP administrator tool. In the DHCP Microsoft Management Console (MMC), right-click on the DHCP root node of the tree and select Manage Authorized Servers. Click on the Authorize button and type in the fully qualified domain name (FQDN) or IP address of the RIS server. Confirm that this is the server you want to authorize, and you are set.

You might wonder why you would need to use the DHCP MMC console to authorize an RIS server. Windows 2000 requires DHCP servers to be authorized in Active Directory as well before they can begin distributing IP addresses to clients, similar to the requirements for RIS. Because RIS is dependent on DHCP, it makes sense to use a similar authentication scheme for bringing new RIS servers into an Active Directory network. That said, we find the last method of authorization ties in with DHCP.

The last method is the easiest. If you install RIS onto an authorized DHCP server, you do not have to take any further steps to authorize RIS. The authorization will be passed along from DHCP to RIS because the server is already authorized in Active Directory.

In order to authorize an RIS server, the account you are logged on with must be a member of the Enterprise Admins security group.

13

Troubleshooting RIS Authorization

If you are having trouble getting an authorized RIS server to respond to client requests, it might be because the changes haven't yet taken effect in Active Directory. You can speed up the process, though, by opening a command prompt and typing the following:

```
secedit /refreshpolicy /MACHINE_POLICY
```

You might remember that command from our discussion of Group Policy implementation in Chapter 10, where we needed to make Group Policy settings we had changed take effect immediately.

Managing RIS Client Options with Group Policy

For an additional measure of security, Windows 2000 enables the administrator to configure options that define the behavior of the Client Installation Wizard. Specifically, the options that can be configured are the choice options presented to users when they invoke RIS through F12.

The choice options are configured through the Remote Installation Services node of the User Configuration container in the Group Policy Editor. Because this is Group Policy, you can apply these settings at the site, domain, or Organizational Unit (OU) level. You might want to use the Default Domain Policy, or you might want to configure different policy options for different OUs. No matter where you choose to apply the policy, you edit it the same way. Open the Group Policy Editor and navigate to the Remote Installation Services node, as described earlier. In the pane on the right side of the editor, right-click on Choice Options and click on Properties. You will see a dialog box like that in Figure 13-22, which shows the following client options:

- *Automatic Setup*—Set to Don't Care by default, which means it inherits its settings from the parent container. Eventually, through inheritance, this policy will be defined as Allow or Deny.

- *Custom Setup*—Denied by default. Allows users to install custom RIPrep-created images.

- *Restart Setup*— Denied by default. Determines if a setup that failed to complete for whatever reason will be allowed to be restarted.

- *Tools*—Denied by default. Allows access to maintenance and troubleshooting tools such as disk utilities and antivirus software. An administrator might make these types of tools available for troubleshooting purposes.

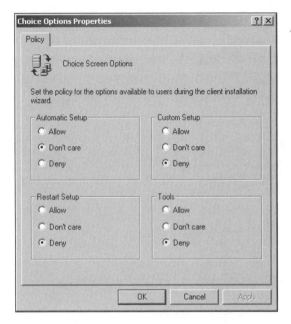

Figure 13-22   An administrator can configure client choice options for additional RIS security

Managing RIS Configuration Settings

The strongest security settings you can configure for RIS lie within the Active Directory Users and Computers administrative tool. Through this utility, you can perform the following tasks as they relate to RIS:

- Configure client support
- Define a computer naming convention
- Grant computer account creation rights
- Prestage computers

Configuring Client Support

In order to configure client support, which includes whether RIS should respond to clients and whether the RIS server should respond to unknown computers, open Active Directory Users and Computers. Next, open either the Domain Controllers or Computers folder (depends on the type of server on which you installed RIS), right-click on your RIS server, and choose Properties. Click on the Remote Install tab, which will bring up a property sheet like that in Figure 13-23.

13

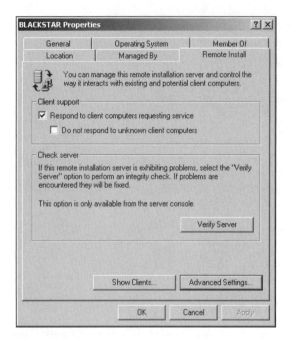

Figure 13-23   The Remote Install property sheet contains RIS server configuration settings

Defining a Computer Naming Convention

In addition to configuring the client support, you can choose Show Clients to search the Active Directory for known RIS client computers. For more security settings, however, click on the Advanced Settings button, which brings up the property sheet shown in Figure 13-24. Through this property sheet, you can define a computer naming convention for RIS clients. In most cases, you will not want users to come up with their own computer names when installing Windows 2000 Professional. If they do, you'll end up with a network full of nonstandard names that make administrative life difficult. Through Advanced Settings, you can determine not only what the naming convention will be, but also where in Active Directory the computer account will be created.

Note that if you choose a naming convention and an Active Directory location for the computer accounts, the user account under which the Client Installation Wizard is run must have the necessary permissions to add computer accounts to the domain.

Granting Computer Account Creation Rights

In order to be able to use the Client Installation Wizard to install Windows 2000 Professional into a domain, a user needs to have Read permission to the OU that has been defined as the Active Directory location for the new computer account. The user also must have permissions to create Computer objects.

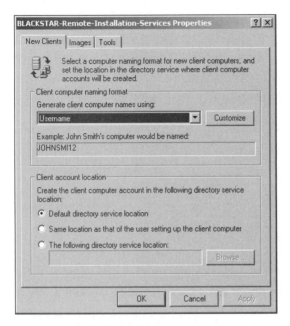

Figure 13-24   The Advanced Settings property sheet contains additional settings to tighten RIS security

In order to ensure a user has Read permission to the required OU, first click on View and select Advanced Features if it is not already selected in Active Directory Users and Computers. Next, right-click on the desired OU (such as Computers) and choose Properties. Then, click on the Security tab. Highlight Authenticated Users and verify that a check appears in the Read box under the Allow column, at minimum.

To allow a user permission to create Computer objects, you will need to use the Delegation Of Control Wizard. Right-click on the OU that will hold the computer account and choose Delegate Control. Select a group or user and click on Next. You will see a dialog box like that in Figure 13-25. Rather than delegate control of everything in this folder, which are far too many permissions for the simple task the user needs to complete (adding their computer account), choose the Only The Following Objects In The Folder option. Select Computer Objects from the list and click on Next. Choose Read and Write permissions, which will automatically select related permissions throughout the list, as in Figure 13-26.

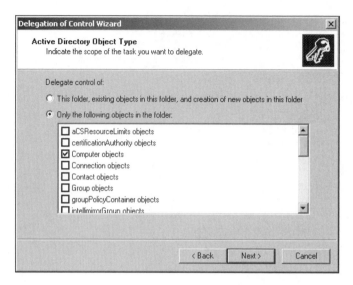

Figure 13-25   The Delegation of Control Wizard allows you to delegate Computer object creation to other users and groups

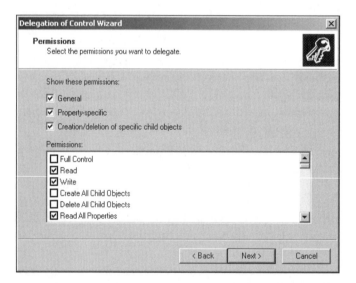

Figure 13-26   Within the Delegation of Control Wizard, you can choose the level of permissions you want the users or groups to have. Click on Next and then finish the wizard. At this point, the users and groups you selected will be able to add computer accounts to this OU

Prestaging Computers

If you do not wish to delegate control for users to add their own computers to an OU, you can use a process called **prestaging** to create computer accounts in advance and to ensure that each computer name is unique. Prestaging uses the computer's Globally Unique Identifier (GUID), which is stored in the BIOS of NetPC- or PC98-compatible computers, to identify the computer. The GUID is then stored with the computer account in Active Directory, ensuring that the specific computer that has the correct GUID will be the only computer to use the computer account. This is an excellent security measure. For example, suppose you know the username and password for a user who—as a potential RIS client—is authorized to add computers to a domain. You can run the Client Installation Wizard and access the RIS server, and you can even set up a domain computer, where you can start accessing network resources easily. It doesn't matter who you are, or what machine you're configuring; it can be a system you've brought from home, or you could be someone from the outside who really shouldn't be accessing the network but just got your very own domain computer through RIS. With prestaging, an administrator doesn't have to grant computer account creation rights to users.

In addition, by tying the computer's GUID to the computer account, an administrator can ensure that someone doesn't "borrow" a valid computer account for his or her own use. That way, you know that a specific computer is using a specific computer account at all times, reducing a potential security risk.

CHAPTER SUMMARY

In this chapter, you learned about Windows 2000 Server's Remote Installation Services, an optional utility that allows a compatible RIS client computer to connect to an RIS server and install the Windows 2000 Professional OS. Some of the key topics included the following:

13

- RIS can install only Windows 2000 Professional. It cannot be used to install Windows 2000 Server, Windows NT, or Windows 9*x*.

- RIS is dependent on Active Directory, Group Policy, DNS, and DHCP.

- An RIS client must support the Preboot Execution Environment (PXE) either through the system BIOS or the network adapter.

- A select number of network adapters are supported by the RIS boot disk, which is used to emulate a PXE environment.

- RISetup.exe is used to create CD-based installation images.

- RIPrep.exe is used to create custom images that can contain Windows 2000 Professional as well as third-party applications.

- RIS servers must be authorized through DHCP before they can respond to client requests.

❏ An administrator can prestage computers for increased security.

❏ If computer accounts are not prestaged, a user must have computer object creation permissions to complete Windows 2000 Professional setup successfully.

❏ An administrator can use Group Policy to determine which client installation options will be available to the user.

❏ RIPrep cannot be used to image a computer with multiple hard-disk partitions.

❏ The Windows 2000 Professional installation directory must be on the boot partition for RIPrep to succeed.

❏ The image process erases all information currently on the RIS client computer's hard disk.

ACTIVE DIRECTORY REPLICATION

After completing this chapter, you will be able to:

♦ Describe how the Windows 2000 domain controllers replicate data to each other

♦ Explain how Windows 2000 minimizes the amount of data that is replicated

♦ Explain how Windows 2000 prevents unnecessary data being copied across the network

♦ Describe what happens when simultaneous updates occur on a single object

♦ Describe the processes that Active Directory uses to prevent replication from swamping WAN links

If you are new to Active Directory, and if you have been paying close attention to the information in this book, you have probably already formulated lots of questions. In Chapter 2, you were introduced to the new terminology of Windows 2000 and to various components that have an effect on Active Directory. Now we are going to put some of that new terminology into practice, and at the same time we will answer some of the most pressing questions you might have regarding Active Directory.

INTRODUCTION TO ACTIVE DIRECTORY REPLICATION

Active Directory allows changes to occur at any domain controller, which is in contrast to Microsoft Windows NT 4 and earlier, where every change must occur at the Primary Domain Controller (PDC). In earlier versions, these changes are then replicated out to Backup Domain Controllers (BDCs) that contain read-only copies of domain data. It's fairly easy to understand the older model: Changes occur in one place and one place only, and they are then effectively copied everywhere else. In Windows 2000, changes can happen anywhere—so how is that information replicated (or copied) everywhere on the network? The answer is a complex mix of property versioning and in-memory tables that will be unraveled in this chapter.

Because a change can occur at any domain controller (DC), Active Directory has a problem. Let's say we make a change to a user's last name at a DC at the head office in Houston, Texas. The user actually works five blocks away and is authenticated by a local DC. What changes are sent from the DC in the head office to the local office? Does it make sense to send the entire copy of the directory? Maybe the DC should send all the information it has regarding the user. Microsoft has been careful to make sure that unnecessary data is not replicated on the network. As you will soon see, Microsoft's design goals are slightly different depending on whether the user's DC is on the same TCP/IP (IP) subnet as the DC in the head office.

When a change occurs at a DC in Windows 2000, the change causes the DC to let its partners know it has accepted a change. That triggers a replication process (we'll dig deep into this process later). This occurs for *every* change. So, let's take a scenario with three DCs. A change occurs at one, and the DC sends a message saying, "I've got a change" to a partner DC. That DC makes the change. Then *both* DCs let the third DC know that they have accepted changes. Is the change sent from both controllers? If it is, does the third controller write that change twice? What would prevent it from writing the change twice? We'll be taking a close look at the resolution process and how Active Directory keeps itself efficient.

As you will see, a distinct path is cut through your network. DCs in Active Directory do not actually replicate with every other DC. Instead, we have the concept of **replication partners**. (We'll define some terms in a moment.) If you work on a large network, you might have more than 100 DCs, and you might be thinking that it will take a lot of work to maintain those partners. What happens if you have a system crash in the middle of the day—does replication stop working? Actually, no; replication can heal itself in these circumstances. What's more, it's a totally hands-off process. Understanding this process will help you decide whether you should override what the system is trying to do.

A Windows 2000 network has two parts (actually, all BackOffice applications also have two parts, the logical model and the physical model). The first part is the logical model, which is a representation of how you want things to work, without regard to the physical nature of your network. For instance, you want to make sure you are able to support your administrative structure—and you might make decisions based on the system administrators' requirements. On the other hand, you ignore the physical aspects of your network at your peril. You simply cannot ignore the fact that your connection to a branch office is a T1 (1.54MB per second) link. You must take into account the amount of bandwidth available at any given point in the day. Active Directory wants to move data around your network at any time, so it is up to you to let it know where those slow links are, and how often they can be utilized.

The good news is that we address all of these questions, as well as many others, in this chapter. Active Directory provides an astonishing amount of automation, and you can also tweak it to your heart's content. In this chapter, we are going to explain this process and show you the tools you can use to look at what is really going on under the covers.

Learning Active Directory replication can be a daunting task. You must learn a lot of new terminology, and getting a handle on the precise process is difficult if you are totally new to it. In order to help you fully *see* what's going on, we have decided to show you the entire process in graphic form as figures. Of course, at first glance you might find it a bit overwhelming; however, in trying to decide how best to describe what is undoubtedly a complex process, a picture often speaks 1,000 words. Therefore, not only do we fully describe what is going on each step of the way, but the figures in this chapter provide a visual representation of what we describe. They start fairly simply, and then become more complex as they go on.

Before you can understand the process, you'll need to learn some new terminology. In fact, if you are learning about Active Directory replication for the first time, it is essential that you read this entire chapter and make sure that you understand the terminologies described in the next section. If, however, you are already familiar with the terminology and with what each part does, and you simply need a refresher on Active Directory replication, you might want to skip forward to the figures that explain the process.

Elements of Active Directory Replication

Once you have a clear understanding of the following terms, you will be ready to jump in and see the replication process. Believe it or not, the important terms described in this section cover just about everything you will need to know about Active Directory replication—so let's make sure we have good definitions for them.

Below is a list of terms we will use in our discussion of replication. Following the list is a detailed description of each term. The terms are:

- Domain controller (DC)
- Originating update
- Replicated update
- Update Sequence Number (USN)
- Replication partners

- High-watermark table

- Up-to-date vector table

- Property Version Numbers (PVN)

- Propagation dampening

- Knowledge Consistency Checker (KCC)

- Site links

- Convergence/latency

Domain Controller

Some of this information was covered briefly at the beginning of this chapter. It is repeated here for good reason, because the concept of DCs has changed quite drastically. Microsoft Windows NT also has a concept of domain controllers. In earlier versions, there are two types: Primary Domain Controllers (PDCs) and Backup Domain Controllers (BDCs). From a user perspective, these two types do basically the same thing—they authenticate you when you log on to the network. That is, you are first prompted for a user name and password, and then the name and password you type are checked against a database to make sure you really are who you say you are.

From the system administrator's point of view, the roles of these two types of DCs are very different. PDCs have a read/write version of the security database on them, while BDCs just have a read-only version. This means that, whenever administrators want to change a password or add a new user account, they have to connect to the PDC—no matter where it is on the network. Of course, this process is "invisible" in that administrators never actually have to choose the PDC specifically—but under the covers, that is what's going on.

This process causes some scalability issues. Think about this situation: The PDC for a domain is in the head office in Houston. You are a system administrator sitting in Northern Virginia making the change. Your computer has to connect to the PDC 3,000 miles away! Although the wonders of a network mean this connection can happen in a matter of seconds, it also causes network traffic to traverse many different pieces of cable and to cross probably several routers. It works, but it is not ideal.

With Windows 2000, Microsoft has addressed this problem by adopting what is called a **multi-master** approach. In this case, all DCs hold a read/write copy of the database. Likening this setup to Microsoft Windows NT, one would have to say that each DC in a Windows 2000 network is a PDC.

This approach solves the problem of scalability that applies to earlier versions. It does so by allowing administrators to make changes—such as user name changes—at a DC that is local to them. The administrator no longer has to send data across long distances to do simple administrative tasks. Of course, the approach also introduces another problem: If changes can happen anywhere on a network, then how do all the other DCs find out about those changes so they are up to date? That's the subject of this chapter—you'll understand the process after you get through all the information here.

Originating Update

We have already said that, in a Windows 2000 network, changes can occur at any DC. That is not to say that all changes are created equally. Two types of changes can occur, and the effects of each type of change are recorded in different places. The first type of change is an **originating update**. Put simply, an originating update is the first time a change is made to a property in Active Directory.

Think about this example: You have two DCs, and you log on as administrator and make a change to a user's password. That change must be written to the database. This is the first time that Active Directory knows of the change. At this point, no other DC is aware of what you are doing. Therefore, this is the originating update.

Replicated Update

Following from the previous definition, we have what is known as a **replicated update**, the second type of change. A replicated update is a change made to Active Directory that did not originate at that copy. Once a change has been successfully written to the first DC, the change must be sent to other DCs. When that change is sent, it will be written to the respective copies of Active Directory. Because the change did not originate at the DC, the change is considered to be a replicated update.

As you'll see later in this chapter, this subtle difference can cause other mechanisms to kick in. In some ways, DCs respond in the same manner to both originating updates and replicated updates. On the other hand, this difference can cause unique events.

> Don't be misled by the terms **originating update** and **replicated update**. They are merely efforts to explain that a change occurs somewhere in Active Directory for the first time, and is then copied everywhere else. It need not—necessarily—be what is traditionally thought of as a write. For instance, the deletion of an object is technically also a write, because the change causes new data (in this case, a deletion) to be written to the Directory. If you are connected to a DC and you delete an object, that action would be considered an originating update, in the context the term is used here.

Update Sequence Number

Every domain controller has to keep track of the number of changes it has made to its own copy of Active Directory. An Update Sequence Number (USN) is a 64-bit number that keeps track of changes as they are written to copies of the Active Directory. As changes are made, this number increments by one.

The number increments for several reasons, not least of all because doing so gives the DC a mechanism to let other DCs know it has made a change. The USN is one of the fundamental building blocks of Active Directory replication. This number *is unique to each DC*. This means that it is not shared among DCs. As time goes on, you will inevitably see that each DC has a different USN. You might have one DC with a USN of 400, and another with a USN of 5. This is not a problem—remember, the USN starts at 1 and increments by one for every change made. If you have a DC with a USN of 400, then this DC may have been online for a long time. A DC with a USN of 5 might be new. USN values can also change if a DC has been restored from backup.

It is not important that all DCs have the same number of changes, only that the USN increments by one for each change. Make sure that you understand this concept—if you don't, then you have missed a key element used in replication.

 The USN increments for *every* change made at a DC, including both originating updates and replicated updates. It does not matter where the change came from—this number will increment by one for each occurrence. You might wonder what happens when this number grows to its maximum size—after all, a 64-bit number is finite. You needn't worry: A 64-bit number means that you could write 10,000 changes per second and not run out of numbers for 66 million years. Anyone want to take a bet that there will be a new version of Windows 2000 on the market before then?

Replication Partners

Every DC can accept a change, and it then replicates the change around your network. Sounds simple, doesn't it? But, how is a server in London going to contact and replicate with a server in Houston? It probably won't. A **replication partner** defines a direct replication relationship. That is, if a DC sends data directly to another DC, the two DCs are said to be replication partners.

It is a key point to remember that in Windows 2000, every DC does not talk to every other DC. Instead, you end up with many little hops that make sure data is propagated everywhere. A single DC might replicate directly with one or several different partners. Those partners, in turn, will have different partners that they talk to, and so on. In the end, data is replicated throughout the network.

If you think about your network for a moment, you will see that this process makes perfect sense. First, unless you work on a very small network with few DCs in a single location, all of your DCs will not have a fast connection to every other DC. Consider remote offices, or DCs in foreign countries. It really does not make sense for a single DC to talk to every other one. Best let Active Directory build its own replication topology, as we'll discuss in a moment.

High-Watermark Table

Now you know that DCs band together into units called *replication partners*. But how does one controller know that a change has been made to a partner, and that the change needs to be replicated? It does this by using two tables that are stored in memory at each DC. One of these tables is the **high-watermark table**.

A high-watermark table stores the name of each of the DC's replication partners, along with the last known USN value for that DC.

> The statement we've just made is not quite accurate. Instead of the server name, the value in the high-watermark table is actually the Globally Unique Identifier (GUID) of the copy of Active Directory stored on a DC. Because GUIDs are 128-bit numbers that look like this:
>
> `a762f268-0dgg-11e4-b5f6-00b0c61e0543`
>
> we decided to simplify their representation. Although a GUID is an interesting piece of information, it does complicate things when writing about Active Directory replication. Just keep in mind that the actual server name is not stored in these tables.

The high-watermark table is used to make sure that only the necessary number of changes are sent during replication. (This process will be illustrated later.) The important thing to remember is that this table stores a record for *each replication partner only*.

> It is worth noting that Active Directory replication is *pull* only. Data is never pushed out. That is, a DC always asks for data to be replicated—the data is never forced upon the DC.

Up-to-Date Vector Table

The up-to-date vector table lists every DC on the network, along with the USN of the last originating update made on that DC. Let's analyze that statement a little bit.

We just looked at the high-watermark table, and it seems to contain similar information. But actually it doesn't—and this area can quickly become confusing to those who are new to Active Directory replication. Let's contrast these two tables and see where they differ.

In the case of the high-watermark table, the type of write (originating or replicated) that causes the USN to increment is not an issue. It does not matter. A change occurs, the USN increments, and it is now different—period. Also, entries are made only for those DCs that are replication partners, not for every DC in the domain. That is the extent of the USN when applied to the high-watermark table.

In the case of the up-to-date vector table, the type of write that occurs *is* important. This table contains an entry for every DC in the domain, along with the USN at the time of the last originating update. (If you don't remember the difference between an originating update and a replicated update, then refer back to our definition earlier in this chapter.) Essentially, the up-to-date vector table keeps a record of the last time a change was first made at each DC.

14

The purpose for these tables will quickly become clear later, when we present an example that illustrates Active Directory replication.

Property Version Numbers

Much of what you have seen so far consists of efforts to offer different levels of uniqueness. For instance, suppose you have recorded that the last change at a server was the one-hundredth change that occurred there. If the server indicates that it now has had 102 changes, it is obvious that two more have occurred since the last time you heard from the server. In order to work properly, Active Directory needs more information than the simple fact that there was a change. It is not enough that you know *where* something changed, or how many times a server has accepted a change—you also need to know how many times a *specific property* has changed. The reasons will become clear later, as we drill down to the replication process.

The Property Version Number (PVN) is a value that is appended to every property within Active Directory. It traces the number of times a specific property has changed. Properties start with a version of 1. If a change is made to the property, then it increments to version 2. This number is used to make sure that two replicated changes arriving at a DC have a method of working out precedence. A higher version number always "beats" a lower version number.

 There are always exceptions to the rule. In the event of a restore operation, it is possible to override this default behavior. However, ordinarily the PVN is a significant tool that you should not override. See Chapter 9 for details on restoring Active Directory and overriding PVNs.

Propagation Dampening

Propagation dampening is a term used to describe the process that Active Directory uses to ensure that changes don't endlessly loop around a Windows 2000 network. The basic principle of replication is a change to Active Directory. As you have seen, such a change causes the USN to increment, which in turn causes a DC to signal its replication partners. Any change—replicated or originating—causes the USN to increment. So, even the process of receiving a replicated update will cause this trigger to fire. Obviously this process is not ideal, because it could trigger a storm of replications on your network, flooding it with traffic.

To understand fully how Active Directory performs propagation dampening, you need to have a good understanding of all the other terms defined in this section. Furthermore, to explain it in paragraphs of text might make for some dry reading. We'll cover this topic in detail later in the chapter.

Knowledge Consistency Checker

By now you should be aware that replication within Active Directory is a controlled process. Instead of broadcasting changes into the network for everyone to hear, DCs replicate their changes with replication partners. Administering all those links would be a lot of work—but, fortunately, the process is largely automatic.

The Knowledge Consistency Checker (KCC) is a background service that creates links between your DCs. These links are used for replication. It is possible (but not recommended) to override the KCC, but doing so complicates your Windows 2000 network design. What's more, the KCC periodically goes back and reevaluates its replication topology. If changes have occurred on a network (perhaps a new DC has been brought online, or an old one has crashed), then the KCC will recalculate an optimal path and reconfigure Windows 2000 automatically. It is highly recommended that you allow the KCC to build your links.

You might well imagine that this is one of those smoke-and-mirror items you hear about sometimes—you know, like when a vendor tells you that something is automatic, but you really have to do most of the work yourself. Well, for once the hyperbole is accurate. The KCC really does work in the background, making sure that replication is efficient on your network.

 The KCC service runs on DCs. However, you won't see an entry for it on the process list, because the KCC runs in the context of the Local Security Authority (LSA). The KCC links together DCs using a proprietary algorithm. This algorithm creates a two-way ring topology that offers fault tolerance to the replication process. Furthermore, the KCC ensures that the DCs it connects are never more than three hops away from each other.

Site Links

A site link is a connector that can be configured between two Active Directory sites. These links have values assigned to them that include a **cost**. This cost is simply a number: The larger the number, the higher the cost. The KCC uses this information when calculating the route that replication should take. For instance, suppose two routes exist from DC A to DC B, and the former has a cost of 2, whereas the latter has a cost of 6. The KCC will favor the first route because it is "cheaper."

Convergence/Latency

Convergence is term used to describe a network in which all DCs are 100 percent up to date: There are no more changes to be replicated. In a Windows 2000 world, this state is something akin to Nirvana. Don't be worried if you never quite reach it (or reach it and can't maintain it for very long). The goal is not necessarily to have no replication taking place, but to ensure that replication is working efficiently.

Latency, on the other hand, describes the inherent delay in replication. When a change is replicated, a communication line must be set up between DCs, packets of data must be sent and analyzed, and changes must be sent and written to Active Directory. All this takes time—albeit a relatively small amount of time. This delay is called *latency*. Latency is not always a problem, and it occurs all the time. In fact, sometimes you'll cause latency deliberately—for example, when you are connecting different sites (more on this later).

On the other hand, you do not want too much latency. Striking a balance between too much and too little is the job of the system designers, who should pay close attention to minimizing latency (but not to eliminating it).

We have used many new terms in this chapter. Don't worry if you can't memorize them straight away. When you begin to see how they are used, they will make more sense. Although the list is not exhaustive, you now have been introduced to all the concepts you need to understand how replication works.

THE REPLICATION PROCESS ILLUSTRATED

The terms defined so far in this chapter are the key to your understanding of how replication works within Windows 2000. However, we do realize that reading a list of terms and their definitions is not the optimal way to learn something. You need to know about the *process* of replication. In the following section, you will see replication working in a series of figures.

What follows is a scenario at the InsideIS network. We have a fairly small network at our business, but it includes all the elements you need to learn about Active Directory replication. Let's begin by taking a look at our network. In Figure 14-1, you see our simple network: four DCs named after our four favorite places (Basildon, Dallas, Houston, and London). Each DC is on the same subnet, and therefore, by definition, they are on the same site. Each has fast connectivity to every other DC.

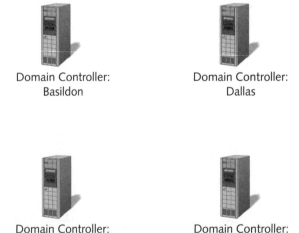

Domain Controller:
Basildon

Domain Controller:
Dallas

Domain Controller:
Houston

Domain Controller:
London

Figure 14-1   Inside IS domain with four DCs

In Windows 2000, every DC in a domain has replication partners with which it shares information. These partnerships form a web that eventually allows every DC to learn about every change that occurs. Let's draw in the replication partners for each of these DCs, as shown in Figure 14-2.

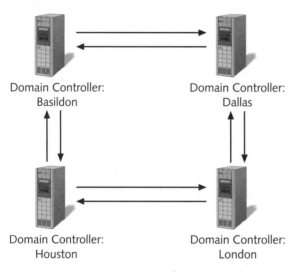

Domain Controller:
Basildon

Domain Controller:
Dallas

Domain Controller:
Houston

Domain Controller:
London

Figure 14-2   Domain controllers and replication partners

In order to help you fully understand what this figure is showing, Table 14-1 details what is shown there.

Table 14-1   Domain controllers and their replication partners

Domain Controller	Replication Partners
Basildon	Dallas and Houston
Dallas	Basildon and London
Houston	Basildon and London
London	Dallas and Houston

Earlier in this chapter we talked about *convergence* and *latency*. In a fully converged network, every change that has been made in Active Directory has been successfully replicated to every DC. Latency is the amount of delay before this replication takes place. In the example, we have a fully converged network: That is, everything is perfect (for the moment).

Figure 14-3 fills out our network diagram to show all the elements we will need for the rest of this chapter. First, we added the USNs to each of the servers. Remember that the USN increments by one for each change the DC accepts. At first glance, you might think that all DCs would have the same number—after all, each DC ends up knowing about every change, so it stands to reason that each DC would eventually have the same USN.

14

However, many things can cause DCs to have different USNs. For the moment, we are going to assume that each DC has been up for a different amount of time. London was brought online first, and Basildon was brought online last. Therefore, London has had to make more changes than Basildon, and its USN has incremented a greater number of times.

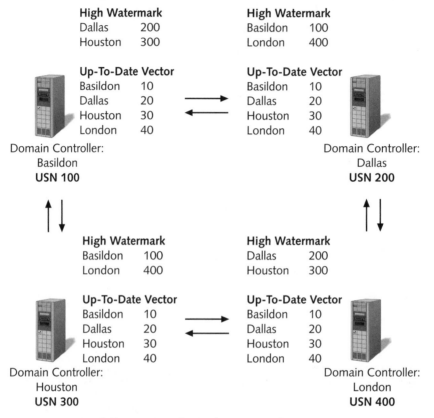

High Watermark
Dallas	200
Houston	300

Up-To-Date Vector
Basildon	10
Dallas	20
Houston	30
London	40

Domain Controller:
  Basildon
  USN 100

High Watermark
Basildon	100
London	400

Up-To-Date Vector
Basildon	10
Dallas	20
Houston	30
London	40

Domain Controller:
  Dallas
  USN 200

High Watermark
Basildon	100
London	400

Up-To-Date Vector
Basildon	10
Dallas	20
Houston	30
London	40

Domain Controller:
  Houston
  USN 300

High Watermark
Dallas	200
Houston	300

Up-To-Date Vector
Basildon	10
Dallas	20
Houston	30
London	40

Domain Controller:
  London
  USN 400

Figure 14-3   A fully converged Windows 2000 domain

We also added the high-watermark table and the up-to-date vector table to each DC. As defined earlier in this chapter, the high-watermark table lists the USNs for each replication partner. Figure 14-2 shows that each DC has two partners, so there are two entries in each DC's high-watermark table.

The up-to-date vector table, you'll recall, contains an entry for every DC in the domain, along with the USN value of the last time the DC performed an originating write. So, there are four entries for each DC. Because this table is concerned only with originating writes, the USN number in this table does not match the actual USN number of a DC.

With this information in hand, we are ready to complicate things a little. We have two administrators we'll call righthand and lefthand, and it should come as no surprise to learn that lefthand doesn't know what righthand is doing—and vice versa.

In our next step, shown in Figure 14-4, lefthand opens the Windows 2000 administration tools and makes a change to the **Description** property for Siobhan, who is a user on our network. Lefthand doesn't care which DC processed the change, and in our case the property change is first made on the London DC.

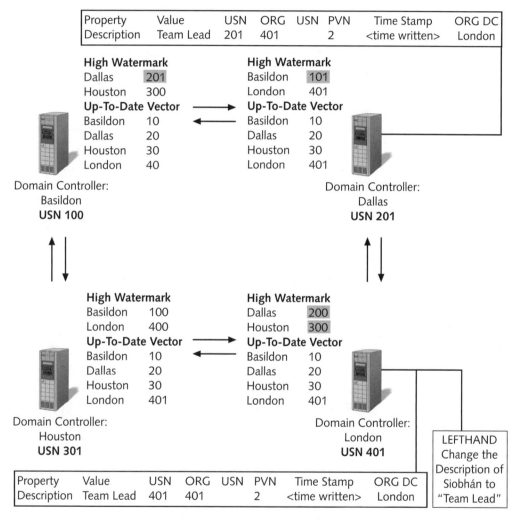

Property	Value	USN	ORG	USN	PVN	Time Stamp	ORG DC
Description	Team Lead	201	401		2	<time written>	London

High Watermark
Dallas   201
Houston   300
Up-To-Date Vector
Basildon 10
Dallas   20
Houston   30
London   40

High Watermark
Basildon 101
London   401
Up-To-Date Vector
Basildon 10
Dallas   20
Houston   30
London   401

Domain Controller:
  Basildon
  USN 100

Domain Controller:
  Dallas
  USN 201

High Watermark
Basildon 100
London   400
Up-To-Date Vector
Basildon 10
Dallas   20
Houston   30
London   401

High Watermark
Dallas   200
Houston   300
Up-To-Date Vector
Basildon 10
Dallas   20
Houston   30
London   401

Domain Controller:
  Houston
  USN 301

Domain Controller:
  London
  USN 401

LEFTHAND
Change the Description of Siobhán to "Team Lead"

Property	Value	USN	ORG	USN	PVN	Time Stamp	ORG DC
Description	Team Lead	401	401		2	<time written>	London

Figure 14-4   Changing a user property

This simple change has actually caused quite a few changes. Let's take a look at what we have added to our figure. Our administrator lefthand changed a property in the DC called London. Because a change is being made on that server, the USN of that server increments by one: The USN for London is now 401. But there is more to it than that—

this is an originating write, so London also writes its current USN in its up-to-date vector table. London's entry in that table now reads

    London 401

 This is a common area of confusion: Why didn't that up-to-date vector simply increment by one? The up-to-date vector table simply stores the USN value of a DC *at the time of an originating update*. The table does not attempt to track the number of originating updates that have occurred at the DC—only the USN at the time they occurred.

Figure 14-4 also shows the data that has changed. (This data is somewhat simplified for the purposes of the book—for instance, the ORG DC field should really be the DC GUID. However, that would confuse the issue, so we changed the value to the server's name.)

Note that the PVN of the **Description** property is 2. When the property was created, the PVN was 1; but now the property has changed, so this is version 2. You will see how this comes into play in a moment.

Because there has been a change at the London DC, this DC must send a message to each of its replication partners saying, "I have a change." They will then pull that change from London. Figure 14-5 shows what the picture looks like when this change replicates to both Dallas and Houston.

A lot just happened. The changes that occurred at the Dallas and Houston DCs are similar, so we will use Dallas as our example. First, the change was written to the DC, which in Dallas caused the USN number to increment to 201. Because the change originated in London, the up-to-date vector for London was also updated. This change was not an originating write at Dallas: It was a replicated write. Therefore, the up-to-date vector for Dallas did not change.

The high watermark for London also changed, because the high watermark records the last USN number that Dallas knew about from London. Because this number is now different, an update occurred to reflect the new value.

You should note the data that was replicated to Dallas. The USN number of the write has changed to reflect the USN number at Dallas when this change was made. However, the ORG USN number remained unchanged. Also, the PVN did not change.

The values in London's high-watermark table also changed. They now reflect the new USNs of both its replication partners.

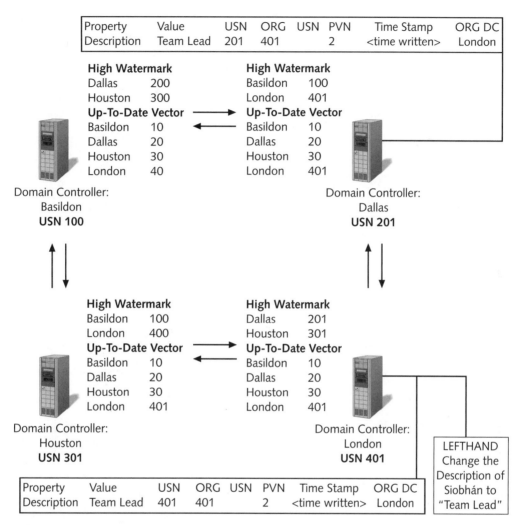

Property	Value	USN	ORG	USN	PVN	Time Stamp	ORG DC
Description	Team Lead	201	401		2	<time written>	London

High Watermark
Dallas   200
Houston   300
Up-To-Date Vector ⟶
Basildon   10   ⟵
Dallas   20
Houston   30
London   40

High Watermark
Basildon   100
London   401
Up-To-Date Vector
Basildon   10
Dallas   20
Houston   30
London   401

Domain Controller:
   Basildon
   USN 100

Domain Controller:
   Dallas
   USN 201

High Watermark
Basildon   100
London   400
Up-To-Date Vector ⟶
Basildon   10   ⟵
Dallas   20
Houston   30
London   401

High Watermark
Dallas   201
Houston   301
Up-To-Date Vector
Basildon   10
Dallas   20
Houston   30
London   401

Domain Controller:
   Houston
   USN 301

Domain Controller:
   London
   USN 401

Property	Value	USN	ORG	USN	PVN	Time Stamp	ORG DC
Description	Team Lead	401	401		2	<time written>	London

LEFTHAND
Change the
Description of
Siobhán to
"Team Lead"

14

Figure 14-5   Change is replicated to Dallas and Houston

Now, things are going to get interesting. The change is safely made at Dallas and Houston, but Basildon has not seen it yet. Basildon is a replication partner for both Dallas and Houston, and it can get the change from either; but, of course, one of them will be first. In this case, we will assume that Dallas informs Basildon of the change, and that Basildon then pulls it from Dallas. When this occurs, we will have the circumstance shown in Figure 14-6.

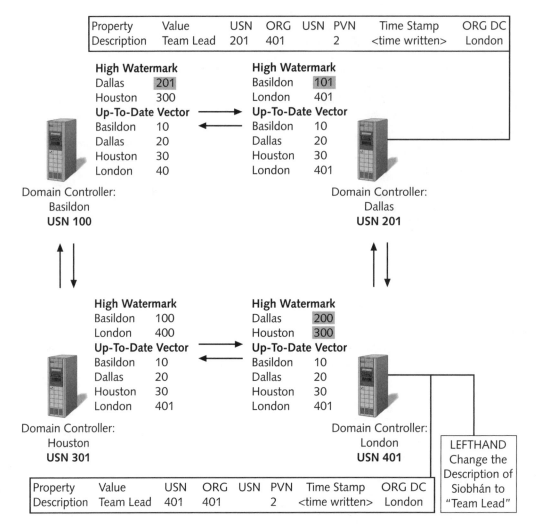

Property	Value	USN	ORG USN	PVN	Time Stamp	ORG DC
Description	Team Lead	201	401	2	<time written>	London

High Watermark
| Dallas | 201 |
| Houston | 300 |

High Watermark
| Basildon | 101 |
| London | 401 |

Up-To-Date Vector
Basildon	10
Dallas	20
Houston	30
London	40

Up-To-Date Vector
Basildon	10
Dallas	20
Houston	30
London	401

Domain Controller:
Basildon
USN 100

Domain Controller:
Dallas
USN 201

High Watermark
| Basildon | 100 |
| London | 400 |

High Watermark
| Dallas | 200 |
| Houston | 300 |

Up-To-Date Vector
Basildon	10
Dallas	20
Houston	30
London	401

Up-To-Date Vector
Basildon	10
Dallas	20
Houston	30
London	401

Domain Controller:
Houston
USN 301

Domain Controller:
London
USN 401

LEFTHAND
Change the
Description of
Siobhán to
"Team Lead"

Property	Value	USN	ORG USN	PVN	Time Stamp	ORG DC
Description	Team Lead	401	401	2	<time written>	London

Figure 14-6   Change is replicated to Basildon

Let's examine what occurred at Basildon. The USN for Basildon incremented by one to 101. Replication also caused changes to both the high-watermark and up-to-date vector tables. To help you keep track of these changes, let's make a quick list of everything that changed in Basildon:

- USN of Basildon
- High-watermark table entry for Dallas
- Up-to-date vector for London
- High-watermark entry for Basildon stored at Dallas

The change came from Dallas, but Houston wants to replicate to Basildon, too. What's more, it wants to replicate the very same information. Let's zero in on that conversation, as shown in Figure 14-7.

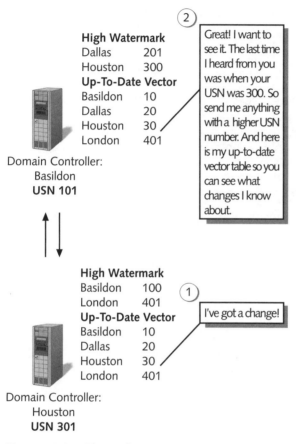

Figure 14-7   The replication conversation

Basildon had quite a bit to say, but where did it get all that information? First, it looked into its high-watermark table and noted that the last time it spoke with Houston, the USN for Houston was 300. So, Basildon asked for changes over 300. It then packaged its up-to-date vector table and sent the table to Houston. The up-to-date vector stores a list of all the originating writes that Basildon knows about. Houston will need this to enforce propagation dampening. Let's see how that works by taking a look at what Houston does when it gets this data from Basildon, as shown in Figure 14-8.

14

Okay, now I have Basildon's up-to-date vector table. Basildon only asked for changes over 300. Because my USN is 301, I know that change to 301 caused us to get out of sync. All I have to do is search through my replica and find the property with a USN of 301. Okay–found it! The ORG DC was London (read from the property), and the ORG USN was 401. Before I replicate, let me check Basildon's up-to-date vector table to see if it already knew about the change. Hey, Basildon already had it! Basildon, I don't have any data for you, but please update your high watermark for me!

Domain Controller:
Houston
USN 301

Figure 14-8   Propagation dampening at Houston

It may look like a long conversation is going on at Houston, but the upshot is that redundant data was not sent to Basildon. You can see our domain in Figure 14-9. Note that the high-watermark table at Basildon has been updated to reflect this conversation.

Now for the tricky part. When Dallas replicated the data to Basildon, the USN number of Basildon incremented. As a result, Basildon will enter the change process itself: It will tell Houston, "I have a change," and Houston will ask Basildon for that change. This process was shown in Figures 14-7 and 14-8. Of course, no data is exchanged, but you should know that the process is triggered.

Once you have been through the replication process a few times, it will become second nature. Of course, we have not covered every eventuality. Let's throw something a bit more complex into the mix.

Replication Conflicts Illustrated

So far in this discussion, we have gone from a fully converged network to a network in which a change was being made. We ended up with a fully converged network again. Now we will have each of our administrators make a change, and see what happens.

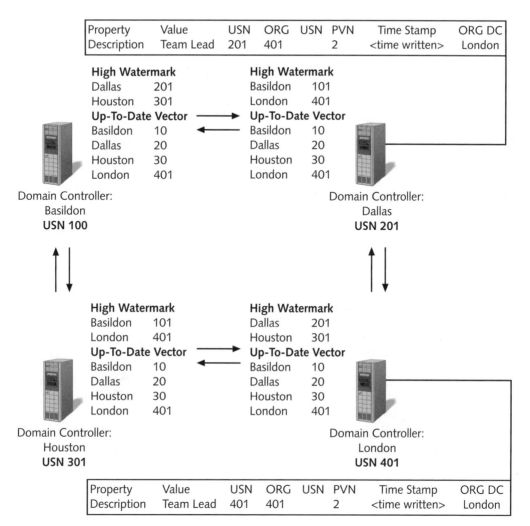

Property	Value	USN	ORG USN	PVN	Time Stamp	ORG DC
Description	Team Lead	201	401	2	<time written>	London

High Watermark
Dallas   201
Houston   301
Up-To-Date Vector
Basildon   10
Dallas   20
Houston   30
London   401

High Watermark
Basildon   101
London   401
Up-To-Date Vector
Basildon   10
Dallas   20
Houston   30
London   401

Domain Controller:
Basildon
USN 100

Domain Controller:
Dallas
USN 201

High Watermark
Basildon   101
London   401
Up-To-Date Vector
Basildon   10
Dallas   20
Houston   30
London   401

High Watermark
Dallas   201
Houston   301
Up-To-Date Vector
Basildon   10
Dallas   20
Houston   30
London   401

Domain Controller:
Houston
USN 301

Domain Controller:
London
USN 401

Property	Value	USN	ORG USN	PVN	Time Stamp	ORG DC
Description	Team Lead	401	401	2	<time written>	London

Figure 14-9   A fully converged InsideIS network

In the following example, the administrator in London—lefthand—will update the **Description** property of a user object called Mike. At the same time, the administrator in Basildon—righthand—will make a change to the same property. In Figure 14-10, you can see how things look as the changes are made.

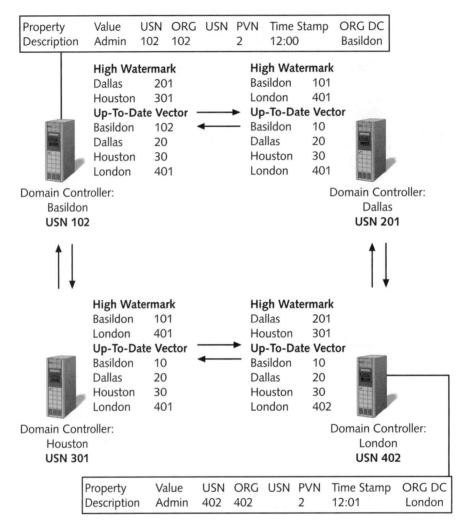

Property	Value	USN	ORG USN	PVN	Time Stamp	ORG DC
Description	Admin	102	102	2	12:00	Basildon

High Watermark
Dallas   201
Houston   301
Up-To-Date Vector
Basildon   102
Dallas   20
Houston   30
London   401

High Watermark
Basildon   101
London   401
Up-To-Date Vector
Basildon   10
Dallas   20
Houston   30
London   401

Domain Controller:
Basildon
USN 102

High Watermark
Basildon   101
London   401
Up-To-Date Vector
Basildon   10
Dallas   20
Houston   30
London   401

Domain Controller:
Houston
USN 301

High Watermark
Basildon   101
London   401
Up-To-Date Vector
Basildon   102
Dallas   20
Houston   30
London   401

Domain Controller:
Dallas
USN 201

High Watermark
Dallas   201
Houston   301
Up-To-Date Vector
Basildon   10
Dallas   20
Houston   30
London   402

Domain Controller:
London
USN 402

Property	Value	USN	ORG USN	PVN	Time Stamp	ORG DC
Description	Admin	402	402	2	12:01	London

Figure 14-10   Two changes made on the same property

As you have seen, DCs replicate with their replication partners. A partner can (and probably will) have more than one replication partner. Changes that arrive at a DC are dealt with one at a time. In our example, Basildon and London have the same replication partners. For the purposes of this example, we will use Houston to illustrate how replication conflicts are resolved.

A replication conflict occurs when a change is made to a single property at about the same time on two different DCs. In our case, we are back with our trusty **Description** property. Because we've already discussed some of this process, let's jump ahead. In Figure 14-11, you can see that Basildon has successfully replicated the change to Houston (beating London to the punch).

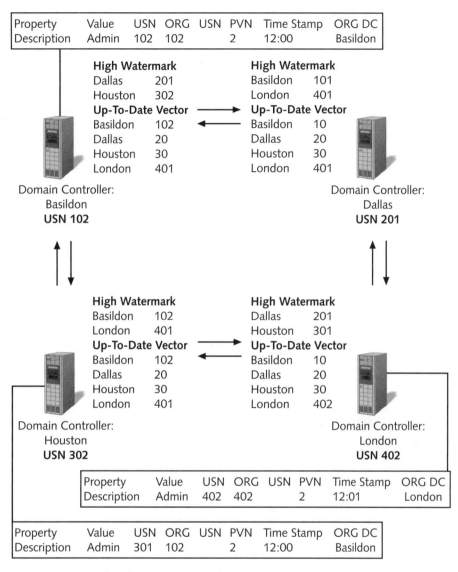

Property	Value	USN	ORG	USN	PVN	Time Stamp	ORG DC
Description	Admin	102	102		2	12:00	Basildon

High Watermark
Dallas   201
Houston   302
Up-To-Date Vector
Basildon   102
Dallas   20
Houston   30
London   401

High Watermark
Basildon   101
London   401
Up-To-Date Vector
Basildon   10
Dallas   20
Houston   30
London   401

Domain Controller:
Basildon
USN 102

Domain Controller:
Dallas
USN 201

High Watermark
Basildon   102
London   401
Up-To-Date Vector
Basildon   102
Dallas   20
Houston   30
London   401

High Watermark
Dallas   201
Houston   301
Up-To-Date Vector
Basildon   10
Dallas   20
Houston   30
London   402

Domain Controller:
Houston
USN 302

Domain Controller:
London
USN 402

Property	Value	USN	ORG	USN	PVN	Time Stamp	ORG DC
Description	Admin	402	402		2	12:01	London

Property	Value	USN	ORG	USN	PVN	Time Stamp	ORG DC
Description	Admin	301	102		2	12:00	Basildon

Figure 14-11   The change arrives at Houston

The following items have changed since Figure 14-10:

- The USN of Houston incremented by one

- The high-watermark table changed at Houston

- The high-watermark table changed at Basildon

- The up-to-date vector table changed at Houston

- The property changed at Houston

Now, let's cause a conflict. Houston has the change from Basildon and now accepts the change from London. First, it looks at the high watermark for London and asks for anything with a USN higher than 401. It also sends its up-to-date vector table so London can perform propagation dampening.

In this case, as far as London knows, propagation dampening need not take place. London doesn't yet know about the change made at Basildon, so it is going to replicate its own data. Once this analysis has taken place, the updated property will be replicated. The rest of this work occurs at Houston.

Figure 14-12 (shown on page 385) shows what our situation looks like once the data has been sent from London to Houston.

Houston now has another change to the same data. To figure out whether it should make this change in Active Directory, it uses a three-step process. If the first step fails, it moves on to the next step. These three steps are as follows:

1. Compare PVNs

2. Compare date and time information

3. Compare Active Directory GUIDs

Let's apply this process to our example so we can see how it works. First, Houston compares the PVN of the information it just received from London with the PVN of the property it just wrote. If the London PVN is higher than the value from Basildon, then the game is over: The London data wins. In this case, the PVNs are the same.

Next, Houston compares the date and time of the two sets of information. If they are the same (within one second of each other), then Houston will move on to the third and final parameter. In our case, however, the change in London happened one minute after the one in Basildon. Therefore, the London data overwrites the change made at Basildon.

If necessary, the final step compares the GUIDs of each Active Directory replica. Whichever is higher will win. It is unlikely that this would ever be the determining factor, however, because there is little chance of changes being made within one second of each other.

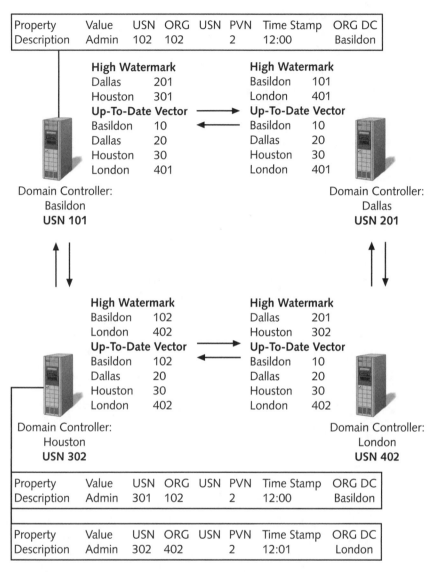

Property	Value	USN	ORG USN	PVN	Time Stamp	ORG DC
Description	Admin	102	102	2	12:00	Basildon

High Watermark
Dallas   201
Houston   301
Up-To-Date Vector
Basildon   10
Dallas   20
Houston   30
London   401

High Watermark
Basildon   101
London   401
Up-To-Date Vector
Basildon   10
Dallas   20
Houston   30
London   401

Domain Controller:
Basildon
USN 101

Domain Controller:
Dallas
USN 201

High Watermark
Basildon   102
London   402
Up-To-Date Vector
Basildon   102
Dallas   20
Houston   30
London   402

High Watermark
Dallas   201
Houston   302
Up-To-Date Vector
Basildon   10
Dallas   20
Houston   30
London   402

Domain Controller:
Houston
USN 302

Domain Controller:
London
USN 402

14

Property	Value	USN	ORG USN	PVN	Time Stamp	ORG DC
Description	Admin	301	102	2	12:00	Basildon

Property	Value	USN	ORG USN	PVN	Time Stamp	ORG DC
Description	Admin	302	402	2	12:01	London

Figure 14-12   Data replicated from London to Houston

Just for the sake of completeness, Figure 14-13 (shown on page 386) illustrates what our figure will look like once everything is nicely converged again. When convergence is achieved, all changes are written to all DCs.

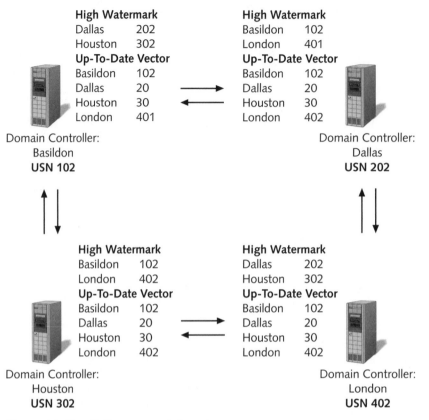

Figure 14-13 Fully coverged domain

INTERSITE AND INTRASITE REPLICATION

We need to discuss one final topic. In order to simplify what is, in all honesty, a somewhat complex task, we used a fairly simple example earlier in this chapter. It included a few DCs that each had fast connectivity (10Mbps or more) between them. Also, our DCs were in the same domain and in the same subnet, and therefore they could replicate whenever they wanted. Of course, life is never that easy, so we need to fill in the blanks.

For a better real-world view of replication, we need to take into consideration the effects of slow links (links slower than 10Mbps) on replication. Obviously, replication across these links cannot happen with the same frequency as it can across fast links. Windows 2000 helps by defining both physical aspects of your network (by IP subnet) and then allowing you to apply costs and a schedule that dictate when replication can occur. IP subnets are grouped into sites.

Windows 2000 sites were discussed in Chapter 2. A **site** is a group of well-connected DCs. This group is defined by IP subnets. Active Directory replication works in slightly different ways depending upon the location of the DCs to which the data needs to be replicated.

Replication within a site (**intrasite replication**) happens as quickly as possible. The focus of Microsoft's design is to get the data replicated quickly. Because the DCs are well connected, bandwidth is not an issue. For **intersite replication** (replication between DCs in different sites), replication is geared toward preserving bandwidth. Intersite replication has the following qualities:

- Data is compressed before it is sent.

- Replication occurs on a schedule.

Replication between sites occurs through **bridgehead servers** (also defined in Chapter 2). Basically, there is a connection point between the two sites—this connection point is between a server in one site and a server in the other. Each server acts as a **bridgehead** (hence the name "bridgehead servers") within its site. Active Directory data is replicated between the two bridgeheads. Once the bridgehead server knows about the changes, replication within each respective site occurs normally (as discussed in our example in this chapter).

CHAPTER SUMMARY

❑ In this chapter, we took a detailed look at Active Directory replication. We started with a simple overview of the Windows 2000 components that participate in the process. These components are:

- Domain controller (DC)

- Originating update

- Replicated update

- Update Sequence Number (USN)

- Replication partners

- High-watermark table

- Up-to-date vector table

- Property Version Numbers (PVN)

- Propagation dampening

- Knowledge Consistency Checker (KCC)

- Site links

- Convergence/latency

14

❏ Each of these components has a role to play in replication. Once we had defined these terms, we took a detailed look at two replication scenarios. First, we noted that replication traffic is not broadcast across the network. Instead, each DC has what is known as a replication partner (or partners)—and it replicates only with these partners. Replication partners can be chosen manually, but you are better off letting the KCC do this for you. In order for the KCC to work, you must define site links with Active Directory, essentially associating costs with slow links. The KCC will examine these site links and the sites you have defined in Active Directory, and will use a proprietary algorithm to work out the optimal path of communication (or replication partners).

❏ If a DC goes offline or a new DC is installed on the network, the KCC will notice this event on its next cycle. If necessary, it will redefine replication partners for DCs. In any case, the KCC does this by default every 30 minutes. It is a good idea to let the KCC do its work unhindered.

❏ We next showed a single change and how it was replicated throughout a network. Starting with a fully converged network, we saw a change made at one DC ripple out and be copied to all DCs in the domain. This process directly affects two tables stored in the memory of every DC: the high-watermark table and the up-to-date vector table. We also observed that the USN of each DC incremented as the change replicated.

❏ We saw that this form of multi-master replication has some problems. Because a change made at a controller causes the controller to want to replicate, you could end up with storms of changes that would hurt the performance of your network. The process that is in place to stop this problem is called propagation dampening. We examined how it works and what mechanisms are involved in the resolution.

❏ We looked at the process that takes place when a change is made to the same property at two different DCs, at about the same time. Eventually, these changes will clash at a DC and need to be resolved.

❏ The three tie-breaker mechanisms are:

- Comparing PVNs

- Comparing times and dates

- Comparing Active Directory GUIDs

❏ These steps act as a filter. The first comparison is applied; if that fails to resolve the issue, then the second is applied; and so on. Because no GUID can be duplicated, this system guarantees that a conflict can be resolved.

❏ Finally, we discussed the difference between intrasite replication and intersite replication. Intrasite replication refers to replication that takes place within a single site. Intersite replication occurs across multiple sites. Intersite replication differs from intrasite in that the data being replicated is compressed before being sent (intrasite replication data is not compressed). Also, replication between sites occurs on a fixed schedule.

15

SECURITY

After completing this chapter, you will be able to:

♦ Describe why security is important in Windows 2000

♦ Define auditing in Windows 2000

♦ Describe how auditing in Windows 2000 differs from that in Microsoft Windows NT 4

♦ Name the log file that contains all auditing entries

♦ Describe the three key pieces of information that auditing can provide

♦ Describe how auditing policies are integrated into Group Policy

♦ Know the order in which policies are applied on a Windows 2000 computer

♦ Know how to configure and implement auditing policies on a Windows 2000 system

♦ Describe available policy options available for files, folders, Active Directory objects, and printers

♦ Describe and define the purpose of security templates

♦ Describe and use the Security Configuration and Analysis tool

Few tasks are more important than making sure your Windows 2000 network environment is secure. Windows 2000 ships with many different tools that are designed to help you configure, implement, and support your security infrastructure, and we will look at the key tools in this chapter.

Security works at many different levels. You can't click on a single button to achieve a secure network. In fact, in order to ensure that invalid users do not access data on your network, you must form a comprehensive plan for how you will approach the issue, and then follow through with vigilance and enforcement.

Securing a network is a question of balance. The more secure your network needs to be, the more work you probably will create for yourself—it will take you longer to design your security plans, to implement your plans, and to maintain your policy. A network that is *too* secure might generate more support calls or prevent you from achieving the goal of making your network invisible to your users. On the other hand, a network that is not secure enough could create havoc.

Security is about preventing unwanted actions from occurring on your network. It includes preventing unauthorized access to resources or documents, validating users or groups if necessary, and making them accountable for the operations they perform. Security is a vital part of your initial network design, driving such factors as the creation of user accounts, groups, and Organizational Units (OU); delegation of authority; placement of domain controllers; replication strategies; and so on.

Fortunately, Microsoft has provided several tools to help you take control of your network. The flexibility of these tools means you can have a very secure network, or a less secure one. The balance is largely due to administrative overhead. The network should be as secure as you need it to be—but no more, because it will take time to monitor the network and maintain the policies you put in place.

When we think of security, we often think about two key areas: Who can access the network (user accounts), and what can a user do while on the network (resource management). In simple terms, does the user have a valid username and password? And, does the user have sufficient rights on the network to access the files and shares he or she needs? These concerns have not changed much from previous versions of Microsoft Windows NT, but the method by which these restrictions are achieved has changed. By leveraging the new feature set of Windows 2000, Microsoft has developed a scalable, manageable, and robust security infrastructure. With some careful design and implementation guidelines, and armed with a good understanding of how they work, you should be able to implement a policy that covers all areas of concern.

But, of course, security involves more than simply deciding what needs to be secure and then following through with assigning permissions. You also need to monitor your configuration. In fact, monitoring is a key consideration, and this area can increase both the cost and labor involved in making sure your network is secure. Security is a balance between convenience and administrative workload. The more secure you make your network, the more work you as an administrator will have to do up front, and also as you move forward.

The policies you put in place will need to be monitored and maintained. They should be reviewed periodically to make sure you are achieving the goals you set. This review will involve using familiar tools such as Event Viewer, and less familiar tools such as the Security Configuration and Analysis Console. Checking your security options should become one of your daily (or weekly) administrative tasks (along with maintenance chores such as checking the success or failure of backup operations).

Because Windows 2000 offers many tools and methods of securing a network, you need to be introduced to the range of tools and how they can be used. The security requirements for your organization will vary. Therefore, it is impossible for us to detail every option you will want to use. By introducing you to the features of each option, however, we can help you decide which tool to use, and how easy or difficult it will be for you to achieve the level of security you require.

WHAT IS AUDITING?

As a system administrator, you will want to know what is going on in your network. But how can you do this when your network is dispersed within your organization, and probably across different countries? The answer is the built-in auditing function of Windows 2000.

Auditing has been available for quite some time in Microsoft Windows NT 4. However, because Windows 2000 has more features and different methods of maintaining user accounts and various other objects within Active Directory, you will find that the configuration interface (and the number of functions that can be audited) has changed. We will look at how you use the auditing functions; before we do, however, let's examine what can be audited, and what the repercussion of auditing can be.

Auditing is the ability to keep a record of certain events and activities. In fact, any activity that involves a Windows 2000 security object can be audited. These events are displayed in the Security Log of the local machine. Security Logs will be covered in more detail later in this chapter. For now, all you need to know is that you can view the Security Log in the Computer Management utility.

By default, the Security Log is empty, because by default Windows 2000 does not perform any auditing. This behavior does not mean that all the security mechanisms are not in place and working—it simply means that a log of these events is not being written. You can think of a log as a bank statement; it details everything you have asked it to track. By default, it tracks nothing.

It is a good idea to audit important events on your system—so why is the default *not* to audit? The problem is, auditing an event takes processing time, and a log can also consume quite a bit of CPU time and hard disk space. In fact, auditing every event is a good way to cripple a machine.

We need a sensible implementation of auditing. We will look at some of the events you might want to audit during this discussion. But first, let's consider the types of information you can expect to see in the Security Log.

15

 You should remember reading about Event Viewer and the various logs it displays in Chapter 8. If not, then you might want to go back and look at that discussion before continuing. This chapter concentrates entirely on the Security Log, but many other useful logs available on domain controllers will also be of interest to you.

Three pieces of key information are recorded for audited events in the Security Log. These pieces of information are:

- The action that was being performed
- The user who performed the action
- The failure or success of the event and when it occurred

It's important to remember that these events are recorded at the location the events took place. So, let's say you have a share on a system, and access to this share has been limited to a small group of people. Someone from outside this group tries to access the share, and you have turned on auditing to capture this event. The event will be recorded at the server that is denying the access—in this case, the server where the share is located.

The dispersed nature of these log files means you must come up with a process for keeping track of them all. In this case, it might be a good idea to archive the log files, so the data in them is never lost. Then, you can peruse them at your leisure.

 It is worth noting that not everyone can look at Security Logs. You need special permissions in order to read and configure them. The minimum permission you will need is the Manage Auditing And Security Log user right on the computer you want to access. In addition, the files for auditing must be stored on an NTFS partition. Although legitimate reasons can exist for storing data on FAT32 or even FAT partitions, it is generally better to overcome those restrictions and make the switch to NTFS as soon as possible.

Of course, it is entirely possible to read the log files of a remote computer from your own system. To do so, just follow these steps:

1. Choose Start | Programs | Administrative Tools | Computer Management to open the Computer Management console.

2. Click on System Tools and then click on Event Viewer to display the available log files in the right-hand panel. Notice the Computer Management (Local) entry at the top of the left-hand panel. The significant part is *Local* in parentheses—it tells you that you are currently looking at the log files for the local machine.

3. Right-click on Computer Management (Local) and select Connect To Another Computer to bring up the Select Computer dialog box. You can select another computer from this list, or type the name of the system you want to connect to in the Name text box.

4. You will be connected to the remote machine. Click on System Tools and Event Viewer to view the log files for the remote machine.

Planning Your Audit Policy

You should consider several things before deciding on your auditing policy. First, what events do you really want to audit? The options are quite amazing, from every successful (or unsuccessful) attempt to use a printer, to the successful logon of every client. Auditing them all would generate a lot of data! So, you should audit only a subset of this data.

Second, you must decide which computers you will audit. It is unlikely that you will be concerned with every computer in your environment. For instance, is it really necessary to audit every event on each Windows 2000 Professional computer? Probably not. Identify those machines that you want to know about up front.

Two types of events can be audited: the success of an action and the failure of an action. In determining which events you are interested in, you should also decide whether you are interested in just the successful attempts that relate to the event, whether you are interested in the failures, or both.

Although this might not sound like a significant difference, it will dictate the types of information you can gain from the collected data. For instance, if you want to find out how many people are accessing a shared resource—perhaps a printer—then you will audit successful attempts. On the other hand, if you are more interested in security breaches (and attempts at breaches), then auditing failures would be more pertinent. When you audit logon attempts, this information can become even more important.

Auditing failed logons is a common usage. However, you'll be amazed how many of your users type the wrong password each morning. They'll even do it multiple times. Don't be surprised at this phenomenon—it is unavoidable.

You should review your audit logs (the Security Log in Event Viewer) regularly. If you do not look at them at the beginning of each day, then you may miss a trend that is developing on your network. Make the review of the log files part of your daily routine. Without review, the collected data has no benefit.

When you are thinking about events you want to audit, be careful not to be too indiscriminate. Many different events take place, and auditing too many of them can place an unnecessary load on your server. Also, because reviewing the logs should be part of your everyday routine, reviewing them will take a long time if you have audited many different parameters.

Generally speaking, successful attempts occur more frequently than failed events. Keep this in mind as you are determining what to audit. We're not saying you should not keep an eye on success events; but you should be clear about the reasons you are auditing an event. Will you really use the data for something? Don't collect data simply for the sake of doing it.

15

If you want to see trends over time, then you will have to archive the log files periodically. **Archiving** means making a copy of an event log for review at a later date. Many auditing options are available, such as overwriting events that are a certain number of days old, or overwriting after the log file reaches a certain size. If you use either of these options, then the records in the log are overwritten. This step prevents you from seeing a trend that might develop over a period of days, weeks, or months.

It is also a good idea to audit the events of the Everyone and Administrators group. By auditing the Everyone group, you can track the events associated with anyone who can access resources on your network. This audit is in contrast to tracking user groups, which may or may not include all users as members. Tracking the Administrators group allows you to track all events caused by administrators on your network. Doing so will enable you to see at a glance what your administrators have done.

Your environment may contain many servers, and you might wonder how you can configure each of them to audit certain events. In previous versions of Microsoft Windows NT, you configured these settings on a machine-by-machine basis. In the Windows 2000 world, Microsoft has incorporated these settings into Group Policy. In order to understand how these settings work, you should have a good understanding of Group Policy.

As you will see as you work your way through this chapter, many configuration options can be controlled from Group Policy. Actually, Group Policy lies at the heart of your auditing strategy. It will enable you to configure a group of settings in one place, and then have them applied to multiple machines in your organization.

Local Policies and Domain Policies

We should make one last point before we dig into the specifics of what can be achieved with the security options of Windows 2000. Because policies and settings have been around for quite some time, it is useful to know how the old policies interact with the new, and what makes the current policies different than those that came before. What follows is a very brief recap of some of the finer points of Group Policy and how they relate to auditing in Windows 2000.

We have already stated that your security policies can be applied through Group Policy. This is significant, because it defines the level at which these policies can be assigned. If you recall from Chapter 10, these policies can be applied at three levels: the site, the domain, or the Organizational Unit. The acronym SDOU is worth remembering—it not only defines at what levels policies can be applied, but it also defines the precedence for multiple policies.

Other than applying policies through Group Policy, you can use two additional methods to set them at a computer. The first is called a **local policy**. As you might guess, such a policy is set at a single machine, and it affects only that one machine. Second, you might have older policies hanging around from your Windows NT 4 days. They can still be applied to Windows 2000 machines, although this practice is not recommended.

Why should you never use older style system policies on Windows 2000 machines? The answer is subtle, but very significant. In the older style policies, changes were made to the Registry of the clients, meaning that a physical change was made to the Registry. The value for a key was changed from one value to another value. This feature was known as **tattooing**.

Tattooing actually gave you less control over what was happening on a machine. With the newer policies, if a policy is not applied for some reason, then the original Registry setting still exists and takes its place.

Group Policy is better than the old style system policies for a few other good reasons. For one thing, NT 4 system policies are contained in a single file, NTCONFIG.POL. This file must take into account all the different policies you want to apply. It can become quite huge. Second, the sheer number of policy settings that can be applied now has increased substantially.

Local policies are stored on the local machine. Group policies are stored in both the Active Directory and on each domain controller. They are replicated from one domain controller to another by the File Replication Service. These details are covered in Chapter 10.

You may be thinking that multiple policies can be applied, and it might be tricky to figure out which one will be applied and which one won't. Let's clear up this question before we go any further. The following list shows each policy that exists. They are given in descending order, which means the policy at the top of the list is applied first. If the next policy includes a conflicting setting, then the next policy wins:

- System policies (Windows NT 4)
- Local policies
- Site policies
- Domain policies
- OU policies

One of the simplest examples is the wallpaper on a system. Let's say a different default wallpaper is assigned in each policy. This wallpaper has the name of the policy written on it. First, the wallpaper would read *system policies*; then it would change to *local policies*, and so on. By the time everything had been calculated, the wallpaper would read *OU policies*, because these policies always end up winning when there is a conflict.

You may wonder how you can tell which policies have been assigned to a computer. Later in this chapter, we will look at a tool called the Security Configuration and Analysis Console, which handles this task.

We hope this brief recap will help you troubleshoot any issues you might have when setting auditing policy through Group Policy in Windows 2000. Now, let's look at how you configure auditing in Windows 2000 through Group Policy.

15

CONFIGURING GROUP POLICY

Configuring auditing is a two-step process. First, you must enable auditing, which means objects can be audited on your system. Doing so does not turn on auditing, however, because far too many auditing events exist. Turning them all on would have a bad effect on your computer. Instead, a second step allows you to go in and select the specific objects and events about which you want to gather auditing information.

Because these security options are configured through Group Policy, it should come as no surprise to find that you will need to access the Group Policy snap-in to make these changes. Nine event categories can be audited from within Windows 2000. These categories can have many different events assigned to them; so once you have enabled a category, you must then configure the specific events you want to capture. Figure 15-1 shows the categories as they appear in the Group Policy console.

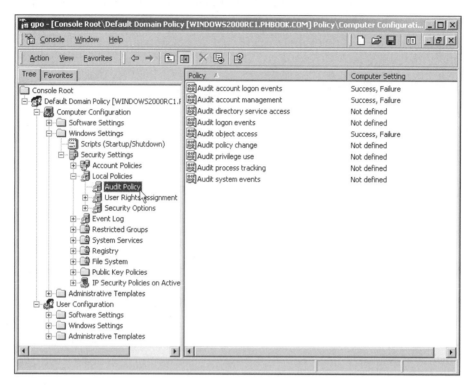

Figure 15-1   The types of events that can be audited in Windows 2000

Table 15-1 gives a brief explanation of what each category covers. We will look at more specific events associated with some of these categories later in this chapter.

Table 15-1   Definitions for auditing categories

Category Name	Definition
Account Logon Events	Records the event when a domain controller receives a request to validate a user account.
Account Management	Audits changes made by administrators to user accounts or groups. These changes include renaming, creating, or deleting accounts. This category will also record an entry when password changes take place.
Directory Service Access	Records an event if a user accesses an object in Active Directory. This setting is configured on a per-object basis.

Table 15-1   Definitions for auditing categories (continued)

Category Name	Definition
Logon Events	Audits specific users' logging on and logging off a system. This event also allows you to audit users who are making (or canceling) a connection to a server.
Object Access	Similar to Directory Service Access. More specifically, however, this setting allows you to audit access to files, folders, or printers. It is set at a per-resource level, so you will need to configure it for each share, file, or printer.
Policy Change	Records events relating to changes in auditing policies, user rights, or user security options.
Privilege Use	Records an event when users exercise one of the rights they have been assigned. These events can quickly fill a Security Log. This setting does not include events for logging on or off, because they are audited in another category.
Process Tracking	Tracks actions performed by a program on the server. You might use this option to track the events of a third-party application, although it is only of specialized interest.
System Events	Tracks some significant system events, such as the restarting of a Windows 2000 system. This setting also records events that are specific to the Security Log, such as the log's being full, or events being deleted from the log.

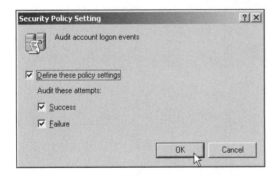

Figure 15-2   The Security Policy Setting dialog box

Before you can go down to the object level and allow events to be audited, you must first turn on auditing for that category. The Security Policy Setting dialog box is shown in Figure 15-2. As you can see, you can configure relatively few options at this level: auditing of successes, failures, or both. Once you have configured this dialog box, you can choose some events to be audited.

Policy changes made in Group Policy can take time to propagate throughout the domain. If you make a change in Group Policy, then you have three choices: You can wait for the change to propagate, restart the computer (causing the Group Policy objects to be read), or force the new settings to be applied. You do this by using the command-line utility secedit. Use the following syntax:

```
secedit /refreshpolicy machine_policy
```

AUDITING FILES AND FOLDERS

Because it is beyond the scope of this book to cover every auditing event that you might want to record, we have chosen to discuss file and folder access. These items can be audited only if the Object Access option has been enabled with either Success or Failure.

As you will see, when you get down to the object level, many different events can be audited. For instance, at the file and folder level there are no fewer than 13 specific events. In order to explain the levels at which auditing can be performed, we will list each of the entries that can be enabled for the auditing of file and folder usage. Figure 15-3 shows these options.

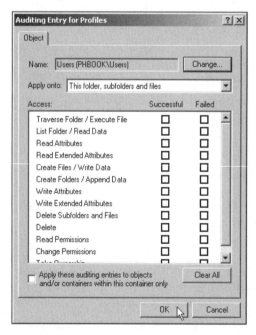

Figure 15-3   The Auditing Entry dialog box

Although we have said this more than once already, it is worth restating that it is not a good idea to turn on all the options. Try to be discerning and work out what information will be useful for you to know.

Table 15-2 explains what the file- and folder-level events mean. You have a fine level of granularity you can use for auditing files and folders. You can also choose whether the settings you configure should apply only to the current files and folders, or whether the folders and files stored in subfolders should inherit the settings. This choice is important because you can easily create too many entries in the Security Log by mistake. Note that by default, settings made in a folder are inherited by all subfolders.

Table 15-2 Auditing categories for files and folders

Category Name	Definition
Traverse Folder/Execute File	Records an event if a user moves through folders to gain access to a folder or share. Also records an event when a program runs.
List Folder/Read Data	Records an event when a user views the folder names or file names. Also records an event when a file is read.
Read Attributes	Records an event when a user displays the attributes of a file or folder.
Read Extended Attributes	Records an event when a user displays the extended attributes of a file or folder.
Create Files/Write Data	Records an event when a file is created in a folder, or when the data in a file is changed.
Create Folders/Append Data	Records an event when a folder is created in a folder, or when a file has data appended to it (without overwriting the file).
Write Attributes	Records an event when an attribute on a file or folder changes.
Write Extended Attributes	Records an event when an extended attribute on a file or folder changes.
Delete Subfolders And Files	Records an event when a file or folder *within a folder* is deleted.
Delete	Records an event when a file or folder is deleted.
Read Permissions	Records an event when a user views the permissions or owner of a file or folder.
Change Permissions	Records an event when permissions of a file or folder are changed.
Take Ownership	Records an event when someone takes ownership of a file or folder.

15

Some of these options might have limited value to you—so many auditing options exist that it can be difficult to choose between them. Along with files and folders, you should learn about auditing two other areas. First we will look at Active Directory objects, and then we will look at printers. The basic principles are the same, but the events that can be audited change.

AUDITING ACTIVE DIRECTORY OBJECTS

No fundamental differences exist between configuring auditing for Active Directory objects and configuring auditing for files and folders. In order to audit Active Directory objects, you must have enabled auditing for the Directory Services Access object. Once you have done this, you can configure the specific events you want to audit.

When auditing Active Directory objects, you can configure auditing for specific objects such as users, computers, groups, or OUs. These objects cover a broad sweep and can generate a lot of data. We will look at configuring some of them later in the chapter. In the meantime, let's examine the types of events that you can audit when working with Active Directory objects. Because there are 43 options, Table 15-3 lists only those that are most commonly used.

Table 15-3   Auditing categories for Active Directory objects

Category Name	Definition
Full Control	Records an event when any type of access is made to the object
List Contents	Records the viewing of objects stored within the audited object
Read All Properties	Records viewing of any attribute
Write All Properties	Records the change of any attribute
Create All Child Objects	Records the creation of any object within an audited object
Delete All Child Objects	Records the deletion of any object within an audited object
Read Permissions	Records the viewing of the permissions for an audited object
Modify Permissions	Records the change of the permissions for an audited object
Modify Owner	Records an event when a user takes ownership of an audited object
Create Printer Objects	Records the creation of a Printer object within an audited object
Delete Printer Objects	Records the deletion of a Printer object within an audited object
Create User Objects	Records the creation of a User object within an audited object
Delete User Objects	Records the deletion of a User object within an audited object
Create Shared Folder Objects	Records the creation of a shared folder within an audited object
Delete Shared Folder Objects	Records the deletion of a shared folder within an audited object

You can choose many additional options when auditing Active Directory objects. Some of them are good for security options, whereas others can simply act as a record of what is occurring on your network—such as administrators doing their jobs.

It is also worth noting that these settings can also be configured for inheritance. By default, all settings are inherited by child objects.

AUDITING PRINTERS

You might also want to audit access to printers. For instance, you may want to audit access to printers that are sensitive—such as those in secure areas of your building, or those that belong to directors or managers.

Once again, the general guidelines are much the same as you have seen before. In order to audit printers, you must enable auditing for object access. Once you have done this, you can configure the events you want to record. These events are defined in Table 15-4.

Table 15-4 Auditing categories for printers

Category Name	Definition
Print	Records the printing of a file
Manage Printers	Records changes made to the printer settings, such as pausing or sharing a printer
Manage Documents	Records changes made to job settings, such as pausing, restarting, moving, or deleting documents
Read Permissions	Records the viewing of printer permissions
Change Permissions	Records changes made to printer permissions
Take Ownership	Records an event when a user takes ownership of the printer

TIPS FOR AUDITING

15

You can audit so many things, you could be forgiven for getting somewhat confused about best practices. With that in mind, we will discuss some things to consider when deciding upon your auditing policy.

If you are worried about hackers or other unauthorized users getting into your network, then it is a good idea to audit failed logons. These logons will inform you when users try to log on with bad passwords. Keep in mind that hackers have programs that can repetitively try different passwords on a user account. Combined with lockout policy on your Windows 2000 network, this event can give very useful information.

If you suspect that someone is using an account without permission, then it can be useful to audit successful logon attempts. In this case, you will look for logins that happen after hours, or when the owner of the account is absent.

If you suspect users are trying to access files or folders to which they do not have permission, then you should audit failure of object access. As detailed in the previous paragraph, if you think access is being gained through a legitimate account, then you might want to audit successful attempts, also.

SECURITY TEMPLATES

Until now, we have looked at some of the options that can be configured for auditing. As you have seen, these options are very powerful, and there are many to choose from. Setting up each option can be time consuming, however, and doing so requires an intimate knowledge of all the available options. Wouldn't it be nice if Microsoft provided some default settings we could use?

Well, Microsoft did just that! These settings are called **security templates**. Security templates are merely collections of settings that alter auditing or security settings. These templates can then be imported into a Group Policy Object (GPO) and applied to sites, domains, or OUs.

Security templates are actually text files with an .inf file extension. Because they are text files, it is possible to cut and paste sections between templates, or to edit the files directly (although doing so is not recommended). Not only can these files be imported into GPOs, they can also be exported. Exporting is useful when you need to back up a security configuration on a machine. If you export the security settings made in the local policy on a machine, you can then import the policy into similarly configured machines, or use it to restore a machine's lost security settings.

Microsoft has provided several preconfigured template files. You can use these files as they are, or edit them to make any adjustments you see fit. In the following section, we will discuss some of these templates and how you can use them.

Preconfigured Security Templates

The preconfigured templates that ship with Windows 2000 are based around computer roles and scenarios. These combinations cover such instances ranging from standalone servers operating in a low-security environment to domain controllers in a high-security environment.

Before you use these templates, it is important that you make a thorough analysis and evaluation of their effectiveness. You should learn the details of what each contains, and then test the templates in a lab. Failure to do so can cause problems on a network due to unexpected behavior.

It probably comes as no surprise to find out that Microsoft ships many templates with Windows 2000. As you can see in Figure 15-4, 13 templates are predefined. You can find them in the *<systemroot>*\Security\Templates folder. Let's take a moment to define briefly what each is intended to do. Don't forget, we mentioned earlier that these templates were designed based on roles and scenarios. Table 15-5 defines the role for which each template was designed.

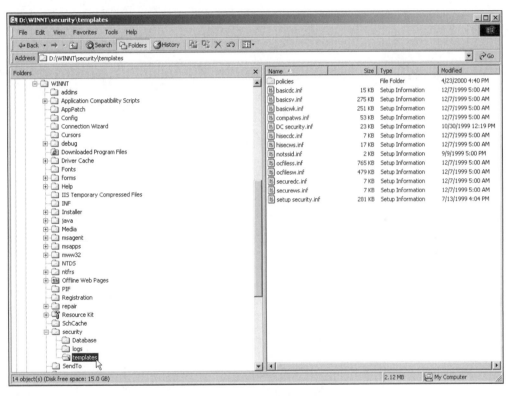

Figure 15-4   Security templates shipped with Windows 2000

Table 15-5   Defining security templates

Template Name	Role Definition
basicdc.inf	Default security settings for a domain controller
basicsv.inf	Default security settings for a standalone (or member) server
basicwk.inf	Default security settings for a Windows 2000 Professional system
compatws.inf	Security settings that make the Professional server backward compatible with Microsoft Windows NT 4
DC security.inf	Default settings (updated) for domain controllers
hisecdc.inf	High-security settings for a domain controller
hisecws.inf	High-security settings for a Windows 2000 Professional system
notssid.inf	Removes the Terminal Server SID assigned to a Windows 2000 Server
ocfiless.inf	Optional component file settings on servers
ocfilesw.inf	Optional component file settings on Windows 2000 Professional
securedc.inf	Secure domain controller settings
securews.inf	Secure Windows 2000 Professional settings
setup security.inf	Default settings applied after installation (installation defaults)

With the exception of three of the above templates—ocfiless.inf, ocfilesw.inf, and notssid.inf—you may have noticed that the others share some naming similarities. These names indicate the level of security (or scenario) that each template has been designed to achieve. It is useful to define these four scenarios for your future reference:

- *basic*—Any template with the term **basic** in its name was designed to return a system to the default settings if they have been changed. Such a template acts as a default starting point. It is worth noting that these templates do not alter user rights on a system; applications might have altered these rights, and undoing them would cause problems. If a system has a problem that you feel is due to a change that has been made to security settings, then use the basic templates.

- *compat*—Templates with **compat** in their names are actually "compatible" templates. Windows 2000 systems have some settings that are different from those you might have seen in previous versions. For instance, by default in Windows 2000, users logging in to a Windows 2000 Professional system are Power Users on that system. These security templates prevent this type of behavior—in this example, by removing all users from the Power Users group.

- *secure*—Any template with **secure** in its name is a recommended template for a system. These templates enforce changes to all areas except files, folders, and Registry keys. They do not make changes to these areas because, by default, the areas are secured.

■ *hisec*—Templates with **hisec** in their names are highly secure. These templates are aimed at network communications. They configure security settings for both network traffic and protocols. These settings will prevent a Windows 2000 system from communicating with any down-level clients, including Windows 9*x* and Microsoft Windows NT 4 systems.

Viewing Security Templates Configurations

All this talk about each of the available templates is pretty interesting, but let's look at what they contain. As you can imagine, examining every setting in each of these templates is daunting. So instead, we will walk you through the process you can use to view and edit these templates.

In the following example, you will create a new Microsoft Management Console (MMC) containing the Security Template snap-in. You will use this snap-in extensively when configuring the security templates. Don't forget, the MMC is very flexible. In this example you will end up with a new MMC with this single snap-in included, but it would be very easy to add the snap-in to any other console you use regularly. Follow these steps:

1. Open a blank MMC. To do so, choose Start | Run and type "MMC". Press Enter. The MMC will open with an empty Console Root.

2. Click on the Console menu and select Add/Remove Snap-In to open the Add/Remove Snap-In dialog box. This dialog box lists the snap-ins that are currently being displayed. This is a new MMC, so the entries are blank.

3. Click on Add to display the Add Standalone Snap-In dialog box. This dialog box displays all the available snap-ins on your system. Scroll down the list until you find the Security Templates snap-in. Click on it to select it. Click on Add. You should see the snap-in displayed in the Add/Remove Snap-In dialog box.

4. Click on Close to close the Add Standalone Snap-In dialog box. Click on OK to exit the Add/Remove Snap-In dialog box. Doing so returns you to the MMC. It should now resemble the MMC shown in Figure 15-5.

5. Double-click on Security Templates in the left-hand panel to display the path to the security template files on your system. Double-click on the path to see a list of all of the templates. Double-click on the first entry—basicdc—to see the group of settings that have been used in this template. By clicking on each of these groups, you can see the specific settings that have been made, as shown in Figure 15-6.

15

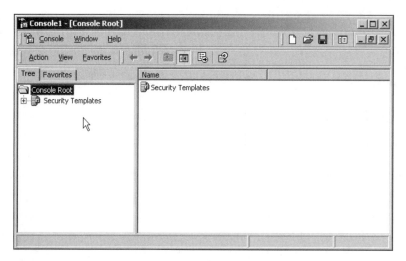

Figure 15-5   An MMC containing the Security Templates snap-in

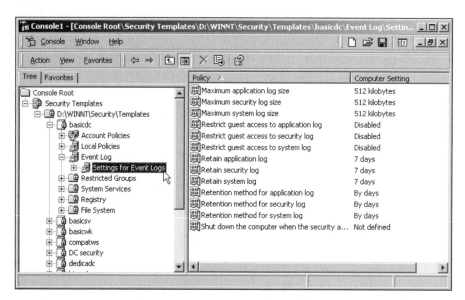

Figure 15-6   The configured settings for the basicdc security template

6. To save this MMC for later use, click on the Console menu and select Save As. Type the name you want to use for the new MMC. By default, the new MMC files are stored in the Administrative Tools folder for the currently logged-on user. As a result, your new console will show up on the Start | Administrative Tools menu. Type "Security Templates" and click on OK.

It is possible to edit the templates that currently exist, or to create entirely new templates from within the Security Templates Console. To do so, simply right-click on the path name in the left-hand side of the console and choose New Console. You will be prompted for a name and description. Once this step is done, an INF file is created to contain your template settings, and an entry is displayed in the Security Templates Console.

Using Security Templates with GPOs

The final piece of this puzzle is using the security templates with Group Policy. In order to apply one of the templates to a GPO, you will have to import the settings into local policies or nonlocal GPOs. Because the settings are preconfigured, configuring groups of computers or users is very easy. Importing the template settings into a GPO means that anyone who is a member of the GPO will be affected by the settings.

In the following example, we will use the Active Directory Users and Computers snap-in to apply a security template to a GPO. In the example, we have already created a new GPO for this purpose. Be careful when performing this example on a live system—you could inadvertently lock down (or undo) security settings that your administrators want in place. Follow these steps:

1. To open the Active Directory Users and Computers Console, choose Start|
   Programs|Administrative Tools and select Active Directory Users And
   Computers.

2. If you are using a production system, you may want to create a test OU for
   this example. To do so, click on your domain name and select New
   |Organizational Unit. You will be prompted for a name; enter "Security test"
   and click on OK. The new OU will be displayed in the left-hand panel.

3. To import one of the security templates so it is applied to this OU (and to
   any members of this OU), right-click on the new OU and select Properties
   from the menu. Select the Group Policy tab, shown in Figure 15-7.

4. To create a new GPO, click on the New button. An entry is shown in the dialog box. The default name for new GPOs is New Group Policy Object.
   Change this name to Security Test by typing "Security Test" and pressing Enter.

5. To import the settings, click on the policy you just created and select Edit to
   bring up the Group Policy Console. Double-click on Computer
   Configuration and then double-click on Windows Settings to display the
   screen shown in Figure 15-8.

15

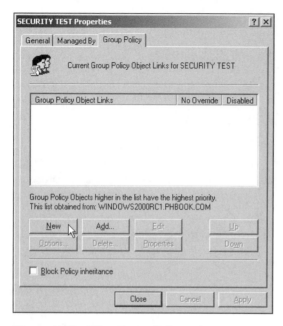

Figure 15-7 The Group Policy tab

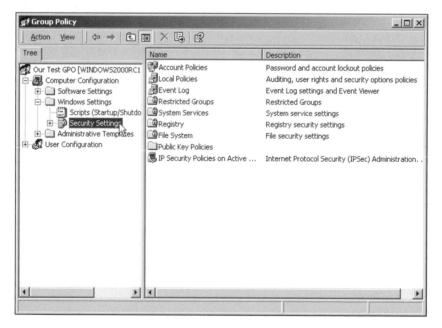

Figure 15-8 The Group Policy Console

6. To import your template, right-click on Security Settings and choose Import Policy. (Note that the Export List option exports the current settings to an INF file.) Doing so opens the Import Policy From dialog box, which lists all the available INF files. For the purposes of this example, you will simply import the basicdc.inf. Select it and click on OK.

Security templates are a key part of your enterprise's security policy. You can create a set of configurations in one place and then reuse them throughout your organization. Because you do so via Group Policy, you can target sites, domains, and OUs with ease. This ability enables you to apply the settings to many different computers at one time.

THE SECURITY CONFIGURATION AND ANALYSIS TOOL

The security settings on a single computer can be quite difficult to track. In fact, with Windows 2000, this difficulty can be accentuated because you can set so many additional options.

Realizing this potential problem, Microsoft came up with an MMC console snap-in called the Security Configuration and Analysis tool. This tool has several different uses: It can help you define the settings suitable for a workstation or server, and it allows you to analyze the effects of applying security templates to a system.

This tool is shown in Figure 15-9. As you can see, the MMC interface is immediately recognizable. You will be using this tool later in this chapter.

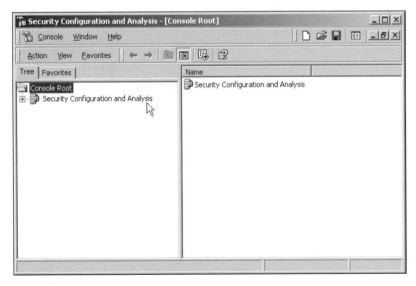

Figure 15-9   The Security Configuration and Analysis tool

15

The Security Configuration and Analysis tool works by creating a database on the local workstation or server. This is one of the tool's drawbacks—because the database is stored locally, you must be at the machine to make it work. In some cases, this requirement might prevent you from using this tool. In networks where all systems are part of a domain, you can use the security templates applied at the GPO level to configure workstations, because the Security Configuration and Analysis tool is impractical.

Once you have created a local database, you can import security templates and have them applied to the workstation. The tool includes options to export and combine multiple templates to create a complete security configuration. Because these templates can be added one at a time, you can see the effects of layering one security template upon another. Where a conflict exists between templates being applied, the last one applied takes precedence. As they are imported, the security settings are applied to the system.

The analysis options of the Security Configuration and Analysis tool allow administrators to view the current settings on a system. Security settings are dynamic, because different users and applications require different levels of security. It is possible for a properly configured system to become noncompliant. This tool allows you to analyze the current settings and see which settings have changed.

Performing an analysis is an important part of your security plan. It is easy to overlook systems that are not part of the domain. Without the occasional review, you will not know what affect routine work is having on your systems. Although it can be difficult to visit every workstation, you should at least take representative samples and analyze them. A lab environment can be used—but you must make sure the lab computers closely resemble those in use on desks around your enterprise.

If you find a discrepancy between the settings on the current system and a security template, then you have several options. You can either accept the changes that the security template is about to apply, or you can accept the current settings and leave them alone. You can also arbitrarily return the system to the state defined by the template. Doing so will overwrite any settings that differ from those in the security template. This choice is useful if a system is not compliant with the security standard you have set for your enterprise.

Alternatively, you can change the settings for a system by importing another template. As you saw earlier in this chapter, many templates exist. If the role of a system changes—perhaps a standard server is being installed as a domain controller—you can easily use this tool to apply a new template.

Once the system database is properly configured and all conflicting security settings are resolved, you can apply the settings to the system. Note that this step is not performed until you specifically want it to be. The settings and conflicts displayed within the tool are simply those generated within the database. Changes made to the settings are database entries—you can decide either to apply them to the system or to ignore them.

CHAPTER SUMMARY

❐ In this chapter, we looked at some of the options that can help you ensure that your network and systems are secure. We started our discussion by examining auditing. The auditing options in Windows 2000 allow you to trace events in your enterprise from a central location. This task is an essential part of system administration.

❐ You learned that events and activities are recorded in the Security Logs of the machines at which they occur. You can view the log using the Computer Management tool. Auditing is turned off by default, because it can put quite a strain on the server on which it is configured by eating both CPU time and disk space.

❐ You should review the Security Logs on your systems on a regular basis. No amount of auditing will secure your systems if you are not paying attention. It is a good idea to review the logs at the start of each day.

❐ Microsoft has provided an easy way to configure servers without having to visit each one. Auditing options can be applied through Group Policy.

❐ Several types of policy can be applied to a system, including local policies, site policies, domain policies, and Organizational Unit policies. Additionally, Group Policy can be applied at several different levels: site, domain, or OU. These levels are known by the acronym SDOU. The old-style Microsoft Windows NT 4 policies can still be applied, but it is a good idea to make an immediate switch to the newer Windows 2000 policy types.

❐ We then looked at the different categories of events and activities that can be configured on a system. You can choose from many different categories, and you should choose only those that are important to you.

❐ We saw that the file and folder level is one of the most common areas for auditing. Auditing at this level allows you to view many different events, such as the reading of a file, or the fact that a specific user has accessed a share.

❐ We also examined the options available when auditing access to Active Directory objects. Doing so allows the system administrator to track both the creation and deletion of objects, or the exercising of other security permissions.

❐ You may also want to audit printers in the enterprise. Printers are a valuable resource; they also represent an area of possible concern for security reasons. We saw that it is possible to record several types of events, including users who change permissions on printers or who change job settings.

15

❑ You learned that it is important to configure security settings at each system. You can do so through preconfigured security templates. These templates are provided by Microsoft. They can be used as is, or you can configure them to better suit your environment. We saw that templates are in place for standalone servers, domain controllers, and Windows 2000 Professional systems. Templates allow for three levels of security: normal, high security, and secure.

❑ These templates can be imported into GPOs, and are then applied to objects that are members of the GPO. This process allows for the widespread application of security settings in the enterprise—preventing you from having to visit each system. It also lets you make changes to security settings in one place and have them applied globally.

❑ Finally, we looked at the Security Configuration and Analysis tool. This tool allows you to view the security settings that are currently being applied to a machine so the settings can be compared to a desired state. It then displays the discrepancies. You can make necessary changes to the security settings and apply them to the system.

❑ The Security Configuration and Analysis tool is of limited use for systems that are part of a domain, because the tool requires that you have physical access to the system. However, it is useful for standalone systems.

A

EXAM OBJECTIVES FOR MCSE CERTIFICATION

Exam #70-217: Implementing and Administering a Microsoft Windows 2000 Directory Services Infrastructure

Installing and Configuring Active Directory

Objective	Chapter: Section	Hands-on Project(s)
Install forests, trees, and domains • Automate domain controller installation	Chapter 5: Installing Active Directory	Project 5-1 Project 5-2 Project 5-3 Project 5-4
Create sites, subnets, site links, and connection objects	Chapter 6: Creating a Site	Project 6-1 Project 6-2 Project 6-3 Project 6-4
Configure server objects. Considerations include site membership and global catalog designation.	Chapter 6: Implementing Organizational Units	Project 6-5
Transfer operations master roles	Chapter 6: Operations Masters	Project 6-5
Verify and troubleshoot Active Directory installation	Chapter 9: Active Directory Maintenance & Recovery	Project 9-2
Implement an organizational unit (OU) structure	Chapter 6: Implementing Organizational Units	Process described in text

Installing, Configuring, Managing, Monitoring, and Troubleshooting DNS for Active Directory

Objective	Chapter: Section	Hands-on Project(s)
Install and configure DNS for Active Directory • Integrate Active Directory DNS zones with existing DNS infrastructure • Configure zones for dynamic updates and secure dynamic updates • Create and configure DNS records	Chapter 4: Installing and Configuring DNS for Active Directory	Project 4-1 Project 4-2 Project 4-3 Project 4-4 Project 4-5
Manage, monitor, and troubleshoot DNS	Chapter 4: Monitoring and Troubleshooting DNS for Active Directory	Project 4-6

Configuring, Managing, Monitoring, Optimizing, and Troubleshooting Change and Configuration Management

Objective	Chapter: Section	Hands-on Project(s)
Implement and troubleshoot Group Policy • Create and modify a Group Policy object (GPO) • Link to an existing GPO • Delegate administrative control of Group Policy • Configure Group Policy options • Filter Group Policy settings by using security groups • Modify Group Policy prioritization	Chapter 10: Implementing Group Policy	Project 10-1 Project 10-2
Manage and troubleshoot user environments by using Group Policy	Chapter 11: Managing User Environments with Group Policy	Project 11-2 Project 11-3 Project 11-4 Project 11-5
Install, configure, manage, and troubleshoot software by using Group Policy	Chapter 12: Deploying and Managing Software by Using Group Policy	Project 12-1 Project 12-2 Project 12-3 Project 12-4
Manage network configuration by using Group Policy	Chapter 10: Group Policy Planning	Process described in text
Configure Active Directory to support Remote Installation Services (RIS) • Configure RIS options to support remote installations • Configure RIS security	Chapter 13: Deploying Windows 2000 Using Remote Installation Services	Project 13-1 Project 13-2 Project 13-3 Project 13-4 Project 13-5 Project 13-6

Managing, Monitoring, and Optimizing the Components of Active Directory

Objective	Chapter: Section	Hands-on Project(s)
Manage Active Directory objects • Move Active Directory objects • Publish resources in Active Directory • Locate objects in Active Directory • Create and manage objects manually or by using scripting • Control access to Active Directory objects • Delegate administrative control of objects in Active Directory	Chapter 7: Administering Active Directory	Project 7-1 Project 7-2 Project 7-3 Project 7-4 Project 7-5 Project 7-6 Project 7-7
Monitor, optimize, and troubleshoot Active Directory performance and replication	Chapter 14: Active Directory Replication	Process described in text
Back up and restore Active Directory • Perform an authoritative and a nonauthoritative restore of Active Directory • Recover from a system failure • Seize operations master roles	Chapter 9: Basic Backup Principles Backup and Restore Security	Project 9-1 Project 9-2

Configuring, Managing, Monitoring, and Troubleshooting Security in a Directory Services Infrastructure

Objective	Chapter: Section	Hands-on Project(s)
Apply security policies by using Group Policy	Chapter 10: Group Policy Implementation Chapter 11: Controlling User Environment Through Administrative Templates	Project 11-6
Create, analyze, and modify security configurations by using the Security Configuration and Analysis snap-in and the Security Templates snap-in	Chapter 15: Security Templates The Security Configuration and Analysis Tool	Project 15-3 Project 15-4 Project 15-5 Project 15-6
Implement an audit policy	Chapter 15: Auditing Files and Folders Auditing Active Directory objects Auditing Printers Tips for Auditing	Project 15-1 Project 15-2
Monitor and analyze security events	Chapter 8: Event Logs	Project 8-1 Project 8-2 Project 8-5 Project 8-6

B

HANDS-ON EXERCISES

CHAPTER 1 KEY TERMS

Active Directory (AD) — Microsoft's new directory service. Active Directory stores information about network resources and allows users to search for and access those resources.

Active Directory Schema — Defines which objects can be stored in Active Directory and what attributes are associated with those objects. The Active Directory schema can be modified. This process is known as extending the schema.

Active Directory Services Interface (ADSI) — A programming interface that allows developers to access and control Active Directory.

attributes — Every object in Active Directory has one or more properties. These properties are known as the object's attributes.

Backup Domain Controller (BDC) — These Windows NT domain controllers are used for fault tolerance (in case the PDC goes offline) and for load balancing (to allow users to log in to the network through multiple systems). The BDC contains a read-only version of the database and cannot modify the objects contained within the database.

directory — A collection of data that is related to other pieces of data. Also known as a database.

domain — A logical collection of users and computers that share a common security profile.

domain controller (DC) — In Windows 2000, the PDC/BDC model no longer exists. Instead, the systems that control Active Directory are known simply as domain controllers. Each DC has a read/write version of the database and uses multimaster replication to replicate data.

Domain Name Service (DNS) — The naming system used for naming Active Directory domains. DNS is also the naming system used for the Internet, allowing for an easy transition between internal networks and the Internet.

Encrypted File System (EFS) — Allows users to lock down and encrypt files and folders on their system so that others cannot read them.

Group Policy — A new feature that allows you to secure and maintain Windows 2000 systems.

Internet Connection Sharing (ICS) — A technology that allows multiple computers in an organization to use a single connection to the Internet. All requests to and from the Internet are routed through the system running ICS.

Internet Information Server (IIS) — A built-in Web server that supports Active Server Pages. A new feature that allows you to control the amount of processing time a Web site receives, which is known as process throttling.

Lightweight Directory Access Protocol (LDAP) — An industry standard protocol for accessing directory information. Microsoft used LDAP as the main communication protocol for Active Directory.

metadata — The properties of an object are also known as the metadata of the object.

Microsoft Management Console (MMC) — A fully customizable tool for performing many of the Windows 2000 Administrative tasks. MMC uses snap-ins for each administrative tool and gives the administrator a common interface to work with.

mixed mode — When both Windows 2000 and Windows NT domain controllers exist, the network is said to run in mixed mode.

native mode — When all systems on the network are Windows 2000 and use Active Directory for authentication and lookup, the network is said to run in native mode. Once the mode is changed from mixed to native, it cannot be reversed.

network operating system — An operating system designed for file, print, and application sharing. These operating systems are optimized for server-based tasks.

nontransitive trust — One of the trust relationships used in Windows NT. In a nontransitive trust, trust relationships are not inherited. For example, if Domain A trusts Domain B, and Domain B trusts Domain C, then Domain A will not trust Domain C.

objects — Every resource that exists in Active Directory (user, group, computer, share, printer, etc.) is known as an object.

Organizational Unit — A container in Active Directory for grouping Active Directory objects that require similar configuration. Departments (Payroll or HR) and locations (Seattle or New York) are common divisions for defining organizational units.

Primary Domain Controller (PDC) — A Windows NT server that controls the directory (the user and group information). This is the only server that can modify any of the objects stored within the database. It will then replicate changes to the Backup Domain Controllers.

Remote Installation Services (RIS) — RIS is a service that simplifies the initial installation of Windows 2000 Professional systems. It uses the Pre-Boot Execution Environment (PXE) read-only ROM chip to connect the system to the RIS server. The operating system is then automatically installed.

replication — The process of sharing any changes to Active Directory objects between the domain controllers.

total cost of ownership (TCO) — A term describing the amount of money a product costs to purchase, implement, and support.

transitive trust — A trust in which multiple trusts are inherited by other trusts. For example, if Domain A trusts Domain B, and Domain B trusts Domain C, then Domain A will trust Domain C.

trust — A relationship that is set up between two domains, allowing the users from one domain to access the resources in the other.

Windows 2000 Advanced Server — Microsoft's enterprise version of Windows 2000 Server. It includes all the options available in Windows 2000 Server but includes scalability options such as network load balance and clustering.

Windows 2000 Datacenter Server — Microsoft's most advanced and powerful NOS in the Windows 2000 server family. Designed for data-warehousing implementations, it supports a large amount of memory (64 GB) and up to 32 processors. This version of Windows 2000 is only available for purchase with the high-end server hardware.

Windows 2000 Professional — The Windows 2000 version designed for the business desktop. The replacement for Windows NT Workstation.

Windows 2000 Server — Microsoft's new entry-level network operating system. The replacement for Windows NT Server.

Windows Scripting Host (WSH) — A powerful scripting language that can be used to script many common and tedious administrative tasks.

CHAPTER 1 REVIEW QUESTIONS

1. What is the main reason for using Active Directory?

    a. Keeping track of network resources and enabling users to access this data

    b. Keeping track of resource usage on the network

    c. Keeping track of user information, such as phone numbers

    d. None of the above

2. With Windows NT, Microsoft introduced the concepts of Profiles and Policies. What does Windows 2000 use to define settings on systems in the network?

    a. Kerberos

    b. Access Control Lists

    c. Discretionary Access Control Lists

    d. Group Policy

3. Which industry standard did Microsoft choose to use when they developed Active Directory for Windows 2000?

    a. LDAP

    b. SMTP

    c. POP3

    d. IMAP4

4. A new feature in Windows 2000 allows for multiple computers to share the same Internet connection. What is the name of that feature?

   a. Internet Proxy

   b. Internet Line Sharing

   c. Shared Internet Connection

   d. Internet Connection Sharing

5. With Windows NT, Microsoft used the NetBIOS naming convention to keep track of systems and resolve their names to addresses. Which naming convention did Microsoft use with Windows 2000?

   a. NetBEUI

   b. NetBIOS

   c. DNS

   d. WINS

6. With Windows NT, all domain information was stored on all domain controllers, but only the Primary Domain Controller maintained the read/write version of the database. This information was then replicated to all the Backup Domain Controllers. If the PDC were to go offline, changes could not be made on the BDCs. This has changed in Windows 2000 because of which of the following?

   a. Multimaster authentication

   b. Multimaster replication

   c. Multimaster controllers

   d. Multimaster database

7. Active Directory requires that which of the following be installed, in order to function?

   a. WINS

   b. DHCP

   c. DNS

   d. NIS

8. A new feature in Windows 2000 allows users to protect their documents from being read. This is done using which feature?

   a. Disk Encryption System

   b. Encrypted Disk System

   c. File Encryption System

   d. Encrypted File System

9. Windows 2000 Professional supports up to four processors out of the box. True or False?

    a. True

    b. False

10. When Active Directory is installed in a Windows 2000 domain, the domain controllers (DCs) can operate in one of two modes. When only Windows 2000 systems are present, which mode does Microsoft recommend that you use?

    a. W2K mode

    b. WinNT mode

    c. Native mode

    d. Mixed mode

11. Many organizations currently use drive-mirroring technologies such as Ghost and DriveCopy to simplify workstation deployment and failure recovery. Microsoft included a feature in Windows 2000 that allows you to rapidly deploy Windows 2000 Professional on network systems. What is that new feature?

    a. Remote Installation Services

    b. Remote Boot Services

    c. Remote Imaging Services

    d. Remote Storage Services

12. Which Windows 2000 version or versions support disk quotas?

    a. Professional

    b. Server

    c. Advanced Server

    d. Datacenter Server

13. Which version or versions of Windows 2000 support up to 32 processors?

    a. Professional

    b. Server

    c. Advanced Server

    d. Datacenter Server

14. Which version of Windows 2000 is a replacement for Windows NT Workstation?

    a. Professional

    b. Server

    c. Advanced Server

    d. Datacenter Server

15. Which version or versions of Windows 2000 is/are a replacement for Windows NT Enterprise Edition?

    a. Professional

    b. Server

    c. Advanced Server

    d. Datacenter Server

16. When Active Directory is installed in a Windows 2000 domain, the domain controllers (DCs) can operate in one of two modes. When both Windows 2000 and Windows NT systems are present, which mode does Microsoft recommend that you use?

    a. W2K mode

    b. WinNT mode

    c. Native mode

    d. Mixed mode

17. Which version of Windows 2000 is the replacement for Windows NT Server – Terminal Server Edition?

    a. Professional

    b. Server

    c. Advanced Server

    d. Datacenter Server

18. Which version of Windows 2000 is a replacement for Windows NT Server?

    a. Professional

    b. Server

    c. Advanced Server

    d. Datacenter Server

19. Which feature of Windows 2000 makes adding components to the computer easier than in Windows NT?

    a. Plug and Play

    b. Windows 95/98 and Windows NT drivers work with Windows 2000.

    c. Windows 2000 uses generic drivers that work with all components.

    d. Microsoft introduced a law forcing all manufacturers to create drivers for Windows 2000.

20. Active Directory can store a predefined set of properties for objects and object attributes. What is this called?

   a. The Active Directory list

   b. The Active Directory directory

   c. The Active Directory database

   d. The Active Directory schema

CHAPTER 1 CASE PROJECTS

Case Project 1-1

Your organization would like to purchase a single system with 32 processors and have the processors and memory assigned to individual departments with no overlap. Which version of Windows 2000 does your organization need?

Case Project 1-2

A client of yours would like to implement a Windows 2000 cluster. Which Windows 2000 solution would you recommend?

Case Project 1-3

You are about to install Active Directory into your network. Which naming convention protocol needs to be installed and set up before the installation can be completed?

CHAPTER 2 KEY TERMS

classes — Collections of similar objects in Active Directory. Also known as Metadata.

container — An Active Directory object that can contain other objects, such as a domain or organizational unit.

domain naming master — The domain naming master controls the addition or removal of domains from the forest. Only a single domain naming master can exist for each forest.

Dynamic Domain Name Service (DDNS) — A new version of DNS that is used with Windows 2000. DDNS allows computers running the Windows 2000 operating system to register themselves to the DDNS service and deregister themselves from it.

forest — A collection of trees.

Global Catalog (GC) — A special limited database that stores partial replicas of all the directories of other domains. This allows users from a domain to become aware of resources on other domains without the need for full replication between all domains. By default, the first domain controller installed in the domain becomes the Global Catalog. Additional Global Catalogs can be configured manually.

hostname — The leftmost portion of a fully qualified domain name. This is the actual name of the system as it is accessed on the local network. For example, for the system with the mail.Austin.TexasPinball.com FQDN, the hostname is mail.

infrastructure master — The infrastructure master is responsible for maintaining all interdomain object references. It informs certain objects that other objects have been moved, changed, or modified. Only one infrastructure master can exist within a single domain.

intersite replication — Replication between sites.

intrasite replication — Replication within a site.

Knowledge Consistency Checker (KCC) — A service that generates the replication topology between and among sites.

namespace — A namespace defines the boundaries within a domain name. Any hosts and subdomains within the domain name are known to be part of the domain's namespace.

operations master — Several types of operations in Windows 2000 networks are impractical for multimaster environments. Windows 2000 uses a single DC to make these types of changes. That DC is known as the operations master.

PDC emulator — This operations master is used whenever non-Windows NT systems exist on the network. It acts as a Windows NT PDC for downlevel clients and for Windows NT BDCs. It accepts all password changes and replicates those changes into Active Directory. One PDC emulator can exist within each domain.

relative ID master — The relative ID (RID) master controls the sequence number for the DCs within the domain. The RID is used to recognize each DC in the domain as a DC. One RID master must exist within each domain.

schema master — The schema master controls all the updates and modifications to the schema within the domain. Only a single schema master can exist for each forest.

site — A site is a collection of computers connected via a high-speed network.

subdomain — If the domain name is stripped out of the fully qualified domain name, and more than just the hostname remains, then the portion immediately to the left of the domain name is known as a subdomain. For example, for the system with the mail.Austin.TexasPinball.com FQDN, the subdomain is Austin.

tree — A collection of domains that share a common schema, Global Catalog, and namespace.

CHAPTER 2 REVIEW QUESTIONS

1. What naming resolution is used by default in Windows 2000?

   a. WINS

   b. NIS

   c. DHCP

   d. DNS

2. What is the definition of a domain?

   a. A collection of computers sharing the same operating system

   b. A collection of computers sharing the same resources

   c. A collection of computer, users, and other objects that share the same security boundary

   d. A physical collection of computers

3. What are Organizational Units used for?

   a. Subdivide a domain along administrative boundaries

   b. Define a new security boundary for the domain

   c. Subdivide a domain along geographical boundaries

   d. Create a relationship between two or more forests

4. What is the special version of DNS in Windows 2000 called?

   a. Double DNS

   b. Dynamic DNS

   c. Automatic DNS

   d. Proxy DNS

5. Which operations master communicates with non–Windows 2000 systems for authentication and logon?

   a. Schema master

   b. Domain naming master

   c. Relative ID master

   d. PDC emulator

   e. Infrastructure master

6. Which operation master controls all changes made to the Active Directory schema?

   a. Schema master

   b. Domain naming master

   c. Relative ID master

   d. PDC emulator

   e. Infrastructure master

7. Which operations master maintains all interdomain object references?

   a. Schema master

   b. Domain naming master

   c. Relative ID master

   d. PDC emulator

   e. Infrastructure master

8. Which operations master assigns RIDs to domain controllers in the domain?

   a. Schema master

   b. Domain naming master

   c. Relative ID master

   d. PDC emulator

   e. Infrastructure master

9. Which operations master controls the addition and removal of domains to and from the forest?

   a. Schema master

   b. Domain naming master

   c. Relative ID master

   d. PDC emulator

   e. Infrastructure master

10. Active Directory domains share which of the following characteristics when they exist within the same tree?

    a. Global catalog

    b. Schema

    c. Namespace

    d. All of the above

11. Schema objects and attributes can be deleted from the Active Directory Schema. True or False?

    a. True

    b. False

12. What type of server must exist in a mixed-mode domain to perform the logon process for Windows NT systems?

    a. Global Catalog

    b. PDC emulator

    c. DC

    d. BDC

13. Which operation master or masters can have only one instance per domain?

    a. Schema master

    b. Domain naming master

    c. Relative ID master

    d. PDC emulator

    e. Infrastructure master

14. Which operation master or masters can have only one instance per tree?

    a. Schema master

    b. Domain naming master

    c. Relative ID master

    d. PDC emulator

    e. Infrastructure master

15. What is the definition of a site?

    a. A site is a logical collection of computers sharing the same security boundary.

    b. A site is a physical collection of computers sharing the same security boundary.

    c. A site is a collection of computers connected via a high-speed network.

    d. A site is a geographical collection of computers.

16. Which Active Directory item has attributes associated with it?

    a. A class

    b. An attribute

    c. An object

    d. A user

17. What Windows 2000 component controls the replication topology between and among sites?

    a. Topology Master

    b. Knowledge Consistency Checker

    c. Topology Consistency Checker

    d. Knowledge Master

18. Replication between sites uses a preferred server to transmit the replication information through a single DC. What is this preferred server known as?

    a. Gateway server

    b. Proxy server

    c. Preferred server

    d. Bridgehead server

19. In the fully qualified domain name Mail1.Dallas.Texas.TexasPinBall.com, which is the hostname of the server?

    a. Mail1

    b. Mail1.Dallas

    c. Dallas.Texas

    d. TexasPinBall.com

CHAPTER 2 HANDS-ON PROJECTS

Project 2-1

1. Open the Active Directory Sites and Services MMC Snap-in by choosing **Start | Programs | Administrative Tools | Active Directory Sites and Services**.

2. Click the **Sites** folder under Active Directory Sites and Services if necessary. Choose the **New Site** option from the Action drop-down list.

3. In the New Object – Site Screen text box, enter a name for the remote site.

4. Select the site link for the site and click **OK**. Click **OK** in message saying site has been created.

5. Add the IP subnets to the site.

6. Install a DC into the site.

7. Close the AD Sites and Services console.

Project 2-2

1. Open the Active Directory Sites and Services MMC Snap-in by choosing **Start | Programs | Administrative Tools | Active Directory Sites and Services**.

2. Open the **Inter-Site Transports** folder.

3. Right-click on the appropriate transport protocol and choose the new site link from the drop-down menu.

4. Give the site link a name in the Name dialog box of the New Object – Site Link window.

5. Select the linked sites from the left column in the dialog box and click **Add** to associate them with the link.

6. Click **OK** to complete the site link creation process.

7. Close the AD Sites and Services console.

CHAPTER 2 CASE PROJECT

Case Project 2-1

You are migrating your network from Windows NT to Windows 2000. You install Windows 2000 and Active Directory and upgrade the PDC, but you find that Windows NT systems can no longer authenticate with it. You check to make sure that the network is running in mixed mode, which it is. What could be causing this lack of connectivity with the Windows NT systems?

CHAPTER 3 KEY TERMS

administrative OU model — An OU model based on the administrative structure within the organization.

administrative overhead — The amount of administrative resources (such as systems and people) required to perform administrative tasks.

business unit OU model — An OU model based on the business units within the organization. Similar to the administrative OU model, but on a much higher level.

departmental OU model — An OU model based on the organizational departments within the company, for example: Payroll, Engineering, HR, Public Relations, etc.

geographic OU model — An OU model based on the geographic layout of the organization. This model can take the form of different locations within a city, within a state, within the country, and within the world.

object OU model — An OU model that sees a different OU for every type of object within the domain, for example: users, groups, and printers.

replication overhead — The amount of network and system resources used for replication of information between domain controllers.

replication window — The period of time a site link is available for replication purposes.

CHAPTER 3 REVIEW QUESTIONS

1. Which description defines a site in Active Directory?

   a. Any location that includes one or more domain controllers

   b. Any physical geographic location

   c. Any group of computers connected by a high-speed connection

   d. Any group of computers connected by a low-speed connection

2. Why would a domain controller not be placed at a specific location?

   a. Replication overhead

   b. Administrative overhead

   c. Hardware costs

   d. All of the above

3. What is the definition of a replication window?

   a. The period of time a site link is available for replication purposes

   b. The amount of data that can be replicated over a site link in a specified period of time

   c. The period of time a domain controller is available for replication purposes

   d. The amount of data that can be replicated by a domain controller in a specified period of time

4. Which of the following is NOT a reason for installing a DC in a specific location?

   a. High bandwidth connection to the other sites

   b. Low bandwidth connection to the other sites

   c. To speed authentication

   d. A domain is limited to just one site.

5. A Windows 2000 Active Directory site requires a domain controller to function. True or False?

   a. True

   b. False

6. Which OU model divides Active Directory objects by object type?

   a. Administrative model

   b. Business unit model

   c. Departmental model

   d. Geographic model

   e. Object model

7. Which OU model divides Active Directory by physical location?

   a. Administrative model

   b. Business unit model

   c. Departmental model

   d. Geographic model

   e. Object model

8. Which OU model divides Active Directory by department?

   a. Administrative model

   b. Business unit model

   c. Departmental model

   d. Geographic model

   e. Object model

9. Which OU model divides Active Directory according to the organization's administrative structure?

   a. Administrative model

   b. Business unit model

   c. Departmental model

   d. Geographic model

   e. Object model

10. Which OU model divides Active Directory by the organization's specific business groups?

    a. Administrative model

    b. Business unit model

    c. Departmental model

    d. Geographic model

    e. Object model

11. What is the definition of an Organizational Unit?

    a. A container object spanning a single forest

    b. A container object spanning multiple domains

    c. A container object spanning multiple domain trees

    d. A container object within a single domain

12. Domain groups rather than OUs are used to grant administrative control to Active Directory objects. True or False?

    a. True

    b. False

13. Under normal operating conditions, when compared to a Windows NT network, what does a Windows 2000 network require?

    a. Same bandwidth

    b. Less bandwidth

    c. More bandwidth

    d. Impossible to determine

14. In Windows 2000, trust relationships are automatically created within a domain tree. True or False?

    a. True

    b. False

15. For a domain name to function on the Internet, with whom should it be registered?

    a. It does not need to be registered.

    b. The Internet Ruling Body, or IRB

    c. An ICAAN-accredited registrar

    d. Microsoft.net

16. Windows 2000 trust relationships are nontransitive, while Windows NT trust relationships are transitive. True or False?

    a. True

    b. False

17. If your organization is to be accessed from the Internet, then two different domain names (one internal and one external) must be used. True or False?

   a. True

   b. False

18. With Windows 2000 domains, logon names take on which of the following structures (assuming that the username is joe and the domain is domain.com)?

   a. joe

   b. joe@domain

   c. joe@domain.com

   d. joe.domain.com

19. When planning for a Windows 2000 infrastructure upgrade, what should the first step be?

   a. Draw out the current environment

   b. Lay out the AD sites

   c. Place the DC in the sites

   d. Schedule replication

20. Active Directory integrates closely with WINS. True or False?

   a. True

   b. False

CHAPTER 3 CASE PROJECT

Case Project 3-1

Your organization contains three geographic locations connected by 64K ISDN links. You decided to create three different sites, but users at the remote sites complain of slow authentication and access to AD information. What could be causing the problems?

CHAPTER 4 KEY TERMS

authoritative — The DNS server that has the primary role and can make changes to the zone is known as the authoritative for the zone.

caching-only DNS server — A caching-only server does not maintain a database of hostname to IP address resolutions. It simply resolves client resolution requests and caches that information.

flat namespace — A manual method for resolving names and addresses. The HOSTS file is a common example.

forward lookup query — A client resolution request to resolve a host name to its IP address. This query is sent to the primary DNS server.

forwarding DNS server — A server used to communicate with DNS servers outside the local zone.

full zone transfer — The process of transferring the entire DNS database from the primary server to the secondary server.

fully qualified domain name (FQDN) — The full name of the host, including the hostname, subdomain(s) (if any), and domain. For example, www.widgets.com.

hierarchical namespace — The namespace used in the Internet. It is divided into different domain and subdomain levels.

HOSTS file — A flat namespace file used for manual name resolution.

incremental zone transfer — The process of transferring only the changes in the DNS databases from the primary server to the secondary server.

name resolution — The process of resolving computer-used addresses with human-used names.

nslookup — An application for resolving hostname and IP addresses directly with the DNS server. Also used for troubleshooting purposes.

primary DNS server — The master DNS server for the specified zone. This is the only server that can make changes to the zone entries.

relative distinguished name — A name that is relative to the domain that it exists in. This is normally simply the hostname. For example, the relative distinguished name for www.widgets.com would be www.

reverse lookup query — A client resolution request to resolve a host's IP address to its hostname. This query is sent to the primary DNS server.

root server — A set of servers on the Internet that are the authoritative for the entire Internet DNS namespace.

secondary DNS server — This server (or servers) acts as a backup to the primary DNS server. This server is used as a failover if the primary DNS server cannot be contacted.

Time To Live (TTL) — The length of time a DNS server will cache the results of a query.

zone — A zone is a partitioned portion of the overall DNS namespace.

zone transfer — The process by which changes made on the primary DNS server are replicated to all the secondary DNS servers in the zone.

CHAPTER 4 REVIEW QUESTIONS

1. What does DDNS stand for?

    a. Dynamic DNS

    b. Distributed DNS

    c. Database DNS

    d. Data DNS

2. Which type of resource creates a record for a name server?

   a. SOA

   b. NS

   c. A

   d. PTR

3. Which type of resource creates a record for a mail server?

   a. SOA

   b. PTR

   c. A

   d. MX

4. Which type of resource creates a record for an alias to a hostname?

   a. SOA

   b. CNAME

   c. PTR

   d. A

5. Which type of resource creates a record for a hostname?

   a. SOA

   b. CNAME

   c. PTR

   d. A

6. Which type of resource creates a record for an IP address?

   a. SOA

   b. CNAME

   c. PTR

   d. A

7. Which type of resource creates a service record for a service that exists on a system?

   a. SRV

   b. SVR

   c. A

   d. SOA

8. Your network uses the 192.168.7.0 network. What would be the correct format of the reverse lookup zone name?

   a. 192.168.7.in-addr.arpa

   b. 192.168.in-addr.arpa

c. 7.168.192.in-addr.arpa

d. 168.192.in-addr.arpa

9. Which utility is most commonly used for troubleshooting DNS problems?

   a. Tracert

   b. Nslookup

   c. Dnscfg

   d. Ping

10. Which type of zone maps hostnames to IP addresses?

    a. Standard primary zone

    b. Forward lookup zone

    c. Reverse lookup zone

    d. Active Directory-integrated zone

11. Which type of zone maps IP addresses to hostnames?

    a. Standard primary zone

    b. Forward lookup zone

    c. Reverse lookup zone

    d. Active Directory-integrated zone

12. Which SOA record entry is used by the secondary DNS server(s) to decide whether a zone transfer is required?

    a. TTL

    b. Retry

    c. Refresh

    d. Serial number

13. Which type of DNS server does not contain any zone databases?

    a. Primary

    b. Secondary

    c. Forwarding

    d. Caching-only

14. Which type of DNS server contains a copy of the zone, which it transfers from the zone master server?

    a. Primary

    b. Secondary

    c. Forwarding

    d. Caching-only

15. Which type of DNS server is the master server for the zone and contains the read/write version of the database?

    a. Primary

    b. Secondary

    c. Forwarding

    d. Caching-only

16. What was the original method of resolving names on the Internet?

    a. LMHOSTS file

    b. HOST files

    c. WINS

    d. DNS

17. Which of the following is a fully qualified domain name?

    a. Microsoft.com

    b. www.microsoft.com

    c. www.microsoft

    d. www

18. Which of the following is considered to be a top-level domain?

    a. com

    b. org

    c. edu

    d. All of the above

19. Which of the following clients does DDNS work with? (Choose all that apply.)

    a. Windows 98

    b. Windows NT

    c. Windows 2000

    d. All of the above

20. When testing a DNS server, which type of test queries the local server for the resolution?

    a. Simple query

    b. Iterative query

    c. Forward lookup query

    d. Reverse lookup query

CHAPTER 4 HANDS-ON PROJECTS

Project 4-1

1. Select **Start | Settings | Control Panel**.
2. Double-click the **Add/Remove Programs** applet.
3. Click **Add/Remove Windows Components**.
4. Select **Networking Services** and click **Details**.
5. Select the **Domain Name System (DNS)** option and click **OK**.
6. Click **Next**. If necessary, insert the Windows 2000 Server CD-ROM and then click **OK**.
7. Click **Finish**. Click **Close** in the Add/Remove Programs window and then close the Control Panel.

Project 4-2

1. Select **Start | Programs | Administrative Tools | DNS**.
2. Navigate to the server where the DNS server is to be configured, right-click the server, and choose the **Configure the server** option.
3. When the Wizard appears, click **Next**. You see the Root Server screen, which asks if this is the first DNS server on the network. Make your selection, then click **Next**. You see the Forward Lookup Zone screen, which asks if you'd like to create a Forward Lookup Zone. If you click **Yes**, continue with Step 4. If you choose **No**, skip to Step 8 to finish the wizard.
4. Select the Zone type and click **Next**.
5. Enter a name for the new zone and click **Next**.
6. Select the **Create a new file with this name** or **Use this existing file** option.
7. Enter a name for the file. You see the Reverse Lookup Zone screen, which asks if you'd like to create a Reverse Lookup Zone. If you click **Yes**, you need to select a zone type, and then identify the zone with a network ID or a name. Click **Next**, then repeat Steps 6 and 7. Then continue with Step 8. If you click **No**, skip to Step 8.
8. Click **Finish**.
9. Close the DNS console window.

Project 4-3

1. Select **Start | Programs | Administrative Tools | DNS**.
2. Navigate to the server where the DNS server is to be configured, right-click the server, and choose the **New Zone** option.

3. When the Wizard appears, click **Next**.

4. Select the Zone type and click **Next**.

5. Select either the **Forward** or **Reverse lookup zone** option and click **Next**.

6. Enter a name for the new zone and click **Next**. If necessary, enter the network ID for the new zone.

7. Select the **Create a new file with this name** or **Use this existing file** option.

8. Enter a name for the file and click **Next**.

9. Click **Finish**.

10. Close the DNS console window.

Project 4-4

1. Do not configure any zones.

2. Make sure that the root servers are configured (this should be done by default).

Project 4-5

1. Select **Start | Programs | Administrative Tools | DNS**.

2. Expand the selected server where the new Forward Lookup Zone is to be created. Highlight the **Forward Lookup Zones** container under the server.

3. Right-click on the container and choose the **New Zone** option.

4. When the Wizard appears, click **Next**.

5. Choose the zone type and click **Next**.

6. Enter the name of the new zone and click **Next**.

7. Select the **Create a new file with this name** or **Use this existing file** option.

8. Enter a name for the file and click **Next**.

9. Click **Finish**.

10. Close the DNS console.

Project 4-6

1. Select **Start | Programs | Administrative Tools | DNS**.

2. Highlight the server to be tested.

3. Right-click on the server and choose the **Properties** option.

4. Click on the **Monitoring** tab.

5. Choose the **A simple query against this DNS server** checkbox and click on **Test Now**. If the server passes the test, a PASS notice will appear in the Test Results box.

6. Choose the **A recursive query to other DNS servers** checkbox and click on **Test Now**. If the server passes the test, a PASS notice will appear in the Test Results box.

7. Click **OK** in the Properties page, then close the DNS console.

CHAPTER 4 CASE PROJECTS

Case Project 4-1

Your organization has six internal DNS servers for resolving intranet addresses. Management has decided that only one of the six DNS servers will be allowed to generate queries for Internet name resolutions through the company's firewall. What would you do to ensure that all of the remaining five servers could still resolve Internet addresses?

Case Project 4-2

Your company's only DNS server is configured on the Developer group's development server. The problem is that the development server tends to be rebooted fairly regularly, at which point Internet addresses cannot be resolved. You have been informed that the development server is to remain the primary DNS server, but the problem still needs to be solved. What is a possible solution?

CHAPTER 5 KEY TERMS

circular logging — The process of reusing a set of log files. As a log file fills to capacity, another one is used. When that one is filled, the first log file is overwritten. This does not allow for full recovery of an Active Directory database; noncircular logging is required.

context — The relationship of all domains in a Windows 2000 Active Directory domain tree.

Directory Services Restore Mode — The Directory Services Restore Mode is a safe-mode option that allows an administrator to restore the SYSVOL directory and AD database from a backup. This option is only available on domain controllers.

multi-master domain model — In a multi-master domain model, each DC is a peer. This allows for fault tolerance by allowing any DC to process changes and updates to the AD database.

NetBIOS domain name — A name given to the Active Directory domain to allow for functionality with previous versions of Windows NT.

noncircular logging — The process of creating a new log file when the old one fills up. This method keeps copies of all the transactions done to the database, allowing for up-to-the-minute recovery of the database.

ntds.dit — A Windows 2000 Jet database, which contains the values for the objects within the domain and the values for the domain forest.

systemroot directory — The systemroot directory is the directory where Windows NT is installed. By default, this directory is the \winnt directory.

shared system volume — A series of folders containing the logon scripts and policy objects for both the enterprise and the local domain. The shared system volume must exist on an NTFS 5 partition.

CHAPTER 5 REVIEW QUESTIONS

1. What is the maximum number of objects AD can support?

   a. 1,000

   b. 10,000

   c. 100,000

   d. 1,000,000 +

2. Where is the shared system volume stored?

   a. *%systemroot%*\system32\SYSVOL

   b. *%systemroot%*\System\SYSVOL

   c. *%systemroot%*\SYSVOL

   d. *%systemroot%*\SharedSYSVOL

3. Where is the current ntds.dit file stored?

   a. *%systemroot%*\

   b. *%systemroot%*\NTDS\

   c. *%systemroot%*\System\

   d. *%systemroot%*\System32\

4. Where is the ntds.dit file used by dcpromo.exe stored?

   a. *%systemroot%*\

   b. *%systemroot%*\NTDS\

   c. *%systemroot%*\System\

   d. *%systemroot%*\System32\

5. Which program is used to install AD on a system and promote it to a domain controller?

   a. ADPromo.exe

   b. DCPromo.exe

   c. ADSetup.exe

   d. This cannot be done. Windows 2000 must be reinstalled in Domain Controller Mode.

6. What is the Directory Services Restore Mode used for?

    a. To promote a member server to a DC

    b. To demote a DC to a member server

    c. To restore AD from a backup

    d. To back up AD

7. By default, when AD is installed, the Windows 2000 domain is set to run in native mode. True or False?

    a. True

    b. False

8. Which of the following statements about the shared system volume is true?

    a. The shared system volume must be installed on any NTFS partition.

    b. The shared system volume must be installed on any FAT32 partition.

    c. The shared system volume must be installed on the boot partition.

    d. The shared system volume must be installed on an NTFS 5 partition.

9. If DNS is not installed when the Active Directory Installation Wizard is executed, then it will ask you if you would like DNS installed. True or False?

    a. True

    b. False

10. Which logging method allows for backup of all AD transactions?

    a. Circular logging enabled

    b. Circular logging disabled

    c. All logging options accomplish this.

    d. This is not possible with AD.

11. How would you recover from a lost Directory Services Restore Mode password?

    a. Use the passrec.exe utility.

    b. Delete the HKEY_LOCAL_MACHINE\System\CurrentControlSet\Services\DSRM\ Password key.

    c. Reinstall Active Directory.

    d. This password cannot be recovered.

12. How would you change the AD logging to circular?

    a. Change the logging properties in the Active Directory snap-in.

    b. Reinstall AD and choose the Circular Logging check box.

    c. Edit the Registry and set the Registry key HKEY_LOCAL_MACHINE\System\CurrentControlSet\Services\NTDS\ Parameters\CircularLogging value to 0.

   d. Edit the Registry and set the Registry key
HKEY_LOCAL_MACHINE\System\CurrentControlSet\Services\NTDS\
Parameters\CircularLogging value to 1.

13. What occurs if dcpromo.exe is executed on a system already configured as a domain controller?

   a. Nothing. The program fails.

   b. AD is reinstalled.

   c. AD is removed.

   d. The domain name can be changed.

14. Which of the following is true?

   a. Windows 2000 and AD use the shared-master domain model.

   b. Windows 2000 and AD use the multi-master domain model.

   c. Windows 2000 and AD use the no-master domain model.

   d. Windows 2000 and AD use the single-master domain model.

15. As in Windows NT, if a member server is to become a domain controller, the operating system must be reinstalled. True or False?

   a. True

   b. False

16. Which of the following replication methods does not occur when the domain is switched into native mode?

   a. NETLOGON continues to run.

   b. The domain uses AD multi-master replication.

   c. Windows NT DCs can no longer join the domain.

   d. All DCs can now perform directory updates.

CHAPTER 5 HANDS-ON PROJECTS

Project 5-1

1. Select **Start | Run**.

2. In the Open field, type **dcpromo**, and click **OK**.

3. When the Wizard appears, click **Next**.

4. In the Domain Controller Type window, choose the **Domain controller for a new domain** option, and click **Next**.

5. In the Create Tree or Child Domain window, choose the **Create a new domain tree** option, and click **Next**.

6. If a message box appears saying that the DNS server cannot be contacted, click **OK**.

7. Choose the **Install and Configure DNS** option, then click **Next**.

8. Choose the **Default permissions for users and groups** option, then click **Next**.

9. Choose the **Create a new forest of domain trees** in the Create or Join Forest window, and click **Next**.

10. Enter the full DNS name of the new domain, and click **Next**.

11. Enter the NetBIOS name that is to be assigned to this domain, then click **Next**.

12. Select the locations where the database and log files are to be stored, and click **Next**.

13. Choose the location for the shared system volume and click **Next**.

14. In the Directory Services Restore Mode Administrator Password window, choose a password that is to be used when you need to restore your Active Directory information, and click **Next**.

15. A summary screen will appear, informing you of all the options you selected. Click **Next** to start the installation.

16. A progress indicator will appear. When the installation is complete, the Completing the Active Directory Installation Wizard window will appear. Click the **Finish** button.

17. A dialog box will appear, notifying you that the system must be rebooted for the changes to take effect. Click **Restart Now** to complete the installation.

Project 5-2

1. For this project the students should work in pairs, and this project should be executed on the second computer. Select **Start|Run**.

2. In the Open field, type **dcpromo**, and click **OK**.

3. When the Wizard appears, click **Next**. A message box will appear, saying that the Domain is a Global Catalog server, so you should make sure users can access other Global Catalog servers. Click **OK**.

4. The Remove Active Directory window will appear. Make sure that the This server is the last domain controller in the domain option is NOT selected, and click **Next**.

5. Enter an Administrator's password and confirm it. Click **Next**.

6. A summary screen will appear. Click **Next** to begin the domain controller demotion.

7. When the demotion is completed, click **Finish**.

8. A dialog box will appear, notifying you that the system must be rebooted for the changes to take effect. Click **Restart Now** to complete the installation.

Project 5-3

1. For this project the students should work in pairs, and this project should be executed on the second computer. Select **Start|Run**.

2. In the Open field, type **dcpromo**, and click **OK**.

3. When the Wizard appears, click **Next**. A message box will appear, saying that the Domain is a Global Catalog server, so you should make sure users can access other Global Catalog servers. Click **OK**.

4. The Remove Active Directory window will appear. Make sure that the This server is the last domain controller in the domain option is selected, and click **Next**. Supply a network username and then click **Next**.

5. Enter an Administrator's password and confirm it. Click **Next**.

6. A summary screen will appear. Click **Next** to begin the domain controller demotion.

7. When the demotion is completed, click **Finish**.

8. A dialog box will appear, notifying you that the system must be rebooted for the changes to take effect. Click **Restart Now** to complete the installation.

Project 5-4

1. Select **Start | Programs | Administrative Tools | Active Directory Domains and Trusts**.

2. Select the domain to be managed.

3. Right-click and choose the **Properties** option.

4. On the General tab, click the **Change Mode** button.

5. Click the **Yes** button to change the mode from Mixed to Native. Click **OK** in the Properties page, then click **OK** in the operation successful message.

6. Close the Active Directory Domains and Trusts console.

CHAPTER 5 CASE PROJECT

Case Project 5-1

You have finally been given the go ahead to install Windows 2000 AD on your network. You have planned out the installation, installed and configured DNS, and installed a domain controller. Some users are complaining that they cannot access the domain. You realize that those people are all running non-Windows 2000 systems. You verify that the NetBIOS domain name that you entered during the AD setup process is correct, but the users still cannot access the domain. What could be the cause of this problem, and what would be a solution to solve it?

CHAPTER 6 KEY TERMS

connection object — Windows 2000 DCs represent the inbound replication through this special object.

cost — A value given to a site link that defines the relative speed of the link in relation to the other links within the network.

DEFAULTIPSITELINK — The default site link created by Windows 2000 that is used to establish the replication process of the AD service.

domain naming master — The domain naming master controls the addition or removal of domains from the forest. Only a single domain naming master can exist for each forest.

Global Catalog (GC) — A special limited database that stores partial replicas of all the directories of other domains. This allows users from a domain to become aware of resources on other domains without the need for full replication among all domains. By default, the first domain controller installed in the domain becomes the Global Catalog. Additional Global Catalogs can be configured manually.

infrastructure master — The infrastructure master is responsible for maintaining all interdomain object references. It informs certain objects that other objects have been moved, changed, or modified. Only one infrastructure master can exist within a single domain.

intersite replication — Replication between sites.

intrasite replication — Replication within a site.

Knowledge Consistency Checker (KCC) — A service that generates the replication topology between and among sites.

operations master — Several types of operations in Windows 2000 networks are impractical for multi-master environments. Windows 2000 uses a single DC to make these types of changes. That DC is known as the operations master.

PDC emulator — This operations master is used whenever non-Windows NT systems exist on the network. It acts as a Windows NT PDC for downlevel clients and for Windows NT BDCs. It accepts all password changes and replicates those changes into Active Directory. One PDC emulator can exist within each domain.

relative ID master — The relative ID (RID) master controls the sequence number for the DCs within the domain. The RID is used to recognize each DC in the domain as a DC. One RID master must exist within each domain.

schema master — The schema master controls all the updates and modifications to the schema within the domain. Only a single schema master can exist for each forest.

site link — Sites are connected by site links. These site links are low bandwidth or unreliable/occasional connections between the sites.

transport — The type of transport used to replicate the directory information between the DCs. There are two different transports to choose from: synchronous RPC over a routed TCP/IP connection, or asynchronous Simple Mail Transfer Protocol (SMTP) connection over the underlying mail transport network.

CHAPTER 6 REVIEW QUESTIONS

1. Which site is automatically created by Windows 2000 Active Directory?

   a. Default-Site

   b. First-Site

   c. First-Default-Site

   d. Default-First-Site

2. OUs are designed to contain only user and group objects. True or False?

   a. True

   b. False

3. Which administrative tool is used to administer the schema master?

   a. Active Directory Users and Computer

   b. Active Directory Domains and Trusts

   c. Active Directory Sites and Services

   d. Active Directory Schema Manager

4. Which administrative tool is used to administer the relative ID master?

   a. Active Directory Users and Computer

   b. Active Directory Domains and Trusts

   c. Active Directory Sites and Services

   d. Active Directory Schema Manager

5. Which administrative tool is used to administer the domain naming master?

   a. Active Directory Users and Computer

   b. Active Directory Domains and Trusts

   c. Active Directory Sites and Services

   d. Active Directory Schema Manager

6. Which administrative tool is used to administer the PDC emulator master?

   a. Active Directory Users and Computer

   b. Active Directory Domains and Trusts

   c. Active Directory Sites and Services

   d. Active Directory Schema Manager

7. Which administrative tool is used to administer the infrastructure master?

   a. Active Directory Users and Computer

   b. Active Directory Domains and Trusts

   c. Active Directory Sites and Services

   d. Active Directory Schema Manager

8. What is used to define explicit replication routing?

   a. Site link bridge

   b. Site trust relationship

   c. Domain link bridge

   d. Routing link bridge

B

9. What is the definition of a site in Windows 2000?

   a. A group of computers sharing the same security information

   b. A group of computers sharing the same IP subnet

   c. A group of computers connected by a low-speed connection

   d. A group of computers connected by a high-speed connection

10. Which administration utility is used to create and manage sites?

    a. Active Directory Users and Computer

    b. Active Directory Domains and Trusts

    c. Active Directory Sites and Services

    d. Active Directory Schema Manager

11. What is the main reasoning behind implementing sites?

    a. To set up security boundaries

    b. To set up a replication schedule

    c. To simplify administration

    d. To compress replication data

12. Manually created connection objects will remain in place until manually deleted. True or False?

    a. True

    b. False

13. The lower the site cost, the faster the site is deemed to be. True or False?

    a. True

    b. False

14. When a new site link is created, what is the default cost assigned to it?

    a. 0

    b. 1

    c. 50

    d. 100

15. When are site link bridges transitive?

    a. In a nonrouted network

    b. In a routed network

    c. All the time

    d. Never

16. Choose the two types of transports available for site links.

    a. SMTP

    b. ESMTP

   c. IP

   d. TCP

17. You can only have a single Global Catalog server in each domain. True or False?

   a. True

   b. False

18. Which transport does the DEFAULTIPSITELINK use?

   a. Synchronous RPCs over SMTP

   b. Synchronous RPCs over TCP/IP

   c. Asynchronous SMTP

   d. Asynchronous TCP/IP

19. OUs are created and managed using which utility?

   a. Active Directory Users and Computer

   b. Active Directory Domains and Trusts

   c. Active Directory Sites and Services

   d. Active Directory Schema Manager

20. Which utility is used to configure whether a server is a Global Catalog server?

   a. Active Directory Users and Computer

   b. Active Directory Domains and Trusts

   c. Active Directory Sites and Services

   d. Active Directory Schema Manager

CHAPTER 6 HANDS-ON PROJECTS

Project 6-1

1. Select **Start | Programs | Administrative Tools | Active Directory Sites and Services**.

2. Right-click on the **Sites** folder and choose the **New Site** option.

3. Enter a name for the new site. Select a site link object, and click **OK**.

4. Click **OK** to complete the site creation.

5. Close the AD Sites and Services console.

Project 6-2

1. Select **Start | Programs | Administrative Tools | Active Directory Sites and Services**.

2. Expand the Sites folder, right-click on **Subnets**, then choose the **New Subnet** option.

3. Enter the IP address for the network.

4. Enter the subnet mask for the network.

5. Choose the site to be associated with this subnet.

6. Click **OK** to create the subnet.

7. Close the AD Sites and Services console.

Project 6-3

1. Select **Start | Programs | Administrative Tools | Active Directory Sites and Services**.

2. Expand the Sites folder, then choose the **Inter-Site Transports** folder.

3. Choose the desired transport protocol. Right-click on the protocol and choose **New Site Link**.

4. Enter the name of the new link.

5. From the left pane, choose the sites that this link is to connect.

6. Click **Add** to add them to the site link.

7. Click **OK** to create the site link.

8. Close the AD Sites and Services console.

Project 6-4

1. Select **Start | Programs | Administrative Tools | Active Directory Sites and Services**.

2. Expand the Sites folder, then expand the **Default-First-Site-Name** folder.

3. Expand the **Servers** folder.

4. Choose the DC that is to be moved to the other site.

5. Right-click on the DC and choose the **Move** option.

6. Choose the Target site from the list.

7. Click **OK** to move the DC.

8. Close the AD Sites and Services console.

Project 6-5

1. Select **Start | Programs | Administrative Tools | Active Directory Sites and Services**.

2. Expand the Sites folder, then expand the site in which the server exists.

3. Expand the **Servers** folder.

4. Choose the server that is to become a GC server.

5. Choose the NTDS Settings in the right pane.

6. Right-click and choose **Properties**.

7. If necessary, check the **Global Catalog** option.

8. Click **OK** to configure the server as a GC server.

9. Close the AD Sites and Services console.

Project 6-6

1. Select **Start | Programs | Administrative Tools | Active Directory Sites and Services**.

2. Expand the Sites folder, then expand the **Inter-Site Transports** folder.

3. Choose the transport to be used for the site links.

4. Right-click and choose **Properties**.

5. Unselect the **Bridge all site links** option in the General tab.

6. Click **OK** to configure the site link bridge.

7. Close the AD Sites and Services console.

Chapter 6 Case Project

Case Project 6-1

Your organization is made up of two locations, HeadOffice and Sales. All the servers are installed in the HeadOffice location. The two locations are connected by slow links. Users at the Sales office complain about the speed of the network. What is the easiest way to alleviate some of the slow network issues?

Chapter 7 Key Terms

Access Control List (ACL) — A list of everyone who has been granted access to an object and the actions that users or groups can perform on those objects.

actions — Similar to permissions. Actions outline what users can do when they gain access to an object.

common objects — Objects that have been defined in the Active Directory schema. Examples are user accounts, contacts, groups, printers and shared folders.

delegation of control — The process of delegating some administrative tasks to different individuals.

extensible — The ability of developers and applications to create their own objects within Active Directory makes Active Directory extensible.

Globally Unique Identifier (GUID) — Similar to a SID, except that this ID is completely unique within the network.

inheritance — The ability for different containers and objects in Active Directory to inherit their permissions from their parent object. This simplifies the administration of permissions.

leaf object — An object with no objects contained within it.

LostAndFound container — A container used to stored orphaned objects.

orphaned object — Any child object whose parent object was either moved or no longer exists.

permissions — A set of rules used to control access to resources on the server and network.

publishing — The process of making Active Directory objects available for viewing.

security identifier (SID) — A unique ID given to every object in Active Directory. This SID is used to identify the object, and it allows objects with the same name to exist in the database.

special permissions — A completely customized set of permissions that can be assigned to a user or group.

standard permissions — A predetermined set of permissions that can be assigned to a user or group.

CHAPTER 7 REVIEW QUESTIONS

1. Which utility is used to move member servers from one domain to another?

   a. MoveTree

   b. MoveServer

   c. NetDom

   d. Active Directory Users and Computers

2. Which application is used to grant administrative permissions to a user or group?

   a. Active Directory Users and Groups

   b. Active Directory Delegation Utility

   c. Delegation of Control Wizard

   d. Delegation of Permissions Wizard

3. Which property list contains user and group permissions for objects?

   a. Access Control List

   b. Access Control Group

   c. Access Control Permissions

   d. Access Control Rights

4. Which Identifier is unique within the entire forest?

   a. SID

   b. GUID

  c. SUID

  d. GID

5. Which utility is used to move objects between domains?

  a. MoveObject

  b. MoveParent

  c. MoveChild

  d. MoveTree

6. What sort of data should you not publish in Active Directory?

  a. Static data (data that rarely changes)

  b. Dynamic data (data that always changes)

  c. Small amounts of data

  d. Useful information

7. Which of the following are standard permissions?

  a. Read

  b. Change

  c. Delete

  d. Full Control

8. The Active Directory schema is not extensible. True or False?

  a. True

  b. False

9. Which options are available to you when you choose to disable the Allow Inheritable Permissions From Their Parent To Propagate To This Object option?

  a. Copy

  b. Remove

  c. Modify

  d. Cancel

10. Which of the following is not a common object in Active Directory?

  a. User

  b. Group

  c. Conference room

  d. Contact

11. What is the term for an object that does not contain other objects?

  a. Standard object

  b. Leaf object

B

    c. Branch object

    d. Child object

12. By default, which permission is granted to a newly created object?

    a. Everyone: No Access

    b. Everyone: Read

    c. Everyone: Modify

    d. Everyone: Full Control

13. Once the Active Directory schema is extended, the new objects and attributes can be deleted at any time. True or False?

    a. True

    b. False

14. You moved a container object from one domain to another. However, when you check the container object, you realize that the leaf objects within it were not moved. Where are they located?

    a. In the root of the old domain

    b. In the root of the new domain

    c. In the LostAndFound container of the old domain

    d. In the LostAndFound container of the new domain

15. Which of the following does an object in a Windows 2000 domain require?

    a. Unique name

    b. Unique description

    c. Unique name and description

    d. None of the above

CHAPTER 7 HANDS-ON PROJECTS

Project 7-1

1. Select **Start | Programs | Administrative Tools | Active Directory Users and Computers**.

2. Navigate to the container in which you would like the Windows NT printer created.

3. Right-click the container and choose the **New | Printer** option from the drop-down menu.

4. Enter the UNC name of the printer (for example, \\server\printer).

5. Click **OK** to create the printer.

6. Close the Active Directory Users and Computers console.

Project 7-2

1. Select **Start | Programs | Administrative Tools | Active Directory Users and Computers**.

2. Navigate to the container in which you would like to search for the Windows NT printer.

3. Right-click the container and choose the **Find** option.

4. In the Find list box, select **Printers**.

5. Enter the name of the printer in the Name field, and click **Find Now** to search for the printer.

6. Close the Active Directory Users and Computers console.

Project 7-3

1. Select **Start | Programs | Administrative Tools | Active Directory Users and Computers**.

2. Select the container in which you would like to create the user. Right-click the container, choose **New | User**.

3. Enter the desired information (such as first name, middle initial, last name, and user login name), and click **Next**.

4. Enter the user's password and confirm it. Choose any other options for this account (User must change password at next logon, User cannot change password, Password never expires, or Account is disabled). Click **Next**.

5. Click **Finish** to create the user.

6. Close the Active Directory Users and Computers console.

Project 7-4

1. Select **Start | Programs | Administrative Tools | Active Directory Users and Computers**.

2. Navigate to the container in which the user that you would like to enable resides. Click the user object to select it.

3. Right-click the selected user and choose the **Copy** option from the drop-down menu.

4. The Copy Object – User window appears. Enter the required information and click **Next**.

5. Enter the password (if any) and confirm it. Select any other desired options and click **Next**.

6. Click **Finish** to complete the user account copy.

7. Close the Active Directory Users and Computers console.

Project 7-5

1. Select **Start | Programs | Administrative Tools | Active Directory Users and Computers**.

2. Right-click the domain or container in which you would like to create the Organizational Unit, and choose the **New | Organizational Unit** option from the drop-down menu.

3. Enter the name of the new Organizational Unit.

4. Click **OK** to create the Organizational Unit.

5. Close the Active Directory Users and Computers console.

Project 7-6

1. Select **Start | Programs | Administrative Tools | Active Directory Users and Computers**.

2. Navigate to the domain in which the Organizational Unit resides.

3. Right-click the Organizational Unit and choose the **Delegate Control** option from the drop-down menu.

4. Click **Next**.

5. Click **Add**.

6. Select the desired users and/or groups, and click **Add**.

7. Click **OK**.

8. Click **Next**.

9. Choose the tasks that you would like to grant these users and/or groups permissions to perform.

10. Click **Next**.

11. Click **Finish**.

12. Close the Active Directory Users and Computers console.

Project 7-7

1. Select **Start | Programs | Administrative Tools | Active Directory Users and Computers**.

2. Navigate to the domain or container in which the Organizational Unit resides.

3. Right-click the Organizational Unit and choose the **Delete** option from the drop-down menu.

4. Click **Yes** to confirm the deletion of the Organizational Unit.

5. Close the Active Directory Users and Computers console.

Chapter 8 Key Terms

alerts — Alerts are used to configure the system to react to the status and state of different objects and object levels. For example, using alerts can generate system messages, start a log file, or start an application.

Application Log — The Application Log records events for applications that exist on the system. Not all applications write to the Application Log; they need to be developed to do so. The Application Log is useful for troubleshooting a failure of a specific application.

baseline — A measurement or snapshot of how the server will operate when things are running normally.

counter logs — Simple ways of creating templates for your performance-monitoring tasks.

counters — A counter is used to measure the various aspects of an object. For example, the Processor object has counters to measure Processor Time and Interrupts/Second.

Desktop Management Interface (DMI) — The predecessor to WMI. It allowed for a loose collection of generic function calls for gathering data from different systems.

Directory Service log — The Directory Service log is used to record all messages generated by Active Directory.

DNS Server log — The DNS Server log records all events that are generated by the Domain Name System (DNS) operations on a DC.

error event — This type of message records the failure of a component or application. An error event message usually means that something major has failed on the system.

File Replication Service log — The File Replication Service log records all messages with regards to the file replication process.

hard page fault — A hard page fault occurs when a process attempts to gain access to data that is not held in memory.

information event — This type of message records the successful operation of a task or application.

instances — Some systems have many duplicate objects. These are known as instances. Dual processor systems, for example, have two different Processor objects or two different Processor instances. Using the different instances allows the objects to be measured together or individually.

object — An object is a system resource. Objects can include the network interface, memory, processor, or hard disks. A System Monitor object is different from an Active Directory object.

paging — When a system is running low on physical memory, it writes out to the hard disk. This process is known as paging.

perfmon — A built-in tool for monitoring a Windows 2000 system. Also known as System Monitor.

queue — When a server or a component in a server begins to fall behind, some tasks have to wait before they are processed. The "line" in which these tasks wait to be processed is known as the queue.

response time — A measurement of elapsed time from the beginning of a process to its conclusion.

Security Log — The Security Log records successful and failed attempts at accessing objects and resources on the system. It responds to auditing events that are configured via the Computer Management MMC snap-in and Group Policy settings.

signature — Similar to a baseline but also includes the level of performance of a normal day.

System Log — The System Log is the location to which all messages generated by the system are stored.

System Monitor — A built-in tool for monitoring a Windows 2000 system. Also known as perfmon.

throughput — The number of processes and tasks that are done on the system within a given amount of time.

trace logs — Trace logs allow you to configure samples of data to be collected from providers on the system.

Update Sequence Numbers (USN) — A value replicated between systems to ensure that all the updated data is replicated between replication partners. Ensures that all the data is synchronized.

warning event — This type of message records a warning about an event that may or may not be significant, but that does not affect the operation of the component or application that has generated it.

Web-Based Management Instrumentation (WBEM) — Same as WMI. Microsoft decided to adopt the WBEM initiative, but named it WMI instead.

Windows Management Instrumentation (WMI) — A Microsoft standard for monitoring and collecting data from a wide range of computers running Windows 2000.

CHAPTER 8 REVIEW QUESTIONS

1. Which tool is used to view the replication partners for a DC using the command line?

   a. REPADMIN

   b. REPLMGR

   c. Active Directory Replication Monitor

   d. Active Directory Replication Administrator

2. Which graphical tool is used to view the replication partners for a DC?

   a. REPADMIN

   b. REPLMGR

   c. Active Directory Replication Monitor

   d. Active Directory Replication Administrator

3. Which counter should you use to figure out if your system has run out of physical RAM and how much of the hard disk it's using to store information?

   a. % Paging

   b. Paging/Second

   c. % Usage

   d. Page Usage/Second

4. Which tool is used to read the logs on the local Windows 2000 system?

   a. System Monitor

   b. Event Logger

   c. Event Manager

   d. Event Viewer

5. Which tool is used to read the logs on a remote Windows 2000 system?

   a. System Monitor

   b. Event Logger

   c. Event Manager

   d. Event Viewer

6. Using System Monitor, what can you configure to page you, should the system processor exceed 95% utilization?

   a. Counter logs

   b. Alerts

   c. Trace logs

   d. Page logs

7. Which of the three events logs records an event that does not affect the system?

   a. Information

   b. Warning

   c. Error

8. Which of the three events logs records an event that does affect the system?

   a. Information

   b. Warning

   c. Error

9. Which of the three events logs records an event that could affect the system?

   a. Information

   b. Warning

   c. Error

10. When the system cannot keep up with all the different processes that request to be executed, the tasks are stored in a _____.

    a. Queue

    b. Throughput

    c. Response time

    d. List

11. As mentioned, the Disk object statistics can be inaccurate when using which of the following server components?

    a. SCSI drives

    b. IDE drives

    c. SCSI controllers

    d. RAID 5 controllers

12. What is the definition of response time?

    a. The amount of time it takes the system to process the data

    b. The amount of time it takes a process to start

    c. The amount of time it takes a process to finish

    d. The amount of time it takes the process to execute

13. What is the definition of a queue?

    a. A group of processes that are waiting to be executed

    b. A group of processes that have been executed

    c. The amount of time it takes a process to execute

    d. The amount of data that is processed on the network

14. What is the definition of throughput?

    a. The amount of data that is processed by the system

    b. The amount of data that is processed by a service

    c. The amount of data that is processed in a specified amount of time

    d. The amount of data that is processed by an application

15. Which three components make up the data System Monitor can process?

    a. Processes

    b. Instances

    c. Objects

    d. Counters

16. Once you have configured a log with all of your desired objects, counters, and instances, you have the ability to save them collectively as what?

    a. Counter log

    b. Trace log

    c. Alert log

    d. Database log

17. You suspect that Exchange 2000 services are failing. Which event log would you search to find the Exchange 2000 logs?

    a. Application Log

    b. Security Log

    c. System Log

    d. Directory Service log

18. You suspect that a hacker is attempting to gain access to unauthorized systems and files on your network. You check the Security Log and find it empty. What is the most likely reason?

    a. The hacker has cleared the Security Log.

    b. The Security Log does not monitor access to files and systems, only to applications.

    c. A hacker is not attempting to access your systems.

    d. Auditing has not been turned on via the Computer Management MMC snap-in and Group Policy settings.

19. When the system runs out of physical memory and starts using the hard disk, it is _____.

    a. Swapping

    b. Paging

    c. Queuing

    d. Mapping

20. What is the default maximum size for each of the event logs in Windows 2000?

    a. 256K

    b. 512K

    c. 1024K

    d. 2048K

CHAPTER 8 HANDS-ON PROJECTS

Project 8-1

1. Select **Start | Programs | Administrative Tools | Performance**.

2. Right-click in the right pane, and choose the **Add Counter** option.

3. Choose a performance object.

4. Select the counters to monitor.

5. If multiple instances exist, choose the desired instance.

6. Click **Add** to add the counter.

7. Repeat for any other desired performance objects and counters.

8. Click Close to close the Add Counters dialog box.

9. Close the Performance console.

Project 8-2

1. Select **Start | Programs | Administrative Tools | Performance**.

2. In the left pane, select the **Performance Logs and Alerts | Counter Logs** container.

3. Right-click **Counter Logs** and choose the **New Log Settings** option.

4. Enter a name for the new counter log and click **OK**.

5. Click **Add** and choose the counter or counters that you would like added to the log, then click **Add** again, and then click **Close**.

6. Specify the logging interval by entering the number in the Interval field, and the units for the interval (seconds, minutes, hours, or days) in the Units field.

7. Click the **Log Files** tab.

8. Enter the log file information, including name, location, size, and type.

9. Click the **Schedule** tab.

10. Enter the start/stop information for the counter log.

11. Click **OK**.

12. Close the Performance console.

Project 8-3

1. Select **Start | Programs | Administrative Tools | Performance**.

2. In the left pane, select the **Performance Logs and Alerts | Trace Logs** container.

3. Right-click **Trace Logs** and choose the **New Log Settings** option.

4. Enter a name for the new trace log, and click **OK**.

5. To log system provider events, select the **Events logged by system provider** radio button and select the desired providers to be used for the trace log.

6. To log nonsystem providers, select the **Nonsystem providers** radio button.

7. Click **Add**, then select the providers, then click **OK**.

8. Click the **Log Files** tab.

9. Enter the log file information, including name, location, size, and type.

10. Click **Schedule** and enter the start/stop information for the trace log.

11. Click **OK**.

12. Close the Performance console.

Project 8-4

1. Select **Start | Programs | Administrative Tools | Performance**.

2. In the left pane, select the **Performance Logs and Alerts | Alerts** container.

3. Right-click in the right pane and choose the **New Alert Settings** option.

4. Enter a name for the new alert and click **OK**.

5. Optional: Enter a comment for the alert.

6. Click **Add**, select the desired counter, click **Add**, and click **Close**.

7. Select the counter.

8. To cause an alert when the counter is either over or under the limit, select the **Over** or **Under** option from the value drop-down list, and enter the limit in the Limit field.

9. Specify the logging interval by entering the number in the Interval field, and the units for the interval (seconds, minutes, hours, or days) in the Units field.

10. Select the **Action** tab.

11. To log an entry: Check the **Log an entry in the application event log** check box.

12. To send an alert: Check the **Send a network message to** check box, and enter the username or group name in the field.

13. To start a performance log: Check the **Start performance data log** check box, and choose the appropriate log type.

14. To run an external program: Check the **Run this program** check box, and enter the path and name of the program.

15. Click the **Schedule** tab. To assign the external program command line switches: Click **Command Line Arguments**, choose the desired switches, and click **OK**.

16. To automatically start the alert: Choose the **At** radio button and enter a date and time.

17. To never stop the alert: Choose the **Manually** option.

18. To stop the alert after a set number of seconds, minutes, hours, or days: Choose the **After** radio button and enter the number of units the system is to wait before stopping the counter log.

19. To stop the alert on a specific date and time: Choose the **At** option and enter the desired date and time.

20. Click **OK**.

21. Close the Performance console.

B

Project 8-5

1. Select **Start | Programs | Administrative Tools | Event Viewer**.
2. In the left pane, highlight the log that you would like to view.
3. In the right pane, double-click the event that you would like to view.
4. You can navigate to the previous and following events by clicking on the up and down arrow buttons respectively.
5. To finish, click **OK**.
6. Close the Event Viewer.

Project 8-6

1. Select **Start | Programs | Administrative Tools | Event Viewer**.
2. Right-click **Event Viewer (Local)** and choose the **Connect to another computer** option.
3. Enter the name of the remote computer, or click **Browse** to navigate to it.
4. Select the computer name. Click **OK**.
5. Close the Event Viewer.

CHAPTER 8 CASE PROJECTS

Case Project 8-1

One of your systems has started to perform poorly. When you check the Windows Task Manager you realize that the system is running with the CPU at 84% utilization. You also notice that the hard disks are "thrashing" (or being accessed repeatedly). You suspect that there is not enough physical memory (RAM) in the system. What would you do to confirm your theory?

Case Project 8-2

One of your systems paged you on Saturday night (using an alert), informing you that it had run out of disk space. The lack of disk space had caused this mission-critical system to "blue screen." You immediately drove to the office, installed an extra hard drive, and rebooted the system. The system, however, had been offline for several hours, making it inaccessible to your organization's clients worldwide. Monday morning you were asked to be present at an emergency meeting. In the meeting it was decided that the failure that occurred on the weekend could not be repeated, and that a solution must be found. It is your job to find a way to detect when a system is starting to get overloaded and running out of resources. What is your best course of action?

CHAPTER 9 KEY TERMS

authoritative restore — A process of restoring a Windows 2000 DC, in which the restored data is given precedence over the current Active Directory data on the network and is then replicated to all the other DCs. This method is normally used when objects in Active Directory have been deleted and need to be restored.

checkpoint file — A file that informs Active Directory which portion of the transaction log has been committed to the database and which has not.

Directory System Agent (DSA) — An agent that makes the data within Active Directory available to an application.

Extensible Storage Engine (ESE) — The underlying engine that physically stores the Active Directory data.

fully committed transaction — Any transaction that has been written to the database.

garbage collection — A process that runs every 12 hours on DCs and cleans up the transaction logs, getting rid of entries that are no longer of use.

non-authoritative restore — A process of restoring a Windows 2000 DC, in which the restored data is then overwritten by Active Directory replication.

online backup — The process of backing up the system without shutting down any of the services. The operating system and applications remain running during the backup process.

patch files — Used during an online backup to store any transactions that need to be written to the database (after the database has been backed up).

rolling back — The process of undoing changes that have not been fully written to the database.

system state data — Information about the system that is required for recovering the system during a failure. This information includes the Active Directory data, the system Registry, DNS, Certificate Server, and File Replication Service settings.

tombstone — A marker for marking deleted objects in Active Directory as deleted. This gives Active Directory time to replicate this change throughout the network.

tombstone lifetime — The amount of time a tombstone remains active in Active Directory. The default is 60 days.

transaction — A change being made to the database.

transaction log — A disk-based file that stores a list of all the transactions that have been applied to the Active Directory database. All transactions are recorded here before being written to the database.

CHAPTER 9 REVIEW QUESTIONS

1. Active Directory uses two backup files when disk space on the system runs out. What are the names of these files?

   a. RES1.LOG

   b. RES2.LOG

B

c. RES1.BAK

d. RES2.BAK

2. Where are transactions written before they are committed to the Active Directory database?

a. EDB.RES

b. EDB.LOG

c. EDB.CHK

d. EDB.CMT

3. What is some of the critical system data that is stored in the system state data? (Choose all that apply.)

a. The Registry

b. Boot files

c. DNS data

d. All of the above

4. What is the default value of the tombstone lifetime in Windows 2000?

a. 15 days

b. 30 days

c. 60 days

d. 90 days

5. What kind of a restore is performed when you want the restored data to take precedence over the existing data?

a. Offline

b. Full

c. Non-authoritative

d. Authoritative

6. What kind of a restore is performed when you want the restored data to be replaced by the existing Active Directory data, using Active Directory replication?

a. Offline

b. Non-authoritative

c. Full

d. Authoritative

7. What is the default size of the Active Directory log files?

a. 1 MB

b. 5 MB

c. 10 MB

d. 20 MB

8. How often does the log cleanup occur on DCs?

   a. Every hour

   b. Every 3 hours

   c. Every 6 hours

   d. Every 12 hours

9. Which logging method creates a new log file when the old one is filled up?

   a. Circular logging

   b. Continuous logging

   c. Infinite logging

   d. None of the above

10. Which files should be placed on their own hard disks?

    a. NTDS.DIT

    b. Windows 2000 files

    c. Boot files

    d. Registry files

11. When an object is deleted in Active Directory, a marker is put in its place. What is that marker called?

    a. Deletion marker

    b. Tombstone

    c. Deletion flag

    d. Dead Object marker

12. When an object is deleted in Active Directory, a marker is put in its place to ensure:

    a. That fragmentation does not occur.

    b. That the object can be undeleted.

    c. That fragmentation does occur.

    d. That the fact that the object has been deleted is replicated to the other DCs.

13. Each DC cleans up its old data (such as committed log files) using which process?

    a. DC cleanup

    b. Garbage collection

    c. Garbage cleanup

    d. Log File cleanup

14. Which logging method overwrites log files when they fill up?

    a. Circular logging

    b. Continuous logging

c. Infinite logging

d. None of the above

15. What are the three layers of the Active Directory model?

a. Directory System Agent

b. Directory Storage Agent

c. Flexible Storage Engine

d. Extensible Storage Engine

e. The database layer

16. Which layer of the Active Directory model physically stores the AD data?

a. Directory System Agent

b. Flexible Storage Engine

c. Extensible Storage Engine

d. Directory Storage Agent

e. The database layer

17. Which layer of the Active Directory model processes the data hierarchically?

a. Directory System Agent

b. Flexible Storage Engine

c. Extensible Storage Engine

d. Directory Storage Agent

e. The database layer

18. Which layer of the Active Directory model controls security in the Directory?

a. Directory System Agent

b. Flexible Storage Engine

c. Extensible Storage Engine

d. Directory Storage Agent

e. The database layer

19. Which file contains pointers to the transactions that have not yet been committed to the database?

a. EDB.LOG

b. EDB.CHK

c. EDB.PAT

d. EDB.PNT

20. Which file is used during the backup process to store the transactions that have not been committed yet, although the database has already been backed up?

  a. EDB.LOG

  b. EDB.CHK

  c. EDB.PAT

  d. EDB.PNT

CHAPTER 9 HANDS-ON PROJECTS

Project 9-1

1. Select **Start | Programs | Accessories | System Tools | Backup**.
2. Click **Backup Wizard**.
3. Click **Next**.
4. Choose one of the three options: Backup everything on my computer, Backup selected files, drives, or network data, or Only back up the System State data.
5. Click **Next**.
6. If you chose Back up selected files, drives, or network data in Step 4, choose the information that is to be backed up and click **Next**.
7. Select the Backup media type and the corresponding Backup media or file name, and click **Next**.
8. For Advanced options, click **Advanced** to select the Backup Type, to verify the backup, to use hardware compression, to append or replace existing data, to enter a label for the backup set and media, and to indicate whether to schedule the backup.
9. Click **Finish** to start the backup.
10. After the backup is complete, click **Close**.
11. Close the Backup utility.

Project 9-2

1. Select **Start | Programs | Accessories | System Tools | Backup**.
2. Click **Restore Wizard**.
3. Click **Next**.
4. Select the backup set to restore, and click **Next**.
5. For advanced features, click **Advanced** to select the restoration location and whether to replace files.
6. Click **Finish** to start the restore.
7. Click **Close**.
8. Close the Backup utility.

Project 9-3

1. Select **Start|Run**.

2. Type in **Regedt32** and click **OK**.

3. In the HKEY_LOCAL_MACHINE hive, navigate to System\CurrentControlSet\Services\NTDS\Parameters.

4. Add a new Value (from the Edit menu) with the name of **CircularLogging**.

5. Click **OK**.

6. Enter a string of **1**.

7. Click **OK**.

8. Close the Registry Editor.

Project 9-4

1. Select **Start|Run**.

2. Type in **Regedt32** and click **OK**.

3. In the HKEY_LOCAL_MACHINE hive, navigate to System\CurrentControlSet\Services\NTDS\Parameters.

4. Add a new Value (from the Edit menu) with the name of **CircularLogging**.

5. Click **OK**.

6. Enter a string of **0**.

7. Click **OK**.

8. Close the Registry Editor.

CHAPTER 9 CASE PROJECTS

Case Project 9-1

A junior administrator is on a work practicum with your organization. He has limited experience with Windows 2000 and Active Directory. On an especially busy day, you leave him alone in his office to answer the help desk while you are putting out some network fires. When you get back to the office, you notice that he is especially quiet and has a strange green tinge to his skin. After you grill him for answers for several minutes, he finally admits that he screwed up. Apparently, a manager called him, requesting that he delete a group in Active Directory that is no longer being used. He insisted that the manager wait for your return, but to no avail. He finally buckled under the pressure and ended up deleting an entire OU from the Active Directory domain. You calm him down and explain that you can simply recover last night's backup and recover the data. The two of you go to the server room and happily recover the lost OU on a backup DC that is reserved for situations such as this. After the DC is recovered, you show him that the deleted OU is back. However, when you try to make a change to the OU, AD returns an error. You refresh the display and, to your horror, the OU has disappeared again. What needs to be done to recover the OU?

Case Project 9-2

One of the hard disks in your DCs failed, and a complete backup does not exist. You explain this to your manager, but he tells you that he read somewhere that the Active Directory database is transactional and that it should be able to do an up-to-the-minute recovery using the backup copy of the database from last night's backup. You notice that the failed disk contained both the Active Directory database files and the transaction log files. Can the system be recovered, and, if not, how can you configure it to avoid this type of failure in the future?

CHAPTER 10 KEY TERMS

administrative templates — Built-in templates for providing a source for Group Policy to generate the policy settings that you can configure.

asynchronous processing — This type of processing allows policies to be processed without waiting for the outcome of other policies.

Group Policy namespace — The namespace covered by a specified GPO.

Group Policy Objects (GPO) — A collection of Group Policy settings.

local Group Policy Objects — Local GPOs exist on each Windows 2000 system, and by default only the settings under the Security node of the Group Policy apply.

monolithic design — This type of design uses a few very large GPOs and is often implemented at the site or domain level. The GPOs apply to all users and computers on the network, regardless of OU membership.

non-local Group Policy Objects — Non-local GPOs are stored on the domain within Active Directory.

Remote Installation Services (RIS) — A new Windows 2000 service for installing Windows 2000 Professional systems over the network.

return on investment (ROI) — A measure of the amount of time it takes in saved administrative resources to pay back for a product (in this case, Windows 2000).

segmented design — This type of design is associated with decentralized administrative control, because that type of environment is more likely to have multiple administrators and delegated control over Group Policy.

synchronous processing — This type of processing waits until one action is complete before beginning another.

total cost of ownership (TCO) — A measure of the amount of money a particular product costs (in this case, Windows 2000) to install, operate, and support.

CHAPTER 10 REVIEW QUESTIONS

1. Which of the following is a characteristic of a monolithic GPO design?

   a. Many small GPOs

   b. Multiple individual GPOs

   c. Few large GPOs

   d. One single GPO

2. Which of the following is a characteristic of a segmented GPO design?

   a. Many small GPOs

   b. Multiple individual GPOs

   c. Few large GPOs

   d. One single GPO

3. Which type of GPO is stored on the individual systems?

   a. Server

   b. Client

   c. Local

   d. Non-local

4. Which type of GPO is stored on the domain?

   a. Server

   b. Client

   c. Local

   d. Non-local

5. Which of the following tasks cannot be delegated?

   a. Managing GPOs

   b. Filtering GPOs

   c. Managing GPO links

   d. Editing GPOs

6. In which order are Group Policy settings applied during the logon process?

   a. Local, site, OU, domain

   b. Local, site, domain, OU

   c. Domain, site, OU, local

   d. Domain, site, local, OU

7. Which utility is used to delegate GPO editing?

   a. Group Policy snap-in

   b. GPO Editing snap-in

   c. Active Directory Users and Computer

   d. Active Directory Domains and Trusts

8. Which utility is used to delegate GPO creation?

   a. Group Policy snap-in

   b. GPO Editing snap-in

   c. Active Directory Users and Computer

   d. Active Directory Domains and Trusts

9. Which utility should be used to associate security settings with an entire site in your organization?

   a. Active Directory Users and Computers

   b. Group Policy snap-in

   c. Active Directory Sites and Services

   d. Group Policy Association snap-in

10. When you refresh a Group Policy, Folder Redirection is excluded. True or False?

    a. True

    b. False

11. A No Override setting is set only on which of the following?

    a. Site

    b. Domain

    c. OU

    d. Link

12. A Group Policy setting has three different states. Which of the following is not one of the states?

    a. Enabled

    b. Disabled

    c. Configured

    d. Not configured

13. You can use the EditSec tool to refresh Group Policy immediately. True or False?

    a. True

    b. False

14. When Group Policy detects a slow link, which of the following does not apply?

    a. Folder Redirection is turned on.

    b. Software Installation is turned off.

    c. Internet Explorer maintenance is turned off.

    d. Security Settings are always processed, regardless of link speed.

B

15. What is the default setting for a Group Policy setting?

    a. Enabled

    b. Disabled

    c. Configured

    d. Not configured

16. The process of associating a GPO with an object is known as _____.

    a. Joining

    b. Linking

    c. Matching

    d. Grouping

17. What should be used to ensure that a Group Policy setting is applied throughout the domain?

    a. No Override

    b. Block Policy Inheritance

    c. Allow Policy Inheritance

    d. Allow Override

18. Which of the following is a definition of synchronous processing?

    a. All processing takes place at once.

    b. All processes are processed one at a time.

    c. Only one process can be executed for every instance of the object.

    d. None of the above

19. Which of the following is a definition of asynchronous processing?

    a. All processing takes place at once.

    b. All processes are processed one at a time.

    c. Only one process can be executed for every instance of the object.

    d. None of the above

20. Administrative templates created with the Windows NT 4.0 System Policy Editor can be read and changed with the Windows 2000 System Policy Editor. True or False?

    a. True

    b. False

CHAPTER 10 HANDS-ON PROJECTS

Project 10-1

1. Select **Start | Programs | Administrative Tools | Active Directory Users and Computers**.

2. Right-click on the domain and choose the **New | Organizational Unit** option.

3. Enter a name for the new OU, then click **OK**.

4. Right-click on the OU and choose the **Properties** option.

5. Select the **Group Policy** tab.

6. Click **New**.

7. Enter a name for the new GPO.

8. Click **Close**.

9. Close the Active Directory Users and Computers console.

Project 10-2

1. Select **Start | Programs | Administrative Tools | Active Directory Users and Computers**.

2. Right-click on the OU and choose the **Properties** option.

3. Select the **Group Policy** tab.

4. Highlight the GPO created in Hands-on Project 10-1, and click **Properties**.

5. Select the **Security** tab.

6. Click **Add** to add users and computers to which this GPO should apply, then click **OK**.

7. Specify the desired permissions.

8. Click **OK**, then click **OK** again.

9. Close the Active Directory Users and Computers console.

CHAPTER 10 CASE PROJECTS

Case Project 10-1

You are the lead administrator for a medium-sized company. Your organization has purchased a competitor. The competitor's network will be joined with yours, but they do not have any full-time administrators on-site. Instead, they contract an IT firm to do the network support for them. While you do not want to give the IT firm full access to your Active Directory tree, you need to grant them some rights. What would be the best course of action to accomplish this?

Case Project 10-2

You inherit a Windows 2000 network, and you realize that the password policy has not been modified from the default settings. From your experience, you know that the default security is not secure enough for most installations. What do you need to do to secure the password settings?

B

CHAPTER 11 KEY TERMS

computer template — An administrative template that controls the configuration of a computer.

File Replication service (FRS) — The replacement to the Windows NT Directory Replication service. This service replicates the entire SYSVOL directory tree across all Windows 2000 domain controllers.

folder redirection — A new feature of Windows 2000 that is essentially the process by which the operating system changes the location of certain Windows 2000 folders from the local hard drive to a specified network share. The folders that can be redirected include: Application Data, Desktop, My Documents, My Pictures, and Start Menu.

logoff script — A script that executes when the user logs off the system.

logon script — A script that executes when the user logs on to the system. This script runs under the account with which the user is associated.

shutdown script — A script that runs when the computer is being shut down. It is executed under the Local System account.

startup script — A computer script that is executed under the Local System account during the computer startup process, before the user logon screen is displayed.

user template — An administrative template that controls the configuration of a user.

Windows Scripting Host (WSH) — A scripting host that allows for the execution of VBScript (.vbs) and JavaScript (.js) natively on 32-bit Windows platforms.

CHAPTER 11 REVIEW QUESTIONS

1. Windows 2000 folder redirection allows an administrator to redirect any folder on the system to a network share. True or False?

   a. True

   b. False

2. Which of the following folders cannot be redirected using the Windows 2000 folder redirection service?

   a. My Documents

   b. Documents and Settings

   c. Start Menu

   d. Desktop

3. What is the DOS-based Windows Scripting Host file?

   a. CScript.exe

   b. WScript.exe

   c. Jscript.exe

   d. VBScript.exe

4. What is the Windows–based Windows Scripting Host file?

   a. CScript.exe

   b. WScript.exe

   c. Jscript.exe

   d. VBScript.exe

5. Which script is applied to the computer when it first starts up?

   a. Boot

   b. Login

   c. Startup

   d. Begin

6. Which script is applied to the computer when it is turned off?

   a. Login

   b. Startup

   c. Shutdown

   d. Down

7. In which order do the Windows 2000 scripts execute?

   a. Logon, logoff, startup, shutdown

   b. Logon, startup, shutdown, logoff

   c. Startup, logon, logoff, shutdown

   d. Logon, startup, shutdown, shutdown

8. Which file extension does WSH 1 use?

   a. .ws

   b. .wsh

   c. .wsf

   d. .ws1

9. Which file extension does WSH 2 use?

   a. .ws

   b. .wsh

   c. .wsf

   d. .ws2

10. With version 2 of WSH, the .vbs and .js files are replaced by the .WSF file. True or False?

    a. True

    b. False

11. Which Registry hive is modified by the computer policies?

    a. HKEY_CURRENT_USER

    b. HKEY_LOCAL_MACHINE

    c. HKEY_CLASSES_ROOT

    d. HKEY_USERS

12. Microsoft has included a variable that directly relates to the name of the user who is currently logged on to the system. This variable can be used with FRS. What is this variable?

    a. username

    b. user

    c. %username%

    d. %user%

13. Custom administrative templates have which of the following extensions associated with them?

    a. .adm

    b. .tmp

    c. .txt

    d. .inf

14. Which of the following two languages are supported in WSH?

    a. JavaScript

    b. Java

    c. VBScript

    d. REXX

15. Which file in WSH version 1 is used simply for formatting the output of a script?

    a. WSH

    b. WSF

    c. WS

    d. WS1

16. Which of the following are entries that are used when creating administrative templates?

    a. POLICY

    b. SECTION

     c. CLASS

     d. CATEGORY

17. Double-clicking on a .VBS file will execute it. True or False?

     a. True

     b. False

18. Which of the following administrative templates exists only under User Configuration?

     a. Network

     b. System

     c. Control Panel

     d. Windows Components

19. Although only JavaScript and VBScript are supported natively by WSH version 2, it is possible to install other languages, such as Perl. True or False?

     a. True

     b. False

20. GPO has a "miscellaneous" category for policies. What is the name of that category?

     a. Control Panel

     b. System

     c. Network

     d. Windows Components

CHAPTER 11 HANDS-ON PROJECTS

Project 11-1

1. Select **Start | Programs | Administrative Tools | Active Directory Users and Computer**.

2. Right-click on the domain, and choose the **Properties** option.

3. Select the **Group Policy** tab.

4. Click **New** to create a new Group Policy, then name the new Group Policy.

5. Highlight the Group Policy and click **Edit**.

Project 11-2

1. In the Group Policy utility, navigate to the Desktop object (**User Configuration | Administrative Templates | Desktop**).

2. Double-click the **Disable adding, dragging, dropping, and closing the Taskbar's toolbars** option.

3. Choose the **Enabled** option and click **OK**.

4. Double-click on the **Don't save settings at exit** option.

5. Choose the **Enabled** option and click **OK**.

Project 11-3

1. In the Group Policy utility, navigate to the Active Desktop object (**User Configuration|Administrative Templates|Desktop|Active Desktop**).

2. Double-click the **Active Desktop Wallpaper** option.

3. Choose the **Enabled** option.

4. Enter a path and a name for the wallpaper file.

5. If necessary, choose the wallpaper style.

6. Click **OK**.

Project 11-4

1. In the Group Policy utility, navigate to the System object (**Computer Configuration|Administrative Templates|System**.

2. Double-click the **Disable Autoplay** option.

3. Choose the **Enabled** option.

4. Choose to disable Autorun on either all drives or on CD-ROM drives, from the drop-down menu.

5. Click **OK**.

Project 11-5

1. In the Group Policy utility, navigate to the Control Panel object (**User Configuration|Administrative Templates|Control Panel**.

2. Double-click the **Disable Control Panel** option.

3. Choose the **Enabled** option and click **OK**.

Project 11-6

1. In the Group Policy utility, navigate to the Logon/Logoff object (**User Configuration|Administrative Templates|System|Logon/Logoff**.

2. Double-click the **Disable Logoff** option.

3. Choose the **Enabled** option and click **OK**.

4. Close the Group Policy utility, click **OK** in the domain Properties page, and then close the Active Directory Users and Computers console.

Chapter 11 Case Projects

Case Project 11-1

Your organization donates one of its labs on the weekends to a local school. The school brings in a group of students to learn all about computers. The problem is that several of the students have "learned too much." You find that when you return to the lab on Monday morning, you have to completely rebuild the lab. How can you configure the lab network (all systems are running Windows 2000) so that the students cannot modify the desktop?

Case Project 11-2

In looking for a way to back up user data, your organization has decided that purchasing a backup agent program for each workstation is simply too costly. You are therefore given a project to find another solution, using the fewest resources possible. You need to back up data such as the user's My Documents, Start Menu, and Application Data files. How would you accomplish this with Windows 2000?

Chapter 12 Key Terms

change and configuration management — A collection of ideas and strategies for reducing TCO and increasing ROI.

distribution phase — The process of distributing applications to your users and systems from central distribution points.

distribution point — A network share or shares from which users can install software.

hard costs — The actual cost of the hardware and software for systems.

installation phase — In this phase, the software is rolled out across the organization to all users and computers that are configured to receive it.

IntelliMirror — A Windows 2000 feature that seeks to increase the availability of Windows 2000-based computers while decreasing total cost of ownership.

Internet Information Server (IIS) — Microsoft's built-in Web server.

just-in-time (JIT) — The technology that allows applications to be available to users whenever they log on to a system or launch an application, no matter where or when they log in.

offline folders — A Windows 2000 feature that allows users to ensure that important documents that are usually stored on the server are made available to them if the server is offline, the network is unavailable, or the system is no longer connected to the network.

Outlook Web Access (OWA) — A component of Exchange Server that allows users to access their e-mail accounts via the Internet.

patching applications — The process of upgrading or fixing applications that have already been installed, without the need to reinstall them. This is similar to applying a hot fix or a service pack in Windows 2000.

pilot phase — In the pilot phase, a pilot program is performed. A pilot program is a trial run deployed first in a lab environment and then to a subset of users, for the express purpose of troubleshooting and debugging any application issues prior to the full deployment.

preparation phase — The preparation phase of software management consists of the initial information collection process, including the analysis of the organization's structure to determine its software requirements.

soft costs — The cost of IT infrastructure. These costs include the cost for the support team and for the employees using the systems.

targeting phase — The targeting phase of software management consists of the creation of Group Policy to create and/or modify Group Policy Objects, in order to target the software to specific users and groups.

transforms — Transforms, which are the MST files that Windows Installer uses, are used to customize the installation of applications, changing them from their default behavior.

universal naming convention (UNC) — An industry standard naming convention for accessing network resources. UNC takes the form of \\server\share. For example, to access the users folder on the server named mainserver, the UNC would be \\mainserver\users.

ZAP file — A ZAP file contains settings relevant to controlling a program's appearance and behavior. It is similar to the old INI files and is used in non-Windows Installer packages.

Zero Administration Windows (ZAW) — The predecessor to IntelliMirror, Microsoft's original initiative to create a managed desktop environment under Windows.

CHAPTER 12 REVIEW QUESTIONS

1. Which phase of software management involves testing the software installation in a controlled environment?

   a. Preparation

   b. Distribution

   c. Targeting

   d. Pilot

   e. Installation

2. Which phase of software management involves analysis of the network to determine the software requirements?

   a. Preparation

   b. Distribution

   c. Targeting

   d. Pilot

   e. Installation

3. Which phase of software management involves the creation of GPOs to deploy the software to the appropriate users?

a. Preparation

b. Distribution

c. Targeting

d. Pilot

e. Installation

4. Which phase of software management involves the actual installation of the software to the targeted group of users or computers?

a. Preparation

b. Distribution

c. Targeting

d. Pilot

e. Installation

5. Which phase of software management involves the sharing of the installation packages on network servers?

a. Preparation

b. Distribution

c. Targeting

d. Pilot

e. Installation

6. Microsoft has produced and sells a product whose features far exceed what can be done with GPOs and IntelliMirror. What is that product?

a. Microsoft Exchange Server

b. Microsoft System Management Server

c. Microsoft SQL Server

d. Microsoft ISA Server

7. A non-Windows Installer package has which extension when it is deployed with Software Installation?

a. .ini

b. .zip

c. .zap

d. .msf

8. Which file extension does a Microsoft Windows Installer file use?

a. .zap

b. .msf

c. .msi

d. .inf

9. What is the term used to describe the network share in which Windows Installer packages are placed before being deployed out to users and computers?

a. mount point

b. share point

c. install point

d. distribution point

10. A soft cost is described as any cost associated with software purchases and upgrades. True or False?

a. True

b. False

11. When you are patching an application, which of the following modifications can be performed by Windows Installer?

a. Hardware settings

b. Services

c. Files

d. Registry entries

12. Which phase of the software deployment strategy is usually not completed?

a. Preparation

b. Distribution

c. Targeting

d. Pilot

e. Installation

13. Which of the following is a requirement of Software Installation on a Windows 2000 system?

a. Active Directory

b. DVD drive

c. 512 MB of RAM

d. 2 GB of disk space

14. Which extension does a transform file use?

    a. .mst

    b. .msi

    c. .msf

    d. .mso

15. An assigned package is a package that is automatically installed on users' systems. They do not get the option not to install the package. True or False?

    a. True

    b. False

16. A published package is a package that is automatically installed on users' systems. They do not get the option not to install the package. True or False?

    a. True

    b. False

17. Which two components of WinINSTALL are included with Windows 2000?

    a. Watcher

    b. Software Console

    c. INSTALLConsole

    d. Discover

18. What is the correct order of the software deployment phases?

    a. Installation, preparation, targeting, distribution, pilot

    b. Preparation, installation, pilot, distribution, targeting

    c. Installation, pilot, targeting, distribution, preparation

    d. Preparation, distribution, targeting, pilot, installation

19. Which application is used to patch an existing .MSI package?

    a. VERITAS Discover

    b. VERITAS Repair Console

    c. VERITAS Software Console

    d. VERITAS Patch

20. What are .MSI modifications known as?

    a. Patches

    b. Modifications

    c. Changes

    d. Transforms

CHAPTER 12 HANDS-ON PROJECTS

Project 12-1

1. Insert the Windows 2000 Server CD into the CD-ROM drive. If Auto run starts, exit the program.

2. Navigate to the **\valuadd\3rdparty\mgmt\winstle** folder.

3. Double-click on the **SWIADMLE.MSI** file.

Project 12-2

1. Select **Start | Programs | VERITAS Software | VERITAS Discover**.

2. Click **Next**.

3. Enter a name for the application for which you are building the installation.

4. Choose a path on the system for the .msi file.

5. Click **Next**.

6. Choose a drive where Discover can store temporary files.

7. Click **Next**.

8. In the left pane, choose the drive or drives to be scanned, and click **Add**.

9. Click **Next**.

10. In the left pane, choose any files or folders to be excluded from the scan, and click **Add**.

11. Click **Next**.

12. Once the scan is completed, click **OK**, then navigate to and select the installation file.

13. Select **Start | Programs | VERITAS Software | VERITAS Discover**.

14. Ensure that the **Perform the "After" snapshot now** radio button is selected.

15. Click **Next**.

16. Click **OK**, then click **OK** again.

Project 12-3

1. Select **Start | Programs | Administrative Tools | Active Directory Users and Computers**.

2. Choose a test OU.

3. Right-click on the OU and choose the **Properties** option.

4. Choose the **Group Policy** tab.

5. Choose a GPO and click **Edit**.

6. Navigate to the Software installation container under **User Configuration | Software Settings**.

7. Right-click **Software installation** and choose **New | Package**.

8. Navigate to the created .msi file and click **Open**.

9. Choose the **Published** option and click **OK**.

Project 12-4

1. Select **Start | Programs | Administrative Tools | Active Directory Users and Computers**.

2. Choose a test OU.

3. Right-click on **OU** and choose the **Properties** option.

4. Choose the **Group Policy** tab.

5. Choose a GPO and click **Edit**.

6. Navigate to the Software Installation container under **User Configuration | Software Settings**.

7. Right-click **Software installation** and choose **New | Package**.

8. Navigate to the created .msi file and click **Open**.

9. Choose the **Assigned** option and click **OK**.

CHAPTER 12 CASE PROJECTS

Case Project 12-1

At a weekly departmental meeting, it is made clear that a large portion of a couple of IT support staff members' time is spent simply fixing broken applications. Many of your users are only computer literate enough to be dangerous, and they tend to delete files that they feel are not needed, thereby breaking applications on their systems. Your organization has looked at products such as Microsoft's SMS, but the cost of the product and the subsequent infrastructure and support costs make it impossible for you to implement. You therefore need to find an inexpensive solution for automatically checking applications and reinstalling missing files, or the entire application, should the need arise. What Windows 2000 technology can you use to accomplish this?

Case Project 12-2

You did such a fine job solving the "file-deleting user" problem that your manager decided to give you another project. This project entails automating the installation of applications on users' systems. The catch is that you do not want to install all applications on all systems by default, only the ones that the users require. How would you accomplish this?

CHAPTER 13 KEY TERMS

Boot Information Negotiation Layer (BINL) — A server-side service that provides a default set of screens to the user.

Client Installation Wizard — The client-side component of RIS. This component is downloaded to the client and communicates with RIS.

Pre-Boot Execution Environment (PXE) — An industry standard for enabling a compliant client PC to gain basic TCP/IP network connectivity automatically.

prestaging — A process used to create computer accounts in advance of installation and to ensure that each computer name is unique.

Remote Installation Services (RIS) — A Windows 2000 service for quickly installing Windows 2000 Professional on systems using the PXE protocol.

RIPrep — A utility used to create Windows 2000 Professional images with customized settings and locally installed desktop applications.

RISetup — A utility used to configure RIS and create Windows 2000 Professional images.

Single Instance Store (SIS) — A service that reduces disk space requirements for RIS images by combining duplicate files.

Trivial File Transfer Protocol Daemon (TFTPD) — A service used by RIS to download the initial client files necessary to begin the Windows 2000 Professional installation.

CHAPTER 13 REVIEW QUESTIONS

1. Which application should you use when creating a network-based installation of Windows 2000?

   a. Winnt32.exe

   b. RIPrep.exe

   c. Winnt.exe

   d. RISetup.exe

2. In which application can an RIS boot disk be created?

   a. RIPrep.exe

   b. RISDisk.exe

   c. RISetup.exe

   d. RBFG.exe

3. Which of the following files can be found on an RIS boot disk?

   a. Ntldr

   b. Boot.ini

   c. RISDISK

   d. Ntdetect.com

4. When you install RIS on a Windows 2000 system, which of the following file system or file systems is required?

   a. FAT16

   b. FAT32

   c. NTFS

   d. CDFS

5. When you want to authorize an RIS server for increased security on the network, which utility do you use?

   a. Active Directory Users and Computers

   b. Active Directory Domains and Trusts

   c. The DNS snap-in

   d. The DHCP snap-in

6. RIS includes a service that saves the disk space required by the images by eliminating duplicate files. What is the name of the service?

   a. SRS

   b. SIS

   c. BINL

   d. TFTPD

7. Which of the following is NOT a requirement for installing RIS?

   a. Active Directory

   b. Domain Name System

   c. Dynamic Host Configuration Protocol Service

   d. Windows Internet Naming Service

8. Which of the following standards must a client computer meet in order to use RIS? Choose all that apply.

   a. NetPC

   b. MPC

   c. PC98

   d. PC97

9. If a system does not meet the required standards and the network card is not PXE-compliant, it might still be possible to use RIS with it. True or False?

   a. True

   b. False

10. RIS cannot be installed if the server is running a Distributed File System (DFS) volume. True or False?

    a. True

    b. False

11. What is the minimum processor required for running RIS?

    a. Pentium 166

    b. Pentium 200

    c. Pentium Celeron 400

    d. Pentium III 650

12. What is the term used when the administrator configures the computer accounts in Active Directory before the systems are installed?

    a. Preconfiguration

    b. Precreation

    c. Premodification

    d. Prestaging

13. For which operating systems can RIPrep be used to create images? Choose all that apply?

    a. Windows NT Workstation

    b. Windows NT Server

    c. Windows 2000 Professional

    d. Windows 2000 Server

14. When an image creation fails, where does RIPrep log its status and error messages?

    a. RIPrep.log

    b. RIPrep.err

    c. RIPrep.aud

    d. RIPrep.txt

15. What does RIS use the Trivial File Transfer Protocol Daemon for?

    a. Uploading the entire Windows 2000 image to the client

    b. Uploading the files necessary to begin the Windows 2000 Professional installation to the client

    c. Uploading the files needed for the Client Installation Wizard

    d. Authenticating with Active Directory

16. Which of the following does the Boot Information Negotiation Layer (BINL) *not* do?

    a. Listen to DHCP/PXE requests

    b. Verify logon credentials with Active Directory

    c. Redirect clients to the appropriate files needed for the installation during the Client Installation Wizard

    d. Download all files necessary to begin the Windows 2000 Professional installation

17. RIS can be installed if the server is running an Encrypted File System (EFS) volume. True or False?

    a. True

    b. False

18. What is the name of the bootstrap program that displays the message for the user to press F12 for Network Service?

    a. Bootstrap.exe

    b. Netboot.exe

    c. Startrom.exe

    d. Netdetect.exe

19. Which file contains the installation information about the image's source computer, such as the installation directory and the HAL type?

    a. RIPrep.dat

    b. Bootcode.dat

    c. Lmirror.dat

    d. HAL.dat

20. Which file contains the boot sector information for the client computer?

    a. RIPrep.dat

    b. Bootcode.dat

    c. Lmirror.dat

    d. HAL.dat

CHAPTER 13 HANDS-ON PROJECTS

Project 13-1

1. Select **Start | Settings | Control Panel**.

2. Double-click **Add/Remove Programs**.

3. Click the **Add/Remove Windows Components** button from the left pane.

4. Select the **Remote Installation Services** checkbox.

5. Click **Next**. If necessary, insert the Windows 2000 Server CD-ROM and then click **OK**.

6. Click **Finish**.

7. Reboot the server if necessary. Open the **Add/Remove Programs** applet again if necessary.

8. In the Add/Remove Programs applet, select the **Add/Remove Windows Components** button from the left pane, select the **Configure Remote Installation Services** option, and click **Configure**.

9. Click **Next**.

10. Enter the folder path where you want the root of the Remote Installation Services operating system images to reside, and click **Next**.

11. If you want the RIS to start immediately, select the **Respond to client computers requesting service** check box, and click **Next**.

12. Enter the path to the Windows 2000 Professional installation files, and click **Next**.

13. Enter a name for the folder that will be created to store the operating system image, and click **Next**.

14. Enter a friendly description for this operating system image, and click **Next**.

15. Click **Finish**.

16. Click **Done** when the Remote Installation Services Setup Wizard tasks are completed, then close the Add/Remove Programs applet and the Control Panel.

Project 13-2

1. Select **Start | Programs | Administrative Tools | Active Directory Users and Computers**.

2. Navigate to the server where you would like to enable RIS, right-click on it, and choose the **Properties** option.

3. Click the **Remote Install** tab.

4. Select the **Respond to client computers requesting service** check box, if necessary, and click **OK**.

5. Close the Active Directory Users and Computers console.

Project 13-3

1. Select **Start | Programs | Administrative Tools | Active Directory Users and Computers**.

2. Navigate to the server running RIS, right-click on it, and choose the **Properties** option.

3. Click the **Remote Install** tab.

4. Click the **Advanced Settings** button.

5. Select the **Images** tab, then click the **Add** button.

6. Indicate whether a new answer file is being used for an existing image, or create a new image from the Windows 2000 Professional installation files, and select the **Add a new installation image** option.

7. Click **Next**.

8. Follow the steps in the Remote Installation Services Setup Wizard.

9. Click **OK** in the Remote Installation Services Properties window, then click **OK** in the server Properties page.

10. Close the Active Directory Users and Computers console.

Project 13-4

1. Install Windows 2000 Professional on a reference system using RIS.

2. Install any applications that are to be duplicated in the image.

3. Configure the system as required.

4. Shut down all services and applications.

5. Run the RIPrep.exe application from the RemoteInstall\Admin\i386 share on the RIS system. Your share name might be different.

6. Click **Next**.

7. Enter the name of the RIS server that you would like to host the image, and click **Next**.

8. Enter the folder name where the image will be stored, and click **Next**.

9. Enter a friendly description for the image, and click **Next**.

10. Click **Next**.

11. To copy the image to the RIS server, click **Next** in the Programs or Services are Running screen, click **Next** in the Review Settings screen, and then click **Next** to start copying.

Project 13-5

1. Insert a blank, formatted 1.44 MB floppy disk, connect to the RIS server's \RemoteInstall\Admin\i386 share, and run the rbfg.exe file.

2. Click **Create Disk**. Click **No** when asked if you'd like to create another disk.

3. Click **Close** in the Windows 2000 Remote Book Disk Generator window.

Project 13-6

1. Shut down the system.

2. Insert the Remote Boot Disk and turn on the system.

3. Press the **F12** button to boot from the network.

4. Press **Enter** to begin the Client Installation Wizard.

5. Enter a username, a password, and the DNS name for the domain, and press **Enter**.

6. Choose the Automatic Setup, Custom Setup, Restart a Previous Setup Attempt, or Maintenance and Troubleshooting Tools option, and press **Enter**.

7. Select the image that you would like to use, and press **Enter**.

8. Press **Enter**.

CHAPTER 13 CASE PROJECTS

Case Project 13-1

Your organization has purchased a large number of new systems. You are looking for the best and quickest way of installing Windows 2000 Professional on these systems. Your organization has not tested any technologies such as Ghost and therefore will not purchase such technologies. You check the systems and confirm that they are PXE-compliant. What would be the best way to accomplish your goals?

Case Project 13-2

After you quickly installed Windows 2000 Professional on all the new systems, management decided to do the same to the older, non–Windows 2000 systems. You check them out and realize that they are not PXE-compliant. How would you go about installing Windows 2000 Professional on the systems, using RIS?

CHAPTER 14 KEY TERMS

convergence — A term used to describe a network in which all DCs are 100% up to date. That is to say, there are no more changes to be replicated.

high-watermark table — A table stored at the DC, which stores the name of each of the DC's replication partners, along with the last known USN value for that DC.

latency — A term describing the inherent delay in Active Directory replication.

originating update — An originating update is the first time a change is made to a property in Active Directory.

propagation dampening — A term used to describe the process used by Active Directory to ensure that changes don't endlessly loop around a Windows 2000 network.

Property Version Number (PVN) — A value that is appended to every property within Active Directory and traces the number of times a specific property has been changed.

replicated update — A replicated update is a change made to Active Directory that did not originate at that copy.

replication partners — A group of DCs that replicate Active Directory data among themselves.

Update Sequence Number (USN) — A 64-bit number that keeps track of changes as they are written to copies of Active Directory.

up-to-date vector table — A table that stores a list of every DC on the network, along with the USN of the last originating update made on that DC.

CHAPTER 14 REVIEW QUESTIONS

1. When replication partners are automatically calculated, what is the maximum number of hops that can exist between them?

   a. 2

   b. 3

   c. 4

   d. 5

2. What is the term used to describe the delay associated with Active Directory replication?

   a. Latency

   b. Convergence

   c. Replication latency

   d. Replication delay

3. What is the term used to describe a network in which no more Active Directory changes need to be replicated?

   a. Latency

   b. Convergence

   c. Replication latency

   d. Replication delay

4. What is a group of DCs that replicate Active Directory data to each other called?

   a. Replication group

   b. Replication block

   c. Replication pair

   d. Replication partners

5. Which of the following are the two types of Windows 2000 replication updates?

   a. Originating update

   b. First update

   c. Replicated update

   d. Duplicated update

6. By what value does an Update Sequence Number (USN) increment?

   a. 1

   b. 2

   c. 3

   d. 4

7. Which table is used to store the USN value only for each DC with which a DC replicates?

   a. Up-to-date vector table

   b. USN table

   c. High-watermark table

   d. KCC table

8. Which table is used to store the USN value at the time of the last originating update for each DC within the domain?

   a. Up-to-date vector table

   b. USN table

   c. High-watermark table

   d. KCC table

9. Active Directory replication uses a pull technology, rather than push. True or False?

   a. True

   b. False

10. Active Directory replication that occurs between DCs in a site is known as _____.

   a. Remote replication

   b. Intersite replication

   c. Intrasite replication

   d. Local replication

11. Active Directory replication that occurs between DCs in different sites is known as _____.

   a. Remote replication

   b. Intersite replication

   c. Intrasite replication

   d. Local replication

12. What keeps track of how many times a record has been modified?

   a. USN

   b. VPN

    c. PVN

    d. KCC

13. When all Active Directory replication between sites is directed through a specific server, what is the name given to that server?

    a. Gateway server

    b. Bridge server

    c. Controller server

    d. Bridgehead server

14. What is the Windows 2000 Active Directory replication model called?

    a. Multi-master

    b. No-Master

    c. Single-Master

    d. None of the above

15. With multiple DCs replicating with multiple other DCs, it is possible for replication data to be replicated repeatedly. What did Microsoft include in Windows 2000 to solve this problem?

    a. Propagation dampening

    b. Propagation termination

    c. Propagation resistance

    d. Propagation control

16. What does the acronym USN stand for?

    a. Universal Sequence Number

    b. Unique Sequence Number

    c. Update Sequence Number

    d. Upgrade Sequence Number

17. The higher the cost of a site link, the more attractive it is to Active Directory replication. True or False?

    a. True

    b. False

18. When replicated between two different sites, data can be compressed. True or False?

    a. True

    b. False

19. When replication takes place within a site, replication can be scheduled. True or False?

    a. True

    b. False

20. There are two tables stored on each DC that assist in Active Directory replication. What are they called?

    a. Up-to-date vector table

    b. USN table

    c. High-watermark table

    d. KCC table

B

CHAPTER 15 KEY TERMS

archiving — The process of making a copy of an event log for review at a later date.

basic scenario — Any template designed to return the system to the default settings if any have been changed.

compat scenario — This template is a compatible template that makes the system compatible with previous versions of Windows.

hisec scenario — These templates are designed to secure systems for network communication.

local policy — A Group Policy set to a single, local machine.

secure scenario — This template is the recommended template for a system. It enforces all the suggested security features.

security template — A collection of prebuilt templates that alter auditing and security settings.

system policy — A Group Policy set to a group of systems over the network.

tattooing — A feature in which the value of a key is changed from one value to another, and the original value is not stored.

CHAPTER 15 REVIEW QUESTIONS

1. Which security template should be used to ensure that these security settings will work with previous versions of Windows?

    a. Basic

    b. Compat

    c. Secure

    d. Hisec

2. Which security template should be used to provide the highest security to the system?

    a. Basic

    b. Compat

    c. Secure

    d. Hisec

3. Which security template should be used to return a system to its default security settings?

   a. Basic

   b. Compat

   c. Secure

   d. Hisec

4. Which security template should be used to secure a system with the recommended settings?

   a. Basic

   b. Compat

   c. Secure

   d. Hisec

5. Which extension is associated with the security templates?

   a. .cfg

   b. .sec

   c. .dat

   d. .inf

6. You specify which events to audit in the object's properties, but the Security event log remains blank. What might be the reason for this?

   a. Audit events are located in the audit logs, not the Security Logs.

   b. While the events to be audited are configured, auditing is not enabled on the system.

   c. The auditing service has incorrect credentials and cannot connect to the logging service.

   d. None of the above

7. Once the Security Templates are created, which tool would you use to apply them to servers on the network?

   a. Security Templates snap-in

   b. Security Configuration and Analysis snap-in

   c. Active Directory Users and Computers

   d. Security Policies snap-in

8. Once the security templates are created, which tool would you use to test how they will affect the servers on the network?

   a. Security Templates snap-in

   b. Security Configuration and Analysis snap-in

    c. Active Directory Users and Computers

    d. Security Policies snap-in

9. What is the correct syntax for forcing the Group Policy changes to propagate?

    a. Secedit /refresh machine_policy

    b. Secedit /propagate machine_policy

    c. Secedit /forcerefresh machine_policy

    d. Secedit /refreshpolicy machine_policy

10. Where are the predefined security templates stored?

    a. *Systemroot*\System32\Security

    b. *Systemroot*\Security\Templates

    c. *Systemroot*\System32\Templates

    d. *Systemroot*\Templates\Security

11. Which utility is used to create and modify the security templates?

    a. Security Templates snap-in

    b. Security Management snap-in

    c. Active Directory Users and Computers

    d. Security Policies snap-in

12. When policy changes are made in Group Policy, which of the following is not an option for speeding up the time it takes to propagate the changes through the network?

    a. Wait for the change to propagate.

    b. Reboot the system.

    c. Use Secedit to force the propagation.

    d. There is nothing that can be done.

13. When Windows 2000 is first installed, which events are audited automatically?

    a. No events are audited.

    b. Only successful audits.

    c. Only unsuccessful audits.

    d. All events are audited.

14. You should turn on all auditing events (both successes and failures) on your network to ensure that no unauthorized access is gone undetected. True or False?

    a. True

    b. False

15. It is a requirement in your organization to archive all log files for future reference. What is the best way of doing this without creating a few, very large log files?

    a. Save the .evt files and store them off the network (such as on a CD-ROM disk).

    b. Increase the audit log file size to 2 GB.

    c. Do nothing. Windows 2000 automatically archives the data.

    d. None of the above

CHAPTER 15 HANDS-ON PROJECTS

Project 15-1

1. Select **Start | Programs | Administrative Tools | Domain Security Policy**.
2. Expand Security Settings, expand Local Policies, and then select **Audit Policy**. Double-click the audit policy that is to be enforced.
3. Indicate whether to audit successes, failures, or both, and click **OK**.
4. Close the Domain Security Policy console.

Project 15-2

1. Open the Active Directory Sites and Services console. Right-click on the object that you would like to audit, and choose the **Properties** option.
2. Select the **Security** tab.
3. Click **Advanced**.
4. Select the **Auditing** tab.
5. To add a user or group, click **Add**, select the user/group, click **OK**, select the access to audit, click **OK**, and then click **OK** in the Access Control Settings page.
6. To remove a user or group, highlight the user/group and click **Remove**.
7. Click **OK**.
8. Click **OK**.
9. Close the Active Directory Sites and Services console.

Project 15-3

1. Select **Start | Run**.
2. Type in **MMC** and click **OK**.
3. Select **Add/Remove Snap-in** from the Console menu.
4. Click **Add**.
5. Select **Security Templates** and click **Add**.

6. Select **Security Configuration and Analysis**, then click **Add**.

7. Click **Close**.

8. Click **OK**.

9. Select the **Save** option from the Console menu.

10. Enter a name for the MMC console, and click **Save**.

Project 15-4

1. Select the Security Templates snap-in configured in Hands-on Project 15-3.

2. Double-click on the default path folder.

3. Right-click on the security template that you would like to change, and choose the **Save As** option.

4. Enter a new name for the template, and click **Save**.

5. Double-click on the newly created template.

6. Modify the security settings.

Project 15-5

1. Select the Security Templates snap-in configured in Hands-on Project 15-3.

2. Right-click on the default path folder, and choose the **New Template** option.

3. Enter a name and description for the new security template, and click **OK**.

4. Double-click on the newly created security template.

5. Modify the security settings.

Project 15-6

1. Select the Security Templates snap-in configured in Hands-on Project 15-3.

2. Right-click **Security Configuration and Analysis**, and choose the **Open database** option.

3. Enter a database name to open, and click **Open**.

4. Right-click on **Security Configuration and Analysis**, then select **Import Template**. Select the template to import and click **Open**.

5. Right-click **Security Configuration and Analysis**, and choose **Configure Computer Now**.

6. Enter the error Error log file path and click **OK**.

7. Close the MMC Console.

CHAPTER 15 CASE PROJECTS

Case Project 15-1

You suspect that a hacker is attempting to access your network by using a password attack on your domain. You need to configure auditing so that it captures any relevant information about the hacker. Your organization will be taking legal action against the hacker and would like as much information as possible. How would you configure your system to capture this information?

Case Project 15-2

After taking a class on Windows 2000 security, one of the junior administrators decides to apply the hisec predefined security template on all the servers in your organization. Users start to complain that they cannot access any of the Windows 2000 servers. After a bit of research, you realize that the systems that cannot access the Windows 2000 servers are all non-Windows 2000 systems. How would you make sure that these non-Windows 2000 systems can access the servers again?

Glossary

access control entry (ACE) — An entry within an Access Control List that grants or denies permissions to users or groups for a given resource.

Access Control List (ACL) — Contains a set of access control entries that define an object's permission settings. ACLs enable administrators to explicitly control access to resources.

Active Directory — The Windows 2000 directory service that replaces the antiquated Windows NT domain structure. Active Directory forms the basis for centralized network management on Windows 2000 networks, providing a hierarchical view of network resources.

Active Directory Service Interface (ADSI) — A directory service model implemented as a set of COM interfaces. ADSI allows Windows applications to access Active Directory, often through ActiveX interfaces such as VBScript.

Active Directory Users and Computers — The primary systems administrator utility for managing users, groups, and computers in a Windows 2000 domain, implemented as a MMC snap-in.

address (A) record — The most basic type of resource record on a DNS server. Every client that registers with DNS has an associated A record that maps its name to its IP address.

assigned applications — Applications that are always available to the user, even if the user attempts to uninstall them. Through the Software Installation utility in Group Policy, administrators can assign applications to users.

asynchronous processing — Occurs when one task waits until another is finished before beginning. It is typically associated with scripts—for example, a user logon script that does not run before the computer startup script has completed. This is the default behavior in Windows 2000.

attribute — The basic unit of an object. An attribute is a single property that, through its values, defines an object. For example, the account name is an attribute of a standard user account.

auditing — A security process that tracks the usage of selected network resources, typically storing the results in a log file.

authentication — The process by which a user's logon credentials are validated by a server so that access to a network resource can be granted or denied.

AXFR — A DNS term that refers to a request from a primary server to one or more secondary servers for a full zone transfer.

Backup Domain Controller (BDC) — A Windows NT 3.*x* and 4 server that contains a backup copy of the domain security accounts manager (user account and security information). BDCs take load from the Primary Domain Controller by servicing logon requests. Periodic synchronizing ensures that data between the PDC and BDCs remains consistent.

baseline — A term associated with performance monitoring. A baseline is the initial result of monitoring by which all future results are measured.

bridgehead server — The contact point for the exchange of directory information between Active Directory sites.

caching — The process by which name resolution query results are stored in order to speed up future name resolution for the same destinations.

checkpoint file — Indicates the location of the last information successfully written from the transaction logs to the database. In a data recovery scenario, the checkpoint file indicates where the recovery or replaying of data should begin.

circular logging — The process by which a full log file is overwritten with new data, rather than a new log file being created. Circular logging conserves disk space but can result in data loss in a disaster-recovery scenario.

computer configuration — The portion of a Group Policy Object that allows for computer policies to be configured and applied.

container — An object in Active Directory that is capable of holding other objects. An example of a container would be the Users folder in Active Directory Users and Computers.

convergence — The process of stabilization after network changes occur. Often associated with routing or replication, convergence ensures that each router or server contains consistent information.

counters — The metrics that are used in performance monitoring. Counters are what you are actually monitoring. An example of a counter for a CPU object would be %Processing Time.

CScript — The command-line executable for Windows Scripting Host.

dcpromo — The command-line utility that is used to promote a Windows 2000 server to a domain controller.

delegation — The process of offloading the responsibility for a given task or set of tasks to another user or group. Delegation in Windows 2000 usually involves granting permission to someone else to perform a specific administrative task, such as creating computer accounts.

directory — A database that contains any number of different types of data. In Windows 2000, the Active Directory contains information about objects in the domain such as computers, users, groups, and printers.

directory service — Provides the methods of storing directory data and making that data available to other directory objects.

Directory System Agent (DSA) — Makes data within Active Directory accessible to applications that want it, acting as a liaison between the directory database and the applications.

disk quota — An administrative limit set on the server storage space that can be used by any particular user.

distinguished name — The name that uniquely identifies an object, using the relative distinguished name, domain name, and the container holding the object. For example, the distinguished name CN=WWillis, CN=Inside-Corner, CN=COM refers to the WWillis user account in the inside-corner.com domain.

Distributed File System (Dfs) — A Windows 2000 service that allows resources from multiple server locations to be presented through Active Directory as a contiguous set of files and folders, resulting in greater ease of use for users of network resources.

distribution point — The network shared location for software to be stored for the purpose of making it available for installation to users.

domain — A collection of Windows 2000 computers, users, and groups that share a common directory database. Domains are defined by an administrator.

domain controller (DC) — A server that is capable of performing authentication. In Windows 2000, a DC holds a copy of the Active Directory database.

domain local group — Can contain other domain local groups from its own domain, as well as global groups from any domain in the forest. Domain local groups can be used to assign permissions for resources located in the same domain as the group.

Domain Name System (DNS) — A hierarchical name resolution system that resolves host names into IP addresses and vice versa.

Dynamic Domain Name System (DDNS) — An extension of DNS that allows Windows 2000 Professional systems to automatically register their A records with DNS at the time they obtain an IP address from a DHCP server.

Dynamic Host Configuration Protocol (DHCP) — A service that allows an administrator to specify a range of valid IP addresses to be used on a network, as well as exceptions. These addresses are automatically given out to computers configured to use DHCP as they boot up on the network, saving the administrator from having to configure static IP addresses on each individual network device.

Encrypted File System (EFS) — A Windows 2000 feature that allows files and folders to be encrypted on NTFS partitions, protecting them from being read by other people.

Extensible Storage Engine (ESE) — The Active Directory database engine. ESE is an improved version of the older Jet database technology.

File Replication Service (FRS) — A service that provides multi-master replication between specified domain controllers within an Active Directory tree.

File Transfer Protocol (FTP) — A standard TCP/IP utility that allows for the transfer of files from an FTP server to a machine running the FTP client.

firewall — A hardware and software security system that functions to limit access to network resources across subnets. Typically, a firewall is used between a private network and the Internet to prevent outsiders from accessing the private network and to limit the Internet services that users of the private network can access.

flat namespace — A namespace that cannot be partitioned to produce additional domains. Windows NT 4 and earlier domains were examples of flat namespaces, as opposed to the Windows 2000 hierarchical namespaces.

folder redirection — A Windows 2000 feature that allows special folders such as My Documents on local Windows 2000 Professional system hard drives to be redirected to a shared network location.

forest — A grouping of Active Directory trees that have a trust relationship between them. Forests can consist of noncontiguous name-spaces; and

unlike domains and trees, forests do not have to be given a specific name.

forward lookup query — A DNS name resolution process by which a host name is resolved to an IP address.

fully qualified domain name (FQDN) — A DNS domain name that unambiguously describes the location of the host within a domain tree. An example of an FQDN would be the computer www.inside-corner.com.

Global Catalog (GC) — Contains a partial replica of every Windows 2000 domain within the Active Directory, enabling users to find any object in the directory. The partial replica contains the most commonly used attributes of an object, as well as information on how to locate a complete replica elsewhere in the directory, if needed.

Global Catalog Server — The Windows 2000 server that holds the Global Catalog for the forest.

global group — Can contain users from the same domain as the group. Global groups can be added to domain local groups in order to control access to network resources.

Globally Unique Identifier (GUID) — A hexadecimal number supplied by the manufacturer of a product, which uniquely identifies the hardware or software. A GUID is in the form of 8 characters followed by 4, by 4, by 4, by 12. For example, {15DEF489-AE24-10BF-C11A-00BB844CE637} is a valid format for a GUID (braces included).

Group Policy — The Windows 2000 feature that allows for policy creation that affects domain users and computers. Policies can be anything from desktop settings to application assignment to security settings and more.

Group Policy Editor — The MMC snap-in that is used to modify the settings of a Group Policy Object.

Group Policy Object (GPO) — A collection of policies that apply to a specific target, such as the domain itself (default domain policy) or an OU. GPOs are modified through the Group Policy Editor to define policy settings.

hierarchical namespace — A namespace, such as that used with DNS, that can be partitioned in the form of a tree. This feature allows great flexibility in using a domain name, because any number of subdomains can be created under a parent domain.

host ID — The portion of an IP address that defines the host, as determined by the subnet mask. For example, if a host has an IP address of 192.168.1.20 and a subnet mask of 255.255.255.0, the host ID would be 20.

HOSTS — A static file that was the primary means for TCP/IP name resolution prior to DNS. The HOSTS file contains a list of host-to-IP-address mappings; it had to exist on every host computer that participates on a network. It has been replaced by the more manageable DNS service on all but the smallest of networks.

image — The installation source for Windows 2000 Professional and any optional applications created through the RIS RIPrep utility.

inheritance — The process by which an object obtains settings information from a parent object.

IntelliMirror — A collection of Windows 2000 technologies that provide for a comprehensive change and control management system.

IXFR — A DNS process by which a primary DNS server requests an incremental zone transfer from one or more secondary servers.

JavaScript (JScript) — An active scripting language that can be used in Windows 2000 with the Windows Scripting Host to run more complicated scripts than were available in the past through batch files.

just-in-time (JIT) — Technology that allows software features to be updated at the time they are accessed. Whereas in the past missing application features had to be installed manually, JIT technology allows the features to be installed on the fly as they are accessed, with no other intervention required.

Kerberos — An Internet standard security protocol that has largely replaced the older LAN Manager user authentication mechanism from earlier Windows NT versions.

Knowledge Consistency Checker (KCC) — A Windows 2000 service that functions to ensure that consistent database information is kept across all domain controllers. It attempts to ensure that replication can always take place.

latency — The delay that occurs in replication from the time a change is made to one replica until that change is applied to all other replicas in the directory.

Lightweight Directory Access Protocol (LDAP) — The Windows 2000 protocol that allows access to Active Directory. LDAP is an Internet standard for accessing directory services.

LMHOSTS — A static file used for NetBIOS name resolution. Similar to a HOSTS file, LMHOSTS had to exist on every individual computer on a network, making it increasingly difficult to keep up to date as the size of networks grew. LMHOSTS was essentially replaced by WINS on Windows networks prior to Windows 2000.

local-area network (LAN) — A network in which all hosts are connected over fast connections (4Mbps or greater for Token Ring, 10Mbps or better for Ethernet).

local group policy objects — Objects that exist on the local Windows 2000 system and take precedence over site-, domain-, and OU-applied GPOs.

Mail Exchanger (MX) record — A DNS record that defines an e-mail server.

Microsoft Management Console (MMC) — An extensible management framework that provides a common look and feel to all Windows 2000 utilities.

mixed mode — Allows Windows NT 4 domain controllers to exist and function within a Windows 2000 domain. This is the default setting when Active Directory is installed, although it can be changed to native mode.

multi-master replication — A replication model in which any domain controller will replicate data to any other domain controller. This is the default behavior in Windows 2000. It contrasts with the single-master replication model of Windows NT 4, in which a PDC contained the master copy of everything and BDCs contained backup copies.

name resolution — The process of resolving a host name into a format that can be understood by computers. This format is typically an IP address, but it could also be a MAC address on non-TCP/IP networks.

namespace — A collection of resources that have been defined using some common name. The DNS namespace is hierarchical and can be partitioned, whereas Windows NT 4 and earlier used a flat namespace.

native mode — The mode in effect when all domain controllers in a domain have been upgraded to Windows 2000 and no more NT 4 domain controllers exist. An administrator explicitly puts Active Directory into native mode, at which time it cannot be returned to mixed mode without removing and reinstalling Active Directory.

NetBIOS — An application programming interface (API) used on Windows NT 4 and earlier networks by services requesting and providing name resolution and network data management.

network ID — The portion of an IP address that defines the network, as determined by the subnet mask. For example, if a host has an IP address of 192.168.1.20 and a subnet mask of 255.255.255.0, the network ID would be 192.168.1.

network operating system (NOS) — A generic term that applies to any operating system with built-in networking capabilities. All Windows operating systems beginning with Windows 95 have been true network operating systems.

non-local Group Policy Objects — GPOs that are stored in Active Directory rather than on the local machine. These can be site-, domain-, or OU-level GPOs.

nslookup — A TCP/IP utility used in troubleshooting DNS name resolution problems.

NTFS — The Windows NT/2000 file system that supports a much more robust feature set than FAT16 or FAT32 (used on Windows 9x). It is recommended that you use NTFS whenever possible on Windows 2000 systems.

object — A distinct entity represented by a series of attributes within Active Directory. An object can be a user, computer, folder, file, printer, and so forth.

object identifier — A number that uniquely identifies an object class or attribute. In the United States, the American National Standards Institute (ANSI) issues object identifiers, which take the form of a x.x.x.x dotted decimal format. Microsoft, for example, was issued the root object identifier of 1.2.840.113556, from which it can create further sub–object identifiers.

operations master — A Windows 2000 domain controller that has been assigned one or more of the special Active Directory domain roles, such as schema master, domain naming master, PDC emulator master, infrastructure master, and relative ID master.

Organizational Unit (OU) — An Active Directory container object that allows an administrator to logically group users, groups, computers, and other OUs into administrative units.

package — A collection of software compiled into a distributable form, such as a Windows Installer (.msi) package created with WinINSTALL.

parent-child trust relationship — The relationship in which a child object trusts its parent object, and a parent object is trusted by all child objects under it. Active Directory automatically creates two-way trust relationships between parent and child objects.

patching — The process of modifying or updating software packages.

ping — A TCP/IP utility that tests for basic connectivity between the client machine running ping and any other TCP/IP host.

policy — Settings and rules that are applied to users or computers—usually Group Policy in Windows 2000 and System Policy in Windows NT 4.

Pre-Boot Execution Environment (PXE) — A set of industry standards that allows for network commands to be run on a client computer before it has booted up in a traditional manner. PXE is used with RIS in Windows 2000 to install Windows 2000 Professional images on client computers.

Primary Domain Controller (PDC) — A Windows NT 4 and earlier server that contained the master copy of the domain database. PDCs authenticate user logon requests and track security-related changes within the domain.

Public Key Infrastructure (PKI) — Industry standard technology that allows for the establishment of secure communication between hosts based on a public key–private key or certificate-based system.

published applications — Applications that appear in Add/Remove Programs and that can be optionally installed by the user. Through the Software Installation utility in Group Policy, administrators can publish applications to users.

Registry — A data repository stored on each computer that contains information about that computer's configuration. The Registry is organized into a hierarchical tree and is made up of hives, keys, and values.

relative distinguished name (RDN) — The part of a DNS name that defines the host. For example, in the FQDN www.inside-corner.com, www is the relative distinguished name.

Remote Installation Services (RIS) — A Windows 2000 optional component that allows for the remote installation of Windows 2000 Professional onto compatible client computers.

replica — A copy of any given Active Directory object. Each copy of an object stored on multiple domain controllers is a replica.

replication — The process of copying data from one Windows 2000 domain controller to another. Replication is a process managed by an administrator, and it typically occurs automatically whenever changes are made to a replica of an object.

Request for Comments (RFC) — Official documents that specify Internet standards for the TCP/IP protocol.

resource records (RR) — Standard database record types used in DNS zone database files. Common types of resource records include Address (A), Mail Exchanger (MX), Start of Authority (SOA), and Name Server (NS), among others.

return on investment (ROI) — A business term that seeks to determine the amount of financial gain that occurs as a result of a certain expenditure. Many IT personnel today are faced with the prospect of justifying IT expenses in terms of ROI.

reverse lookup query — A DNS name resolution process by which an IP address is resolved to a host name.

root server — A DNS server that is authoritative for the root zone of a namespace.

router — A dedicated network hardware appliance or server running routing software and multiple network cards. Routers join dissimilar network topologies (such as Ethernet to Frame Relay) or simply segment networks into multiple subnets.

scalability — A measurement (often subjective) of how well a resource (such as a server) can expand to accommodate growing needs.

schema — In Active Directory, a description of object classes and attributes that the object class must possess and can possess.

schema master — The Windows 2000 domain controller that has been assigned the operations master role to control all schema updates within a forest.

security identifier (SID) — A number that uniquely identifies a user, group, or computer account. Every account is issued an SID when created, and if the account is later deleted and re-created with the same name, it will have a different SID. Once a SID is used in a domain, it can never be used again.

security templates — Collections of standard settings that can be applied administratively to give a consistent level of security to a system.

Single Instance Store (SIS) — An RIS component that combines duplicate files to reduce storage requirements on the RIS server.

single-master operations — Certain Active Directory operations that are allowed to occur in only one place at any given time (as opposed to being allowed to occur in multiple locations simultaneously). Examples of single-master operations include schema modification, PDC elections, and infrastructure changes.

site — A well-connected TCP/IP subnet.

site link — A connection between sites. Site links are used to join multiple locations.

slow link — A connection between sites that is not fast enough to provide full functionality in an acceptable timeframe. Site connections below 512Kbps are defined as slow links in Windows 2000.

snap-in — A component that can be added or removed from an MMC console to provide specific functionality. The Windows 2000 administrative tools are implemented as snap-ins.

Software Installation — A Group Policy component that allows administrators to optionally assign or publish applications to be available to users and computers.

Start of Authority (SOA) record — The first record created on a DNS server. The SOA record defines the starting point for a zone's authority.

static IP address — Also called a static address. A network device (such as a server) is manually configured with an IP address that doesn't change, rather than obtaining an address automatically from a DHCP server.

store — The physical storage of each Active Directory replica. A store is implemented using the Extensible Storage Engine.

subnet — A collection of hosts on a TCP/IP network that are not separated by any routers. A basic corporate LAN with one location would be referred to as a subnet when it is connected by a router to another network, such as that of an Internet service provider.

subnet mask — Defines where the network ID ends and the host ID begins in an IP address. Subnet masks can result in very basic to very complex network configurations, depending on their value.

synchronous processing — Occurs when one task does not wait for another to complete before it begins, but rather runs concurrently. Synchronous processing is typically associated with scripts in Windows 2000, such as when a user logon script runs without waiting for the computer startup script to finish.

system policies — Windows NT 4 Registry-based policy settings, which have largely been replaced in Windows 2000 by Group Policy. System policies can still be created using poledit.exe, however, for backward compatibility with non–Windows 2000 clients.

Systems Management Server (SMS) — A product in Microsoft's BackOffice server line that provides more extensive software distribution, metering, inventorying, and auditing than is possible strictly through Intellimirror.

TCP/IP — Transmission Control Protocol/Internet Protocol. TCP/IP is the standard protocol for communicating on the Internet and is the default protocol in Windows 2000.

Time To Live (TTL) — The amount of time a packet destined for a host will exist before it is deleted from the network. TTLs are used to prevent networks from becoming congested with packages that cannot reach their destinations.

total cost of ownership (TCO) — A change and control management concept that many IT professionals are being forced to become more aware of. TCO refers to the combined hard and soft costs (initial price and support costs) of owning a given resource.

transitive trust — An automatically created trust in Windows 2000 that exists between domain trees within a forest and between domains within a tree. Transitive trusts are two-way trust relationships.

tree — A collection of Windows 2000 domains that are connected through transitive trusts and that share a common Global Catalog and schema. Domains within a tree must form a contiguous namespace.

Universal group — A new Windows 2000 security group that can be used anywhere within a domain tree or forest. The only caveat is that Universal groups can be used only when Windows 2000 has been converted to native mode.

Update Sequence Number (USN) — A 64-bit number that keeps track of changes as they are written to copies of the Active Directory. As changes are made, this number increments by one.

user configuration — The portion of a Group Policy Object that allows for user policy settings to be configured and applied.

user profile — Contains settings that define the user environment, typically applied when the user logs on to the system.

Visual Basic Script (VBScript) — An active scripting language that can be used in Windows 2000 with the Windows Scripting Host to run more complicated scripts than have been available in the past through batch files. VBScript has been in the news frequently lately due to its use in creating e-mail viruses.

well-connected — A network that contains only fast connections between domains and hosts. The definition of *fast* is somewhat subjective and may vary from organization to organization.

wide-area network (WAN) — Multiple networks connected by slow connections between routers. WAN connections are typically 1.5Mbps or less.

Windows Internet Naming Service (WINS) — A dynamic name resolution system that resolves NetBIOS names to IP addresses on Windows TCP/IP networks. With Windows 2000, WINS is being phased out in favor of DNS.

Windows Management Instrumentation (WMI) — A Windows 2000 management infrastructure for monitoring and controlling system resources.

Windows Scripting Host (WSH) — Enables the running of VBScript or JavaScript scripts natively on a Windows system, offering increased power and flexibility over traditional batch files.

WinINSTALL — An optional utility that ships with Windows 2000 server and that can be used to create Windows Installer packages.

WScript — The Windows interface to the Windows Scripting Host.

X.500 — A set of standards developed by the International Standards Organization (ISO) that define distributed directory services.

zone — A subtree of the DNS database that can be managed as a single, separate entity from the rest of the DNS namespace.

zone file — The DNS database, traditionally stored as a text file on the primary server and replicated to secondary servers. With Windows 2000, the zone file can be optionally integrated into Active Directory.

zone transfer — The DNS process by which zone information is replicated between primary and secondary servers.

Index

MCSE CoursePrep
ExamGuide/StudyGuide
Exam #70-217

Implementing and Administering a Microsoft Windows 2000 Directory Services Infrastructure

TABLE OF CONTENTS

PREFACE

The *MCSE CoursePrep ExamGuide* and *MCSE CoursePrep StudyGuide* are the very best tools to use to prepare for exam day. The *CoursePrep ExamGuide* and *CoursePrep StudyGuide* provide you ample opportunity to practice, drill, and rehearse for the exam!

COURSEPREP EXAMGUIDE

The *MCSE CoursePrep ExamGuide for Exam #70-217*, included with this book, provides the essential information you need to master each exam objective. The *CoursePrep ExamGuide* devotes an entire two-page spread to each certification objective for the exam, helping you understand the objective and giving you the bottom-line information—what you really need to know. Memorize these facts and bulleted points before heading into the exam. In addition, there are several practice test questions for each objective on the right-hand page. That's hundreds of questions to help you practice for the exam! The *CoursePrep ExamGuide* provides the exam fundamentals and gets you up to speed quickly. If you are seeking even more opportunity to practice and prepare, we recommend that you consider our total solution, the *CoursePrep StudyGuide*, which is described below.

COURSEPREP STUDYGUIDE

For those really serious about certification, we offer an even more robust solution—the *MCSE CoursePrep StudyGuide for Exam #70-217* (ISBN 0-619-03471-8). This offering includes all of the same quality material you get with the CoursePrep ExamGuide, including the unique two-page spread, the bulleted memorization points, and the practice questions. In addition, you receive a password valid for six months of practice on CoursePrep, a dynamic test preparation tool. The password is found in an envelope in the back cover of the *CoursePrep StudyGuide*. CoursePrep is a Web-based pool of hundreds of sample test questions. CoursePrep exam simulation software mimics the exact exam environment. The CoursePrep software is flexible and allows you to practice in several ways as you master the material. Choose from Certification Mode, to experience actual exam-day conditions, or Study Mode, to request answers and explanations to practice questions. Custom Mode lets you set the options for the practice test, including number of questions, content coverage, and ability to request answers and explanation. Follow the instructions on the inside back cover to access the exam simulation software. To see a demo of this dynamic test preparation tool, go to www.courseprep.com.

FEATURES

The *MCSE CoursePrep ExamGuide* and *MCSE CoursePrep StudyGuide* include the following features:

Detailed coverage of the certification objectives in a unique two-page spread. Study strategically by really focusing on the MCSE certification objectives. To enable you to do this, a two-page spread is devoted to each certification objective. The left-hand page provides the critical facts you need, while the right-hand page features practice questions relating to that objective. You'll find the certification objectives and sub-objectives clearly listed in the upper-left corner of each spread.

An overview of the objective is provided in the ***Understanding the Objective*** section. Next, ***What You Really Need to Know*** lists bulleted, succinct core facts, skills, and concepts about the objective. Memorizing these facts will be important for your success when taking the exam. ***Objectives on the Job*** places the objective in an industry perspective, and tells you how you can expect to incorporate the objective at work. This section also provides troubleshooting information.

Practice Test Questions on each right-hand page help you prepare for the exam by testing your skills, identifying your strengths and weaknesses, and demonstrating the subject matter you will face on the exam and how it will be tested. These questions are written in a similar fashion to real MCSE exam questions. The questions test your knowledge of the objectives described on the left-hand page and also the information on pages 1–502 in this book. Answers to the practice test questions are found at the back of this guide.

Glossary of Acronyms and Abbreviations: The world of networking, perhaps more than any other computer-related discipline, uses a language all its own, which is comprised largely of acronyms. You will find a complete list of all acronyms used in this guide, along with their meanings, at the back of the book.

Section 1

Installing, Configuring, and Troubleshooting Active Directory

1.1   Install Active Directory

WIZARD • DCPROMO • SRV

UNDERSTANDING THE OBJECTIVE

Installing **Active Directory** is a straightforward process, but it does have some requirements. Run DCPROMO to launch the **AD** installation wizard, and answer the wizard's questions. You can create a new domain, tree, or forest using the wizard.

WHAT YOU REALLY NEED TO KNOW

◆ To successfully run DCPROMO, you must have a DNS server that supports SRV records and, optionally, dynamic updates.

◆ If a configured DNS server is not found, the wizard installs DNS on that computer.

◆ The wizard allows you to create an additional domain controller for an existing domain, a new child domain, a new domain tree, or a new forest.

◆ Only computers running Windows 2000 Server, Advanced Server, or Datacenter Server can become AD domain controllers.

◆ To become an AD domain controller, a computer must have a partition formatted with **NTFS** v.5 for Sysvol, and it is recommended that it has at least 1 **GB** of free space. **TCP/IP** must be one of your network protocols.

◆ For a new domain controller in a new forest, you must have local administrative permissions. To install an additional domain controller in an existing domain, you must be a domain administrator in that domain.

◆ You must be an enterprise administrator to create a child domain or a new domain tree.

OBJECTIVES ON THE JOB

The most frequent source of problems encountered when running DCPROMO is a missing or misconfigured DNS server or one that does not meet the minimum requirements. Also, it is a good idea to place the AD database (NTDS.dit) and log files on separate physical drives, preferably **RAID** arrays. This improves **I/O** performance and provides fault tolerance. The wizard also creates setup log files in the %systemroot%\debug folder. Use these if you encounter errors. After the wizard completes the configuration, it reboots the server. The server is now a domain controller. It is highly recommended that your DNS server support dynamic updates. You can also use the wizard to remove AD from a server. When upgrading a Windows NT domain, first upgrade the **PDC** to Windows 2000.

PRACTICE TEST QUESTIONS

1. **You are running Windows NT 4.0 SP4 DNS and wish to install AD. What should be your first step?**
   a. Run the AD Installation Wizard on Windows 2000 Server.
   b. Upgrade Windows NT 4.0 DNS Server to Windows 2000 Server with DNS.
   c. Install SP5 to allow DNS to accept dynamic updates.
   d. Move the DNS service to a BDC, upgrade the original Windows NT server to Windows 2000, run DCPROMO, and install DNS.

2. **You are creating a new child domain, but the AD Installation Wizard continues to fail with an error message that states you have insufficient permissions. What should you do?**
   a. Run DCPROMO as a local administrator.
   b. Run DCPROMO as a domain administrator.
   c. Run DCPROMO as a member of the enterprise administrators group.
   d. Ensure that the Domain Naming FSMO master is online.

3. **Upon running the AD Installation Wizard, a series of error messages causes the wizard to fail. How would you diagnose the problem?**
   a. Check Event Viewer.
   b. Open the DCPROMO.LOG file and look for error messages.
   c. Open the DCPROMOUI.LOG file and look for error messages.
   d. All of the above

4. **Which of the following network protocols must be installed in order to install AD?**
   a. NWLink
   b. NetBEUI
   c. TCP/IP
   d. IPX/SPX

5. **The AD Installation Wizard fails and states that there is no partition formatted with NTFS v.5. Which partition must be NTFS v.5?**
   a. The partition containing the %systemroot% partition
   b. The partition that will contain the NTDS.dit file
   c. The partition that will contain the AD log files
   d. The partition that will contain the Sysvol folder

6. **You run the AD Installation Wizard on a network that does not have a configured DNS server. What happens to the wizard?**
   a. It stops and gives you the option to configure DNS, or it has the wizard install and configure DNS.
   b. It quits and gives a DNS error message.
   c. It quits and gives an unrelated error message.
   d. The AD Installation Wizard fails to run at all.

1.2   Create sites

SITES • OBJECTS • REPLICATION

UNDERSTANDING THE OBJECTIVE

Although AD is a logical design, sites are created to map your physical network topology. Sites allow you to control AD replication among domain controllers between sites. Sites also allow AD to efficiently answer client requests for services by providing the client with a list of services on servers that are in close proximity.

WHAT YOU REALLY NEED TO KNOW

- ◆ Sites are defined as one or more highly connected IP subnets. Basically, sites are **LANs** separated by **WANs**.

- ◆ The AD Sites and Services snap-in can be used to create and manage sites, site links, and site bridges.

- ◆ A default site is created with the name Default-First-Site-Name. It contains all domain controllers that have not been placed into other sites.

- ◆ To define a site, you must associate one or more IP subnets with a site name. You can then create site links between sites to control AD replication traffic.

- ◆ The **KCC** uses sites to develop an intrasite replication topology.

- ◆ After sites have been defined, any new domain controllers automatically become members of their respective site.

- ◆ Domain controllers in the Default-First-Site-Name site must be manually moved to the site in which they actually belong.

- ◆ **GPOs** can be placed on sites so that users in a certain physical location have a common desktop environment or common software applications.

OBJECTIVES ON THE JOB

Many infrastructure designers make the mistake of modeling AD based on their physical network topology. AD is a purely logical design that can, but shouldn't necessarily, model your physical network. Instead, sites can be used for that purpose. A site is simply an object stored in AD that has one or more IP network IDs associated with it. For example, sites are used to provide clients with a nearby domain controller when logging on or a nearby Global Catalog server when querying AD. You place domain controllers in sites so that the KCC can automatically build and adjust intrasite connection agreements between domain controllers. A site can contain one or more domains, or a single domain can span several sites. There is no correlation between domains and sites, unless you design it that way. Group policies can be applied at the site level, but require enterprise administrator credentials because GPOs placed on a site can potentially affect many domains.

PRACTICE TEST QUESTIONS

LAN Magic is an international consulting firm in the process of designing its AD structure. LAN Magic's environment consists of eight Windows 2000 domain controllers, 18 Windows 2000 member servers, and 900 Windows 2000 Professional workstations. These computers are located in five locations within four cities in North America: Chicago, Denver, New York, and Seattle. Seattle has two facilities, each at an opposite end of the city. Each of the five locations is connected to the others via a 10 Mbps ATM backbone, which is 65% utilized during daytime hours.

1. How many sites would you recommend to LAN Magic?
   a. One
   b. Four
   c. Five
   d. Nine

2. What could you do to prevent replication from saturating the ATM backbone?
   a. Place all the domain controllers in one physical location.
   b. Place all the member server objects in one site.
   c. Place all the domain controller objects in one site.
   d. Position the member servers geographically to best balance the traffic load.

3. How can you prevent new domain controller objects from being placed into the Default-First-Site-Name site? (Choose all that apply.)
   a. Define additional sites with a name and associate IP subnets with the sites.
   b. Move at least one domain controller into each site. This automatically places all new domain controllers into their respective sites.
   c. Delete the Default-First-Site-Name site, which unbinds the domain controllers and allows them to be moved into their respective sites.
   d. Rename the Default-First-Site-Name site to an actual site name.

4. A newly created domain controller object defaults to the Default-First-Site-Name site when its object should have been created in the Denver site. What could have caused this? (Choose all that apply.)
   a. The Denver site name had a typo and was actually spelled Danver.
   b. The Denver site had no subnets associated with it.
   c. The domain controller had an incorrect network ID.
   d. The KCC hasn't yet updated the site topology.

1.3 Create subnets

IP • SITES • SUBNETS • REPLICATION

UNDERSTANDING THE OBJECTIVE

Defining a site consists of creating a site name and then associating one or more IP subnets with it. By associating IP subnets, site-aware applications such as Exchange 2000 can function properly. Associating IP subnets with sites also allows DNS to provide a client with the IP address of the server in that client's site, when the client queries for network services such as Kerberos. Lastly, replication among domain controllers within a site is handled differently from intersite replication.

WHAT YOU REALLY NEED TO KNOW

◆ By default, no IP subnets are defined. Only the Default-First-Site-Name site exists.

◆ You should create site names using the Active Directory Users and Computers tool.

◆ It is important to create one or more IP subnets and associate them with the appropriate site. The site must exist before the subnet can be properly associated with it.

◆ An IP subnet consists of a network ID (e.g., 10.0.0.0) and a subnet mask (e.g., 255.0.0.0). Windows 2000 stores this using **CIDR** notation, such as 10.0.0.0/8.

◆ When clients query DNS, they submit their IP address in the query packet. DNS uses this to identify the site to which the client belongs.

◆ DNS scans the zone file for a server in the client's site that is providing the required network service and passes back the IP address to the client.

OBJECTIVES ON THE JOB

By associating subnets with sites, AD becomes aware of the physical location of clients and servers. This is recorded in DNS and in the configuration partition of the AD database. You can verify site awareness by opening the DNS snap-in and expanding the zone file. DNS uses site-specific subdomains to store SRV records of servers providing network services in that site, such as an **LDAP** server. If a site is not properly defined with IP subnets, clients and servers default to the Default-First-Site-Name site. This can result in logon authentications and LDAP queries occurring across WAN links. Location tracking is enabled on subnets to allow users to browse or query the physical network structure for resources, such as printers.

PRACTICE TEST QUESTIONS

1. **How many subnets can be associated with one site?**
   - a. Four
   - b. Six
   - c. Eight
   - d. Unlimited

2. **If a client's IP address is 10.0.1.22/16, to what network does the client belong?**
   - a. 10.0.1.0
   - b. 10.0.0.0
   - c. 10.0.1.22
   - d. 10.0.1.1

3. **What must occur before a subnet can be created and associated with a site?**
   - a. A site name must be created.
   - b. All domain controllers must be moved into the Default-First-Site-Name site.
   - c. You must run ipconfig /registersite.
   - d. The DNS forward lookup zone must be set to allow dynamic updates.

4. **Which of the following tasks can you not complete with Active Directory Sites and Services? (Choose all that apply.)**
   - a. Moving clients into sites
   - b. Moving member servers into sites
   - c. Moving domain controllers into sites
   - d. Creating site links

5. **A client's site membership is determined by _____.**
   - a. its domain membership
   - b. its host ID
   - c. its network ID
   - d. an administrator manually configuring the client's site membership field

6. **After a subnet has been associated with a site, a subnet's association can be changed.**
   - a. True
   - b. False

7. **When a roaming laptop, configured with Windows 2000 Professional as a DHCP client, moves to another subnet, what happens?**
   - a. The client's site membership changes as its network ID changes.
   - b. The client's site membership remains unchanged.
   - c. The client's object must be manually moved into the other site.
   - d. The client's object automatically moves into the other site.

1.4 Create site links

REPLICATION • SITES • IP • SMTP • KCC

UNDERSTANDING THE OBJECTIVE

The KCC calculates the replication topology for both intrasite and intersite replication. However, for intersite replication, the KCC uses site links that are defined by administrators to calculate the replication technology. Site links allow administrators to manage replication between sites by giving the ability to schedule replication, set a replication frequency, and give costs to the site links. The KCC uses this information to determine when, how, and how often to replicate between sites.

WHAT YOU REALLY NEED TO KNOW

- ◆ A site link can use one of two protocols to facilitate replication: **SMTP** or **RPC/IP**.
- ◆ SMTP can only be used between two sites if they reside in different domains. SMTP provides asynchronous communication.
- ◆ RPC/IP can be used in any situation in which sites are connected via reliable WAN links. **RPCs** are a form of synchronous communication.
- ◆ With site links, you can set a replication interval, replication cost, and replication schedule.
- ◆ The minimum replication interval is 15 minutes; the maximum interval is 10,080 minutes.
- ◆ The replication cost value can range from 1 to 32,767. If multiple site links exist, the least costly link is used for replication.
- ◆ A replication schedule consists of the times of the week when replication can occur.
- ◆ Replication traffic is compressed.

OBJECTIVES ON THE JOB

Two or more sites must participate in a site link. For example, if your company maintains a Frame Relay cloud, you may create one site link and associate with it all sites connected to the cloud. By default, the KCC views all site links as transitive. For example, if Site A is connected to Site B, and Site B is connected to Site C using the same transport (RPC/IP or SMTP), the KCC may configure a direct connection agreement between a domain controller in Site A and Site C. If you have a reliable, underutilized WAN structure, you can also configure the KCC to ignore site link schedules. This reduces the latency of replicating changes to domain controllers in other sites.

MediaMinds is an international marketing firm with offices in seven locations: Aberdeen, Los Angeles, New York, Frankfurt, London, Paris, and Tokyo. MediaMinds' 3800 employees are spread across these locations, with the largest offices in New York and London. Currently, the Information Technology Group (ITG) is planning domain controller placement and how it will affect the company's WAN links. The company's WAN structure is depicted below:

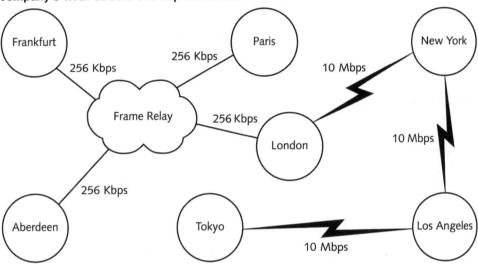

1. How many site links would you create if each link averaged 85% utilization?
    a. Seven
    b. Two
    c. Three
    d. Four

2. If you decided to set the cost of the 10 Mbps links at 100, what cost would you set for the 256 Kbps frame connections?
    a. 10,080
    b. 3900
    c. 512
    d. 256

3. What transports are available for intersite replication? (Choose all that apply.)
    a. RPC/IP
    b. SMTP
    c. POP
    d. FTP

1.5 Creating site link bridges

TRANSITIVE • SITES • BRIDGING • REPLICATION • ISTG

UNDERSTANDING THE OBJECTIVE

By default, all site links are considered transitive. Therefore, the KCC establishes direct connection agreements with domain controllers in other sites. However, due to internal firewalling or routing configurations, domain controllers sometimes cannot communicate directly with domain controllers on other sites. In such cases, site transitiveness should be disabled and site bridging enabled where necessary. Site bridges create replication paths using two or more site links to better mirror a routed environment.

WHAT YOU REALLY NEED TO KNOW

- ◆ Site transitiveness is enabled by default through the *Bridge all site links* option. This option can be disabled for a specific transport (RPC/IP or SMTP).

- ◆ When *Bridge all site links* is enabled, you do not have to create site link bridges.

- ◆ Each site link in a bridge needs to have a site in common with another site link in the bridge.

- ◆ The cost of using a site link bridge is the sum of the costs of the individual site links in the bridge.

- ◆ In large environments consisting of many sites, it is advantageous to disable the *Bridge all site links* option and create site bridges manually.

- ◆ Site link bridges adhere to the replication schedules and intervals of the site links in the bridge.

OBJECTIVES ON THE JOB

One domain controller in each site holds the role of **ISTG**. The KCC running on the ISTG is responsible for calculating a replication schedule for intersite replication. The ISTG creates connection agreements between Bridgehead servers in each site. A Bridgehead server is the entry and exit point for replication between sites and is chosen automatically by the KCC. A Bridgehead server exists for each naming context in each site. If too many sites exist, the KCC is unable to calculate a replication schedule using the entire schedule of the site links. By disabling the *Bridge all site links* option, an administrator can manually create the connection agreements between domain controllers.

PRACTICE TEST QUESTIONS

1. **A site link bridge consists of _____. (Choose all that apply.)**
   a. two or more site links
   b. the sum of the site link costs
   c. two or more sites
   d. a common site

2. **What are some of the attributes of site link transitiveness? (Choose all that apply.)**
   a. A site can communicate directly with another site.
   b. It is disabled by default.
   c. Site link bridges are required.
   d. It is enabled by default.

3. **Site A is linked to Site B using a site link named LinkAB. Site B is linked to Site C using LinkBC. LinkAB has a replication schedule of Monday to Friday, 8:00 p.m. to 8:00 a.m., with a replication interval of 30 minutes. LinkBC's replication schedule is Sunday to Saturday, 7:00 p.m. to 6:00 a.m., with a replication interval of 60 minutes. What is the replication schedule between Site A and Site C?**
   a. Sunday to Saturday, 7:00 p.m. to 6:00 a.m., every 60 minutes
   b. Monday to Friday, 8:00 p.m. to 8:00 a.m., every 30 minutes
   c. Sunday to Saturday, 7:00 p.m. to 8:00 a.m., every 90 minutes
   d. Monday to Friday, 8:00 p.m. to 6:00 a.m., every 60 minutes

4. **At minimum, how many site links must be in a site link bridge in order to create the bridge?**
   a. One
   b. Two
   c. Three
   d. None

5. **LinkAB has a cost of three, LinkBC has a cost of six, and LinkCD has a cost of seven. What is the cost of site link bridge AC?**
   a. Three
   b. Six
   c. Nine
   d. 16

6. **You have just begun creating sites and site links for a small company. You check the Event Viewer on several of the domain controllers in one of the sites and notice numerous AD replication error messages. Several of the other sites are also exhibiting the same problem; however, other domain controllers seem to be replicating correctly. How would you solve this problem? (Choose all that apply.)**
   a. Disable the *Bridge all site links* option.
   b. Add the necessary site link bridges.
   c. Adjust the internal routing tables to allow direct communication between sites.
   d. Adjust the packet filter rules on the internal firewalls.

OBJECTIVES

1.6 Create connection objects

REPLICATION • SITES • KCC

UNDERSTANDING THE OBJECTIVE

Connection objects are created automatically or manually between domain controllers. They signify a pull replication agreement between two domain controllers using a given transport protocol: RPC/IP or SMTP. The KCC creates and deletes connection objects automatically for intrasite replication. The ISTG is responsible for creating inbound intersite connection objects on Bridgehead servers. Manually created connection objects can assist in reducing replication latency.

WHAT YOU REALLY NEED TO KNOW

◆ Connection objects are required for replication. Intrasite replication occurs whenever changes are detected. Changes are then replicated on a store-and-forward basis.

◆ The KCC automatically adds and removes connection objects based on the intrasite topology.

◆ The KCC automatically creates a direct connection object so two domain controllers are never more than three hops, or 15 minutes (3 hops x 5 minutes), away from each other. This keeps replication latency at a minimum while minimizing the number of connection objects.

◆ Without site links, connection objects between sites would not be created by the ISTG.

◆ Manually created connection objects are used by the KCC whenever possible.

◆ The KCC runs on each domain controller. Each domain controller uses the same algorithm and so calculates the same topology.

OBJECTIVES ON THE JOB

Although it may appear that you can alter the transport protocol on an intrasite connection object, you cannot. Intrasite replication always uses RPC/IP. You can also change the schedule dictating when the connection object is available for replication. The KCC always creates two bi-directional connection objects between two domain controllers. Manually adding connection objects when the KCC is running can result in redundant connection and potentially increased replication traffic. Use the REPLMON utility to view and troubleshoot connection agreements. RPCs use dynamic ports, which can make firewall configuration difficult. If replication must occur over public networks, consider creating a **VPN** tunnel to the remote network.

PRACTICE TEST QUESTIONS

1. **What is the primary reason for creating manual connection objects?**
   a. To reduce replication latency
   b. To create redundant connections for failover purposes
   c. To force the KCC to use these connection objects
   d. To create bi-directional replication between two domain controllers

2. **What can you define on a connection object? (Choose all that apply.)**
   a. Transport protocol
   b. Schedule
   c. Cost
   d. Frequency

3. **How does the KCC handle manually created connection objects?**
   a. Uses them and ignores automatically generated connection objects
   b. Uses them and deletes redundant, automatically generated connection objects
   c. Uses them with the automatically generated connection objects, preferring the most efficient connection
   d. Ignores them, except when an automatically generated connection object doesn't exist

4. **Which of the following cannot be configured on a connection object between two domain controllers in the same site? (Choose all that apply.)**
   a. Transport protocol
   b. Schedule
   c. Cost
   d. Frequency

5. **You remove a domain controller from a site. How will the KCC likely respond? (Choose all that apply.)**
   a. It marks the connection object as orphaned.
   b. It deletes the connection object.
   c. It readjusts other connection objects.
   d. The connection object now points to the domain controller in the other site.

6. **What is the role of the ISTG?**
   a. It appoints a Bridgehead server in each site.
   b. It monitors the inbound connections on the Bridgehead server and creates them as required.
   c. It creates push connection objects.
   d. It monitors the KCC on each domain controller in a site.

7. **What is the role of the Bridgehead server?**
   a. It pushes all replication changes from one site to another.
   b. It pulls replication changes from other sites.
   c. It establishes inbound connection objects.
   d. It establishes outbound connection objects.

1.7 Create Global Catalog servers

DOMAIN CONTROLLER • REPLICATION • UNIVERSAL GROUPS

UNDERSTANDING THE OBJECTIVE

A **GC** server performs two important roles in an AD environment. First, it stores the membership of universal groups in a forest. Second, it maintains a replica list of all the objects in an AD forest, as well as a subset of the attributes of these objects. This is useful when users attempt a forest-wide LDAP query looking for objects in other domains.

WHAT YOU REALLY NEED TO KNOW

- ◆ A GC is always a domain controller. You can configure as many GCs as necessary.
- ◆ Generally, a GC is placed in every site.
- ◆ GCs are contacted during logon to determine if the user is a member of any universal groups (native mode only).
- ◆ GCs replicate with other GCs in the forest by using intersite or intrasite replication.
- ◆ Forest-wide searches are answered by GCs because they store a replica of all objects in the entire forest, whereas domain controllers that are not GCs only know of all the objects in their domain.

OBJECTIVES ON THE JOB

GCs play an immensely important role in a Windows 2000 AD environment. One of the main features of AD is the ability to query for objects or attributes of an object rather than to browse. A user who issues an LDAP query for an object in his or her domain has his or her query answered by a domain controller in that domain. However, the GC answers LDAP queries for objects in other domains. It is important to note that even though the GC knows of all the objects in the forest, it doesn't know of all the attributes of every object. The GC does not store certain attributes because they are rarely queried upon and would increase replication traffic. You can specify additional attributes for the GC to store by using the AD Schema snap-in. In native mode, the GC also stores the membership of universal groups. An authenticating domain controller queries a GC to enumerate the universal groups of which a user is a member, if any. If the GC cannot be contacted, logon fails and the user is logged on with cached credentials. Therefore, it is important to appoint enough GCs to ensure that logons occur quickly and efficiently. Placing a GC at each site improves logon performance, but it also increases replication traffic across the WAN link.

PRACTICE TEST QUESTIONS

1. **What occurs if all Global Catalog servers are unavailable in an AD forest in native mode? (Choose all that apply.)**
   a. Logons fail.
   b. Universal groups are unavailable.
   c. Forest-wide searches fail.
   d. Domain-wide searches fail.

2. **What type of server can become a Global Catalog server?**
   a. A member server
   b. An AD-integrated DNS server
   c. A domain controller
   d. An NT 4.0 PDC

3. **What items are stored on a Global Catalog server? (Choose all that apply.)**
   a. Global Group memberships
   b. Domain Local Group memberships
   c. Universal Group memberships
   d. Built-in Group memberships

4. **To improve logon performance, it is recommended that Global Catalog servers be placed _____.**
   a. in every site
   b. in every domain
   c. on every domain controller
   d. on the RID master

5. **With which FSMO role is the global catalog incompatible?**
   a. Schema Master
   b. Domain Naming Master
   c. RID Master
   d. Infrastructure Master

6. **What are some of the ramifications of placing a global catalog at each site? (Choose all that apply.)**
   a. Increased replication traffic
   b. A larger NTDS.dit file
   c. A larger partition to hold the Sysvol folder is required.
   d. More powerful domain controllers are required.

7. **Additional attributes can be stored on a Global Catalog server.**
   a. True
   b. False

1.8 Move server objects between sites

SITES • REPLICATION • DOMAIN CONTROLLER • NTDS

UNDERSTANDING THE OBJECTIVE

Server objects represent domain controllers in AD. Using the Active Directory Sites and Services tool, you can move server objects between sites to better position domain controllers for replication and authentication.

WHAT YOU REALLY NEED TO KNOW

◆ If you reposition domain controllers, it may also be necessary to move server objects.

◆ Move server objects into the site in which the actual domain controller resides.

◆ When you change the IP address of a domain controller and physically move it to another site, that domain controller's server object must be moved manually to the new site.

◆ When new domain controllers are added to AD, their server objects automatically show up in the appropriate site, but only if the site exists.

◆ If a site doesn't exist, server objects for newly added domain controllers are placed under the Default-First-Site-Name site.

◆ Use the Active Directory Sites and Services tool to move server objects.

OBJECTIVES ON THE JOB

Moving server objects to other sites is usually done when you are physically repositioning domain controllers in your enterprise. For example, you have added another 60 users to a remote site office and wish to redeploy an existing domain controller to that location. You first change the TCP/IP settings of that domain controller to match those of the site. Next, you must manually move the server object representing that domain controller into the new site by using the Active Directory Sites and Services tool. If your sites have already been predefined, newly created domain controllers automatically join the existing site. If your sites have not been defined, newly created domain controllers join the Default-First-Site-Name site.

PRACTICE TEST QUESTIONS

MediaMinds is an international marketing firm with offices in seven locations: Aberdeen, Los Angeles, New York, Frankfurt, London, Paris, and Tokyo. MediaMinds' 3800 employees are spread across these locations, with the largest offices in New York and London.

Recently, the company added 720 employees in its seven locations, and employees have noticed deterioration in logon performance. In response, the Information Technology Group (ITG) is planning to add domain controllers and redeploy several existing domain controllers. The following domain controllers will be added:

DC Name	Location
MM-AB-DC15	Aberdeen
MM-LA-DC16	Los Angeles
MM-PA-DC17	Paris
MM-NY-DC18	New York

The following domain controllers will be redeployed:

DC Name	Current Location	New Location
MM-FF-DC11	Frankfurt	London
MM-PA-DC09	Paris	New York

1. Upon moving MM-FF-DC11, an administrator notices that the server's object remains in the Frankfurt site. What would you do next?
   a. Manually move MM-FF-DC11 to the London site.
   b. Delete the MM-FF-DC11 server object and re-create it in the London site.
   c. Leave MM-FF-DC11 in the Frankfurt site and let the KCC automatically move it at the next interval.
   d. Rename the server object to MM-LO-DC11 and move it to the London site.

2. You have renamed the domain controller's host name from MM-PA-DC09 to MM-NY-DC09 by running the AD Installation Wizard. What is the result of these actions?
   a. The MM-PA-DC09 server object remains in the Paris site and an MM-NY-DC09 object is created in the New York site.
   b. The MM-PA-DC09 server object is removed from the Paris site and an MM-NY-DC09 object is created in the New York site.
   c. The MM-PA-DC09 server object is automatically moved to the New York site by the KCC.
   d. The MM-PA-DC09 server object is automatically moved to the New York site by the KCC and renamed MM-NY-DC09.

OBJECTIVES

1.9   Transfer operations master roles

FSMO • SCHEMA • RID • DOMAIN NAMING • INFRASTRUCTURE • PDC

UNDERSTANDING THE OBJECTIVE

A domain controller can host one or more of the five operations master roles, formerly called **FSMO** roles. As more domain controllers are added to a domain or a forest, you may wish to transfer and balance these roles across multiple domain controllers.

WHAT YOU REALLY NEED TO KNOW

- ◆ The five operations master roles are Schema Master, Domain Naming Master, **RID** Master, Infrastructure Master, and PDC Emulator.
- ◆ Only one Schema Master and one Domain Naming Master can exist per forest.
- ◆ Only one RID Master, one Infrastructure Master, and one PDC Emulator can exist in each domain.
- ◆ You can transfer any of the roles to any domain controller provided that the destination domain controller can handle the performance load. The exception is the Infrastructure Master, which cannot be located on a domain controller that is acting as a Global Catalog server.
- ◆ The first domain controller in the forest hosts all five operations master roles.
- ◆ The first domain controller in a domain hosts the RID Master, Infrastructure Master, and PDC Emulator roles.
- ◆ As additional domain controllers are added, transfer the roles to the domain controllers best suited to handle the role.

OBJECTIVES ON THE JOB

After you have located the tool to accomplish the task, transferring the operations master roles is a straightforward process. Transferring roles is usually done when a domain controller will be removed permanently from the network or for performance purposes. Transferring a domain controller's roles before removing it helps you avoid having to seize those roles in the future. You can also transfer any of the roles using the NTDSUTIL.exe command-line utility.

PRACTICE TEST QUESTIONS

1. **To transfer the Schema Master role, which tool must you use?**
   a. Active Directory Sites and Services
   b. Active Directory Domains and Trusts
   c. Active Directory Users and Computers
   d. Active Directory Schema snap-in

2. **To transfer the Domain Naming Master role, which tool must you use?**
   a. Active Directory Sites and Services
   b. Active Directory Domains and Trusts
   c. Active Directory Users and Computers
   d. Active Directory Schema snap-in

3. **To transfer the PDC Emulator role, which tool must you use?**
   a. Active Directory Sites and Services
   b. Active Directory Domains and Trusts
   c. Active Directory Users and Computers
   d. Active Directory Schema snap-in

4. **To transfer the RID Master role, which tool must you use?**
   a. Active Directory Sites and Services
   b. Active Directory Domains and Trusts
   c. Active Directory Users and Computers
   d. Active Directory Schema snap-in

5. **To transfer the Infrastructure Master role, which tools can you use? (Choose all that apply.)**
   a. NTDSUTIL.exe
   b. REGSVR32.exe
   c. Active Directory Users and Computers
   d. DUMPFSMO.exe

6. **To unhide the Schema snap-in, what command must you use?**
   a. SNAPADD.exe/SCHEMA
   b. REGSVR32.exe SCHMMGMT.dll
   c. NTDSUTIL.exe/ADDSCHEMA
   d. REGSRV32.exe SCHMMGMT.dll

7. **Which operations master role conflicts with the global catalog when located on the same domain controller?**
   a. RID Master
   b. Domain Naming Master
   c. PDC Emulator
   d. Infrastructure Master

1.10 Verify Active Directory installation

NTDS • SYSVOL • DCPROMO • DCPROMO.LOG

UNDERSTANDING THE OBJECTIVE

After installing AD using the AD Installation Wizard (DCPROMO), the changes made by the installation should be verified. The installation creates folders, data files, and log files in various directories under %systemroot%. The installation also adds several AD administration tools.

WHAT YOU REALLY NEED TO KNOW

- ◆ Three administrative tools are added: Active Directory Users and Computers, Active Directory Sites and Services, and Active Directory Domains and Trusts.
- ◆ The installation creates several folders under the %systemroot% directory: Sysvol, Ntfrs, and Ntds.
- ◆ The Sysvol folder contains group policies and the group policy template.
- ◆ The Ntds folder contains the AD database file (NTDS.dit), log file (EDB.log), checkpoint file (EDB.chk), and reserve space files (RES1.log, RES2.log).
- ◆ The Ntfrs folder contains the file replication service database, which is responsible for replicating the Sysvol folder among domain controllers.
- ◆ Two log files are created during the installation under the %systemroot%\debug folder: DCPROMO.log and DCPROMOIU.log. The two files capture the steps performed and input received by the Installation Wizard, including error messages.
- ◆ Two Event Viewer logs are added: the directory service log and the file replication service log.

OBJECTIVES ON THE JOB

After DCPROMO successfully installs AD on a domain controller, the domain controller reboots. Subsequently, you should verify the changes made during the installation and investigate any error messages. The DCPROMOIU.log file captures all the status information during the promotion or demotion, from start to finish. You can increase the level of logging to this file by modifying a registry value. Review the DCPROMOIU.log file and the more concise DCPROMO.log file and search for any error events. Additionally, open Event Viewer and review the newly created directory service and **FRS** logs. Review any error or warning messages. If you encounter errors, search Microsoft's TechNet to discover the cause of, and resolution to, the problem. Open the three AD administrative tools and confirm that all the required objects and sites exist. It is also a good idea to verify that the domain controller has registered itself and its services in DNS.

PRACTICE TEST QUESTIONS

MediaMinds is in the process of installing five new domain controllers to support AD. Two of the domain controllers are newly acquired four-way Pentium III-700 servers with 512 MB of RAM and 60 GB of disk space. Both are running Windows 2000 Server. The other three domain controllers are former NT 4.0 member servers that were upgraded to Windows 2000 Server. All three are dual-processor Pentium II-400s with 256 MB of RAM and 30 GB of disk space.

DCPROMO was run on all five servers. Upon completing and rebooting, one of the newly acquired PIII-700s and two of the upgraded PII-400s reported errors.

1. **How would you begin troubleshooting the errors on the PIII-700 server?**
    a. Confirm that the NTDS.dit file was indeed located in the Ntds folder.
    b. Review the application log in the Event Viewer.
    c. Open the DCPROMOIU.log file and search for the keywords "status error."
    d. Review the directory service log in Event Viewer for any warning or error messages.

2. **You notice a warning event in the directory service log in Event Viewer. Unfortunately, the description field of the warning message is blank. How would you proceed in determining the problem? (Choose all that apply.)**
    a. Search Microsoft's Knowledge Base for the event ID.
    b. Using Notepad, open the DCPROMOIU.log file and search for the keyword "error."
    c. Open the EDB.log file in the Ntds folder and search for the keyword "error."
    d. Open the system log in Event Viewer and look for any warnings or errors messages.

3. **On the two PII-400s, you notice that many of the objects in MediaMind's AD haven't replicated to these two servers. Where would you look to identify the source of the problem?**
    a. In the %systemroot%\ntfrs\jet\ntfrs.jdb file
    b. In the directory service log in Event Viewer
    c. In the file replication service log in Event Viewer
    d. In the system log in Event Viewer

4. **On the two PII-400s, you notice that many of the group policies in MediaMind's AD haven't replicated to these two servers. Where would you look to identify the source of the problem?**
    a. In the %systemroot%\ntfrs\jet\ntfrs.jdb file
    b. In the directory service log in Event Viewer
    c. In the file replication service log in Event Viewer
    d. In the system log in Event Viewer

1.11 Implement an Organizational Unit (OU) structure

OU • OBJECT • CONTAINER • ACTIVE DIRECTORY USERS AND COMPUTERS

UNDERSTANDING THE OBJECTIVE

One of the most beneficial aspects of AD is the ability to create a logical network management structure, which is accomplished through the use of **OU**s. A company's OU structure is largely hidden to end users, and thus can take on any structure that meets the organization's needs.

WHAT YOU REALLY NEED TO KNOW

- ◆ An OU is a type of container object. Objects such as users, computers, printers, shared folders, and other OUs can be created within an OU.
- ◆ Although group policies cannot be placed onto container objects, they can be placed onto OUs.
- ◆ The domain controller's OU exists by default. All other OUs must be created manually.
- ◆ Several containers exist by default: Builtin, Computers, ForeignSecurityPrincipals, and Users.
- ◆ OUs allow for network administration to be delegated among IT support staff. Instead of staff having permissions throughout the domain, staff can be delegated permissions to OUs.

OBJECTIVES ON THE JOB

The ability to create a logical network structure is one of the biggest advantages of using AD. With an OU structure, you can group objects by function, department, division, location, task, etc. It is much easier to manage a 60,000-user network when you can organize users into OUs. However, your OU structure shouldn't necessarily mirror your physical structure unless it is appropriate. Sites are used for that purpose. Unlike other directory services, an AD OU structure is relatively hidden from end users. This gives administrators and designers the flexibility to create a structure that meets the exact needs of the organization without burdening end users with network complexities. An OU structure also allows permissions to be delegated to network staff at the OU level. For example, a Help Desk group can be delegated the ability to reset passwords on the SalesUsers OU. Permissions can be delegated with whatever granularity is desired. When a new AD domain is created, one OU and four containers exist by default: the Domain Controller's OU, and the Builtin, Computers, ForeignSecurityPrincipals, and Users containers.

PRACTICE TEST QUESTIONS

1. **Which sentence(s) accurately describes an OU? (Choose all that apply.)**
   a. An OU is an object that can contain other objects.
   b. An OU is a non-leaf object that can contain other objects.
   c. An OU is an object upon which group policies can be placed.
   d. An OU is an object that can be delegated permission to other objects.

2. **What must a user specify when logging into AD?**
   a. The domain name only
   b. The domain name and user's OU
   c. The site and OU name
   d. The OU only

3. **An administrator can create containers in AD using the Active Directory Users and Computers tool.**
   a. True
   b. False

4. **An OU named Sales exists in the mediaminds.com domain. What is the OU's distinguished name?**
   a. dc=com,dc=mediaminds,dc=sales
   b. cn=sales,dc=mediaminds,dc=com
   c. ou=sales,dc=mediaminds,dc=com
   d. dc=sales,dc=mediaminds,dc=com

5. **A container named Users exists in the mediaminds.com domain. What is the container's distinguished name?**
   a. dc=com,dc=mediaminds,dc=users
   b. cn=users,dc=mediaminds,dc=com
   c. ou=users,dc=mediaminds,dc=com
   d. dc=users,dc=mediaminds,dc=com

6. **Which of the following facts about containers is false?**
   a. OUs cannot be created in containers.
   b. Containers cannot be created in OUs.
   c. Containers cannot be deleted.
   d. Containers cannot have permission delegated to them.

7. **Which of the following facts about OUs is false? (Choose all that apply.)**
   a. OUs cannot be created in other OUs.
   b. OUs cannot be moved.
   c. Containers cannot be created in OUs.
   d. OUs cannot be created in containers.

OBJECTIVES

1.12 Back up Active Directory

BACK UP • SYSTEM STATE • NTDS.DIT

UNDERSTANDING THE OBJECTIVE

To ensure that AD can survive system failures, it is critical to back up AD. Furthermore, backups ensure that accidentally deleted objects can be restored. You can achieve AD backups by using the Windows 2000 Backup program or third-party backup software.

WHAT YOU REALLY NEED TO KNOW

- ◆ AD is an online transactional database. Backup software must be able to backup AD while it is running and take into account transaction logging.

- ◆ The Windows 2000 Backup program can back up AD while it is running, without stopping AD. It backs up transactions in the AD database.

- ◆ Select System State in the Windows 2000 Backup program to guarantee that AD is backed up. System State also backs up other key components on a domain controller, such as the Registry, COM+ database, system and boot files, Certificate Services, Sysvol, and Clustering Service information.

- ◆ Restore the System State information when restoring AD on a failed domain controller.

- ◆ The Windows 2000 Backup program cannot remotely back up System State information.

OBJECTIVES ON THE JOB

Traditional backup software cannot be used to back up AD because it never stops running. Most backup software skips over open files and, therefore, skips the AD database files. If you are going to use third-party backup software, you will likely have to purchase an "agent" in order to back up AD. Otherwise, you can use the Windows 2000 Backup program. By selecting System State on a domain controller, you instruct the Backup program to back up AD, which includes the NTDS.dit, EDB.log, and EDB.chk files. Each domain controller should be backed up independently. Backups should occur on a daily basis. By performing regular backups, you will be able to recover your domain controller from a system failure, if necessary. To restore AD, you must restore the System State information. This is known as a non-authoritative restore. You are also able to perform authoritative restores. This type of restore is necessary in the case of a deleted object, such as an OU. You can schedule backups to occur automatically using the Backup Wizard. The Scheduled Tasks tool manages backup schedules.

PRACTICE TEST QUESTIONS

1. **Which backup program comes standard with Windows 2000?**
   a. NT Backup
   b. ArcServeIT Lite
   c. Backup Exec Lite
   d. Backup

2. **Why can't traditional backup software be used to back up AD? (Choose all that apply.)**
   a. AD is always running.
   b. The backup software must be able to back up individual transactions.
   c. Because open files are skipped.
   d. An agent is required.

3. **How can you schedule the backup to occur automatically?**
   a. Use the AT command.
   b. Use the WinAT tool.
   c. Use Backup's Task Scheduler.
   d. Schedule a Cron job.

4. **On which domain controllers should System State be backed up?**
   a. The PDC Emulator
   b. The Global Catalog server
   c. Any operations masters
   d. All domain controllers

5. **On a domain controller, what does backing up System State include? (Choose all that apply.)**
   a. Registry
   b. %Systemroot%\System32
   c. Active Directory
   d. Sysvol

6. **When objects are accidentally deleted from AD, you must perform which type of restore?**
   a. Authoritative
   b. Non-authoritative
   c. Full
   d. Incremental

7. **How often should System State be backed up in a medium-sized company?**
   a. Weekly
   b. Monthly
   c. Daily
   d. Hourly

1.13 Perform an authoritative restore of Active Directory

NTDSUTIL • RESTORING AN OBJECT • REPLICATION

UNDERSTANDING THE OBJECTIVE

Under normal circumstances, restoring AD means restoring System State information on a domain controller. When the domain controller is restarted, the other domain controllers replicate missing AD changes and bring that domain controller back up-to-date. When an object is deleted, however, System State must be restored and the deleted object marked for authoritative restore. This forces the object to be replicated to all domain controllers and prevents AD replication from deleting the object because its version information is considered old.

WHAT YOU REALLY NEED TO KNOW

◆ A restore due to system failure is considered a non-authoritative restore.

◆ A deleted object must be restored authoritatively to allow it to replicate to all other domain controllers and prevent replication from deleting the object.

◆ It is important to boot the server into Directory Services Restore Mode to begin the authoritative restore process.

◆ System State information can be restored using Backup.

◆ Know the NTDSUTIL.exe commands to mark objects for authoritative restore. Use the object's fully distinguished name when referring to the object.

OBJECTIVES ON THE JOB

Replication changes are tracked using stamp information, which includes a version number, timestamp, and GUID. In the case of a non-authoritative restore, objects with old stamp information are restored. AD then replicates the necessary changes to bring those objects up-to-date. In the case of an authoritative restore, you must mark objects as current using the NTDSUTIL.exe utility. This prevents replication from overwriting those objects by increasing the version number by 100,000 for each day between the backup and the restore period. While the domain controller is in Directory Services Restore Mode, the AD database is offline on that domain controller. Upon restoring System State information, be sure to run NTDSUTIL.exe.

PRACTICE TEST QUESTIONS

1. **What is the purpose of an authoritative restore?**
   a. To restore deleted objects
   b. To restore failed domain controllers
   c. To restore DNS information
   d. To restore the NTDS.dit file

2. **What must you do before restoring System State information?**
   a. Reboot into Directory Services Restore Mode
   b. Reboot into Safe mode
   c. Reboot into Safe mode with Network Support
   d. Stop the AD service

3. **After restoring System State information, what should *not* be done?**
   a. Start the AD service
   b. Reboot
   c. Use the **net accounts /sync** command
   d. Log off

4. **Immediately after restoring System State information, what should be done?**
   a. Reboot
   b. Log off and log on as a domain administrator
   c. Use NTDSUTIL.exe to mark the object for authoritative restore
   d. Start the AD service

5. **You wish to mark the Sales OU in the *microsoft.com* domain for authoritative restore. What is the correct syntax?**
   a. restore subtree cn=sales,cn=microsoft,cn=com
   b. restore subtree dc=com,dc=microsoft,ou=sales
   c. restore subtree dc=sales,dc=microsoft,dc=com
   d. restore subtree ou=sales,dc=microsoft,dc=com

6. **You reboot the server after restoring System State information and notice that the restored objects have suddenly disappeared. What is the likely cause?**
   a. You did not mark the objects for authoritative restore.
   b. You did not increment the object version numbers.
   c. You did not increment the object numbers by 100,000.
   d. You were not in Directory Services Restore Mode when you marked the objects for authoritative restore.

7. **What three properties form an object's stamp?**
   a. Version number
   b. USN
   c. GUID
   d. Timestamp

OBJECTIVES

1.14 Recover from a system failure

BACKUP • RESTORE • CRASH • EMERGENCY REPAIR

UNDERSTANDING THE OBJECTIVE

System failures can occur for various reasons, including malfunctioning devices or device drivers, system file or DLL conflicts, mis-configuration, or unsupported hardware. Fortunately, Windows 2000 provides many tools for recovering from system failures. Before attempting a complete system restoration from backup, use these tools to try to revive a failed system.

WHAT YOU REALLY NEED TO KNOW

◆ An **ERD** can be created using the Backup program. It contains system files, the partition boot sector, and startup environment information. It does not back up the registry or system files. Keep the ERD up-to-date to reflect recent system changes.

◆ To use the ERD, boot the system using the Windows 2000 installation CD. When prompted, choose the emergency repair process by pressing **R**.

◆ Another method for recovering a failed system is through the Windows 2000 Advanced Options menu. Press F8 at system boot to bring up the menu. From here, you can boot using the following methods: safe mode, safe mode with networking, safe mode with command prompt, boot logging, **VGA** mode, last known good configuration, directory services restore mode, or debugging mode.

OBJECTIVES ON THE JOB

System failures on servers and domain controllers can result in significant downtime and cost. Restoring a server from backup is usually a tactic of last resort due to the time required to perform the restore. By keeping an up-to-date ERD, you can quickly recover a failed system if the failure results from a damaged boot sector or from a corrupted system file or startup files. If you use an out-of-date ERD, you may have to reapply recent configuration changes. The options available in the Advanced Options menu offer other methods for recovering a failed system and should be tried before using the ERD. Booting in safe mode boots the system using minimal drivers and services, and bypasses the majority of the Registry. Safe mode with networking is similar but also enables networking. Safe mode with command prompt boots the system to a command prompt instead of to the Windows desktop. Boot logging boots the system and logs all loaded and unloaded drivers and services to %windir%\ntbtlog.txt. This can help identify devices or services that may be causing the failure. VGA mode boots Windows 2000 using a standard VGA driver. The last known good configuration boots into your previous configuration settings, but only if you have not already logged into the system. Debugging mode starts Windows 2000 and sends debugging information to another computer using a serial cable. Another option is to boot the server using winnt32.exe/cmdcons, which installs the Recovery Console. Using the Recovery Console you can stop and start services, format drives, read and write to NTFS volumes, and perform many other tasks.

PRACTICE TEST QUESTIONS

After arriving at work one morning, you notice that a Windows 2000 domain controller has a blue screen with a stop message of 0x000000072. Repeated attempts to reboot the server result in the same stop message. After consulting Microsoft's TechNet, you determine that the stop message is the result of a configuration change performed two days earlier. Since that day, you have rebooted the server and logged into the console several times without problems.

The ERD was last updated three weeks ago. Your last full tape backup of the server was last night.

1. How can the ERD be used in this repair?
   - a. Boot the failed server using the ERD.
   - b. ERD can be used after booting with the Windows 2000 CD.
   - c. ERD can be used after booting with a DOS boot disk.
   - d. ERD can be used after restoring last night's backup.

2. Which of the following does the ERD *not* store?
   - a. System files
   - b. Partition boot sector
   - c. Registry
   - d. Startup environment

3. What would be your first task in trying to revive the failed server?
   - a. Press F8 and enable boot logging.
   - b. Press F8 and boot using safe mode.
   - c. Boot with the Windows 2000 CD and do a repair using the ERD.
   - d. Press F8 and use the last known good configuration.

4. You enable boot logging and notice a particular service driver failing to load. How would you disable this driver?
   - a. Boot the server using winnt32.exe /cmdcons.
   - b. Press F8 and boot using safe mode with command prompt.
   - c. Press F8 and boot using safe mode.
   - d. Boot with a NTFSDOS boot disk.

5. If you hadn't logged into the server following the configuration changes, what approach would you have used to fix the failed server?
   - a. Press F8 and use the last known good configuration.
   - b. Boot the server using winnt32.exe /cmdcons.
   - c. Boot with the Windows 2000 CD and do a repair using the ERD.
   - d. Press F8 and enable boot logging.

1.15 Troubleshoot Active Directory

EVENT VIEWER

UNDERSTANDING THE OBJECTIVE

AD is a reliable and extensible directory service. However, with an organization's infrastructure depending on a well-functioning AD, problems must be diagnosed and fixed quickly. Therefore, it is important to develop the skills needed to troubleshoot AD problems quickly and efficiently.

WHAT YOU REALLY NEED TO KNOW

- ◆ AD logs informational, warning, and error messages to the directory service log in Event Viewer.

- ◆ Using the Event ID number, source, category, or description information from Event Viewer messages, you can consult Microsoft's TechNet to determine the source and a fix for the message.

- ◆ Failures or errors in DNS can cause problems in AD. If you suspect DNS, test the DNS server using the NSLOOKUP.exe utility.

- ◆ When using NSLOOKUP in interactive mode, enter ls –t srv domainname to determine if the service records of domain controllers are being registered in the appropriate sites.

- ◆ If you suspect AD replication is not performing correctly, consult the file replication service log in Event Viewer. This log displays messages if, for example, group policies are failing to replicate to other domain controllers.

- ◆ AD problems can also stem from failed operations master servers, such as the PDC Emulator, RID Master, or Infrastructure Master.

OBJECTIVES ON THE JOB

Microsoft provides numerous logs, tools, and methods for troubleshooting AD problems. The following is a list of support tools to assist in diagnosing and solving AD problems. Most of these tools are available from the \support\tools\2000rkst.msi file on the Windows 2000 CD.

EseUtil – Repairs, checks, compacts, moves, and dumps the directory database files.

NtdsUtil – Has many of the same features as EseUtil, plus the ability to manage operations masters (seize or transfer roles).

Ldp – Views AD object metadata, including security descriptors and replication metadata.

Replmon – Monitors and views AD replication status. Also useful for forcing replication and triggering the KCC to recalculate its replication topology.

RepAdmin – Checks replication consistency between replication partners and monitors replication status.

NLTest – Checks that the locator and secure channel are functioning correctly.

NetDom5 – Checks and reconfigures trust relationships.

PRACTICE TEST QUESTIONS

1. **Which two Event Viewer logs can be useful for troubleshooting Active Directory-specific problems?**
   a. %systemroot%\debug\dcpromo.log
   b. Directory Service log
   c. File Replication Service log
   d. System log

2. **What information from an Event Viewer message would you use to search Microsoft's Knowledgebase? (Choose all that apply.)**
   a. Event ID
   b. Computer
   c. User
   d. Description

3. **What NSLOOKUP command would you use to query for service records in the _microsoft.com_ domain?**
   a. ls –d microsoft.com
   b. set query=srv, set domain=microsoft.com
   c. ls –d srv microsoft.com
   d. ls –t srv microsoft.com

4. **You notice that group policies and logon scripts are failing to replicate to other domain controllers in the domain. What tool should be used first to determine the source of the problem?**
   a. Event Viewer – file replication service log
   b. Repadmin
   c. Replmon
   d. NLTest

5. **Which GUI-based tool allows you to monitor replication, trigger replication, and view your replication topology?**
   a. RepAdmin
   b. LDP
   c. Replmon
   d. Netdom5

6. **You attempt to run NLTest, but get a File not found message. Why?**
   a. You failed to install the Windows 2000 Resource Kit.
   b. You did not install NLTest into %systemroot%\system32.
   c. You did not enter the command: regsvr32 nltest.dll.
   d. You failed to install the Windows 2000 Support Tools.

7. **Which tool can be used to seize operations master roles?**
   a. RepAdmin
   b. Active Directory Users and Computers
   c. Replmon
   d. NTDSutil

Section 2

Installing, Configuring, Managing, Monitoring, and Troubleshooting DNS for Active Directory

2.1 Install DNS for Active Directory

DCPROMO • ADD/REMOVE WINDOWS COMPONENTS • DNS INSTALLATION

UNDERSTANDING THE OBJECTIVE

AD uses DNS to locate computers that provide services (such as domain controllers) and to translate the host names and **FQDN**s to IP addresses. Without DNS, AD can't be installed. DNS can be installed either before or during the installation of AD.

WHAT YOU REALLY NEED TO KNOW

◆ If a domain controller is created (via DCPROMO) in a new forest and DNS is not already properly installed, you are prompted to install it as part of the AD Installation Wizard. If you are joining an existing domain, tree, or forest, the wizard assumes that DNS is already properly configured on the network.

◆ If DNS is not properly configured on a soon-to-be domain controller, AD will not install properly, if at all. DNS *must* be properly configured and tested before you attempt an AD installation.

◆ Non-Windows 2000 DNS servers can be used, as long as they support SRV records. Dynamic update support and **IXFR**s are highly recommended, but not required.

◆ In most cases, Microsoft recommends using Windows 2000-based DNS servers for AD information, even if other DNS servers are used for other purposes.

◆ DNS servers should have static IP addresses so clients can always locate them.

◆ Dynamic update support must be enabled after the zone is created. Zones are static by default.

◆ The Active Directory Installation Wizard (if desired) automatically installs DNS, creates a forward lookup zone with the same name as the zone being created, configures it as an AD integrated zone, and configures it for secure dynamic updates.

OBJECTIVES ON THE JOB

DNS is critical to the functioning of AD. If you are not already familiar with DNS, it is imperative that you study it. Before using a non-Windows 2000 DNS server, consider the implications of your decision. Before implementing any DNS solution, consider understanding all of the DNS issues with a "Designing Active Directory" course (MCSE exam #70-219). For more information, consult the *MCSE Guide to Designing a Microsoft Windows 2000 Directory Service* by Michael Palmer (Course Technology, 2001).

PRACTICE TEST QUESTIONS

1. **Your boss decides that AD will save the company a lot of money and wants to know what requirements the DNS server must meet. The requirements are: (Choose all that apply.)**
   a. dynamic update
   b. reverse lookup support
   c. BIND compliance
   d. support for service records
   e. support for PTR records
   f. incremental zone transfers

2. **DNS must be installed before you begin the AD Installation Wizard.**
   a. True
   b. False

3. **AD requires DNS to function.**
   a. True
   b. False

4. **To install DNS before you start the AD Installation Wizard, use:**
   a. Control Panel, Network
   b. Control Panel, Services
   c. Control Panel, Active Directory
   d. Control Panel, Add/Remove Programs

5. **AD works with which of the following types of DNS servers? (Choose all that apply.)**
   a. Most Linux DNS servers
   b. Most UNIX DNS servers
   c. Windows NT 4.0 DNS servers
   d. Windows 2000 DNS servers
   e. Novell DNS servers

6. **By default, Windows 2000 zones are dynamic.**
   a. True
   b. False

2.2   Integrate AD DNS zones with non-AD DNS zones

BIND • AD INTEGRATED ZONES • DNS REPLICATION

UNDERSTANDING THE OBJECTIVE

DNS exists on many platforms, including UNIX, Linux, Novell, Windows NT 4.0, and Windows 2000. The Windows 2000 DNS server is RFC-compliant, and therefore can operate with any other RFC-compliant DNS server, including those just listed.

WHAT YOU REALLY NEED TO KNOW

◆ BIND stands for Berkeley Internet Name Daemon and is the standard implementation of DNS on Linux/UNIX machines.

◆ AD integrated zones only exist on Windows 2000-based computers because only they have AD, but they can send and receive updates with other DNS servers.

◆ DNS replication replicates data from master name servers to secondary name servers, which in turn may act as master name servers to other secondary name servers. The ultimate source of information in standard DNS is the primary DNS server, of which there may only be one per zone. In other words, there is only one place where changes are made.

◆ When an AD integrated zone is used, DNS data is replicated along with all other AD data, not as part of DNS replication. With this type of zone, changes can be made at any DNS server that is also configured with the same zone type and the changes are replicated to all other DNS servers. In other words, it uses multimaster replication.

◆ An AD integrated zone may be seen as the primary server to update other DNS servers, or as a secondary server to be updated by other DNS servers. Note that in either case, only one of the Windows DNS servers in the zone needs to be specified as the primary or secondary server—it replicates with all other Windows 2000 DNS servers for that zone.

OBJECTIVES ON THE JOB

DNS is the primary name resolution method used on the Internet today. As such, most companies already have a DNS server. You must decide whether you want to continue to use your existing DNS server(s) or use Windows 2000 DNS servers, or both. In most cases, the simplest approach is to use Windows 2000 DNS servers for all of the AD information and your existing DNS servers for name resolution as they are currently configured, which is typically for Internet access to and from your external servers. Work carefully with your existing DNS administrator before implementing Windows 2000 DNS servers and AD.

PRACTICE TEST QUESTIONS

1. **AD integrated zones can exist on DNS servers in which of the following operating systems?**
   a. Windows 2000
   b. Windows NT
   c. Linux
   d. UNIX
   e. Novell

2. **When using an AD integrated zone, the data is replicated to other Windows 2000 DNS servers servicing the zone using standard DNS mechanisms.**
   a. True
   b. False

3. **When using an AD integrated zone, the data is replicated to non-Windows 2000 DNS servers servicing the zone using standard DNS mechanisms.**
   a. True
   b. False

4. **When data is updated in DNS, it can be replicated from _____ DNS servers to _____ DNS servers. (Choose all that apply.)**
   a. primary, secondary
   b. secondary, primary
   c. master, secondary
   d. master, primary
   e. AD integrated zones on Windows 2000, AD integrated zones on Windows 2000
   f. AD integrated zones on Windows 2000, primary
   g. AD integrated zones on Windows 2000, secondary
   h. primary, AD integrated zones on Windows 2000
   i. master, AD integrated zones on Windows 2000

5. **When using standard primary and secondary zones, data can be updated at:**
   a. the primary DNS server
   b. any secondary DNS server
   c. both
   d. neither

2.3   Configure zones for dynamic updates

DYNAMIC UPDATES • ZONES • DDNS

UNDERSTANDING THE OBJECTIVE

Although DNS servers support either dynamic or static updates, implementation of the dynamic update capability is done on a per-zone basis, not a per-server basis. Generally, all of the zones associated with AD (both forward and reverse) should be configured to allow dynamic updates to drastically reduce administrative overhead.

WHAT YOU REALLY NEED TO KNOW

◆ Dynamic updates are enabled on a per-zone basis.

◆ If the zone is configured as an AD integrated zone, secure dynamic updates may be configured.

◆ When secure dynamic updates are allowed, you can specify the users or groups that are allowed to update DNS.

◆ Secure dynamic updates can be applied at the zone or individual resource record levels.

◆ Both reverse and forward lookup zones may be configured for dynamic updates.

◆ You can force a client to update its records in DNS (such as after making it dynamically updateable) by typing ipconfig/registerdns on the command line.

OBJECTIVES ON THE JOB

In a pure Windows 2000 network, **DDNS** can completely eliminate the need for **WINS** servers, because all updates to computer names and IP addresses can be handled by DNS. In mixed-mode environments (Windows 2000 servers and Windows NT and 9x clients), WINS is still needed for **NetBIOS** resolution in most cases. Zones associated with resources accessible on the Internet are often not dynamic, making them harder to hack from the outside. However, those associated with AD generally are dynamic in order to greatly reduce the overhead of creating, changing, and removing AD and PTR records whenever a machine is added or removed or an IP address is changed. This is especially true for domain controllers, because they make many entries in DNS that must be accurate for AD to function.

PRACTICE TEST QUESTIONS

1. **When creating a DNS zone for resources available on the Internet, the zone should be:**
   a. primary
   b. secondary
   c. AD integrated
   d. static
   e. dynamic
   f. secure dynamic

2. **Secure dynamic updates can be configured with which of the following zone types?**
   a. Primary
   b. Secondary
   c. AD integrated

3. **Secure dynamic updates can be applied to which of the following? (Choose all that apply.)**
   a. DNS servers
   b. Zones
   c. Resource records

4. **By default, all DNS zones in Windows 2000 are set to allow dynamic updates.**
   a. True
   b. False

5. **Dynamic updates apply to:**
   a. forward lookup zones
   b. reverse lookup zones
   c. both
   d. neither

2.4 Manage replication of DNS data

PRIMARY DNS SERVER • SECONDARY DNS SERVER • MASTER DNS SERVER • ACTIVE DIRECTORY INTEGRATED ZONE

UNDERSTANDING THE OBJECTIVE

DNS replication can be performed using one of three methods, two of which are standard DNS methods and one of which is unique to Windows 2000. The standard DNS replication mechanisms are **AXFR**s and IXFRs. If a zone is an AD integrated zone, DNS data is replicated with standard AD mechanisms and with the AD data.

WHAT YOU REALLY NEED TO KNOW

◆ In a standard DNS zone, there is one master source of information (one writeable copy of DNS information), stored in a primary zone file. All other copies of the DNS data are stored in secondary zone files, which are read-only. The primary DNS server is a single point of failure for making updates to DNS (although not for name resolution).

◆ All DNS servers that support an AD integrated zone are writeable. Updates made at any of these servers are replicated to all other DNS servers for that zone. This eliminates the single point of failure for making DNS updates and allows updates to be spread across multiple DNS servers.

◆ All DNS servers support AXFRs; only newer DNS servers (Windows 2000 and BIND 8.2.1) support IXFRs.

◆ A master DNS server is a server that updates another DNS server for a given zone. It may be either the primary name server for the zone or another secondary name server.

◆ Any DNS server that serves an AD integrated zone can act as a primary DNS server to any other DNS server, which then acts as a secondary DNS server for that zone.

◆ Windows 2000 DNS servers are RFC-compliant and can therefore share information with Novell, UNIX, Linux, and Windows NT 4.0-based DNS servers, among others. The other server can be either a primary or secondary DNS server, as can the Windows 2000 server.

OBJECTIVES ON THE JOB

DNS is probably the most critical network service in Windows 2000. Without it, AD doesn't work. With any service this critical, constant access to the data is vital. This level of access is achieved by replicating the DNS data to other servers. In all but the smallest of networks, in which only one server exists, a second DNS server should be considered mandatory. Understanding DNS replication is essential to making sure that the data is replicated in a timely manner and that updates can be accomplished as needed. Whenever a Windows 2000 DNS server is used to store AD data, you should strongly consider using AD integrated zones.

PRACTICE TEST QUESTIONS

1. **Windows 2000 DNS servers can replicate with non-Windows 2000 DNS servers.**
    a. True
    b. False

2. **The server that replicates with a secondary DNS server is called a _____.**
    a. source name server
    b. parent name server
    c. child name server
    d. master name server

3. **A major difference between primary DNS servers and secondary DNS servers is that primary name servers are _____, whereas secondary name servers are _____.**
    a. dynamic, static
    b. static, dynamic
    c. updateable, read-only
    d. read-only, writeable

4. **Which of the following are major differences between standard DNS zones and AD integrated zones? (Choose all that apply.)**
    a. Standard zones are static, whereas AD integrated zones are dynamic.
    b. Standard DNS zones are replicated by standard DNS means, whereas AD integrated zone data is replicated with AD data.
    c. Standard DNS uses AXFR, whereas AD uses IXFR.
    d. In standard zones, only the primary DNS server is writeable; in AD integrated zones, all DNS servers that serve the zone (in AD integrated mode) are writeable.

5. **Which of the following is an advantage of using IXFR over AXFR?**
    a. Less bandwidth is used to replicate changes.
    b. More bandwidth is used to replicate changes, but less bandwidth is used in initial replication.
    c. IXFR-enabled zones require less disk space to store changes.
    d. IXFR-enabled zones require more disk space to store changes, but less bandwidth to replicate the changes.

2.5   Monitor and troubleshoot DNS

NSLOOKUP • DNS MMC CONSOLE • SYSTEM MONITOR

UNDERSTANDING THE OBJECTIVE

DNS is crucial to the functioning of AD. Therefore, you must ensure that your DNS servers are accessible, functioning properly, and able to handle the load created by dynamic updates and queries. To verify that your DNS server is functioning properly, you can use either the command-line utility NSLOOKUP or the DNS **MMC**. To monitor the load created on your server by dynamic updates and queries, you can use the System Monitor snap-in.

WHAT YOU REALLY NEED TO KNOW

- ◆ NSLOOKUP is a command-line utility that can be used in either interactive or noninteractive mode. Interactive mode allows you to look up multiple pieces of information and specify advanced parameters. Noninteractive mode allows you to specify a name and view your server's name-to-IP-address mapping information.
- ◆ The DNS MMC can be used to monitor DNS.
- ◆ The MMC can also be used to repeat either the simple or recursive test at a user-defined interval, which allows you to see when the DNS server stopped (or started) working properly.
- ◆ Common causes of DNS problems include: not enabling dynamic updates, an incorrect IP address for the server specified in TCP/IP properties, an unplugged network cable, and out-of-date information in DNS.
- ◆ System Monitor is used to monitor the performance of any portion of the system, including DNS.

OBJECTIVES ON THE JOB

The best planned and implemented DNS strategy won't do any good if the DNS server is down or unable to keep up with the demands placed on it. To test the functionality of DNS, use either the DNS console or NSLOOKUP from any computer that has the desired DNS server configured as its primary DNS server. If you use the DNS console, you can choose to specify an interval to have the test repeat. To verify that the server can stand up to the load being placed on it, use System Monitor. For more information on the counters used to monitor DNS performance, go to Windows 2000 Server Help. There you will find more than 60 counters and an explanation on how they may be used to monitor performance. There is also a link called "Server planning for DNS" that discusses capacity planning issues relative to DNS.

PRACTICE TEST QUESTIONS

1. **The command NSLOOKUP www.microsoft.com entered on a command line returns _____.**
   - a. an IP address, based on data in WINS
   - b. the path to the Web server at microsoft.com
   - c. an IP address, based on data in DNS
   - d. four ICMP responses to the request to prove the server is up

2. **NSLOOKUP is a GUI utility.**
   - a. True
   - b. False

3. **NSLOOKUP continues to query a DNS server for information until the desired information is returned.**
   - a. True
   - b. False

4. **The DNS console can repeatedly query a DNS server to let you determine when a DNS server started or stopped working.**
   - a. True
   - b. False

5. **The DNS console offers _____ test(s) to monitor a DNS server.**
   - a. one
   - b. two
   - c. three
   - d. four

6. **To determine how well a DNS server is performing, use _____.**
   - a. Computer Management
   - b. Event Viewer
   - c. DNS console
   - d. System Monitor

7. **If out-of-date information is found to be in the DNS for your system, the fastest way to get it updated is to _____.**
   - a. execute the registerdns command
   - b. reboot
   - c. execute the ipconfig/registerdns command
   - d. update the DNS information directly using the DNS console

Section 3

Configuring, Managing, Monitoring, Optimizing, and Troubleshooting Change and Configuration Management

3.1 Create a Group Policy Object (GPO)

SITE • DOMAIN • OU • SOFTWARE DEPLOYMENT

UNDERSTANDING THE OBJECTIVE

GPOs give administrators an immense amount of control over a user's environment. From desktop settings to security permissions, GPOs can be applied selectively to deliver customized and secure environments to users. Additionally, GPOs can be used to deploy and remove software from users.

WHAT YOU REALLY NEED TO KNOW

- ◆ GPOs can remove icons, secure desktops, apply security settings, customize user environments, and much more. This can all be done remotely.

- ◆ Software using the Microsoft Installer technology can be deployed using GPOs. Software can be deployed to users or computers.

- ◆ GPOs are stored in AD and can be linked to a site, a domain, or an OU. Group policies are physically stored in the Sysvol folder and replicated to all other domain controllers in the domain.

- ◆ The local GPO is processed first. Next, site GPOs are processed, followed by domain-level GPOs and finally OU-level GPOs. If conflicts exist, the last GPO applied wins. Otherwise, settings from site, domain, and OU GPOs are combined to give the user their effective environment.

- ◆ Only members of the Enterprise Admins group can create site GPOs. Domain Admins can create domain and OU GPOs.

- ◆ By default, GPOs are created and edited on the domain controller holding the PDC Emulator operations master role. They are replicated to all other domain controllers in the domain.

- ◆ Site GPOs are created using the Active Directory Sites and Services tool, whereas domain and OU GPOs are created using the Active Directory Users and Computers tool.

OBJECTIVES ON THE JOB

Group policies are represented by GPOs in AD and are stored in the System container under Policies. GPOs are identified and stored using a unique GUID. Group policies are physically stored in the Winnt\Sysvol\Sysvol\Domainname\Policies folder and replicated to other domain controllers. Each GPO is comprised of computer settings and user settings. If no settings are made to either the user or computer section, that section can be disabled to allow for faster processing of the GPO. Group policies make changes to the local Registry under HKEY_CURRENT_USER\ Software\Policies and HKEY_LOCAL_MACHINE\Software\Policies. A local GPO is created using the Group Policy MMC snap-in. Group policies can be used to enforce desktop settings, set a common wallpaper, and deploy software to users, to name a few applications. If you want to restrict who receives the group policy settings, consider applying the group policy to an OU or using permissions to specify which users and groups receive the group policy.

PRACTICE TEST QUESTIONS

MediaMinds is an international firm specializing in marketing consulting. MediaMinds has offices in Boston, New York, and Miami, each employing between 200 and 300 people working in various departments such as sales, ad design, and so on.

MediaMinds is planning to use group policies to customize and enforce its users' environment. Furthermore, group policies will be used to deploy software to users and computers. MediaMinds' OU structure is departmentally based (sales, HR, etc.) with location-based OUs (Boston, New York, etc.) inside each.

1. MediaMinds wants to remove the Run command from sales users in all locations. Where should the GPO be linked?
   a. At the domain
   b. At each site
   c. At the Sales OU
   d. At each location OU

2. MediaMinds wants to deploy an application to all users in Boston. Where should the GPO be linked?
   a. At the domain
   b. At each location OU
   c. At the Boston site
   d. At each Boston OU

3. An administrator at MediaMinds wants to create a site GPO for Miami. Which tool should he use?
   a. Active Directory Users and Computers
   b. Active Directory Domains and Trusts
   c. The Group Policy snap-in
   d. Active Directory Sites and Services

4. How can an administrator verify that a domain GPO has been replicated to all domain controllers?
   a. By opening the Winnt\Sysvol folder and confirming that a folder exists based on the GPO's GUID
   b. By using the Active Directory Users and Computers tool
   c. By using the Active Directory Domains and Trusts tool
   d. By using the Active Directory Sites and Services tool

5. An administrator at MediaMinds wants to create a site GPO for the New York OU, which is beneath the HR OU. Which tool should he use?
   a. Active Directory Users and Computers
   b. Active Directory Domains and Trusts
   c. The Group Policy snap-in
   d. Active Directory Sites and Services

3.2 Link an existing GPO

GPO • LINK • SITE • DOMAIN • OU

UNDERSTANDING THE OBJECTIVE

GPOs provide an immense amount of flexibility in managing and enforcing user environments. GPOs can be created at the site, domain, and OU level. Rather than creating duplicate GPOs, administrators can link to existing GPOs in AD. The permission to link can be delegated to administrators at the OU level, for example.

WHAT YOU REALLY NEED TO KNOW

- ◆ All GPOs, whether created at the site, domain, or OU level, are stored in AD.
- ◆ Linking to existing GPOs reduces the number of GPOs with duplicate settings.
- ◆ When a GPO is modified, all linked GPOs reflect that modification.
- ◆ This can prove dangerous when the administrator making changes to a GPO is unaware that the GPO has been linked.
- ◆ It is important to determine if a site, domain, or OU has been linked to a GPO before modifying it.
- ◆ Use the Active Directory Sites and Services tool to link a GPO to a site.
- ◆ Use the Active Directory Users and Computers tool to link a GPO to a domain or OU.
- ◆ When deleting a GPO, selecting Remove the Link from List removes only the link to the GPO. Selecting Remove the Link and Delete the Group Policy object permanently removes the link and deletes the GPO from AD.

OBJECTIVES ON THE JOB

Because GPOs are stored in AD under the System\Policies container, it may be advantageous to link to existing GPOs rather than create new ones. This reduces the number of GPOs with duplicate settings. However, this can also create several problems. If a GPO is modified, all links to that GPO reflect that modification. For example, an administrator may modify a GPO that has been linked to by several OUs. The linked OUs receive this modification, which may result in inappropriate settings being applied to the OUs. Before modifying a GPO, determine whether any sites, domains, or OUs have been linked to it. Also, if a GPO is deleted, all links to the GPO are also removed. Again, first determine if any sites, domains, or OUs have been linked to the GPO before deleting it.

PRACTICE TEST QUESTIONS

MediaMart is an international firm specializing in marketing consulting. The company has offices in Dallas, Houston, and Denver, each employing between 400 and 800 people working in various departments, such as human resources, finance, and so on.

MediaMart is planning to use group policies to customize and enforce its users' environment. Furthermore, group policies will be used to deploy software to users and computers. The company's OU structure is location-based (Dallas, Houston, etc.) inside each.

1. You want to remove the My Network Places icon from the desktop of users in the Sales OU. You create a GPO for the Sales OU under the Denver OU. What is the best method for applying the GPO to all other Sales OUs in all other locations?
   a. Create duplicate GPOs on each Sales OU in every location OU.
   b. Link the existing GPO to each Sales OU.
   c. Copy and paste the GPO to each Sales OU.
   d. Link each Sales OU to the GPO's GUID in the System\Policies container.

2. You are the administrator of the Denver OU. Your users begin complaining that they are missing certain desktop icons. What is the most likely cause of the problem?
   a. Another administrator modified a GPO that was linked to the Denver OU.
   b. A new GPO was created on the Houston OU.
   c. Another GPO link was created.
   d. A site GPO was removed.

3. You wish to apply certain Internet Explorer settings to users in the Dallas OU. Where would you create the GPO link? (Choose all that apply.)
   a. The Dallas OU
   b. The Dallas site
   c. The Domain
   d. On each department in the Dallas OU

4. Which tool is used to link a GPO to a site?
   a. Active Directory Users and Computers
   b. The Group Policy snap-in
   c. Active Directory Domains and Trusts
   d. Active Directory Sites and Services

3.3   Delegate administrative control of group policy

DELEGATION WIZARD • PERMISSIONS • OU

UNDERSTANDING THE OBJECTIVE

Using a well-designed OU structure, administrators can delegate the permission to link to existing GPOs. This is useful if a local OU administrator who lacks domain administrative permissions wants to use an existing GPO and apply it to his or her OU. Additionally, the permission that allows a user to create and modify GPOs can be delegated to nonadministrators.

WHAT YOU REALLY NEED TO KNOW

◆ By default, only Domain Administrators, Enterprise Administrators, Group Policy Creator owners, and the operating system can create new GPOs.

◆ If Domain Administrators want nonadministrative users to create GPOs, they must add those users to the Group Policy Creator Owner security group using the Active Directory Users and Computers tool.

◆ By giving nonadministrative users read and write access to the gPLink and gPOptions properties on a particular site, domain, or OU, they can manage the GPOs linked to that site, domain, or OU.

◆ Use the Delegation Wizard to delegate control of GPOs to nonadministrative users.

OBJECTIVES ON THE JOB

A well-designed OU structure can assist administrators in delegating control over OUs to qualified, nonadministrative users. This is useful in situations in which a branch office, represented by an OU in AD, has one or more users responsible for the network at that office. Control can also be delegated at the site and domain level. You must be a member of the Enterprise Admins security group to delegate permissions at the site level.

PRACTICE TEST QUESTIONS

1. **What must be done to give nonadministrative users the ability to create GPOs?**
    a. Add the user to the Group Policy Creator Owner security group.
    b. Add the user to the Domain Admins security group.
    c. Add the user to the Enterprise Admins security group.
    d. Run the Delegation Wizard.

2. **What must be done to give nonadministrative users the ability to link GPOs to a particular OU?**
    a. Add the user to the Group Policy Creator Owner security group.
    b. Add the user to the Domain Admins security group.
    c. Add the user to the Enterprise Admins security group.
    d. Run the Delegation Wizard on that OU.

3. **By default, who has the ability to create GPOs and delegate permissions at the site level?**
    a. the Domain Admins security group
    b. the Enterprise Admins security group
    c. the local Administrator group
    d. the Domain and OU Admins security group

4. **By default, who has the ability to create GPOs and delegate permissions at the domain and OU level?**
    a. the Domain Admins security group
    b. the Enterprise Admins security group
    c. the local Administrator group
    d. the Domain and OU Admins security group

5. **Which permissions are required for a user to link a GPO to an OU? (Choose all that apply.)**
    a. Read and Write on gPLink
    b. Read and Write on GPOLink
    c. Read and Write on gPOptions
    d. Read and Link on gPLink

6. **How can you confirm the changes made to an OU by the Delegation Wizard?**
    a. View the advanced permissions on the OU.
    b. View Event Viewer's security log.
    c. View the standard permissions on the OU.
    d. View the Delegation Wizard permission log.

7. **Why delegate the permission to link a GPO to an OU? (Choose all that apply.)**
    a. Allows local, qualified, nonadministrators to link to policies
    b. Allows policies to be applied that are appropriate for the OU
    c. Allows users to apply the settings they need to their computers
    d. Removes the ability for local OU administrators to create GPOs, but leaves them the ability to link to them

3.4 Modify group policy inheritance

GROUP POLICIES • EVALUATION • CONFLICT RESOLUTION

UNDERSTANDING THE OBJECTIVE

Differing, and sometimes contradictory, group policies can be created and applied to the local computer, the site, the domain, and OUs. In such environments, it is important to understand how AD processes group policies and resolves any group policy conflicts.

WHAT YOU REALLY NEED TO KNOW

◆ When a computer starts up, the computer configuration settings from all group policies are applied in order.

◆ When a user logs on, the user configuration settings from all group policies are applied in order.

◆ The local group policy is processed first. Each Windows 2000 computer has one local group policy.

◆ Site-level group policies are processed next. If multiple group policies exist at the site level, they are processed from the bottom of the list to the top, with the top policy having the highest priority.

◆ Domain-level group policies are processed next. If multiple group policies exist at the domain level, they are processed from the bottom of the list to the top, with the top policy having the highest priority.

◆ OU-level group policies are processed last. If multiple group policies exist at the OU level, they are processed from the bottom of the list to the top, with the top policy having the highest priority.

◆ If multiple nested OUs exist and each OU has several group policies applied, the group policies on the OU closest to the user or computer object are processed last.

◆ By default, group policies are processed synchronously.

◆ OU administrators can enable the Block Policy Inheritance option and block all group policies from above.

OBJECTIVES ON THE JOB

If no group policy conflicts exist, the user's effective setting is a combination of all group policies. Setting a particular group policy to No Override prevents other group policies from overriding that group policy. It also overrides the Block Policy Inheritance option. For example, an OU administrator may enable the Block Policy Inheritance on a particular OU. However, a domain administrator may enable the No Override option on a group policy at the domain level. This nullifies the block at the OU level.

PRACTICE TEST QUESTIONS

1. **Which is the correct order in which group policies are inherited?**
   a. Site, domain, OU, local
   b. Domain, OU, local, site
   c. OU, domain, site, local
   d. Local, site, domain, OU

2. **Tim creates a group policy called Sales_Policy for the Sales OU that disables the Run command and hides the My Network Places icon. Chad creates a group policy for the domain called Domain_Policy that enables the Run command. What is the user's effective setting?**
   a. Run command is enabled; My Network Places is hidden.
   b. Run command is disabled; My Network Places is not hidden.
   c. Run command is enabled; My Network Places is not hidden.
   d. Run command is disabled; My Network Places is hidden.

3. **Tim creates a group policy called Sales_Policy for the Sales OU. Chad creates a group policy for the domain called Domain_Policy. Tim enables the Block Policy Inheritance option. Chad enables the No Override option. Which policy takes precedence?**
   a. Sales_Policy
   b. Domain_Policy

4. **Tim creates a group policy called Sales_Policy for the Sales OU. Chad creates a group policy for the domain called Domain_Policy. Joe creates a site policy called Denver_Policy. Tim enables the Block Policy Inheritance option. Chad enables the No Override option. Joe enables the No Override option. Which policy takes precedence?**
   a. Sales_Policy
   b. Domain_Policy
   c. Denver_Policy

5. **Tim creates a group policy called Sales_Policy for the Sales OU. Within the Sales OU, Mike creates a group policy for a child OU called SalesSupport_Policy. Chad creates a group policy for the domain called Domain_Policy. Which policy takes precedence?**
   a. Sales_Policy
   b. SalesSupport_Policy
   c. Domain_Policy

6. **Four group policies exist on the Sales OU in the order specified: Software_Policy, Restriction_Policy, Desktop_Policy, and Security_Policy. Software_Policy is listed first, followed by the others in order. Which is the last policy to be processed?**
   a. Software_Policy
   b. Restriction_Policy
   c. Desktop_Policy
   d. Security_Policy

3.5   Filter group policy settings by associating security groups to GPOs

SECURITY GROUPS • SELECTIVELY APPLY GROUP POLICIES

UNDERSTANDING THE OBJECTIVE

Applying group policies at the site, domain, or OU level can result in unintended consequences. If GPOs are not filtered, users and computers may be incorrectly affected by GPOs. This can result in inappropriate settings and restrictions being applied to users or computers.

WHAT YOU REALLY NEED TO KNOW

◆ A security group requires Read and Apply Group Policy permissions to receive a group policy's settings.

◆ By denying Read or Apply Group Policy permissions, a group policy is not applied to a security group's members, regardless of whether the members have permissions in other security groups.

◆ Group policies only affect user and computer objects in a particular site, domain, or OU.

◆ The location of the security group has no effect on filtering through that security group.

◆ Except for the Software Installation and Folder Redirection, filtering is based on the entire group policy, not on subsets of it.

◆ Filtering cannot be applied selectively to the user or computer portion of a group policy. It must be applied to the entire group policy.

OBJECTIVES ON THE JOB

Filtering group policies is useful when you want to control which users and computers receive a GPO. For example, you have an OU named Sales. Within the Sales OU reside sales users, tech support staff, and various computer objects. A GPO is applied to the Sales OU. Through filtering, you can selectively apply the GPO to all users in the OU except the sales users. This is accomplished by placing all the sales users in a security group and denying Read and Apply Group Policy permissions to the security group. You can filter the scope of a group policy using Active Directory Users and Computers, Active Directory Sites and Services, and the Group Policy snap-in.

PRACTICE TEST QUESTIONS

LAN Magic is an application service provider (ASP) specializing in desktop support. LAN Magic has offices in Calgary, Edmonton, Vancouver, and Toronto. They have an Active Directory domain named lanmagic.net.

Currently, LAN Magic creates separate OUs in the lanmagic.net domain for each client. Within each OU reside the user and computer objects of LAN Magic clients.

LAN Magic recently received a help desk contract from ABC Widgets Corp. LAN Magic has created a separate OU called ABC in the lanmagic.net domain for all ABC objects.

1. **Three hundred user objects, 300 computer objects, and 12 security groups are created in the ABC OU. A desktop restriction GPO has been applied to the ABC OU for the 12 payroll staff contained within. What is the best way to ensure that only the payroll staff receives the GPO?**
   a. Create one security group for all 300 user objects. Deny the Read and Apply Group Policy permissions to the security group.
   b. Create one security group for the 12 payroll staff. Allow the Read and Apply Group Policy permissions to the security group.
   c. Create several security groups. Deny the Read and Apply Group Policy permissions to the payroll security group.
   d. Create several security groups. Deny the Read and Apply Group Policy permissions to all the security groups except for the payroll group.

2. **What permissions are required to successfully apply a GPO? (Choose all that apply.)**
   a. Read
   b. Write
   c. Apply Group Policy
   d. Apply

3. **The Sales security group is located in the HR OU, but the members of the Sales group are located in the Sales OU. You apply a GPO to the Sales OU. What is the simplest way to ensure that all the Sales users receive the GPO settings?**
   a. Grant the Read and Apply Group Policy permissions to the Sales group.
   b. Create a new group called Sales2 in the Sales OU. Add all the Sales users into this group. Grant the Read and Apply Group Policy permissions to the Sales2 group.
   c. Move the Sales group to the Sales OU. Grant the Read and Apply Group Policy permissions to the Sales group.
   d. Grant the Read and Apply Group Policy permissions to the Sales OU.

3.6   Modify group policies

GROUP POLICIES • GPO • MODIFY

UNDERSTANDING THE OBJECTIVE

Over time, a GPO will likely have to be modified to meet the ever-changing needs of the organization. Knowing how to modify GPOs to bring about the desired result is an important skill.

WHAT YOU REALLY NEED TO KNOW

◆ Only members of the Enterprise Admins security group can modify site GPOs. Domain Admins and Enterprise Admins can modify domain and OU GPOs.

◆ By default, GPOs are edited on the domain controller holding the PDC Emulator operations master role. Modifications are replicated to all other domain controllers in the domain.

◆ Site GPOs are modified using Active Directory Sites and Services. Domain and OU GPOs are modified using Active Directory Users and Computers.

◆ You should carefully monitor the effect of the GPO after modifications are made to ensure that setting changes are applied.

◆ The total number of revisions and the date/time stamp of the last modification are tracked on each GPO. This is viewable under the General tab on a GPO.

◆ The Edit button allows you to modify a GPO. This button opens the Policy Editor.

◆ GPO modifications are applied to a user or computer every 90 minutes with a 30-minute variance, the next time a user logs on (for user setting changes) or a computer reboots (for computer setting changes), or when the SECEDIT/REFRESHPOLICY command-line utility is used.

OBJECTIVES ON THE JOB

As the needs and the structure of the organization change, so too will group policies. Consider making incremental changes over time rather than drastic changes, especially when those changes further restrict users' actions. Make users aware of changes being made via e-mail before implementing those changes. Users hate surprises. Also, consider adding a group policy with the new changes rather than modifying an existing one, just in case other administrators have linked to it. Then, filter the group policy via permissions so that only a select group of beta testers receive the changes. When the changes are fully tested, modify the permissions so that all users in a site, domain, or OU receive the new group policy.

PRACTICE TEST QUESTIONS

1. **An administrator wants to modify a site GPO. What tools can be used? (Choose all that apply.)**
   a. Active Directory Sites and Services
   b. Active Directory Domains and Trusts
   c. Active Directory Users and Computers
   d. The Group Policy snap-in

2. **How can a group policy be manually refreshed?**
   a. SECEDIT /REFRESHPOLICY
   b. SECEDITOR.exe
   c. NTDSUTIL.exe
   d. GPRESULT.exe

3. **How can the user settings of a group policy be manually refreshed?**
   a. SECEDIT /REFRESHPOLICY USER_POLICY
   b. SECEDITOR.exe refresh=userpolicy
   c. NTDSUTIL.exe
   d. GPRESULT.exe /Refreshpolicy User_Policy

4. **What options exist for each GPO setting? (Choose all that apply.)**
   a. Not configured
   b. Enabled
   c. Disabled
   d. Configured

5. **What is the easiest method to track modifications to a GPO?**
   a. ADSI
   b. VBScript
   c. System Policy Editor
   d. The General tab on each GPO

6. **By default, who can modify a site-level GPO?**
   a. Domain Admins
   b. Enterprise Admins
   c. Local Administrators
   d. Server Operators

7. **By default, who can modify a domain-level GPO? (Choose all that apply.)**
   a. Domain Admins
   b. Enterprise Admins
   c. Local Administrators
   d. Server Operators

3.7 Control user environments by using administrative templates

ADMINISTRATIVE TEMPLATES • COMPUTER CONFIGURATION • USER CONFIGURATION

UNDERSTANDING THE OBJECTIVE

Administrative templates are used within group policies to control and restrict users' desktops, including removing icons and desktop options. Within a group policy, the Computer Configuration area and the User Configuration area each have a set of three administrative templates. Microsoft provides three default administrative templates for each area: Conf.adm, Inetres.adm, and System.adm.

WHAT YOU REALLY NEED TO KNOW

- ◆ Making changes using the administrative templates under the Computer Configuration area of a group policy allows an administrator to control Windows components as well as system, network, and printer settings.

- ◆ Making changes using the administrative templates under the User Configuration area of a group policy allows an administrator to control Windows components as well as the start menu, taskbar, desktop, Control Panel, network, and system settings.

- ◆ Although the administrative template settings under Computer Configuration and User Configuration may appear similar, they actually contain complementary settings rather than duplicate settings.

- ◆ Most settings have three options: not configured, enabled, and disabled.

- ◆ Additional administrative templates can be created and imported into a group policy.

- ◆ Two Registry.pol files are created under %systemroot%\sysvol that apply the template settings to the local registry.

- ◆ Administrative template settings are applied to the local Registry under HKEY_LOCAL_MACHINE and HKEY_CURRENT_USER.

OBJECTIVES ON THE JOB

Administrative templates provide administrators with an immense amount of control over users' desktops. Everything from desktop restrictions to Internet Explorer settings can be configured using administrative templates. In addition to the three default .adm files, custom .adm files can be created and imported into group policies. For more information, search the Microsoft Windows 2000 Help Files for "Advanced topic: creating custom .adm files."

PRACTICE TEST QUESTIONS

LAN Magic is an application service provider (ASP) specializing in desktop support. LAN Magic has offices in Calgary, Edmonton, Vancouver, and Toronto. They have an Active Directory domain named lanmagic.net.

Currently, LAN Magic creates separate OUs in the lanmagic.net domain for each client. Within each OU reside the user and computer objects of LAN Magic clients.

LAN Magic is looking at administrative templates as a tool to control what changes a user can make to his or her desktop environment.

1. LAN Magic wants to remove the Run command from the desktop of everyone in the domain. However, the TechSupport OU must be exempt from this policy because they require the use of the Run command. Which steps must be completed to best accomplish this task? (Choose all that apply.)
   a. Create a GPO on the TechSupport OU. Under the User Configuration area, disable the administrative template setting "Remove Run Command from Start Menu."
   b. On the TechSupport OU, select Block Policy Inheritance.
   c. Create a GPO at the domain level. Under the User Configuration area, enable the administrative template setting "Remove Run Command from Start Menu."
   d. On the domain GPO, filter the GPO to not apply to the TechSupport OU.

2. Which of the following Windows components cannot be configured through administrative templates without a custom .adm file?
   a. NetMeeting
   b. Windows Explorer
   c. Windows Installer
   d. Outlook Express

3. Which of the following are default .adm files supplied by Microsoft? (Choose all that apply.)
   a. System.adm
   b. Configure.adm
   c. Inetres.adm
   d. Policy.adm

4. LAN Magic wants to control the behavior of the Windows Installer system for everyone in the domain. However, the TechSupport group must be exempt from this policy. Which steps must be completed to best accomplish this task? (Choose all that apply.)
   a. Create a GPO on the TechSupport group. Under the User Configuration area, enable the administrative template setting "Disable Rollback."
   b. On the TechSupport group, select Block Policy Inheritance.
   c. Create a GPO at the domain level. Under the User Configuration area, enable the administrative template setting "Disable Rollback."
   d. On the domain GPO, filter the GPO to not apply to the TechSupport group.

3.8   Configuring security using group policies

GROUP POLICIES • SECURITY SETTINGS • IPSEC

UNDERSTANDING THE OBJECTIVE

Through the use of group policies, security settings can be placed on computer and user objects. These settings can range from account policies and restricted groups to file system security and **IPSec** policies.

WHAT YOU REALLY NEED TO KNOW

◆ You can modify the following under the Computer Configuration\ Security Settings area of a group policy: account policies, local policies, event logs, restricted groups, system services, Registry, file systems, public key policies, and IPSec policies.

◆ You can modify public key policy security settings under the User Configuration area of a group policy.

◆ Account policy settings include password policy, account lockout policy, and Kerberos policy.

◆ An account policy can only be set at the domain level. The only exception is if you set an account policy on an OU, those settings apply to the local security settings on all workstations and servers in the OU. If differing account policies are required, multiple domains must be used.

◆ Local policy settings include audit policy, user rights assignment, and security options.

◆ Preconfigured security templates can be imported to provide additional or reduced security settings. You can create and modify security templates using the Security Templates snap-in.

◆ To analyze and configure local security, use the Security Configuration and Analysis snap-in.

◆ To apply security settings to a site, domain, or OU, use the Group Policy snap-in, Active Directory Users and Computers, or Active Directory Sites and Services.

OBJECTIVES ON THE JOB

A vast number of security settings exist that can be used to secure computers. For example, an organization can set a minimum character password policy, secure several Registry keys, disable the Computer Browser service, and define an IPSec policy. In addition, the following can be accomplished using security settings: setting a password policy, account lockout policy, Kerberos policy, or audit policy; assigning user rights, security options, or event log settings; restricting groups; enabling and disabling system services; securing Registry keys and file/folders with NTFS permissions; and defining public key and IPSec policies.

PRACTICE TEST QUESTIONS

1. **Which of the following can be accomplished using group policy security settings? (Choose all that apply.)**
   a. Deleting the Guest account
   b. Setting an audit policy
   c. Restricting the Log On Locally right
   d. Defining Data Recovery Agents

2. **Using the Group Policy snap-in and viewing the local computer policy, what is meant by the Effective Setting column?**
   a. The actual settings of the local policy
   b. The actual security settings after local, site, domain, and OU policies have been applied
   c. The actual settings of the domain policy
   d. The actual settings of the site policy

3. **Within the security settings of a group policy, what can be configured in the account policies area? (Choose all that apply.)**
   a. Password policy
   b. Account lockout policy
   c. Kerberos policy
   d. IPSec policy

4. **What tool(s) can be used to create preconfigured security templates? (Choose all that apply.)**
   a. Security Configuration and Analysis
   b. Security Templates
   c. SECEDIT.exe
   d. Group Policy snap-in

5. **Account policies can be applied to a(n) _____. (Choose all that apply.)**
   a. domain
   b. OU
   c. site
   d. container

6. **Local policies can be applied to _____. (Choose all that apply.)**
   a. Windows 2000 Domain Controllers
   b. Windows 2000 member servers
   c. Windows 2000 Professional workstations
   d. Windows NT 4.0 workstations

7. **In which Security Settings area would you grant a security group the ability to log on locally?**
   a. User Rights Assignment
   b. Security Options
   c. Registry
   d. Account Policy

3.9 Assign script policies to users and computers

GROUP POLICIES • LOGON, LOGOFF, STARTUP, AND SHUTDOWN SCRIPTS

UNDERSTANDING THE OBJECTIVE

Scripts allow administrators to perform tasks, such as mapping network drives, assigning printers, cleaning up temporary folders, and much more. Scripts can be DOS batch files, VBScript files, and JScript files, to name a few. Windows 2000 group policies allow for logon, logoff, startup, and shutdown scripts. Assigning these scripts to users or computers gives administrators a great deal of flexibility in configuring user environments and system settings.

WHAT YOU REALLY NEED TO KNOW

- ◆ Logon and logoff scripts can be assigned to users through group policies.
- ◆ Startup and shutdown scripts can be assigned to computers through group policies.
- ◆ Logon and logoff scripts are stored in %Systemroot%\Sysvol\Domainname\Policies\{Guid}\User\Scripts.
- ◆ Startup and shutdown scripts are stored in %Systemroot%\Sysvol\Domainname\ Policies\{Guid}\Machine\Scripts.
- ◆ Valid script extensions include .vbs, .js, .bat, .cmd, and .exe.
- ◆ The FRS replicates scripts to other Windows 2000 domain controllers in the same domain. If applicable, use the LBRIDGE.cmd utility to replicate these scripts to the NT 4.0 **BDC** acting as the export server.

OBJECTIVES ON THE JOB

A logon script can still be assigned to a user object. To do so, open the user object, select the Profile tab, and enter the script name in the Logon Script field. This is similar to the way logon scripts were assigned in a Windows NT 4.0 network. Legacy clients must still receive their logon script using this method. However, using group policies, we can assign startup, shutdown, logon, and logoff scripts to users and computers in a site, domain, or OU. Logon and logoff scripts are useful for configuring a user's environment, including assigning drive letter mappings. Startup and shutdown scripts are useful for cleanup of temporary folders and system configuration changes, to name a few. The scripts are stored under the Sysvol folder and replicated to all domain controllers in the domain. Remember to test your scripts prior to assigning them to users or computers.

PRACTICE TEST QUESTIONS

1. **What types of scripts can be assigned through group policies? (Choose all that apply.)**
   a. Startup
   b. Boot
   c. Shutdown
   d. Logon
   e. Reboot
   f. Logoff
   g. Software Installation

2. **What types of scripts can be assigned to a user? (Choose all that apply.)**
   a. Startup
   b. Logon
   c. Shutdown
   d. Logoff

3. **What types of scripts can be assigned to a computer? (Choose all that apply.)**
   a. Startup
   b. Logon
   c. Shutdown
   d. Logoff

4. **Which of the following are not valid script extensions? (Choose all that apply.)**
   a. .exe
   b. .dll
   c. .pl
   d. .cmd
   e. .vbs
   f. .js
   g. .bat
   h. .sys

5. **Where are user scripts stored on domain controllers?**
   a. %Systemroot%\Sysvol\Domainname\Policies\{Guid}\User\Scripts
   b. %Systemroot%\Sysvol\Domainname\Policies\{Guid}\Machine\Scripts
   c. %Systemroot%\Ntfrs\Domainname\Policies\{Guid}\User\Scripts
   d. %Systemroot%\Ntfrs\Domainname\Policies\{Guid}\Machine\Scripts

3.10 Deploy software by using group policy

GROUP POLICIES • DEPLOY SOFTWARE PACKAGES • MSI

UNDERSTANDING THE OBJECTIVE

One of the most powerful features of group policies is the ability to deploy software to users and computers in a site, domain, or OU. Software packages written using Microsoft Installer (.msi) technology can be assigned to users or computers, or published to users. Software deployed using group policies can also be upgraded or removed.

WHAT YOU REALLY NEED TO KNOW

◆ To deploy a software package, the package must have a Microsoft Installer (.msi) file. If the package does not come with an .msi file, a .zap file may be created and used.

◆ Another option is to repackage the software program into an .msi file using third-party products such as Veritas' WinINSTALL. A basic edition of this product is included on the Windows 2000 CD.

◆ Packages can be assigned to both users and computers, or they can be published to users only.

◆ When a package is assigned to a user, it is advertised under the Start | Programs menu the next time the user logs on. The advertised application follows the user regardless of where the user sits. The first time the application is selected or the file extension is invoked, the application is installed.

◆ When a package is assigned to a computer, it is installed when the computer restarts.

◆ A package that has been published to a user appears under Control Panel | Add/Remove Programs. The user must install the application from this location. The application may also be installed when the file extension of the application is invoked.

◆ Multiple Microsoft Transformation (.mst) files can be associated with a package to customize the package, such as providing a localized language version. This must be done at the time of assignment or publication of the package.

◆ Software packages can be filtered through users or security groups. Software packages are filtered independently from the group policy.

OBJECTIVES ON THE JOB

The new .msi file format offers several advantages over the traditional SETUP.exe installation file. These files, when assigned, are resilient; that is, if any of the components are removed or corrupted, the application replaces those components from the original deployment folder. It is important that the original shared folder used for the deployment remains available for the life of the application. If the shared folder is unavailable when an application attempts to repair itself, the user is prompted for the application CD. Another feature offered by .msi files is clean installation and clean removal. MSI-based applications, when removed, will remove all files, folders, and Registry settings relating to the application. Recently released Microsoft applications and many third-party vendors now ship .msi setup files with their applications.

PRACTICE TEST QUESTIONS

LAN Magic is an application service provider (ASP) specializing in desktop support. LAN Magic has offices in Calgary, Edmonton, Vancouver, and Toronto. They have an Active Directory domain named lanmagic.net.

Currently, LAN Magic creates separate OUs in the lanmagic.net domain for each client. Within each OU reside the user and computer objects of LAN Magic clients.

LAN Magic is considering the use of group policies to deploy software, namely Microsoft Office 2000, WinZip, and Adobe Acrobat Reader. There are currently 600 users in the ABC OU. These 600 users are broken into five security groups: Sales, Marketing, HR, MFG, and Administration.

1. LAN Magic wants to install Microsoft Office 2000 to the HR users. Furthermore, they want Office installed prior to the users logging on to their workstations. Given the above case information, what is the best option?
    a. Create a group policy on the ABC OU and publish the Microsoft Office 2000 package under User Configuration. Filter the package by granting the Read permission to the HR security group.
    b. Create a group policy on the domain and assign the Microsoft Office 2000 package under Computer Configuration. Filter the package by removing the Read permission for Authenticated Users and granting the Read permission to the HR security group.
    c. Create a group policy on the ABC OU and assign the Microsoft Office 2000 package under User Configuration. Filter the package by granting the Read permission to the HR security group.
    d. Create a group policy on the ABC OU and assign the Microsoft Office 2000 package under User Configuration. Filter the package by removing the Read permission for Authenticated Users and granting the Read permission to the HR security group.

2. LAN Magic wants to install WinZip and Adobe Acrobat Reader to the workstations of HR users. Given the above case information, what is the best option?
    a. Create a group policy on the ABC OU and assign WinZip and Adobe Acrobat Reader as two packages under Computer Configuration. Create a security group containing all Sales computers. Filter the package by removing the Read permission for Authenticated Users and granting the Read permission to the security group.
    b. Create a group policy on the ABC OU and assign WinZip and Adobe Acrobat Reader as one package under Computer Configuration. Create a security group containing all Sales computers. Filter the package by removing the Read permission for Authenticated Users and granting the Read permission to the security group.
    c. Create a group policy on the ABC OU and publish WinZip and Adobe Acrobat Reader as two packages under Computer Configuration. Create a security group containing all Sales computers. Filter the package by removing the Read permission for Authenticated Users and granting the Read permission to the security group.

3.11 Maintain software by using group policy

GROUP POLICIES • DEPLOY SERVICE PACKS, UPGRADES • REMOVE SOFTWARE

UNDERSTANDING THE OBJECTIVE

Software maintenance can be accomplished using group policies. Specifically, software initially deployed using group policies can be upgraded, repaired, and removed. Administrators can specify whether packages must be upgraded, or whether upgrades are optional. Furthermore, packages initially installed using group policies can be optionally or forcibly removed.

WHAT YOU REALLY NEED TO KNOW

- ◆ An upgrade or hot fix can only be deployed using group policies if an .msi file is supplied.
- ◆ Another alternative is to apply an .msp (Microsoft Patch) file to the shared distribution folder. This updates the distribution files. The package can then be marked for redeployment through a group policy.
- ◆ An upgrade can only upgrade packages that were previously deployed using group policies.
- ◆ Upgrades can either be optional or required.
- ◆ To deploy upgrades, remove the original package first or directly upgrade over the original package.
- ◆ Group policies can remove packages only if the package was initially deployed using group policies.
- ◆ Packages can be immediately removed, or you can allow current users to continue using the software and prevent new installations.
- ◆ Upgrades can be published or assigned.

OBJECTIVES ON THE JOB

Software maintenance is an ongoing task in any network environment. Vendors routinely release service packs, hot fixes, upgrades, and patches. Applying these to already-deployed software packages can largely be accomplished using group policies.

PRACTICE TEST QUESTIONS

1. **What kind of upgrade packages can be deployed using group policies?**
   a. .msi packages
   b. .msp packages
   c. .vbs packages
   d. .exe packages

2. **After a distribution folder has been upgraded with an .msp file, what must be done next?**
   a. The package must be marked for redeployment.
   b. The package must be marked for removal.
   c. The .msp file must be assigned or published.
   d. The .msp file must be deployed as an upgrade.

3. **You publish a package to upgrade another application on users' computers. However, under the Upgrade tab, you fail to see the old application to be upgraded. What is the likely cause?**
   a. The .msi files cannot upgrade 16-bit applications.
   b. You cannot publish an upgrade.
   c. The application was deployed using a .zap extension.
   d. The application was not deployed using group policies.

4. **After an upgrade using a group policy, users complain that the application fails to run and returns numerous error messages. What is the most likely cause?**
   a. The upgrade was built using a repackaging tool.
   b. The upgrade was not meant to overwrite the existing package, but to replace it.
   c. The package did not install with elevated permissions.
   d. The application was deployed using a .zap extension.

5. **You attempt to create a group policy to remove WordPad, but it fails. What is the most likely cause of the problem?**
   a. WordPad does not adhere to the MSI standard.
   b. WordPad was deployed using a .zap file.
   c. WordPad was not deployed using group policies.
   d. You do not have sufficient permissions to remove WordPad.

6. **You modify a group policy to remove a package that was installed via a group policy six months ago. Afterward, you notice that users still have access to the application and are continuing to use it. What is the most likely cause of this? (Choose all that apply.)**
   a. The users reinstalled the application from a shared folder.
   b. The group policy conflicted with another group policy.
   c. The option to remove the package immediately was not selected.
   d. The users cancelled the uninstallation when the group policy was applied.

3.12 Configure deployment options

DEPLOYMENT OPTIONS • SOFTWARE PACKAGES

UNDERSTANDING THE OBJECTIVE

In addition to publishing or assigning a package, numerous other software deployment options can be configured. These options include categorizing software packages, associating file extensions, and setting the user interface options.

WHAT YOU REALLY NEED TO KNOW

◆ Under the Deployment tab, the options available include:

- *Auto-install this application by file extension activation*—A published application can be installed when the user opens a file with the appropriate extension. This is also known as document invocation.

- *Uninstall this application when it falls out of the scope of management*—If the group policy that initially deploys an application no longer applies (because the policy is removed, a user object is moved, or a computer object is moved), the application is uninstalled.

- *Do not display this package in the Add/Remove Programs Control Panel*—After an application has been installed (via assignment or publishing), it is not shown in the list of installed applications under Add/Remove Programs. This can prevent accidental removal of the application by the user.

- *Remove previous installs of this product for users, if the product was not initially installed by Group Policy-based Software Installation*—Can assist in removing previous copies of the application. (It is found by pressing the Advanced button under the Deployment tab.)

◆ Under the Modifications tab is a list of transformations that will be applied to the application. A transformation consists of an .mst file. Consult the vendor's documentation on how to create an .mst file. To create an .mst file for Microsoft Office 2000, consult the Microsoft Office 2000 Resource Kit.

◆ Under the Categories tab, you can add the application to one or more categories.

OBJECTIVES ON THE JOB

One of the most interesting deployment options is known as document invocation. By associating an extension with a published application, the application installs if a user attempts to open a file with that extension. If you deploy multiple applications with the same extension, you may define a precedence order.

PRACTICE TEST QUESTIONS

1. **You want to prevent Microsoft Word from automatically installing itself if the user opens a file with a .doc extension. What should you do?**
   a. Disable the *Auto-install this application by file extension activation* option.
   b. Disable the *Document invocation* option.
   c. Remove the extension from under the File Extensions tab under Software Installation Properties.
   d. Change the application precedence order by moving Microsoft Word to the top of the list.

2. **You removed a group policy that deployed Microsoft Project 2000 to the Sales OU. Users can no longer access Microsoft Project 2000. What is the most likely cause of the problem?**
   a. Removing the group policy disabled Project 2000.
   b. Removing the group policy removed the permission for users to run Project 2000.
   c. Removing the group policy hid Project 2000 from users.
   d. The option to *Uninstall this application when it falls out of the scope of management* was selected.

3. **Users are complaining that when they open a .jpg file, a third-party photo-editing application installs. Microsoft Photo Paint is supposed to install when users open a .jpg file. You check the group policy and notice that both applications have been properly published. What can you do to prevent this problem?**
   a. Assign the third-party application.
   b. Change the application precedence order.
   c. Assign Microsoft Photo Paint.
   d. Remove the third-party application deployment package.

4. **Users are complaining that too many programs are being published under Control Panel, Add/Remove Programs and that scrolling down the list is taking too long. What can you do to remedy the situation?**
   a. Split up the applications, assigning some and publishing others.
   b. Create and assign the applications to categories.
   c. Incrementally publish the applications over a period of months.
   d. Filter the applications using security groups.

5. **Users are frequently uninstalling applications deployed using group policies. How can you easily prevent this from happening?**
   a. Deny the Write security permission on the deployment package.
   b. Remove the users from the Power Users local group on each workstation.
   c. Enable the *Do not display this package in Add/Remove Programs* option on each package.
   d. Assign the application to the computer instead of the user.

3.13 Troubleshoot common problems that occur during software deployment

TROUBLESHOOT • PERMISSIONS • ANSWER FILES

UNDERSTANDING THE OBJECTIVE

Developing your knowledge surrounding common software deployment problems can assist you in troubleshooting those problems when they occur. Problems can vary from users not receiving the correct software package(s) to the applications themselves not operating properly. Understanding the software installation process is key to effective troubleshooting.

WHAT YOU REALLY NEED TO KNOW

- ◆ You can only deploy packages that contain an .msi or .zap software installation file. If you deploy a package that contains only a Setup.exe installation file, it will fail.

- ◆ Be aware of the physical location of the distribution server. Avoid installing packages across WAN links. If WAN links are an issue, try deploying to a site and selecting a local distribution server.

- ◆ If a deployment fails, check to see that the users have Read permission on the distribution share.

- ◆ If the share is located on an NTFS volume, ensure that users have Read permission to the folder and its contents.

- ◆ Check the group policy to verify that the users have Read permission on the software installation package itself.

- ◆ If a package fails to appear under Start | Programs, check to see if the package has been assigned but not published.

- ◆ If a package does not deploy, ensure that the user or computer object is located in the correct OU and that the group policy has been applied to that OU.

OBJECTIVES ON THE JOB

Many of the problems arising from software installation fall under the umbrella of permissions. Check the permissions of the shared folder containing the distribution files. Check that the user has the appropriate NTFS permissions within that share. Also check that the user has at least Read permission on the package itself within the group policy. Another frequent source of installation errors is when an answer file used for unattended software installations contains errors or omissions. This can cause the package installation to fail midway through deployment. Check the syntax of the answer file to ensure it is correct.

PRACTICE TEST QUESTIONS

LAN Magic is an application service provider (ASP) specializing in desktop support. LAN Magic has offices in Calgary, Edmonton, Vancouver, and Toronto. They have an Active Directory domain named lanmagic.net.

LAN Magic is currently using group policies to deploy software, namely Microsoft Office 2000, WinZip, and Adobe Acrobat Reader.

1. LAN Magic administrators create a shared folder called Office2000 and leave the default share permissions on the shared folder. A group policy is created that publishes the Office 2000 application. In order to prevent all users from receiving the application, the Allow Read permission is removed from the Authenticated Users group on the software package permissions inside the group policy. The package fails to deploy. How would you fix this problem?
   a. Grant the Authenticated Users group the Allow Read permission to the software installation package.
   b. Grant the Accounting security group the Allow Read permission to the software installation package.
   c. Grant the Accounting security group Read permission to the Office2000 shared folder.
   d. Grant the Accounting security group Full Control permission to the Office2000 shared folder.

2. LAN Magic administrators create a shared folder called Office2000 and leave the default share permissions on the shared folder. The share resides on an NTFS volume. The Everyone group has been denied Read NTFS permission to the folder and its contents. The Accounting group has been granted Read NTFS permission to the folder and its contents. The package fails to deploy. How would you fix this problem? (Choose all that apply.)
   a. Remove the Everyone group from the access control list of the folder and its contents.
   b. Grant the Accounting group Full Control permission to the folder and its contents.
   c. Remove the Deny Read permission for the Everyone group.
   d. Grant the Accounting security group Full Control permission to the Office2000 shared folder.

3. WinZip is deployed to the Sales OU. Brian's computer object is in the Sales OU. Brian's user object is in the Accounting OU. Brian fails to receive the package. What is the cause?
   a. The package was assigned to the user.
   b. The package was published to the computer.
   c. Brian's computer was turned off when the package was deployed.
   d. The package was assigned to the computer.

3.14 Manage network configuration by using group policy

**GROUP POLICIES • NETWORK CONFIGURATION SETTINGS •
SLOW LINK • OFFLINE FILES**

UNDERSTANDING THE OBJECTIVE

Group policies can be used to manage client network configuration settings. Administrators can configure offline files, network and dial-up connections, and how group policies are applied over slow network connections, all within group policies. Settings can be configured under both the Computer Configuration node and User Configuration node of a group policy.

WHAT YOU REALLY NEED TO KNOW

- ◆ Under Computer Configuration\Administrative Templates\Network, administrators can control the behavior of offline files and network and dial-up connections.

- ◆ Offline file settings include: enable offline files, synchronize offline files before logging off, default cache size, event logging level, and many more.

- ◆ Network and dial-up connection settings include: allow configuration of connection sharing.

- ◆ Under Computer Configuration\Administrative Templates\System\Group Policy, you can enable group policy slow-link detection. This allows administrators to limit what portions of a group policy are applied when a slow-link is detected (e.g., < 500 **Kbps**).

- ◆ Using slow-link detection, software installation policy processing can be canceled when a slow link is detected to prevent installations from occurring over WAN connections.

- ◆ Under User Configuration\Administrative Templates\Network, administrators can also control the behavior of offline files and network and dial-up connections.

- ◆ Group policy slow-link detection can also be enabled through User Configuration\Administrative Templates\System\Group Policy.

OBJECTIVES ON THE JOB

The group policy slow-link detection feature can be enabled to detect a slow link. You can specify the connection speed in Kbps to define a slow link. This is useful for detecting when clients are authenticating to Active Directory over a **PPP** or VPN connection. Administrators can then configure portions of the group policy not to apply when a slow link is detected. For example, by enabling the Computer Configuration\Administrative Templates\System\Group Policy\Software installation policy processing option, you can prevent software installations from occurring over a PPP or VPN connection. Numerous other network settings can be enabled or disabled through group policies. Under User Configuration\Administrative Templates\Network\Network and Dial-up Settings, administrators can restrict what TCP/IP and **RAS** configuration changes users are allowed to make.

PRACTICE TEST QUESTIONS

LAN Magic is an application service provider (ASP) specializing in network support. LAN Magic has offices in Seattle, Denver, New York, and Tucson. They have an Active Directory domain named lanmagic.net.

LAN Magic is currently using group policies to deploy software, namely Microsoft Office 2000, WinZip, and Adobe Acrobat Reader. Group policies are also being used to enforce desktop environments and network configurations.

1. Currently, LAN Magic users dial into the corporate network or connect via a VPN. Dial-up users are limited to 56 Kbps connections to the corporate network, whereas VPN users can connect at speeds up to 1.544 Mbps. Users have begun to complain that Microsoft Office 2000 attempts to install whenever they connect via dial-up or VPN. What is the best solution to prevent this problem?

   a. Set the firewall packet filters to block TCP and UDP ports 1024–5000.
   b. Assign the group policy to computers rather than to users within the OU.
   c. Filter the software installation of the group policy to exclude users who dial into the corporate network or connect via a VPN.
   d. Set the group policy slow-link detection feature to detect links slower than 2 Mbps. Enable the software installation policy processing option and configure it to prevent software deployments when a slow link is detected.

2. Offline files have been implemented throughout LAN Magic. Recently, network performance has been suffering and users are complaining. Specifically, users are complaining that logon and logoff performance is poor. What two options can be configured to alleviate this problem?

   a. Disable the *Synchronize all offline files before logging off* option.
   b. Decrease the default cache size.
   c. Disable the offline files feature.
   d. Enable the *Files not cached* feature.

3. After running a protocol/traffic analyzer, you notice that much of the network traffic is from the refreshing of group policies. What can be done to mitigate this problem? (Choose all that apply.)

   a. Enable the *Apply Group Policy for computers asynchronously during startup* option.
   b. Enable the *Apply Group Policy for users asynchronously during logon* option.
   c. Enable the *Disable background refresh of Group Policy* option.
   d. Adjust the *Group Policy refresh interval for computers* option.

4. Where can administrators restrict RAS and TCP/IP settings?

   a. User Configuration\Administrative Templates\Network
   b. Computer Configuration\Administrative Templates\Network\Network and Dial-up Settings
   c. Computer Configuration\Administrative Templates\Network
   d. User Configuration\Administrative Templates\Network\Network and Dial-up Settings

OBJECTIVES

3.15 Deploy Windows 2000 by using RIS

RIS • NETWORK-BASED INSTALLATIONS • BOOTABLE NETWORK CARDS

UNDERSTANDING THE OBJECTIVE

Deploying Windows 2000 Professional across the network usually requires a computer with a networked, bootable operating system in order to connect to a distribution server. Using **RIS**, this is no longer necessary. By utilizing **NICs** with the Pre-Boot Execution chipset (**PXE**), a computer void of any operating system can boot directly from the NIC and connect to the distribution server.

WHAT YOU REALLY NEED TO KNOW

◆ RIS clients require a NIC that is PXE version .99c or later.

◆ RIS clients do not require an operating system or partitions. RIS replaces any existing partitions with one partition and installs Windows 2000 Professional.

◆ To install the RIS, DNS, DHCP, and AD must be installed on the network.

◆ The RIS can be installed on any Windows 2000 Server, Advanced Server, or Datacenter Server computer through Control Panel | Add/Remove Programs | Add/Remove Windows Components.

◆ After the RIS has been installed, it must be configured using the RISETUP.exe utility. The utility also copies the i386 folder from the Windows 2000 Professional CD to an NTFS volume on the RIS server.

◆ Before use, a RIS server must be authorized in AD. This can be accomplished using the DHCP snap-in.

◆ Enabling the *Respond to client computers requesting service* option allows the RIS server to respond to RIS clients.

OBJECTIVES ON THE JOB

Several options can be configured on a RIS server using the Active Directory Users and Computers tool. After clicking the *Respond to client computers requesting service* option, you can specify *Do not respond to unknown client computers.* This forces the RIS server to respond only to clients presenting a valid GUID for a computer object in AD. After clicking the Advanced button, administrators can specify a naming convention for RIS clients as well as a location where the RIS client's computer object appears in AD. RIS installations can be automated through the use of an answer file. RIS answer files can be created using SETUPMGR.exe and usually end with a .sif extension. Answer files can then be associated with existing images on the RIS server. Placing appropriate NTFS permissions on the answer files prevents users from accessing unauthorized images.

PRACTICE TEST QUESTIONS

1. **Which of the following are prerequisites to installing RIS? (Choose all that apply.)**
   a. AD
   b. WINS
   c. DNS
   d. DHCP

2. **What utility is initially used to configure the RIS?**
   a. DCPROMO.exe
   b. NTDSUTIL.exe
   c. RISETUP.exe
   d. RIPREP.exe
   e. RBFG.exe

3. **Which of the following are prerequisites for the RIS server? (Choose all that apply.)**
   a. Windows 2000 Server, Advanced Server, or Datacenter Server
   b. NTFS volume with 2 GB of free space
   c. 800 x 600 resolution
   d. 256 MB of RAM

4. **You have met all the prerequisites and installed the RIS server. However, the service fails to start. What is the most likely cause of the failure?**
   a. AD is offline.
   b. DNS is not functioning.
   c. DHCP scope is disabled.
   d. The RIS server is not authorized in AD.

5. **Which tool is used to authorize a RIS server in AD?**
   a. Active Directory Users and Computers
   b. DHCP snap-in
   c. RIS snap-in
   d. DNS snap-in

6. **Which of the following methods can be used to create a RIS answer file? (Choose all that apply.)**
   a. Notepad
   b. WordPad
   c. Active Directory Users and Computers
   d. SETUPMGR.exe

7. **How can a RIS image be secured to prevent unauthorized users from installing it?**
   a. Apply the appropriate NTFS permissions to the answer file.
   b. Apply the appropriate permissions to the computer object in AD.
   c. Filter which users and groups can utilize RIS using the Active Directory Users and Computers tool.
   d. Filter which users and groups can utilize RIS using the RIS snap-in.

3.16 Install an image on a RIS client computer

RIS IMAGE INSTALLATION • CLIENT COMPUTER

UNDERSTANDING THE OBJECTIVE

After a RIS server has been properly configured with the appropriate images and set to respond to clients, a RIS client can initiate a RIS installation. RIS clients are computers with PXE-compliant network cards that can connect to a RIS server and download a Windows 2000 Professional image. Installing Windows 2000 Professional via RIS is another option to using third-party imaging products such as Ghost. The primary benefit of RIS is that the user can initiate and complete the RIS installation process without a visit from technical support personnel.

WHAT YOU REALLY NEED TO KNOW

- ◆ It is important to ensure that the PXE-compliant network card is set as a bootable device in the computer's BIOS. One way to notice this is if the user does not receive a prompt (for example, press any key, or F12) to boot off of the network when the computer starts, it is likely that the network card is not set as a boot device.

- ◆ DHCP issues the RIS client IP addressing information.

- ◆ When the RIS client queries DNS for the RIS server, the RIS client connects to the RIS server and is presented with a logon screen. It is imperative for the user to log on with his or her appropriate domain credentials so that the RIS server can authenticate the user to AD.

- ◆ The menu options presented to the user are configurable through group policies.

- ◆ You can specify which RIS server answers a particular RIS client by matching the GUID of the RIS client to a RIS server. This can be set in the client's AD computer object.

- ◆ After the image begins to download, all information on the RIS client is lost. A RIS answer file (.sif) supplies the answers necessary for the installation to proceed unattended. Customized .sif files can be created using SETUPMGR.exe and associated with a RIS image.

OBJECTIVES ON THE JOB

Using group policies, administrators can give users different RIS menu options. The automatic setup option allows the user to run a completely automated installation of Windows 2000 Professional. The custom setup option lets the user override the automatic computer name assignment and default computer account location. The restart setup option allows a user to restart a failed RIS installation. The tools menu allows administrators to post tools on a RIS server (for example, to flash a computer's **BIOS**) that other authorized users may use. Certain non-PXE-compliant network cards can use RIS, provided that a RIS boot disk is created. Use the RBFG.exe utility to create the RIS boot disk. Be warned: Only a select number of non-PXE-compliant network cards are supported.

PRACTICE TEST QUESTIONS

LAN Magic is an application service provider (ASP) specializing in network support. LAN Magic has offices in Seattle, Denver, New York, and Tucson. They have an Active Directory domain named lanmagic.net.

LAN Magic has decided to use RIS as a method of deploying Windows 2000 Professional. LAN Magic has 800 Pentium II client computers with 3Com network cards.

1. Clients are complaining that they are not receiving a prompt to boot off of the network when the computer starts. What could be the problem? (Choose all that apply.)
   a. The network cards are non-PXE-compliant.
   b. The network cards are not enabled as a boot device in the computer's BIOS.
   c. The RIS server is set not to respond to unknown clients.
   d. The network card was unable to contact a DHCP server.

2. You notice that 100 of the computers have PXE .99a. What should you do first?
   a. Upgrade the network cards to PXE .99b.
   b. Run RBFG.exe.
   c. Upgrade the network cards to PXE .99c.
   d. Flash the PXE ROM.

3. You notice that newly installed RIS clients have their computer object name show up in Active Directory based on the user name of the person who initiated the installation. How would you remedy this?
   a. Rename the computer object.
   b. Configure the RIS server to generate a custom computer name.
   c. Configure the RIS server to create the computer object outside of the computer's container in Active Directory.
   d. Configure a group policy to allow custom setups.

4. You create a RIS boot disk using RBFG.exe. However, the computer continues to fail to connect to the RIS server. What is the most likely problem?
   a. The network card is not supported through RBFG.exe.
   b. The network card has a PXE version prior to version .99c.
   c. The DHCP server is down.
   d. The DNS server is down.

5. What is one way a client can determine the GUID of its network card?
   a. Call the vendor.
   b. View the DHCP lease in the DHCP scope.
   c. Connect to a RIS server.
   d. Boot into the computer's BIOS.

3.17 Configure remote installation options

GROUP POLICIES • AUTOMATIC SETUP • CUSTOM SETUP • RESTART SETUP • TOOLS

UNDERSTANDING THE OBJECTIVE

After a user logs on to a RIS server, the user can be presented with up to four menu options: automatic setup, custom setup, restart setup, and tools. These options are configured using group policies.

WHAT YOU REALLY NEED TO KNOW

♦ Automatic setup allows the user to run a completely automated installation of Windows 2000 Professional. Windows 2000 Professional installs using the naming convention and computer account location predetermined by the RIS server. The user has no opportunity to view or change the installation defaults.

♦ The custom setup option allows the user to override the automatic computer name assignment and default computer account location. By default, these are predetermined by the RIS server. However, the user has no opportunity to view or change any of the other setup information.

♦ The restart setup option allows the user to restart a failed RIS installation without having to re-enter the previously supplied information.

♦ The tools option allows the user to select one or more of the listed third-party tools. These tools may perform tasks such as flashing the computer's BIOS. These tools must be installed on the RIS server in order to be available.

♦ Three settings exist for each of the four options: Allow, Deny, and Don't Care. Allow makes the option available. Deny removes the option. Don't Care has no effect; instead, the setting is inherited from the site, domain, or OU. By default, only automatic setup is enabled.

OBJECTIVES ON THE JOB

By configuring RIS options through group policies, administrators have the flexibility to give different users and groups different RIS choices. For example, a group policy on the Help Desk OU sets all four options to Allow. This gives help desk personnel the ability to override RIS settings, restart a RIS installation, or use any of the tools.

PRACTICE TEST QUESTIONS

1. **Which RIS menu options can be configured using group policies? (Choose all that apply.)**
   a. Custom setup
   b. Default setup
   c. Debug setup
   d. Automatic setup
   e. Tools
   f. Maintenance
   g. Restart setup
   h. Unattended setup

2. **What does the custom setup option allow a user to do? (Choose all that apply.)**
   a. Specify a different location for the Windows 2000 Professional installation files.
   b. Create a new answer file.
   c. Override the .sif file defaults.
   d. Change the computer's name.
   e. Change the computer account location.
   f. Supply custom TCP/IP information to the automated setup.

3. **Which of the following are valid settings for each of the four options? (Choose all that apply.)**
   a. Deny
   b. Inherit
   c. Override
   d. Allow
   e. Block
   f. Don't Care
   g. Ignore

4. **What is the purpose of the Don't Care setting?**
   a. The RIS client can decide whether to use it.
   b. The client's Active Directory security is not taken into account.
   c. The setting is not configured, but can be configured through other group policies.
   d. The setting is configured on each RIS server individually but not in Active Directory.

5. **What purpose does the tools option serve?**
   a. Allows software vendors to write tools specific to RIS
   b. Allows access to the RIS administration tools
   c. Allows access to the Active Directory administration tools
   d. Allows access to the command-line tools

3.18 Troubleshoot RIS problems

PRESTAGING • DHCP • DNS • UNDERSTANDING HOW RIS WORKS

UNDERSTANDING THE OBJECTIVE

Although RIS is not a very complex service to configure, it does require numerous services to be enabled and properly configured. Understanding the RIS process is key to effectively troubleshooting RIS problems.

WHAT YOU REALLY NEED TO KNOW

◆ If RIS problems occur, it is important to verify the following:

- Ensure that the version of PXE is .99c or later. To determine the network card's PXE version, attempt to boot from the network card. The version of the PXE ROM appears on the screen.

- Ensure that DHCP is installed, configured, and authorized. If the DHCP server is on another subnet, ensure that DHCP packets can reach the DHCP server.

- Ensure that DNS is configured and enabled.

- Ensure that Active Directory is functioning correctly and that the RIS service has been installed, configured, and authorized.

- Check that the RIS has the *Respond to client computers requesting service* option enabled. Clear the D*o not respond to unknown client computers* option, unless the client computer has been prestaged.

◆ If prestaging client computers, it is important to verify the following:

- Confirm that the GUID is correct and that "-" and "{}" are included in the correct locations. Confirm the GUID on the client computer. Most new PCs allow you to view the GUID through the computer's BIOS.

- If you have prestaged a client but the client continues to get service from another RIS server, wait for Active Directory replication to complete. This may take up to 15 minutes within a site.

◆ By default, Remote Installation Services uses the Welcome.osc file to manage the client installation image choices. For multiple language installation image options, you need to replace the default Welcome.osc file with the Multilng.osc file.

OBJECTIVES ON THE JOB

The Windows 2000 Event Viewer on the RIS server may also yield clues as to why a RIS client is failing to connect to a RIS server. Specifically, check for warning or error messages relating to the **BINL**, DHCP, DNS, or AD services. Also, try stopping and starting the various services under Start | Program | Administrative Tools | Services.

PRACTICE TEST QUESTIONS

1. **You determine that RIS clients cannot connect to a RIS server because they cannot contact a DHCP server. You determine that the DHCP server is located on a remote subnet. Which two solutions best remedy this problem?**
   a. Install a DHCP relay agent on the local subnet.
   b. Configure a DHCP server on the local subnet.
   c. Configure the local router to forward BOOTP packets.
   d. Move the RIS client to the subnet where the DHCP server is located.

2. **You want to modify the language installation choices. What must be done?**
   a. Replace Welcome.ocx with Multilng.ocx.
   b. Install the RIS on a computer running Windows 2000 Server—Multilanguage Edition.
   c. Select which languages to display using the RIS language option.
   d. Replace Welcome.osc with Multilng.osc.

3. **What is the best method of quickly locating RIS error messages in Event Viewer?**
   a. Create a filter that searches for BINL in the description field.
   b. Create a filter that searches for BINL in the description field of error and warning messages.
   c. Create a filter that searches for RIS in the description field.
   d. Create a filter that searches for RIS in the description field of error and warning messages.

4. **You suspect that you have incorrectly prestaged a RIS client. You want to confirm the client's GUID. What is the quickest method?**
   a. Open the computer, remove the network card, and look on the PXE ROM label.
   b. Boot the computer and simulate a RIS installation.
   c. Boot into the computer's BIOS.
   d. Call the vendor.

5. **You determine that you have correctly entered the client's GUID, yet the client cannot contact a RIS server. Other non-prestaged clients are also experiencing the same problem. What is the most likely cause of the problem?**
   a. The RIS server is down.
   b. The DHCP server is down.
   c. The DNS server is down.
   d. The *Respond to client computers requesting service* option has not been enabled.

6. **You determine that you have correctly entered the client's GUID, yet another RIS server services the client. What is the cause?**
   a. AD has not yet replicated the client's GUID to all domain controllers.
   b. The client entered incorrect authentication credentials using RIS.
   c. The client manually selected another RIS server.
   d. The initial RIS server is offline.

3.19 Manage CD-based images for performing remote installations

CD-BASED IMAGES • RIS • RISTNDRD.SIF

UNDERSTANDING THE OBJECTIVE

All RIS servers require a CD-based image. Multiple answer files may use the same CD-based image.

WHAT YOU REALLY NEED TO KNOW

◆ RIS *only* installs Windows 2000 Professional, *not* Server, NT 4.0, or any other operating system.

◆ RIS and the image(s) it installs must be located on a separate volume from the operating system, which is formatted as NTFS and has enough free space for RIS and the image(s) it places there (typically, 2 GB or more of free space).

◆ The default answer file created for you by RIS is called Ristndrd.sif.

◆ Ristndrd.sif can be modified to meet your needs by manually editing it or using Setup Manager, as with any other unattended installation file.

◆ *Danger: In the [RemoteInstall] section, if the repartition parameter is not specified or is set to "Yes," all partitions on the client computer are deleted and replaced with a single, new NTFS partition. If it is set to "No," the parameters in the answer file are used instead.*

◆ Multiple answer files are associated with a CD-based image by using Active Directory Users and Computers.

◆ By default, all of the answer files that are associated with the CD-based image are available to everyone; to restrict them to those you want to have access, give the Read & Execute NTFS permissions to those who should be able to use the image and remove them from everyone else. Applying these permissions to groups is a great way to make sure that those in sales get the image appropriate for their situation and hardware configuration, and not engineering's.

◆ If you have technicians who install the majority of the machines for the users, consider giving the technicians NTFS permissions to all of the answer files and still giving permissions to the appropriate groups, in the event a technician is not available.

◆ The NTFS permissions approach works because the client must log on after they press F12 to start the Client Installation Wizard.

◆ It deploys only the operating system, although to any supported HAL.

OBJECTIVES ON THE JOB

If there are many kinds of computers on a network, a CD-based image makes sense, as it is essentially an unattended installation, allowing any kind of supported computer to be installed. It is not the fastest installation method, but it is the one that offers the broadest support for different kinds of computers on the network.

PRACTICE TEST QUESTIONS

1. **Which of the following NTFS permissions is needed in order to use an answer file?**
   a. Full Control
   b. Modify
   c. Read & Execute
   d. Read
   e. Write

2. **A CD-based image is the fastest way to deploy Windows 2000 Professional to 100 similarly configured computers.**
   a. True
   b. False

3. **The tool used to configure a RIS server is _____.**
   a. RIS Configuration
   b. RBFG.exe
   c. Computer Management
   d. Active Directory Sites and Services
   e. Active Directory Users and Computers

4. **If the RemoteInstall section is not placed in an answer file used by RIS, it _____.**
   a. repartitions the drive and formats it NTFS
   b. repartitions the drive and formats it FAT32
   c. reformats the system partition NTFS
   d. reformats the boot partition NTFS
   e. installs on the existing partition using the existing file system

5. **Using RIS, which operating systems can be deployed?**
   a. Windows 95/98
   b. Windows NT 4.0 Workstation
   c. Windows NT 4.0 Server
   d. Windows 2000 Professional
   e. Windows 2000 Server
   f. Windows 2000 Advanced Server

6. **The default answer file created by RIS is called _____.**
   a. Unattend.txt
   b. Unattend.sif
   c. Ris.sif
   d. Ristndrd.txt
   e. Ristndrd.sif
   f. Default.txt
   g. Default.sif

7. **By default, answer files can only be accessed by _____.**
   a. administrators
   b. power users
   c. technicians
   d. everyone

3.20 Manage RIPrep images for performing remote installations

RIPREP IMAGES • RIS • SOURCE COMPUTER • DEFAULT USER PROFILE • REMOTE INSTALLATION PREPARATION WIZARD

UNDERSTANDING THE OBJECTIVE

RIPrep images are "ready-to-run" images. They can contain not only the operating system, but also applications, and they are very useful when you need to deploy software with the operating system (and don't want to do so later with group policies) when all of your systems are similar.

WHAT YOU REALLY NEED TO KNOW

◆ RIPrep images allow both Windows 2000 Professional and software to be deployed at the same time.

◆ RIPrep images copy only the files and registry keys that are necessary (in the source image and added by devices added by **PnP**).

◆ RIPrep images configure the source computer (the one from which the image is made) exactly as desired (though you may skip the installation of software if it will later be done by GPOs).

◆ *Only one partition will be imaged*, so install everything (operating system and applications) on one partition.

◆ Typically, the computer is installed and configured by an administrator, so only the administrator has the correct profile settings.

◆ You must use the Remote Installation Preparation Wizard to create RIPrep images; you can't use any other program to create this special image type.

◆ A RIPrep image can't be created until a CD-based image is created on the RIS server.

◆ The Remote Installation Preparation Wizard removes all computer-specific information from the image (such as **SIDs**, the computer name, and so on) and creates an answer file for the image.

◆ To run the RIPrep image, execute the following command on the source computer: \\RIS_Server\reminst\admin\i386\riprep.exe. If you want the image on multiple machines, you must either run the wizard again for each machine or manually copy the image to each RIS server.

OBJECTIVES ON THE JOB

If all of your computers are similar, consider deploying Windows 2000 using RIPrep images, as the installation is faster and uses less bandwidth. Consider using this solution if you need to deploy software with the OS, but remember that if the software is deployed this way, it cannot be managed by group policies later on.

PRACTICE TEST QUESTIONS

Betty, the network administrator for a network of libraries, is concerned with the logistics of getting new machines quickly installed and ready for public use as they are obtained. Each computer needs Windows 2000 installed to make it secure, as well as some proprietary software for library use. Each member library has a server with RIS installed. All libraries belong to the same domain.

1. The proprietary library applications need to be deployed as simply as possible, but can't be installed by Windows Installer. They need to be deployed with the operating system to make this process as simple as possible. How can Betty do this?
   a. She can use a CD-based image.
   b. She can use a RIPrep-based image.
   c. She can do an unattended installation.
   d. This is not possible.

2. Most of the libraries only have 10 Mb Ethernet, and patrons need to be able to access resources as well. Betty is concerned about bandwidth utilization, and she doesn't have the staff to install each new computer, Windows 2000, and all of the applications manually. Which solution is best for Betty, given these limitations?
   a. She can use a CD-based image.
   b. She can use a RIPrep-based image.
   c. She can do an unattended installation.
   d. She can use group policies.

3. How can an image with the required setup be created? (List the steps in order.)
   a. Copy the Administrator's user profile to the Default User Profile.
   b. Install the necessary applications.
   c. Run the Remote Installation Preparation Wizard.
   d. Install Windows 2000.
   e. Grant the Everyone group permission to use the profile.

4. What is the file name of the Remote Installation Preparation Wizard?
   a. RipWiz.exe
   b. Sysprep.exe
   c. Riprep.exe
   d. Ripw.exe
   e. Riprepw.exe

3.21 Configure RIS security

AVOID LICENSING VIOLATIONS AND INAPPROPRIATE INSTALLATIONS

UNDERSTANDING THE OBJECTIVE

If anyone could simply boot their computer and install a copy of Windows 2000 Professional, companies could face licensing issues. Security is an integral part of RIS necessary to avoid inappropriate Windows 2000 Professional deployments.

WHAT YOU REALLY NEED TO KNOW

◆ Once installed, the RIS server must be authorized in Active Directory in order for the RIS to start. Similar to authorizing a DHCP server, the DHCP snap-in is used to authorize RIS servers. If the RIS server is also a DHCP server, this step is not required.

◆ By default, users cannot join computers to a domain. In order for RIS to be successful, administrators should delegate this permission to the users and groups that utilize RIS. Use the Delegation Wizard to delegate the permission Join a Computer to a Domain.

◆ Check that the RIS has the *Respond to client computers requesting service* option enabled. Check the *Do not respond to unknown client computers* option to prestage client computers.

◆ Using group policies, configure the four menu choices: automatic setup, custom setup, restart setup, and tools. Filter the group policy by users and groups to ensure that only authorized users have access to the menu options.

◆ To ensure that only selected users access a particular RIS image, secure the .sif file using NTFS permissions. The .sif files are stored under the RemoteInstall\Setup\English\Images\Win2000.pro\i386\templates directory. (Note: Never remove the administrator permissions on .sif files. This prevents the RIS from accessing the files.)

OBJECTIVES ON THE JOB

RIS is a powerful tool used to assist companies in deploying Windows 2000 Professional. However, users may purposely or inadvertently abuse the service by deploying unauthorized images to the computers. In a worst-case scenario, a corporate user brings a computer from home to the office and installs an unauthorized copy of Windows 2000 Professional. By utilizing the methods previously noted, this problem can be prevented. You can also view a list of clients who have installed RIS images through Active Directory Users and Computers.

PRACTICE TEST QUESTIONS

1. **How can an administrator view a list of installed RIS clients?**
   a. Active Directory Users and Computers, RIS Server Properties, Remote Install tab, Show Clients
   b. SMS 2.0
   c. The RIS MMC snap-in
   d. Not supported

2. **What permission must be delegated to users for RIS to work?**
   a. Create a Computer Object
   b. Join a Computer to a Domain
   c. Start a RIS Session
   d. Connect to a RIS Server

3. **What must be done before a RIS can successfully start?**
   a. Active Directory must be installed.
   b. DNS must be installed.
   c. DHCP must be installed.
   d. The RIS must be authorized in Active Directory.

4. **How can users be prevented from downloading the wrong RIS image?**
   a. Not supported
   b. NTFS permissions on the Unattend.txt files
   c. NTFS permissions on the .sif files
   d. NTFS permissions on the .inf files

5. **How can a RIS server be configured to respond to only select RIS clients?**
   a. Authorization in Active Directory
   b. GUID-to-computer mapping
   c. IP-to-computer mapping
   d. GUID prestaging

6. **Where are .sif files stored?**
   a. RemoteInstall\Setup\English\Images\Win2000.pro\i386\templates
   b. RemoteInstall\Setup\English\Win2000.pro\i386\templates
   c. RemoteInstall\Setup\Images\Win2000.pro\i386\templates
   d. RemoteInstall\Setup\English\Images\Win2000.pro\i386\

7. **Which of the following menu choices should be disabled for most users using group policies? (Choose all that apply.)**
   a. Custom
   b. Tools
   c. Manual
   d. Automatic

3.22 Authorize a RIS server

RIS REQUIREMENTS • DHCP CONSOLE • ACTIVE DIRECTORY • DNS

UNDERSTANDING THE OBJECTIVE

Authorization of the RIS server means that it can process incoming client requests (after it is configured to do so). Authorizing the RIS server entails several important requirements worthy of review.

WHAT YOU REALLY NEED TO KNOW

◆ The requirements to use RIS fall into three categories: network, server, and client.

◆ The network requirements are: a DHCP server, a DNS server, and Active Directory.

◆ The server requirements are: a minimum of 2 GB of hard drive space for the CD-based image, RIS, any RIPrep images desired, and it should be located on an NTFS partition or volume that is neither the system nor the boot partitions (or volumes). For best performance, this partition or volume should be on a separate hard drive or RAID array.

◆ The client requirements are: hardware sufficient for the installation of Windows 2000 Professional and network boot capability, including a Pre-Boot Execution Environment PXE boot ROM, version .99c or higher. If the PXE requirement and/or network boot requirement can't be met, a floppy disk created by the remote boot floppy generator (RBFG.exe) with a compatible network card may be used instead.

◆ Only Enterprise Administrators can authorize a RIS server (just like the requirement to authorize a DHCP server).

◆ The users who perform the installations must have the ability to create a computer account in Active Directory. By default, each user can create 10 user accounts.

◆ If more than 10 computer accounts are needed (for example, for technicians), use the Delegation of Authority Wizard to delegate the creation of computer objects to that user or group.

OBJECTIVES ON THE JOB

Until the RIS server is authorized in Active Directory, it will be of no use to anyone on the network. Be sure to properly install and configure RIS and authorize it in Active Directory before trying to use it.

PRACTICE TEST QUESTIONS

1. **To authorize a RIS server in Active Directory, use the _____ MMC console.**
    a. Active Directory Users and Computers
    b. Active Directory Sites and Services
    c. Active Directory Domains and Trusts
    d. DHCP
    e. DNS

2. **The network requirements to implement RIS include which of the following? (Choose all that apply.)**
    a. DHCP
    b. RRAS
    c. AD
    d. NTFS volumes
    e. DNS

3. **The server requirements to implement RIS include which of the following? (Choose all that apply.)**
    a. 1 GB of free disk space
    b. 2 GB of free disk space
    c. 4 GB of free disk space
    d. NTFS partition/volume
    e. FAT/FAT32 partition/volume
    f. Same partition as the operating system
    g. Separate partition from the operating system

4. **The client requirements to implement RIS include which of the following? (Choose all that apply.)**
    a. Hardware on the HCL
    b. Hardware capable of running Windows 2000 Server
    c. Hardware capable of running Windows 2000 Professional
    d. A floppy disk drive
    e. PXE boot ROM .98b or higher
    f. PXE boot ROM .99c or higher

5. **Which group can authorize a RIS server in Active Directory?**
    a. Domain Administrators
    b. Enterprise Administrators
    c. Schema Administrators
    d. Power Users
    e. RIS Administrators
    f. DHCP Administrators
    g. DNS Administrators

6. **How many computer objects can a user create without granting permissions?**
    a. Zero
    b. One
    c. Five
    d. 10
    e. 25
    f. No limit

3.23 Prestage RIS client computers for added security and load balancing

GUID • MAC ADDRESS

UNDERSTANDING THE OBJECTIVE

RIS clients can be prestaged to specify which RIS server services a given client and to prevent unauthorized computers from being installed with RIS.

WHAT YOU REALLY NEED TO KNOW

◆ If a computer is assigned a specific RIS server, only that RIS server delivers an image to that client. If another RIS server gets the request, it forwards it to the appropriate RIS server.

◆ If the RIS server is set to "Do not respond to unknown clients," then only the clients that are prestaged with it get images; all others are ignored. If all RIS servers are configured in this manner, only the approved clients can get images from RIS.

◆ To prestage a client, you need to know its GUID, if it is booting from the NIC or its **MAC** address, or if it is booting from a RIS startup disk.

◆ The PXE specification requires that each NIC have a GUID; generally, this information can be obtained from the computer's BIOS or on a label either inside or outside the case.

◆ If the computer is installed from a RIS startup disk, the MAC address is used, with enough leading zeroes to make it a 32-character number. For Ethernet, this means 20 leading zeroes. This provides the GUID that prestaging requires.

OBJECTIVES ON THE JOB

Although this idea offers benefits in theory, it requires quite a bit of work to actually implement. The requirement that you must know (or discover) the GUID or MAC address of each of the clients you want to install can be very time consuming. Consider placing a RIS server and a DHCP server on each subnet and not passing DHCP packets through your routers to ensure that only local RIS servers service local RIS clients. The DHCP servers could be reduced in number and more centrally located after the deployment, if necessary.

PRACTICE TEST QUESTIONS

Vickie, the network administrator of a chain of home decorating stores, is concerned that a RIS server in one store may supply the image for a computer in another store, causing the computer to be installed over the WAN. She wants to prevent this from happening under all circumstances, and has enlisted your help to make sure the deployment goes smoothly and to answer her questions.

1. **How can you guarantee that all clients will be installed from a local RIS server and not across the WAN?**
   a. Configure RIS to reply only to local clients.
   b. Prestage all of the clients.
   c. Place a DHCP server on each subnet.
   d. Disconnect the WAN while the clients are being installed.

2. **What information must Vickie have to implement the method described in Question 1? Many of the machines are capable of booting directly from the network and will be installed in that manner.**
   a. Each computer's MAC address
   b. Each computer's asset tag
   c. Each computer's GUID
   d. Each computer's IP address

3. **For the machines that can't boot directly from the network and will be installed using a floppy disk, what must be known to implement the method described in Question 1?**
   a. Each computer's MAC address
   b. Each computer's asset tag
   c. Each computer's GUID
   d. Each computer's IP address

4. **What tool is used to prestage the computer accounts with that information, assuming it has already been gathered?**
   a. Computer Management
   b. RIS Manager
   c. Active Directory Sites and Services
   d. Active Directory Users and Computers
   e. Active Directory Domains and Trusts

5. **What should be done if the computer's GUID cannot be found?**
   a. Type "IPCONFIG/ALL" at a command prompt.
   b. Begin the Client Installation Wizard.
   c. Call the computer's manufacturer.
   d. Call Microsoft for technical support.
   e. Choose "Find" in Active Directory Users and Computers to have it gather a list of all of the GUIDs on the network.

Section 4

Managing, Monitoring, and Optimizing the Components of Active Directory

OBJECTIVES

4.1 Move Active Directory objects

ACTIVE DIRECTORY USERS AND COMPUTERS • ADMT

UNDERSTANDING THE OBJECTIVE

All AD objects exist in a single location at any given time. For example, if a user moves from one physical location to another, the user's associated user object may also need to be moved. This is so appropriate group policies are applied, appropriate users have delegated authority over the user, and so on. Any AD object can be moved as needed within a domain. If an object needs to be moved between domains, then other tools such as **ADMT**, ClonePrincipal, and MoveTree must be used.

WHAT YOU REALLY NEED TO KNOW

◆ To move an object within a domain, use Active Directory Users and Computers. The simplest way to move users and groups between domains is with ADMT, which can be downloaded free from Microsoft. It allows you to move security principals between domains, both within the same forest (intra-forest) and between forests (inter-forest), as well as from Windows NT 4.0-based domains to Windows 2000 domains.

◆ Any use of ADMT requires that the target domain be in native mode.

◆ ADMT can copy users and groups between forests and move users, groups, and computers between domains within a forest.

◆ ADMT can perform trial migrations, in which errors are checked but nothing is actually copied or moved.

◆ ClonePrincipal is a series of VB scripts for copying users from one domain to another domain in a different forest. They usually need to be edited for the specific environment in which they will be used.

◆ NetDom is a command-line utility that establishes and maintains trusts (both one-way and two-way), as well as adds and removes computer accounts and moves computer accounts between domains.

◆ MoveTree is a command-line utility that moves objects within a forest.

OBJECTIVES ON THE JOB

Users, computers, groups, and many other objects often need to be relocated as their physical locations change, business units are reorganized, and so on. AD is designed to be flexible, as business needs change. The primary tool for accomplishing these moves within a domain is Active Directory Users and Computers. Moving security principals between domains is more complicated, as new SIDs are created whenever a new security principal is created in a domain. To preserve all of the permissions that the object previously had, a new attribute called SIDHistory tracks the old SIDs that the object had when it was moved between domains. In all cases, every object (security principal or not) has a GUID assigned when it is created. This GUID never changes until the object is deleted, when the GUID is retired.

PRACTICE TEST QUESTIONS

1. **Which tools are used to move objects within a domain?**
   - a. Active Directory Users and Computers
   - b. ADMT
   - c. ClonePrincipal
   - d. Netdom
   - e. MoveTree

2. **Which tools are used to move objects between domains within a forest? (Choose all that apply.)**
   - a. Active Directory Users and Computers
   - b. ADMT
   - c. ClonePrincipal
   - d. Netdom
   - e. MoveTree

3. **Which tools are used to move objects from one domain to another in a different forest? (Choose all that apply.)**
   - a. Active Directory Users and Computers
   - b. ADMT
   - c. ClonePrincipal
   - d. Netdom
   - e. MoveTree

4. **A security principal is _____.**
   - a. a user
   - b. a group
   - c. a computer
   - d. any object

5. **A GUID is used for _____.**
   - a. all objects without SIDs
   - b. all objects with SIDs
   - c. all objects, whether or not they have SIDs

6. **A SID is generated when _____. (Choose all that apply.)**
   - a. a user is created in a domain
   - b. any group is created in a domain
   - c. an OU is created in a domain
   - d. a user is moved between domains
   - e. a computer account is created in a domain
   - f. a contact is created

4.2 Publish resources in Active Directory

ACTIVE DIRECTORY USERS AND COMPUTERS • SHARED FOLDER • PRINTER • APPLICATION • GROUP POLICY

UNDERSTANDING THE OBJECTIVE

When a resource is published in AD, the object can be located more easily. The mechanism varies depending on the type of object you are looking for, but the goal is the same: to make finding resources easier for users. Shared folder and printer objects are two of the more popular types of objects to locate, but applications can also be published in AD. It is important to understand how to get the resource in AD.

WHAT YOU REALLY NEED TO KNOW

- ◆ Resources to be published should be relatively static, so that there is less replication traffic.
- ◆ Published resources allow administrators and users to locate resources, even if the physical locations of those resources change.
- ◆ Printers are automatically published in AD if they are shared on a Windows 2000-based computer that is part of a domain. Likewise, they are automatically removed if the printers are no longer shared.
- ◆ Printer locations can be created to allow users to find printers physically located near them or in any other location they desire. This requires two or more IP subnets (and the corresponding AD subnet objects), a subnet object for each site, a location value specified for each subnet object and a matching value for each printer, and location tracking, which is enabled in group policies.
- ◆ A printer or a shared folder can be created in Active Directory Users and Computers for a printer or share that exists on any Microsoft-based OS that supports sharing (such as Win 9x, NT, and 2000), as long as the UNC path is known. Printers may also be published using the PUBPRN.vbs script.
- ◆ Applications (and their associated extensions) can be published in AD, allowing applications to be located and installed from a nearby server.

OBJECTIVES ON THE JOB

One of the biggest wastes of user time is attempting to locate resources when there are many servers, shares, and printers available. The goal of any directory service, including AD, is to make locating resources faster, easier, and more intuitive. As an administrator, knowing how to publish resources for your users results in greater user productivity and fewer calls to the help desk.

PRACTICE TEST QUESTIONS

The administrator of the North American region of Acme Inc. wants to make locating resources easier for her users. She has found that users are printing multiple copies of the same document on several different printers all over the network, because they can't find printers near them. She also frequently gets calls from users asking for help finding files and has realized that sending a technician to the desk of each user who needs software installed is time-consuming, expensive, and maintenance-intensive. She has considered installing all of the possible software applications that people use on all of the network computers, but has found that to be cost-prohibitive.

1. **What has to be done so that users can locate the printers physically near them?**
   a. Enable location tracking.
   b. Enable location tracking and create and configure subnet and printer objects.
   c. Enable location tracking and create and configure site and printer objects.
   d. Enable location tracking and create and configure site, subnet, and printer objects.

2. **What is a good strategy for helping users find rarely accessed files?**
   a. Publish applications in AD.
   b. Create a shared folder object and then enter a description and keywords to make searching for it easier.
   c. Create a shared file object and then enter a description and keywords to make searching for it easier.
   d. Map drives to all of the resources the user ever needs, and then search for files and folders (including the mapped drives) to locate the desired resource.

3. **What is a good method of distributing software applications only to those users who need them, without sending a technician to each user's computer?**
   a. Publish applications via a group policy at the appropriate site, domain, or OU level.
   b. Publish applications via shared folder objects, and then control share and NTFS permissions.
   c. This is not possible in Windows 2000.

4.3   Locate objects in Active Directory

MY NETWORK PLACES • SEARCH FOR PRINTERS • ADD/REMOVE PROGRAMS

UNDERSTANDING THE OBJECTIVE

The information stored in AD is of no value unless it can be searched and the desired resource located. It is important to focus on how to locate the resources that users need. Many possible methods exist for finding information on users, contacts, shares, and printers; you must also focus on knowing what results are produced by each method.

WHAT YOU REALLY NEED TO KNOW

◆ If printer locations have been properly configured, the location defaults to your location (based on your computer's IP address), and then you can search for nearby printers.

◆ Use Add/Remove Programs, which is located in the Control Panel, to view applications published to you (the user).

◆ Applications can be installed with no user intervention when you try to open a file that contains an extension that is unknown locally, but for which an application that can open the file has been properly published in AD using group policies. This is called "installation by document invocation" or "document activation."

OBJECTIVES ON THE JOB

To take advantage of AD's features that make it easier to locate resources, the appropriate objects must exist. However, users must know how to search through those objects for the things they need, or the feature is useless. This objective is primarily focused on two groups: help desk personnel and end users. As a member of the help desk, it is important to have the knowledge and ability to teach users how to access these resources. This results in fewer calls for help in finding files and printers or installing software. As an end user, the ability to find resources without help is empowering and a great productivity enhancer.

PRACTICE TEST QUESTIONS

1. **What methods can a user employ to find and install a desired printer? (Choose all that apply.)**
   a. Ask the help desk for the print server name and the printer's share name, and then enter it in the Add Printer Wizard.
   b. Using the Add Printer Wizard, choose "Find a printer in the Directory" when you choose to install a network printer.
   c. To search for a printer, use Start, Search, For Printers, then right-click the printer of your choice, and choose Install.
   d. To search for a printer, use Start, Search, For Printers, then right-click the printer of your choice, and choose Connect.
   e. Browse for it in My Network Places; when it is found, right-click it and choose Install.

2. **What ways are there to easily locate resources in Windows 2000? (Choose all that apply.)**
   a. Open My Network Places, choose Entire Network, Directory, right-click on any domain, and choose Find. Choose the type of object you are looking for (often the Shared Folders object), and then choose to look in the directory (instead of the domain you selected).
   b. Map network drives to all of the shares that a user will ever need, search for them using Start, Search, For Files or Folders, and then look in My Computer.
   c. Open Active Directory Users and Computers, right-click on the object you would like to search in, and then choose Find. In the Find box, select the type of object you wish to locate and where to look.

3. **How can users employ the tools included with Windows 2000 to help with software deployment and maintenance? (Choose all that apply.)**
   a. Group policies can deploy and maintain software. Users can install applications using Add/Remove Programs located in the Control Panel.
   b. When users open a file of unknown type, the associated application automatically installs by document activation.
   c. RIS can be used to deploy images of software applications.

4.4   Create and manage accounts manually or by scripting

LDIFDE • CSVDE • ACTIVE DIRECTORY USERS AND COMPUTERS • ADSI

UNDERSTANDING THE OBJECTIVE

In a small network, creating accounts individually is not a large task. However, as the number of users grows, or in environments in which multiple platforms are in use, it is useful to understand an efficient method of creating large numbers of objects from existing data.

WHAT YOU REALLY NEED TO KNOW

◆ **ADSI** is a set of interfaces used to access various directories.

◆ ADSI uses LDAP to access AD.

◆ VBScript, Java, Visual Basic, C, and C++, among others, may be used with ADSI to automate the creation, modification, and removal of AD objects. Knowledge of scripting in VBScript or Java is required.

◆ **LDIFDE** and **CSVDE** are tools used for creating multiple objects from a text file in a process called "bulk import." Both are command-line tools.

◆ CSVDE uses data in text format with fields separated by commas to create new accounts. It can only create them, not remove or change them.

◆ LDIFDE uses text data in **LDIF** to create, modify, and remove objects in AD. LDIF is a draft standard for a common file format for importing and exporting data between directories that support LDAP.

◆ Active Directory Users and Computers is the primary tool provided with Windows 2000 to create, manage, modify, and remove most objects in AD.

◆ Active Directory Users and Computers allows you to manipulate the following object types: users, groups, published printers, published shared folders, computers, and contacts. It is a **GUI**-based tool.

OBJECTIVES ON THE JOB

When creating large numbers of users from data that exists in other systems (including potentially proprietary systems, which are often in use by HR departments), the data to script the creation of those users becomes paramount to the success of AD. This capability is also very important in test labs, in which many users must exist for capacity planning, performance analysis, and so on. In small, simple environments, Active Directory Users and Computers will probably be the primary tool used to manage most of the objects in AD.

PRACTICE TEST QUESTIONS

The IT manager of a movie studio wants to investigate the possibility of using Windows 2000 to allow access to resources by producers, directors, actors, and others who are often on location throughout the world. Currently, the studio doesn't have a coordinated company-wide network, but instead has several departmental LANs and ad-hoc networks that are created and removed while filming is taking place on location. For payroll purposes, the Accounting and HR departments share a proprietary database of all employees and contractors, which is capable of importing and exporting data in ASCII format. They also have an LDAP-compliant e-mail system.

1. Is there a way to leverage the existing database of employees and contractors maintained by HR, without programming to create new users? If so, what program can be used?
   - a. Yes, LDIFDE can be used.
   - b. Yes, CSVDE can be used.
   - c. Yes, ADSI can be used.
   - d. No, Active Directory Users and Computers can be used, but all data must be entered manually.

2. Is there a way to leverage the existing e-mail application to create new users and groups, and if so, what program can be used?
   - a. Yes, LDIFDE can be used.
   - b. Yes, CSVDE can be used.
   - c. Yes, ADSI can be used.
   - d. No, Active Directory Users and Computers can be used, but all data must be entered manually.

3. Is there a way to manipulate the data in the database or e-mail program programmatically and import the data into AD, and if so how? (Choose all that apply.)
   - a. Yes, LDIFDE can be used.
   - b. Yes, CSVDE can be used.
   - c. Yes, ADSI can be used in conjunction with VBScript.
   - d. Yes, ADSI can be used in conjunction with C.
   - e. No, Active Directory Users and Computers can be used, but all data must be entered manually.

4. After objects exist in AD, what is the simplest way to change passwords, move objects, and update current address and phone number information?
   - a. LDIFDE
   - b. CSVDE
   - c. ADSI
   - d. Active Directory Users and Computers

4.5   Control access to Active Directory objects

DACL • ACE • PERMISSIONS • INHERITANCE • BLOCKING INHERITANCE

UNDERSTANDING THE OBJECTIVE

Just as there are permissions in the NTFS that control access to files and folders, and permissions that control access to printers, so there are permissions that control access to AD objects. Although many of the terms are the same for file, folder, printer, and AD object access, it is critical to understand that file, folder, and printer permissions are completely separate from AD permissions.

WHAT YOU REALLY NEED TO KNOW

◆ Permissions relate to the ability to access an object and, optionally, the attributes within the object.

◆ Permissions are stored in the **DACL** for each object. The DACL is made up of individual **ACE**s, meaning that a specific security principal is granted or denied a specific permission or set of permissions.

◆ Permissions can be inherited from parent objects, as with the file system, and flow down the hierarchy until blocked.

◆ Unchecking the check box "Allow inheritable permissions from parent to propagate to this object" blocks permissions. At this point, the permissions set on that object flow down until similarly blocked. When permissions are blocked, the existing permissions may be copied as a starting point for the new permissions assignment, or all permissions may be removed and a fresh set assigned.

◆ The top of the permissions inheritance hierarchy is the domain.

◆ Once set, inherited permissions can't be changed unless all of the permissions flowing into the object are blocked. However, specific permissions can be denied that had been allowed higher in the hierarchy, and as deny permissions win over allow permissions, the effect is that specific permissions are denied. Both permissions (allow and deny) continue to flow down until blocked.

◆ A security principal's permissions to an AD object (such as a printer) do not necessarily correspond to that security principal's permissions on the resource the AD object represents, such as the shared printer.

◆ To view permissions in Active Directory Users and Computers, you must choose View, and then Advanced Features.

OBJECTIVES ON THE JOB

Access to objects of any type is critical to the functioning of an enterprise. However, if permissions are too broad, security can be compromised, leading to the intentional or accidental loss of data. Security should be approached with the big picture in mind, not relying on any one specific set of permissions to lock down the network.

PRACTICE TEST QUESTIONS

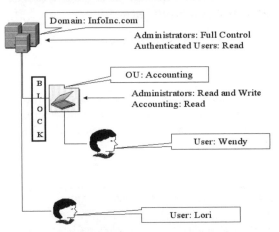

Use the figure displayed here to answer the questions below. Note that permissions have been blocked at Accounting, with the only permissions being those listed. Sandy is a member of the Administrators group and David belongs to the Accounting group.

1. **What permission(s) does David have to Wendy?**
   a. Read
   b. Read and Write
   c. Full Control
   d. not enough information

2. **What permission(s) does David have to Lori?**
   a. Read
   b. Read and Write
   c. Full Control
   d. Not enough information

3. **What permission(s) does David have to Accounting?**
   a. Read
   b. Read and Write
   c. Full Control
   d. Not enough information

4. **What permission(s) does Sandy have to Wendy?**
   a. Read
   b. Read and Write
   c. Full Control
   d. Not enough information

5. **What permission(s) does Sandy have to Lori?**
   a. Read
   b. Read and Write
   c. Full Control
   d. Not enough information

4.6   Delegate administrative control of objects in Active Directory

DELEGATION OF CONTROL WIZARD • TASKS • TASKPADS

UNDERSTANDING THE OBJECTIVE

One of the major improvements that AD offers over Windows NT 4.0 Directory is the ability to control permissions on a more granular level. With this finer level of control, the ability to control who can do what to which objects becomes far more important and time consuming. The Delegation of Control Wizard makes this task much simpler.

WHAT YOU REALLY NEED TO KNOW

- ◆ The Delegation of Control Wizard can be run at the domain or OU levels, but not at the user, group, printer, or other noncontainer, or leaf, level.

- ◆ Administrative control can be delegated at the leaf object level by manually controlling the permissions that one object has to another object. However, the permissions must be set and maintained on each object with this approach, and there are many permissions that must be set correctly, increasing the possibility of errors.

- ◆ All delegated permissions, at any level, should be properly documented so that security can be analyzed and maintained.

- ◆ Tasks that can be delegated to other security principals depend on the level at which you are delegating (domain vs. OU), and include common activities, such as adding, modifying, and deleting users and groups, changing users' passwords, and joining a computer to a domain.

- ◆ If the predefined tasks don't meet a specific need, custom tasks can be created. To specify a custom task, specify the object type(s) that will be affected (or all existing and new objects in the container) and then specify the permission(s) that you want to delegate. Permissions are split into three categories: general permissions that apply to all objects, permissions that apply to only certain types of objects, and permissions that are necessary to create and/or delete specific types of objects.

- ◆ Delegated permissions generally follow the same inheritance rules as any other permission assignment.

- ◆ Custom MMC Consoles and Taskpads can be created and distributed to make it easier to provide the tools necessary for those with delegated authority.

OBJECTIVES ON THE JOB

In a small environment, there is little, if any, delegation of control to anyone. As the size of the network grows, however, the ability to delegate limited administrative control over specified objects to others plays a larger role and becomes more important in maximizing the usefulness of AD while minimizing the costs associated with maintaining it.

PRACTICE TEST QUESTIONS

1. **Permissions should generally be delegated at the _____ level to ease administration.**
    a. site
    b. domain
    c. OU
    d. leaf object

2. **The simplest way to assign some of your administrative authority to others is:**
    a. Delegation of Power Wizard
    b. Delegation of Control Wizard
    c. Delegation of Authority Wizard
    d. Setting individual permissions on the desired objects

3. **The wizard that allows you to delegate administrative authority to others can be run at which levels? (Choose all that apply.)**
    a. Site
    b. Domain
    c. OU
    d. Leaf object

4. **The tool used to access the wizard allowing you to delegate some administrative power to others is accessed through which of the following tools?**
    a. Active Directory Users and Computers
    b. Active Directory Domains and Trusts
    c. Active Directory Sites and Services
    d. Computer Management
    e. There is no default tool for this; a custom MMC must be created.

5. **Taskpads and MMCs can be created to _____.**
    a. provide easier access to the tools necessary for those with delegated authority to perform the tasks they have been given
    b. allow administrators access to the wizard to delegate authority
    c. allow users to search AD, as all of the searching capabilities only exist inside MMCs
    d. manage inherited permissions

6. **Only predefined tasks can be delegated to others; an administrator must do all other tasks.**
    a. True
    b. False

4.7   Monitor domain controller performance

PERFORMANCE CONSOLE • NTDS OBJECT

UNDERSTANDING THE OBJECTIVE

Monitoring domain controller and Active Directory performance is similar to monitoring the performance of any other Windows 2000-based system. There are a few more things to watch for, but essentially standard performance monitoring techniques are adequate.

WHAT YOU REALLY NEED TO KNOW

- ◆ The primary tool for monitoring performance in Windows 2000 is the Performance console.
- ◆ The Performance console is broken down into two major categories: System Monitor and Performance Logs and Alerts.
- ◆ System Monitor allows you to view real-time or stored data in either a chart format or a more traditional report format.
- ◆ Performance Logs and Alerts allows you to gather data and store it for future analysis. Typically, you choose to gather data during peak usage times, such as shift changes when backups are occurring, and scheduled AD replication intervals, if such replication is scheduled.
- ◆ Common counters to watch are:
  - Processor: % Processor Time
  - Physical Disk: Disk Queue Length
  - Logical Disk: Disk Queue Length
  - Physical Disk: % Disk Time
  - Memory: Pages/sec
  - Memory: Committed Bytes
- ◆ The **NTDS** object is the object for all AD-related information. Counters are available to analyze inbound and outbound replication traffic (both within and between sites), number of updates, cache utilization for directory-related queries, and synchronization request information, among many others. There are also counters for viewing utilization of various AD interfaces, such as LDAP, **SAM** (for down-level clients), and **XDS** (for administration). Kerberos vs. **NTLM** (down-level) authentication information can be monitored with this object as well.

OBJECTIVES ON THE JOB

Monitoring performance is critical for any administrator. This is especially true when it comes to server monitoring. The most important servers of all, in terms of basic infrastructure access, are the domain controllers. Standard monitoring techniques should be employed, in addition to monitoring the NTDS object to analyze the impact that AD is having on the system.

PRACTICE TEST QUESTIONS

1. The most important object for monitoring the performance of AD is _____.
    a. AD
    b. NTDS
    c. DR
    d. Repl
    e. DirRep

2. The object used to monitor how well the CPU is handling the load placed on it is _____.
    a. Processor
    b. Process
    c. CPU
    d. % Processor Utilization

3. Which of the following objects is related to hard drive performance? (Choose all that apply.)
    a. Disk
    b. Drive
    c. DiskPerf
    d. LogicalDisk
    e. PhysicalDisk

4. One of the most useful counters for monitoring memory utilization is _____.
    a. Memory
    b. RAM
    c. Cache
    d. Pages/sec

5. The tool used to monitor performance in Windows 2000 is _____.
    a. PerfMon
    b. Performance Monitor
    c. Performance console
    d. System Logs and Alerts

6. Which of the following components is part of the Performance console? (Choose all that apply.)
    a. System Monitor
    b. Reports
    c. Logs
    d. Alerts
    e. Performance Logs and Alerts
    f. Chart

OBJECTIVES

4.8 Maintain domain controller performance

SITES • INTRASITE AND INTERSITE REPLICATION • REPLICATION BRIDGEHEADS

UNDERSTANDING THE OBJECTIVE

In addition to monitoring the performance of domain controllers, a major responsibility of an administrator is to maximize that performance. The key to good performance over WAN links in AD is the appropriate use of sites.

WHAT YOU REALLY NEED TO KNOW

- ◆ A site is one or more well-connected (high bandwidth, low cost) IP subnets.
- ◆ By default, all computers in a domain belong to the site "Default-First-Site-Name."
- ◆ Sites are typically created when WAN links are involved.
- ◆ Sites play a major role in AD replication, **DFS**, FRS, and logon validation.
- ◆ Intrasite replication always uses RPC over IP, and it cannot be scheduled. When a change occurs on a server, it notifies its replication partners, which in turn get the updates and notify their partners, and so on. The KCC attempts to keep each domain controller connected to at least two other domain controllers and at the same time makes sure that domain controllers are no more than three hops from any other domain controller.
- ◆ Urgent replication takes place intrasite when the following events occur: an account is locked out, the state of the RID manager changes, or an **LSA** secret is changed. In addition, for mixed-mode domains, account lockout policy updates and interdomain trust password changes also trigger urgent updates. Urgent updates are replicated faster than other updates and preferentially update the PDC FSMO.
- ◆ Intersite replication must be RPC over IP-based for replication within a domain, whereas it may be RPC over IP- or SMTP-based between domains. It can be scheduled and multiple routes for updates can be prioritized with costs.
- ◆ A replication bridgehead is a domain controller in a site that replicates to another domain controller in another site.

OBJECTIVES ON THE JOB

The appropriate creation and use of sites in a forest is a major way to optimize WAN bandwidth. As scheduling is possible, AD updates can be set for times when WAN bandwidth demands are lighter, such as overnight and on weekends.

PRACTICE TEST QUESTIONS

Marching Band Inc. has four locations—a manufacturing plant and three sales locations—which are all linked by T-1 lines. Each location needs access to data in all of the other locations. During the day, bandwidth utilization has been reaching 80 percent, reducing performance for critical business decisions, whereas utilization at night is usually less than 10 percent. A single domain has been implemented for the company, and domain controllers exist at all locations. Each location has at least two domain controllers (for redundancy), with the largest location (the manufacturing plant) having the most, at eight.

1. **How many sites currently exist with the default Windows 2000 installation?**
   a. Zero
   b. One
   c. Three
   d. Four

2. **Should more sites be created, and if so, how many?**
   a. No, the default is fine.
   b. Yes, you should create a site in which to place all of your resources because sites are not automatically created.
   c. Yes, you should have one site for manufacturing and one for sales.
   d. Yes, you should have four sites, one for each location in the company.

3. **What are the benefits of creating multiple sites? (Choose all that apply.)**
   a. Replication can be scheduled between sites.
   b. Sites help reflect the organizational structure of the company.
   c. Costs can be set to prioritize replication paths.
   d. There are no benefits to creating multiple sites for a small company; they only exist for large companies with hundreds of sites.

4. **After creating the necessary sites, is there anything else you must do to take advantage of them?**
   a. No, the defaults are fine.
   b. Yes, create site links.
   c. Yes, create site link bridges.
   d. Yes, move the domain controller objects into the correct sites.

5. **Is there any way to control which servers replicate with which other servers in the different sites?**
   a. No, it is determined by the system and can't be changed.
   b. Yes, by editing the Registry.
   c. Yes, by creating bridgehead servers.
   d. Yes, by making the desired servers Global Catalog servers.

4.9   Troubleshoot domain controller performance

PERFORMANCE CONSOLE • SITES • REPLICATION TRAFFIC

UNDERSTANDING THE OBJECTIVE

To troubleshoot problems, an understanding of the Performance console is critical, as is an understanding of WAN bandwidth usage in AD replication. A few tips for improving performance based on those guidelines are presented here, as are a few tips on monitoring replication.

WHAT YOU REALLY NEED TO KNOW

◆ Processor: % Processor Time should be less than 80 percent. If not, consider adding another CPU, upgrading the CPUs you have, or moving the largest consumer of CPU time (as seen in the Performance console or Task Manager) to another machine.

◆ Both Physical Disk: Disk Queue Length and Logical Disk: Disk Queue Length should be less than 2; and Physical Disk: % Disk Time should be less than 90 percent. If they're not, consider adding a hard drive and spreading frequently accessed data across them, adding a RAID 0 (striped) or RAID 5 (stripe set with parity) volume and redistributing data, and/or separating the physical drives that hold the system and boot partitions from the volume(s) that hold(s) the page file.

◆ Memory: Pages/sec should be less than 20. If not, excessive paging is occurring, meaning that you don't have enough physical RAM. Consider adding more RAM or removing the top consumers of RAM until this value falls below 20.

◆ Memory: Committed Bytes should be less than the total bytes of physical RAM. If not, carefully monitor the cache object and the pages/sec to see if a problem exists.

◆ For best performance, Microsoft recommends, at a minimum, placing the operating system, AD logs, and the AD database on separate physical drives (therefore, three drives are necessary). Ideally, the operating system is on a mirrored volume, the AD log files are on a separate mirrored volume, and the AD database file is on a RAID-5 volume (therefore, at least seven drives are necessary).

◆ If WAN bandwidth is an issue, consider implementing sites and replication bridgeheads.

◆ To monitor replication traffic, use the Performance console with the NTDS object and/or use Active Directory Replication Monitor (REPLMON.exe). The Performance console gives you the big picture and overall statistics, whereas Replication Monitor gives you greater detail on the specifics of replication.

OBJECTIVES ON THE JOB

The issues discussed here are critical to the success of any administrator. Replication monitor, specifically, can be a great aid to understanding what has and hasn't replicated and which domain controllers are replication partners.

PRACTICE TEST QUESTIONS

1. **To maximize the performance of a heavily utilized domain controller, the hard drives should be configured in what manner?**
   a. Place all files in one partition and format it as NTFS.
   b. Place the operating system on one hard drive and the AD database and log files on a second hard drive.
   c. Place the operating system on one hard drive, the database on a second hard drive, and log files on a third hard drive.
   d. Place the operating system and log files on a mirrored volume and place the database on a RAID-5 volume.
   e. Place the operating system on a mirrored volume, the log files on a separate mirrored volume on separate dedicated hard drives, and the database file on a RAID-5 volume on dedicated hard drives.

2. **If Pages/sec is at 150 and Physical Disk: % Disk Time is at 95 percent, what is the most likely bottleneck?**
   a. Disk
   b. Network
   c. Memory
   d. Processor

3. **What is the maximum acceptable average value for Processor: % Processor Time?**
   a. 50
   b. 67
   c. 80
   d. 90
   e. 100

4. **The main component of Active Directory designed to control AD-related WAN traffic is _____.**
   a. site
   b. domain
   c. organizational unit
   d. WAN Traffic Manager
   e. SMTP

5. **The best tool for determining the amount of traffic caused by AD is _____.**
   a. Task Manager
   b. Performance console
   c. Replication Monitor
   d. Netdom

6. **The best tool for determining which objects haven't yet been replicated between two domain controllers is _____.**
   a. Task Manager
   b. Performance console
   c. Netdom
   d. Replication Monitor

4.10 Monitor Active Directory components

PERFORMANCE CONSOLE • NTDS OBJECT

UNDERSTANDING THE OBJECTIVE

Monitoring domain controller and Active Directory performance is similar to monitoring the performance of any other Windows 2000-based system. There are a few more things to watch for, but essentially standard performance monitoring techniques are adequate.

WHAT YOU REALLY NEED TO KNOW

◆ The primary AD components are forests, trees, domains, organizational units, objects, and sites. There is little to monitor at the forest, tree, and organizational unit levels, as most activity takes place at the object level, within domains, and replication can be controlled via sites.

◆ The Performance console is the primary tool for the big picture on how AD is performing.

◆ All of the counters described below are found in the NTDS object. Each has both a "since boot" and a "per second" variation to view traffic since the last reboot and to view current traffic. Each also has both an inbound and an outbound variation. To conserve space, all possible permutations of each are not listed.

◆ **DRA** Inbound (or Outbound) Bytes Total: Sum of compressed and uncompressed bytes incoming or outgoing, or number of bytes on the network.

◆ DRA Inbound (or Outbound) Bytes Not Compressed (Within Site): Total amount of intrasite traffic in either direction; especially important if sites are not used and WAN links exist.

◆ DRA Inbound (or Outbound) Bytes Compressed (Between Sites, After Compression): Amount of traffic in either direction on the wire, usually on WAN links. Compare with the next counter to get an estimate of the impact on WAN traffic of implementing sites.

◆ DRA Inbound (or Outbound) Bytes Compressed (Between Sites, Before Compression): Amount of traffic in either direction before compression, not actually on the wire. Compare with the previous counter to view how well the traffic is compressed and to get an estimate of the impact on WAN traffic of implementing sites.

◆ DRA Inbound (or Outbound) Objects/sec (no "since boot" counter exists for this counter): Number of objects replicating per second; useful in determining the level of AD updates that are occurring on the network.

OBJECTIVES ON THE JOB

A thorough understanding of AD components and the Performance console is a great boon to any administrator who is trying to analyze the impact of AD on the network infrastructure.

PRACTICE TEST QUESTIONS

1. **The number of servers that replicate data between any two given sites within the same domain is:**
   a. one
   b. two
   c. four
   d. There is not enough information provided.

2. **The number of servers that replicate data between themselves within a site within the same domain (assuming multiple domain controllers exist at the given site) is:**
   a. zero
   b. one
   c. two
   d. There is not enough information provided.

3. **To determine the total WAN traffic involved in AD replication in a two-site network, add the values of which of the following counters together? (Choose all that apply.)**
   a. DRA Inbound Bytes Total
   b. DRA Outbound Bytes Total
   c. DRA Inbound Bytes Not Compressed (Within Site)
   d. DRA Outbound Bytes Not Compressed (Within Site)
   e. DRA Inbound Bytes Compressed (Between Sites, After Compression)
   f. DRA Outbound Bytes Compressed (Between Sites, After Compression)
   g. DRA Inbound Bytes Compressed (Between Sites, Before Compression)
   h. DRA Outbound Bytes Compressed (Between Sites, Before Compression)

4. **To determine the total LAN traffic involved in AD replication to and from a single server within a site, add the values of which of the following counters together? (Choose all that apply.)**
   a. DRA Inbound Bytes Total
   b. DRA Outbound Bytes Total
   c. DRA Inbound Bytes Not Compressed (Within Site)
   d. DRA Outbound Bytes Not Compressed (Within Site)
   e. DRA Inbound Bytes Compressed (Between Sites, After Compression)
   f. DRA Outbound Bytes Compressed (Between Sites, After Compression)
   g. DRA Inbound Bytes Compressed (Between Sites, Before Compression)
   h. DRA Outbound Bytes Compressed (Between Sites, Before Compression)

5. **To estimate the number of changes occurring on any given domain controller at any given point in time, use which of the following counters (taking into account the number of replication partners the domain controller has):**
   a. DRA Inbound Objects/sec
   b. DRA Outbound Objects/sec
   c. DRA Inbound Bytes Total
   d. DRA Outbound Bytes Total

OBJECTIVES

4.11 Maintain Active Directory components

ACTIVE DIRECTORY SITES AND SERVICES • SITES • SITE LINKS • SITE LINK BRIDGES

UNDERSTANDING THE OBJECTIVE

In addition to monitoring the performance of the domain controllers in a domain, a major responsibility of an administrator is to maximize that performance. The key to good performance over WAN links in AD is the appropriate use of sites.

WHAT YOU REALLY NEED TO KNOW

- ◆ All sites need to be joined together by site links, or else AD will not replicate changes to or from servers in that site.
- ◆ By default, Windows 2000 creates a site named "Default-First-Site-Name" and a site link named "DefaultIPSiteLink."
- ◆ All sites are bridged by default, meaning that the site links are transitive, allowing changes in one site to be replicated through as many sites as necessary to reach the final destination site. If the IP network isn't fully routed, this feature may be disabled, in which case site link bridges must be explicitly created to link the sites together.
- ◆ Site links join two or more sites together, whereas site link bridges join two or more site links together.
- ◆ Sites, site links, and site link bridges are configured by transport (RPC over IP or SMTP).
- ◆ Multiple site links are created to join individual sites together when different schedules or costs are required.
- ◆ Subnet objects link one or more physical IP subnets with the site objects. A subnet object is always associated with one and only one site.
- ◆ Client computers know their IP address and check with AD to find out which subnet object they belong to. They can then find out which site the subnet object is linked with to find resources, such as domain controllers, within their own sites. If a client can't locate the desired resource in its own site, it randomly looks at all other options on all other sites equally; there is no prioritization of sites. A resource can be anywhere, including in the client's site.
- ◆ Domain controllers automatically belong to the Default-First-Site-Name site unless the appropriate site and subnet objects were created before the domain controller was installed. Domain controllers should be moved into the site where they are physically located, if they do not already reside there.

OBJECTIVES ON THE JOB

Understanding site configuration and setup is one of the most important AD configuration tasks for administrators that have multiple physical configurations. Creating the appropriate sites and site links saves WAN bandwidth and increases performance.

PRACTICE TEST QUESTIONS

Small Bank Inc. has two primary locations—a headquarters and a document processing center—and 12 branch offices. Each branch office has its own domain controller, whereas the two primary locations have three domain controllers each. The branch offices are linked to the headquarters with 128 Kbps fractional T-1 links, and the headquarters and the document processing center are linked with a T-1 line. All branch offices are in the same time zone and are open from 9:00 a.m. to 5:00 p.m., Monday through Friday, and from 9:00 a.m. to 1:00 p.m. on Saturday. The headquarters is open from 8:00 a.m. to 6:00 p.m., Monday through Friday. The document processing center is open 24 hours a day, Monday through Saturday, but most of the work is done overnight on weeknights. The bank's network administrator has recently deployed Windows 2000 in the default configuration and has noticed a significant reduction in performance.

1. **How many sites does Windows 2000 create by default?**
   a. Zero
   b. One
   c. One for each physical location

2. **How many sites should exist for optimal performance?**
   a. One
   b. Two
   c. Three
   d. 12
   e. 14

3. **How many site links does Windows 2000 create by default?**
   a. Zero
   b. One
   c. One for each pair of sites

4. **How many site links are needed based on the number of sites?**
   a. One
   b. Two
   c. 12
   d. 13
   e. 14

5. **How many site link bridges does Windows 2000 create by default?**
   a. None, all sites are transitively bridged.
   b. One for the default site link.
   c. One for each pair of site links.

6. **Based on the number of site links, how many site link bridges are needed?**
   a. Zero
   b. One
   c. Two

4.12 Troubleshoot Active Directory components

LOSTANDFOUND • ACTIVE DIRECTORY SITES AND SERVICES • ACTIVE DIRECTORY REPLICATION MONITOR

UNDERSTANDING THE OBJECTIVE

Troubleshooting AD requires many possible solutions to many problems. Fortunately, most problems stem from replication issues. The LostAndFound container is also populated due to replication issues. This objective focuses primarily on forcing replication and understanding when LostAndFound gets objects in it. Experiment with Replication Monitor and understand its capabilities.

WHAT YOU REALLY NEED TO KNOW

◆ To view the LostAndFound container, use Active Directory Users and Computers, and then make sure that the Advanced view is selected.

◆ The LostAndFound container is populated when an object is created in or moved to a container on one domain controller while, at the same time, another administrator deletes the same container. In such a case, as replication occurs, the newly created or moved object gets orphaned as the container is removed, so the object is relocated to LostAndFound and the new location is replicated.

◆ To force two domain controllers to replicate, use Active Directory Sites and Services. Navigate to the DC that you want to receive the updates, select NTDS settings, choose the connection object that represents the source of the data (i.e., the updated DC), and choose Replicate Now. In other words, you are pulling the changes to the outdated DC. Active Directory Replication Monitor can be used to view any of the following information: the domain controllers in a domain, the replication topologies, the Global Catalog servers in the forest, existing trust relationships, and the bridgehead servers either in the current site or throughout the forest.

◆ Active Directory Replication Monitor can be used to force the KCC to run immediately to verify that the appropriate connection objects exist. You can also force a synchronization of each of the directory partitions (schema, configuration, and domain or domains for a Global Catalog server) with other servers, including those in other sites. This is a powerful option that can have a dramatic impact on available bandwidth.

◆ Active Directory Replication Monitor can be used to force an update of its directory information from another domain controller, in much the same manner that it can be done with Active Directory Sites and Services.

OBJECTIVES ON THE JOB

To ensure that AD functions properly, you should schedule periodic checks of the LostAndFound container. Forcing replication and waiting for it to complete can fix many other problems in AD.

PRACTICE TEST QUESTIONS

1. The LostAndFound container gets populated when:
   a. an object is created and then deleted immediately.
   b. an object is created or moved into a container that is simultaneously being deleted on another domain controller.
   c. any object is deleted, acting much like a recycle bin for AD objects.
   d. a container object is deleted, with the contents of the container going into LostAndFound.

2. To view the contents of the LostAndFound container, you need to:
   a. open Active Directory Sites and Services.
   b. open Active Directory Sites and Services and be sure it is in the Advanced view.
   c. open Active Directory Users and Computers.
   d. open Active Directory Users and Computers and be sure it is in the Advanced view.

3. To force two domain controllers to replicate with each other, you can use: (Choose all that apply.)
   a. Active Directory Sites and Services
   b. Active Directory Domains and Trusts
   c. Active Directory Users and Computers
   d. Active Directory Schema
   e. Active Directory Replication Monitor

4. The capabilities of Active Directory Replication Monitor include: (Choose all that apply.)
   a. viewing all Global Catalog servers in the forest
   b. viewing all FSMO holders in the forest
   c. forcing the KCC to immediately execute
   d. viewing the replication topology
   e. creating a user account
   f. creating a trust to an NT 4.0 domain
   g. viewing the bridgehead servers in the forest
   h. forcing a synchronization of selected directory partitions with other servers
   i. forcing a synchronization of all directory partitions with other servers

5. The purpose of the KCC is to:
   a. make sure that all data is correctly replicated.
   b. make sure that the necessary connection objects exist and create them if they don't.
   c. make sure that the schema is up to date by verifying it with the Schema FSMO.
   d. make sure the configuration directory partition is up to date by verifying it with the Domain Naming FSMO.

OBJECTIVES

4.13 Manage and troubleshoot intersite replication

REPLICATION SCHEDULE • REPLICATION INTERVAL • REPLICATION BRIDGEHEAD SERVER

UNDERSTANDING THE OBJECTIVE

Replication within and between sites, and their similarities and differences, are integral to the exam. Understanding how replication takes place within and between sites is critical to managing intersite performance and troubleshooting problems that may arise. Sites are the biggest WAN bandwidth improvement in Windows 2000.

WHAT YOU REALLY NEED TO KNOW

◆ Replication between sites can be scheduled, but not within sites.

◆ Logon traffic is directed to any domain controller in the site, whether or not it is in the same physical location.

◆ Replication between sites is controlled by three factors: cost, replication schedule, and replication cost. These factors are defined on the site link.

◆ A site link defines the replication parameters for two or more sites that are grouped together into one site link.

◆ The cost determines the route taken between two sites, and the cheapest route is always taken. Costs range from 1 to 32767.

◆ The replication schedule defines when replication can take place.

◆ The replication interval defines how often within the replication schedule replication takes place. You can choose from once every 15 minutes (the default) to once every 10,080 minutes (once a week).

◆ A replication bridgehead server is the preferred replication partner for a site. Typically, they are defined for each site. If a site spans a firewall, the firewall server should be the preferred bridgehead for replication to function properly.

◆ If replication is not occurring as expected, verify that the site is linked to a site link object, or replication does not occur.

◆ Replication between sites can take place using RPC over IP or SMTP, but SMTP can only be used when replicating between domains (to a GC server in another domain).

OBJECTIVES ON THE JOB

The simple rule for site creation is: create a site for each location connected by a WAN link. A new site is not necessary if a high-speed WAN link with a large amount of available bandwidth links the two sites, but this is very rare. Keep in mind that a T-1 line is *not* high speed—it is 1.5 percent of a 100 Mbps LAN. After sites are created, verify that replication between them is working properly with Active Directory Replication Monitor and/or the NTDS object in System Monitor.

PRACTICE TEST QUESTIONS

1. **Replication between sites is affected by: (Choose all that apply.)**
   a. amount of data to replicate
   b. time of day
   c. day of the week
   d. replication interval
   e. cost
   f. available bandwidth

2. **Replication within a site can be scheduled.**
   a. True
   b. False

3. **Which tool can be used to verify that replication is occurring as expected?**
   a. Active Directory Replication Monitor
   b. Netdom
   c. Active Directory Migration Tool
   d. Active Directory Sites and Services

4. **The cost associated with a site link ranges from _____ to _____.**
   a. 1, 100
   b. 1, 1000
   c. 1, 10,000
   d. 1, 16,384
   e. 1, 32,767
   f. 1, 65,536

5. **Replication between domain controllers in the same domain between sites can take place over which of the following protocols? (Choose all that apply.)**
   a. LDAP
   b. NetBIOS
   c. DNS
   d. RPC
   e. DCOM
   f. Sockets
   g. Named pipes
   h. SMTP

6. **Replication between domain controllers in different domains between sites can take place over which of the following protocols? (Choose all that apply.)**
   a. LDAP
   b. NetBIOS
   c. DNS
   d. RPC
   e. DCOM
   f. Sockets
   g. Named pipes
   h. SMTP

4.14 Manage and troubleshoot intrasite replication

KCC • CONNECTION OBJECTS • ACTIVE DIRECTORY REPLICATION MONITOR

UNDERSTANDING THE OBJECTIVE

Replication between domain controllers within the same site cannot be scheduled; updates are gathered and applied every five minutes, assuming changes are occurring. The links between the domain controllers are automatic, although they can be overridden.

WHAT YOU REALLY NEED TO KNOW

- ◆ The replication topology within a site is automatically generated by the KCC.
- ◆ The KCC creates connection objects to provide fault tolerance by creating at least two connection objects for each server.
- ◆ The KCC is designed for good performance and low latency, creating as many connection objects as necessary to ensure that no two servers are more than three hops apart.
- ◆ Additional connection objects can be manually created if the default behavior of the KCC is not adequate for the performance desired.
- ◆ Manually created connection objects are not automatically removed by the KCC.
- ◆ Replication within a site uses a notification scheme wherein a domain controller that has updates notifies its replication partners that it has updates, which the partners then retrieve.
- ◆ Replication within a site uses uncompressed traffic to reduce the load on the CPU, whereas replication between sites uses compressed traffic. The data is compressed to 10 to 15 percent of the original size.
- ◆ Replication between two domain controllers can be forced to occur immediately by using Active Directory Sites and Services. Navigate to the DC that you want to *receive* the updates, select NTDS settings, choose the connection object that represents the *source* of the data (i.e., the updated DC), and choose Replicate Now. In other words, you are *pulling* the changes to the outdated DC.
- ◆ Replication can be monitored with Active Directory Replication Monitor, System Monitor, and Performance Logs and Alerts. The NTDS object contains the counters necessary for monitoring replication.

OBJECTIVES ON THE JOB

AD automatically configures links between domain controllers within a site, and the defaults are generally sufficient, unless fine-tuning is desired. You may want to force replication to make an update replicate quickly to a desired domain controller and/or to verify that replication is taking place as expected. This may be necessary for remote sites to ensure they are quickly updated with a new user, group, etc., especially if there isn't a local administrator to make the changes locally.

PRACTICE TEST QUESTIONS

1. **A connection object is created by _____.**
   a. the KCC
   b. broadcast
   c. DNS
   d. WINS

2. **Replication within a site uses _____.**
   a. cost
   b. notifications
   c. schedules
   d. broadcasts

3. **To force replication, _____ should be used.**
   a. Active Directory Users and Computers
   b. Active Directory Domains and Trusts
   c. Active Directory Schema
   d. Active Directory Sites and Services

4. **AD data is compressed when it is replicated within a site.**
   a. True
   b. False

5. **The KCC creates connection objects such that: (Choose all that apply.)**
   a. Domain controllers are no more than one hop apart.
   b. Domain controllers are no more than two hops apart.
   c. Domain controllers are no more than three hops apart.
   d. Domain controllers are no more than four hops apart.
   e. There is at least one connection per domain controller.
   f. There are at least two connections per domain controller.
   g. There are at least three connections per domain controller.
   h. There are at least four connections per domain controller.

6. **The following tools are often used to verify that replication is taking place as expected: (Choose all that apply.)**
   a. Active Directory Sites and Services
   b. System Monitor
   c. Active Directory Domains and Trusts
   d. Performance Logs and Alerts
   e. Active Directory Replication Monitor

Section 5

Configuring, Managing, Monitoring, and Troubleshooting Security in a Directory Services Infrastructure

5.1 Apply security policies by using group policy

SECURITY TEMPLATE • SECURITY POLICIES • PERSISTENT

UNDERSTANDING THE OBJECTIVE

Security templates allow you to manage your security policies centrally and then have them propagated to all of your servers and clients, assuming they are using Windows 2000.

WHAT YOU REALLY NEED TO KNOW

- ◆ You can view and manage your security settings using the MMC snap-in Security Configuration and Analysis.

- ◆ Using the MMC snap-in Security Templates, you can edit existing security templates (located in \WINNT\Security\Templates*.inf).

- ◆ After your desired security configuration has been tested and saved to a security template (*.inf) file, you can use GPOs to distribute the policy.

- ◆ Account policies (such as minimum password length, password history, and so on) can be set only at the domain level. If they are set anywhere else, they are ignored.

- ◆ To distribute the policy, open the desired GPO, and then expand the following: Computer Configuration, Windows Settings, and Security Settings. Right-click Security Settings, choose Import Policy, and select the policy you wish to import (and distribute).

- ◆ To manually set Security settings (without templates), set the desired individual policies in the GPO.

- ◆ Security settings are persistent, unlike other GPO policies, meaning that they remain in the Registry (and therefore in effect) even after the GPO has been removed.

- ◆ It is good practice to implement the policy on a local machine first and test it thoroughly before implementing it on a wider scale through GPOs.

OBJECTIVES ON THE JOB

Security is a key component of most network administrators' job descriptions today. It is critical that security policies are properly designed to define what the necessary policies are in any given environment. Applying these security policies in the past was somewhat difficult, but by using GPOs, this problem has largely been eliminated (as long as all of your computers are using Windows 2000). Be sure to properly test the policies before wide-scale distribution of them is begun to ensure that you do not lose connectivity and that your applications still function as expected.

PRACTICE TEST QUESTIONS

The network administrator for an airport is concerned with making sure that only authorized personnel can use the airport's computers. She has decided that running Windows 2000 on all systems is the best way to secure her network.

1. **Does Windows 2000 allow her to distribute from a central location the security policies she has defined?**
   a. No, she must edit each computer's security policy directly.
   b. Yes, by using GPOs she can manage all of the servers.
   c. Yes, by using GPOs she can manage all of the clients.
   d. Yes, by using GPOs she can manage all of the Windows 2000-based systems in the entire network.

2. **Are there predefined templates that she can use as a starting point for implementing security policies?**
   a. Yes, there are several predefined templates.
   b. No, she must create any template(s) that may be needed.

3. **Is there a way to compare current security policies on a machine with an existing template?**
   a. Yes, use the Security Templates snap-in.
   b. Yes, use the Security Configuration and Analysis snap-in.
   c. Yes, look in the GPOs for policies, and then compare that to how the machine behaves.
   d. No, there is no easy way to do so.

4. **How can she create her own templates?**
   a. By using the Security Templates snap-in
   b. By using the Security Configuration and Analysis snap-in
   c. By creating a new GPO
   d. By using Active Directory Users and Computers

5. **After a security policy is applied, the changes remain even if the GPO is removed.**
   a. True
   b. False

6. **Can she have different password policies for users in different parts of her domain?**
   a. Yes, she can change the password policies anywhere by making the change in the desired GPO.
   b. Yes, she can have different policies for different users within an OU by modifying the user's properties in Active Directory Users and Computers.
   c. No, password policies must be set at the domain level.
   d. No, password policies must be set at the forest level.

5.2   Create security configurations by using Security Configuration and Analysis and security templates

SECURITY CONFIGURATION AND ANALYSIS • SECURITY TEMPLATES •
SECURITY DATABASE

UNDERSTANDING THE OBJECTIVE

Security Policies, implemented using Security Configuration and Analysis and security templates, are a very powerful method of controlling the security policies necessary to secure your network. Predefined templates offer the ability to provide various predefined levels of security. You can customize these templates and create new templates based on a machine configured exactly as you wish.

WHAT YOU REALLY NEED TO KNOW

- ◆ The Security Templates snap-in allows you to view and modify the predefined templates, as well as any that you have created.

- ◆ The security templates are stored in \WINNT\Security\Templates by default, but other paths may be specified, including network paths.

- ◆ Predefined templates include basic, compatibility, secure, and high secure. The templates come in some combination of the three versions: *wk.inf for Professional-based computers, *sv.inf for member servers, and *dc.inf for domain controllers.

- ◆ The basic template upgrades the security on an upgraded computer to match the security of a cleanly installed computer (which doesn't happen by default). All three versions are available.

- ◆ The compatibility template lowers overall system security so that applications that may not run properly with higher levels of security will run. To reiterate, you get broader security at the cost of lower security. This is available only for Windows 2000 Professional-based machines.

- ◆ The secure template makes the computer more secure by managing account policies, auditing, and modifying some Registry entries. This is available only for Windows 2000 Professional-based machines and domain controllers.

- ◆ The high secure template builds on the security that the secure template provides and adds the requirement that all network communications be digitally signed and encrypted. These capabilities only exist in Windows 2000, meaning that all down-level machines are not able to communicate with this computer. This is available only for Windows 2000 Professional-based machines and domain controllers.

OBJECTIVES ON THE JOB

Implementing the security policies that you have documented is most easily accomplished by using the Security Configuration and Analysis snap-in. You can compare a machine's current computer settings to a standard that you wish to use (stored in a template) and then update the machine to the template's level of security.

PRACTICE TEST QUESTIONS

1. **The available security templates are: (Choose all that apply.)**
   a. Basic
   b. Original
   c. Compatible
   d. Standard
   e. Secure
   f. Very secure
   g. High secure

2. **In a mixed environment consisting of Windows 95, 98, NT, and 2000-based computers, you should use the high-secure template to maximize security on the network.**
   a. True
   b. False

3. **The primary tools provided by Microsoft to configure the desired level of security on a computer running Windows 2000 include: (Choose all that apply.)**
   a. Computer Management
   b. Active Directory Users and Computers
   c. Event Viewer
   d. Security Configuration and Analysis
   e. Security Checker
   f. Security Templates

4. **To edit a security template to provide the settings necessary in your environment, use:**
   a. Notepad
   b. WordPad
   c. Security Configuration and Analysis
   d. Security templates
   e. Edit

5. **To view how your computer compares to a predefined security template, you should use:**
   a. Computer Management
   b. Security Configuration and Analysis
   c. Security Checker
   d. Security templates

6. **Security templates are available for: (Choose all that apply.)**
   a. Windows 95/98
   b. Windows NT Workstation
   c. Windows NT Server
   d. Windows NT Server domain controller
   e. Windows 2000 Professional
   f. Windows 2000 Server
   g. Windows 2000 Server domain controller

5.3 Analyze security configurations by using Security Configuration and Analysis and security templates

SECURITY CONFIGURATION AND ANALYSIS

UNDERSTANDING THE OBJECTIVE

The previous two objectives have defined what the security templates are, what they are for, and how to deploy them using group policies. This objective focuses on using Security Configuration and Analysis to compare the security settings on your machine with those defined in a template to see how they are the same or different.

WHAT YOU REALLY NEED TO KNOW

- ◆ To begin an analysis, you must create an MMC that has the Security Configuration and Analysis snap-in added, then right-click Security Configuration and Analysis, and choose Open database to create a new database. Give it a name and click Open to create it. Select the template you want to compare it against, and then choose Open.

- ◆ To compare it to other templates, right-click Security Configuration and Analysis, choose Import Template, and then choose the new template.

- ◆ To analyze the current settings versus the template, right-click Security Configuration and Analysis and choose Analyze Computer Now. Provide a path for the log file that is automatically generated, which lists the similarities and differences.

- ◆ There are two ways to examine the output: reviewing the log or viewing the output graphically with Security Configuration and Analysis.

- ◆ Differences between the log and the current configuration may be viewed by searching for the word "mismatch."

- ◆ The graphical view shows each setting, the value in the template, and the current value on the computer. Each setting shows one of three possible values: green check (they are both the same), red X (they are different [mismatch]), or no icon (the value is not set in the template, so the local value is relevant). To change the effective template settings, double-click the item and make changes as needed.

- ◆ To make the template settings the current settings for the computer, right-click Security Configuration and Analysis and choose Configure Computer Now.

- ◆ To save the database settings (the combination of the original template settings and any changes that have been made to it) to a new template file, right-click Security Configuration and Analysis and choose Export Template.

OBJECTIVES ON THE JOB

This tool is often used on the job to find out how the security settings on a given machine differ from a standard—either a predefined standard from Microsoft or a company standard stored in a security template. It can also be used while new policies are being developed to test them and see the impact they have on applications and day-to-day operations.

PRACTICE TEST QUESTIONS

1. **The output of Security Configuration and Analysis can be viewed using which of the following? (Choose all that apply.)**
   a. Notepad
   b. SNMP Traps
   c. Computer Management
   d. Security Configuration and Analysis

2. **Values that are updated in Security Configuration and Analysis can be exported to a template file.**
   a. True
   b. False

3. **The current database settings can be applied to a computer using which of the following methods? (Choose all that apply.)**
   a. Apply the log.
   b. Use Security Configuration and Analysis.
   c. Use group policies.
   d. Use Computer Management.

4. **After a security template is opened and the analysis has taken place, a new template can't be used unless a new instance of Security Configuration and Analysis is started.**
   a. True
   b. False

5. **You must create a security database before an analysis can take place.**
   a. True
   b. False

6. **When differences are noted in the log file, they are flagged using _____.**
   a. Difference
   b. Flag
   c. Mismatch
   d. Error

OBJECTIVES

5.4 Troubleshoot/modify security configurations by using Security Configuration and Analysis and security templates

SECURITY CONFIGURATION AND ANALYSIS • GPO • SECURITY TEMPLATES

UNDERSTANDING THE OBJECTIVE

Whether the security configuration is done at the local machine or is distributed via a GPO or series of GPOs, you may need to change your security settings from time to time, or troubleshoot problems with those security settings. Although GPO troubleshooting is not covered here, it is still important to be sure that the correct policies are applied. This objective focuses on how to troubleshoot that configuration.

WHAT YOU REALLY NEED TO KNOW

◆ Individual security templates can be viewed and modified with the Security Templates snap-in.

◆ The net effect of the security policies distributed by GPOs can be viewed using Security Configuration and Analysis. To determine the individual GPOs that were applied, use the Resource Kit utility GPRESULT.exe.

◆ If the security settings applied impair functionality or compromise security, apply the settings to a test computer, disconnect it from the network (so group policies are not refreshed as you make changes, overwriting your test configuration with the settings that need to be updated), and use Security Configuration and Analysis to view the policies in effect on that workstation.

◆ Make changes and test the functionality of those changes using the test machine with Security Configuration and Analysis until the machine is configured exactly as desired. Export those settings to a new security template to save them. Reconnect the test computer to the network.

◆ Update any GPOs that need to be updated with portions or all of the security template just created, filter the GPO to apply to a small number of test computers, and verify that the net effect of the deployed policies is as expected.

◆ Minimize the number of GPOs that deploy security policies to minimize the amount of time that must be spent troubleshooting security conflicts between GPOs.

OBJECTIVES ON THE JOB

Security configurations can make certain applications install incorrectly or function incorrectly, impair users' ability to complete their assigned tasks, and so on. The best way to review and fix these problems is with Security Configuration and Analysis. Use this tool in conjunction with the Security Templates snap-in and the standard GPO troubleshooting tools to provide the desired balance between security and functionality.

PRACTICE TEST QUESTIONS

1. **Put the following steps that should be taken to troubleshoot security configuration in the proper order.**
   a. View the test computer's configuration with Security Configuration and Analysis.
   b. Update GPOs as necessary.
   c. Export the correct settings to a security template.
   d. Apply the settings to a test computer.
   e. Disconnect the test computer from the network.
   f. Make changes to the test computer's configuration with Security Configuration and Analysis. Test the changes and repeat until desired changes are obtained.
   g. Verify that the correct settings were applied from the GPO(s) to one or more test computers.
   h. Verify that the correct settings were applied from the GPO(s) to one or more test computers.

2. **The purpose of GPRESULT.exe is to:**
   a. View the GPO(s) that is/are being applied to a given user and computer.
   b. Force an immediate update of all GPOs that apply to a given user or computer.
   c. Rearrange the order in which GPOs are applied.
   d. Modify the GPO(s) that is/are being applied to a given user or computer.

3. **To make security policy troubleshooting as simple as possible, you should: (Choose all that apply.)**
   a. Create as many GPOs as possible, each focused on a single policy.
   b. Apply group policies at the lowest level possible.
   c. Apply group policies at the highest level possible.
   d. Create the fewest GPOs possible, grouping all security policies together that apply to a given group of users and/or computers.

4. **To view the net effect of all the security policies applied to a given user or computer, use:**
   a. GPRESULT.exe
   b. Security Configuration and Analysis
   c. Security Templates
   d. Group Policy Editor

5.5   Implement an audit policy

GPO • SACL • ACCESS

UNDERSTANDING THE OBJECTIVE

It is important to understand how to implement an audit policy. An audit policy must first be developed, and then implemented, either locally or via GPOs. Implementing auditing is easiest when GPOs are used, but this often requires more up-front effort to develop the policy.

WHAT YOU REALLY NEED TO KNOW

◆ You may deploy audit policies on one computer or on many computers at once via GPOs.

◆ Audit policies should be set for all computers in a domain, with very targeted group policies (local policies) set for those computers that hold confidential information, are domain controllers, or are other potential targets for attack.

◆ A **SACL** is used to configure auditing. A DACL (sometimes referred to as **ACL**) is used for resource access (permissions).

◆ The Audit Directory Service Access and Audit Object Access policies must be configured before AD or resources can be audited; the other audit policies require no further action or prerequisites.

◆ Audit object access must be enabled to audit access to files, folders, and printers. Files and folders must reside on NTFS volumes in order to audit them.

◆ Audit directory services access must be enabled to audit access to any object in AD.

◆ The success and/or failure of any event may be audited.

◆ The Audit account logon events policy is used to audit domain controller validations of users; it applies to domain controllers only (if used in a domain).

◆ The Audit logon events policy is used to audit whenever someone logs on to a computer (i.e., accesses its resources) locally or across the network. *Do not confuse it with the Audit account logon events policy.*

◆ The Audit account management policy is used to audit whenever a user or group is created, modified, or deleted.

◆ Audit policy change is used to audit changes to user rights (not permissions), audit policies, and/or password and logon settings (e.g., account lockout, minimum and maximum password length, and so on).

◆ The audit privilege use policy is used to track the exercise of user rights (other than logon/logoff) and when administrators take ownership of objects (though not AD objects; they are covered by the account management policy).

OBJECTIVES ON THE JOB

Auditing is a key element of security. An audit policy needs to be devised that collects all relevant data needed to ensure the security of the network, but does not produce so much data that it can't be effectively analyzed for potential security breaches. Finding that balance comes from practice, intuition, and a disciplined approach to configuring and reviewing the security logs.

PRACTICE TEST QUESTIONS

The network administrator of Band Instruments Inc. is concerned about network security. She has applied NTFS permissions and applied account and password policies, but still suspects some unauthorized access to information. She often gets reports of files being deleted, which the owner had nothing to do with.

1. **Is there a way to find out who is accessing various network resources in Windows 2000?**
   a. No, you must use a third-party tool.
   b. Yes, you can use audit policies.

2. **How can the network administrator apply the necessary audit policies? (Choose all that apply.)**
   a. Manually, at each individual computer with Computer Management
   b. Manually, at each individual computer with local policies
   c. Automatically, through system policies
   d. Automatically, through group policies

3. **Is there a policy that allows her to track the deletion of files and the person responsible?**
   a. No, there is no way to track file deletions.
   b. Yes, she may use the Audit privilege use policy.
   c. Yes, she may use the Audit object access policy.
   d. Yes, she may use the Audit file access policy.

4. **Aside from enabling a policy, what else must be done to audit file deletions?**
   a. Nothing, once the policy is enabled, you are ready to go.
   b. You must ensure that the files are on NTFS volumes.
   c. You must ensure that the files are on FAT or FAT32 volumes.
   d. You must ensure that the files are on NTFS volumes and you must choose to audit the files you want to track.
   e. You must ensure that the files are on FAT or FAT32 volumes and you must choose to audit the files you want to track.

5. **Is there a way to track who accesses the computer where most of the deletions occur?**
   a. No, you must audit all computers or none of them.
   b. Yes, use the Audit account logon policy.
   c. Yes, use the Audit logon events policy.
   d. Yes, use the Audit directory service access policy.

6. **Where is the auditing information stored? (Choose all that apply.)**
   a. In the Security Event Log
   b. In the SACL
   c. In the DACL

5.6 Monitor security events

EVENT VIEWER • FILTER • FIND

UNDERSTANDING THE OBJECTIVE

Understanding how to locate the events that are important as defined in a security policy is crucial to ensuring the integrity of your network. This objective focuses on how to locate security events. The previous objective focused on how to generate the events in the first place, and the next one covers how to understand the meaning of the events.

WHAT YOU REALLY NEED TO KNOW

- ◆ The Event Viewer snap-in is used to view all event logs, including the security log.
- ◆ Access to the security log is limited to administrators, although anyone can view the system and application logs.
- ◆ Administrators are the only ones allowed to set up, maintain, or remove auditing.
- ◆ Event logs may be saved for future use, trend analysis, and historical context.
- ◆ Event viewer may be configured to display all the records in the log or to filter the records displayed based on user-defined criteria.
- ◆ When you are done, be careful to filter by choosing All Records so that important events don't pass unnoticed. Some administrators prefer to use Find instead, so that all records remain visible.
- ◆ Both Find and Filter offer the following criteria: event types (Information, Warning, and Error [for all logs except security] or Success audit and Failure audit [for the security log only]), event source, category, event ID, user (if any), and computer.
- ◆ The Filter option allows the following additional criteria: first to last events or a specified date and time range.
- ◆ The Find option offers one additional criterion: description.
- ◆ The description, user, and computer are probably the most useful criteria, as they allow you to search the description of the event for any text you desire, as well as for a user involved (such as a file deletion) or the computer on which the event occurred.

OBJECTIVES ON THE JOB

Monitoring security events should be a daily priority for every administrator. Many administrators set aside time each day to review the security logs, backup and anti-virus logs, and so on, to be sure that the network is performing as expected, and to fix any problems as soon as possible after they occur. This practice becomes even more important as more servers are added to the network.

PRACTICE TEST QUESTIONS

1. **Which of the following criteria are available with the Find option but not with the Filter option?**
   a. Description
   b. User
   c. Computer
   d. Date range
   e. Event type
   f. Category

2. **Which of the following criteria are available with the Filter option but not with the Find option?**
   a. Description
   b. User
   c. Computer
   d. Date range
   e. Event type
   f. Category

3. **The tool used to view auditing output is:**
   a. Computer Management
   b. Event Viewer
   c. Active Directory Users and Computers
   d. Security Configuration and Analysis

4. **The log that contains auditing output is:**
   a. audit
   b. system
   c. security
   d. application
   e. Active Directory

5. **The security log can be viewed by:**
   a. guests
   b. domain users
   c. power users
   d. backup operators
   e. administrators

6. **Event logs can be saved so they can be viewed and analyzed in the future.**
   a. True
   b. False

OBJECTIVES

5.7   Analyze security events

EVENT VIEWER • EVENT PROPERTIES

UNDERSTANDING THE OBJECTIVE

After the data has been collected on audited events, it must be interpreted. Typically, viewing the event properties does this. Making sense of the output is the goal of this objective. This objective also focuses on key information to look for as that analysis is performed.

WHAT YOU REALLY NEED TO KNOW

- ◆ For most security-related events, focus particularly on the user field, the computer field, and the description.

- ◆ The user field informs you of the user who attempted the action in question (logon, logoff, file creation or deletion, etc.).

- ◆ The computer field informs you of the computer in question; for example, the domain controller that validated the logon.

- ◆ The description field lets you know the details of what happened; for example, the file that was accessed, the action that was attempted on the file, and so on.

- ◆ You should note the date and time the event occurred to determine if there is a pattern, such as repeated attempts to log on or certain times of day that attacks occur. This enables you to determine where to tighten security.

- ◆ Many threats occur from ignorance and/or sabotage from users on the network, as well as those who may try to hack in from the outside. You should audit the Everyone group, and not a restrictive group, to ensure that you see what everyone is doing (both inside and outside).

- ◆ Generally, both successes and failures should be audited so you can determine attempted intrusions, unauthorized file additions and removals, and so on, as well as determine which accounts may be compromised or which users may be causing problems on the network.

OBJECTIVES ON THE JOB

All of the auditing that Windows 2000 makes possible is useless unless (and until) an administrator reviews the logs for intrusions and other unauthorized actions. Once found, the administrator can take corrective steps to secure the resource and prevent further problems. This is one of the key security-related duties of an administrator, and it should be taken very seriously to keep the network as secure as possible in a given environment. The administrator is ultimately responsible for the network and the data on it, both from internal and external threats.

PRACTICE TEST QUESTIONS

1. For maximum security, which types of events should be audited? (Choose all that apply.)
   a. Information
   b. Warning
   c. Error
   d. Success audits
   e. Failure audits

2. Which of the following fields are generally most important in determining breaches of security? (Choose all that apply.)
   a. Date
   b. Time
   c. Category
   d. Description
   e. User
   f. Event ID
   g. Computer
   h. Event source

3. Which tool is used to view auditing entries?
   a. Event Viewer
   b. Security Configuration and Analysis
   c. Computer Management
   d. Local Security Policy

4. Threats to the network can come from which of the following sources?
   a. Users on the network
   b. Administrators
   c. Outside users
   d. All of the above

5. When auditing, which group should be audited?
   a. Users
   b. Administrators
   c. Everyone
   d. Authenticated users
   e. Network
   f. Creator/owner

Section 1.0

Objective 1.1

Practice Questions:

1. b
2. c
3. d
4. c
5. d
6. a

Objective 1.2

Practice Questions:

1. c
2. a, c
3. a
4. b, c

Objective 1.3

Practice Questions:

1. d
2. b
3. a
4. a, b
5. c
6. a
7. a

Objective 1.4

Practice Questions:

1. d
2. b
3. a, b

Objective 1.5

Practice Questions:

1. a, b, d
2. a, d
3. d
4. b
5. c
6. a, b

Objective 1.6
Practice Questions:
1. a
2. a, b
3. c
4. a, c, d
5. b, c
6. b
7. b

Objective 1.7
Practice Questions:
1. a, b, c
2. c
3. c
4. a
5. d
6. a, b, d
7. a

Objective 1.8
Practice Questions:
1. d
2. b

Objective 1.9
Practice Questions:
1. d
2. b
3. c
4. c
5. a, c
6. b
7. d

Objective 1.10
Practice Questions:
1. d
2. a, b
3. b
4. c

Objective 1.11

Practice Questions:

1. b, c
2. a
3. b
4. c
5. b
6. d
7. a, b

Objective 1.12

Practice Questions:

1. d
2. a, b, c, d
3. c
4. d
5. a, c, d
6. a
7. c

Objective 1.13

Practice Questions:

1. a
2. a
3. b
4. c
5. d
6. a
7. a, c, d

Objective 1.14

Practice Questions:

1. b
2. c
3. b
4. a
5. a

Objective 1.15

Practice Questions:

1. b, c
2. a, d
3. d
4. a
5. c
6. d
7. d

Section 2.0
Objective 2.1
Practice Questions:
1. d (All others are optional.)
2. b
3. a
4. d
5. a, b, c, d, e (All support SRV records.)
6. b

Objective 2.2
Practice Questions:
1. a
2. b
3. a
4. a, c, e, g, h, i
5. a

Objective 2.3
Practice Questions:
1. e
2. c
3. a, b, c
4. b
5. c

Objective 2.4
Practice Questions:
1. a
2. d
3. c
4. b, d
5. a

Objective 2.5

Practice Questions:

1. c
2. b
3. b
4. a
5. b
6. d
7. c

Section 3.0

Objective 3.1

Practice Questions:

1. c
2. c
3. d
4. a
5. a

Objective 3.2

Practice Questions:

1. b
2. a
3. a, b
4. d

Objective 3.3

Practice Questions:

1. a
2. d
3. b
4. a
5. a, c
6. a
7. a, b

Objective 3.4

Practice Questions:

1. d
2. d
3. b
4. c
5. b
6. a

Objective 3.5
Practice Questions:
1. d
2. a, c
3. a

Objective 3.6
Practice Questions:
1. a, d
2. a
3. a
4. a, b, c
5. d
6. b
7. a, b

Objective 3.7
Practice Questions:
1. a, c
2. d
3. a, c
4. c, d

Objective 3.8
Practice Questions:
1. b, c, d
2. b
3. a, b, c
4. a, b, c, d
5. a, b
6. a, b, c
7. a

Objective 3.9
Practice Questions:
1. a, c, d, f
2. b, d
3. a, c
4. b, c, h
5. a

Objective 3.10
Practice Questions:
1. d
2. a

Objective 3.11
Practice Questions:
1. a
2. a
3. d
4. b
5. c
6. b, c

Objective 3.12
Practice Questions:
1. a
2. d
3. b
4. b
5. c

Objective 3.13
Practice Questions:
1. b
2. a, c
3. a

Objective 3.14
Practice Questions:
1. d
2. a, b
3. c, d
4. d

Objective 3.15
Practice Questions:
1. a, c, d
2. c
3. a, b
4. d
5. b
6. a, b, d
7. a

Objective 3.16
Practice Questions:
1. a, b
2. b
3. b
4. a
5. c

Objective 3.17
Practice Questions:
1. a, d, e, g
2. d,e
3. a, d, f
4. c
5. a

Objective 3.18
Practice Questions:
1. a, c
2. d
3. b
4. c
5. d
6. a

Objective 3.19
Practice Questions:
1. c
2. b
3. e
4. a
5. d
6. e
7. d

Objective 3.20
Practice Questions:
1. b
2. b
3. The correct order is: d, b, a, e, c
4. c

Objective 3.21
Practice Questions:
1. a
2. b
3. d
4. c
5. d
6. a
7. a, b

Objective 3.22

Practice Questions:

1. d
2. a, c, e
3. b, d, g
4. c, f
5. b
6. d

Objective 3.23

Practice Questions:

1. b
2. c
3. a
4. d
5. b

Section 4.0

Objective 4.1

Practice Questions:

1. a
2. b, d, e
3. b, c, d
4. d
5. c
6. a, d, e

Objective 4.2

Practice Questions:

1. c
2. b
3. a

Objective 4.3

Practice Questions:

1. b, d
2. a, c
3. a, b

Objective 4.4

Practice Questions:

1. b
2. a
3. c, d, e
4. d